# MODERN BANK MANAGEMENT

# MODERN BANK MANAGEMENT

**PAUL F. JESSUP**
University of Minnesota

**WEST PUBLISHING CO.**
St. Paul   New York   Los Angeles   San Francisco

COPYRIGHT © 1980 By WEST PUBLISHING CO.
50 West Kellogg Boulevard
P.O. Box 3526
St. Paul Minnesota 55165

Printed in the United States of America

**Library of Congress Cataloging in Publication Data**

Jessup, Paul F
  Modern bank management.

  Bibliography: p.
  Includes index.
  1.  Bank management.  I.  Title.
HG1615.J467              332.1'068              79-27255
ISBN 0-8299-0330-5

1st Reprint—1980

Voor Anneke met waardering voor haar geduldige steun

# CONTENTS

# PREFACE

It has been an arduous process, but I have enjoyed researching and writing this book. I welcome the opportunity thus to present what I hope is a comprehensive, readable book that also conveys some of the excitement and opportunities of modern banking.

Throughout *Modern Bank Management* I cite the research contributions of numerous banking scholars. I do so not to encumber the book with footnotes but to alert readers to the usefulness of such applied research for bankers and others concerned about banking and public policy. Often I cite the principal conclusions of researchers who suitably caveat their research designs. While I have tried to cite their results within the intended context, I encourage interested readers to refer to the original studies.

While it incorporates much of recent banking research, this book also contains statements that can become bases for further testing. Such research would be a welcome outcome. Any scholarly book raises questions at the same time it provides answers and ways to answer questions.

Many people typed portions of this manuscript; I acknowledge the assistance of Yvonne Duperon, Joyce Hegstrom, Debra Holmen, Vi Johnson, Pam Jonckowski, LuAnne Moe, and Mary Trandem.

I am also indebted to the helpful staff members of the libraries of the Federal Reserve Bank of Minneapolis and the University of Minnesota.

Some banking officials and scholars read all or portions of draft versions of this manuscript, and they suggested constructive improvements. I gratefully acknowledge the assistance of Douglas Austin, David Durst, Richard Stolz, and Roger Stover. I am solely responsible for any errors in the final manuscript.

Various graduate students read draft chapters of this manuscript, and they suggested ways by which I could improve the final version. I appreciate their constructive comments and questions.

My wife and children patiently accepted my personal commitment to this lengthy writing project, which immediately followed my completion of a companion casebook. I appreciate their support of my endeavors, and I commit myself now to spending more time with them.

Minneapolis, Minnesota                                                                              P.F.J.
February 1980

# 1
# OBJECTIVES

*Modern Bank Management* seeks to:

- use a unifying managerial perspective to introduce and examine banking—a vital, vibrant industry
- build systematically toward a comprehensive view of bank management and expansionary banking systems
- specify the changing environment within which modern bankers make diverse decisions
- demonstrate how banks and their supervisory agencies can use research to help plan banking structure and strategies

To achieve its objectives, *Modern Bank Management* assumes that most of its readers are either new to banking or specialists within one part of banking.

## UNIFYING MANAGERIAL PERSPECTIVE

To develop a solid understanding of banking, one needs to adopt broad perspectives and then add specialized information.

Chapter 2 describes why modern bankers must be able to manage their firms within the context of rapid changes. These bankers use computer-based systems to assist them in their management decisions and to help process an expanding variety of transactions. They make their decisions subject to a myriad of changing laws and regulations, and they face new demands for social accountability.

Chapter 3 introduces a portfolio concept of bank management. From this perspective, a bank is a cluster of financial assets and liabilities, and it commits most of its human and physical resources to the managing and servicing of its total portfolio. A bank's balance sheet summarizes the composition and financing of the total portfolio at a specific time. As it

manages its portfolio over time, a bank generates revenues and incurs
expenses, which it reports in its income statement. Portfolio management
involves short-run and long-run decisions about funds flows. Recent
developments in portfolio theory can provide useful insights for modern
bankers.

A bank is a complex organization embedded within the nation's
banking, financial, and socioeconomic systems. Chapter 4 summarizes the
principal components of a bank's decision environment, and it illustrates
how this changing environment affects many management decisions.

Although their portfolio composition and decision environment differ
from those of most other firms, banks can use many of the management
systems used by successful nonbanking firms. Chapter 5 shows how bankers
thus use modern management systems. (Flow charts, in particular, provide a
structured summary of many bank decision processes.) A bank's senior
officers focus primarily on planning and control systems, and so Chapter 5
focuses on how to set bank objectives and evaluate bank performance. Each
bank has objectives and policies to guide its personnel in their daily
decisions, and its directors and senior officers have access to detailed reports
by which to evaluate their bank's performance over time. Other interested
parties—such as bank supervisors, stockholders, and community
residents—also monitor and evaluate bank performance.

Chapters 3 through 5 also provide a framework for later, more
specialized, chapters. The portfolio perspective, for example, emphasizes
interrelationships within a portfolio and funds-flow management over time.
A bank can use this perspective to analyze the structure and flow of its
portfolio(s), and an expansionary banking organization can extend this
perspective to analyze its portfolio of holding-company affiliates and its
multinational activities. Banking organizations similarly can apply concepts
and techniques of systems management to many of their specialized
activities.

## BUILDING A COMPREHENSIVE VIEW OF BANK MANAGEMENT

Chapters 6 through 14 focus on the management of bank deposits, cash
items, investments, and loans. These chapters examine how, subject to
constraints, a bank makes strategic decisions concerning each element of its
total portfolio. Throughout these chapters, one must keep in mind that most
bank portfolio decisions involve complex interrelationships. For example, if
it competes for government deposits, a bank has to hold investment
securities that it can pledge as collateral for these deposits. If it competes for
corporate deposits, a bank has to plan to meet borrowing requests of these
depositors. Before a bank lending officer rejects a loan request from an
established customer, the officer must assess the probability that the
customer will terminate deposit account(s) and other relationships with the
bank and transfer them to an institution more willing to meet the loan
request.

Chapter 15 demonstrates how bank capital decisions relate to the current and expected future composition of a bank's total portfolio; and Chapter 16 demonstrates how bank trust departments, in various legal capacities, manage funds for diverse clients.

Chapters 17 through 21 examine strategies by which banking organizations expand into new domestic and international markets. Chapter 17 describes why most banks face statutory and regulatory restrictions on multioffice expansion. The subsequent four chapters then focus on how banking organizations work to expand via branching, bank holding companies, and multinational banking systems.

In its concluding, integrating, chapter, *Modern Bank Management* summarizes the probable future directions of banking and bank management.

## CHANGING ENVIRONMENT WITHIN WHICH BANKERS MAKE DECISIONS

Each bank is embedded within a set of external systems that include the:

- competitive system
- banking system
- financial system
- socioeconomic system

Modern bankers must understand their current operating environment and anticipate how technological developments and public-policy decisions will lead to probable changes in their environment. They need to develop contingency plans for probable changes that include:

- expanded "banking" activities by nonbank financial institutions
- further advances in electronic funds transfer systems (EFTS)
- gradual elimination of interest-rate prohibitions and ceilings on various categories of deposits
- revised requirements for membership in the Federal Reserve System
- revision of the Glass-Steagall Act that bans bank underwriting of most municipal revenue bonds
- refinements in recent consumer protection legislation, especially as it relates to consumer loans and home mortgage loans
- possible selective credit controls by which the federal government tries to channel bank loans into "socially productive" uses
- new attempts to measure and monitor bank risks and capital adequacy
- reduced legislative and regulatory barriers to bank expansion via branching and multibank holding companies
- increased expansion by bank holding companies into nonbanking activities
- continued expansion of multinational banking

*Modern Bank Management* demonstrates why such changes are likely to occur, and it presents strategies by which banks can prepare for such changes.

## USING RESEARCH TO PLAN BANKING STRUCTURE AND STRATEGIES

There has been an explosion of banking research in the 1970s. Banking scholars—associated with academic institutions, banking organizations, and/or governmental banking agencies—have focused their research on two often interrelated topics:

- public-policy decisions that affect the environment within which banks operate
- strategies and decisions as to how bankers can profitably manage risks within a rapidly changing environment

*Modern Bank Management* summarizes the principal results of much of this recent research and demonstrates how bankers can use such results in their strategic planning. Footnotes throughout the book alert readers to convenient sources that provide more detailed analyses of specialized topics.

## SUMMARY

To demonstrate the vitality and opportunities of modern banking, this book seeks to: provide a unifying managerial perspective, build toward a comprehensive view of banking, specify the changing environment within which banks operate, and demonstrate the applicability of research to banking decisions.

# 2
# MODERN BANKING: A PREVIEW

Banking, one of the nation's largest industries, is rapidly changing. Many banks now aggressively lend to consumers, and they use innovative procedures to help finance business and industry—both domestic and foreign. These new lending practices shatter the traditional portrait of solemn bankers who cautiously lend to select local businessmen and farmers.

Consumers increasingly use bank credit cards, drive-in and remote TV tellers, and direct deposit of payroll checks to their bank accounts. Modern technology thus challenges traditional images of austere bank lobbies, in which bank tellers, behind high partitions, serve lines of customers.

Modern banking demands new professional skills involving computers and decision analysis. Many banks recruit and rapidly promote persons with these skills, such that women and members of minority groups constitute a growing proportion of bank officer and staff positions. Thus the "banking fraternity" increasingly comprises persons of diverse skills and backgrounds.

## PERVASIVENESS OF CHANGE

New technology provides opportunities for modern bankers. Banks use computers to process traditional paperwork quickly and accurately, and to assist in management decisions. They use computer technology to expedite interregional funds transfers and to offer their customers convenient ways to deposit and withdraw funds via telephone or computer terminals placed in retail stores. Banks also use computer-based procedures to help analyze deposit accounts and loan applications. Large banks use computerized systems to detect potential abuses of their credit cards and to provide senior officials—responsible for multimillion dollar transactions—timely information about national and international financial markets.

American banks have long been subject to special laws and regulations. A bank has to meet specific legal and regulatory requirements not only to begin operations, but to maintain its daily operations. It has to hold specific percentages of its deposits as noninterest-earning reserves; it cannot make certain types of loans; and it cannot pay interest on checking accounts. If it wants to enter new domestic or foreign markets, a bank faces a maze of legal and regulatory hurdles. Modern bankers therefore must understand the current—and probable future—legal and regulatory environment that so pervades their daily operations and future strategies.

Banks face new demands for social accountability. Bank lending policies affect local economic development. Bank officers traditionally have been community leaders whose personal values influence community attitudes toward local development and fund-raising activities. Some bankers go beyond these traditional community roles; they seek to involve their banks in such matters as consumer information, advancement of minorities, and revitalization of urban areas. Other bankers may not personally subscribe to such goals, but increasingly they face new laws and regulations associated with such goals.

## BANKING DECISIONS: A BANKER'S DAY

Almost daily there are news reports about banking, including such terms as federal funds, negotiable certificates of deposit, Eurodollars, bank holding companies, and electronic funds transfer systems. Nonbankers thus quickly learn that banking, like many businesses and professions, has its specialized activities and vocabulary.

It is convenient to distinguish between two categories of banks. The first consists of medium-sized banks having total deposits ranging from $25 to $100 million. These banks usually are located in suburbs or rural cities. The second category consists of large money-center banks that generally have deposits ranging upward of $1 billion. These banks typically are headquartered in downtown areas of very large cities.

Both medium-sized banks and money-center banks offer checking accounts, savings accounts, consumer loans, mortgage loans, and credit cards. Managers of medium-sized banks make decisions that are a subset of the more extensive set of decisions made by money-center banks competing nationally—and internationally—for large customers. Money-center banks, through their correspondent departments, also provide diverse services to medium-sized and small banks.

### DAILY DECISIONS: A MEDIUM-SIZED BANK

An illustrative medium-sized bank is located in a growing rural city. Most of its officers and staff have been with the bank for many years. Its directors include some bank officers and some local nonbanking business and professional people. Most of its stockholders reside in the community.

On a typical morning the bank president opens the local newspaper and sees the latest balance sheet (report of condition) of a nearby bank. Referring to the prior year's balance sheet, the president quickly computes the percentage change in total deposits at the competing bank and then compares the percentage increase with that of the president's own bank in the same period. This comparison indicates whether the competing bank has been growing more rapidly and thus possibly increasing its share of bank deposits in the community. Scanning the rival bank's balance sheet to develop insights into that bank's strategies, the president asks a staff member to analyze further the new information. By thus using some basic ratio analysis, the banker monitors developments among banks in his community.

Later the banker meets with the senior lending officers to review loan applications, especially those that are nonroutine because of their large sums, unusual repayment schedules, or unusual proposed collateral. The president asks the lending officers their recommendations concerning each application. When the recommendation is to make a loan, the president wants to confirm that the proposed loan meets legal and regulatory guidelines and is consistent with the bank's lending policy. When the recommendation is to deny a loan request, the president asks whether such a denial will likely result in losing a valued customer. The president and chief lending officers use this joint review procedure prior to presenting their recommendations to the directors' loan committee.

After meeting with the loan officers, the president meets with the cashier, whose duties include controlling the bank's cash in the vault and at the tellers' windows, and managing the bank's investments. The cashier gives the president a report that summarizes recent and probable future deposit flows at the bank, lists the bank's short-term investments that mature in the coming days, and lists the cashier's current recommendations for new short-term investments. Based on the report, the president and cashier agree to have the bank sell $200,000 in federal funds. This transaction involves an overnight loan to another bank, and the lending bank receives interest on this loan. If agreeable to both parties, this federal funds transaction may be renewed the following day. The cashier also reports that a large correspondent bank recently reviewed the bank's bond portfolio and recommended that the bank sell some long-term U.S. Treasury bonds and reinvest in some medium-term municipal bonds. The cashier agrees with the recommendation and proposes some specific bond transactions for the president to review in the next day or so.

At noon the president attends a luncheon meeting with some local business officials. They discuss economic prospects, banking developments, and their pending involvement in a fund-raising campaign for the community hospital.

In the early afternoon the president has appointments with bank customers who want to discuss their loan and deposit relationships with the bank. The president also walks through the bank and chats with various employees. Later, on meeting with the senior vice-president, who has just analyzed the report submitted recently by federal bank examiners to the bank's board of directors, the two officers review criticisms of several

past-due loans and of some operating procedures. They then prepare a
specific response to present to the board of directors at its next meeting.

Late in the afternoon the president browses through some new banking
magazines. Several articles summarize recent studies of the financial-
services industry. These articles discuss such subjects as liberalized
branching laws, electronic funds transfer systems, and broader lending and
deposit powers for savings and loan associations. Several other articles
report how specific banks improved their operations. The president notes
useful ideas to discuss with various officers in subsequent days.

After dinner the president is a guest speaker in a noncredit evening
class in business and economics. Speaking on "Consumerism and Banking," the president summarizes how recent consumer-credit regulations
affect bankers and consumers. Class questions about banking follow the
speech. Afterwards, driving home, the president reflects on the bank's
recent growth and how various key decisions contributed to its success.

## DAILY DECISIONS: A LARGE MONEY-CENTER BANK

The illustrative money-center bank has its head office downtown in a large
city, and it has an extensive network of banking offices (branches)
throughout the metropolitan area. The bank was founded in the late 1800s
and has grown both by internal expansion and by acquisition of other banks.
A bank holding company, the stock of which is widely held and listed on a
stock exchange, owns the bank and some bank-related affiliates that engage
in mortgage banking, consumer lending, and investment advisory services.
Many of the bank's senior officers have been with it for many years, and
most of its junior officers are college graduates who have participated in the
bank's management training program.

Most of this bank's officers and employees have specialized duties;
and, within policy limits, they often make decisions involving large sums of
money. (Its traders in foreign currencies or in government securities, for
example, make many transactions involving millions of dollars each day.)
Senior management, responsible for general policies and for many inter-
departmental decisions, often requires committee recommendations and
staff reports to aid its decisions.

The bank uses a specialized, hierarchical, decision system to conduct
its loan activities. Junior officers, supervised by a senior officer, comprise
lending groups that specialize in loans to specific industries or regions. One
group, for example, focuses on loans to petroleum companies, another to
utilities, and another to medium-sized businesses in the bank's metropolitan
area. The senior officer of each group has authority to make a loan if it is
consistent with bank policy and does not exceed a specified dollar amount
that is that officer's maximum lending authority. That officer confers with a
superior officer about loan requests that deviate from policy or exceed the
lending authority. This higher officer, in turn, has authority to make
decisions about some unusual loan requests. In exceptional cases, where an
officer lacks authority or is uncertain as to the decision, he or she refers the
loan requests to the executive loan committee comprised of top management

and, possibly, some directors. By means of this decision structure, senior officials keep informed of amounts of routine loans made or denied at lower levels and become directly involved in exceptional loan requests not decided at lower levels. Nevertheless, the senior officials, as well as the directors, are legally responsible for all loans made by the bank—including those made by the junior officers.

Each of the bank's metropolitan branches also makes loans in its neighborhood. Most of these loans are to consumers, homeowners, and small businesses; and they are for comparatively small amounts. One or more officers in each branch can act on loan requests that meet the bank's policy guidelines. Requests that deviate from the guidelines are referred to specialist groups or senior loan officers at the head office. The types of loans made at a suburban branch office thus are similar to those made by a medium-sized suburban bank. The procedures differ, however, in that branch lending officers refer exceptional items to the head office, while senior officials of a medium-sized bank directly participate in all large loan decisions.

Specialists make most of the daily investment decisions in the money-center bank. Teams of officers and employees monitor, almost continuously, major flows of funds in and out of the head office and the branches. Other specialists monitor the bank's short-term investments and liabilities—especially those scheduled to become due within hours or days. For example, the bank holds millions of dollars of U.S. Treasury bills and municipal securities that are soon due for redemption. Also, the bank has outstanding millions of dollars of time deposits that it must soon redeem. Many times within a day the bank buys and sells federal funds as a means of managing its funds flows and as a service to smaller banks that have accounts with it. Alerted to schedules of maturing assets and liabilities, senior officers in this division make frequent decisions about how and when to reinvest large sums of money. The officers who make these major funds-flow decisions do so subject to policies and limitations set by top management. As with loan decisions, top management and directors can delegate decision authority; but they are accountable for all such decisions.

Managers of the neighborhood branches seldom make investment decisions. They regularly inform the head office of recent and probable funds flows at their branches. The head-office specialists incorporate this information into their estimated funds flows for the entire branch system, and they continuously make short-term and long-term investment decisions for the entire system.

Managers of the neighborhood branches focus on operating details involving personnel, customer accounts, and loans. They also seek new business accounts in their neighborhoods and participate in community betterment activities. They have limited flexibility, however, in local marketing strategies, because head-office specialists decide marketing policies and advertising budgets for the entire branch system.

Senior management focuses on long-range planning for the complex organization; it sets policies for component specialized departments; and it monitors key decisions made by departmental officers. Also, senior management makes major decisions involving long-run commitments of the bank's human and financial resources. Illustrative of such decisions are:

- where and when to add new branches to its metropolitan network
- whether to commit substantial resources to new systems of unmanned electronic tellers in nonbank locations throughout the metropolitan area
- whether to open additional branches abroad, and, if so, where and when
- how much reliance the bank should place on the Eurodollar market as a source of funds over time
- whether to raise additional capital funds for the bank, and, if so, how and when

Senior management also is responsible for organizational responses to new legislation and regulations affecting, for example, bank hiring and promotion policies, advertising, and lending practices.

Senior managers of the money-center bank thus direct a complex organization in a rapidly changing environment. New employees of this bank develop specialized skills. Yet they also benefit from a broad understanding of banking and of principal decisions common to most banking organizations. Within this general framework they then conduct their specialized activities.

## SUMMARY

The rapid pace of legal, regulatory, social, and technological change affects banks and their customers. To introduce bank decision-making in a changing environment, this chapter highlights a typical day at a medium-sized bank and at a large money-center bank. Often one reads new stories about selected activities of large city banks. While these money-center banks account for a majority of bank deposits, most of the approximately 14,400 banks in the United States are medium-sized and small banks that are based in various-size population centers. Many activities of medium-sized banks represent a microcosm of the complex operations of large money-center banks. Therefore it is often useful first to understand management systems appropriate for a medium-sized bank and then to extend this understanding to more complex banking systems.

# 3
# BANK PORTFOLIOS

A portfolio is a cluster of assets, but the portfolio concept can be extended to encompass a cluster of assets and associated liabilities. People and firms construct portfolios of financial assets from which they expect financial returns. They also make decisions as to how much debt they will use to finance part of a portfolio.

A bank exemplifies a financial portfolio. Loans and investment securities constitute most of its assets. These assets generate interest income that typically accounts for over 90 percent of a bank's total revenue.

Deposits and borrowed funds account for most of a bank's total liabilities, which in turn finance a large proportion of its total assets. From a bank's view, deposits with it are liabilities; but from the depositors' view such deposits are among their most liquid assets. They view their funds in checking accounts as money.

## PORTFOLIO COMPOSITION

A balance sheet summarizes the principal components of a bank's total portfolio at a specific time.

### BALANCE SHEET OF A MEDIUM-SIZED BANK

Exhibit 3-1 is an illustrative *report of condition* (balance sheet) of a medium-sized bank. This report divides the bank's total assets, liabilities, and capital into various categories; and it states the total dollar amounts in each category at the time of the report. Although such a report divides a bank's portfolio into various categories, each category itself encompasses many subcategories.

*Cash and due from banks* summarizes the amounts of: currency and coin that the bank has in its own vault; balances that it holds as deposits at

**EXHIBIT 3-1**

**Report of Condition of Illustrative Medium-sized Bank: Year-end 1977**

**(Thousands)**

| ASSETS | | LIABILITIES, SUBORDINATED DEBENTURES, AND EQUITY CAPITAL | |
|---|---|---|---|
| Cash and due from banks | $ 4,513 | Demand deposits | $14,281 |
| U.S. Treasury securities | 4,706 | Time and savings deposits | 27,418 |
| Obligations of federal agencies | 2,178 | Total Deposits | 41,699 |
| Other securities | 6,541 | Federal funds purchased and | |
| Federal funds sold | 1,750 | other liabilities | 990 |
| Loans, net | 24,990 | Total Liabilities | 42,689 |
| Bank premises and equipment | 847 | | |
| Other assets | 646 | Common stock | 800 |
| | | Surplus | 1,300 |
| | | Undivided profits | 1,300 |
| | | Capital reserves | 82 |
| | | Total Equity Capital | 3,482 |
| | | Total Liabilities, subordinated De- | |
| Total Assets | $46,171 | bentures and Equity Capital | $46,171 |

*Source:* This illustrative medium-sized bank reflects composite data derived from Table A (Nation), *Bank Operating Statistics,* 1977.

other banks; and checks that it is in the process of presenting to other banks for their payment.

*Investments* is a summary category for the various marketable securities owned by the bank. Most of these securities are debt instruments issued by the U.S. Treasury; federal agencies, such as the Federal Home Loan Bank System; and various state and local governmental units, such as cities and school districts. A bank's investments differ by issuer, maturity, stated rate of interest, and marketability. Management of the investments portfolio is a specialized, ongoing process.

*Loans* and discounts account for over half the total assets of most banks. (Discounts are seldom used, and so this book uses the term "loans" to summarize this category of assets.) Bank loans contain many sub-categories, such as, by type of borrower: commercial and industrial, agricultural, real estate, to individuals, and other. There are other ways to subclassify the loans, such as, secured or unsecured, insured or uninsured, and repayment schedule. A bank usually has a large proportion of its skilled personnel administer its various loans.

*Bank premises and equipment* constitute a small part of a bank's total assets. Laws and regulations prohibit a bank from owning most types of physical assets not directly used for a bank's operations or not specifically leased to the bank's clients. Although many banks purchase their buildings and equipment and depreciate them over time, some banks choose to lease the fixed assets they use. On average, a bank's fixed assets account for less than 2 percent of its total assets.

Deposits constitute most of a bank's liabilities, and there are two principal categories: demand and time.

*Demand deposits* are subject to immediate withdrawal or transfer by a depositor. Withdrawals or transfers are usually by check, and so demand deposits are popularly called checking accounts. A bank's report of condition may subclassify the total demand deposits by principal categories of holders: individuals, partnerships, and corporations (*IPC*); the U.S. government; and states and political subdivisions. IPC deposits represent an aggregation of demand deposits held by diverse owners. A bank devotes substantial physical and human resources to managing and processing the flows of funds in and out of its demand deposits.

*Time and savings deposits* are not legally subject to withdrawal or transfer on demand, and owners of these deposits cannot write checks directly against them.[1]

A savings deposit represents an open account relationship between a depositor and a bank. The depositor has a passbook or receives periodic statements which record the deposits, withdrawals, and current balance in the account. Although a bank legally can require a depositor to give 30-days notice before withdrawing funds from a savings account, in practice a bank almost always waives this requirement.

In contrast to a savings account, other time deposits have specific maturity dates. Legally, a bank need not redeem a time deposit before its maturity date, and in practice it seldom does so. The infrequent cases in which a bank redeems a time deposit prior to its maturity usually reflect special circumstances and also result in interest penalties for the depositor.

As with demand deposits, a bank's time and savings deposits often are categorized by their holders: individuals, partnerships, and corporations (IPC); the U.S. government; and states and political subdivisions.

*Capital* is the other principal item on a bank's report of condition. It consists of stockholders' equity, which reflects paid-in capital plus the accumulation of earnings retained over time.

## BALANCE SHEET OF A LARGE MONEY-CENTER BANK

Exhibit 3-2 is an illustrative report of condition of a large money-center bank. This report has the same basic categories as that of the medium-sized bank. Its composition differs, however, in its magnitudes and in its greater variety of financial assets and liabilities.

---

1. Since November 1978, a bank can offer its customers an automatic transfer service whereby the bank will automatically transfer funds from a customer's savings account to his or her checking account whenever the checking account balance falls below a *preagreed* level. A customer who uses this service thus earns interest on funds in a savings account up to the time that the bank automatically transfers the funds to the noninterest-earning checking account. Also, in some states a bank can offer NOW accounts, time-deposit accounts that in practice can function like checking accounts.

**EXHIBIT 3-2**

**Report of Condition of Illustrative Regional Money-Center Bank:  Year-end 1977**

**(Thousands)**

| ASSETS | | LIABILITIES, SUBORDINATED DEBENTURES AND EQUITY CAPITAL | |
|---|---|---|---|
| Cash and due from banks | $174,160 | Demand deposits | $323,741 |
| U.S. Treasury securities | 79,383 | Time and savings deposits | 430,951 |
| Obligations of federal agencies | 23,578 | Deposits in foreign branches | 51,877 |
| Other securities | 102,232 | Total Deposits | 806,569 |
| Trading account securities | 4,953 | Federal funds purchased | 90,691 |
| Federal funds sold | 50,832 | Other borrowed money and other | |
| Loans, net | 511,466 | liabilities | 29,575 |
| Direct lease financing | 6,015 | Total Liabilities | 926,835 |
| Bank premises and equipment | 16,244 | | |
| Other assets | 25,320 | Subordinated debentures | 6,600 |
| | | Capital stock | 13,200 |
| | | Surplus | 24,400 |
| | | Undivided profits | 21,900 |
| | | Reserves for contingencies and other capital reserves | 1,248 |
| | | Total Equity Capital | 60,748 |
| | | Total Liabilities, Subordinated | |
| Total Assets | $994,183 | Debentures and Equity Capital | $994,183 |

*Source:* This illustrative regional money-center bank reflects composite data for 425 large banks (each with total assets above $300 million) in the United States—*minus* the aggregate data for the nation's 20 largest banks. This illustrative balance sheet is derived from Table A (Nation) and Table A (Twenty Largest Banks), *Bank Operating Statistics*, 1977.

Cash and due from banks, investments, loans, and bank premises are principal categories of assets. Within these categories, however, a large money-center bank has many subcategories. Its total loans include large sums lent to financial institutions, brokers and dealers in securities, and multinational borrowers. Such loans are less prevalent among medium-sized banks.

Some large money-center banks act as dealers in securities issued by federal, state, and/or local governmental units. As a dealer, a bank sometimes takes a large position in a security in which it makes a market. Even as a nondealer, a large bank actively buys and sells various securities that it specifically designates as *trading account securities*. Principles and techniques of portfolio management are especially useful to the specialists who manage a bank's trading account securities.

*Federal funds sold* involves short-term (often overnight) loans of funds to other banks and financial institutions. A bank generally sells federal funds when it has a temporary excess of funds in its account at its Federal Reserve Bank. It then lends some of these funds—often in million-dollar increments—to another bank that willingly pays interest for overnight use of these funds. Medium-sized banks also lend federal funds, but not in the quantity or with the frequency customary to large money-center banks.

A large money-center bank's deposit composition is more complex than that of a medium-sized bank. A large bank has extensive IPC demand deposits, many of which are large deposits of corporations headquartered far from the bank. Large banks in California, Illinois, and New York, for example, actively solicit and service accounts of large firms located throughout the nation. A large money-center bank's demand deposits also include substantial correspondent deposits (which are deposit liabilities to other banks) and substantial foreign deposits associated with the bank's extensive network of foreign offices and relationships.

*Short-term borrowings* represent a large bank's diverse short-term nondeposit liabilities. This broad category can include federal funds purchased (borrowed), security repurchase agreements, and promissory notes.

## INITIAL PORTFOLIO PERSPECTIVES

Reports of condition of large money-center banks reflect greater sums and variety than do those of medium-sized banks. At this stage more details about various components are not as important as is an early grasp of how to view any bank as a complex financial portfolio.

There are many interrelationships among a bank's various assets, liabilities, and capital. A bank typically lends to its depositors or to those who are likely to become depositors. A bank pledges many of its investment securities as collateral for deposits of the U.S. government and of state and local governments. A bank's capital often affects the types and amounts of loans that it makes and the types and amounts of deposits it attracts. Seldom is one part of a bank's report of condition independent of other parts. Most bank decisions must explicitly recognize interdependencies among various components of a bank's total portfolio and the financing of the portfolio.

A convenient way to compare balance sheets of various banks or groups of banks is to recast their principal items as ratios. To illustrate, Exhibit 3-3 reports summary balance-sheet ratios of the banks reported in Exhibits 3-1 and 3-2. This format quickly highlights differences in the portfolio composition of the two illustrative banks. It also demonstrates the need to recognize portfolio differences among banks—especially among banks of vastly dissimilar size.

A bank's report of condition summarizes its current financial structure, which in turn reflects a series of past lending, investing, and financing decisions. This current position provides an important basis for decisions about the future composition of the portfolio. A bank, for example, that has an unusually high proportion of loans to total deposits cannot readily take actions that will further increase this ratio. Constrained by today's portfolio composition, which reflects past decisions, the bank has to reevaluate its

**EXHIBIT 3-3**

**Ratio Comparisons Between the Two Illustrative Banks**

| Selected Balance-Sheet Ratios | Illustrative Medium-Sized Bank | Illustrative Regional Money-Center Bank |
|---|---|---|
| Percent of Total Assets | | |
| Cash and due from banks | 9.8 | 17.5 |
| U.S. Treasury securities | 10.2 | 8.0 |
| Obligations of federal agencies | 4.7 | 2.4 |
| Other securities | 14.2 | 10.3 |
| Trading account securities | . . . . . | 0.5 |
| Federal funds sold | 3.8 | 5.1 |
| Loans, net | 54.1 | 51.4 |
| Direct lease financing | . . . . . | 0.6 |
| Bank premises and equipment | 1.8 | 1.6 |
| Other assets | 1.4 | 2.5 |
| Total | 100.0 | 99.9 |
| | | |
| Percent of Total Deposits | | |
| Demand deposits | 34.2 | 40.1 |
| Time and savings deposits | 65.8 | 53.4 |
| Deposits in foreign branches | . . . . . | 6.4 |
| | | |
| Other Ratios | | |
| Total deposits to Total assets | 90.3 | 81.1 |
| Net loans to Total deposits | 59.9 | 63.4 |
| Equity capital to Net loans | 13.9 | 11.9 |
| Equity capital to Total assets | 7.5 | 6.1 |

*Source:* Computed from Exhibits 3-1 and 3-2.

loan policies and investigate ways to increase its deposit and/or nondeposit sources of funds. Its past decisions and present position thus relate to most of a bank's decisions about its future strategies.

## REPORTING AGGREGATE PORTFOLIO RESULTS

A bank holds financial assets in order to generate interest revenues, and it incurs various expenses to finance and administer its asset portfolio. Over time the flows of various revenues and expenses result in net income (or losses). A bank usually distributes part of its net income as dividends to its stockholders, and it retains the other part to increase its capital accounts.

Exhibit 3-4 is an illustrative *consolidated report of income* for a medium-sized bank.

The bank obtains over 90 percent of its *total operating income* from its loans and investments. It receives interest and fees from its loans and

**EXHIBIT 3-4**

## Consolidated Report of Income of Illustrative Medium-sized Bank

### (Thousands)

| | |
|---|---:|
| Operating Income | |
| Interest and fees on loans | $2,191 |
| Interest on federal funds sold | 95 |
| Interest on U.S. Treasury securities | 317 |
| Interest on federal agency securities | 157 |
| Interest on other securities | 320 |
| Income from fiduciary activities | 25 |
| Income from service charges | 165 |
| Other income | 62 |
| Total Operating Income | 3,332 |
| Operating Expenses | |
| Salaries and employee benefits | 621 |
| Interest on time and savings deposits | 1,466 |
| Other interest expense | 36 |
| Occupancy expense | 186 |
| Provision for possible loan losses | 92 |
| Other expenses | 415 |
| Total Operating Expenses | 2,816 |
| Income before income taxes and securities gains or losses | 516 |
| Applicable income taxes | 96 |
| Income before securities gains or losses | 420 |
| Securities gains (losses), net | 9 |
| Net income | $ 429 |

*Source:* This illustrative medium-sized bank reflects composite data derived from Table B (Nation), *Bank Operating Statistics*, 1977.

interest from its investments. Less than 10 percent of the bank's total operating income comes from such other sources as service charges on deposit accounts, trust department income, and various other commissions and fees.

The bank's *total operating expenses* include various subcategories, the largest of which is the interest it pays on deposits as a way to compete for funds to help finance its asset portfolio. Employee expenses and occupancy expenses account for another large part of total operating expenses. The bank needs personnel and facilities to manage and process its loans, investments, and deposit accounts. A bank's interest expense and its employee and occupancy expenses overshadow its various other operating expenses.

A bank's total operating income minus its total operating expenses leaves its operating earnings. A bank then deducts applicable income taxes from its operating earnings; and it adjusts its after-tax earnings for possible gains or losses from securities transactions and for possible extraordinary income or expenses. The final outcome is the bank's *net income* for the reporting period. The bank usually distributes part of its net income as dividends and retains the remainder.

The principal categories of revenues and expenses for a large money-center bank are similar to those of most medium-sized banks. Interest and fees from loans and investments provide about 90 percent of total operating income. Revenues from its trust department, trading account activities, and foreign branches provide most of the remaining total income. A large money-center bank's principal expense item is interest on deposits and on the money it borrows. Its next major expense items usually involve employee and occupancy expenses. As do almost all banks, a large money-center bank reports an expense item called *provision for loan losses*. After it then provides for taxes and nonoperating transactions, the bank reports its net income available for retention or distribution as dividends.

In summary, most of a bank's revenues come from its loans and investments, and most of its expenses arise from financing and managing its portfolio. A bank's periodic income statements report the aggregate financial results of past decisions. Senior officials, by evaluating past outcomes, gain insights concerning their current decisions that, in turn, will affect reported results of future periods.

## MONITORING PORTFOLIO CHANGES

Portfolio management requires a longer-run perspective than that provided by a bank's recent financial reports. Bank officers examine past trends in various components of their firm's report of condition and report of income. These officers also work with projected (pro forma) financial reports prepared by junior officers and members of the bank's staff. By using specific planning assumptions, these *pro forma reports* project the probable composition and financing of a bank's future portfolio. For example, a bank's staff uses specific assumptions about past trends and expected events to generate a pro forma report of condition. By comparing this pro forma report to the latest actual report, the staff members observe that the dollar amount of loans is expected to increase sharply—as will the ratio of loans to total assets. Senior management and the staff then review the assumptions used for the projections. If the assumptions seem valid, then senior management is likely to examine the bank's current policies. It may decide to curtail the expected growth in loans, explore additional ways to finance this expected loan demand, or develop a combination of some curtailment and some new financing. Bankers thus can use pro forma statements to help them make strategic decisions about the long-run composition and financing of a bank's portfolio.

A sources and uses of funds statement is another device that enables bank officials to review past and projected changes in the bank's portfolio. A *sources and uses of funds statement* systematically summarizes major changes in a bank's report of condition, and it relates these changes to some items from the bank's report of income. A detailed sources and uses of funds statement includes various noncash expenses, such as depreciation and provision for both possible loan losses and deferred income taxes. It also shows detailed subcategories of the capital account. Most large, publicly traded banks include a recent sources and uses of funds statement in their annual reports.

A sources and uses of funds statement also can summarize changes during periods of less than a year (such as quarters) and during periods encompassing many years. A bank's senior management can request its staff to prepare statements spanning the most recent 5-year and 10-year periods. This information quickly provides a long-run perspective of past changes in a bank's report of condition.

Sources and uses of funds statements not only summarize past changes but provide insights into future changes in a bank's portfolio. A bank's senior officers, for example, request the staff to prepare pro forma reports of condition and of income. Further, the officers may want to examine alternate projections for the coming year. The staff then constructs a pro forma sources and uses of funds statement by using a recent actual report of condition, and a pro forma report of condition and report of income. This technique, which highlights expected changes in the bank's portfolio, can provide useful information for planning decisions.

Funds flow management is at the heart of most banking decisions. Senior officers spend long hours evaluating various long-run policies and strategies related to funds flows and portfolio composition. They analyze various ways that their bank can obtain and use deposits and nondeposit funds. They project their bank's capital needs and examine various ways to obtain capital. They also establish policies and review procedures to guide and control ongoing portfolio activities, such as investment transactions and loan decisions. Subsequent chapters more fully specify various aspects of managing the flows of funds in and out of a bank's portfolio.

## APPLYING PORTFOLIO PRINCIPLES TO BANKING DECISIONS

This section introduces five principles of portfolio management and illustrates their application to bank strategies and decisions. The five principles are:

- rates of return
- risk
- diversification
- hedging
- leveraging

### RATES OF RETURN

A rate of return is a measure of the net benefits that flow to a specific commitment of resources. Although it focuses on financial benefits and resources, a rate-of-return measure can be broadened to include such intangible items as "goodwill." The rate-of-return concept applies both to realized (past) returns and to expected (future) returns.

### Past Returns

Past rates of return provide measures by which to evaluate a bank's aggregate performance. A bank's *rate of return on total assets* is defined as its annual net income divided by its total assets.[2] A bank's *rate of return on total capital* is the annual net income divided by total capital accounts. Bankers can look for unusual items and trends among a series of past annual returns on assets or capital. They also can compare their bank's rates of return on assets, and on capital, to those of similar banks.

Bankers obtain additional insights by examining past returns on components of their bank's total portfolio. A bank's rate of return on loans is a recent year's total interest and fees on loans divided by the total dollar amount of outstanding loans. Its rate of return on U.S. Treasury securities is its annual interest income from these securities divided by the dollar amount of such securities held by the bank. Past returns on other categories of loans and investments are similarly calculated. Senior management can then analyze various return measures over time and among similar banks.

In addition to evaluating returns on a bank's total portfolio and its principal components, bankers often want to know the returns from a past strategy or decision. To develop a new source of profits, an illustrative bank decided to introduce a credit-card system that required large outlays of time and money. To evaluate the success of this major decision, the bank wants to know its return on investment, which is the flow of cash flows from the credit-card system relative to the initial investment in the system. Although it is difficult to measure precisely its investment outlays and subsequent cash flows, the bank thus tries to evaluate its realized return from this strategic decision.[3] The rate-of-return concept also applies to other banking decisions, such as the return on a specific purchase of some bonds and the return on a specific loan.

### Expected Returns

While past returns enable one to evaluate past performance, expected returns help set standards by which to evaluate future performance. A bank can include target rates of return among its objectives. It can, for example, specify that it wants its rates of return on assets and on capital to be among the top third of similar banks. As time passes, it then evaluates whether it has achieved its target returns. Similarly, a bank can set rate-of-return

---

2. The denominator in a rate-of-return measure can reflect balance-sheet items as of different times, such as the beginning of a period, end of a period, or average for a period. Thus one has to understand which figure is used and why.

3. To compute multiperiod rates of return, one specifies the investment outlay(s) and the subsequent net cash flows and then uses the present-value formula to compute the internal rate of return from the investment.

objectives for categories of loans and investments, and it can set rate-of-return objectives for specific investment and loan decisions.

Bankers also can use expected returns to help them select from among alternative strategies and decisions. Management of an illustrative bank wants the bank to increase its return on total loans. Therefore it encourages its staff to identify and analyze strategies that will help the bank to achieve this objective. The staff is likely to outline at least four strategies:

- Increase the bank's explicit interest rate for many new loans. Competition and legal ceilings, however, will limit the bank's flexibility to raise its explicit rates.
- Repackage some new loans in ways that will increase the bank's total return from them. For example, the bank can request some borrowers to pay explicit fees for loan-related services.
- Reduce loan processing costs and thus increase the bank's profit margin on such loans. One way is to use statistical screening procedures to quickly classify loan applications into three categories: accept, reject, or uncertain, and then have officers and staff focus on the applications that are initially classified as uncertain.
- Examine ways to change the mix of the total loan portfolio, primarily by increasing the proportion of high-return loans. Before changing its loan mix, however, the bank will want to examine the total return from its relationships with various borrowers and the probable changes in costs and risks associated with nominally high-return loans.

By thus having its staff analyze various strategies, senior management positions itself to select a strategy—or combination of strategies—that will likely contribute to higher returns on the loan portfolio.

## Computational Caveats

Computation of a specific rate of return requires careful definition of the net benefits (the numerator) and the commitment (the denominator). To illustrate, a bank's return on capital is basically its annual net income divided by total capital accounts. Yet in some cases the calculation may involve another income measure, such as income before securities gains or losses, or net income before extraordinary items. Also, instead of total capital accounts the calculation may focus on related definitions of capital, such as equity capital.

Some rate-of-return measures involve complex enumeration of the benefits. It is not easy to enumerate the benefits from a bank's major decisions, such as to inaugurate a credit-card system or to open many new offices. (Similarly, it is not easy to enumerate the resource commitments of such decisions.) Still, senior management tries to get good approximations of the flow of benefits from complex strategic decisions.

Computation of expected returns also involves uncertainty about future outcomes. A bank, for example, expects a 9-percent return from a specific loan. There is, however, a possibility that the borrower will not repay the loan as scheduled and that the bank will lose all or part of the amount it lends. The uncertainty of future outcomes is even greater when a bank initiates a major new venture, such as opening a network of foreign branches. Although they work with expected rates of return from such ventures, senior management realizes that diverse future events will affect the future return from the venture, and that the actual return may differ substantially from the expected return. Senior management therefore tries to focus on the risks associated with banking decisions.

## RISK

A risk of decision-making is that the actual outcome(s) will differ from the expected outcome(s). Financial decisions focus on rate-of-return outcomes, and so their risk is that an actual rate of return differs from the expected rate of return. Banks, too, focus on returns and risks; but banks differ from most nonbank financial decision-makers in three principal ways.

### Banking Risks

In most of its loan and investment decisions, a bank cannot expect to obtain a rate of return higher than the contractual interest rate. Yet it faces possible lower returns from any of its loans and investments that *default* in that they fail to meet their contractual obligations to pay timely interest and/or repay the principal. Because its maximum return usually is limited, a bank tries to be confident that the actual return will be close to the contractual (expected) return. It carefully screens and monitors its loans, and it requires contractual agreements that reduce the likelihood of loan default. Thus, by seeking to avoid and control problem loans, a bank tries to be confident that it will obtain the contractual rate of return. Similarly, a bank tries to avoid investments that may default.

As can most people and nonbanking firms, a bank can become illiquid and/or insolvent. A bank uses short-term liabilities to finance most of its portfolio, and most of its deposits are subject to withdrawal on demand or on short notice. Because it knows that it faces irregular funds outflows, a bank holds some short-term assets that it can sell quickly at little, if any, loss. It thus seeks to avoid *illiquidity* by preparing for periods when net cash outflows exceed its expectations. Because it uses fixed liabilities—not stockholders' capital—to finance most of its portfolio, a bank cannot afford to incur many losses (negative returns) that reduce the value of its assets. A bank becomes *insolvent* when the total dollar value of its assets is less than the total dollar amount of its liabilities. Even the hint of a bank's pending insolvency can be a self-fulfilling prophecy. To try to protect themselves, some depositors will withdraw their funds from the bank. These unusual outflows will compound the bank's liquidity problems and will likely hasten its insolvency. People and nonbanking firms also can become illiquid or insolvent, but most of them do not rely on short-term liabilities to the extent that banks do.

Bank deposits, especially demand deposits, are the major part of the nation's money supply. Bank depositors expect to be able to withdraw their funds when needed, and they settle most of their financial transactions by checks. Because bank deposits are important to their owners and to the nation's economic system, legislatures have developed laws and regulations that are intended to reduce the probability of losses (negative returns) by banks and by bank depositors. Banking statutes and regulations try to prevent banks from making risky loans and investments, and bank supervisory agencies monitor bank exposure to risks. The Federal Reserve Act provides for a central bank to reduce the illiquidity risks of individual banks and the banking system, and the Federal Deposit Insurance Corporation provides added protection for bank depositors. Financial decisions by individuals and nonbanking firms also are subject to laws and regulations, but seldom to the same extent as those made by banks.

### Risk Analysis and Control

Risk analysis requires a careful assessment of the possible outcomes from a specific decision or series of decisions. Often such analysis is informal, as when a loan officer tries to predict the chances that a specific borrower will default or when an investment officer tries to predict the chances that a specific municipality will default on its bonds. There are also formal risk-analysis procedures, as when a management-sciences team develops a complex statistical model to predict the probability of default on specific categories of loans or investments. Some large banks use advanced simulation techniques to test the distribution of possible returns from strategic decisions, such as the opening of new offices or the introduction of a costly new service. Simulation techniques enable senior managers to examine the distribution of possible future returns from decisions they may make today.

A bank uses some general procedures to control its risks. It avoids categories of loans and investments for which the probabilities of negative returns are high. It insures against some types of possible losses, and it uses control systems to reduce possible losses due to inept or criminal actions. Two other risk-control procedures, diversification and hedging, are presented later in this chapter.

There are other ways by which a bank can control its risks of negative returns from specific decisions. Before it grants a loan request, a bank usually requires detailed financial information from an applicant. A lending officer reviews this information and then scrutinizes it if he or she has any initial reservations about the request. As part of a loan agreement, a bank usually requires a borrower to inform the bank of subsequent events that could jeopardize the borrower's continued ability to meet the conditions of the loan agreement. A bank often requests a borrower to pledge collateral that can be sold to repay the loan in the event that the borrower defaults. When it lends to corporate customers, a bank often insists on specific covenants whereby, for example, the borrower agrees not to pay unusually high salaries, bonuses, and dividends, and not to merge or sell major assets without the bank's prior consent. Later chapters more fully discuss the diverse risk-control procedures that banks use.

## DIVERSIFICATION

Modern portfolio theory extends its return-risk framework to provide new insights into diversification, a principle that most banks have long applied to management of their loans, investments, and deposits.

No matter how carefully a bank scrutinizes a loan, there is a possibility that the borrower will default and that the bank then will not receive its expected return. While this is true for any one loan, if a bank lends to many different borrowers, then most of the loans will provide their expected returns and only some will not. The weighted average of these individual loan returns accounts for the realized return from the total loan portfolio. By thus diversifying its loan portfolio, a bank can be confident that—despite some individual losses—its actual portfolio return will approximate the expected return. The bank knows that returns from some loans will not meet expectations and that these adverse outcomes are an expected "cost" of its lending activities.

Portfolio theory alerts financial managers to the need to examine interrelationships among components of a portfolio. A bank's loan portfolio may contain loans to many borrowers, so that each borrower accounts for a small percentage of the total loan portfolio. Yet if many of these borrowers are vulnerable to similar economic events, then the portfolio probably has inadequate diversification. (Many large banks have faced major losses arising from large real estate loans made in recent years. These banks lent funds to various borrowers, many of whom were similarly vulnerable to periods of high interest rates and slack demand for real estate properties.) As a counter illustration, a loan portfolio, even if it does not represent many different borrowers, can be well diversified if the borrowers are not highly vulnerable to similar economic events.

Banks try to develop and offer new types of loans. One motivation is the quest for profitable new loans; a second motivation is to diversify further the total loan portfolio.

Banks also diversify their investments portfolios. Most banks hold U.S. Treasury securities, federal agency securities, and bonds issued by various municipalities. When trying to decide whether to buy, sell, or hold a specific bond issue, a bank's investment manager evaluates the bond's expected return, its risk, and its projected relationship to other bonds in the portfolio. Although U.S. Treasury securities may account for a large part of its total bond portfolio, a bank diversifies its other investments among those of many different issuers, so that a default, although unlikely, will not have a major impact on the portfolio return(s). Also, a bank diversifies the maturities of its investments in order to reduce the portfolio's vulnerability to interest-rate fluctuations.

Most banks try to have many different depositors, no one of which accounts for a large part of the bank's total deposits. If it thus can diversify its deposit base, a bank is less vulnerable to a sudden large withdrawal by a major depositor. Also, a bank with a broad deposit base is unlikely to face simultaneous withdrawal requests by many depositors. As some of its depositors withdraw funds, others deposit funds, and so the bank can reasonably predict its net funds flows.

In recent years many banks have developed new sources of deposit and nondeposit funds, thus enabling them further to diversify their sources of funds and the maturity structure of their various liabilities.

The diversification principle pervades banking policies and decisions. Some banking laws specify that a bank cannot legally lend any one borrower an amount that exceeds 10 percent of the bank's capital and surplus. Bank supervisory agencies insist that banks diversify their loan and investment portfolios; and within a bank, senior officials set and review diversification guidelines for assets and liabilities.

Even though it diversifies its loans, investments, and deposits, a bank cannot expect to obtain some unusually high returns to help offset some unusually low returns. Also, because it uses short-term liabilities to finance much of its total portfolio, a bank cannot readily absorb many unusually large losses. Therefore, to screen out and control possible losses, a bank continues to scrutinize and monitor its loans and investments.

## HEDGING

Hedging is a procedure by which a financial manager controls the risk of one transaction by engaging in an offsetting transaction. Banks engage in both specific and general hedging strategies.

Each day large banks serve multinational firms and international travelers who want to buy and sell foreign currencies. On any one day, a bank's international banking department may service its customers by buying large amounts of a specific foreign currency from them, and these transactions may result in the bank's accumulating a large position in the currency. If the value of this currency were to fall sharply, the bank would likely incur a negative return. To control this risk, the bank hedges its position by selling similar amounts of the currency at a fixed price for future delivery. By thus offsetting its transactions, a bank can hedge all or part of a currency position.

Large banks view their role as serving their international clients, and they usually avoid major speculative (unhedged) transactions in foreign currencies. Therefore most banks have internal guidelines as to how much of each foreign currency they will hold in an unhedged position. Failure to adhere to such guidelines has contributed to embarrassingly large foreign-exchange losses by some banks. Although it virtually eliminates the chance of loss, hedging also removes the possibility of unusual gains from having unhedged positions in currencies that rise in value.

In addition to their hedging of foreign-exchange transactions, banks use general hedging techniques in their financial transactions.

American banks historically have hedged their structure of liabilities and assets. They incurred short-term deposit liabilities (primarily demand deposits), and they offset these short-term liabilities by making short-term loans, primarily to commercial, industrial, and agricultural borrowers. By thus basically matching the maturity structure of its assets with that of its liabilities, a bank could try to avoid illiquidity by simply relying on funds from its maturing short-term assets to offset unusual deposit outflows. Because of events that often were beyond the control of individual banks, this hedging strategy at times did not provide adequate liquidity; and so Congress created a central bank (the Federal Reserve System) that would provide additional liquidity to the banking system.

Since the 1950s banks have lengthened the maturities of their liabilities and their assets. They now compete for various types of funds that are not subject to short-term withdrawal, and they hold longer-term business loans, mortgage loans, and municipal securities. Thus a bank can now seek to hedge the average maturities of its diverse liabilities and assets.

Large banks recently have begun to use floating interest rates as a new way to hedge risks of some financial transactions. To illustrate, if it makes a large 5-year loan at a fixed interest rate and yet continuously relies on short-term funds to finance the loan, then a bank incurs an interest-rate risk. The loan, for example, is made at 9 percent, which is the competitive rate for such 5-year loans when the loan agreement is signed. At the same time, the bank is paying interest rates of about 7 percent on its principal sources of short-term funds. The difference between the expected 9 percent interest rate and the 7 percent cost of funds provides the bank with an expected *spread* of 2 percentage points on the transaction.[4] If, however, subsequent interest rates unexpectedly rise, then the bank will continue to receive a 9 percent annual interest return on the loan; but its costs of short-term funds may rise to, say, 11 percent. The bank then will have a negative spread of 2 percentage points on the transaction; and, if it persists, such a negative spread will lower the net return from the loan.

To avoid this interest-rate risk, the bank can try to negotiate a *floating interest rate* whereby it offers to lend funds at an interest rate related to its fluctuating cost of short-term funds. For example, the bank offers to lend the funds for a 5-year period, but at an annual interest rate that is always one percentage point above the bank's cost of funds. Thus, at the time the illustrative loan is made, the initial interest rate is 8 percent; but if the bank's cost of funds goes to 11 percent, then the loan rate will be adjusted to 12 percent.

When it uses floating-interest-rate loans, a bank transfers the risk of fluctuating interest rates from itself to the borrower. Some borrowers accept this risk as a condition of obtaining a loan or in order to obtain a loan having an interest rate that is initially lower than that for a fixed-rate loan. Because it is difficult to calculate precisely a bank's cost of short-term funds, most floating-rate loan agreements link the rate to a standardized rate, such as the prime rate that the bank charges its large, most creditworthy borrowers. To date most floating-rate loans have been made to large corporate borrowers.

---

4. Simplifying somewhat, this spread, or difference, between the bank's expected interest return and its expected percentage cost of funds can be viewed as its expected net return from the transaction. If the expected interest return is fixed but the percentage cost of funds can vary, then the actual spread—or net return—can differ from the expected net return.

A bank also incurs an interest-rate risk if it relies on long-term funds with fixed interest costs to finance short-term loans with fluctuating interest rates. For example, in a period of generally high interest rates, a bank issues 20-year debentures with a fixed interest rate of 9 percent. It also has many short-term lending and investment opportunities that yield 11 percent. If interest rates later fall sharply, unless the bank has the right to redeem its debentures prior to maturity, it will have to continue paying 9 percent interest on them. Meanwhile its interest income from short-term loans and investments drops to, say, 7 percent. Simplifying somewhat, the bank then has a negative spread of 2 percentage points. To avoid this interest-rate risk, a bank can try to issue floating-rate debentures, with an interest rate pegged, for example, to a specific spread above the rate on 90-day Treasury bills. This way the bank transfers at least some of the risk of interest-rate fluctuations from itself to the owners of the floating-rate debentures.

This brief introduction to how banks can hedge with floating-rate instruments necessarily simplifies the issues. A bank does not have a direct correspondence between its specific uses and sources of funds, and it has many complex interrelationships within its total portfolio. To date banks have used floating-rate assets and liabilities for a small part of their total portfolio. Yet bank use of floating-rate instruments will likely increase in coming years—especially if interest rates become historically high and erratic.

## LEVERAGING

Leveraging refers to the relationship whereby a firm's fixed costs act like a lever such that small changes in the firm's revenues can result in magnified changes in its net income.

There are two principal procedures by which a firm can increase its fixed costs as a proportion of its total costs. One procedure is called *financial* (or capital-structure) *leverage,* whereby a firm uses increasing proportions of borrowed funds, having fixed repayment terms, to finance its portfolio of assets. The second procedure is called *operating leverage,* whereby a firm increases the fixed proportion of its total production expenses. It can modify these various "fixed" expenses only in the long run.

Small changes in total operating revenue can have major impact on the net income of a firm that has a high proportion of fixed costs. If its revenues increase and most of its costs are fixed, than a large part of the increased revenues flows through to the firm's net income. Conversely, if its revenues decrease and it must continue to meet its fixed costs, then the firm's net income can decline sharply. Thus, over time, the net income of a highly leveraged firm (one with a high proportion of fixed costs) will be more volatile than that of a firm that uses little leverage and yet faces similar fluctuations of revenues.

Financial managers look to leverage as one means of increasing a firm's net income. As long as investors and lenders confidently expect a firm's revenues to cover its fixed costs, then the firm's stockholders will likely benefit from leverage. Yet leverage also poses hazards for the firm's stockholders. During adverse periods the firm must continue to meet its fixed costs, and so its net income is likely to decline sharply. Even if it continues to be able to service its fixed costs, the firm will likely have less flexibility to make new financial decisions. At an extreme, if its revenues and other resources become inadequate to service its fixed costs, then the firm may go bankrupt, with losses to its stockholders. Even if its stockholders are willing to accept the hazards of leverage, a firm will likely find that potential lenders insist on higher interest rates if asked to finance an increasingly larger proportion of the firm's assets.

Banks lend to diverse firms that use leverage. Loan officers evaluate the cost structure of loan applicants, and they focus on an applicant's ability to service its debts. If a loan officer concludes that an applicant has too much leverage, then he or she is likely to refuse the loan and advise the firm to reduce its fixed costs, for example, by relying less on debt and more on stockholders' equity. Banks also monitor the financial reports of their current borrowers in order to detect and forestall moves toward high leverage. There is seldom a clear answer as to how much leverage is too much for a specific firm. The answer depends on how owners and lenders each assess the potential returns and risks to them from various degrees of leverage.

While they monitor the use of leverage by their borrowers, banks also assess their own use of leverage. Banks are highly leveraged firms. Most banks rely on deposits to finance almost 90 percent of their total assets. To compete for deposits, a bank pays explicit interest on time deposits and implicit interest, in the form of convenience and free services, on demand deposits. Thus in its quest for deposits a bank incurs substantial interest expenses and employee and occupancy expenses, all of which are rather "fixed" in the short run. The bank cannot easily pare these expenses in response to a sudden decline in its operating revenues. Concern about bank leverage underlies the Banking Act of 1933, which prohibits banks from paying interest on demand deposits. Some proponents of the prohibition say that, without it, some banks might commit themselves to paying high interest rates that they then could not pay during periods of economic adversity.

Its depositors are among a bank's major creditors. Yet most depositors do not try to assess the risk (possible negative returns) of leaving funds with various banks. They expect banks to have the financial resources to meet their deposit liabilities. Also, they know that banks are subject to government supervision, and that if a bank's resources become inadequate then the supervisory agencies will try to protect the depositors. Most bank depositors have their funds fully insured (up to $40,000) by a federal agency, the Federal Deposit Insurance Corporation.

While most depositors are unconcerned about bank leverage, bank supervisory agencies seek to prevent bank failures. These agencies commit major resources to trying to evaluate and monitor the use of leverage by individual banks and by the banking system.

Investors and securities analysts also focus on bank use of leverage. During the 1960s and early 1970s many large banks, or their parent holding companies, sought to broaden the market for their securities; they turned to public capital markets as a major source of additional funds. At first many investors probably viewed banks as conservative institutions closely monitored by conservative supervisory agencies. Moreover there had been no major bank failures since the 1930s.

Any euphoria about bank securities was dispelled by some major bank failures in the 1970s and by reports that the federal supervisory agencies listed some other large banks as problem banks. Investors and securities analysts could no longer assume that bank securities were virtually riskless, and so they began to focus more attention on the potential hazards—as well as the potential benefits—of bank use of leverage. Similarly, large uninsured depositors and other bank creditors could no longer assume any bank to be risk free. Many of these depositors and investors now try to learn whether the fixed costs of some banks make them especially vulnerable to adverse economic periods. As a consequence, senior officers of large banks now have to assess how large investors and depositors—as well as supervisory agencies—are likely to respond to a bank's use of various degrees of leverage. These assessments have become key factors in bank capital-planning decisions.

## PORTFOLIO SUPPORT ACTIVITIES

A bank needs capable people to conduct most of its portfolio activities. Bank personnel make ongoing decisions that affect their bank's financial structure and flows. Tellers, for example, initially service customers transactions that are next processed by various employees who are usually unseen by customers. Loan officers and investment officers make and review decisions that affect their bank's portfolio. Some senior employees make daily loan or investment decisions that involve large sums of money.

Most banks know how important their employees are to their financial operations, and they actively seek to recruit and retain capable personnel. Large banks, especially, have recruiting programs and in-house training programs. These banks encourage their employees to extend their skills by attending banking classes and institutes. Each bank has one or more officers whose responsibility it is to establish and review employee compensation programs and working conditions. In recent years unions have tried to organize bank employees, most of whom are not members of a union.

A bank's physical facilities, although they account for a small proportion of total assets, provide ongoing support for the bank's financial transactions. Where permitted, banks have networks of offices that are designed to attract and retain customers. These banks view the locations and decor of their offices as key parts of their deposit-acquisition strategies. Banks also invest in diverse equipment to help their employees process transactions. This equipment ranges from adding machines and coin-counting machines to advanced computer systems. Large banks in particular commit substantial resources to computer systems that can be used to expedite routine transactions and to help bank officers structure and analyze various decisions. To help offset their various computer costs, large banks often provide specialized computer services to smaller banks.

## SUMMARY

This chapter introduces how portfolio concepts apply to banking. Later chapters build on this introductory portfolio perspective.

A report of condition summarizes the composition of a bank's portfolio at a specific time. Each major part of the portfolio is comprised of subparts, and seldom is one part independent of the others. Most banking decisions must explicitly recognize key interrelationships among components of the portfolio.

A consolidated report of income summarizes a bank's principal categories of revenues, expenses, and net income over time. Interest from loans and investments provides most of the revenues, and interest paid on deposits and employee and occupancy costs constitute most of the expenses.

Bankers use information from reports of condition and reports of income, as well as from pro forma reports and sources and uses of funds statements. They thus develop insights into the outcomes of past decisions and—importantly—into possible future outcomes of current decisions.

Modern portfolio theory provides insights into how to evaluate and structure diverse banking decisions. By using return-risk analysis, managers develop a basis for evaluating past outcomes and for choosing from among alternative strategies and decisions.[5] Diversification and hedging are strategies by which a bank can control some of its portfolio risks. A bank can use leveraging to magnify its stockholder returns, but in doing so it will also increase various risks to the firm, its stockholders, and others.

A broad portfolio perspective, although it focuses on financial structures and flows, recognizes the importance of a bank's personnel, facilities, and systems. Senior management focuses on bank goals, policies, and strategies; and various employees, often with extensive mechanical support, implement the strategies and process the funds flows in and out of the bank.

---

5. This chapter introduces risks and risk-control procedures from the viewpoint of a bank's management. Another perspective is that of risks associated with the banking system. See, for example, John J. Mingo, Stephen A. Rhoades, and Benjamin Wolkowitz, "Risk and Its Implications for the Banking System," (A two-part article), *The Magazine of Bank Administration,* February 1976, pp. 52-58, and March 1976, pp. 43-47.

# 4

# A BANK'S SYSTEMS ENVIRONMENT

Modern bankers operate in a complex, rapidly changing environment. Exhibit 4-1 portrays a bank within a series of encompassing systems, and it identifies the principal components of these systems.

## THE COMPETITIVE SYSTEM

Banks compete with nearby banks for accounts of local people, firms, and governmental units. Banks face laws and regulations that restrict the services they can offer, interest they can pay, and, in some cases, prices they can charge. Therefore they emphasize nonprice competitive strategies, such as advertising, convenience, and professional performance.

### NONBANK DEPOSITORY INTERMEDIARIES

Many banking services are similar to those offered by such nonbank depository firms as savings and loan associations, credit unions, and mutual savings banks. With minor exceptions, these intermediaries do not offer checking accounts; but they engage in other deposit and lending services that are directed toward consumers.

*Savings and loan associations* (S&Ls) offer time and savings accounts similar to those offered by banks. On some types of deposits, S&Ls legally can pay higher interest rates than can banks. S&Ls also make many residential mortgage loans. Thus, in these depository and lending activities, most banks compete against nearby S&Ls.

*Credit unions* are mutual nonprofit associations that provide banking types of services for their members, who have to share a common bond, such as their place of work. Credit unions offer their members diverse types of deposit accounts and consumer and home mortgage loans. Many large firms and public agencies sponsor credit unions for their employees, who then have the added convenience of using a payroll deduction plan to make

**EXHIBIT 4-1**

## A Bank's Decision Environment: A Systems Perspective

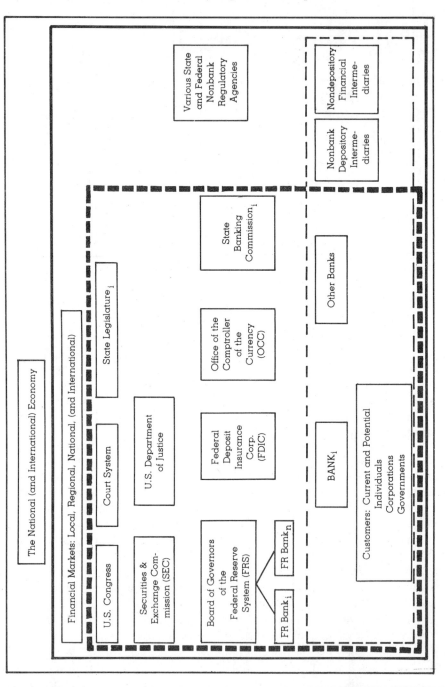

direct deposits and/or loan repayments at their credit union. Compared to banks, many credit unions pay higher interest on deposits and charge lower interest on loans. Therefore, as they assess their local competitive system, bankers must consider current and probable future actions of nearby credit unions.[1]

*Mutual savings banks* offer many banking services, and they are owned by their depositors.[2] Although they are found in about 17 states, mutual savings banks are most prevalent in the northeastern United States. Mutual savings banks offer various time and savings deposits; and they make diverse investments and loans, including consumer loans and home mortgage loans. In contrast to a credit union, a mutual savings bank does not require a depositor or borrower to be a member in order to use its services. Banks located near one or more mutual savings banks must consider them as additional components in the local competitive system.

## NONDEPOSITORY FINANCIAL INTERMEDIARIES

Some nondepository financial intermediaries also offer some types of banking services. These local nondepository intermediaries include small loan companies, insurance agencies, brokerage firms, large retail stores, and, in rural areas, components of the federal farm credit system.

Small loan companies generally cannot accept deposits or investment funds of local customers. They are, however, active lenders to consumers, especially to those who cannot qualify for installment loans from banks. Small loan companies focus on a riskier category of borrowers, and they typically charge higher rates than do banks. Nevertheless, small loan companies and banks do compete for some customers who are eligible to borrow at either institution. Most cities have small loan company offices, and bankers consider these offices when they enumerate their competitors for small loans.

Insurance agents representing diverse life insurance companies operate in most communities that have a bank. Although life insurance companies are not depository institutions, they offer whole-life and endowment policies featuring systematic saving by policy owners. These policies also provide for policy loans, whereby policyholders have contractual rights to borrow from their insurance company, usually at rates of 5 to 6 percent. Policyholders often borrow for special purposes, such as to buy a car or to make a downpayment on a home. In recent years many policyholders have chosen to borrow at 5 or 6 percent and then reinvest the funds in bonds and short-term investments that yield upwards of 8 percent. Life insurance companies, represented by extensive agent networks, thus compete for

1. Peggy Brockschmidt, "Credit Union Growth in Perspective," *Monthly Review* (Federal Reserve Bank of Kansas City), February 1977, pp. 3-13. David S. Kidwell and Richard L. Peterson, "A Close Look at Credit Unions," *The Bankers Magazine,* January-February 1978, pp. 71-80.

2. Technically, the term "bank" applies both to (1) stockholder-owned banks (often called commercial banks) and to (2) mutual savings banks. For brevity and convenience, this book uses "bank" only for those in category (1) and uses "mutual savings bank" for those in category (2).

savings dollars; and they actively lend not only to policy owners but also to mortgage borrowers throughout the country.

Brokerage firms, through their networks of offices, offer various investment services to residents of most large communities. Instead of depositing their long-term funds with a bank or nonbank depository intermediary, people may choose to invest in stocks and bonds. They can do so either directly or indirectly by purchasing shares of investment companies that hold diversified portfolios of stocks and/or bonds. Two special types of investment companies have recently become popular with investors. One type manages portfolios of municipal bonds, the interest payments of which are exempt from federal income taxes. The second type, commonly called money-market mutual funds, manages portfolios of short-term investments such as Treasury bills, commercial paper issued by large well-known corporations, and negotiable certificates of deposit issued by large banks. These money-market mutual funds enable investors to participate in diversified portfolios of high-quality liquid securities that often provide higher returns than do deposits with banks and nonbank depository intermediaries.[3] Retail brokerage firms thus offer various services that compete for savings dollars. They do not actively lend to individuals, except to those who have a margin account.

Most large retail stores provide credit plans for eligible customers. Many people find it more convenient to use a retailer's credit plan than to borrow from a bank or other lending institution.

Agents of the Federal Farm Credit Banks operate in most rural areas. These agents seek and process various agricultural loans for units such as a Federal Land Bank, Federal Intermediate Credit Bank, or Bank for Cooperatives. The units of the Federal Farm Credit Banks have increased their share of total agricultural lending in recent years, while banks in rural areas have accounted for declining proportions of such loans.

## MULTIDIMENSIONAL—AND CHANGING—COMPETITION

A bank operates within a competitive system that is more complex than that outlined in the preceding paragraphs and in Exhibit 4-1. Marketing surveys, regulatory policies, and court decisions all view banks as multiservice firms that face various competitors. Even if it identifies all competitors that offer some similar services, a bank is unlikely to weight them equally when it specifies the competitive system within which it operates. It probably views nearby banks and nonbank depository intermediaries as its principal competitors and therefore develops strategies to compete against them. It assigns less weight to nondepository intermediaries and to distant banks and nonbank depository intermediaries.

A large bank offers extensive services and operates over a wide geographical area. Therefore it operates within a competitive system that

---

3. Paul F. Jessup and Mary Bochnak, "Money Market Mutual Funds: Their Impact on Banks," *The Magazine of Bank Administration,* September 1977, pp. 28-32.

contains many banking and nonbanking firms. Yet even such an expansive competitive system is a logical extension of that summarized in Exhibit 4-1.

A bank operates within a competitive system that changes over time as banks modify their services and as other firms change their services.[4] S&Ls and credit unions, for example, increasingly offer deposit accounts that are similar to checking accounts. Nonbanking firms pioneered nationwide credit card systems, and banks subsequently developed their own regional and national credit card systems.

Laws and regulations shape the competitive system in which banks operate. Banks and nonbank financial intermediaries must receive a charter before they begin operations, and once open they are supervised closely by special governmental agencies. Other financial-service firms, such as small loan companies and insurance companies, have more flexibility to open and move their offices, but they too face some governmental supervision of their operations. Thus a bank operates within a competitive system that itself is part of a broader system that also includes banking laws and regulations.

## THE BANKING SYSTEM

The United States contains about 14,400 banks, any one of which is a small part of the nation's banking system.

The United States has a *dual banking system,* whereby each bank has either a state charter or a federal charter. Once chartered, a bank can apply to switch charters from state to national, or vice versa. Whichever its charter, a bank is subject to some state and federal laws and regulations.[5] Almost all state banks, for example, are also subject to supervision by the Federal Deposit Insurance Corporation and/or by the Federal Reserve System. State banks are subject to such federal legislation as the Bank Merger Act and the Bank Holding Company Act. Similarly, national banks must adhere to certain laws of the state in which they operate. For example, a national bank cannot have branches in a state that prohibits branching by its state-chartered banks. This dual banking system apparently is unique among industrialized nations. Some observers view it as a logical and vital extension of the federal system of government; others view it as a disorganized patchwork of overlapping laws and institutions.

Exhibit 4-1 summarizes the key regulatory and legislative components of America's complex banking system.

---

4. Chris Binger-Saul, "How Much of a Threat Are Nonbanks?: Nonbank Financial Institutions' Services and Performance," *The Magazine of Bank Administration,* July 1978, pp. 32-37 ff. Doris E. Harless, *Nonbank Financial Institutions,* Federal Reserve Bank of Richmond, 1975. Jean M. Lovati, "The Changing Competition Between Commercial Banks and Thrift Institutions for Deposits," *Review* (Federal Reserve Bank of St. Louis), July 1975, pp. 2-8.

5. Emmette S. Redford, "Dual Banking: A Case Study in Federalism," and Frank Wille, "State Banking: A Study in Dual Regulation," both in *Law and Contemporary Problems,* Autumn 1966, pp. 749-773 and pp. 733-748, respectively.

The *Office of the Comptroller of the Currency* (OCC), headed by the Comptroller of the Currency (a public official appointed by the President) is part of the U.S Treasury. The National Bank Act of 1863 created the OCC, which has power to grant federal banking charters and has the responsibility to supervise federally chartered (national) banks. About 4,700 of the nation's banks have federal charters. All have the word "national" in their legal title, although some abbreviate their complete title to terms such as N.A. (National Association). The OCC, headquartered in Washington, D.C., has regional offices throughout the United States.[6]

Each state also has an agency that charters and supervises its state banks. Exhibit 4-1 depicts this situation schematically with the item titled "State Banking Commission$_i$," where i represents any one of the 50 separate state bank supervisory agencies with its specific title and adminis- trative responsibilities.

People wanting to organize a new bank must obtain either a federal charter from the OCC or a state charter from the banking commission of the state in which the proposed bank is to be located. Without a charter from one of these two agencies, a proposed bank cannot begin operations. Once it has a national or state charter, a bank can later apply to switch charters.

The *Federal Reserve System* (FRS) is another major part of the banking system. The Federal Reserve Act of 1913 created the FRS, the key elements of which are the:

- Board of Governors, headquartered in Washington, D.C.
- twelve Federal Reserve Banks, located in various sections of the country
- member banks

The Board of Governors has seven members appointed by the President, and, working through the Federal Open Market Committee, it is responsible for the nation's monetary policy. Each Federal Reserve Bank serves member banks in its designated Federal Reserve District (Exhibit 4-2). All national banks must be members of the FRS, and state banks can choose whether or not to be members. About 1,000 state banks are members, and this includes almost all large state banks. Member banks receive benefits, such as access to the check-clearing facilities of the FRS and the privilege of borrowing from their Federal Reserve Bank. Membership, however, involves a cost because member banks must maintain required reserves (deposits) at their Federal Reserve Bank; and they do not receive any explicit interest on these required reserves. Although it has no chartering powers, the FRS has important bank supervisory powers, especially over state member banks and all bank holding companies.[7]

---

6. For a summary of recent developments in the OCC, see David H. Jones, "Sweeping Changes in the Comptroller's Office," *The Bankers Magazine,* Autumn 1976, pp. 55-61.

7. For more complete information about the FRS, see *The Federal Reserve System: Purposes and Functions,* Board of Governors of the Federal Reserve System, September 1974. Also, Lester V. Chandler, "The Future of the Federal Reserve System: If Any," *Journal of the Midwest Finance Association,* 1976, pp. 1-13.

## EXHIBIT 4-2

## Map of Federal Reserve Districts

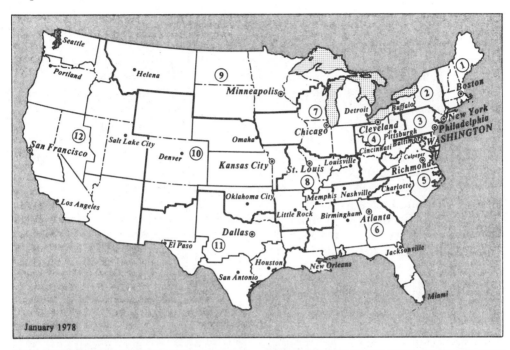

January 1978

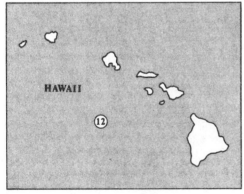

## LEGEND

—— Boundaries of Federal Reserve Districts

—— Boundaries of Federal Reserve Branch
    Territories

⭐ Board of Governors of the Federal
    Reserve System

◉ Federal Reserve Bank Cities

• Federal Reserve Branch Cities

· Federal Reserve Bank Facility

*Source: Federal Reserve Bulletin*

The *Federal Deposit Insurance Corporation* (FDIC) insures deposits in almost all American banks. Currently it insures deposits up to $40,000 per account. The U.S. Congress created the FDIC when it passed the Banking Act of 1933. The FDIC has a three-person Board of Directors. The Comptroller of the Currency is always one of the directors, and the President of the United States appoints the other two.

The FDIC technically supervises all banks it insures. In practice it relies primarily on the OCC to supervise national banks and on the FRS to supervise its state member banks. (All banks in these two categories are insured by the FDIC.) This coordination of federal bank supervision allows the FDIC to focus its supervisory resources on state nonmember banks, almost all of which choose to be insured by the FDIC. In addition to its insuring and supervisory functions, the FDIC has the responsibility to liquidate insured banks that fail. It does not have chartering powers. The FDIC has headquarters in Washington, D.C., and regional offices throughout the United States.

Exhibit 4-3 summarizes how American banks are often categorized according to their principal federal bank supervisory agency. The four categories are:

- national
- state member
- insured nonmember (state)
- noninsured (state)

In addition to their federal supervision, state member and insured nonmember banks are also subject to supervision by the state in which they are located—as are any noninsured state banks.

Each state has extensive banking statutes that apply to bank: chartering, supervision, reporting, branching, ownership, and operations. Few people want to be experts in these extensive laws that vary among states. Yet bankers and students of banking need a general understanding of current and probable future banking laws, especially those of states in which they are most interested. Officials of state banks make frequent decisions in the context of specific state banking laws. Officials of national banks also are alert to current or probable future banking laws of states in which their banks operate. They know that some state laws can directly affect their operations (such as branching) and that state laws can help or handicap state banks against which they compete.

Federal banking statutes also are a key element of the banking system. These laws provide for national banks, and they create the current structure of federal bank supervisory agencies. Congress has passed and amended other milestone banking legislation, such as the Banking Act of 1933, the Bank Merger Act, and the Bank Holding Company Act. Later chapters summarize how these federal laws apply to banking strategies and decisions.

The court system at times has to adjudicate federal and state banking laws. Several proposed bank mergers have resulted in landmark decisions by

**EXHIBIT 4-3**

**Banks Categorized by Principal
Federal Bank Supervisory Agency**

| Category of Banks | Principal Federal Bank Supervisory Agency | Number of Banks (Midyear 1978) | Percent of Total Bank Deposits (Midyear 1978) |
|---|---|---|---|
| National[1] | Office of the Comptroller of the Currency (OCC) | 4,616 | 55 |
| State Member[2] | Federal Reserve System (FRS) | 1,005 | 17 |
| Insured Non-member | Federal Deposit Insurance Corporation (FDIC) | 8,760 | 26 |
| Noninsured[3] | None | 317 | 2 |
| Total | | 14,698 | 100 |

[1] All national banks are members of the FRS and are insured by the FDIC.
[2] All state member banks are insured by the FDIC.
[3] All noninsured banks are state chartered. They are typically small in deposit size, and they are located in about 28 states. Some noninsured banks are associated with foreign banking organizations.
*Source:* Computed from *Federal Reserve Bulletin*, August 1979, p. A17.

the U.S. Supreme Court. Courts also have had to interpret how various legislation defines branch banking and determine the extent to which national banks must adhere to specific state laws.

The U.S. *Department of Justice* has specific responsibilities to review proposed bank mergers and acquisitions by bank holding companies. Also, bankers, like other businesspeople, try to avoid actions that the Justice Department might view as anticompetitive.

Bankers are aware that they make decisions in a context of a complex banking system (like that summarized in Exhibit 4-1). They try to keep informed about principal changes in this system. At times they read about proposals to restructure the three federal bank supervisory agencies, either by reassigning various powers and responsibilities among the agencies or by consolidating the agencies into one unit.[8] Similarly, they learn about such proposals as whether to strengthen or dismantle the dual banking system, and whether to implement a policy of interstate banking. If such proposed changes occur, they will alter substantially the decision environment in which each bank operates.

## THE FINANCIAL SYSTEM

The banking system is embedded in a broader financial system that also includes intermediaries and markets. Banks, S&Ls, credit unions, and mutual savings banks accept deposits and in turn lend or invest these funds.

---

8. For a summary of some recent proposals, see Lucille S. Mayne, "Restructuring the Federal Bank Regulatory System," *The Bankers Magazine*, September-October 1978, pp. 70-74.

They thus channel funds from depositors to borrowers, and so serve as financial intermediaries.

## FINANCIAL MARKETS

Many financial transactions do not involve intermediation. Instead, they occur directly between lenders and borrowers, as, for example, when investors buy bonds issued by the U.S. Treasury or by large corporations. Other transactions occur daily among investors who directly buy and sell common stocks that represent corporate ownership. These transactions occur in financial markets that also constitute a major part of the nation's financial system.

There are several convenient ways to classify financial markets. One classification is:

- money markets
- capital markets
  debt
  equity

*Money markets* involve transactions in debt instruments—usually of high-quality borrowers—that mature within one year. *Capital markets* involve transactions in debt or equity instruments having maturities beyond one year or, as with common stock, having no specified maturity. A second useful classification is:

- local
- regional
- national
- international

Although they escape sharp delineations, these four geographical categories provide additional insights into financial markets.

## BANKS AND FINANCIAL MARKETS

Both as owners and issuers of securities, banks make frequent decisions in the context of complex financial markets. Exhibit 4-4 summarizes key areas in which banks thus participate.

Banks invest in the following principal categories of money-market instruments:

- U.S. Treasury securities
- federal agency securities
- commercial paper
- negotiable certificates of deposit (CDs)

## EXHIBIT 4-4

### Bank Participation in Domestic Financial Markets: A Preview

| Instruments | Banks as: Investors | Banks as: Issuers |
|---|---|---|
| Money-market Instruments | | |
| U.S. Treasury securities | Yes | ..... |
| Federal agency securities | Yes | ..... |
| Commercial paper | Yes | ..... |
| Negotiable certificates of deposit (CDs) | Yes | Yes |
| Longer-term Debt Instruments | | |
| U.S. Treasury securities | Yes | ..... |
| Federal agency securities | Yes | ..... |
| Municipal bonds | Yes[1] | ..... |
| Corporate debentures | No | Yes[3] |
| Common Stock | No[2] | Yes[3] |

[1] Municipal obligations that will soon mature and that are large issues by major issuers can be classified as money-market instruments. Because most municipal obligations do not meet these criteria, this Exhibit does not include this category among its list of major money-market instruments.

[2] Primarily because of legal and regulatory restrictions, banks seldom invest directly in common stock. Bank trust departments, however, frequently invest in common stocks and corporate debentures on behalf of clients. In the aggregate, bank trust departments are major investors in American stock markets.

[3] All banks have common stock outstanding, and many issue debentures. A bank's securities are often owned, all or in part, by a parent holding company that in turn issues common stock, debentures, and in some cases commercial paper, that trade in national or regional financial markets.

A common feature of these money-market instruments is that they mature within one year and often within even shorter periods.

There is a nationwide market for the first three instruments, which are debt obligations of prime federal or corporate borrowers. *Federal agency securities* are those, for example, of the Federal Farm Credit Banks and the Federal National Mortgage Association. Unlike U.S. Treasury securities, debt instruments of federal agencies are not backed by the full faith and taxing power of the federal government. Most investors, however, doubt that the U.S. Congress will allow any federal agency to default on its debt.

Many banks invest in *negotiable certificates of deposit* (CDs), which are large-denomination, time-deposit liabilities of the nation's largest banks. There is typically a national market for negotiable CDs issued by large banks in California, Illinois, and New York. Investors and dealers in these CDs are located throughout the country. In contrast, large banks in some other states also issue negotiable CDs, but the market for these CDs is usually more regional than national.

Banks also invest in long-term debt instruments issued by: the federal government, its agencies, state and local governments, and their agencies.

Issues of the U.S. Treasury and federal agencies trade in national markets. Municipal bonds, depending primarily on the size of the issuer and of the specific issue, trade in national, regional, or local markets. For example, large issues of a major state trade in the national market, while, in contrast, the long-term bonds of a public school district in a small city trade infrequently in a local or possibly regional market. Banks seldom purchase long-term corporate bonds or debentures. Some banks and/or their parent holding companies do, however, issue subordinated debentures that—depending primarily on the size of the issuer—trade in national, regional, or local financial markets.

Because of laws and regulations, banks own virtually no common stock. All banks have common stock outstanding that is owned either by investors or by parent holding companies, the shares of which are owned by investors. There is a national—in some cases, international—market for stock of America's largest banks and bank holding companies. Shares of some large banking organizations are listed on foreign stock exchanges as well as on the New York Stock Exchange. Others are actively traded in the national over-the-counter (OTC) market. Shares of smaller regional and local banking organizations are bought and sold in local OTC markets, and shares of the nation's small banks usually are closely held and inactively traded.

Although banks do not directly own much common stock, bank trust departments invest in common stocks on behalf of diverse clients. For many years there was little public information about the investment policies and practices of bank trust departments. Because of recent special studies and new reporting requirements, outsiders now can learn more about the role of bank trust departments in the nation's financial markets.

Exhibit 4-4 summarizes the principal investment instruments by which banks participate in financial markets. Most of these investments involve impersonal transactions, and banks are only one major category of participants. In contrast, most bank loans involve long-run, personalized relationships between banks and their borrowers. With minor exceptions, there are no active markets in which banks buy and sell loans. Federal funds transactions contain elements of both money-market investments and loan transactions. Federal funds transactions are for short periods, and they take place in active regional and national markets. Banks are the principal participants in federal funds transactions.

Some banks also participate in financial markets as dealers and underwriters. These dealer banks maintain inventories of government securities in which they make markets. Many other banks act as agents for their customers who want to buy or sell government securities. Most large banks also underwrite and deal in municipal securities—primarily *general obligation* (GO) *bonds,* for which payments of principal and interest are backed by the full faith and taxing power of the issuer. (GO bonds contrast to revenue bonds that are backed only by some assigned revenues, for example from a tollroad or a municipal transportation system.) Either individually or in syndicates these banks bid for new municipal issues that they then hold for investment or for resale to other investors. The Banking Act of 1933 prohibits banks from underwriting or dealing in most corporate securities, and it prohibits them from having affiliates that engage in these investment-banking activities.

American banks traditionally have participated only in domestic financial markets. Starting in the 1960s, a rapidly growing number of American banks began to participate in financial markets of foreign countries and in international capital markets that straddle various countries. The explosive growth of the Eurodollar market is a prime example. This market, based primarily in London, straddles national boundaries. By the late 1960s many large American banks actively used the Eurodollar market as a source of funds and as a major factor in their reserve-management decisions.

Banks have long provided detailed operating information to their principal bank regulatory agencies. As they have become more active participants in financial markets, banks have encountered increasing demands for fuller public disclosure of their activities. These demands were triggered as banks and bank holding companies became issuers of debentures and common stock during the 1960s. Institutions and individuals invested in these securities, many of which were actively bought and sold in public markets.

The *Securities and Exchange Commission* (SEC) is the federal agency that supervises securities markets in the United States. Increasingly, it insists that banking organizations provide full, fair, and timely public disclosure of corporate information—as it also requires of nonbanking corporations that have publicly traded securities and at least 300 stockholders. The federal banking agencies also have moved toward fuller public disclosure of information about banks they supervise. These new disclosure standards and sources of banking information can be useful to bankers, securities analysts, investors, and others who want to examine the performance of specific banks or the banking system. Many large banking organizations thus find themselves increasingly accountable to participants in markets in which their securities are bought and sold.

## THE SOCIOECONOMIC SYSTEM

The banking and financial systems are parts of a socioeconomic system that reflects public goals and values.

The Employment Act of 1946 is a keystone of America's socioeconomic system. This legislation, enacted by elected officials, presumably reflects a consensus of public values. The Act declares maximum employment, production, and purchasing power to be national economic goals. These goals are not precisely defined; they may be incomplete; and they may at times conflict with one another. Despite such potential weaknesses, these legislated goals provide the basis for national economic policy.

## MONETARY POLICY AND PROCEDURES

The Employment Act provides guidelines to the Federal Reserve System (FRS), which conducts monetary policy by using three principal instruments:

- reserve requirements
- discount window
- open-market operations

Bank decisions are sensitive to each of these instruments.

Because they earn no explicit interest on required reserves, many state banks decide not to become members of the FRS. National banks at times convert to state charters in order to have the option to withdraw from membership. Member banks, subject to required reserves of the FRS, often seek nondeposit sources of funds, such as federal funds, that are not subject to required reserves.

Member banks have the privilege of borrowing from the discount window of their Federal Reserve Bank. To decide whether to borrow and, if so, how much to borrow, banks consider the current and probable future levels of the discount rate charged by the Federal Reserve Bank. Also, they assess nonrate factors, such as the perceived administration of the discount window. Their Federal Reserve Bank at times publicly posts a discount rate, but it discreetly informs member banks that it expects them not to borrow at the discount window except for "suitable" reasons.

Almost daily the Manager of the System Open Market Account, on behalf of the FRS, conducts open-market operations, usually by buying or selling U.S. Treasury securities. Open-market operations affect the financial markets in which banks participate as investors, dealers, and/or agents. Banks make investment decisions for themselves and their clients based, at least in part, on their assessments and expectations about open-market operations by the FRS.

During the late 1960s and early 1970s, the FRS experimented with interest rate ceilings as a new instrument of monetary policy. Many large banks were aggressively offering negotiable certificates of deposit (CDs) in order to raise funds to lend to key clients. To try to limit the growth of such loans, the FRS refused to raise the ceiling rates that banks could pay, even though rates on other money-market instruments began to exceed those offered on CDs. As their CD rates became less competitive with money-market alternatives, banks found it difficult to sell new CDs; and many owners of CDs refused to renew them as they matured. Faced with major deposit runoffs during periods of strong loan demand, many large banks sought other sources of funds not subject to interest rate ceilings. They quickly found federal funds, Eurodollars, and, temporarily, nondeposit promissory notes. In retrospect, because of such alternate sources of funds, interest rate ceilings proved to be a troublesome—but not notably effective—instrument of monetary policy.

Monetary policy, probably unevenly and with varying delays, affects member banks, nonmember banks, and other participants in financial markets. On grounds of economic efficiency and equity there are periodic proposals to subject all banks to reserve requirements as set by the FRS and to extend required reserves to nonbank depository intermediaries that offer deposit services similar to those of banks. Such proposals, if implemented, will affect current competitive relationships among banks and other financial intermediaries.

## FISCAL POLICY AND PROCEDURES

The goals of the Employment Act also apply to government fiscal policy, which includes taxation and management of the public debt.

Diverse tax laws affect many bank decisions. Banks are major investors in municipal securities, the interest from which is exempt from federal income taxes. Large banking organizations have astute tax planners who outline for management the probable tax consequences of decisions in areas such as holding company structure, leasing, and international operations.

The U.S. Treasury, as part of its tax-collection and debt-management procedures, has a *Treasury Tax & Loan* (TT&L) *account* at almost all banks. Taxpayers can pay certain taxes—such as income taxes withheld for employees and corporate income taxes—directly to their bank, which then debits the taxpayer's account and credits the TT&L account. Subscriptions to some issues of U.S. Treasury securities also are eligible for direct deposit in TT&L accounts and remain there until subsequently transferred to the Treasury's account at Federal Reserve Banks. Treasury and banking spokespersons state that use of TT&L accounts is less disruptive than would be the case if major tax payments and subscriptions to all new Treasury issues were debited by transfers from bank accounts and immediately credited to the Treasury's account at the Federal Reserve Banks.

## OTHER PUBLIC POLICIES

Antitrust policy is another key element of the socioeconomic system. The United States has a tradition of public distrust of concentrated economic power—especially concentrated financial power. The U.S. Congress, reflecting public values, passed the Sherman Act (1890) and the Clayton Act (1914), each of which applies generally to American business. As banks became subject to more federal laws and regulations, many officials believed that banks should be subject to special standards consistent with banking's special public role and regulated status. A result was federal legislation, the Bank Merger Act of 1960. A rapid series of major bank mergers followed the Act. In a landmark action the U.S. Department of Justice sued to prevent a proposed merger between two large Philadelphia banks. Instead of relying only on the Bank Merger Act, the Justice Department also invoked the Clayton Act. In an historic decision, the Supreme Court upheld the Justice Department's contention that general antitrust laws apply to banks. Subsequently the Bank Merger Act was amended, but it continues to be part of the mainstream of American antitrust policy.

Consumerism and individual rights have become more vocal features of the socioeconomic system. Banks and other businesses must comply with equal opportunity laws and affirmative action policies. Similarly, employee working conditions undergo increased federal and state scrutiny as part of the Occupational Safety and Health Act (OSHA), passed by Congress in 1970. Recent truth-in-lending types of laws directly affect banks and other financial intermediaries. Because of growing public discussion of individual privacy, banks and other financial firms have had to reexamine traditional procedures used to gather and release credit information about people and firms.

As the American economy has become more integrated with other national economies, public policy has set new guidelines for multinational firms. To illustrate, federal legislation provides the Commerce Department, the U.S. Treasury, and the FRS with various powers to monitor and control various overseas financial activities of American firms, including the large banks.

## SUMMARY

This chapter introduces the principal external systems within which a bank operates. Exhibit 4-1 schematically summarizes these systems, each of which is complex and changing over time. Bankers and students of banking benefit from a basic understanding of these systems—especially as they relate to specific banking strategies and decisions.

Each bank operates within a competitive system that includes diverse financial firms that commit substantial resources to redesign and extend their depository and lending services. Bankers are alert to the development of "banking" services—such as check-like accounts—by other intermediaries. These competitive developments affect strategic decisions by individual banks and the banking industry, and they force review of traditional concepts of "banking" services and "banking" markets.

The banking system is a complex, changing network of banks, bank supervisory agencies, and banking laws. A bank operates with either a federal or state charter, and this basic choice is a keystone of the dual banking system. At the federal level, the principal bank supervisory agencies are the: Office of the Comptroller of the Currency, Federal Reserve System, and Federal Deposit Insurance Corporation. Each state also has an agency that supervises its state-chartered banks. Detailed federal and state statutes affect daily banking operations; and they affect banking strategies in areas such as branching, mergers, and holding companies. This legislative maze leads to lengthy court cases, in which the U.S. Department of Justice often is a participant.

A bank and the banking system are embedded in a broader financial system that contains diverse financial markets and participants. Its investment transactions—for example in U.S. Treasury securities and municipal bonds—link a bank to various components of the money and capital markets. Banks also issue instruments, such as negotiable CDs and common stock, that are bought and sold in financial markets. The Securities and Exchange Commission increasingly insists that large banks meet the public-reporting standards that apply to publicly traded nonbanking corporations. Although boundaries are imprecise, bankers and public officials often find it useful to classify financial markets geographically, ranging from local to international markets. Bankers can use this geographical perspective to help them develop market-penetration strategies.

A bank is a profit-oriented firm operating within a socioeconomic system that reflects a consensus of public goals and values. The Employment Act of 1946 and various tax and antitrust laws reflect public policies that affect banks and most other American businesses. Various legislatures recently have passed laws designed to protect the rights of consumers, employees, and members of minority groups, Most of these public laws apply to banks.

As they examine how their bank fits into broader systems, modern bankers develop perspectives that they can then apply to the design and implementation of management systems and strategies.

# 5
# BANK DECISION SYSTEMS

Senior officials misallocate their time if they make many routine decisions within their firm. They can, however, set policies that identify decisions to be classified as "routine," that provide guidance to personnel making those decisions, and that establish procedures to monitor and review the decisions. By thus delegating many routine decisions, senior officials can allocate more of their time to strategic decisions that involve large long-run commitments of bank resources.

This chapter examines how senior banking officials can structure decision processes within their firm. It focuses on:

- developing management decision perspectives
- structuring for bank decisions
- setting bank objectives
- evaluating bank performance

Subsequent chapters demonstrate that most banking decisions fit into this systematic framework.

## MANAGEMENT DECISION PERSPECTIVES

Not only is a bank embedded in external systems, it is itself an organization comprised of various interrelated components. To manage effectively, the senior officers need systematic views of their firm's external environment and its internal components.[1]

Exhibit 5-1 schematically summarizes the multiple perspectives useful to senior management. These officials direct the activities of their bank over time, but they do not administer the detailed daily operations of various

---

1. Paul F. Jessup, "A Systems Approach to Bank Management," *The Bankers Magazine*, Winter 1971, pp. 93-101.

**EXHIBIT 5-1**

**Management Decision Perspectives**

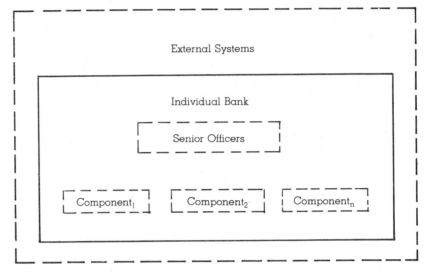

*Note*: Chapter 4 summarizes various external systems.

components within the bank. Senior officers, for example, set and review loan policies and investment policies. They do not, however, monitor each loan decision made by a lending officer nor do they monitor each transaction made by the investment department.

A bank's organization chart summarizes the firm's major components. Most large banks have such divisions as loans, investments, operations, and trust. Each principal component in turn has subcomponents. A large bank's loan division, for example, has subdivisions that specialize in loans categorized by geographical region and/or by types of borrowers. Not all large banks have similar organization charts, and many small and medium-sized banks have implicit organization charts. At any time an organization chart summarizes the formal structural components and interrelationships among these components. Over time the senior officials restructure the organization to provide for growth and change.

Senior officers evaluate past and possible future activities of their bank and its components in the context of the bank's external systems. For example, how does the deposit growth of their bank compare to that of nearby banks? How does the recent profit performance of their bank compare to that of other similar banks? While such comparisons of past outcomes provide insights, senior officials especially seek to understand probable future developments. If, for example, they expect the banking system to phase out paper checks and replace them with electronic payments transactions, then senior officials will focus on strategies appropriate for this futuristic banking system. Knowing that their industry is sensitive to

**EXHIBIT 5-2**

**Planning and Control Systems:
A Model Framework**

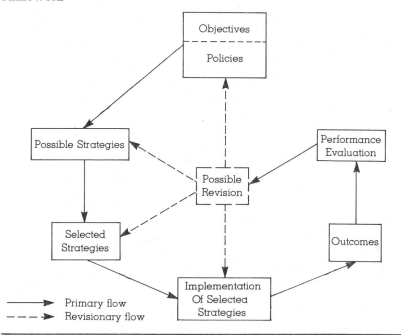

economic and social policies, bankers seek to understand—and at times to influence—the changing socioeconomic system within which their firms operate.

## ORGANIZATIONAL DECISION SYSTEMS

Exhibit 5-2 schematically summarizes the decision process within most organizations. This framework applies to a total banking organization, such as a large bank or a bank holding company, and to its principal components, such as departments responsible for check processing, loans, or international banking. The framework also can be applied to specific units or projects within a bank.

Senior management at times reviews a bank's *objectives* as specified, either formally or informally, by the bank's organizers and preceding managers. A bank often has a statement that summarizes its general objectives in such terms as profitability, safety, and service. Also, it usually has specific objectives for the bank and its component units. Illustrative measurable objectives include rates of return, growth rates, and shares of markets. In some banks the managers, and often the employees, of component units provide senior management and its staff with a set of objectives by which they agree their units will be evaluated.

Senior officials and their staff regularly reexamine the bank's *policies,* which are long-term guidelines closely associated with objectives. A large regional bank, for example, has long had a policy to emphasize services for large business firms in its area. It thus views itself primarily as a *wholesale* bank, with the financial and managerial resources necessary to provide corporate clients with large specialized loans, advanced cash-management systems, multinational banking expertise, and pension fund management. This wholesale bank views its principal competitors as major money-center banks and other large banks in its region.

Another large bank has had a long-standing policy of having foreign correspondent banks service many of the overseas banking needs of its corporate customers. Over time, however, competing banks develop new services for multinational firms. Therefore the bank's senior officials at times have to reexamine the policy of relying on foreign correspondent banks rather than opening foreign branches that can directly service its customers.

Senior management similarly reviews major portfolio policies, such as maximum amounts and types of loans, amounts and types of capital, and use of nondeposit funds. Within the context of these general policies, junior managers develop and review the policies of their units or projects.

Bank managers and staff specialists continually seek to *identify and evaluate possible strategies* by which to implement bank objectives and policies. They strive to identify banking needs of current and potential customers, and they keep informed about innovative services offered by, and procedures used by, other banks and nonbank financial intermediaries.

Assume that a large wholesale bank, which previously focused on serving corporate customers, reexamines its policy and decides to increase its *retail* business of servicing individual customers. Its officers and staff then identify various possible strategies by which to increase their bank's retail business. These possible strategies include:

- acquiring through merger one or more retail-oriented banks
- establishing a network of new branches to attract new retail customers
- redirecting the bank's marketing efforts toward retail customers
- committing major resources to a new consumer-oriented credit-card system
- developing networks of electronic banking terminals to service retail transactions

Combinations of these illustrative strategies are also possible.

Because of legal barriers and resource limitations, not all these possible strategies are equally feasible—at least in the short run. If it already accounts for a large share of bank deposits within its area, then the bank is unlikely to receive regulatory approval to acquire other banks in the area. State laws may prevent the opening of any branches or restrict the locations at which the bank can open branches. Even if branching is legally feasible, the bank's financial and personnel resources will limit the rate at which the bank can open and staff new retail branches. Legal and resource impediments similarly can limit rapid expansion via new credit cards or electronic banking facilities.

Bank officials analyze the feasibility of possible strategies and then evaluate the expected returns and risks of feasible strategies. Modern computer systems and management science techniques facilitate such analyses of alternate strategies. Senior management uses these analyses, along with other discussions and insights, to *select strategies* judged most effective for achieving the bank's objectives and policies.

Senior officials usually do not *implement selected strategies*. They delegate the implementation to managers of units within the bank. Because they delegate operating authority yet retain responsibility, the senior officials have to monitor and evaluate decisions by subordinates. They focus on the *outcomes* as systematically recorded by the bank's operating units. Measurable outcomes include revenues, costs, error rates, and employee absenteeism and turnover. Senior officials and their staff can then compare these actual outcomes against the objectives set for the relevant operating unit and the bank.

*Performance evaluation* provides the control mechanism for the management system outlined in Exhibit 5-2. Senior officials and their staff try to explain major differences between expected and realized performance. In cases where they conclude that the expected performance had been unrealistic, they will *revise* the future performance objectives of the unit and/or revise the policies or strategies that most directly affect the unit's performance. In cases where they conclude that subordinate managers incompetently implemented selected strategies, senior management will likely revise the authority and compensation of such managers. At the extreme, they will authorize reorganization of poorly performing units and removal of their officers.

External and internal constraints apply to all the components of the management system outlined in Exhibit 5-2. Laws, regulations, and competition limit the feasible range of most bank objectives, policies, strategies, and operations. Merger, branching, and holding company laws constrain a bank's objectives concerning size, rate of expansion, and form of expansion. Laws and regulations similarly constrain the purposes, amounts, and repayment terms of bank loans; and they limit the types and maturities of securities that banks can own. In addition to such external constraints, senior officials often specify internal constraints that reflect, for example, the risk aversion of the bank's principal stockholders. Subsequent chapters build in detail on this initial perspective of constrained management decision making.

Senior officials of most large banks focus on the planning and control components of the management system outlined in Exhibit 5-2.[2] The

---

2. A related view of organizational decision systems is presented by Herbert E. Johnson, "Comprehensive Corporate Planning for Commercial Banks," *The Magazine of Bank Administration*, January 1978, pp. 20-25.

principal *planning* components involve the bank's objectives, policies, and major strategies. The principal *control* components are performance evaluation and possible revision of plans.

## SETTING BANK OBJECTIVES

Each bank and bank holding company has objectives by which senior officials direct the firm and evaluate its performance. Large and medium-sized banks often have written statements of organizational objectives. Small banks also have objectives, but often these are informally structured in the minds of owner-managers.

Managers of a bank's component units set objectives by which to evaluate the performance and personnel of their units. They know that senior management also will evaluate them based on how well their units perform compared to their stated objectives.

### PROFIT AND VALUATION OBJECTIVES

American banks are part of an economic system that expects private firms to focus on long-run profits. Most banks therefore focus on profitability as a principal corporate objective, but they recognize that profitability is subject to various interpretations and constraints.

A bank that seeks to *maximize long-run profits* will avoid actions that temporarily increase short-run profits but jeopardize its long-run existence or its long-run profits. Its management avoids venturesome decisions that can result in *either* unusually high short-run profits *or* bankruptcy. (This objective does not preclude some—probably diversified—venturesome decisions.) Its management sets policies that are intended to build and maintain long-run profitable relationships with customers. These policies permit occasional decisions that are known to be unprofitable or marginally profitable in the short run, but that, by accommodating valued customers, are expected to contribute to long-run profits.

Although it provides a useful perspective for management policies and decisions, a goal of long-run profit maximization is not readily measurable. Therefore banks often specify profit goals for a coming time period such as three years or five years. To illustrate, after they have reviewed projections about the general economy and their bank's principal markets, a bank's senior officials adopt a profit plan the goal of which is to steadily increase annual profits by 10 percent a year over the coming five years. Although it is not a long-run maximizing process, this five-year plan sets measurable objectives for the bank and provides guidelines for profit planning by component units within the bank. In addition to using the profit plan within the organization, senior management may announce the profit objectives to shareholders and the press.

A bank can set *profitability* (rate-of-return) objectives, such as its return on total assets and return on equity capital. For example, a bank's senior officials decide that their bank should have among its objectives that returns on assets and on equity capital be among the top 50 percent of all banks that are similar in asset size. If its total assets are $75 million, then the bank's return objectives will be to exceed the following percentages:[3]

|  | *Rate-of-Return (1977)* |
|---|---|
| on average assets | 1.01 |
| on average equity capital | 13.24 |

Unless it believes the near future will differ substantially from the recent past, then a bank can base its target returns on recent realized returns for similar banks, as illustrated above. In another case, a new team of senior officers concludes that its bank's recent returns are well below average, and so it sets as a specific objective to improve the returns by having them approach or exceed the average, within, say, three years.

Bank stockholders are interested in long-run profit maximization, profit planning, and rate-of-return measures—but principally as these items affect market valuation of their shares. The stockholders focus on expected returns and risks of their bank stock, and they compare these expectations to those for other investment opportunities. Bank stockholders expect their returns to consist partly of dividends and partly of price changes of their stock. They also assess various risks associated with their returns from a stock, such as the probability of total loss and the expected volatility of returns from the stock. Other factors also enter the market valuation of a firm's stock.[4]

Officials of a large, publicly traded bank have little control over how investors value their firm, but they try to understand investor expectations about the firm. For example, what do investors apparently expect to be the bank's profit growth, variability of profits, dividend payout, and capital structure? By trying to understand these market expectations, management has some additional guidance as it sets and reviews bank objectives and policies.

## PROFIT-RELATED OBJECTIVES AND CONSTRAINTS

Some banks state that, in addition to profit objectives, their objectives include such items as safety, service, and growth. These items seldom are primary objectives; instead they relate to, and often constrain, the profit objective(s).

---

3. The ratios are (1) net income to average assets and (2) net income to average equity capital. (The average refers to the use of an average figure from three of a bank's balance sheets that span a year.) The return ratios are unweighted averages of individual bank ratios for insured commercial banks with total assets within the range of $25.0-99.9 million. For all banks, regardless of asset size, the respective ratios are 0.96 and 12.01. *Bank Operating Statistics: 1977* (Federal Deposit Insurance Corporation), National Totals, Table D.

4. Financial theory does not fully specify—at least operationally—the valuation of the firm. It hypothesizes that a key element in the valuation process is the discounted stream of expected future profits (or dividends) from the firm. Therefore the objective of maximizing the current wealth (stock price) of the firm's owners is closely linked to management decisions that affect the expected magnitude and timing of future profits (or dividends).

## Safety

Managers of profit-oriented firms try to avoid failure, an outcome that is inconsistent with long-run profitability. They therefore try to set policies and make decisions that will contribute to long-run profitability while keeping low the probability of failure. The financial officers carefully plan funds flows, and they evaluate probable returns and risks associated with leveraging and with rapid expansion into new areas.

Bankers similarly have strong incentives to manage their firms so that they are safe for their creditors (mostly depositors) and are perceived to be safe by current and potential depositors. Even without elaborate regulation, banks would seek to diversify their deposits, maintain what they judge to be adequate short-term assets to meet withdrawals, try to hold a diversified portfolio of low-risk investments and loans, and have an adequate capital base provided by stockholders. Despite such cautious policies, at times some banks will fail, either because of errors in the implementation of the policies and/or because of economic conditions beyond their control.

A bank can set safety of its depositors as a primary objective, but this will lead to policies that limit its profitability. This bank, toward an extreme, will: accept only time deposits that are not legally withdrawable on demand; hold an extra margin of short-term assets to meet even extremely unlikely deposit withdrawals; invest primarily in short-term U.S. Treasury securities and possibly make some federally insured loans; and have equity capital that substantially exceeds that of banks its size and even that expected by its supervisory agencies. A bank that follows these conservative policies is unlikely to rank high in profitability, community service, or growth.

## Service

Banks provide diverse services to the public, but they develop and price their services in ways that likely will contribute to their long-run profit objectives. When they evaluate which services to offer and what prices to charge, banks try to assess current and probable future demand for the services and current and probable future actions by competing banks and other firms. If it blatantly fails to provide a variety of competitively priced services, then a bank fosters local-market conditions that encourage entry by a newly organized bank or a new branch of a competing bank. Current competition and the threat of new competition thus stimulate most profit-oriented banks to provide their customers and communities with an appropriate variety of competitively priced banking services.

Some banks direct their services toward specialized categories of customers. Historically some local unions organized banks that would service primarily union members. Recently some groups have organized banks that would service primarily such minority groups as Blacks, Indians, and professional women. These organizers probably judge that established banks inadequately service these specific groups and that specialized banks can profitably fill this void. Yet, to obtain regulatory permission to begin a new specialized bank, these organizers must demonstrate not only a need for but also the expected profitability of their proposed bank.

### Growth

Most organizations, banks included, emphasize growth. Financial theory assumes that firms emphasize long-run growth of profits and that their shareholders focus on how profit growth is likely to be translated into growing dividends and stock prices. Within this framework of profit growth, however, management and stockholders also consider related objectives, such as growth in total resources and growth in shares of specific markets. To illustrate, a management team may set as five-year objectives that its bank will increase its total assets at a rate of 10 percent per year and that it will increase its share of total deposits held by all banks in its area. Although such growth objectives usually are in the context of long-run profit objectives, management at times willingly foregoes some profitability and profit growth in order to achieve other growth objectives. Moreover, one can imagine cases where the senior officials receive greater monetary and psychic rewards by engineering growth of their firm's size, subject to satisfactory profit growth, in contrast to maximizing long-run profits when this objective is associated with less rapid growth in size.

### Constrained Profit Objectives

In summary, most banks, and bank holding companies, specify long-run profitability and maximizing the value of their firm as principal objectives. Safety, service, and growth are secondary objectives consistent with long-run profit maximization. Although banks vary in the weights that they assign to secondary objectives, neither a bank's stockholders nor its supervisory agencies are likely to allow a bank to emphasize one or more secondary objectives to the extent that this impairs the bank's long-run profitability.

## EVALUATING BANK PERFORMANCE

Exhibit 5-3 schematically summarizes various parties that evaluate bank performance. Some, such as senior management and bank supervisory agencies, have access to detailed—usually timely—information by which to monitor and evaluate the performance of a bank and its principal components. Others, such as stockholders and community residents, base their evaluations on generally available public information, which for banking is extensive.

### INTERNAL EVALUATION

A bank's *board of directors* usually consists of some senior officers and other persons who are major customers, stockholders, and/or community

**EXHIBIT 5-3**

**Bank Performance Evaluators:
A Framework**

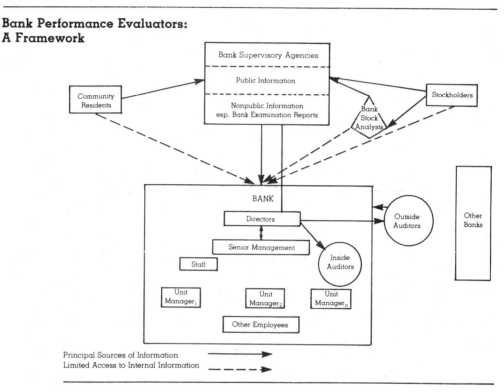

leaders. These directors are legally responsible for the actions of a bank and its representatives. This responsibility is awesome. The directors of a large complex banking organization cannot keep fully informed of all actions for which they are responsible. They can help set broad policies, and they can insist on procedures that adhere to stated policies.[5]

The board of directors and its committees have access to detailed internal reports about the performance of the bank and its component units. Although senior management and its staff prepare many of these internal reports, the directors also have access to reports by inside auditors, outside auditors, and bank supervisory agencies. These audit reports and examination reports give directors a supplementary perspective of the performance of their bank's officers and other employees. While they thus can help directors to meet their responsibilities, these reports are not generally available to persons outside the bank.

Senior management has access to detailed financial information about the performance of the bank and its component units. It receives frequent reports about funds flows in and out of the bank; balance-sheet accounts such as deposits, loans, and problem loans; unused loan commitments (credit lines) to customers; various revenues and expenses; and risk exposure

5. Ronald G. Burke, "Bank Directors Face Stronger Role," *The Magazine of Bank Administration,* September 1978, pp. 28-31. B. D. Chaps, "If I Were a Bank Director . . .," *The Magazine of Bank Administration,* September 1977, pp. 18-21.

of bond trading accounts and foreign currency accounts. Senior management usually receives this information as summary reports compiled from a continually updated computerized information base.

In addition to the flow of short-run reports, senior management receives reports that summarize the bank's long-run performance. Often these reports compare realized outcomes to internal objectives and budgets, and they compare long-run performance measures to those of other banks.

Staff reports inform senior management about how a bank's performance compares to objectives specified in a long-run profit plan. These reports evaluate trends in major categories of revenues and expenses, both for the total bank and for its major component units. By alerting management to areas where profitability measures and growth rates depart markedly from long-run objectives, these reports trigger remedial action and/or revised objectives and strategies.

## AUDITS

Inside auditors have the responsibility and power independently to review the performance of all units within a bank. To detect possible fraud and thefts, the audit staff regularly verifies cash accounts, securities holdings, and bookkeeping entries. (For example, most bank customers have at times received by mail a form stating their deposit or loan balance at a specific date and requesting the customer to verify the balance and to address any reported discrepancy to a post office box accessible only to the audit staff. This procedure permits the audit staff to verify, usually on a sampling basis, bookkeeping entries in the bank's various operating units.) Moreover, to try to prevent losses, the auditors scrutinize operating procedures in order to develop secure systems for vulnerable areas. Reports by internal auditors provide senior management and directors with independent verifications and recommendations about bank operating procedures.[6]

Large banks and many medium-sized banks also periodically commission outside audits. Although their procedures are similar to those used by the internal auditors, outside auditors often specialize in bank audits and so have developed expertise and systems by which to evaluate a client bank's operating practices and its internal audit procedures. Outside audits are infrequent compared to the almost continuous auditing that occurs within large and medium-sized banks. To develop their reports, outside auditors have unconditional authority to review a bank's records and practices. They treat their findings as confidential; and, like inside audits, their reports go to senior management and to the board of directors, especially to its audit committee.[7]

---

6. Walter S. Fisher, "Building a Better Audit Program," *The Magazine of Bank Administration,* August 1977, pp. 17-21. Donald J. O'Reilly, "The Role of the Bank Internal Auditor in the 80's," *The Magazine of Bank Administration,* July 1978, pp. 47-48, 50.

7. A multibank holding company typically has a centralized audit staff that substitutes for inside auditors in its medium-sized affiliate banks and provides an extra review of inside audit procedures in its large affiliate banks. These internal audits seldom preclude outside audits.

## BANK EXAMINATIONS

Federal and/or state supervisory agencies examine each bank, usually at least once each year. The Office of the Comptroller of the Currency (OCC) has examiners who visit national banks; Federal Reserve examiners visit state banks that are members of the Federal Reserve System (FRS); examiners of the Federal Deposit Insurance Corporation (FDIC) visit state banks that are not members of the FRS.[8] State banking agencies also examine their state banks, and often they coordinate their examinations with those of the appropriate federal banking agency.

Although details differ, the various supervisory agencies use similar procedures to examine banks. A team of field examiners usually arrives unannounced as a bank is about to open. The bank provides the examiners with work space and gives them access to its books and vaults. An examination is not an audit. The examiners verify a bank's on-premises cash and securities, and they confirm the amounts of cash and securities that the bank has on deposit or in safe-keeping with its correspondent banks and/or its Federal Reserve Bank. They do not, however, seek to verify, in detail, all of a bank's investments and loans. What examiners want to verify is that the deposits, loans, and investments comply with laws and regulations. They check, for example, that the bank is not paying interest rates which exceed regulatory ceilings. Examiners often use sampling procedures to confirm that a set of specific loans has rates, collateral, and repayment terms which comply with the law. For example, they check that loans used to purchase or carry securities comply with the Federal Reserve System's Regulation U, which sets a maximum percentage that banks and others can lend against the value of listed and many unlisted securities used as collateral. Examiners also check that the amount of loans to a borrower does not exceed a legal maximum percentage of a bank's capital accounts.

Bank examiners also evaluate the quality of the loan portfolio. They review past-due loans to estimate which are likely to be repaid, and when. Where repayment is very improbable, the examiners will require the bank to charge off the loan. In cases where eventual repayment is likely, the examiners will classify loans as substandard or doubtful. By thus rating the quality of the loans, bank examiners provide the bank's senior officers and directors with an independent evaluation of current and potential performance of the loan portfolio.

Examiners review other parts of a bank's portfolio and its support activities. Although they are not auditors or management consultants, examiners may note ways by which a bank can, for example, improve its internal audit procedures, credit files (systematic information about borrowers), and/or security procedures. The examiners will include such observations and recommendations in their final report.

---

8. There are overlapping examination powers among federal banking agencies. All national banks are members of the FRS and are insured by the FDIC. In practice, these two agencies usually accept the reports prepared by the examining staff of the OCC. Technically, these agencies can insist on separate examinations by their staffs.

After they complete the initial parts of their examination, the field examiners often discuss their initial findings with the bank's senior officers and possibly with the directors. This discussion procedure allows the various parties to clarify and possibly resolve minor differences before the field examiners write a report, which they submit to their supervisory examiners for review. After this review and possible editing, the final examination report is filed in the supervisory agency; a copy is sent to the board of directors of the examined bank. It provides the directors with a detailed, independent evaluation of the bank's activities. It alerts them, for example, to: specific cases in which the bank does not comply with laws and regulations; problem loans; inadequate safeguards; and possible needs for additional capital. By documenting what the examiners judge to be a bank's specific problems, the report also communicates the examiners' implicit evaluation of senior management. (At times, an examination report bluntly cites inadequacies of a bank's management.) The board of directors then reviews the examination report and invites the senior officers to respond to it. The directors then evaluate the views of the examiners and of senior management before deciding what remedial actions, if any, to take.

Because examiners' reports often contain detailed criticisms of a bank's activities, customers, and employees, bank supervisory agencies treat them as highly confidential and require bank directors to do likewise. These evaluations, while done by outsiders, are mainly for use by the supervisory agencies and by directors and senior management of an examined bank. The general public has no access to these reports.

Field examinations traditionally have been the heart of the examination process. Field examiners usually visit each bank at least annually; they are likely to visit problem banks, as determined by preceding examinations, more frequently; and they promptly visit banks that report changes in controlling shareholders and management. This scheduling process focuses examination resources on small and medium-sized banks, among which, until recently, have occurred most problems, control changes, and failures.

In recent years, there have been some newsworthy failures and near failures by large banks. These events have triggered revision of bank examination priorities and procedures.[9] Even if the probability of a large bank getting into difficulties is small, the social costs of such a failure can well exceed that of more numerous failures of small banks scattered throughout the country. Moreover, recent aggressive practices by some large banks may have increased their probability of future failure over what it was in the past. As discussed in later chapters, these practices occur in such areas as loans, capital-structure leveraging, holding company expansion, multinational banking, and foreign-currency transactions.

Bank supervisory agencies consequently now seek fuller and prompter information about major risk exposures in large banks. They require more frequent, detailed reports from these banks; and they use *early warning*

---

9. Howard D. Crosse, ''A Fresh Approach to Bank Examinations,'' *The Bankers Magazine*, May-June 1978, pp. 39-42.

*systems,* which are computerized analytical systems, to scan the reports for trends and ratios that provide early signs of pending problems. When it is thus alerted to possible problems, the appropriate supervisory agency(ies) can commit additional resources to prompt, detailed examination of the bank. As with bank examination reports, the supervisory agencies do not publicize the procedures and specific predictions of these computerized early warning systems. Although they are in developmental stages, these early warning systems will likely become major components of future bank supervisory and examination procedures.[10]

## EXTERNAL EVALUATION BY INVESTORS AND COMMUNITY RESIDENTS

Bank stockholders have a direct interest in evaluating their bank's performance, especially as it compares with that of other banks and other investment opportunities. Some of a bank's major stockholders also are directors; and, in these dual roles, they help set policies and monitor performance. In contrast, most stockholders can influence their bank's policies only indirectly, such as in annual meetings when they vote on proposed directors and proposed changes in corporate bylaws. (Often, however, their participation consists of signing and returning proxies solicited by current management.) These nondirector stockholders rely on generally available public information by which to evaluate their bank-stock investment(s).

Stockholders who want to evaluate their bank's performance likely begin with the bank's recent annual report, or that of its parent holding company.[11] Most large banks publish elaborate annual reports. The chairman of the board of directors or the president introduces the report with a message that summarizes the firm's recent progress and problems and outlines its future plans. Subsequent sections survey the economic environment and highlight the bank's new services, expansion programs, and civic involvement. After these verbal and pictorial sections, there are extensive accounting reports with their accompanying footnotes. These reports include balance sheets, income statements, and sources and uses of funds statements. This accounting information, especially when it is analyzed over time and compared to that of other banks, provides basic information for stockholders who want to evaluate bank financial performance.

Bank stockholders and the general public have access to detailed documents that banks file with supervisory agencies. Banks with many

---

10. The OCC uses its National Bank Surveillance System, and the FDIC and some of the Federal Reserve Banks have experimented with their own versions of computerized surveillance systems. Some state banking agencies, such as the Illinois State Banking Commission, also have begun to incorporate computerized early-warning systems into the procedures by which they monitor and examine banks.

11. Many banks, especially large ones, are owned by bank holding companies, which in turn have public stockholders. In these cases the parent holding company provides most of the detailed stockholder information about the holding company and its affiliate bank(s) and bank-related firms. Although one needs to be aware of this structural nuance, for brevity the following paragraphs usually refer to banks.

public stockholders regularly file supplementary accounting reports with their supervisory agencies, that then make these reports publicly available. Until recently stockholders of a closely held bank were lucky to receive abridged balance sheets and income statements. Under new policies, federal bank supervisory agencies now make publicly available, usually for a modest charge, the complete Consolidated Report of Condition (balance sheet) and Consolidated Report of Income of any insured bank. In addition to their periodic reports, banks irregularly file special reports that are fully or partially available to stockholders and other interested parties. These reports include prospectuses or offering circulars for new securities and applications for mergers and holding company affiliations.

A bank's public reports focus on its corporate achievements. Stockholders who want to evaluate expected returns and risks of investment alternatives must analyze diverse corporate reports. Few stockholders have the time or training for such in-depth analysis, and so they turn to convenient sources, such as *Business Week, Forbes,* and *Fortune,* which periodically publish summary performance measures of large banks. An interested investor can use these summary measures to develop initial performance comparisons among large banks. .

As bank-stock ownership broadened in the 1960s, brokerage firms and institutional investors added bank-stock analysts to their research staffs. These professionals analyze extensive banking information in order to compare past performance and to make predictions about probable future performance of various bank stocks. Their judgments become part of the ongoing information system by which investors make decisions about which bank stocks to buy and sell. These investment analyses and decisions provide a collective market evaluation of a bank's past and probable future performance. Thus a bank's senior management can benefit from professional outside evaluation of its performance and prospects if it monitors how investors view the bank and how they will likely respond to publicized changes in the bank's policies and strategies.

Various residents evaluate the performance of banks located in and near their community. Most are customers or potential customers, but not stockholders; and they focus on how well a bank serves them, their friends, and their community. Personal experience often dominates their evaluations. For example, many residents may have experienced loan rejections by a local bank, and they know of friends who have had similar experience with the bank. They also know that their local bank pays lower interest on savings accounts that that advertised by distant banks, and they joke about its brief "bankers' hours." In the short run, residents of such a community cannot do much to change such banking practices. (Some can, if they choose, establish accounts with more distant banks.) In the long run, new owners may acquire control of the bank and revise its past policies. Also, another banking organization may evaluate the local market and judge it profitable to enter the community with a new bank or branch. If so, when it applies to enter, it will base its case at least partly on its willingness to provide improved banking services in the community. Another possibility is that a group of local residents will seek to obtain a charter for a new community bank; and it too will emphasize how its proposed bank will better service the local community.

Residents of some communities forcefully demand changes of specific banking practices they judge detrimental to them and their community. To illustrate, critics charge that some bank and other financial institutions practice redlining when they review mortgage loan applications. *Redlining* refers to the practice of some lenders who, at least implicitly, take a city map and draw red lines around deteriorated neighborhoods and around neighborhoods they judge to be rapidly deteriorating. These lenders then refuse to make mortgage and home improvement loans in these redlined districts, which they believe to be high-risk areas. Opponents charge that this practice accelerates neighborhood deterioration because it hinders concerned citizens from buying and improving homes in redlined areas. Citizens groups at times organize to oppose redlining practices in their areas. One tactic is to insist that the aggregate dollar amount of home mortgage loans that a bank or S&L makes in each neighborhood should approximate the total deposits it derives from the neighborhood. Although there are valid questions whether and how a financial intermediary should implement such a guideline, there is no question that some citizens and their elected representatives are focusing attention on alleged redlining practices. Recent laws and regulations require banks and other lenders to file detailed geographical information about their home mortgage loans, and community activists will likely use this new source of information to try to evaluate the "community performance" of local banks.

## BANK PERFORMANCE MEASURES

To evaluate their bank's performance, bank directors and senior officers can:

- examine trends in their bank's performance measures
- compare actual outcomes to (budgeted) performance objectives
- compare their bank's performance measures to publicly available measures of the performance of rival banks

These bankers and other parties—such as supervisory agencies, investors, and community residents—also can compare a bank's performance to that of "similar" banks, as categorized for example by their deposit size and/or location, and to "exceptional" banks, as categorized, for example, by their superior financial performance. These comparative standards are conveniently available from bank supervisory agencies, banking trade associations, and specialized firms.

### BANK OPERATING STATISTICS

Anyone who wants to evaluate a bank's performance should turn to *Bank Operating Statistics,* an annual publication of the FDIC. *Bank Operating*

*Statistics (BOS)* is a compendium of tables prepared from balance sheets (Consolidated Report of Condition) and income statements (Consolidated Report of Income) of all insured banks. *BOS* groups banks as follows:

- national totals (for all banks)
- by state
- where appropriate, by economic areas within a state[12]

*BOS* further subclassifies the national and state groupings by bank asset size. For each group of "similar" banks, by location and/or by asset size, *BOS* provides a set of four tables that report the group's:

- assets, liabilities, equity capital (aggregate dollar amount), and annual percent change
- income, expenses (aggregate dollar amount) and annual percent change
- selected balance sheet ratios
- selected income, expense, and rate-of-return ratios (some of which combine income or expense items with balance sheet items)

Readers who review *BOS* will quickly appreciate its format and its usefulness for evaluating bank performance. (The Appendix on pages 568-569 reprints Tables C & D of the National Totals.) A person who wants to evaluate a specific bank can, for example, compare its ratios with average ratios of similar-sized banks within its state and with average ratios of all banks in its economic area within the state.

Assume, for example, that a bank in Randolph County, Indiana, has total assets of $30 million at year-end 1977 and that its reported net income for the year accounts for 0.87 percent of its year-end total assets. This rate-of-return outcome is below the national average of 1.01 for banks with total assets in the range of $25-100 million (Appendix, Table D)[13]. Moreover, the bank's outcome is below the average ratio of 1.04 for banks in its size category in Indiana and below the average ratio of 0.99 for all banks in its nine-county economic area within Indiana. These initial comparisons do not prove that this bank has performed poorly. They do, however, alert management and other observers to analyze further the reasons why this bank's return on assets differs substantially from that of "similar" banks. As summarized in *BOS* (Explanatory Notes), "there can be a number of reasons a particular bank's results might differ significantly from the average calculated for each group of similar-sized banks." Yet "such comparisons can be useful to a bank reviewing its policies and performance."

12. The area definition most frequently used is "the State Economic Area (SEA), described by the Bureau of the Census as a county or group of counties, within a State, that are homogeneous in general livelihood and socioeconomic characteristics." *Bank Operating Statistics: 1977,* (Explanatory Notes), Federal Deposit Insurance Corporation.

13. For strict comparison, the denominator of the ratio for the illustrative bank should be an average figure from its reports of condition from December 1976, June 1977, and December 1977. This would be consistent with the procedures used in *BOS*.

*BOS* is probably the most convenient and comprehensive source of statistics by which one can evaluate a bank's comparative performance. (One drawback is that *BOS* often involves a year's publication lag, so that, for example, the *BOS* for 1979 is not available until late 1980.) The *Annual Report* for the FDIC and the *Federal Reserve Bulletin*, published monthly by the Board of Governors of the Federal Reserve System, contain tables that report balance sheet, income, and expense items of various categories of banks, but in general these tables are more aggregate than those of *BOS*.

Two other publications provide information that supplements that in *BOS. Summary of Deposits in All Commercial and Mutual Savings Banks*, an FDIC publication, reports the amounts of deposits, by type of deposit, in banks grouped by geographical areas. To illustrate, Table 2 of the *Summary of Deposits* reports various deposit totals in all banks in Randolph County, Indiana (Exhibit 5-4). With this information and its own report of condition, a bank in this county can compute its "share" of various categories of deposits. If it obtains similar information for various periods, it can compute changes in its market shares over time, and also changes in market shares of its rival banks. All three federal banking agencies contribute information for *Assets and Liabilities: Commercial & Mutual Savings Banks* (and Report of Income), which is published and distributed by the FDIC. Compared to *BOS*, this publication provides more details about balance sheet, revenue, and expense items; but it does not disaggregate its information as finely by location and asset-size categories.

## PEER GROUP DATA FROM THE NATIONAL BANK SURVEILLANCE SYSTEM

The OCC provides each national bank with a copy of its National Bank Surveillance System (NBSS) report. A national bank can use its NBSS report to compare its performance to that of a "peer group" of national banks that are similar, based on their asset size, location (rural or urban), and branching status (whether they have branches). A national bank's NBSS report contains extensive performance measures about a bank's and its peer group's balance sheet, income items, expenses, rates of return, and growth rates. The report contains annual figures for a five-year period; and, for some items, it flags a bank's departure from the median figure for its peer group.

To extend the previous example, assume that the $30 million bank in Randolph County, Indiana, is a national bank with branches in a rural area. During the period 1971-1976, this bank's peer group had a median return on average assets that ranged from 0.95 to 1.05.[14] Thus the illustrative bank's recent return on average assets (0.87) falls below the median figure for its

---

14. From Figures 1 and 2 in Dale Arahood, "NBSS Measures of Banking Industry Performance: A Long-Term View," *The Magazine of Bank Administration*, September 1978, pp. 40-46. This article defines the peer groups, provides tables of peer group medians for selected performance measures, and analyzes aggregate peer-group trends and performance.

## EXHIBIT 5-4

### Excerpt of Amount of Bank Deposits, by Type, Grouped by County June 30, 1978

| State County | Banks | Banking Offices | Total Deposits | Demand IPC | Savings IPC | Other Time IPC | Public Funds Demand | Public Funds Time & savings |
|---|---|---|---|---|---|---|---|---|
| | —Number of— | | | Amount of Deposits (in Thousands of Dollars) | | | | |
| INDIANA | | | | | | | | |
| • | | | | | | | | |
| • | | | | | | | | |
| • | | | | | | | | |
| PULASKI | 3 | 5 | $ 76,916 | $15,530 | $20,580 | $31,734 | $3,424 | $ 5,290 |
| PUTNAM | 4 | 7 | 134,115 | 26,334 | 28,684 | 59,750 | 5,952 | 12,314 |
| RANDOLPH | 8 | 13 | 119,552 | 26,376 | 24,841 | 52,626 | 7,016 | 7,851 |
| RIPLEY | 8 | 11 | 140,300 | 25,215 | 37,660 | 61,433 | 6,769 | 8,428 |
| RUSH | 5 | 11 | 88,758 | 20,509 | 11,020 | 45,292 | 3,440 | 7,847 |
| • | | | | | | | | |
| • | | | | | | | | |
| • | | | | | | | | |

*Note*: IPC stands for Individuals, Partnerships, and Corporations

*Source*: From *Summary of Deposits in All Commercial and Mutual Savings Banks: June 30, 1978*, Federal Deposit Insurance Corporation, Table 2, p. 27.

peer group. As with their initial comparisons to similar banks from *BOS*, the bank's officials and/or interested outsiders will want to examine further the reasons why this bank's return on assets departs from that of its peers.

## BAI INDEX OF BANK PERFORMANCE

The Bank Administration Institute (BAI), a nonprofit organization that helps develop professionalism and problem solving within banking, publishes its annual BAI Index of Bank Performance. BAI uses its own computer programs and comprehensive data tapes available from the FRS to compute about fifty ratios for each insured bank. BAI then publishes summary tables of these ratios for all banks and for banks categorized by asset size and/or by state.

The BAI Index also reports the distribution of selected performance ratios. To illustrate, return on assets is a key measure of bank performance. The BAI Index reports two return-on-assets measures: one uses operating income as the numerator and the other uses net income (after securities gains or losses) as the numerator. In 1976, for all U.S. banks the median return on assets was 0.94 using operating income, and 0.98 using net income.[15] The

---

15. "A Look at 1976 Bank Performance," *The Magazine of Bank Administration*, October 1977, pp. 20-24. Also see Donnie L. Daniel, "Utilizing Industry Ratios to Assess and Improve Your Bank Profitability," *The Magazine of Bank Administration*, April 1975, pp. 27-31.

BAI Index further summarizes the distributions of these ratios. For example, with operating income as the numerator, the return on average assets for all banks in 1976 was (in percent):

| | |
|---|---|
| Upper tenth percentile | 1.52 |
| Upper quartile | 1.23 |
| Median | 0.94 |
| Lower quartile | 0.65 |
| Lower tenth percentile | 0.26 |

Based on these figures, 10 percent of all banks had a return on assets of 1.52% or higher, and 25 percent had a return on assets of 1.23% or higher. The BAI Index further disaggregates these percentile and quartile figures for banks categorized by asset size. Thus, for all banks with assets within the range of $25-50 million, the return-on-assets figures were: 1.47, 1.22, 0.97 (median), 0.71, and 0.39. On this basis the return on assets of 0.87 for the illustrative bank in Randolph County, Indiana, is below the median but above that of more than 25 percent of all similar-sized banks in the nation.[16]

The Bank Administration Institute not only publishes its Index of Bank Performance; it provides a service whereby any bank can order a set of performance ratios for its bank and/or for any other U.S. bank. Thus, for a nominal fee, a bank can obtain a set of its ratios, a set of ratios for all banks in its state, and a set of ratios for any other selected bank. The bank's staff then can use these ratios to analyze the bank's performance compared to that of similar and/or rival banks.[17]

## HIGH-PERFORMANCE BANKS

Since 1974, *Banking*, the journal of The American Bankers Association, has reported about High-Performance Banks (HPBs), those which achieve exceptionally high rates of return on equity. To be classified as one of the 1,000 HPBs, a bank has to meet two tests:[18]

- its average rate of return on equity has to be very high over a five-year period
- its rate of return on equity has to be among the top 50% of all banks in the last year of the five-year period

---

16. Although it is for 1977, the illustrative bank's ratio can be compared to these BAI figures for 1976. By interpolation, the illustrative bank's ratio exceeds that of 40 percent of similar banks. The return for the illustrative bank uses net income for the numerator and, strictly speaking, should therefore be compared to the BAI Index figures for net income as a percentage of average assets.

17. Any bank also can obtain detailed analytical reports from a firm like Sheshunoff & Company, which, for a fee, provides such services as a book that contains detailed performance ratios of every bank within a state and custom-tailored reports of a specific bank's ratios compared to those of its designated rival banks.

18. William F. Ford and Dennis A. Olson, "How 1,000 High-Performance Banks Weathered the Recent Recession," *Banking,* April 1978, pp. 36-38 ff.

The 1,000 banks that had the highest five-year average returns and that also met the second test are classified as HPBs. Between 1972 and 1976 these HPBs (about 7% of all banks) had an average return on equity of 20.8%—compared to 12.3% for all other banks.

Two coauthors, in a series of articles, analyze why and how HPBs are able to outperform other banks. In their most recent analysis, they summarize how, *compared to other banks,* HPBs have:[19]

- higher yields on their loan portfolios—primarily because of the HPBs' loan-pricing systems and risk-control procedures
- similar proportions of total loans to total assets
- higher yields from tax-exempt securities and higher proportions of tax-exempt securities to total assets
- lower proportions of nonearning cash assets and of fixed assets
- lower ratios for such expenses as salaries and wages, occupancy costs, other operating expenses, and loan losses

Even these summary characteristics of HPBs suggest ways that a bank can try to move its performance toward that of HPBs.[20]

## FUNCTIONAL COST ANALYSIS

The FRS invites its member banks to participate in its Functional Cost Analysis (FCA) program, which is designed "to develop and maintain a uniform income and cost accounting system as a tool for bank management."[21] The FCA program helps a participating bank to increase its total income and to increase the profitability and efficiency of each function within the bank.

If it chooses to participate in the FCA program, a member bank receives from its Federal Reserve Bank an instruction manual and worksheets that help it to collect systematic information about its assets, income, expenses, and item counts. The manual also provides guidance as to how bankers should use their judgment to allocate expenses like wages and salaries to such specific bank functions as demand deposit activity and installment lending. Where a participating banker chooses not to or cannot allocate some expense items, the FRS uses a computer program to allocate these items based on "experience factors" derived from expense information of other participating banks.

---

19. Ford and Olson, "How 1,000 High-Performance Banks Weathered the Recent Recession."

20. Also see William F. Ford, "Using 'High-Performance' Data to Plan Your Bank's Future," *Banking,* October 1978, pp. 40-41 ff.; and William F. Ford and Dennis A. Olson, "How to Manage High Performance Banks," *Banking,* August 1976, pp. 36-38 ff.

21. *Functional Cost Analysis: 1977 Average Banks,* available from the Federal Reserve Banks. Also see Carla M. Warberg, "Functional Cost Analysis—A New System Approach to Gauging Profitability," *Business Review* (Federal Reserve Bank of Dallas), August 1971, pp. 7-11.

A participating bank later receives from its Federal Reserve Bank a report that summarizes its operations in a standardized FCA format. It also receives FCA averages for two comparison groups:

- "For overall operations, the average figures of a group of banks of similar deposit size and percent of time deposits to total deposits and, where possible, similar functional processing procedures.
- "For functional comparisons, the average figures of a group of banks with similar functional activity or dollar volume, and, where possible, similar functional processing procedures."[22]

If it has participated in the program for two successive years, a bank also receives a year-to-year comparison of its operations. These extensive reports provide a participating bank's officials and staff with additional information by which to evaluate various dimensions of their bank's performance: against stated goals, compared to similar banks, and over time. If they have questions about how to collect data for their bank's report and/or how to interpret the final report(s), these banks can schedule discussion sessions with FRS officers and staff who specialize in the FCA program.

In addition to its detailed reports for participating banks, the FRS publishes annual booklets that summarize aggregate FCA information for participating banks categorized by deposit size and/or Federal Reserve District. These FCA booklets can provide helpful cost-accounting information to participating bankers who choose to supplement the comparative information in their reports and to nonparticipating bankers who understand the objectives, terms, and procedures of the FCA program.

## SUMMARY

A bank's senior officials direct and review diverse decisions made by people throughout their organization. They delegate to junior officers and employees the authority to make routine decisions, subject to corporate policies and review procedures. Such delegation enables senior officials to focus on strategic decisions that affect their bank and its industry.

Specific decision procedures vary among banks and change over time. Instead of becoming immersed in details, managers need a broad understanding of the key components and structure of an ongoing decision system. They need to:

- set objectives
- set policies
- identify and evaluate possible strategies
- select from among feasible strategies

---

22. *Functional Cost Analysis: 1977 Average Banks*, p. ii.

- implement selected strategies
- record outcomes
- evaluate performance
- engage in the revision process

This chapter introduces how such a structured decision system provides a general framework by which to analyze decision processes within most banks.

Banks—as do most business firms—have interrelated objectives. A bank is a profit-oriented firm owned by its stockholders. Its principal objective is long-run profitability such that investors will value highly its shares over time. A bank also has related objectives and constraints. Because a bank's deposits are money and near-money and its liabilities substantially exceed its capital accounts, a bank's senior officials and stockholders realize that bank safety is linked to long-run profitability. Service and growth are additional objectives that generally coincide with long-run profitability. Bank officers and directors must regularly review and reaffirm their firm's objectives, which in turn help set standards by which to evaluate the performance of the bank and its component units.

Bank directors have the legal responsibility to guide their firm and to verify that it adheres to their guidelines. These directors have access to detailed reports prepared by the bank's officers and staff and by auditors and bank examiners. These reports are not generally available to the stockholders or to community residents.

Unless they happen to be on the board of directors, bank stockholders have to rely on publicly available information about their firm. They can study the annual report, in which management summarizes the bank's plans and reviews its recent performance. The annual report also provides detailed financial statements, and, especially in recent years, contains additional statistical information about specialized operating areas within the bank. Stockholders who want more information about their bank also have access to part or all of many documents that banks—or their parent holding companies—file with public agencies, such as the Securities & Exchange Commission and bank supervisory agencies. To avoid becoming overwhelmed with detailed information about specific banks, investors can seek summary professional evaluations by analysts who specialize in bank stocks. While stockholders of large banks have access to detailed public information about their banks, stockholders of most medium-sized and small banks have less information by which to evaluate bank performance.

Community residents, many of whom are current or potential customers, traditionally have had only two choices if a bank did not meet their performance expectations. They could either take their financial business to another institution, or they could try to encourage new competitors to enter the market. The first choice often involves some inconvenience, and the second choice often involves long waits. Recently, however, various citizen groups, such as redlining critics, have actively sought to encourage specific banks to meet the groups' standards of corporate social responsibility.

Bank supervisory agencies and bankers associations publish extensive sets of bank performance measures. Bank officials can compare their bank's performance to that of "similar" banks, as reported by: *Bank Operating Statistics,* the National Bank Surveillance System (NBSS), the BAI Index of Bank Performance, and the Functional Cost Analysis (FCA) program. They also can evaluate their bank's performance compared to that of "exceptional" banks, such as High-Performance Banks. Similarly, with a little practice, students of banking quickly learn how to use ratio analysis to evaluate a bank's performance; and they develop an overall perspective of—and some subtle insights into—a bank's past policies, its strategies, and their associated outcomes.

# 6
# OBTAINING DEMAND DEPOSITS

Historically, only banks offered demand-deposit (checking) accounts; but especially during the 1970s mutual savings banks, credit unions, and other nonbank intermediaries began to offer accounts that are similar to bank checking accounts. This chapter introduces why demand deposits are important to their holders and to banks; and it examines the principal strategies by which banks compete for demand-deposit accounts of households, small businesses, public agencies, large firms, other banks, and foreign clients.

## CONVENIENCE OF DEMAND DEPOSITS

By law a holder of a demand-deposit account can withdraw—on demand—any or all of the funds on deposit in the account.[1] Withdrawals from a demand deposit can take various forms:

- currency and coin
- via negotiable instruments for transferring funds (checks)
- via direct transfers to another account in the financial system

Depositors withdraw currency and coin as convenient media to pay for small transactions. These withdrawals are a small percentage of total dollar withdrawals from demand-deposit accounts.

Checks account for most of the dollar volume of withdrawals and associated funds transfers among account holders. Although banks tradi-

---

1. Technically, a depositor can withdraw on demand only that part of the account that represents funds that the depository institution has had time to collect on behalf of the depositor. To illustrate, a person who today deposits a personal check drawn on a distant bank cannot legally demand the depository bank to honor a withdrawal against this item until the depository bank itself has had time to collect the check on behalf of the depositor. Most banks have rules that govern the collection period for deposited items.

tionally have been the only intermediary legally empowered to offer accounts against which depositors can write checks, in recent years some other financial intermediaries have obtained powers to offer accounts against which depositors can write instruments that are functionally similar to checks; and there are legislative proposals to permit various nonbank intermediaries to offer checking accounts. These actions are eroding the distinction of checking accounts as a service unique to banks.

A growing share of future withdrawals will involve direct funds transfers to other accounts in the financial system. One such procedure is already known to people who use *preauthorized bill-paying services,* whereby they authorize their banks to withdraw funds from (debit) their checking accounts in order to pay directly their periodic bills from firms such as insurance companies and utilities. Banks also directly transfer funds among themselves for their own accounts and as a service for large clients.[2] Most federal funds transactions, for example, are not by check but by specific wire transfers and bookkeeping transfers. Banks similarly serve their customers by using computers linked by wires to expedite large funds transfers among account holders. Thus an illustrative large firm has its major bank account in New York, but it also has a network of bank accounts in regional financial centers, and it directly and rapidly transfers funds among these various accounts.

Although they will be a major growth area in the payments system, direct funds-transfer systems will not be a private preserve for banks. Already other financial intermediaries have begun to offer their customers many features of direct funds transfers. Some S&Ls, mutual savings banks, and credit unions provide services whereby their account holders can directly transfer funds to other accounts within the same institution and to accounts at other institutions including banks. As principal components of a payments system that is subject to rapid technological and legal change, the banking industry and individual banks must plan how to retain their role in the payments system and their access to demand deposits as a major source of funds.


## IMPORTANCE OF DEMAND DEPOSITS

Demand deposits are important to their holders and to the banks in which the deposits are held.

*Money* has two principal functions: it is a medium of exchange and a store of value. Demand deposits, legally subject to negotiable checks or direct transfers, fulfill the first function. They also, but not uniquely, fulfill the second function. Therefore, demand deposits constitute the major part of the nation's money supply, of which currency in circulation accounts for a minor part. There is continuing debate as to the role of time deposits.

2. H. Clay Simpson, Jr., "Money Transfer Services: A Look at the Payment Messages Network," *The Magazine of Bank Administration,* September 1976, pp. *21-24.*

The U.S. Constitution gives the federal government responsibility for the nation's legal tender (money). Government agencies issue currency and coin which account for a small part of the money supply. Demand deposits constitute the major part of the money supply, but these deposits are liabilities of investor-owned banks that are subject to the rewards and risks of a competitive economic system.

Because of its Constitutional responsibility and because of money's economic and social importance, the federal government has assumed broad legislative and regulatory powers over the banking system. The FRS seeks to influence the rate of expansion or contraction of aggregate demand deposits. Bank supervisory agencies try to prevent bank actions that will increase the likelihood of bank failures; and, when insured banks fail, the FDIC acts quickly to give depositors prompt access to their demand deposits. Public policy thus acknowledges the public importance of banking, and it seeks to constrain and guide banking decisions.

While they serve their owners as money, demand deposits are also a major source of funds for banks. Demand deposits accounted for most deposit liabilities of America's banks until 1971, when time and savings deposits first surpassed demand deposits as a percentage of total bank deposits. These trends have continued, and now time and savings deposits account for 64 percent and demand deposits account for 36 percent of total deposits of all banks in the United States. Although they have developed new sources of deposit and nondeposit funds, banks continue to compete for demand deposits. Their competitive strategies, however, are constrained by public policies that reflect concerns about the nation's money supply and the financial power of large banks.

## STRATEGIES TO OBTAIN DEMAND DEPOSITS

Deposits are principal sources of funds for banks. In turn, banks use deposited funds for loans and investments, the interest from which constitutes the major source of bank revenues. Part of these revenues, after various expenses, flow through to bank profits or, occasionally, losses.

Banks logically will bid for deposits that can thus contribute to their profits. In a free-market system, banks will evaluate the expected net returns from current and possible additional loans and investments, and they will then bid for various deposit and nondeposit sources of funds. Although diverse factors can affect its bidding for funds, in a competitive market a bank will pay a price that enables it to make loans and investments the revenues from which, after the price paid and other operating expenses, will contribute to its long-run profitability. In this profit-oriented system, a bank competes against other banks and also against other market participants such as nonbank intermediaries.

Banks logically have two principal procedures by which to bid for deposits. They can offer to pay explicit interest to depositors. They can also pay implicit interest, in such forms as customer convenience, low charges for other banking services, and free premiums.

## PAYING INTEREST: LEGISLATED PROHIBITION

The Banking Act of 1933 prohibits banks from paying—"directly or indirectly, by any device whatsoever"—interest on demand deposits. This legislation thus closes to banks one major procedure by which to bid for deposits.

Many bank failures preceded the Banking Act of 1933, which was passed during a major economic depression. The Act contains diverse provisions that were intended to reestablish confidence in the nation's banking system and to forestall practices judged likely to contribute to bank failures.

Various reviewers have examined the legislative history of the Banking Act of 1933, and they cite two principal reasons for the prohibition of interest on demand deposits:[3]

- to protect banks from destructive competition among themselves
- to protect local borrowers by impeding funds flows to major bidders in large cities

Prior to 1933 some large banks paid interest on large deposit balances. There was concern, however, that the practice would become prevalent and that some aggressive bankers would offer excessively high rates of interest that would in turn lead them to use the deposit funds for high-yielding—but riskier—loans and investments. Not only would these banks thus develop risky portfolios, but other banks, in order to compete for funds, might begin to follow similar strategies. Therefore, to prevent such potentially reckless behavior, a case was made to prohibit all banks from paying interest on demand deposits.

The second principal reason for prohibiting interest payments was the belief that large city banks, with their diverse loan and investment opportunities, could bid directly for deposits from distant residents; and they could bid indirectly for funds by paying interest on balances that small banks held with them. In either case deposit funds would flow from local communities to large cities and thus not be as available to local borrowers. Therefore, to try to keep loan funds available for rural borrowers, a further case was made to prohibit all banks from paying interest on demand deposits.

Theory and subsequent evidence cast doubt on both principal reasons for banning interest payments on demand deposits. The belief that bankers will recklessly pay high rates and then construct risky portfolios rests on the assumption that some banks will act irrationally concerning their long-run survival and profitability. Also, it assumes that bank examiners cannot

---

3. Bryon Higgins, "Interest Payments on Demand Deposits: Historical Evolution and the Current Controversy," *Monthly Review* (Federal Reserve Bank of Kansas City), July-August 1977, pp. 3-11. James M. O'Brien, "Interest Ban on Demand Deposits: Victim of the Profit Motive?" *Business Review* (Federal Reserve Bank of Philadelphia), August 1972, pp. 13-19. Richard E. Towey, "The Prohibition of Interest on Demand Deposits," *Journal of Bank Research,* Winter 1971, pp. 8-16.

effectively monitor and prevent risky portfolios. Several researchers have examined the records of banks that failed prior to 1933, and they conclude that payment of interest on demand deposits and risky portfolio behavior do not generally explain the failures.[4] The belief that large city banks will attract funds from outlying areas may be valid, but theory suggests that society benefits from an integrated, competitive, financial market in which funds can readily flow to high-return (risk-adjusted) projects throughout the economy. Moreover, even if it encourages recycling of funds within local areas, the banning of interest payments on deposits benefits local borrowers, but to the detriment of local depositors, who cannot conveniently try to obtain higher rates outside their local communities.

Even if the principal reasons for it were clearly valid, the prohibition of interest rates on demand deposits has other consequences: it encourages banks to develop new sources of funds on which they can legally pay interest, and it encourages banks to use nonprice strategies to compete for demand deposits.

## CHECK-CLEARING SERVICES

Because they use similar procedures to clear checks deposited or written by their customers, most banks are integral parts of the nation's check-clearing system. Exhibit 6-1 schematically summarizes this system's principal components, and it identifies five paths by which checks flow through the system.

### Intrabank Clearing

At times the recipient of a check has an account at the same bank, perhaps at a different branch, as does the writer of the check. In such cases the bank processes the transaction internally by withdrawing funds from (debiting) the check writer's account and crediting the recipient's deposit account. Path 1 of Exhibit 6-1 identifies such internal clearing of checks.

### Local Clearing Systems

Path 2 depicts the case where the recipient of a check deposits it in a bank near the one used by the check writer. The two banks, for example, are in the same small city or rural county. Nearby banks often have bilateral clearing arrangements whereby at least daily each bank directly presents all the checks received by it and drawn on the other bank. To illustrate, one day Bank A has a bundle of checks totalling $50,000 drawn against Bank B; and Bank B has checks totalling $60,000 drawn against Bank A. In this case the two banks settle with each other by Bank A's giving Bank B a banker's

---

4. George J. Benston, "Interest Payments on Demand Deposits and Bank Investment Behavior," *The Journal of Political Economy,* October 1964, pp. 431-449. Charles F. Haywood and Charles M. Linke, *The Regulation of Deposit Interest Rates,* a study prepared for the Trustees of the Banking Research Fund, Association of Reserve City Bankers, 1968, esp. pp. 11-24.

**EXHIBIT 6-1**

### Check-Clearing Networks

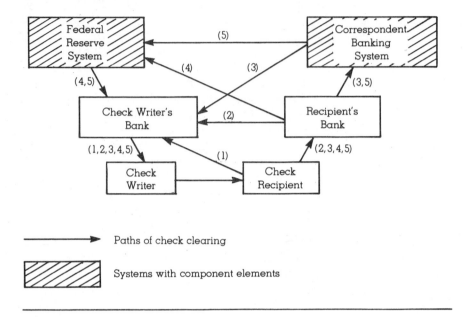

→ Paths of check clearing

▨ Systems with component elements

check or similar instrument for the $10,000 difference. The next day's results may be approximately reverse, with Bank B paying Bank A the difference.

As a logical extension of bilateral clearing arrangements, nearby banks may join a local *clearinghouse*, which involves one convenient location at which representatives of each participating bank meet, often several times a day, to present the checks received by their bank and drawn against the other banks that belong to the clearinghouse. At any one settlement time, some banks will present a greater dollar amount of checks drawn against other members than the other members present to them. The banks will then settle these differences among themselves, typically by instructing the Federal Reserve Bank to transfer the net settlement amounts among the accounts that the participating banks hold with the Federal Reserve Bank. Clearinghouse arrangements not only expedite settlement among banks; they reduce delays in identifying problem checks—such as those drawn against accounts with insufficient funds—so that banks can act promptly to reduce possible losses.

### Nonlocal Clearing Systems

The recipient of a check may deposit it in a bank that is distant from the check writer's bank. Seldom does the recipient bank directly present such a check to the check writer's bank; it clears it through the correspondent banking system, the Federal Reserve System, or some combination of these two systems.

The *correspondent banking system* is an intricate network of relationships between banks. Small and medium-sized banks usually have correspondent relationships with several large banks, called city correspondents, in their region and in the nation's money centers. An outlying bank typically maintains a deposit account with its city correspondent which, in turn, provides various services, such as check clearing, for the outlying bank.

When a customer of an outlying bank deposits a check drawn against a distant bank, the outlying bank will likely forward this check in a bundle of similar items to a city correspondent. This large bank, either directly or through its extensive correspondent associations, will present the check to the bank against which it is drawn and credit the proceeds to the account of the outlying bank. (Path 3 of Exhibit 6-1 depicts this check clearing process.) At times, because of competition or delays in clearing, the city correspondent credits the account for the item before it itself receives the funds from the bank against which the check is drawn.

Correspondent banking is not exclusively between distant banks of substantially different size. Large regional and money-center banks maintain correspondent relationships with similar banks in other regions. In part they do this to expedite clearing of distant checks deposited by their own customers or forwarded to them for clearance by the smaller banks they serve as city correspondents.

The Federal Reserve System (FRS) is another key element of the nation's check-clearing system. The Federal Reserve Act of 1913 authorizes the FRS to take actions that will facilitate funds transfers within the United States. The twelve Federal Reserve Banks therefore provide extensive check-clearing services for their member banks. A member bank that receives checks drawn on distant banks clears at least some of them through the FRS. At least daily it sends such checks to its Federal Reserve Bank or branch (Path 4). Within the same Federal Reserve District, the Federal Reserve Bank will present these checks directly to the banks against which they are drawn and will receive payment from the banks, usually by debiting their accounts at the Bank. The Federal Reserve Bank will forward checks drawn on banks outside its District to the appropriate Federal Reserve Banks for their presentation, collection, and remission of funds to the originating bank.

In clearing checks for its members, each Federal Reserve Bank credits their account based on a schedule of clearing times. For example, a member bank (A) sends to its Federal Reserve Bank a check drawn on another bank (B) in the District. The schedule calls for the Federal Reserve Bank to credit the account of Bank A for the amount of the check at the end of twenty-four hours. At the end of the period, Bank A has this new credit at the Federal Reserve Bank even if the Federal Reserve Bank has not yet presented the check to Bank B.

When, in clearing a check, one bank's account is credited at the Federal Reserve Bank before the other bank's account is debited, the result is *float*.

In essence, the Federal Reserve System provides net credit to the banking system, although the amount of float can fluctuate widely over time and among banks.[5] For example, a snowstorm that blankets a large section of the nation can result in a temporary upsurge of float in the banking system.

Banks that are members of the FRS do not use its facilities to clear all distant checks they receive. They usually clear checks, especially large ones, through the correspondent banking system when this procedure gives them credit for the funds sooner than will the clearing schedule of the FRS. Therefore large correspondent banks often develop extensive courier networks to expedite clearance of large checks. These banks view this service as one way of competing for the correspondent deposit balances of other banks. These city correspondents also offer to clear special items, such as nonpar checks, that the Federal Reserve System, as a matter of policy, refuses to process. (Nonpar checks are drawn against about forty banks— usually small rural institutions—that, under state law, can legally refuse to redeem at par checks presented on behalf of distant recipients. Nonpar banking is in the twilight years of a long, often divisive, history.)

Banks also clear some distant checks through combinations of the Federal Reserve System and the correspondent banking system (Path 5). Banks that are not members of the FRS send many checks to their city correspondents for clearing. When convenient and less costly, these city correspondents will forward some of these checks for clearance through the FRS, of which they are members. Thus, by clearing checks for member banks that are also city correspondents, the FRS often indirectly clears checks for nonmember banks.

## Check-Processing Costs and Cost-Control Developments

A brief introduction cannot do justice to the magnitude and intricacies of the nation's check-clearing system. Specialists estimate that the American banking system processed about 22 billion checks in 1971 and that, based on recent trends, this figure will increase to around 44 billion by 1980.[6] The dollar amounts similarly are staggering. Only by visiting the check-processing department of a Federal Reserve Bank or a city correspondent bank is one likely to conceptualize the amount of human and technical resources used to process so many checks.

Even a brief introduction, however, provides initial insights into the cost structure of processing checks. Processing any check involves costs, although the total cost of clearing a check through several participants (such as in Path 5) is usually higher than the total cost of processing a check within one bank (Path 1). The FRS pays a substantial proportion of the nation's

---

5. Arline Hoel, "A Primer on Federal Reserve Float," *Monthly Review* (Federal Reserve Bank of New York), October 1975, pp. 245-253.

6. James V. Vergari, "Check Processing at the FED in the Electronic Seventies," *The Magazine of Bank Administration*, April 1972, pp. 35-39. J. C. Welman, Jr., "Future Changes in Check Collection," *The Magazine of Bank Administration*, August 1972, pp. 39-40, 51.

total costs of clearing checks. If, as is likely, there are economies of scale in check processing, then many city correspondent banks have the specialized resources and procedures for achieving such scale economies. Moreover, these city correspondents, in competing for business, probably pass on many benefits of their scale economies to the smaller banks that use their check-clearing services. Although there are thus general principles about the costs of clearing checks, it is difficult to define and measure the exact "costs" borne by various participants in the check-clearing process.

There are new general approaches that try to reduce various costs of check processing.

**Regional Check-Processing Centers**   Regional check-processing centers (RCPCs) are clearinghouses that cover broad regions, such as extended metropolitan areas. The FRS has fostered development of RCPCs, the members of which present checks drawn on other participant banks and settle their accounts, usually through the Federal Reserve Bank, at least daily.[7] One cost saving is that checks cleared within outlying RCPCs need not undergo additional handling by a Federal Reserve Bank or by city correspondent banks. Membership in a RCPC is not limited to banks that are members of the FRS.

**Direct-Deposit Systems**   Under direct-deposit systems, people who receive periodic payments from large funds disbursers, such as major employers or the Social Security Administration, can authorize their bank—or a selected nonbank financial intermediary—to receive the payments and to credit them directly to their account. Some of these participants have accounts with Bank X, others with Bank Y, and others with Bank Z. Therefore the payor, instead of writing separate checks to each participant, will send each participating bank a list of the deposit accounts that are to receive payments; a list of the amount to be deposited in each account; and a transfer of funds from the payor to the bank for the total amount. (The listings are likely to be on a computer tape that the bank can then use to expedite the crediting of the payments to the specific accounts.) Although they somewhat reduce the number of checks written and they provide convenience and safety benefits to recipients, direct-deposit systems do not reduce the numbers of checks written by the recipients, some of whom may not have previously used checking accounts.

**Check-Truncation Procedures**   Under current procedures bank customers customarily receive from their bank a monthly statement that also contains their cancelled checks that were cleared during the statement period. Included, for example, will be a cancelled check paid to a credit card company in a distant city. After it received this check, the credit card

7. William Burke, "RCPC's: Transitional Step," *Business Review* (Federal Reserve Bank of San Francisco), July-August 1973, pp. 11-15.

company, through its bank, physically returned the check via one of the paths depicted in Exhibit 6-1.

Instead of this return procedure, advocates of check truncation suggest that such a check be microfilmed and temporarily held by the bank in which the recipient (the credit card company) deposited it. The bank will use modern communications technology to inform the check writer's bank about the check and to obtain a transfer of funds. Thus, at the end of the statement period, the check writer will not receive this physical check; but his or her computerized bank statement will show that the credit card company (identified by name or a code number) has been paid the amount of the check as of a specific day. If subsequent questions arise about this payment, a copy of the original check can be obtained from the bank in which it was deposited. Although truncation is novel compared to traditional check-clearing procedures, some charge-account customers know how they periodically receive an itemized statement of transactions and do not receive copies of the specific charge slips they signed.

There have been initial experiments with check-truncation procedures. One major study (the Atlanta Payments Project) concludes that the most feasible procedure is a localized system in which any check that is drawn on a local participating bank should be truncated at the first participating bank that receives the check. Yet one has to question whether consumers, accustomed to receiving their cancelled checks, will readily accept check-truncation procedures. After testing at the Federal Reserve Banks of Dallas and Richmond, the U.S. Treasury inaugurated (1978) a nationwide program whereby its checks are truncated at the Federal Reserve Bank that first receives them.[8] Instead of forwarding them to the U.S. Treasury, the Federal Reserve Banks store the checks after they record them on computer tape and microfilm and forward the summary information to the U.S. Treasury for its processing. Although it has little initial effect on check recipients and banks, this new government program may portend future check-truncation developments.

**Electronic Funds Transfer Systems**   Electronic Funds Transfer Systems (EFTS) involve advanced communications systems that use electronic impulses to facilitate funds transfers among accounts.[9] In some cases, such as with check truncation, EFTS expedites the check-clearing process; in other cases EFTS supplants—or has the capability to supplant—traditional check-clearing systems.

---

8. "Treasury Checks to Be 'Truncated'," *Voice* (Federal Reserve Bank of Dallas), January 1978, p. 13.

9. "Electronic Funds Transfer: An Introduction," *Ninth District Quarterly* (Federal Reserve Bank of Minneapolis), July 1976, pp. 7-13. Mary G. Grandstaff and Charles J. Smaistrla, "A Primer on Electronic Funds Transfer," *Business Review* (Federal Reserve Bank of Dallas), September 1976, pp. 7-14. Bankers have to keep informed about public policy issues and developments associated with EFTS. See, for example, Wayne B. Lewin, "Interim Report of the National EFT Commission," *The Magazine of Bank Administration*, April 1977, pp. 14-19. Charles J. Smaistrla, "Current Issues in Electronic Funds Transfer," *Review* (Federal Reserve Bank of Dallas), February 1977, pp. 1-7. George C. White, Jr., "Private Sector Alternative," and Benjamin Wolkowitz, "The Fed's Role in EFTS," both in *Issues in Bank Regulation*, Autumn 1977, pp. 6-15.

*Bank wire systems*, which facilitate direct transfer of funds among participating banks, are one form of EFTS. The Federal Reserve Communication System (Fed Wire), operated by the FRS, is an automated communications network that links together the FRS, its member banks and their clients, and some government agencies and RCPCs. Its participants use the Fed Wire to transfer electronically funds and/or bookkeeping entries of U.S. government securities for their own accounts and on behalf of their major clients. Some large banks also jointly own and participate in domestic and international bank wire systems that expedite direct funds transfers.

*Automated clearinghouses* (ACHs) are logical extensions of traditional clearinghouses except that, instead of exchanging bundles of paper checks, the participants exchange payments information that is encoded on computer tapes. ACHs expedite direct-deposit systems in which organizations with large payrolls transmit encoded computer tapes to ACHs, which relay the direct-deposit information—and associated total funds transfers—to participating banks, which then credit the deposits to the appropriate deposit accounts. ACHs similarly expedite preauthorized bill-paying services in which, for example, a large utility transmits to the local ACH an aggregate computer tape that identifies which bank accounts are, by preagreement, to be debited specific amounts on a specific date. The ACH in turn relays this specific debit information to the participating banks.

The FRS has fostered development of regional ACHs, many of which in turn belong to the National Automated Clearinghouse Association that was founded in 1974. Plans are underway to link the regional ACHs into interregional systems and eventually into a national system.[10]

While bank wire systems and ACHs may expedite some transactions associated with their accounts, consumers directly encounter other variants of EFTS.

*Cash dispensers* are limited-service electronic terminals at which bank customers identify themselves, usually with an encoded plastic card, and then withdraw currency—up to specified limits per day—from their deposit accounts or preauthorized credit lines. The customers do not have to write out checks for "cash" or withdrawal slips from savings accounts. To decide whether to install cash dispensers within or near its building, a bank has to evaluate their expected benefits (such as shorter lines at staffed teller windows and extended customer-service hours) compared to the installation and operating cost for the new equipment.

In contrast to cash dispensers, *automated teller machines* (ATMs) provide a larger set of banking services so that participating customers can, for example:

- withdraw currency from their accounts and/or preauthorized credit lines

10. James D. Bergstrom, "Nationwide ACH Payments in 1978: The Future Is Now," *The Magazine of Bank Administration,* June 1978, pp. 32-36, 38. Carl M. Gambs, "Automated Clearinghouses: Current Status and Prospects," *Economic Review* (Federal Reserve of Kansas City), May 1978, pp. 3-16. (The second article also provides a cost-benefit analysis and public-policy analysis of ACH developments.)

- deposit funds to accounts
- transfer funds among accounts
- make loan payments
- confirm the amount(s) in their account(s)

As with cash dispensers, bank customers need an encoded card to gain access to an ATM; and to supplement its staffed teller windows, banks can use ATMs to shorten customer waiting times and offer longer banking hours. Where permitted by law, a bank can evaluate the net benefits of developing a network of off-premise ATMs instead of—or to supplement—a network of brick-and-mortar branches.[11]

*Point-of-sale (POS) systems* extend consumer-oriented EFTS beyond bank customers and their banks; they facilitate direct funds transfers between bank customers and participating retailers. Some banks and nonbank financial intermediaries have developed local or regional POS systems in which they enroll retailers who agree to have a POS terminal in their store. In such systems, participating bank customers have an encoded plastic card by which they can have direct access to a POS terminal or which they present to a sales clerk or other person who administers a store's POS terminal. In the first case (direct access) a store's POS terminal is like an off-premises ATM; in the second case the retail operator is an intermediary between the bank customers and the POS terminal in the store.

Some abbreviated POS systems permit bank customers only to withdraw or deposit cash at the retail location and/or permit the retailer to verify checks by participating bank customers. Advanced POS systems enable bank customers to authorize direct transfers of funds from their accounts to that of the retailer. To illustrate, a bank customer goes through the check-out line at a participating grocery store, and to pay for the items authorizes the check-out clerk to use the POS terminal to transfer funds directly from the customer's account to the store's account at the same bank or, through interbank communications switches, at another participating bank. The customer does not have to spend time writing a check and having it verified by the clerk; the retailer expedites check-out service, promptly receives the funds, and avoids checks drawn against closed accounts or accounts with insufficient funds. The technology for POS systems is available and experiments demonstrate its feasibility. Nevertheless, consumers have not rushed to use POS systems from which they see limited benefits compared to the convenience of writing checks at retail locations.[12]

## SERVICE CHARGES

Banks recover, through service charges on their checking accounts, only a fraction of their costs to process the accounts. This unrecovered difference is

11. Linda Fenner Zimmer, "Cash Dispensers: Automated Tellers Come of Age," *The Magazine of Bank Administration,* May 1978, pp. 19-23.

12. Gary Marple and Blair C. Shick, "Consumers: Forgotten Factors in the EFT Formula," *The Magazine of Bank Administration,* February 1977, pp. 20-25.

an implicit payment to the account holder(s). Other things equal, if it lowers its service charges, a bank can increase its implicit payment to the account holder(s); and, if it raises its service charges, it can decrease the payments. A bank also can structure its service charges to provide higher, or lower, implicit payments to depositors that meet specific conditions, such as those with large balances. Thus a bank can use its service charge policy as a way to engage in implicit price competition for demand deposits.

### Diversity of Service Charges

Most banks have service charge schedules by which they charge a demand-deposit account a *monthly maintenance fee,* such as one dollar, and/or a *per-item fee,* such as ten cents per check written against the account. Service-charge schedules also specify special fees for items like:

- *NSF checks,* which are written against an account with *n*ot *s*ufficient *f*unds and returned by the bank to the check recipient
- *overdraft checks,* which are written against an account with insufficient funds but that, as a service to the check writer, the bank decides to pay and then collect from the check writer
- *stop payment orders,* in which a check writer instructs the bank not to pay a check that has not yet cleared  (A check writer usually stops payment because a check apparently has been lost or because of a dispute with the check's recipient.)

Most service charge schedules waive all or part of the fees for accounts with large minimum or average balances-during a service charge period.

While bank service charge schedules thus have some common features, two studies document the variety of service charge strategies. One study surveys "checking account plans and prices at 113 banks in 23 Texas towns," and it reports that "the prices differ considerably from town to town and, with one or two exceptions, from bank to bank within a town."[13] It further reports that "prices tend to be more variable in the towns where their average is higher, so the depositor has much to gain from shopping." While it thus demonstrates the variety of checking account prices, the study does not try to explain the reasons for the variety. Another study shows how "the ratio of total service charges to average demand deposits varies" among various groupings of banks.[14] The study reports how this service-charge ratio generally is:

- "higher at banks with deposits less than $500 million than at those with deposits above this amount"

13. Dale Osborne and Jeanne Wendel, "The Surprising Variety of Checking Account Prices," *Voice* (Federal Reserve Bank of Dallas), May 1978, pp. 8-16.

14. Eleanor Erdevig, "Deposit Service Charges," *Economic Perspectives* (Federal Reserve Bank of Chicago), November-December 1977, pp. 10-13.

- "substantially higher on personal checking accounts than on commercial checking accounts"
- within similar deposit-size categories, lower for FRS member banks than for nonmember banks

The study further reports that the service-charge ratio has been rising since its low point between 1972 and 1973.

## Free Checking

Although check clearing involves costs for individual banks and the banking system, some banks offer free checking accounts. Proliferation of free checking illustrates how banks compete for demand deposits when they cannot pay interest. It also raises provocative questions about the costs and benefits of continuing to prohibit payment of explicit interest.

A bank offering free checking does not charge qualified depositors any service charges for maintaining the account or for processing each check written against the account. Most banks traditionally offered free checking as a courtesy to some customers, such as churches and charitable organizations. By the early 1960s, however, some banks began to offer free checking to any retail customer who met minor qualifications such as maintaining a minimum balance of $50 to $100 or having a credit line with the bank.

A bank that initially offers free checking probably anticipates that it will more than offset the foregone service charges with revenues generated by many new depositors who also use other services of the bank.[15] Moreover, a bank that initiates free checking in a community often is a new bank that has no legacy of service charge revenues to forego and is anxious to obtain customers whose new business will help offset the bank's fixed costs. An initiating bank often attracts people who previously were customers of other banks, which promptly respond by offering their versions of free checking. Before long, free checking is prevalent throughout the community, so that depositors then have little incentive to switch banks. The banks, however, forego service charge revenues that help offset check-processing costs.

Although it provides some depositor benefits, free checking imposes substantial costs on the banking system and other parts of the economy. People who are eligible for free checking can treat their check writing as a "free good." They incur no per-unit cost per check, so why not, whenever convenient, write small checks to merchants, news carriers, and others? Such activity proliferates the number of checks that must be cleared. The FRS bears substantial costs to clear checks. When it incurs higher check-processing expenses, other things equal, it contributes less revenue to

---

15. Steven J. Weiss, "Commercial Bank Price Competition: The Case of 'Free' Checking Accounts," *New England Economic Review* (Federal Reserve Bank of Boston), September-October 1969, pp. 3-22.

the U.S. Treasury. Banks incur check-clearing costs, but they do not absorb these costs. They pass on at least part of these expenses to their customers, for example by charging higher loan rates than they would without the check-clearing costs. Thus other bank customers indirectly bear part of the clearing costs associated with unrestrained check writing. (Paradoxically, free checking increases the flow of checks at a time when banks seek to reduce the flow by variants of EFTS.) Merchants who process many small checks also incur costs related to delays at check-out counters, delays in check clearing, and possible bad checks. Unrestrained check writing also imposes costs of inconvenience to others, such as the people waiting in a check-out line behind a purchaser who writes a small check that must then be scrutinized by the clerk before being accepted. Thus when one reviews free checking's various costs and benefits, "it is difficult to postulate any circumstances by which, when examined across participating publics, the benefits of free checking can exceed its costs."[16] Therefore there is a need to examine ways to discourage the writing of checks that provide small benefits to writers and impose costs on others. One way is to reexamine the merits of prohibiting interest payments on demand deposits. If this ban were lifted, banks would pay explicit interest; and they would develop competitive service charge schedules that more accurately reflect costs of check processing.

## CUSTOMER CONVENIENCE

Various surveys conclude that many people select a bank because of its proximity to a person's home or work.[17] There are, however, at least two more dimensions of convenience: access to tellers, staff, and officers within a bank; and access to related banking services. An innovative bank develops appropriate strategies for each dimension of customer convenience.

Most people have an account with a bank that is near their home or place of work. Location, therefore, is a key factor in a bank's ability to attract depositors. In states that permit branching, many banks develop networks of branches that are convenient to clusters of people and businesses, especially those that are potentially profitable customers. Branch systems often use survey information and advanced analytical techniques to select sites for new branches. Whether or not branching is permitted, banks seek to provide their depositors convenient access via drive-in and walk-up facilities, parking lots, extended banking hours, bank-by-mail procedures, direct-deposit systems, and, where permitted, off-premise ATMs and/or POS terminals.

To try to differentiate itself from rival banks, a bank can develop procedures to reduce customer waiting time. If a bank believes that many

16. Paul F. Jessup, "How Free is 'Free Checking'?" *The Magazine of Bank Administration*, May 1974, pp. 18-23.

17. "Bank Markets and Services: Summary of Three Surveys of Bank Customers," *Business Conditions* (Federal Reserve Bank of Chicago), May 1967, pp. 6-10.

customers value prompt, courteous service, it will willingly incur higher expenses to staff its tellers' windows, especially in periods of customary peak demand. Any bank can reduce average waiting times by having observant supervisors who monitor waiting-line patterns and experiment with staffing schedules to reduce customer delays. Some large banks use formal analytical procedures to simulate, over time, the patterns of customer arrivals at tellers' windows and to improve the scheduling of, and access to, tellers' windows.[18]

A bank also can develop procedures by which its customers have convenient access to officers and staff. One way is to identify those personnel who most frequently serve the public and then have these people openly seated at desks that are easily accessible to bank customers. Another way is to develop convenience centers within a bank and have these centers staffed by people who can promptly process various transactions and answer diverse questions.

As they publicize with their industry logo of "full-service banking," in addition to checking accounts banks offer related financial services to individuals and to large private and public organizations. Banks view these services as parts of a total service package that helps attract and retain depositors. At the retail level, for example, banks advertise their bank credit cards, consumer loans, and home mortgage loans. Some banks also offer *automatic transfer* (AT) *accounts,* whereby, by prior agreement, a bank automatically transfers funds from a retail customer's savings account to checking account whenever the customer's checking account balance falls below a preagreed level. (The federal banking agencies first permitted these AT accounts in late 1978, and so banks have had limited experience with them.) Large banks also emphasize their expertise with such services as cash-management systems, complex loans, leasing, portfolio management, and international banking. Banks thus stress how their current and potential depositors can conveniently obtain diverse financial services within one organization.

## PROVIDING AND PRICING RELATED BANKING SERVICES

To attract and retain demand deposits, a bank often makes concessions in related services that it can price more flexibly than demand deposits. To illustrate, a bank usually will offer and/or negotiate lower loan rates for its depositors who maintain large balances. Two individuals, for example, each apply for a similar loan from the bank at which they each have demand deposits. A loan officer reviews both applications and concludes that the bank should offer to make each loan. If other factors, such as risk, are similar, but Applicant A has maintained and is expected to maintain demand deposits substantially higher than those of Applicant B, then the loan officer

---

18. James A. Gossen, "BAI Teller Model: A Simulation Approach to Teller Efficiency," *The Magazine of Bank Administration,* November 1972, pp. 33-37. George W. Sheldon and Frederic E. Finch, "Bank Queues: A Comparative Analysis of Waiting Lines," *The Magazine of Bank Administration,* July 1976, pp. 31-35.

will likely offer Applicant A better loan terms, such as a lower rate, a lower downpayment, and/or a longer maturity. If the loan officer does not directly offer the better terms, the loan officer will likely concede them if Applicant A is an astute negotiator.

Banks offer reduced loan rates especially to corporations and municipalities that keep large balances in their checking accounts. One study reports a significant relationship whereby banks, other things equal, charge their business customers lower loan rates the higher the balances that these borrowers keep in their checking accounts.[19] Another study reports how a sample of banks made concessions in lending rates to municipalities that maintained checking accounts with them.[20]

A bank has other ways to reward people who keep noninterest-earning deposits with them. For example, it can rent its safe-deposit boxes at low rates as a way to attract and retain depositors; and it can provide specialized financial planning services to large depositors.

## OTHER NONPRICE STRATEGIES

While they traditionally offered occasional premiums, such as distinctive coin banks, in recent years banks have expanded their offerings to include crystal, flatware, shrubbery, and other household and personal items. Some bank lobbies evoke a bazaar atmosphere in which the bank displays its latest premium offerings. Thus, when they cannot pay explicit interest, banks engage in a form of barter; and, as interest rates rise and the value of funds to both owners and banks increases, the value of the premiums typically increases. The FDIC and various states have had limited success in their attempts to limit premium offerings.

To test the effectiveness of bank premium offerings, one study analyzes the retention rates and deposit balances for samples of 200 new accounts that were attracted by premiums and 200 new accounts not attracted by the premiums.[21] The study concludes that ''new demand deposits opened by bank customers receiving a premium perform as well for the bank during the six months following their opening as those deposits not attracted by such a premium.''

A second strategy is for a bank to develop new services that will usefully distinguish it—at least temporarily—from its principal rivals. Some banks rushed to introduce their own credit cards, not only as a probable source of future revenues but also to attract deposits of card applicants who were not already among the banks' customers. Banks also develop

---

19. Donald P. Jacobs, *Business Loan Costs and Bank Market Structure: An Empirical Estimate of Their Relations,* National Bureau of Economic Research, Occasional Paper 115, 1971.

20. Neil B. Murphy, ''A Test of the Deposit Relationship Hypothesis,'' *Journal of Financial and Quantitative Analysis,* March 1967, pp. 53-59.

21. Robert H. Preston, F. Robert Dwyer, and William Rudelius, ''The Effectiveness of Bank Premiums,'' *Journal of Marketing,* July 1978, pp. 96-101. (The study also examines time-deposit accounts.)

innovative ways to package their services, such as computerized *consolidated statements* that report the recent status and activity of all of a customer's deposit accounts and loans with a bank. Although some banks publicize the customer convenience of consolidated statements, the banks also benefit in that handling and mailing costs are reduced. Also, to *cross sell* its services, a bank can have its staff use visual or computerized procedures to scan the statements to identify groups of customers who do not currently use—but are probable candidates to use—specific services. The marketing staff can then directly advertise these services to the targeted customers.

As a third strategy, a bank tries to develop and project what it judges to be an effective image. Bank officials commit substantial resources to plan and staff their bank's physical facilities, and they often seek unified architectural designs for branch networks and unified wearing apparel for staff who meet the public. Also, as part of their public image, most banks encourage their personnel to participate in community and trade organizations and in civic fund-raising activities.

A fourth strategy is advertising, which publicizes the other marketing strategies. Unable to engage in price competition, banks extensively use advertising budgets as part of their nonprice competitive strategies. In many communities bank advertisements pervade newspapers, billboards, and television programs. A bank thus publicizes its newest premiums and services, or it seeks to publicize the bank's image as personal, friendly, caring, or resourceful.

A fifth strategy involves *direct calling programs* by which a bank's officers and staff personally call on potential and current accounts. At the retail level, banks often participate in programs that receive newcomers to a community. At the wholesale level, a large bank has officials who call on current and potential customers throughout the bank's perceived market area. These callers solicit accounts of outlying banks, corporations, and other large organizations.

Bank marketing officials use their trade journals and trade-association meetings to keep informed about strategies used by banks in other cities. They then evaluate the probable costs and benefits of trying similar strategies in their communities.

## PRINCIPAL SOURCES OF DEMAND DEPOSITS

Banks seek deposits from various customers categorized as follows:[22]

- households
- small businesses

---

22. In its report of condition, a bank reports its total IPC deposits (those of individuals, partnerships, and corporations), an aggregate figure that contains accounts that vary widely by size, location of the holders, and type of holders. Bankers and students of banking gain insights by looking at subcategories of IPC deposits.

- public agencies
- large firms
- correspondent banks
- foreign clients

All banks have deposits from the first three categories; large banks in major financial centers hold most deposits of large firms, correspondent banks, and foreign clients.

Exhibit 6-2 outlines how banks direct their deposit-acquisition strategies toward various categories of customers. For example, to compete for household accounts, banks emphasize convenience and premiums. In contrast, to compete for business and public accounts, banks emphasize their loan policies, check-clearing capabilities, and other special services.

## HOUSEHOLDS

Studies consistently show that heads of households generally choose a bank that is convenient to their home or place of work. One study surveys two medium-sized cities and concludes that the large majority of households use a bank "that is most convenient to them" and that these households "consider only other local banks as possible alternatives to their present banks."[23] Most households that bank by mail similarly use local or nearby institutions. Another study reports similar results from a survey of households in a suburban county.[24] Fifty-eight percent of the households cite convenience to home (47%) or place of work (11%) as the principal reason why they select a particular bank for their household checking account. The third most frequently cited reason is "nice, friendly, like it" (10%). Because most banks emphasize their "friendliness," few banks can use this attribute to distinguish themselves from nearby rivals.

The preceding surveys report two other general conclusions. One, although they use their banks primarily for checking accounts, substantial percentages of households also use the same bank for services like time deposits and loans. Two, although customer loyalty is less strong for households than for business firms, most households do not readily change banks. These results suggest that banks should cross sell their services and they should focus on ways to identify households that are about to open their first account in the community.

No recent studies refute the basic conclusions of the preceding surveys, which predate the spread of "free checking" and services such as bank credit cards and consolidated customer statements. Also, when it evaluates whether to offer a new promotional service, a bank has to estimate whether it is likely to continue attracting nonlocal household depositors as nearby banks respond with their variants of the competitive strategy.

---

23. "Bank Markets and Services: Summary of Three Surveys of Bank Customers," *Business Conditions* (Federal Reserve Bank of Chicago), May 1967, p. 10.

24. Robert D. Bowers, "Businesses, Households, and Their Banks," *Business Review* (Federal Reserve Bank of Philadelphia), March 1969, pp. 14-19.

## EXHIBIT 6-2

### Competing for Demand Deposits: Principal Strategies and Sources

| Sources | Paying Interest | Check-Clearing Services | "Free Checking" | Customer Convenience | Providing and Pricing Related Banking Services | Other Nonprice Strategies |
|---|---|---|---|---|---|---|
| | (Legislated Prohibition) | | | | | |
| Households | | | | 1 | | 2 |
| Small businesses | | | | 1 | 2 | |
| Public agencies | | | | 1 | 2 | |
| Large firms | | 2 | | | 1 | |
| Correspondent banks | | 1 | | | 1 | |
| Foreign clients | | | | | | |

*Note*: Numbers rank the reportedly most effective strategies as related to each source. For greater detail, see text.

## SMALL BUSINESSES

Although they most often cite "quality of services" as their principal criterion by which to select a bank, most small businesses confine their selections to local banks.[25] Business firms are strongly loyal to their primary bank. "It appears that once having selected a primary bank, firms change banks very infrequently—usually only after experiencing a substantial disappointment such as a loan turndown."[26] A probable reason for this loyalty is that a business develops a close relationship with its bank, which thus becomes expert in servicing the firm's special needs. To end such an established relationship involves disruption costs, so most businesses change their primary bank very infrequently.

Many small businesses have accounts at more than one local bank, and they keep informed, usually by direct contact, of prices and policies at other banks in their area. Also, most small businesses have loan relationships with their local bank(s).

The preceding survey results suggest that a bank that seeks local business accounts should focus its solicitations on small businesses that have convenient access to the bank. Also, because customer loyalty is strong, it should consider these tactics:

25. Robert D. Bowers, "Businesses, Households, and Their Banks," *Business Review* (Federal Reserve Bank of Philadelphia), March 1969, pp. 14-19. "Bank Markets and Services: Summary of Three Surveys of Bank Customers," *Business Conditions* (Federal Reserve Bank of Chicago), May 1967, pp. 6-10. Clifton B. Luttrell and William E. Pettigrew, "Banking Markets for Business Firms in the St. Louis Area," *Review* (Federal Reserve Bank of St. Louis), September 1966, pp. 9-12.

26. "Bank Markets and Services: Summary of Three Surveys of Bank Customers," *Business Conditions* (Federal Reserve Bank of Chicago), May 1967, p. 8.

- cement current customer relationships and cross sell these customers
- identify new businesses that have as yet no local bank relationship
- try to become a valuable additional (secondary) bank for businesses that already have a primary bank.

## PUBLIC AGENCIES

All banks are depositories for some local public agencies, such as school districts, community hospitals, and city governments; and almost all banks are depositories for the U.S. Treasury. In addition, large money-center banks actively solicit deposits of state and regional governmental units.

### Local and State Governmental Units

Although there is little survey information about relationships between public agencies and banks, it is likely that most local governmental units have their demand deposits with one or more nearby banks. These local public treasurers cannot earn interest on demand deposits at other banks, and they do not need many special banking services, so why should they incur the inconvenience costs of having demand deposits at nonlocal banks. Moreover, officials of local governmental units often have close civic and social ties with local bankers.

A local governmental unit has few banking needs. It wants its bank(s) to process its accounts efficiently and perhaps to provide some advisory services. When it decides to borrow funds, it expects its depository banks to be willing lenders, either by direct loans or by investing in its newly offered debt instruments. A study of depositor-borrower relationships among a sample of Massachusetts towns and their banks supports this expected behavior pattern.[27]

Large banks compete for part of the demand deposits held by states, regional governmental units, and large cities. These banks have financial and human resources to provide specialized deposit, loan, and other services to large customers. Also, they often have departments or affiliates that underwrite public offerings of debt instruments by large public agencies.

As long as interest rates on other short-term assets were low, public treasurers contentedly held demand deposits that exceeded their transactions needs. By the early 1960s, however, interest rates began to rise and some citizens groups scrutinized the financial practices of public agencies. Under these new conditions most public treasurers have pared their demand deposits in order to invest any excess funds in interest-earning time deposits and money-market instruments. Analytical banks must therefore monitor and evaluate whether the benefits of retaining or attracting such pared public accounts continue to exceed the costs of servicing them.

---

27. Neil B. Murphy, "A Test of the Deposit Relationship Hypothesis," *Journal of Financial and Quantitative Analysis,* March 1967, pp. 53-59.

Many states have laws that require banks to *pledge collateral* against deposits of public agencies. These laws are to protect these special depositors in the event their bank fails. A state can require, for example, that any bank holding its deposits, or those of its political subdivisions, must pledge $110 of U.S. Treasury or other acceptable securities against each $100 of public deposits. If a bank then fails, the public depositors can claim their collateral. In contrast to other depositors, who are general creditors of the bank, the public depositors are secured creditors with preferred claims in the event of liquidation. (With minor exceptions, by law banks cannot similarly secure the claims of other depositors.) To pledge collateral a bank incurs some costs associated with its reduced flexibility to manage its investments portfolio. Analytical bankers therefore evaluate whether certain public deposits warrant these collateralization costs. Also, some banking spokespeople advocate that, as an alternative to pledged collateral, the FDIC should insure all public deposits.

### Treasury Tax & Loan Accounts

The U.S. Treasury has a collateralized Treasury Tax & Loan (TT&L) account at most banks. Business firms can pay certain federal taxes—such as income taxes withheld for employees and corporate income taxes—to one of these banks, which, on instruction, will debit the taxpayer's account and credit the TT&L account. Subscriptions to some issues of U.S. Treasury securities, such as savings bonds, also are eligible for deposit in TT&L accounts.

Treasury and banking spokespeople cite how use of TT&L accounts is less disruptive than would be the case if major tax payments were debited from bank accounts and immediately credited to the Treasury's disbursement accounts at the Federal Reserve Banks. From the inception of the TT&L system in 1917, banks paid no interest on TT&L accounts until 1978. Banks with TT&L accounts did, however, provide various services for the U.S Treasury at little or no cost. For example, they acted as tax collection agents and they sold and redeemed U.S. savings bonds. Throughout this long period the Treasury and the banks implicitly agreed that a bank's earnings from its noninterest-paying TT&L account was to compensate the bank for the services it performed for the Treasury.

As interest rates climbed in the 1960s, the Treasury began to suspect that its noninterest-earning TT&L accounts overcompensated the depository banks, and a Treasury study in 1974 confirmed this belief. Subsequent federal legislation (1977) revises the rules for TT&L accounts and allows the Treasury to earn an explicit return on its temporary cash surpluses. Under the new rules, if it wants to be a TT&L depository, a bank (or a qualifying nonbank intermediary) has to choose one of two ways to process the TT&L account.[28] It can select the *remittance option,* under which it agrees to

---

28. Elijah Brewer, "Treasury to Invest Surplus Tax and Loan Balances," *Economic Perspectives* (Federal Reserve Bank of Chicago), November-December 1977, pp. 14-20. William N. Cox, "Changes in the Treasury's Cash Management Procedures," *Economic Review* (Federal Reserve Bank of Atlanta), January-February 1978, pp. 14-16.

forward—within one day—all its tax and loan receipts to the Treasury's account at the Federal Reserve Bank. Alternatively, it can select the *note option,* under which it agrees that each day it will transfer all of its previous day's tax and loan receipts to an interest-paying note account. The bank further agrees to redeem the note on demand and to pay interest at the publicized repurchase agreement rate. Because the note is not a deposit, the bank does not have to hold required reserves against it. Under either option a bank no longer has use of noninterest-paying TT&L accounts, and so the Treasury has set a schedule of fees that it agrees to pay banks that provide selected tax and loan services for it. In view of these new TT&L procedures, a bank has to decide whether to be a Treasury depository and, if so, which option to choose. These decisions are not irrevocable, so, over time, a bank needs to reevaluate the benefits and costs of its TT&L alternatives.

## LARGE FIRMS

Several surveys focus on the banking relationships of large firms defined, for example, as:[29]

- *Fortune's* listing of the 500 largest firms
- twenty large firms that have assets which range from $46 million to $2 billion, and that have their headquarters in the northeastern United States
- twenty-three firms with net worth above $1 million and with headquarters in or near St. Louis

Although they do not use the same definition of a "large firm," these three surveys report similar results, which in some ways contrast to those of surveys of small businesses and their banks.

Large firms have their primary banking relationship(s) with one or more large banks that usually are located near a firm's headquarters and/or in a major financial center. One of the surveys reports that "the financial condition of a bank is of first importance to more treasurers than is any other selection factor."[30] (Location ranks number two.) The treasurers apparently examine a bank's financial condition as a guide to its ability to make large loans. Corporate treasurers also favor large banks that offer a wide range of services in such areas as collections and payments, short-term investment counselling, and international banking.

Large banks seldom charge explicit fees for the specialized services they provide to large firms. Instead they rely on a barter system whereby they provide services, the total value of which directly relates to the value of

29. William F. Staats, "Corporate Treasurers and Their Depositories," *Business Review* (Federal Reserve Bank of Philadelphia), March 1969, pp. 9-13. Neil B. Murphy, "Large Firms and Their Banks," *New England Business Review* (Federal Reserve Bank of Boston), December 1968, pp. 18-22. Clifton B. Luttrell and William E. Pettigrew, "Banking Markets for Business Firms in the St. Louis Area," *Review* (Federal Reserve Bank of St. Louis), September 1966, pp. 9-12.

30. Staats, "Corporate Treasurers and Their Depositories," p. 11.

the demand deposits maintained by a firm over time. Some commentators document various costs of this implicit pricing system, and they emphasize the benefits of an alternative system whereby banks would explicitly price their various corporate services.[31]

All three surveys report that large firms are strongly loyal to their primary bank(s). As with small businesses, large firms see major disruption costs in changing banks; and so, unless they foresee substantial benefits from doing so, they are reluctant to switch their primary bank(s).

In contrast to small businesses, a large firm often has several primary banking relationships. One of the surveys reports that well over half the firms have major depository relationships with ten or more banks. Moreover, a large firm usually has many secondary accounts with other geographically scattered banks that help clear its checks, process its local payrolls, and often participate in large loans to the firm.

Because large firms seldom switch their primary depository relationships but do have many bank relationships, a large bank should focus on its becoming an additional depository of large firms that do not already have an account with it. One tactic is to develop new specialized services that appeal to large firms that will therefore open a new account relationship with it. The large bank then works to cement and extend these new account relationships.

### Accelerated Funds Collection Systems

Some large banks have specialists who design accelerated check collection systems as a service for current and potential corporate clients. These systems help a client firm to reduce its nonearning assets that are in the process of collection.

To illustrate, a Boston firm has an extensive mail-order business throughout the United States. Initially, its customers all send their payments to the company's headquarters, where the checks are recorded and then delivered to a nearby primary bank for collection via the check-clearing system. Because of the FRS clearing schedule and possible delays in clearing distant checks through other channels, the depository bank defers crediting the retailer's account with collected funds until it, the bank, receives credit for the deposited checks. In this process, the retailer cannot use the uncollected funds for transactions or short-term investments; it has to wait until its bank fully credits its account for the collected items.

An alternative procedure is for the retailer to establish accounts with banks located in regional financial centers throughout the country. It also rents a post office box (*lock box*) near each of these banks, and it authorizes each bank to have access to the nearby box. Then the retailer groups its mail-order customers by region; and, when it bills its customers in each

---

31. Lowell L. Bryan, "Put a Price on Credit Lines," *The Bankers Magazine*, Summer 1974, pp. 44-49. James P. Furniss and Paul S. Nadler, "Should Banks Reprice Corporate Services?" *Harvard Business Review*, May-June 1966, pp. 95-105.

region, it provides them with remittance envelopes that are preaddressed to the firm's post office box in that region. Several times a day a bank employee removes all the envelopes addressed to the retailer's lock box and delivers them to the bank. There other personnel quickly record key information from each check and then sort the checks for rapid clearance within the region, probably through the local Federal Reserve Bank and various clearinghouses.

This regional lock box procedure expedites the retailer's check collection. One, checks mailed from distant points spend less time en route when they go to a nearby regional post office instead of to the firm's headquarters. Two, each regional depository bank quickly records key information (such as payor and amount) from each check and then starts the check's clearing process. The bank later sends the information, often on a computer tape, to the retailer's headquarters where it is processed for accounting purposes. This procedure contrasts to that whereby a firm first records the information and then sends the checks to its bank for clearing. Three, the regional depository banks can clear checks drawn on nearby banks more quickly than can a distant primary bank that has to route the checks back to each region. If it thus expedites its check-collection procedures, the retailer gains prompter access to collected funds in its regional banks. It then arranges for the regional banks to transfer funds quickly by wire to one or more of its primary depository banks so that the firm can use the funds for transactions and/or short-term investments. While it thus benefits by expediting and mobilizing its collection of funds, the firm also incurs costs of compensating the regional depository banks for their services. To compensate them it usually maintains agreed amounts of demand deposits or at times it pays an explicit fee.

Some large banks have specialists who design tailor-made lock-box systems for current and potential customers. These specialists use management-science techniques to analyze the costs and benefits of various combinations of regional lock boxes. Usually the specialists begin by analyzing samples of a firm's current inflow and routing of checks. Then they analyze various delivery schedules of the post office and other couriers and the processing schedules of various large regional banks. With such information, the specialists model various lock-box combinations in order to identify the several combinations that result in the firm's having funds promptly available, and at low cost.[32] To illustrate, the designers may show one firm how a new lock-box system with 5 regional depositories will likely enable it to obtain its funds almost as promptly as its current judgmental system that uses 15 regional depositories. Moreover, the total compensation to the 5 depositories will be substantially less than the total currently paid to the 15 depository banks. Although the designers recommend a specific

32. Robert L. Kramer, "Analysis of Lock Box Locations," *Bankers Monthly,* May 15, 1966, pp. 50-53. Alan Kraus, Christian Janssen, and Alan McAdams, "The Lock-Box Location Problem," *Journal of Bank Research,* Autumn 1970, pp. 50-58. Steven F. Maier and James H. Vander Weide, "The Lock-Box Location Problem: A Practical Reformulation," *Journal of Bank Research,* Summer 1974, pp. 92-95.

5-box system for one firm, their procedures will likely suggest a different combination (by number and location) of lock boxes for another firm based in a different city and receiving checks in a different pattern. Even though a bank's own specialists, based on their analyses, cannot consistently recommend their bank as a regional depository, some large banks choose to offer this service to demonstrate their capability of providing valuable advisory assistance to large firms.[33]

## CORRESPONDENT BANKS

Deposits of other domestic banks account for about 11 percent of total demand deposits in the domestic banking system. Exhibit 6-3 summarizes how these *interbank deposits* generally flow from small and medium-sized banks in outlying areas to large banks in major financial centers. About 175 large banks hold about 85 percent of all correspondent deposits; and about

## EXHIBIT 6-3

### Flows of Correspondent Deposits

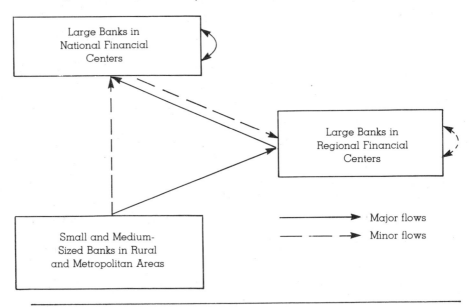

---

33. Specialists who design accelerated check collection systems can apply similar techniques to design *delayed disbursement systems,* by which corporate clients, usually by writing checks against accounts at selected remote banks, can delay the clearing of the checks by their recipients. FRS officials have begun to express their disapproval with some delayed disbursement practices, and they urge banks voluntarily to curtail their participation in such practices or else face new regulations that will curtail such participation.

20 large banks in Chicago and New York account for almost 60 percent of all such deposits.[34]

Interbank deposits are a keystone of the nation's correspondent banking system. Prior to the Federal Reserve Act, outlying banks typically held some legal and/or precautionary reserves in the form of demand deposits with large city banks. An outlying bank thus had cash readily available to meet future deposit withdrawals or loan demands, and at times it earned interest on its deposits with the large bank(s). Since the Federal Reserve Act, however, member banks—which include all national banks—can use only their deposits with Federal Reserve Banks and their vault cash to meet their legal reserve requirements. Most nonmember banks, however, can count at least part of their deposits at correspondent banks toward meeting their state reserve requirements.

Most outlying banks have accounts with several city correspondents, with medium-sized banks maintaining more such accounts than small banks. "Most small banks keep relatively large balances with one or two correspondent banks, generally located in the nearest regional city, and three or four smaller accounts with other banks."[35] Many of the smaller accounts are courtesy accounts based on tradition or personal friendships.

Exhibit 6-4, which summarizes various benefits and costs of correspondent banking, provides a systematic framework by which to introduce the principal dimensions of correspondent banking.

## EXHIBIT 6-4

### Correspondent Banking: A Cost-Benefit Perspective

| | Rural and Metropolitan Banks (Small and Medium-Sized) | City Correspondents (Large) |
|---|---|---|
| Principal Benefits | Access to large resources and specialized services<br>Share in probable scale economies | A major source of demand deposits<br><br>Probable contribution to profits<br><br>Helps defray costs of specialization |
| Principal Costs | Low costs, especially for banks that can count deposits at correspondent banks as part of their required reserves | Need for account analysis |

---

34. Calculated from *Federal Reserve Bulletin*, August 1979, p. A19. An average of daily or weekly figures is probably more representative than are these figures as of September 30, 1978. Using such averages, one author reports that large banks accounted for 88 percent of domestic interbank deposits in late 1969. Robert E. Knight, "Correspondent Banking," *Monthly Review* (Federal Reserve Bank of Kansas City), Part I, November 1970, pp. 3-14.

35. Robert E. Knight, "Correspondent Banking," *Monthly Review* (Federal Reserve Bank of Kansas City), Part I, November 1970, pp. 3-14, Part II, December 1970, pp. 12-24, Part III, December 1971, pp. 3-17. (This quotation is from Part I, p. 9.)

### Benefits and Costs for Outlying Banks

Two large-scale surveys document how outlying banks gain convenient access to the resources and specialized services of their city correspondents.[36] Outlying banks extensively use their city correspondents for clearing checks. They cite ways in which this path is often quicker and more convenient than clearing through the FRS.

Outlying banks also expect their city correspondents to participate in loans with them. An *upstream loan participation* arises when an outlying bank has a valued customer who requests a loan amount that exceeds what the bank can legally or prudently lend to one borrower. In such a case the bank will often ask its city correspondent to participate in the loan. For example, a country bank lends $50,000 to a local farmer and arranges for its correspondent to lend another $100,000 to the same borrower. By one estimate, at least 60 percent of the banks in one Federal Reserve District have arranged such loan participations with correspondents. A *downstream loan participation* arises when an outlying bank faces slack loan demand in its area and then asks its city correspondent to let it participate in a large loan to one of the correspondent's major customers. The outlying bank may also agree to buy some small loans from the city correspondent. Often the outlying bank can obtain higher returns from such downstream loan participations and purchases than it can obtain from short-term investments.

Outlying banks also look to their city correspondents for such other services as computerized bookkeeping, safekeeping of securities, federal funds transactions, investment advice and transactions, and international financial transactions. Other specialized banking services are available—as well as special services like hospitality suites at bankers' conventions and sports and theatre tickets for country bankers visiting the big city.

City correspondents usually do not charge explicit fees for the diverse services they provide to outlying banks. Instead they expect each of their outlying banks to maintain balances that at least compensate for the package of services it uses. Therefore, from the viewpoint of outlying banks— especially nonmember banks—many of the services are "free." Even without the services, they would hold some assets in the form of noninterest-earning demand deposits at large banks. Under the current system they receive free services, instead of explicit interest, on these deposits.

### Benefits and Costs for City Correspondents

If there are scale economies in producing some specialized banking services, then large banks likely achieve such economies. To illustrate, no small bank will specialize in international transactions if it faces infrequent demand for this service. Occasionally, however, a local customer requests some foreign

---

36. Knight, "Correspondent Banking." Also, *A Report on the Correspondent Banking System,* Subcommittee on Domestic Finance, Committee on Banking and Currency, House of Representatives, 88th Congress, 2d Session, December 10, 1964.

currency or a funds transfer to a foreign country. The small bank can readily accommodate this request by using its city correspondent; and, indirectly, it incurs only a per-unit cost that reflects the cost structure of the large bank's specialized international banking department. City correspondents similarly share their likely scale economies and expertise when they assist outlying banks in their portfolio analyses.

Large banks usually benefit from their relationships with smaller banks. One, correspondent deposits are a major source of funds for which large banks pay no explicit interest and yet which they can lend or invest to generate revenues. At least part of these revenues flow through to profits. Two, correspondent deposits contribute to the total size of large banks, which can then cite their size when seeking accounts of other large depositors. Three, by allocating their total costs of specialized services among many users, large banks often can reduce per-unit costs. For example, a large bank can probably have a capable international banking department at lower per-unit cost when it can allocate the department's costs among many users, such as outlying banks as well as large firms.

Large banks need to analyze periodically their account relationships to ensure that the benefits they obtain from correspondent deposits exceed the costs of servicing these accounts. They have to be alert to cases where an outlying bank pares its noninterest-earning correspondent deposits but does not similarly pare the level of services it expects from the city correspondent. One author notes how "larger correspondent banks, confronted with an increasing demand for loans from their own nonbank customers, for loan participations from banks, and for more services from smaller banks, began seriously to analyze the accounts of respondent [outlying] banks to determine the profitability of serving as their correspondents."[37] The author then details various techniques of account analysis, as practiced by large correspondent banks.

Advocates of explicit bank pricing claim that banking and social resources would be distributed more efficiently if correspondent banks would charge explicit prices (fees) for their various services. Banks, especially those that can count their correspondent balances as part of their required reserves, generally oppose such a fee system. Despite such opposition, recent applications of account analysis procedures constitute a major first step toward a system whereby large banks list explicit fees for various services they offer to other banks.

## FOREIGN CLIENTS

Large American banks also hold some deposits of foreign clients that include governments, central banks, and other banks. These deposits total $10 billion (year-end 1977) and account for about 3 percent of total demand deposits in American banks.

---

37. Knight, "Correspondent Banking," Part III, p. 4.

A small number of large banks account for most of these foreign deposits. Thirteen large banks in New York City account for almost 70 percent of such deposits, and large banks in California and Chicago apparently account for most of the remainder.

Foreign banks other than central banks account for most of these deposits. This reflects the practice whereby the world's large banks hold deposits with peer banks in international financial centers. They develop these relationships to expedite international financial transactions, to arrange international loan participations, and to obtain timely information about economic developments in other regions. Thus, these international relationships logically extend the practice whereby large banks in national financial centers maintain some reciprocal correspondent relationships (Exhibit 6-3).

Foreign deposits are very much a preserve of America's largest banks, with their worldwide correspondent relationships and branch networks. These deposits are but one facet of the specialized—but important—subject of multinational banking (Chapter 21).

## SUMMARY

Historically, only banks have offered accounts from which depositors have the right to withdraw or transfer funds on demand. Although depositors mostly use checks to transfer funds from their demand deposits, banks—and some nonbank financial intermediaries—are developing electronic funds transfer (EFT) systems, by which depositors can instruct participating institutions to transfer funds directly to other accounts in the system. These technological and competitive developments will erode the traditional role of checks and the unique place of banks in the payments system.

Owners of demand deposits view them as money. Banks view demand deposits as a basic source of funds, part of which they can lend or invest in earning assets. The Banking Act of 1933 prohibits banks from paying interest on demand deposits. Despite questions about its rationale and economic efficiency, this prohibition still stands. Because they cannot pay explicit interest on demand deposits, banks engage in diverse forms of nonprice competition by which they pay implicit interest to owners of demand deposits.

All banks provide check-clearing services for their depositors. To do so they participate, directly or indirectly, in check-clearing networks that include: clearinghouses, regional check processing centers (RCPCs), the Federal Reserve System (FRS), and the correspondent banking system. To reduce the flow of paper checks, the banking system has developed and now offers:

- direct deposit systems
- check truncation procedures
- bank wire systems
- automated clearinghouses (ACHs)

- cash dispensers
- automated teller machines (ATMs)
- point-of-sale (POS) systems

While some banks offer each of these systems, consumers have not rushed to discontinue their traditional use of paper checks.

Banks also use their service charge policies as a way to pay some implicit interest on demand deposits. Most banks have service charge schedules that include: a monthly maintenance fee, per-item fees, and special fees for items like NSF checks, overdrafts, and stop-payment orders. Seldom, however, do these fees fully cover a bank's costs to process the demand-deposit accounts. Some banks offer free checking to qualifying depositors, but this "free" service often imposes costs on other participants in the payments system.

Customer convenience is another dimension of nonprice competition by banks that try to offer convenient: locations, hours, parking, access to tellers and officers, and packages of services.

Unable—by law—to offer explicit interest on demand deposits, a bank often makes price concessions in related services that it offers to depositors, especially those whose accounts are profitable for the bank. In particular, a customer who has a large inactive checking account will likely get a lower loan rate than will a customer of similar risk, but with a small, active checking account.

To try to get a competitive edge over their rivals, banks frequently offer and advertise novel premiums and services; they project their chosen image; and they use direct call programs to solidify current customer relationships and to solicit new depositors.

The principal sources of demand deposits are:

- households
- small businesses
- public agencies
- large firms
- correspondent banks
- foreign clients

Banks of all sizes compete for accounts in the first three categories; in addition, large money-center banks compete for accounts in the last three categories.

Various studies document that most households and small businesses select a bank that is convenient for them. These studies, and others, also report that businesses (small and large) seldom change their primary banking relationship(s). These survey results can be useful to bankers as they evaluate strategies by which to compete for various categories of depositors.

Banks usually have to pledge eligible securities as collateral for public deposits. Analytical bankers therefore have to review whether the benefits of such deposits exceed their collateralization and processing costs. Also, if it wants to be a depository for the U.S. Treasury, a bank has to select whether it will service the Treasury Tax & Loan (TT&L) account via the remittance option or the note option.

Large firms have their major accounts with one or more primary banks, and they have some additional accounts with secondary banks that provide them with such valuable services as accelerated funds collection systems and processing of strategically located lock boxes.

Correspondent deposits are a basic part of the correspondent banking system, by which medium-sized and small banks receive specialized services from large money-center banks. It is also these large banks, especially those in New York, that account for most of the nation's demand deposits held by foreign clients.

# 7
# OBTAINING TIME DEPOSITS

While they compete for demand deposits, banks also seek time deposits as a principal source of funds. This chapter examines strategies by which banks obtain time deposits via innovations in:

- consumer time deposits, such as consumer certificates of deposit, money-market certificates, and NOW accounts
- negotiable certificates of deposit that are held by large investors, such as large firms and nonprofit organizations

Even as they compete for time deposits subject to current laws and regulations, bankers need to have contingency plans for probable changes in these legal-regulatory constraints.

## INCREASING IMPORTANCE OF TIME DEPOSITS

Time deposits encompass two principal categories. *Savings deposits* have no specified maturity; they involve an account relationship between a depositor and a bank. The bank records all deposits to and withdrawals from such an account, and it provides the depositor with a record in the form of a passbook or a periodic statement of account transactions. *Other time deposits* have specified maturity dates, in some cases with provisions for automatic renewal. Most are in the form of a certificate for a specific amount of dollars that will be subject to withdrawal at a specific date. At times these deposits are in an open account to which additional deposits can be added but from which principal can be withdrawn only at specified future dates, such as the first five days of each month.

In contrast to demand deposits, time deposits are not legally subject to withdrawal on demand. By law, a bank can require depositors to provide up to 30-days notice before they withdraw funds from a time deposit. In practice, a bank stands ready to meet withdrawals from savings accounts on request and to meet withdrawals of other time deposits at their scheduled maturity dates. A bank will strive to honor these current practices and to avoid having to invoke its legal right to require advance notice of withdrawals.

With minor—but growing—exceptions, a customer cannot write a check against his or her time deposit in order to transfer funds directly to another person or institution. To thus transfer funds to a third party, a customer must:

- withdraw and transfer cash
- withdraw funds to obtain a bank check payable to a third party
- withdraw and transfer funds to a demand deposit against which a personal check can be written

Yet under automatic transfer accounts, a depositor can prearrange to have the bank automatically transfer funds from a savings account to a checking account, against which a check can be written. Also, in some states banks can offer NOW (negotiable order of withdrawal) accounts that are savings accounts that function like checking accounts.

Although they have long had powers to accept them, most banks did not solicit time deposits. Many bankers believed that banking's proper function was to accept demand deposits and make short-term loans to commerce and industry. They further believed that banks should not actively seek household demand deposits or time deposits, nor make long-term loans, such as home mortgage loans or consumer loans. Thus other institutions such as mutual savings banks, S&Ls, credit unions, and small loan companies began to provide services that many banks had defined to be outside their domain. In some cities, public-spirited bankers helped establish mutual savings banks to provide safe depositories for household savers that were not serviced by banks.

By the 1950s various banks, especially large banks in downtown areas, began to reexamine their traditional focus on a limited number of wholesale activities. If they retained this focus, then several new factors seemed certain to limit their future growth:

- Their demand deposits were unlikely to grow rapidly as major customers sought to pare such nonearning deposits in order to invest in short-term money-market instruments.
- Many individuals, whose demand deposits the downtown banks had not aggressively sought, were moving to outlying suburbs where banks had begun to provide more retail services.
- Although their sources of funds thus appeared limited, the large banks foresaw continued borrowing demands by their large customers.

Therefore most banks began to reevaluate their earlier policies of not actively seeking time deposits.

**EXHIBIT 7-1**

**Changing Sources of Time Deposits: 1961-77**
**(All Insured Commercial Banks: Figures in Billions)**

|  | Year-end 1961 | Year-end 1977 | 1977 Figure as an Approximate Multiple of 1961 Figure |
|---|---|---|---|
| Savings accounts | $ 64 | $215 | 3x |
| Other time deposits of individuals, partnerships and corporations (IPC) | 10 | 260 | 26x |
| U.S. government | * | * | |
| State and political subdivisions | 5 | 57 | 11x |
| Domestic interbank | * | 7 | . . . . . |
| Foreign clients | | | |
| Governments and central banks | 2 | 8 | 4x |
| Other banks | * | 2 | . . . . . |
| Total† | $ 81 | $549 | |
| Percent of Total Deposits | (33) | (59) | |

*Less than $1 billion.
†Actual reported totals for year-end 1961 and 1977 are $82.8 billion and $550.4 billion, respectively.
Source: *Annual Report of the Federal Deposit Insurance Corporation*, 1961, 1977, Table 109. (Prior to 1961 the FDIC did not report a detailed breakdown of various categories of IPC time deposits.)

Exhibit 7-1 summarizes how the banking system has increased its reliance on time deposits as a source of funds. At year-end 1961, time deposits accounted for 33 percent of total bank deposits; by year-end 1977 they accounted for 59 percent. Moreover, Exhibit 7-1 highlights broad changes in major sources of time deposits. Growth in savings deposits was relatively modest. These deposits, as a part of total time deposits, declined from almost 80 percent (year-end 1961) to 39 percent by year-end 1977. In contrast, there were notable increases in other categories of time deposits.

## SERVICING VARIOUS SOURCES OF TIME DEPOSITS

As with demand deposits, it is convenient to classify principal sources of time deposits as follows:

- households
- small businesses
- public agencies
- large firms
- correspondent banks
- foreign clients

In contrast to the prohibition of interest payments on demand deposits, banks can pay interest on time deposits. The rates they can pay, however, are generally subject to regulatory ceilings. Therefore banks also engage in nonprice strategies, by which they compete among themselves and also against nonbank financial intermediaries and money-market instruments.

## HOUSEHOLDS

The Banking Act of 1933 gives to the FRS the power to define what constitutes "time deposits" and to set maximum rates on time deposits. The statute applies to member banks, and the FRS administers its power through its *Regulation Q* rulings. The Banking Act of 1935 gives the FDIC similar powers over insured nonmember banks, and since 1936 these two federal banking agencies have coordinated their rulings about maximum interest rates on time deposits.

The rationale for ceiling rates on time deposits is similar to that used to prohibit interest payments on demand deposits:

- Some bankers might recklessly bid for time deposits and then construct risky portfolios to try to generate sufficient revenues to pay the promised interest.
- Funds might flow from local areas to major financial centers.
- If their costs of funds are held down, then banks might hold down their loan rates.

Subsequent commentators point out how each of these arguments—while possibly persuasive in the turmoil of a national depression—is suspect and how interest rate ceilings can contribute to economic inequities and inefficiencies.[1]

---

1. Chapter 6, "Paying Interest: Legislated Prohibition." Also, Milton Friedman, "Controls on Interest Rates Paid by Banks," *Journal of Money, Credit, and Banking,* February 1970, pp. 15-32. For a provocative critique of interest-rate ceilings, see Edward J. Kane, "Short-Changing the Small Saver: Federal Government Discrimination Against Small Savers During the Vietnam War," (A Comment) *Journal of Money, Credit, and Banking,* November 1970, pp. 513-522. One researcher uses a statistical model to estimate the "income losses to savers at savings institutions due to interest rate regulation." He estimates that their lost income is over $5 billion between 1968 and 1970. "The arguments brought to the defense of savings deposit rate regulation need to take these losses into account." David H. Pyle, "The Losses on Savings Deposits from Interest Rate Regulation," *The Bell Journal of Economics and Management Science,* Autumn 1974, pp. 614-622. Another study that attempts to measure the costs of interest-rate ceilings on time deposits is by Robert A. Taggart, Jr., and Geoffrey Woglom, "Savings Bank Reactions to Rate Ceilings and Rising Market Rates" *New England Economic Review* (Federal Reserve Bank of Boston), September-October 1978, pp. 17-31.

The Regulation Q ceiling on rates paid on savings deposits was 2½ percent from 1935 through 1956. (For other time deposits the ceiling ranged from 1 to 2½ percent, depending on maturity.) During the early part of this period, the ceiling rate had little impact on bank strategies. Many banks passively accepted, but did not actively seek, household savings deposits; and potential depositors could not readily get higher rates from other financial intermediaries or money-market investments. By the 1950s however, S&Ls and other nonbank financial intermediaries actively sought household savings accounts, and they offered rates that often exceeded the regulatory maximum that could be paid by banks. Some retail-oriented banks also wanted to compete for savings accounts; and so, the federal banking agencies lifted the rate ceiling on savings deposits to 3 percent at the beginning of 1957. After this change in the ceiling rate, the amount of consumer savings deposits at banks grew more rapidly than in preceding years. By year-end 1961, savings deposits accounted for almost 80 percent of all time deposits in banks. Since then, most banks have sought savings deposits, and they have also sought to develop new types of time deposits for household savers.

**Passbook Savings Accounts**

As with their demand deposits, many households keep their savings accounts at a bank that is convenient to their home or place of work. Usually this bank is the same one at which a household keeps its checking account. Banks publicize how their customers thus have the convenience of one-stop banking in which they can obtain various financial services at one location. Because most savings depositors select a bank that is geographically convenient, a bank tries to situate itself in an accessible location. Where branching is permitted, it focuses on placing new branches in strategic locations; and where branching is prohibited or limited, a large downtown bank often promotes revised legislation that will increase its flexibility to establish outlying branches.

While it tries to have convenient locations, any one bank finds it difficult to offer savings accounts that are distinctive from those offered by rival banks. Deposits at almost all banks are insured to legal maximum amounts by the FDIC, and most banks pay similar interest rates (at or near the Regulation Q ceiling) on savings deposits. Most banks similarly emphasize fast, friendly service and convenient hours, and they occasionally offer free premiums to new savings depositors and to current depositors who add to their accounts. Some banks also offer *telephonic transfer systems* by which their depositors who prearrange to do so, can, by telephone, instruct their bank to transfer funds from their savings accounts to checking accounts and vice versa.

Banks that seek household savings deposits compete not only with nearby banks but also with nearby S&Ls and mutual savings banks. Throughout most of the 1950s and 1960s these nonbank intermediaries customarily paid interest rates on savings deposits that exceeded the rates paid by nearby banks. In part, the nonbank intermediaries paid higher rates because, as more specialized financial intermediaries, they could not offer their depositors the convenience of a full set of consumer banking services that includes checking accounts.

Congress codified the customary difference between rates paid by banks and nonbank intermediaries when it passed the Interest Rate Act of 1966. This Act allows the FDIC to specify maximum rates on deposits in federally insured mutual savings banks, and it allows the Federal Home Loan Bank Board to specify maximum rates on deposits (accounts) in S&Ls that it supervises. The Act further requires the three regulatory agencies (FRS, FDIC, and FHLBB) to consult with each other before they change ceiling rates. Because S&Ls and, to a lesser extent, mutual savings banks hold large proportions of home mortgage loans, a reported goal of this Act is to provide these intermediaries—and indirectly the housing industry—a competitive edge in obtaining funds. Therefore the regulatory agencies permit S&Ls and mutual savings banks to pay interest rates up to 5½ percent on savings deposits, while they limit banks to a ceiling rate of 5¼ percent on savings deposits.

Many bankers contend that their banks are placed at a competitive disadvantage by the quarter-point difference in ceiling rates on savings accounts. Most S&Ls and mutual savings banks provide federally insured deposits; they advertise their convenient hours, friendly services, free premiums, and, where permitted, branch locations. Even so, one author examines savings flows between banks and nonbank financial intermediaries, and he observes that banks "have a fairly solid core of depositors who are not sensitive to interest rate differentials."[2]

## NOW Accounts

In 1972, several mutual savings banks first offered NOW accounts, which are a type of savings account against which depositors can write negotiable orders of withdrawal (NOWs) that look and function like checks. A NOW depositor, for example, can write a NOW payable to a store that in turn deposits it in its checking account for clearance like a check. The merchant thus receives a transfer of funds from the payor's interest-earning NOW account.

When they were first introduced, NOW accounts triggered debates among financial intermediaries and among their supervisory agencies. Bankers emphasized how inequitable it was if rival financial intermediaries could offer interest-paying NOW accounts while banks could not offer a similar product to their customers.

Although there was some initial discussion of proposals to ban all NOW accounts, in 1973 Congress passed legislation that permitted controlled experimentation with NOW accounts. In Massachusetts and New

2. Paul S. Anderson, "Savings Flows to Institutions Paying Low Rates," *New England Economic Review* (Federal Reserve Bank of Boston), September-October 1978, pp. 5-16.

Hampshire—the states where such accounts began—mutual savings banks, S&Ls, cooperative banks (state-chartered S&Ls in Massachusetts), and *banks* could offer NOW accounts to individuals. Institutions that offer NOW accounts could not use advertisements or in other ways solicit out-of-state depositors for these accounts. The federal supervisory agencies were to set ceiling rates for NOW accounts, and they set an initial ceiling rate of 5 percent for all NOW accounts. The agencies also were to study how these accounts were offered and used so that they could subsequently recommend whether Congress should extend, terminate, or modify the experiment. This initial NOW account experiment would also provide new information to reassess the broader issues of the probable effects if Congress were to remove the prohibition against explicit interest on demand deposits. In 1976 Congress extended the NOW account experiment throughout New England, and in 1978 it authorized NOW accounts for financial intermediaries in New York.

Several studies examine how banks and nonbank financial intermediaries introduced and managed NOW accounts in New England:[3]

- In Massachusetts and New Hampshire most banks were reluctant to offer NOW accounts, but they then did so in order to stem potential deposit losses to nonbank intermediaries that offered NOW accounts. Many of the banks initially offered "free" NOW accounts, but over time they and the nonbank intermediaries have imposed fees and/or high minimum balances for "free" NOW accounts.[4]
- In contrast, once they could do so, many banks in Connecticut, Maine, Rhode Island, and Vermont promptly offered NOW accounts but with high required minimum balances. These banks thus tried, with apparent success, to retain high-balance accounts even if the nonbank intermediaries offered free NOWs.
- A large proportion (31%) of Connecticut banks increased their service charges and/or minimum-balance requirements on personal checking accounts during the period in which they could first offer NOW accounts.

One author reviews the experiment with NOW accounts in New England, and he draws two lessons for bankers in other regions where NOW accounts

---

3. Ralph C. Kimball, "Recent Developments in the NOW Account Experiment in New England," and "The Maturing of the NOW Account in New England," both in *New England Economic Review* (Federal Reserve Bank of Boston), November-December 1976, pp. 3-19, and July-August 1978, pp. 27-42, respectively. Howard Keen, "Why Bankers Are Concerned about NOW Accounts," *Business Review* (Federal Reserve Bank of Philadelphia), November-December 1977, pp. 3-10. William A. Longbrake and Sandra B. Cohan, "The NOW Account Experiment," *Journal of Bank Research,"* Summer 1974, pp. 71-85.

4. One study reports that "NOW accounts are estimated to have reduced pretax earnings at all commercial banks in Massachusetts and New Hampshire by $6.7 million, or 3.4 percent in 1974, and by $15.9 million or 11.3 percent in 1975." Ralph C. Kimball, "Impacts of NOW Accounts and Thrift Institution Competition on Selected Small Commercial Banks in Massachusetts and New Hampshire, 1974-75," *New England Economic Review* (Federal Reserve Bank of Boston), January-February 1977, pp. 22-38.

may be permitted. "Whether NOW accounts are profitable or unprofitable can depend upon the pricing package that bankers devise"; and the transition period to NOW accounts may not extend beyond several years.[5] In view of various proposals to extend NOW accounts nationwide, each bank needs to do some contingency planning as to its introduction and pricing of NOW accounts.[6]

### Consumer Certificates of Deposit

Unlike savings deposits (and NOW accounts) that in practice are subject to withdrawal on demand, CDs are time deposits with specific maturity dates. If it designs and publicizes a variety of CDs, a bank can thereby segment and broaden its sources of time deposits; and it can try to manage the average maturities of such deposits.

If it does not already pay the ceiling rate, a bank can estimate the probable costs and benefits of raising the rate it pays on savings deposits. As a principal cost, the bank will have to pay the higher rate on *all* its savings deposits—not just on new deposits that the higher rate may attract. The bank can reasonably predict this incremental interest cost, especially as it would apply to its current passbook accounts. In contrast, the bank will find it difficult to confidently predict its incremental benefits from its thus raising its passbook rate. It has to try to estimate the incremental deposits that the bank will attract with its higher rate, and it has to try to estimate the potential profitability of the incremental deposits. Many depositors in rival institutions are unlikely to incur the inconvenience of transferring their accounts to the bank unless it raises its passbook rate substantially above those of its rivals. But then, if they anticipate substantial losses of deposits to the bank, the rival institutions will likely raise the rates they pay on passbook accounts. This competitive process may induce households to save more, but no one depository institution is likely to attract substantial deposits from its rivals.

Thus if it foresees additional interest costs and uncertain benefits from its raising its rate on passbook deposits, a bank will likely evaluate ways that it can offer higher rates *only* to current and new depositors who are willing to

---

5. Keen, "Why Bankers Are Concerned about NOW Accounts," p. 9.

6. A study estimates what might happen to bank earnings if Congress were to extend NOW account powers to financial intermediaries throughout the U.S. The authors provide various estimates based on alternate key assumptions and conclude that:

> . . . a bill which authorizes NOW accounts to be offered nationwide and a 2% interest to be paid on reserves held at Federal Reserve Banks would not have a substantially adverse effect on bank earnings, even if a 5% interest rate is permitted on NOW accounts. This is in large part attributable to our belief, based upon the recent NOW account experience in New England, that rational pricing of NOW account services would occur nationwide. The estimated earnings impacts do not vary substantially with bank size.

Gary G. Gilbert and Alan S. McCall, "The Transitional Impact of Nationwide NOW Accounts on Bank Earnings," *Issues in Bank Regulation,* Winter 1978, pp. 20-31. Also Dwight B. Crane and Michael J. Riley, "Strategies for a NOW-Account Environment," *The Bankers Magazine,* January-February 1979, pp. 35-41.

accept the terms of various CDs with their fixed maturities. Also, it may decide to offer higher rates on longer-term CDs and thus obtain funds it can manage differently than those from passbook accounts and short-term CDs.

CDs of less than $100,000 are subject to Regulation Q ceilings, and these CDs are classified as consumer CDs. Exhibit 7-2 summarizes the

## EXHIBIT 7-2

### Maximum Interest Rates Payable on Time and Savings Deposits at Federally Insured Institutions

Percent per annum

| Type and maturity of deposit | Commercial banks | | | | Savings and loan associations and mutual savings banks | | | |
|---|---|---|---|---|---|---|---|---|
| | In effect July 31, 1979 | | Previous maximum | | In effect July 31, 1979 | | Previous maximum | |
| | Percent | Effective date | Percent | Effective date | Percent | Effective date | Percent | Effective date |
| 1 Savings.......................... | 5¼ | 7/1/79 | 5 | 7/1/73 | 5½ | 7/1/79 | 5¼ | (7) |
| 2 Negotiable order of withdrawal accounts [1]........................ | 5 | 1/1/74 | (8) | .......... | 5 | 1/1/74 | (8) | .......... |
| *Time accounts* [2] | | | | | | | | |
| Fixed ceiling rates by maturity | | | | | | | | |
| 3 30–89 days..................... | 5 | 7/1/73 | (9) | (9) | (8) | .......... | (8) | .......... |
| 4 90 days to 1 year................. | 5½ | 7/1/73 | 5 | (10) | 35¾ | (7) | 5¼ | 1/21/70 |
| 5 1 to 2 years [3]...................} | 6 | 7/1/73 { | 5½ | 1/21/70 | 6½ | (7) | 5¾ | 1/21/70 |
| 6 2 to 2½ years [3]................} | | | 5¾ | 1/21/70 }| | | 6 | 1/21/70 |
| 7 2½ to 4 years [3]................. | 6½ | 7/1/73 | 5¾ | 1/21/70 | 6¾ | (7) | 6 | 1/21/70 |
| 8 4 to 6 years [4]................. | 7¼ | 11/1/73 | (11) | .......... | 7½ | 11/1/73 | (11) | .......... |
| 9 6 to 8 years [4]................. | 7½ | 12/23/74 | 7¼ | 11/1/73 | 7¾ | 12/23/74 | 7½ | 11/1/73 |
| 10 8 years or more [4]............. | 7¾ | 6/1/78 | (8) | .......... | 8 | 6/1/78 | (8) | .......... |
| 11 Issued to governmental units (all maturities)...................... | 8 | 6/1/78 | 7¾ | 12/23/74 | 8 | 6/1/78 | 7¾ | 12/23/74 |
| 12 Individual retirement accounts and Keogh (H.R. 10) plans ( 3 years or more) [5]............... | 8 | 6/1/78 | 7¾ | 7/6/77 | 8 | 6/1/78 | 7¾ | 7/6/77 |
| Special variable ceiling rates by maturity | | | | | | | | |
| 13 6 months (money market time deposits) [6]................ | (12) | (12) | (12) | (12) | (12) | (12) | (12) | (12) |
| 14 4 years or more.................. | (13) | (13) | (13) | (13) | (13) | (13) | (13) | (13) |

1. For authorized states only. Federally insured commercial banks, savings and loan associations, cooperative banks, and mutual savings banks in Massachusetts and New Hampshire were first permitted to offer negotiable order of withdrawal (NOW) accounts on Jan. 1, 1974. Authorization to issue NOW accounts was extended to similar institutions throughout New England on Feb. 27, 1976, and in New York State on Nov. 10, 1978.

2. For exceptions with respect to certain foreign time deposits see the FEDERAL RESERVE BULLETIN for October 1962 (p. 1279), August 1965 (p. 1094), and February 1968 (p. 167).

3. No minimum denomination. Until July 1, 1979, a minimum of $1,000 was required for savings and loan associations, except in areas where mutual savings banks permitted lower minimum denominations. This restriction was removed for deposits maturing in less than 1 year, effective Nov. 1, 1973.

4. No minimum denomination. Until July 1, 1979, minimum denomination was $1,000 except for deposits representing funds contributed to an Individual Retirement Account (IRA) or a Keogh (H.R. 10) Plan established pursuant to the Internal Revenue Code. The $1,000 minimum requirement was removed for such accounts in December 1975 and November 1976, respectively.

5. Accounts maturing in less than 3 years subject to regular ceilings.

6. Must have a maturity of exactly 26 weeks and a minimum denomination of $10,000, and must be nonnegotiable.

7. July 1, 1973, for mutual savings bank; July 6, 1973 for savings and loan associations.

8. No separate account category.

9. Multiple maturity: 4¼ percent, January 21, 1970; single maturity: 5 percent, September 26, 1966.

10. Multiple maturity: July 20, 1966; single maturity: September 26, 1966.

11. Between July 1, 1973, and Oct. 31, 1973, there was no ceiling for certificates maturing in 4 years or more with minimum denominations of $1,000; however, the amount of such certificates that an institution could issue was limited to 5 percent of its total time and savings deposits. Sales in excess of that amount, as well as certificates of less than $1,000, were limited to the 6½ percent ceiling on time deposits maturing in 2½ years or more.

Effective Nov. 1, 1973, ceilings were reimposed on certificates maturing in 4 years or more with minimum denominations of $1,000. There is no limitation on the amount of these certificates that banks can issue.

12. Commercial banks, savings and loan associations, and mutual savings banks were authorized to offer money market time deposits effective June 1, 1978. The ceiling rate for commercial banks is the discount rate on most recently issued 6-month U.S. Treasury bills. Until Mar. 15, 1979, the ceiling rate for savings and loan associations and mutual savings banks was ¼ percentage point higher than the rate for commercial banks. Beginning Mar. 15, 1979, the ¼ percentage point interest differential is removed when the 6-month Treasury bill rate is 9 percent or more. The full differential is in effect when the 6-month bill rate is 8¾ percent or less. Thrift institutions may pay a maximum 9 percent when the 6-month bill rate is between 8¾ and 9 percent. Also effective March 15, 1979, interest compounding was prohibited on money market time deposits at all offering institutions. For both commercial banks and thrift institutions, the maximum allowable rates in July were as follows: July 5, 8.867 (thrifts, 9.0); July 12, 9.164; July 19, 9.255; July 25, 9.473.

13. Effective July 1, 1979, commercial banks, savings and loan associations, and mutual savings banks are authorized to offer variable ceiling accounts with no required minimum denomination and with maturities of 4 years or more. The maximum rate for commercial banks is 1¼ percentage points below the yield on 4-year U.S. Treasury securities; the ceiling rate for thrift institutions is ¼ percentage point higher than that for commercial banks. In July, the ceiling was 7.60 percent at commercial banks and 7.85 percent at thrift institutions.

NOTE. Maximum rates that can be paid by federally insured commercial banks, mutual savings banks, and savings and loan associations are established by the Board of Governors of the Federal Reserve System, the Board of Directors of the Federal Deposit Insurance Corporation, and the Federal Home Loan Bank Board under the provisions of 12 CFR 217, 329, and 526, respectively. The maximum rates on time deposits in denominations of $100,000 or more with maturities of 30-89 days were suspended in June 1970; such deposits maturing in 90 days or more were suspended in May 1973. For information regarding previous interest rate ceilings on all types of accounts, see earlier issues of the FEDERAL RESERVE BULLETIN, the Federal Home Loan Bank Board *Journal*, and the *Annual Report* of the Federal Deposit Insurance Corporation.

Source: *Federal Reserve Bulletin*, August 1979, p. A10.

ceilings that apply to various types of CDs. The basic pattern is that a bank can pay higher rates on consumer CDs with longer maturities. For example, a bank can pay up to 5¼% on savings deposits and on consumer CDs that have an original maturity within 30 to 89 days. In contrast, it can pay up to 7¾% on a CD that matures in 8 years or more.

A *single-maturity CD* involves a contractual agreement between a bank and a customer who deposits a specific dollar amount that will earn a specific rate of interest, but the amount is not subject to withdrawal prior to its maturity date. A customer who makes such a deposit willingly foregoes the withdrawal liquidity of a savings account, usually in return for a higher interest return on the illiquid CD. If the depositor has to redeem the CD prior to its maturity date, then by federal regulation the depositor incurs interest penalties. Therefore, banks advise customers to obtain a CD only with funds that they are unlikely to need prior to the CD's maturity.

In June 1978, the supervisory agencies ruled that banks, S&Ls, and mutual savings banks could offer consumer *money-market certificates of deposit* (MMCDs), the interest rate of which is linked to that of a money-market instrument. These MMCDs must:

- have a maturity of exactly 26 weeks
- have a minimum denomination of $10,000
- be nonnegotiable

The ceiling rate that a bank can offer on its MMCDs is the discount rate on the most recently issued 6-month U.S. Treasury bills. Thus a bank's maximum offering rate on its MMCDs can vary each week as a function of the prior week's discount rate on Treasury bills. Furthermore, the supervisory agencies have ruled that:

- When the Treasury bill rate is 8¾% or less, S&Ls and mutual savings banks can pay one-quarter of a percentage point more than banks can pay on their MMCDs.
- When the Treasury bill rate is between 8¾% and 9%, the S&Ls and mutual savings banks may pay a maximum of 9%.
- When the Treasury bill rate is 9% or more, there is no difference in the maximum rates that banks, S&Ls, and mutual savings banks can pay.

These rulings thus have partially removed the quarter-point interest rate difference enjoyed by S&Ls and mutual savings banks.

The supervisory agencies authorized MMCDs as a way to avert disintermediation by some savers who would otherwise withdraw funds from the depository intermediaries and invest these funds in money-market instruments that were not subject to Regulation Q ceilings. Initial studies indicate that the MMCDs have thus helped avert disintermediation, but they have also increased the interest costs of the intermediaries, as depositors transfer funds from other lower-yielding accounts into the higher-yielding

MMCDs.[7] Thus a bank has to evaluate whether it wants to offer and aggressively promote MMCDs. If most of its rival intermediaries offer them and if its depositors inquire about them, then a bank will likely decide to offer MMCDs. (At year-end 1978, almost eighty percent of all banks offered MMCDs). Even if it thus has them, a bank has to decide whether to publicize quietly or promote aggressively its MMCDs. If it quietly publicizes them, the bank may be able to avert outflows by its interest-sensitive depositors and yet avoid major increases in its advertising and interest costs.

A *multiple-maturity CD* is automatically renewable at maturity without action by the depositor or is payable only after written notice of withdrawal. One popular form is nominally a passbook account to which a depositor can add funds, but from which the depositor can withdraw principal only at specific dates (such as within the first five days of each month) and/or with contractual written notice. Another popular form is a CD written for an initial period, such as four years, that is subject to automatic renewal for another four-year period, but at the interest rate the bank is then paying on four-year CDs. (At an extreme, at least one bank has offered a CD that automatically renews itself throughout the life of the depositor.) Exhibit 7-2 summarizes how multiple-maturity CDs, like single-maturity CDs, are subject to Regulation Q ceilings and conditions. Subject to these constraints, a bank can design a variety of multiple-maturity and single-maturity CDs that it believes will appeal to its current and potential household depositors.

## SMALL BUSINESSES

Most small businesses have an account relationship with a nearby bank. This long-run relationship centers around the checking account that a firm uses for daily transactions and precautionary purposes, and a probable loan agreement between the firm and its bank. At times a small business has cash inflows and/or cash balances that exceed its anticipated short-run cash outflows, but this excess cash may involve small amounts available for short time periods. If it leaves this excess cash in its checking account, the firm earns no explicit interest; but it may receive implicit interest in the form of free services and/or price concessions on other banking services. If it were to try to invest the excess cash in money-market instruments, then the small firm is likely to find that the costs and inconvenience of such small-scale, temporary investments may offset much of the potential interest revenues.

A small firm could earn explicit interest and avoid inconvenience and transactions costs if it could deposit its temporarily excess cash in a passbook savings account at its bank. Yet until 1975 this option was not available because the federal banking agencies ruled that banks could not

---

7. R. Alton Gilbert and Jean M. Lovati, ''Disintermediation: An Old Disorder with a New Remedy,'' *Review* (Federal Reserve Bank of St. Louis), January 1979, pp. 10-15. John M. Godfrey and B. Frank King, ''Money Market Certificates: An Innovation in Consumer Deposits,'' *Economic Review* (Federal Reserve Bank of Atlanta), May-June 1979, pp. 59-64.

open savings accounts for profit-making organizations. The agencies were concerned that these organizations would frequently transfer funds in and out of such accounts and thereby add to bank deposit volatility. In contrast, S&Ls could open savings accounts for profit-making organizations; and so, in 1975, the federal banking agencies authorized banks to open savings accounts for corporations and other profit organizations.

A bank is not permitted to pay interest (current maximum of 5¼%) on more than $150,000 in a business savings account. Even with this constraint, if it offers such accounts, a bank can nurture its relationships with businesses, especially small ones that have limited access to the money markets. An initial survey in one Federal Reserve District reports that there are "significant differences in the importance of these deposits among member banks in various size classes in the five district states."[8] These survey results suggest that, if it has not already done so, a bank needs to examine whether to offer and/or promote passbook accounts to its current and potential small-business clients. A bank also can offer its various CDs to small businesses.

## PUBLIC AGENCIES

Public agencies at times have excess funds for extended periods. For example, unless it has borrowed in anticipation of its tax collections, a local governmental unit collects most of its tax revenues on or before a specific date; and it then gradually disburses these funds over the subsequent period. Also it sometimes sells bonds for a capital-improvement project such as a new school or hospital; and it then holds the bond proceeds until it later disburses payments for completed work.

Public treasurers traditionally kept their temporarily excess funds in noninterest-earning demand deposits at local banks. They did so especially if their state and/or local laws did not authorize the investment of public funds in interest-earning time deposits. However, as taxes and interest rates have risen, most political districts have permitted public treasurers to invest in various interest-earning assets; and public treasurers have become skillful funds managers.[9]

Since 1974 banks have been permitted to offer savings accounts to governmental units. (Prior to then the federal banking agencies prohibited such accounts, for reasons similar to those used to prohibit savings accounts for profit-making organizations.) On governmental time deposits of under $100,000, irrespective of maturity, banks can pay interest rates as high as the regulatory maximum permitted for any federally insured depository institutions, such as S&Ls.

To document that they obtain the highest return available from depository intermediaries, public treasurers often solicit competitive bids for their funds. To illustrate, a treasurer of a rural community projects that the

8. Paul L. Kasriel, "Banks Now Offer Savings Deposit Service to Businesses," *Economic Perspectives* (Federal Reserve Bank of Chicago), September-October 1978, pp. 8-11.

9. Donald G. Simonson and George H. Hempel, "Public Deposit Policies: Trends and Issues," *Issues in Bank Regulation*, Spring 1978, pp. 14-19.

city has $200,000 that it does not need for 180 days. The treasurer will invite several nearby depository institutions, and possibly some distant ones, to bid for the city's time deposit. Other factors equal, the institution offering the highest rate on 180-day CDs will obtain the deposit.

Because it now has to bid for most public time deposits, a bank has to evaluate the costs and expected benefits from specific bids. In addition to the interest that it offers to pay, a second ''cost'' is that the successful bidder will have to pledge collateral for the public deposit, and this required collateralization will constrain the bidder's flexibility to manage its investments portfolio.[10] To decide what interest rate to bid, a bank has to estimate its expected returns if it were to win the bid and then lend and/or invest the funds. Even if it wins the bid, a bank cannot count on a long-run relationship with the public treasurer, who will solicit a new set of bids when he or she next projects a period of excess funds. The advent of these bidding procedures weakens traditional relationships between a bank and its nearby public agencies, many of which solicit bids from large money-center banks that aggressively bid for time deposits of public agencies.

## LARGE FIRMS

As they manage their cash flows, large firms have potential cash balances that exceed what they plan to hold in their noninterest-earning demand deposits. To invest these excess funds in interest-earning assets, corporate treasurers evaluate the risk-return attributes of various money-market instruments, which include negotiable CDs issued by large money-center banks.

### Origins of Negotiable CDs

After the Depression and World War II, most banks had most of their assets invested in U.S. Treasury securities, which they could readily sell and use the proceeds to make short-term loans. These sales were especially feasible as long as the FRS continued its wartime policy of *pegging* interest rates (and market values) of Treasury securities by standing ready to purchase such securities whenever their interest rates might exceed the pegged level, which for long-term bonds was under 2½ percent. With this pegging policy, banks had a ready market in which to sell Treasury securities at little if any capital loss. Also, interest rates on money market instruments were low, so corporate and public treasurers willingly held temporarily excess cash in noninterest-earning demand deposits. In this financial environment, banks had little stimulus to seek new sources of funds.

By the 1950s there were major changes in financial markets. The FRS ended its pegging policy shortly after its 1951 Accord with the U.S. Treasury. No longer could banks rely on selling some of their Treasury securities at little or no loss. Short-term and long-term interest rates began to

---

10. The FDIC insures most bank deposits up to $40,000; but, since authorized by Congress in 1974, it insures public time and savings deposits up to $100,000. Pledging requirements usually apply only to the uninsured portion of public deposits.

rise. Corporate and public treasurers sought to reduce excess cash from their nonearning demand deposits and to invest it in money-market instruments. Meanwhile, many corporate treasurers increased their loan demands and requested longer repayment periods. Some city banks began to examine how they might attract deposits from suburban households and businesses, but often these banks encountered state branching restrictions that impeded their expansion into the suburbs. Therefore large banks, especially those in downtown areas, began to realize that, if they were to meet growing loan demands, they could not rely on selling some of their Treasury bonds and/or on growth in demand deposits. This realization challenged some conventional banking views and practices.

By tradition large banks seldom sought large time deposits. Many bankers viewed such deposits as inconsistent with customary practices by which banks accepted demand deposits and made short-term loans, primarily to businesses and agricultural units. Bankers also believed that if their banks provided interest-paying time deposits, then some large depositors would shift some excess funds from demand deposits to time deposits within the bank, and thus the bank would have to pay interest on funds that it already held as noninterest-paying demand deposits.

By 1961 a major bank apparently concluded that its future growth would be curtailed if it adhered to conventional views of large time deposits. The First National City Bank of New York announced in 1961 that it would issue negotiable certificates of deposit. Negotiability was a key feature. Owners of negotiable CDs could sell them to other parties, who might hold them until maturity or in turn resell them. (In contrast, some small and medium-sized banks had long issued CDs, but they were for small amounts and seldom negotiable.) The new negotiable CDs were designed to compete with other negotiable money-market instruments. At first the negotiable CDs had minimum denominations of $1 million. Some major securities firms promptly began to act as dealers in the negotiable CDs, and an active secondary market for the CDs soon developed.

After the introduction of negotiable CDs, other large money-center banks began to offer negotiable CDs. The banks realized that some of their large depositors might purchase a bank's negotiable CDs by reducing their excess funds in demand deposits within the bank; but they also realized that it was increasingly likely that such depositors would in any case pare their demand deposits and purchase interest-earning money-market instruments, including negotiable CDs of rival money-center banks. Thus to protect their deposit base and to try to attract new large deposits, most large banks began to offer negotiable CDs.

### Managing Negotiable CDs: Investor Perspectives

Principal holders of negotiable CDs include large firms, pension funds, nonprofit organizations, and governmental units.[11] When they have large

---

11. Although they cannot directly buy large-denomination negotiable CDs, small savers can conveniently do so indirectly by purchasing shares of money-market mutual funds, which permit small

amounts of temporarily excess funds, treasurers of such organizations evaluate the expected returns and risks of negotiable CDs and other money-market instruments, such as commercial paper and short-term Treasury and federal agency securities.

When obtained from an issuing bank, CDs involve no commission costs; and banks will tailor CD maturities to meet their buyers' maturity preferences. From a buyer's view, there is little risk associated with negotiable CDs because of their short maturities, their liquidity, and the stature and resources of the issuing banks. Many large investors view negotiable CDs of money-center banks as impersonal money-market instruments that involve similar—although not the same—risks and returns. Therefore potential buyers usually call several banks to learn the rates they offer, and then, subject to their diversification policies, buy the CD of the bank that offers the highest rate at the time.

Many large investors like the risk-return characteristics of negotiable CDs, but they cannot conveniently invest upwards of $1 million as was originally required by large money-center banks. Also many banks, especially in regional financial centers, want to retain or obtain large deposits—even if they do not involve million-dollar transactions. Therefore most large banks now offer negotiable CDs in denominations of under $1 million, but to be exempt from Regulation Q interest-rate ceilings the minimum denomination has to be $100,000.

With many banks issuing negotiable CDs in various denominations, large investors have developed summary systems by which to classify CDs. At first they classified CDs primarily on the basis of their marketability. Large depositors classified as "prime" those CDs known to have very broad and active secondary markets. Such nationwide markets typically developed for CDs issued by the largest money-center banks. Large depositors classified as "nonprime" the CDs having less broad and active secondary markets. Nonprime CDs often were of smaller denominations and issued by large regional banks.

Large investors initially had little fear that a bank issuing negotiable CDs would fail. The subsequent failure of several large banks dispelled this initial complacency, and large investors have become concerned about the risk of loss (default risk) of negotiable CDs—especially since federal deposit insurance applies to only a small part of a negotiable CD. Therefore the term "prime CD" has also come to mean one judged to involve virtually no default risk, while a nonprime CD involves some slight default risk.

Large investors seemingly have the incentive and resources to analyze the default risks, however low, of various CDs, but such analysis requires clear criteria by which to measure a bank's financial strength, and detailed

---

minimum purchases and invest their stockholders' money in portfolios of money-market instruments, a large proportion of which are negotiable CDs. These funds, which also provide various services to expedite purchase and redemption of their shares, have grown rapidly from a zero base in 1970 to over $35 billion in total assets by 1979. Paul F. Jessup and Mary Bochnak, "Money Market Mutual Funds: Their Impact on Banks," *The Magazine of Bank Administration,* September 1977, pp. 28-32.

current financial information about various banks.[12] Because such criteria and information are not readily available, some large investors choose to purchase only CDs issued by a small number of the nation's largest banks. These purchasers reportedly believe that the bank supervisory agencies cannot and will not permit these banks to fail, and therefore only such banks are fail-safe.

Exhibit 7-3 summarizes the risk attributes of prime and nonprime CDs. This two-way classification conveniently summarizes a spectrum of gradations within and between the categories of prime and nonprime, and the range of the spectrum is not very wide.[13] Various investors probably assign different weights to marketability and default risk, and investors may change their weights over time. For example, during the period of uncertainty about a possible default by New York City, investors reportedly became more cautious of negotiable CDs issued by some large New York banks.

When they decide among negotiable CDs of similar maturities, investors generally will accept lower returns from CDs judged to involve lower risks. Thus banks that issue what the market views to be prime CDs often can obtain funds at lower rates than can banks that issue CDs that are viewed as nonprime. If these rate differences persist over time, and if many

**EXHIBIT 7-3**

**Negotiable Certificates of Deposit:
A Summary Risk-Return Classification**

| Summary Classification | —— Risk Attributes —— | | Return | Principal Issuers |
| --- | --- | --- | --- | --- |
| | Secondary Market | Perceived Credit Risk | | |
| Prime | Very broad and active | Virtually none | Closely relates to prime money-market alternatives | Largest money-center banks |
| Nonprime | Less broad and active | Slight, but some | Somewhat higher than for a prime negotiable CD having a similar maturity | Other large, but usually regional, banks |

12. In 1979, a private rating service, Moody's Investors Service, Inc., began to rate the risk of negotiable CDs of large banks. Thus large investors can use these independent ratings to supplement their own risk analyses of negotiable CDs.

13. For a more detailed discussion of the multi-tier market for negotiable CDs, see Dwight B. Crane, "Lessons from the 1974 CD Market," *Harvard Business Review*, November-December 1975, pp. 73-79.

of the nation's largest banks, primarily because of their size, are viewed as issuers of prime CDs, then these prime issuers will maintain a comparative advantage in their cost of CD funds.

### Managing Negotiable CDs: Issuer Perspectives

Large banks also view negotiable CDs as a major source of funds. From a zero base in early 1961, the total dollar amount of negotiable CDs has grown to about $97 billion outstanding at year-end 1978.[14]

**Volatility of Negotiable CDs**   Large banks view negotiable CDs as a potentially volatile source of funds. They expect current and potential holders to evaluate expected risks and returns from various CDs as well as from other money-market instruments. These impersonal, often transitory, CD relationships contrast to the more stable, long-term relationships that banks try to cultivate with most of their customers.

Large banks have encountered unanticipated past periods when total dollar redemptions of their maturing negotiable CDs substantially exceeded the total dollar sales of new CDs. Often these net outflows from one bank reflected shifts of funds to other banks whose CDs offered higher returns and/or perceived lower risks. At times, however, these net outflows reflected FRS monetary policies in which the Board of Governors administered Regulation Q in ways that would intentionally trigger net CD outflows from the banking system.

When negotiable CDs were introduced in 1961, the maximum rates that banks could pay on time deposits ranged from 1 to 3 percent, depending on maturity. Subsequently the FRS revised these ceilings upward to reflect rises in interest rates on other money-market instruments. These upward revisions helped forestall CD runoffs from large banks and enabled American banks to compete for large foreign deposits.

During two periods, however, the FRS did not raise Regulation Q ceilings to levels that would allow negotiable CDs to compete effectively with other money-market instruments. The first period was in late 1966, and the second period included most of 1969 and 1970. During both periods the FRS tried to forestall rapid expansion of bank loans by impeding bank access to sources of funds. In both periods the dollar volume of negotiable CDs declined as holders shifted their funds from maturing CDs to other higher-yielding instruments. Although they thus experienced declines of negotiable CDs, most large banks developed new sources of funds to help offset much of their runoff.[15] Many large banks increasingly turned to the

---

14. These figures are for negotiable CDs of large weekly reporting commercial banks with assets of $750 million or more, as reported in the *Federal Reserve Bulletin,* February 1979, p. A23.

15. A. Gilbert Heebner, "Negotiable Certificates of Deposit: A Reexamination," *The Bankers Magazine,* Summer 1970, pp. 11-18. Donald M. DePamphilis, "The Short-term Commercial Bank Adjustment Process and Federal Reserve Regulation," *New England Economic Review* (Federal Reserve Bank of Boston), May-June 1974, pp. 14-23.

Eurodollar market for funds during both periods, and they actively developed new nondeposit sources of funds during the second period. In retrospect, FRS use of Regulation Q ceilings to forestall bank credit expansion was not very successful.

In June 1970, the FRS suspended interest-rate ceilings on large ($100,000 and over) single-maturity time deposits having maturities of 30-89 days. This suspension gave banks additional funds-flow flexibility in the aftermath of Penn Central's bankruptcy. In 1973 the FRS suspended interest-rate ceilings on all remaining time deposits in denominations of $100,000 or more. By its thus giving banks this interest-rate flexibility to compete for negotiable CDs, the FRS reduces the incentive of large banks to develop and use nondeposit sources of funds. As long as the FRS continues its suspension of interest-rate ceilings on large deposits, banks can focus on how to manage their CD flows in competition with other large banks. There remains, however, a possibility that ceilings will be reimposed, and so forward-planning bankers need to develop contingency plans for such an environment.

**Management Strategies for Negotiable CDs**   When it sells a negotiable CD, a bank can plan to use these funds until the CD's specific maturity date. (If the CD holder needs funds prior to the CD's maturity date, the holder can sell the CD in the secondary market.) Therefore one strategy, especially for banks that do not issue many CDs, is for a bank to hedge each new CD liability by holding a low-risk asset that will mature just prior to the maturity date of the CD. The bank should expect its return on the asset, after administrative expenses, to exceed the rate that it pays on the associated CD.

An issuing bank can view its negotiable CDs as a portfolio of liabilities and then focus on broadly diversifying its CDs among many holders and maturities. This diversification reduces the probability of large-scale redemptions within a brief period. Moreover, the issuing bank expects its CD liabilities to provide almost a continuous source of funds; as some CDs are about to mature, the bank expects to renew them and/or to issue new CDs to obtain funds to redeem the maturing CDs. Yet it cannot expect to refinance continuously all of its maturing CDs, and so it must anticipate and prepare to meet periods of net deposit outflows. These periods can be brief, for example when other banks or intermediaries aggressively bid for funds; and they can be lengthy, for example if the FRS again uses Regulation Q ceilings to encourage CD runoffs.

An issuing bank can emphasize its financial strength and thus try to ensure a continuous inflow of CD funds from investors who are attracted by the bank's low-risk stature. It may even obtain these deposits at rates below those paid by rival institutions which issue CDs that the market judges to involve somewhat higher risk. To pursue this strategy, a bank is likely to maintain high capital ratios and in other ways structure its report of condition to reflect a strong, conservative image. A bank must therefore evaluate whether the probable benefits of low-cost CD inflows exceed the probable costs of a conservative capital and portfolio posture. Moreover, a bank can implement this strategy only if it effectively distinguishes its financial stature from that of other banks. If many banks try to pursue this strategy, then the financial strength of any one bank is not likely to differ substantially from that of its rivals.

As another strategy, especially for large regional banks, a bank can try to issue its negotiable CDs primarily to its established customers. In this way a bank does not try to compete directly with impersonal money-market CDs; instead it views its CDs as an extension of its total relationship with its major clients. Over time the bank offers competitive rates for its clients' temporarily excess funds, and it expects them to deposit most of their money-market funds with it. This strategy deemphasizes the usual impersonal features of negotiable CDs as money-market instruments. Even major money-center banks at times use this type of strategy. When faced with sudden and substantial runoffs of negotiable CDs during 1966 and between 1969 and 1970, some major banks reportedly suggested that holders of maturing CDs might want to renew them and that the issuing bank would likely remember this cooperation in future periods.

An issuing bank can try to become among the largest in the nation so that, because of the bank's sheer size, its negotiable CDs will likely trade in nationwide markets and be viewed as fail-safe investments. To try to enter this top rank quickly, a bank can try to accelerate its growth via a series of major acquisitions and mergers. Large banks in regional financial centers use versions of this strategy when they try to enumerate the public benefits from more liberal branching laws in their states and when they apply to merge with other large banks in their region.

As another strategy, a bank can develop various types of nonnegotiable time deposits as a further way to increase and segment the flows of funds from large depositors. Large money-center banks can use this strategy to diversify further their portfolios of CD liabilities. Large and medium-sized regional banks may choose to emphasize this strategy instead of trying to compete directly against the negotiable CDs of large money-center banks. Large nonnegotiable time deposits (issued in amounts of $100,000 or more) account for about 27 percent of all large time deposits issued by large commercial banks (year-end 1978). Negotiable CDs account for the rest (73 percent) of such large time deposits.

The preceding strategies are not mutually exclusive. Bankers need to evaluate the benefits and costs of variants and combinations of these illustrative strategies.

## CORRESPONDENT BANKS

Time deposits traditionally have been a minor part of the correspondent banking network. At year-end 1961, interbank time deposits were about one percent of total interbank deposits.

In contrast, demand deposits are the cornerstone of the correspondent banking system. Outlying banks maintain demand deposits with city correspondents in order to receive diverse services and to have immediately available funds. Also, nonmember banks often can include their demand deposits with city correspondents as part of their reserves, as required by their state.

Each outlying bank keeps some funds in assets that earn no explicit interest, such as: vault cash; demand deposits at large correspondent banks; and, if a member bank, balances at the Federal Reserve Bank. It holds these assets to fulfill legal requirements and as a way to manage its short-term cash flows. It tries to earn interest on its remaining assets and so lends or invests most of them. In this portfolio context, some outlying banks now evaluate the returns and risks of negotiable CDs compared to those of other money-market instruments. From their low initial base, domestic interbank time deposits increased to over $7 billion by mid-1978. At this level they account for about seventeen percent of total domestic interbank deposits.

Some large correspondent banks may actively solicit purchases of their CDs by outlying correspondents. This practice is unlikely to become widespread, however, as long as most city correspondents rely on demand deposit balances as compensation for services provided to outlying banks and as long as outlying banks have convenient access to the federal funds market in which they can earn interest on overnight loans to other—often large correspondent—banks.

## FOREIGN CLIENTS

America's major money-center banks also have time deposits from foreign entities that include individuals, business firms, governments, central banks, and other banks. These large banks, through their head offices and their networks of foreign branches and affiliates, offer a variety of time deposits, including negotiable CDs, to foreign holders.

For the foreseeable future, America's largest banks will continue to account for most foreign time deposits. Before they commit substantial resources to try to enter this multinational market, other large banks must realistically assess their comparative disadvantages.

- Most large regional banks do not have extensive networks of foreign branches and affiliates. They can try to have one or several strategically located foreign offices, but often they face many competing banks in locations such as London and the Bahamas.
- Many large regional banks issue CDs that are viewed as nonprime even within domestic money markets. Their CDs will rank even lower when they are compared to CDs issued by the world's largest money-center banks.

To try to reduce its comparative disadvantages, a large regional bank can evaluate whether to be a part owner of a major international bank. The regional bank and its coowners, which usually are other large domestic and foreign banks, thus can pool resources in order to compete against the world's largest banks.

## SUMMARY

Most banks traditionally accepted—but did not seek—time deposits. (One outcome was the growth of nonbank financial intermediaries, such as S&Ls and mutual savings banks, that explicitly offered savings accounts to households.) By the 1960s, however, large money-center banks in particular foresaw limited deposit growth if they continued to rely on demand deposits, especially of large firms. Therefore these banks and others began to develop and market new types of time deposits and time-deposit services.

Today most banks offer passbook savings accounts, from which in practice a depositor can withdraw funds on demand; and they offer various single-maturity and multiple-maturity consumer certificates of deposit (CDs). In states where federal law permits, many banks also offer NOW accounts, which are interest-paying savings accounts that function like checking accounts. These NOW accounts blur the traditional boundary between interest-paying savings accounts and noninterest-paying demand deposits, and there is a high probability that Congress will soon allow all banks to offer NOW accounts. Therefore, even where it cannot yet offer NOW accounts, a bank needs to have a contingency plan as to whether it will offer NOW accounts and, if so, with what likely interest rates, minimum balance requirements, and/or service charges. To develop such a contingency plan, a bank can review the experience and strategies of New England financial institutions (bank and nonbank) that first offered NOW accounts.

Banks, and most nonbank financial intermediaries, are subject to laws and regulations that set interest-rate ceilings on consumer savings and time deposits. Under current regulations, S&Ls and mutual savings banks can pay their savings depositors one-quarter of a percentage point more than can banks. Some bankers cite this quarter-point difference in ceilings as unfair, and various commentators cite how interest-rate ceilings lead to economic inefficiencies and inequities. Yet, because of their concern about the possible disruptive effects on the funds flows of nonbank financial intermediaries, and the associated possible impact on the housing market, Congress is unlikely soon to remove interest-rate ceilings on consumer deposits. Thus the supervisory agencies will likely continue to adjust the ceilings and to allow some controlled experimentation with new types of consumer CDs, such as it did with money-market certificates of deposit. Subject to these changing regulations, a bank can analyze various feasible consumer CDs to determine which it should offer and/or aggressively market as a means of helping it manage its deposit flows, interest costs, and maturity structure of CDs.

Whatever its size, a bank competes for savings deposits and other time deposits of nearby households, small firms, and local public agencies. If it pays interest rates that are similar (ceiling rates) to those of its rivals, then it has to focus on such nonprice strategies as convenience and occasional premium offerings.

Certificates of deposit of $100,000 or more are exempt from interest-rate ceilings, and so banks can use explicit price competition when they bid for these CD deposits. These large CDs can be negotiable or nonnegotiable. Large banks, in major or regional money centers, issue negotiable CDs; and investors in these CDs classify them across a narrow spectrum of prime to nonprime, where prime CDs are judged to have minimal default and marketability risks. Whether its CDs are classified as prime or nonprime, an issuing bank has to have contingency plans for a possible runoff among its CDs. In the short run, because of their location and size, many large regional banks cannot expect to have their CDs recognized as prime, and so they have to develop strategies that are consistent with their nonprime classification.

While it can offer a wide range of savings and time deposits, each bank has to evaluate its current and potential sources of such deposits and thus identify those markets in which it has a comparative advantage over other banks and nonbank intermediaries. As it analyzes its time-deposit strategies, a bank also has to evaluate expected returns from its loans and investments, costs of alternative sources of funds, and the volatility of various sources of funds, especially in periods of disintermediation.

# 8

# CASH FLOW MANAGEMENT

Cash flow management is at the heart of bank operating systems. A bank evaluates how various strategies, in areas such as deposits and loans, can affect its patterns of cash inflows and outflows; and it sets and reviews policies to guide the officers who manage its cash flows.

While all economic units manage their cash flows, banks differ from most other units:

- Bank demand deposits, and possibly time deposits, are money that the depositors expect to be free of default risk.
- By law, banks must immediately meet withdrawals or transfers from demand deposits, and they must honor the contractual repayment dates of their liabilities.
- Federal and state laws require banks to hold specific amounts and types of assets as legal reserves against their deposit liabilities.

This chapter examines how, subject to such constraints, banks:

- manage their required reserves
- evaluate the benefits and costs of membership in the FRS
- manage their liquidity

The last section of this chapter introduces why and how large banks, in particular, practice liabilities management and spread management.

## REQUIRED RESERVES

Each bank must meet its legal reserve requirements as a condition for its continuing operation. While it operates subject to its current required reserves, which differ among categories of banks and bank liabilities, it also has to have contingency plans for possible changes in the reserves required of it and its rival depository intermediaries.

## SPECIFYING RESERVE REQUIREMENTS

The Board of Governors of the FRS has statutory powers to specify reserve requirements for all banks that are members of the FRS. (These requirements thus apply to all national banks, which by law must belong to the FRS, and to all state banks that choose to belong to the FRS.) The FRS specifies:

- the categories of liabilities, primarily deposits, that are subject to required reserves
- the assets (balances at Federal Reserve Banks and vault cash) that can be used to meet the reserve requirements
- the percentage relationships between the permissible reserve assets and the liabilities that are subject to required reserves

Over time the FRS can, within limits, change its specifications of required reserves. Most states similarly set reserve requirements for state-chartered banks. In practice most states defer to the FRS requirements as they apply to state member banks, and they focus on requirements for their state-chartered nonmember banks.

## MOTIVATIONS FOR REQUIRED RESERVES

Federal and state laws originally mandated required reserves as a way to protect depositors and banks. In principle, if they always had to hold some short-term, low-risk assets, then banks could use these assets to help meet unexpected deposit outflows. Depositors, in turn, could see that banks thus held liquid assets to help meet unexpected outflows, and so they might have more confidence in individual banks and the banking system. This confidènce factor might help forestall periodic panics, in which many bank depositors rush to withdraw their funds.

Required reserves probably could never have fulfilled their original purpose to protect depositors and banks. If it has to maintain continuously a specific percentage of its deposits in liquid assets and if it suddenly faces unusual deposits outflows, then—unless it has *excess* liquid assets—a bank must move rapidly to convert nonliquid assets, such as long-term loans and investments, to liquid assets in order to replace those that it used to help meet the initial outflows. Thus a pool of liquid assets is a limited buffer if it has to be promptly replenished by selling illiquid assets, especially if such unexpected sales involve substantial losses.

Even if one bank could replenish its required reserves, many banks could not simultaneously do so. They would likely incur substantial losses if many tried quickly to obtain funds from sales of their long-term loans and investments. The FRS, as the central bank, therefore has the responsibility to provide liquidity to the banking system.

Although they do not directly protect depositors and banks, required reserves have evolved into an instrument of monetary policy. The FRS uses its reserve requirements as one way to influence the money supply and financial markets. FRS reserve requirements apply only to member banks, but these banks account for about seventy-two percent of the nation's total bank deposits. FRS monetary policy also is indirectly transmitted to nonmember banks that are subject to state reserve requirements.

The FRS has broad powers to modify its required reserves. It can change its percentage requirements within the present ranges authorized by Congress:

|                                          | Minimum | Maximum |
|------------------------------------------|---------|---------|
| Net demand deposits, reserve city banks  | 10      | 22      |
| Net demand deposits, other banks         | 7       | 4       |
| Time deposits                            | 3       | 10      |
| Borrowings from foreign banks            | 0       | 22      |

The FRS can request the Congress to revise these ranges; and it has, or can usually get, statutory powers to redefine the liabilities that are subject to required reserves and/or the forms in which required reserves must be held.

## CURRENT STRUCTURE OF REQUIRED RESERVES

In 1972 the FRS ended its traditional reserve classification of banks based on their location (reserve city, city, or country); and it specified that "each member bank will maintain reserves related to the size of its net demand deposits." Thus, under its revised Regulation D, the FRS specifies that any member bank that has net demand deposits in excess of $400 million will be classified as a *"reserve city bank"* while any member bank that has net demand deposits of or below $400 million will be classified as *"other."*

The FRS has adopted a system of reserve requirements that relate to a member bank's:

- types of deposit (demand or time)
- amounts of deposits
- maturities of time deposits

Exhibit 8-1 summarizes this multi-tiered structure of reserve requirements, which incorporates the principle of *graduated required reserves,* under which a bank is subject to the percentage required reserves that apply to designated deposit intervals. To illustrate, from Exhibit 8-1, a member bank with $50 million in net demand deposits must hold required reserves of: 7 percent against the first $2 million, 9½ percent against the next $8 million, and 11¾ percent against the incremental $40 million. Exhibit 8-1 also shows how the FRS uses a maturity criterion as well as a dollar criterion to specify reserves required against time deposits.

At times the FRS also specifies reserve requirements for special categories of liabilities. These special categories—usually found only in

## EXHIBIT 8-1

### Member Bank Reserve Requirements[1]

Percent of deposits

| Type of deposit, and deposit interval in millions of dollars | Requirements in effect July 31, 1979 | | Previous requirements | |
|---|---|---|---|---|
| | Percent | Effective date | Percent | Effective date |
| **Net demand[2]** | | | | |
| 0–2 | 7 | 12/30/76 | 7½ | 2/13/75 |
| 2–10 | 9½ | 12/30/76 | 10 | 2/13/75 |
| 10–100 | 11¾ | 12/30/76 | 12 | 2/13/75 |
| 100–400 | 12¾ | 12/30/76 | 13 | 2/13/75 |
| Over 400 | 16¼ | 12/30/76 | 16½ | 2/13/75 |
| **Time and savings[2,3,4]** | | | | |
| Savings | 3 | 3/16/67 | 3½ | 3/2/67 |
| Time[5] | | | | |
| 0–5, by maturity | | | | |
| 30–179 days | 3 | 3/16/67 | 3½ | 3/2/67 |
| 180 days to 4 years | 2½ | 1/8/76 | 3 | 3/16/67 |
| 4 years or more | 1 | 10/30/75 | 3 | 3/16/67 |
| Over 5, by maturity | | | | |
| 30–179 days | 6 | 12/12/74 | 5 | 10/1/70 |
| 180 days to 4 years | 2½ | 1/8/76 | 3 | 12/12/74 |
| 4 years or more | 1 | 10/30/75 | 3 | 12/12/74 |

| | Legal limits | |
|---|---|---|
| | Minimum | Maximum |
| **Net demand** | | |
| Reserve city banks | 10 | 22 |
| Other banks | 7 | 14 |
| Time | 3 | 10 |
| Borrowings from foreign banks | 0 | 22 |

1. For changes in reserve requirements beginning 1963, see Board's *Annual Statistical Digest, 1971–1975* and for prior changes, see Board's *Annual Report* for 1976, table 13.
2. (a) Requirement schedules are graduated, and each deposit interval applies to that part of the deposits of each bank. Demand deposits subject to reserve requirements are gross demand deposits minus cash items in process of collection and demand balances due from domestic banks.
(b) The Federal Reserve Act specifies different ranges of requirements for reserve city banks and for other banks. Reserve cities are designated under a criterion adopted effective Nov. 9, 1972, by which a bank having net demand deposits of more than $400 million is considered to have the character of business of a reserve city bank. The presence of the head office of such a bank constitutes designation of that place as a reserve city. Cities in which there are Federal Reserve Banks or branches are also reserve cities. Any banks having net demand deposits of $400 million or less are considered to have the character of business of banks outside of reserve cities and are permitted to maintain reserves at ratios set for banks not in reserve cities. For details, see the Board's Regulation D.
(c) Effective August 24, 1978, the Regulation M reserve requirements

on net balances due from domestic banks to their foreign branches and on deposits that foreign branches lend to U.S. residents were reduced to zero from 4 percent and 1 percent, respectively. The Regulation D reserve requirement on borrowings from unrelated banks abroad was also reduced to zero from 4 percent.
(d) Effective with the reserve computation period beginning Nov. 16, 1978, domestic deposits of Edge Corporations are subject to the same reserve requirements as deposits of member banks.
3. Negotiable order of withdrawal (NOW) accounts and time deposits such as Christmas and vacation club accounts are subject to the same requirements as savings deposits.
4. The average reserve requirement on savings and other time deposits must be at least 3 percent, the minimum specified by law.
5. Effective November 2, 1978, a supplementary reserve requirement of 2 percent was imposed on time deposits of $100,000 or more, obligations of affiliates, and ineligible acceptances.

NOTE. Required reserves must be held in the form of deposits with Federal Reserve Banks or vault cash.

Source: *Federal Reserve Bulletin,* August 1979, p. A9.

large money-center banks—have included foreign branch deposits, time deposits exceeding $100,000, and specific holding-company liabilities. The FRS at times imposes *marginal reserve requirements,* whereby, for some categories, it requires a higher percentage reserve against deposits that exceed a base amount as of a specific time. To illustrate, during part of 1973 and 1974, if a member bank increased its outstanding time deposits of $100,000 or more beyond a base related to its previous amounts of such deposits, then the bank had to maintain reserves of 11 percent on the incremental amount and 5 percent on the base amount.

Bank officials monitor recent and pending developments in FRS reserve requirements. These bankers realize that the FRS usually has the power—or can obtain additional power from Congress—to redefine what constitutes a bank liability that is subject to reserve requirements. Therefore, as they evaluate strategic decisions about competing for various types of deposit and nondeposit funds, these bankers estimate whether and how the FRS might respecify its reserve requirements.

A nonmember bank similarly adheres to the current reserve requirements of the state in which it operates, and it monitors and tries to forecast possible changes in its state's reserve requirements.

## MEETING RESERVE REQUIREMENTS

To meet its required reserves, a member bank has to adhere to the definitions and computational procedures specified by the FRS.

FRS reserve requirements apply to *net demand deposits,* defined as a bank's:

Gross demand deposits
*Minus*  Cash items in process of collection *and*
Demand deposits due from domestic banks

The definition excludes uncollected cash items because they represent deposit liabilities, subject to reserve requirements, of other banks; and it excludes deposits due from domestic banks because such interbank deposits, by definition, are not part of the money supply. The FRS also sets reserve requirements for ''Savings'' deposits (which includes open-account time deposits such as Christmas and vacation clubs) and other ''Time'' deposits. All member banks have net demand deposits and savings and time deposits that are subject to basic reserve requirements. Only large banks generally have the special categories of deposit and nondeposit liabilities (such as large-denomination time deposits and foreign branch deposits) that may be subject to special reserve requirements.

To meet its reserve requirements, a member bank must hold *eligible reserves* in the form of vault cash and deposits with its Federal Reserve Bank.

To facilitate reserve management by member banks, the FRS specifies some standard operating procedures. It permits each member bank to *average* its reserves over a *reserve period,* defined as a seven-day week ending each Wednesday. The FRS also provides for *lagged reserve accounting,* whereby a bank uses its actual daily balances of two weeks ago to calculate and partly meet its current reserve requirements. To illustrate, in the current period a bank is to hold reserves against an average of its end-of-day deposits in the reserve period two weeks ago. Similarly, to meet partly its current reserve requirements, a bank is to include an average of its end-of-day vault cash during the reserve period two weeks ago. Thus as a bank enters its current reserve period, it conveniently calculates from its ledgers its average deposit balances and its average vault cash of two weeks ago. Once it determines these two average figures, the bank has only its end-of-day reserve balances with its Federal Reserve Bank as a decision variable during the current period. A bank cannot precisely control these balances, which change often as the Federal Reserve Bank debits or credits clearing items to the bank's account. The bank has to try, however, to manage its balances with the Federal Reserve Bank so that the average of its end-of-day balances will approximate the amount required for the current period. (This averaging process allows for wide, if largely offsetting, fluctuations of reserve balances within a reserve period.)[1]

Despite the use of averages and lagged accounting, a bank seldom can manage its reserves so closely that its actual reserves equal its required reserves. Therefore the FRS also provides for a *carry-over allowance,* which permits a bank to carry forward into its next reserve period any reserve deficiency or excess of up to two percent of the total reserves required in the current period. This provision enables a bank to use its eligible excess reserves in one period to help offset a deficiency in the next period. Likewise, within limits, a deficiency in one period can be offset by an excess in the next period.

The FRS can penalize a member bank that has a reserve deficiency of more than two percent in a reserve period. Unless it waives the penalty, the FRS requires a member bank to pay interest on the deficiency. (The rate is set at two percentage points higher than the Federal Reserve Bank's discount rate in effect at the beginning of the month in which the deficiency occurs.) If a bank is consistently deficient in its reserves, the FRS can impose additional sanctions. Member banks choose to avoid penalties and sanctions, and so they manage their reserves consistent with the specified procedures of reserve accounting.

A nonmember bank must meet the reserve requirements specified by its state.[2] Most states distinguish between demand deposits and time deposits as separate categories that are subject to required reserves. States differ, however, in how they define demand deposits that are subject to reserves. Some states exempt certain governmental deposits from reserve requirements, especially if these deposits require pledged assets. Although they thus differ in their definitions of deposit liabilities that are subject to required reserves, many states specify percentage reserve requirements that are similar to those that the FRS sets for its member banks. Also, similar to the FRS, most states allow their banks to average their deposit liabilities and eligible reserves over an accounting period; and states usually allow their state banking agency some flexibility to vary the percentage requirements.

The form of eligible reserves differs substantially between member and nonmember banks. Member banks can count only vault cash and balances

1. For more details and examples of reserve management by member banks, see Robert E. Knight, "Guidelines for Efficient Reserve Management," *Monthly Review* (Federal Reserve Bank of Kansas City), November 1977, pp. 11-23. Also, Stuart G. Hoffman, "Reserves Management Strategy and the Carry-Forward Provision," *Monthly Review* (Federal Reserve Bank of Atlanta), August 1976, pp. 102-109.

2. For a summary enumeration of state reserve requirements, see Robert E. Knight, "Reserve Requirements, Part I: Comparative Reserve Requirements at Member and Nonmember Banks," *Monthly Review* (Federal Reserve Bank of Kansas City), April 1974, pp. 3-20. Also, R. Alton Gilbert and Jean M. Lovati, "Bank Reserve Requirements and Their Enforcement: A Comparison Across States," *Review* (Federal Reserve Bank of St. Louis), March 1978, pp. 22-31.

with Federal Reserve Banks among their eligible reserves. In contrast, nonmember banks generally can include a broader range of assets to meet their eligible reserves. Depending on its state's specific requirements, a nonmember bank usually can include vault cash and demand balances with other banks. Also, in most states a nonmember bank can include its cash items in process of collection among its eligible reserves, and in many states it can include at least part of its securities holdings (especially U.S. Treasury securities) as eligible reserves.

States generally enforce their reserve requirements less strictly than does the FRS. In many states, a nonmember bank does not have to submit periodic reports about its reserve position; it only has to satisfy a visiting examiner that it has been meeting its state requirements. Moreover, in about twenty states, a nonmember bank faces no explicit penalty if it fails to meet its reserve requirements.

Any bank, whether a member or nonmember, plans to adhere to its applicable reserve requirements. Its officials identify the current rules, and then they have one or more employees monitor and manage the bank's eligible reserves so that these reserves approximate the amounts required over time. While a bank's officials delegate many tactical details of reserve management, these officials make the ongoing strategic decision of whether their bank will be subject to FRS or state reserve requirements.

## MEMBERSHIP IN THE FEDERAL RESERVE SYSTEM

A national bank must be a member of the FRS; a state bank can choose whether or not to belong to the FRS. However, a national bank can apply to switch to a state charter and then withdraw from the FRS. Most state banks, while they choose not to belong to the FRS, are insured by and supervised by the FDIC.

### BENEFITS AND COSTS OF FRS MEMBERSHIP

Because it can choose whether or not to belong to the FRS, each bank—including national banks with their option to switch charters—needs to evaluate periodically the benefits and costs of FRS membership.

#### Benefits

A member bank has access to various FRS services:

- check clearing
- currency and coin shipments
- discount window
- safekeeping of investment securities
- wire transfer services

A member bank pays no explicit fees for these services, except that it pays the current discount rate for its borrowings, if any, at the discount window.

While member banks can receive various "free" services from their Federal Reserve Bank, both member and nonmember banks can receive similar services from large correspondent banks that too provide check clearings, currency and coin shipments, safekeeping facilities, and wire transfer services. Through their city correspondents, member and non-member banks also have access to such services as bond portfolio analyses, data processing, international transactions, loan participations, and training workshops. Member banks thus have to participate in the correspondent banking system in order to obtain some services not available from the FRS; and nonmember banks can, from their correspondent banks, obtain almost all services—except access to the discount window—that the FRS provides to its members. To compensate the city correspondents for the services, most banks do not pay explicit fees; they maintain noninterest-earning deposits with the correspondents.

## Costs

As a member of the FRS, a bank incurs a set of obligations. It must:

- adhere to FRS required reserves
- submit to FRS regulations and supervision
- subscribe to stock in its Federal Reserve Bank

A nonmember bank incurs some similar obligations, the costs of which can be lower than those associated with FRS membership:

- A nonmember bank has to meet its state required reserves, but in many states it can include among its eligible reserves: cash items in collection, correspondent balances (with their implicit income in the form of "free" services), and some interest-earning government securities.
- A nonmember bank is subject to regulation and supervision by its state banking agency and, if it is insured, by the FDIC. Over time the cost burden of this supervision is likely to be similar to that of supervision by the FRS, and, in the case of national banks, by the OCC.
- A nonmember bank does not have to subscribe to stock in a Federal Reserve Bank on which it would receive a statutory annual dividend of 6 percent, a return that is below that which banks can otherwise obtain from loans and investments during periods of high interest rates.

Thus, as it analyzes the costs of FRS membership, a bank has to compare these costs to those of nonmembership.

## Comparing Benefits and Costs

Various studies document that for many banks the costs of FRS membership exceed the benefits.

One study compares the profitability of member and nonmember banks in Illinois, which is the only state that has no reserve requirements for its state-chartered banks.[3] It reports that, on average, nonmember banks are more profitable than member banks that are similar in size, location, deposit composition, and growth rates.

In contrast, another study compares the earnings of member and nonmember banks in the Fourth (Cleveland) Federal Reserve District. It concludes that "the earnings of Fourth District member banks as a group were not significantly different from those of nonmembers during 1963-70 where allowance is made for differences in location by state, size, growth, loan to investment composition, and the proportion of total deposits made up of time and savings accounts."[4]

A study adjusts for and estimates the percentage reserve requirements faced by member and nonmember banks in 34 states. It reports that "adjusted cash reserve requirements averaged 7.85 percent for member banks, and 5.90 percent for nonmember banks, a difference of about one-third. This differential has meant millions of dollars in income lost from earning assets sacrificed for the greater cash reserves required for Fed. membership."[5]

Another study analyzes what might occur if nonmember banks had to meet reserve requirements similar to those of member banks. It observes that nonmember banks "hold relatively less nonearning assets and, therefore, more earning assets than their member bank counterparts in every size class." The study then concludes that if nonmember banks had to meet member bank required reserves and if they also were to receive all Federal Reserve services, then the nonmembers would have "to reduce their earning assets by approximately 1.7-3.5 percent of total assets. In terms of net income, this would mean an annual loss to nonmember banks of 5.5-13.0 percent, depending on bank size."[6]

---

3. Lucille Stringer Mayne, *The Cost of Federal Reserve System Membership*, Research Paper No. 2, Department of Economics and Research, The American Bankers Association, 1967. A study of banks in Louisiana, New Mexico, Oklahoma, and Texas similarly concludes that member banks face a cost burden of FRS membership. Edward E. Veazey, "Estimates of the Cost to Member Banks of Reserve Requirements," *Review* (Federal Reserve Bank of Dallas), December 1977, pp. 14-21. A study of banks in the Sixth (Atlanta) Federal Reserve District estimates that member banks in that region similarly bear a cost burden, as measured by earnings foregone as a percentage of actual earnings. It concludes that, on average, the District's largest member banks have the lowest burden and that the very smallest member banks have the highest burden. It further notes, however, that the estimated "burden differential between very small and very large banks is tentative." Stuart G. Hoffman, "The Burden of Fed Membership for Sixth District Banks," and "The Burden of Fed Membership Revisited," *Economic Review* (Federal Reserve Bank of Atlanta), November-December 1978, pp. 126-129, and March-April 1979, p. 23, respectively.

4. Marvin Phaup, "The Effect of Federal Reserve Membership on Earnings of Fourth District Banks, 1963-1970," *Economic Review* (Federal Reserve Bank of Cleveland), January-February 1973, pp. 3-18.

5. Chris Joseph Prestopino, "Do Higher Reserve Requirements Discourage Federal Reserve Membership?," *The Journal of Finance*, December 1976, pp. 1471-1480.

6. Lawrence G. Goldberg and John T. Rose, "The Effect on Nonmember Banks of the Imposition of Member Bank Reserve Requirements—With and Without Federal Reserve Services," *The Journal of Finance*, December 1976, pp. 1457-1469.

Instead of comparing samples of member and nonmember banks, another study analyzes the before and after performance of banks that withdrew from, or joined, the FRS between 1963 and 1969. This study compares the performance of these changing banks to that of similar banks (based on size and location) that did not change their membership status throughout the period. It concludes that "banks withdrawing from the System reduced cash holdings, increased loans, and experienced significantly increased profits," measured as rates of return on assets and capital. Moreover "the profit gains to bank management have been generated without significant increases in service charges or rate reductions on time and savings deposits."[7]

## EROSION IN FRS MEMBERSHIP

Many banks have decided that for them the costs of FRS membership outweigh the benefits. In 1950 member banks accounted for 51 percent of all banks and for 87 percent of all bank deposits; by 1978 these figures declined to 38 percent and 72 percent respectively.[8]

One study analyzes the recent erosion (1960-77) in FRS membership, and it observes that:

- There have been net withdrawals (over 500) from FRS membership.
- Most newly chartered banks have state charters, and over 90 percent of these new banks choose to be nonmembers. (The proportion of nonmembership is lower, however, for newly chartered affiliates of bank holding companies.)
- Some member banks have merged into other banks, thus reducing the number of members.
- The merger process has eliminated some member and nonmember banks as separate entities, but on balance this process has added to deposits of the continuing member banks.
- Nonmember banks, in total, have had more rapid internal deposit growth than have member banks.

The study reviews these trends and concludes that "if the pace of aggregate deposit attrition is to be significantly slowed and possibly turned around in the near future, the burden of System membership must not just be eliminated but must be converted to a net benefit in order to encourage both ongoing nonmembers and *de novo* banks to join the System."[9]

---

7. Gary G. Gilbert and Manferd O. Peterson, "The Impact of Changes in Federal Reserve Membership on Commercial Bank Performance," *The Journal of Finance*, June 1975, pp. 713-719. The coauthors also report that the banks that joined the FRS increased their proportion of assets held in cash and reduced the proportion in loans, but with no significant change in the profit measures.

8. John T. Rose, "Federal Reserve System Attrition Since 1960," *Journal of Bank Research*, Spring 1979, pp. 8-27; and computed from *Federal Reserve Bulletin*, August 1979, p. A17.

9. Rose, "Federal Reserve System Attrition Since 1960," p. 26.

To examine banker attitudes toward the FRS, another study surveys samples of banks, by state, that: recently withdrew from the FRS, never had been FRS members, or are still members. The author of the study sent questionnaires to these samples of banks, and he received responses from about thirty-seven percent of the surveyed banks. All three groups (former members, never members, and current members) indicate that, by wide margins, the most important advantages of membership are access to the discount window and free shipments of currency and coin. All three groups overwhelmingly cite FRS reserve requirements as the major disadvantage of membership. The study concludes that among the banks that withdrew from membership, a majority believed that their earnings would increase and that this was the actual outcome following their withdrawals. It also observes that a large number of the current members "expressed interest in leaving the system."[10]

## ACTIONS AND PROPOSALS TO STEM EROSION OF FRS MEMBERSHIP

Officials of the FRS express concern about the increasing proportions of total banks and total bank deposits that are outside of the FRS. They assert that this nonmembership may impede FRS implementation of monetary policy and that it places an inequitable burden on remaining member banks that have to comply with FRS reserve requirements.[11] Nonmember banks and some analysts question whether nonmembership in fact leads to significant inefficiencies and inequities. Bankers and banking scholars need to monitor, and perhaps participate in this ongoing debate; and they need to monitor proposals that would revise some of the benefits and/or costs of FRS membership.

In recent years the FRS has consistently tried to reduce the burden of FRS membership. It has improved and increased its services for member banks. It now more quickly credits a member bank's account for check-clearing items; it fosters innovations in funds-transfer systems; and it provides a seasonal-borrowing privilege at its discount window. Also, as part of its monetary policy, the FRS has made various percentage and procedural changes in reserve requirements. On balance, these changes have led to a general lowering of reserve requirements and to simplification of reserve-management procedures, especially for small and medium-sized banks. While the FRS has thus increased some benefits and reduced some costs of membership, many banks continue to choose nonmembership, especially when, as nonmembers, they can obtain historically high returns on at least part of their eligible reserve assets.[12] Also, while the FRS has

---

10. Peter S. Rose, "Banker Attitudes Toward the Federal Reserve System: Survey Results," *Journal of Bank Research,* Summer 1977, pp. 77-84. Also by the same author, "Exodus: Why Banks Are Leaving the Fed," *The Bankers Magazine,* Winter 1976, pp. 43-49.

11. *Federal Reserve Bulletin,* August 1978, pp. 636-642, and March 1979, pp. 229-235.

12. Many current and potential member banks also could reduce the net cost of membership if they were to substitute more of the free services provided by the FRS for the similar services provided by city correspondent banks that expect compensation in the form of balances and/or fees. R. Alton Gilbert,

gradually lowered its reserve requirements, some states have also lowered their effective requirements.

Some bankers and banking scholars propose that, to reduce the burden of membership, the FRS should eliminate or sharply curtail its reserve requirements.[13] (A variant of this proposal is that the FRS should at least end its required reserves for time and savings deposits.) Proponents of this proposal cite some monetary studies which indicate that the FRS can conduct its monetary policy via open-market operations and the discount window. Opponents of the proposal usually assert that the FRS should not reduce its instruments of monetary policy and that, unless offsetting measures are taken, elimination of reserve requirements will provide a windfall to bank stockholders.

The FRS also could modify the benefit-cost equation of FRS membership if it were to pay explicit interest on member bank reserves. One author summarizes how such a procedure can result in increased economic efficiency and equity.[14] As a corollary to its paying interest on member bank reserves, the FRS also could institute an explicit pricing schedule for the services that it now provides "free" to member banks. Some economists demonstrate how such a pricing system can result in increased economic efficiency.[15] The FRS has begun to evaluate the merits and feasibility of such a pricing system for its services, and it has published, for comment, a preliminary schedule of such prices.[16] Therefore, bankers need to estimate how such an explicit pricing system, if implemented by the FRS, is likely to affect their use, and possibly offerings, of correspondent banking services.

For two decades FRS officials have proposed federal legislation that would provide for *uniform required reserves,* whereby all banks—members and nonmembers—would have to meet the reserve requirements specified by the FRS, the nation's central bank.[17] Several prominent study commissions also have proposed that all banks conform to similar reserve requirements. Its advocates usually claim that uniform required reserves will

"Utilization of Federal Reserve Bank Services by Member Banks: Implications for the Costs and Benefits of Membership," *Review* (Federal Reserve Bank of St. Louis), August 1977, pp. 2-15; and Bruce J. Summers, "Correspondent Services, Federal Reserve Services, and Bank Cash Management Policy," *Economic Review* (Federal Reserve Bank of Richmond), November-December 1978, pp. 29-38.

13. Deane Carson, "Should Reserve Requirements Be Abolished?," *The Bankers Magazine,* Winter 1973, pp. 12-17. Lucille S. Mayne, "The Deposit Reserve Requirement Recommendations of the Commission on Financial Structure and Regulation: An Analysis and Critique," *Journal of Bank Research,* Spring 1973, pp. 41-51.

14. Ira Kaminow, "Why Not Pay Interest on Member Bank Reserves?," *Business Review* (Federal Reserve Bank of Philadelphia), January 1975, pp. 3-9.

15. W. Lee Hoskins, "Should the Fed Sell Its Services?," *Business Review* (Federal Reserve Bank of Philadelphia), January 1975, pp. 11-17. Preston J. Miller, "The Right Way to Price Federal Reserve Services," *Quarterly Review* (Federal Reserve Bank of Minneapolis), Summer 1977, pp. 15-22.

16. "Fed Publishes Preliminary Pricing Schedule," *Voice* (Federal Reserve Bank of Dallas), January 1979, p. 14.

17. Robert E. Knight, "Reserve Requirements, Part II: An Analysis of the Case for Uniform Reserve Requirements," *Monthly Review* (Federal Reserve Bank of Kansas City), May 1974, pp. 3-15, 24.

contribute to more effective monetary policy and to greater equity among competing financial institutions.[18] Other scholars are skeptical about the extent of such claimed benefits.[19]

The U.S. Congress has begun to review specific proposals that would sharply modify the system of FRS required reserves and services.[20] In summary, these proposals contain most of the following provisions:

- permit the FRS, as the nation's central bank, to set uniform reserve requirements for all transactions (or check-like) accounts offered by all financial institutions. (These requirements would apply to all banks and nonbank financial intermediaries but would not apply to transactions deposits below a specified total, such as $35 million for each institution.)
- reduce and simplify the current structure of reserve requirements
- reduce or remove reserve requirements for time and savings deposits
- permit the FRS to pay interest on reserve balances that member banks keep with it
- allow nonmember banks and nonbank intermediaries to hold at least some of their required reserves in interest-earning assets, possibly as voluntary balances with the FRS
- permit qualifying nonmember institutions also to have access to the FRS discount window
- have the FRS implement an explicit competitive pricing system for its services that would then be available to members and nonmembers

There has been extensive debate about these proposals. While a political consensus has not yet emerged, it is likely that Congress will soon pass legislation with many of the above provisions. Therefore all banks need to keep informed about the progress of these legislative proposals, and they need to plan strategies for a revised system of reserve requirements and FRS services.

---

18. Frank E. Morris, "The Need for a Uniform System of Reserve Requirements," *New England Economic Review* (Federal Reserve Bank of Boston), January-February 1972, pp. 14-18. Dorothy M. Nichols, "Toward More Uniform Reserve Requirements," *Business Conditions* (Federal Reserve Bank of Chicago), March 1974, pp. 3-12.

19. One researcher analyzes various systems of reserve requirements and concludes that none will make it more difficult for the FRS to control the money supply. He therefore suggests that equity among institutions become the principal criterion for selecting an optimal system of required reserves and concludes "that only uniform reserves against demand deposits for all banks, member and nonmember, qualify [as optimal] on grounds of equity and resource allocation" and that "there should not be any reserves required against time deposits." George J. Benston, "An Analysis and Evaluation of Alternative Reserve Requirement Plans," *The Journal of Finance,* December 1969, pp. 849-870. Also, Ira Kaminow, "The Case against Uniform Reserves: A Loss of Perspective," *Business Review* (Federal Reserve Bank of Philadelphia), June 1974, pp. 16-21.

20. *Federal Reserve Bulletin,* July 1978, pp. 605-610 and March 1979, pp. 229-235. Also, "A Way Out of the Fed Membership Impasse," *The Morgan Guaranty Survey,* May 1979, pp. 5-13; and George J. Benston, *Federal Reserve Membership: Consequences, Costs, Benefits and Alternatives,* a study prepared for the Trustees of the Banking Research Fund, Association of Reserve City Bankers, 1978.

## LIQUIDITY MANAGEMENT

Even if it had no legal reserve requirements, a bank would hold some cash so that it could conveniently meet net outflows of funds; and it would have procedures by which it could quickly add to its pool of cash. Liquidity management consists of the analyses and procedures by which a bank thus continuously prepares to meet net cash outflows without having to incur major portfolio-adjustment costs.

Liquidity is a relative term; at any time there is no precise definition or measure of the liquidity of an individual bank or of the banking system.[21] For example, a pool of current and readily available cash can be adequate to meet expected plus some unexpected net cash outflows, but this same pool can be inadequate to meet unpredictably high net cash outflows. Unless it holds most of its assets in cash, a bank cannot rely on its own resources to meet unpredictably large net outflows. If it is a member bank, it can turn to the FRS as a residual source of liquidity.

Once it accepts liquidity as a relative concept, a bank can better manage its liquidity. It has to:

- identify its principal sources of cash inflows and outflows and then decide over which of these it has some short-run control
- develop systems to help it predict and monitor its cash flows
- evaluate the costs and benefits of various procedures by which to adjust its cash flows over time

Thus each bank has to engage in an individualized analysis of its cash flows and ways to manage its cash flows.

### IDENTIFYING THE PRINCIPAL CASH FLOWS

Exhibit 8-2 schematically summarizes the relationships between a bank's cash flows and its principal balance-sheet items, and it thus places liquidity management in the context of a bank's total portfolio.

Exhibit 8-2 identifies six major categories of a bank's balance sheet:

- cash items
- deposit liabilities
- long-term investments and loans
- long-term liabilities and capital
- short-term noncash assets
- short-term nondeposit liabilities

---

21. Bank analysts cite and evaluate "bank-liquidity" measures such as a bank's (or the banking system's) ratios of: cash to total assets, cash plus U.S. Treasury securities to total assets, and loans to deposits (in which instance a higher ratio implies less "liquidity"). Yet invariably these analysts note that these traditional balance-sheet measures of bank liquidity are inadequate because they are too aggregate and they fail to consider cash-flow patterns. Also, James L. Pierce, "Commercial Bank Liquidity," *Federal Reserve Bulletin,* August 1966, pp. 1093-1101.

**EXHIBIT 8-2**

## Cash Flow Management: A Balance Sheet Perspective

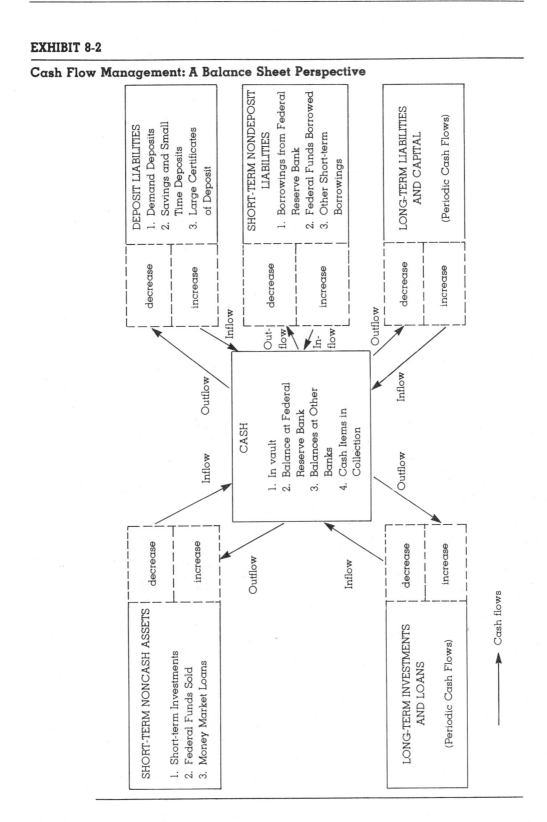

Cash is at the heart of liquidity management. Net increases or decreases in any of the other five categories trigger flows in and out of the pool of cash. In the long run, a bank can reasonably control each of the six categories. In the short run, however, a bank has limited control of changes in its: cash items, deposit liabilities, long-term investments and loans, and long-term liabilities and capital. Therefore, to manage its liquidity, a bank monitors cash flows over which it has little control; and it makes decisions to increase or decrease items over which it has some short-run control: its short-term noncash assets, and its short-term nondeposit liabilities.

## Cash Items

At any time a bank's cash pool consists of:

- vault cash (currency and coin)
- balance at the Federal Reserve Bank, if the bank is a member
- balances at other (correspondent) banks
- cash items in collection

The total amount of cash reflects management decisions and short-run factors that are beyond management's direct control.

To illustrate, a bank begins a day with a level of vault cash that it believes will enable it to meet its expected, and some unexpected, net cash withdrawals by its depositors. Although it expects its vault cash to decline over the day, it plans to replenish it the next day when it expects net currency inflows and a delivery of currency and coin from its city correspondent bank. After it has made this inventory decision about its vault cash, the bank stands ready to meet currency withdrawals throughout the day.[22] If, for whatever reason, currency withdrawals exceed the amount for which it had planned, then the bank must act quickly to replenish its ebbing vault cash. Most likely it will arrange to send a courier to obtain some vault cash from a nearby bank that has an amount that exceeds its short-run needs. The nearby bank thus helps because it knows that it too has days when unexpected currency withdrawals threaten to exceed its available vault cash.

A bank also plans its balances at its Federal Reserve Bank and/or at other banks. These balances ebb and flow as checks, in the clearing process, are debited and credited to the bank's accounts. Although a bank can somewhat select the schedules by which it clears its items, actual clearing times are subject to events outside its control. Thus a bank plans to hold balances that will cover both anticipated and some unanticipated clearing items.

---

22. A member bank can potentially benefit if it holds excess vault cash and then subsequently transfers these funds to its Federal Reserve account, where they can also serve as a reserve-eligible asset in a current reserve period. An author summarizes this "vault cash game," and concludes that, while possible, it is not prevalent. Warren L. Coats, Jr., "Regulation D and the Vault Cash Game," *The Journal of Finance,* June 1973, pp. 601-607.

As an operating strategy, a bank may hold vault cash and correspondent balances that substantially exceed its expected and unexpected needs. It can then conveniently meet almost all cash outflows; but this convenience benefit involves a cost, because the bank earns no returns from this excess cash that, alternatively, could generate returns as investments or loans. Also, it may have to pay a higher premium for insurance coverage of its excess vault cash. Therefore a bank must frequently evaluate the net marginal cost of its holding excess cash.

### Deposit Liabilities

When its deposit liabilities change, so do a bank's cash balances. Net deposit withdrawals, either as currency or as transfers to other banks, reduce the cash balances; and net deposit additions add to the pool of cash. While in the short run it primarily has to respond to its deposit fluctuations, a bank can develop and implement longer-run strategies that affect its deposit volatility.

To illustrate, one bank's strategy is to develop a diversified base of small and medium-sized deposits, which many bankers call *core deposits*. Toward this end it maintains an extensive branch network; it stays open long hours; and it directs most of its marketing toward local depositors. Although funds flow in and out of these individual accounts, in total these flows approximately offset each other over time. Except during unusual periods, such as disintermediation, this diversification strategy enables the bank to confidently predict its total cash flows from deposits.

After it evaluates its competitive environment and resources, a second illustrative bank decides to focus on accounts of professional people and medium-sized firms. Toward this end it emphasizes its expertise and willingness to service the total banking needs of its targeted set of customers. This bank's deposit base is not as diversified as that of the first bank's, and this bank has to stand ready promptly to meet its depositors' loan requests. This deposit-acquisition strategy thus implies that the bank's aggregate short-run funds flows will be more volatile than those of the bank that has a more diverse base of many local depositors.

A large bank generally has diverse retail deposits; and it also competes for demand deposits and time deposits of many large firms, governmental units, other banks, and foreign clients. Although balances in any one account fluctuate over time, fluctuations within the bank's many accounts largely offset each other. Thus the bank's total deposits do not fluctuate as widely as do many of the component accounts. While its broadly diversified deposit base helps reduce erratic cash flows, the large bank remains alert to possible periods of disintermediation, when market interest rates exceed those that it can legally pay to some of its depositors.

### Long-term Investments and Loans

Each business day a bank receives interest and principal payments from some borrowers. Often, as previously agreed, the bank debits a borrower's deposit account for the amount of the payment due. This internal transfer provides no cash to the bank. Yet, in anticipation of the payment, the borrower probably made a deposit; and this anticipatory action previously added to the bank's cash inflows. A bank similarly receives periodic interest payments from issuers of the many long-term bonds that it owns. For convenience, many banks have most of their bonds held in safekeeping by a city correspondent bank that then collects the interest and credits these inflows to the correspondent balances of the outlying banks.

As it evaluates whether and how to change its long-term loans and investments, a bank considers how such changes can affect its liquidity management. For example, to obtain and retain valued customers, a bank plans to meet their bank-loan needs. In some cases a bank and a customer negotiate a formal agreement, whereby, subject to the conditions of the agreement, the bank commits itself to meet the customer's loan requests. In many cases, however, a bank and a valued customer have an informal understanding that both parties view as morally binding throughout normal economic conditions. A bank thus plans to meet its formal and informal loan commitments in response to its customer requests, and so it does not have direct control of part of its short-run loan demand. The bank stands ready to credit the deposit accounts of the borrowers, and it knows that most of these borrowers in turn will draw down their accounts in order to pay their bills.

Similarly, a bank has little short-run flexibility to reduce its outstanding loans. Once it has made a long-term loan, a bank cannot readily convert it to cash. (There are secondary markets for only some types of bank loans.) As long as the borrower meets the contractual loan terms, the bank can only plan on cash inflows according to the scheduled payments of principal and interest.

If it wants to change the cash flows from its loan portfolio, a bank does so by gradually changing the pace at which it makes new loans. To illustrate, if it tightens its lending standards, a bank can pare the rate of increase in new loan commitments and new loans, and thus over time, as the cash inflows from repaid loans exceed the cash outflows of new loans, the bank can reduce the size of its total loan portfolio.

Although there are markets for most of its long-term investments, a bank seldom plans to sell such nonliquid assets as a way to add to its pool of cash. It buys and sells long-term investments based on its analysis of future interest rates, future loan demands, the relative prices of various investment securities, and the tax consequences of possible transactions.

## Long-term Liabilities and Capital

A bank makes infrequent, but major, decisions about its long-term liabilities and capital. These strategic decisions also affect a bank's cash flows. For example, a bank plans to have cash available to meet its scheduled rental payments and its payments of interest and principal on outstanding long-term debt, if any. After it has declared a cash dividend, a bank plans to have cash available on the dividend payment date. While it thus makes periodic cash payments to its long-term creditors and its stockholders, a bank also makes infrequent decisions to increase or decrease its long-term liabilities and/or capital. Such increases in these balance-sheet items involve cash inflows, and decreases involve cash outflows.

### Short-term Noncash Assets and Nondeposit Liabilities

In contrast to the preceding balance-sheet items, a bank has more direct control of changes in its short-term noncash assets, such as federal funds sold, and its short-term nondeposit liabilities, such as federal funds purchased. A bank predicts and monitors the cash flows over which it has limited control, and it manages its short-term assets and liabilities in ways that help offset these cash flows.

### PREDICTING AND MONITORING CASH FLOWS

Once it identifies its principal cash-flow items, a bank designs and implements a cash-planning system, as outlined in Exhibit 8-3. The pool of cash is the sum of the various cash items at a specific time. This sum changes over time in response to cash flows in and out of the pool. Also, a bank can change its pool of cash as it engages in transactions that involve other balance-sheet items.

**EXHIBIT 8-3**

**A Cash-Planning System**

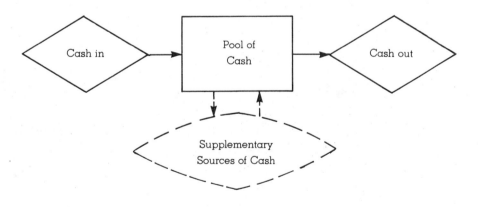

A *cash-planning system* focuses on cash flows within future planning periods. A bank makes some detailed projections of its cash flows for the coming day and week, and it broadly outlines its major cash flows for longer planning periods.

Cash-planning procedures vary among banks. Most medium-sized or small banks have informal cash-planning systems that use some summary worksheets. For these banks, the benefits of an intricate system are unlikely to exceed the costs to implement such a system. In contrast, large banks devote substantial resources to cash-flow planning. Each business day these large banks experience large, often erratic, cash flows. If they closely manage their cash flows, often with the use of computer systems, these banks can operate with a lower pool of nonearning cash than they could without such a system. Thus a large bank can expect that, if it reallocates nonearning cash to additional earning assets, its incremental returns are likely to exceed the incremental costs of a detailed cash-planning system.

A bank's cash flows fall into three principal categories:

- scheduled
- unscheduled, but predictable
- unexpected

While each bank tries to estimate its pending scheduled and unscheduled cash flows, by definition it cannot confidently estimate its unexpected cash flows. Yet it must have plans and contingency plans for each of the three categories.

### Scheduled Cash Flows

A bank can precisely project many scheduled cash inflows and outflows. It knows, for example, the exact payroll schedules of large depositors, such as a university. If it participates in a direct-deposit agreement with such an employer, the bank knows that on or slightly before the scheduled payroll days the employer will transfer funds to the bank, which, in turn, will credit the accounts of its participating depositors. Even if it does not know the exact amount of the scheduled transfer, the bank can closely estimate the amount for cash-planning purposes. Similarly, a bank knows that some of its large depositors, such as local chain stores and automobile dealers, transfer funds to their headquarters or suppliers according to fixed schedules. In addition to some deposit flows, a bank can closely estimate its scheduled inflows from interest income and loan repayments. It also knows the amounts, if any, of CDs and federal funds purchases that it is scheduled to repay in the cash-planning period.

### Unscheduled, but Predictable, Cash Flows

A bank can confidently estimate various unscheduled, but predictable, cash flows. To illustrate, if it processes many direct deposits for employees who have accounts with it, a bank can review and extrapolate past patterns of how these depositors in total reduce their balances until the next payroll date. By examining past patterns, most banks can estimate their outflows of vault cash on Fridays and days prior to national holidays. If it has many small loans, a bank can, without examining the schedule of each loan, reasonably predict its total pending inflows from interest and principal payments. It can also estimate the total dollar amount of such new loans that it will make if it does not change its loan policies. Thus there are many categories of cash flows for which a bank can make a confident prediction, subject to a small range of possible error. A medium-sized bank is likely to base its predictions on judgmental extrapolations of past patterns; a large bank can use various statistical forecasting techniques to make best estimates—and distributions of estimates—of its various cash-flow items.

Deposit fluctuations account for a large part of a bank's daily cash flows. Several studies analyze the deposit fluctuations for samples of banks in different regions and in different time periods.[23] The studies vary in how they calculate *deposit variability*, which is a measure of how much a bank's deposits deviate around an average during a specific time period. The principal, but not unanimous, conclusions of these studies are that:

- Small banks experience more deposit variability than do large banks.[24]
- Rapidly growing banks experience more deposit-variability than do their slower-growing counterparts.
- Deposit composition, such as a bank's proportion of demand deposits and time deposits, affects deposit variability; and various types of deposits experience differing deposit variability.

While it can gain insights from such conclusions, each bank has to analyze its own deposits for unusual fluctuations and then examine ways to predict and/or reduce, for example by diversification, the unusual fluctuations.

### Unexpected Cash Flows

A bank's cash-planning system enables it to prepare for scheduled and for unscheduled, but predictable, cash flows. It is the unexpected cash flows—especially large net outflows—that pose a major challenge to liquidity management.[25]

To reduce its unexpected outflows, a bank can informally request its large depositors and borrowers to forewarn it about pending major changes in their deposit balances and borrowing requests. In this way a bank

---

23. Hugh Chairnoff, "Deposit Variability: A Banker's Headache," *Business Review,* (Federal Reserve Bank of Philadelphia), September 1967, pp. 9-15. Chayim Herzig-Marx, "Holding Companies and Deposit Variability," *Business Conditions,* (Federal Reserve Bank of Chicago), March 1976, pp. 12-15. George G. Kaufman, "Deposit Variability and Bank Size," *Journal of Financial and Quantitative Analysis,* December 1972, pp. 2087-2096. Frederick M. Struble and Carroll H. Wilkerson, "Bank Size and Deposit Variability," *Monthly Review* (Federal Reserve Bank of Kansas City), November-December 1967, pp. 3-9.

24. Kaufman notes (p. 2094) that large banks experience relatively less variability "when variability is measured biweekly or longer, but that they experience greater day-to-day variability."

25. Two coauthors emphasize that "random deposit variability" is a major factor in bank liquidity management. They define this term not as total variability but as that component "that is not readily accountable to seasonal variations and trends in deposit growth at individual banks." William G. Dewald and G. Richard Dreese, "Bank Behavior with Respect to Deposit Variability," *The Journal of Finance,* September 1970, pp. 869-879.

develops an *advance-warning system* by which it learns about large pending transactions that will likely affect its cash flows.

A bank also can develop an *early warning system* whereby bank employees promptly inform senior officers about unexpectedly large transactions. Its tellers, for example, are to report unusual patterns of cash withdrawals so that the bank can act quickly to take offsetting actions, if necessary. Many large banks use computerized systems to monitor various categories of cash flows and then to compare these actual patterns to predicted patterns. If the actual patterns start to deviate substantially from predicted patterns, then bank officials can examine quickly whether to take actions to offset the unexpected trends.

As a third way to prepare for unexpected cash outflows, a bank can choose to hold a buffer of cash in excess of its scheduled and predictable needs. Yet the bank still has to decide how much excess cash is adequate for various possible, but improbable, unexpected net cash outflows. Also, cash is a nonearning asset; and so if it holds excess amounts of cash, the bank foregoes some returns that it could otherwise obtain from earning assets.

As a fourth procedure, a bank structures and manages its short-term, noncash balance-sheet items in ways that will enable it to promptly adjust its cash position. Each bank has to evaluate the principal benefits and costs of its available cash-adjustment procedures.

## EVALUATING CASH-ADJUSTMENT PROCEDURES

To manage its liquidity, a bank first identifies and tries to anticipate its future cash flows. Because it cannot precisely predict its future flows, it also has to evaluate procedures by which it can promptly adjust its pool of cash and its cash flows.

Management of its required reserves is part of a bank's liquidity management. A bank has to meet its reserve requirements, and this process constrains the composition of the bank's short-term assets within each reserve period.

Suppose that a medium-sized member bank suddenly incurs net cash outflows that substantially exceed its expectations. To meet these outflows it reduces its vault cash and its balance at the Federal Reserve Bank. Yet the bank cannot allow its balance at the Federal Reserve Bank to fall so low for so long that the average balance in the current reserve period falls below the amount required to meet its legal reserves. How can the bank now adjust for these unexpected outflows?

First the bank tries to identify the principal unexpected flows and to estimate whether the flows represent temporary events or major changes. For example, if the net outflows reflect some unusual delays in the check-clearing system, the bank will likely expect the delays to be soon overcome or else offset by Federal Reserve open-market operations. If several large withdrawals account for most of the unexpected outflows, bank officials can call these customers and try to learn whether they plan soon to rebuild their deposit balances at the bank. If the outflows seem temporary and subject to short-term reversals, then the cash-adjustment procedures are less complex than they would be for major changes, such as a new period of disintermediation when many depositors reduce their bank balances in order to invest in money-market instruments that are not subject to interest-rate ceilings. Liquidity management focuses on short-term adjustments, but within the context of strategic planning for long-term changes in a bank's cash flows.

## Near-Term Cash Inflows

If it is faced with unexpected temporary outflows of cash, a bank can decide to await near-term cash inflows. It reviews its cash-flow projections to determine whether it expects soon to receive net cash inflows. It especially uses this approach to plan to meet its reserve requirements if it is early in a reserve period. At that time the bank can allow its balances at the Federal Reserve Bank to fall low if it is confident that cash inflows will soon restore its balances to the point that the seven-day average is close to the required amount. Moreover, if it experiences a small (up to two percent) deficiency in the current period and if it had no deficiency in the prior period, then the bank has the additional flexibility to offset the deficit with a surplus in the subsequent period. In contrast, as a reserve period comes toward a close, a bank has less flexibility to count on cash inflows to offset a potential deficit reserve position. It then has to act to supplement its expected cash flows.

## Excess Reserves

For any reserve period a member bank's excess reserves are its actual balances at its Federal Reserve Bank minus the amount of balances that it needs to meet its reserve requirements for the period. If it thus holds excess reserves, a bank can conveniently accommodate unexpected cash outflows by reducing its balance at the Federal Reserve Bank. If its excess reserves are sufficiently large, the bank can thus meet its outflows and still maintain balances that will cover its reserve requirements for the period.

As a strategy a bank can choose to maintain excess reserves in most reserve periods. If it does so, it achieves some convenience benefits; but it incurs the cost of the foregone income that it could have if it invested the excess reserves in short-term earning assets. The extent of this cost is sensitive to the amount of excess balances, level of interest rates, transaction costs, and administrative costs of precise reserve management. If, for example, the amount is small, interest rates are low, and transaction and administrative costs are positive, then the convenience benefits of holding some excess reserves can exceed the cost of such a strategy. On this basis, many small and medium-sized banks decide to hold some excess reserves, especially during periods of low interest rates. Yet it is a strategy that they need frequently to review.

One study analyzes a sample of banks in the Fourth (Cleveland) Federal Reserve District, and it concludes that many banks apparently try to maintain excess reserves.[26] The study also reports that there is a positive nonlinear relationship between excess reserves and bank size, such that, on average, a bank that is five times the size of a second bank will hold a greater dollar amount of excess reserves, but its dollar amount of excess reserves will not be five times that of the smaller bank. This relationship suggests that there are economies of scale in holding excess reserves. For example, a large bank probably incurs lower per-unit transaction costs when it invests its potentially excess reserves in large-denomination money-market instruments.

Although many banks maintain some excess reserves, the average holding of excess reserves has declined in recent decades. In 1948, the average excess reserves of all member banks was about five percent of their required reserves. By 1970 this percentage was less than one. One analyst concludes that "the primary explanation for the decision of banks to hold fewer excess reserves is the upward trend in the interest return that can be obtained on alternative reserve adjustment assets."[27]

## Correspondent Balances

A bank also uses its correspondent balances to help meet unexpected cash outflows. As a member or nonmember, a bank has balances with some large money-center banks that provide it with services such as check clearing and loan participations. A bank knows that its city correspondents expect it to maintain balances that over time will at least compensate the correspondents for the services. Yet while it thus cannot deplete them, a bank has flexibility to reduce temporarily and then later rebuild its correspondent balances.

To obtain reserve-eligible assets, a member bank can have funds transferred from its correspondent account to its account at the Federal Reserve Bank. As it thus reduces its correspondent balance, the bank transmits part of its cash adjustment to the correspondent bank, the reserves of which fall as it transfers funds to the outlying bank's account at the Federal Reserve Bank. The city correspondent views these temporary declines in its deposits and reserves as one small part of its total cash flows. It has a diversified deposit base that enables it to expect some offsetting cash inflows, and it also has convenient access to various cash-adjustment techniques. The city correspondent's specialized skills in liquidity management thus enable it to serve as a convenient buffer for the cash-adjustment procedures of its outlying correspondents.

## Short-term Investments

Banks hold various money-market instruments as precautionary assets against unexpected cash outflows. In contrast to its excess reserves and

---

26. James Barth and Marvin Phaup, "Excess Reserves and Bank Size," *Economic Review*, (Federal Reserve Bank of Cleveland), January 1972, pp. 3-11.

27. J. A. Cacy, "Reserve Adjustment Behavior of Tenth District Banks," *Monthly Review* (Federal Reserve Bank of Kansas City), May 1970, pp. 3-9.

correspondent balances, a bank earns explicit interest on these investments that have low default risk and active secondary markets. The major money-market instruments are U.S. Treasury securities, federal agency securities, commercial paper, and negotiable CDs. Money-market instruments mature in one year or less.

When it faces unexpected cash outflows, a bank can readily sell some of its money-market instruments and receive prompt payment in cash. To expedite such transactions, an outlying bank can leave its money-market instruments in safekeeping with a money-center correspondent bank or, if a member, with its Federal Reserve Bank. When it decides to sell some of its holdings, an officer of the outlying bank calls the custodial institution and instructs it, as agent, to deliver the sold securities to the purchaser or its agent and to credit the sale proceeds to the account of the selling bank.

While it adds to its cash when it sells some of its short-term investments, a bank thus generally shifts the cash-adjustment process to other banks. It obtains cash from purchasers who pay for the securities by reducing their deposits at other banks that, in turn, have to factor these outflows into their ongoing liquidity management. Thus while one or several banks can conveniently adjust their cash position by selling some money-market instruments, many banks cannot simultaneously do so unless the FRS, as the central bank, provides backstop liquidity for the banking system.

Purchases and sales of most money-market instruments involve low, but not zero, transaction costs. Therefore a bank is reluctant to buy such an instrument if it is likely that it may soon have to sell it. The bank anticipates a low net return, after transaction costs, from such a brief holding period. Similarly, if it faces sudden cash outflows, a bank is reluctant to incur the costs of selling some short-term investments, especially if it expects to incur similar costs to reinvest pending cash inflows. Also a bank may find it inconvenient to sell some short-term investments that are pledged against public deposits. Even if it can substitute other assets to meet its pledging requirements, the bank may choose to avoid the minor costs and inconvenience of arranging such substitutions.

To broaden its options to obtain prompt cash from its investment securities, a bank can use *repurchase agreements* by which it sells some of its investments, such as long-term U.S. Treasury securities, to another institution and simultaneously agrees to repurchase the securities at a slightly higher price within a short period. The higher repurchase price provides the second institution with a specific return for its short-term holding. Banks enter into repurchase agreements among themselves and with government securities dealers that use these agreements to help finance their fluctuating inventories of bonds. A bank with temporarily excess cash can thus evaluate the net benefits of buying bonds that are subject to repurchase. It earns an agreed return from this short-term investment vehicle; and, if it needs cash, it can conveniently decide not to renew the agreement.

Banking theory and practice have traditionally emphasized the importance of short-term investments in cash-adjustment procedures. In recent years the traditional emphasis has declined as banks have developed additional procedures by which to manage their liquidity.

### Federal Funds

Federal funds are short-term, usually overnight, loan transactions among banks. They do not involve federal securities nor any physical securities; they involve a series of accounting entries by participants in the transactions. Both member and nonmember banks can conveniently buy and/or sell federal funds.

A member bank earns no return from its excess reserves at its Federal Reserve Bank; and, except for the carry-forward provision, its excess reserves expire at the end of a reserve period. Yet within a reserve period there are some other banks that foresee a need to increase their vault cash and/or reserve balances in order to meet their required reserves. In such cases the surplus bank can choose to lend (sell) some of its excess reserves to banks that are willing to pay interest for the temporary use of the reserves.[28] Both the lending bank and the borrowing bank(s) can benefit from this transaction. The lender converts a noninterest-earning asset (excess reserves) into a short-term interest-earning asset (federal funds sold); the borrower willingly pays the interest in order to avoid more costly cash-adjustment procedures, such as selling short-term securities.

When federal funds transactions are among member banks, a lender of federal funds can instruct its Federal Reserve Bank to transfer funds from its reserve account to that of the borrowing bank. This transaction represents a set of accounting entries. The Federal Reserve Bank debits the lending bank's reserve account and credits the borrowing bank's reserve account. The lending bank records a decrease in one asset (its balance at the Federal Reserve Bank) and an equivalent increase in another asset (federal funds sold). The borrowing bank records an increase in its asset accounts (its balance at the Federal Reserve Bank) and an equivalent increase in its liabilities (federal funds purchased). Unless the loan is extended, the next day the borrowing bank instructs the Federal Reserve Bank to reverse the transaction by debiting its account and crediting the selling bank's account. The two banks similarly reverse their entries of the prior day. The borrower also pays the lending bank interest, usually by a separate check or other funds transfer.

Many banks use federal funds transactions as a cash-adjustment procedure. Often a lender of federal funds receives a higher return, with no transactions cost, than it can obtain from purchases of short-term securities. Meanwhile it has the daily option to decide not to renew a transaction and thus to receive prompt repayment in the form of increased reserve balances.

---

28. For many years the FRS and the OCC differed as to whether federal funds transactions should be viewed as ''borrowings'' and ''loans,'' and thus subject to legal lending limits, or as ''purchases'' and ''sales,'' and thus exempt from such limits. In practice most banks report their federal funds transactions as purchases or sales.

A borrowing bank willingly incurs an interest-paying liability (federal funds purchased) in order to quickly and conveniently supplement its pool of cash, especially in the form of reserve-eligible assets.

Federal funds transactions have grown from a small base to a daily transactions volume of billions of dollars. Large money-center banks account for most of the dollar volume of federal funds transactions. In the aggregate, large money-center banks borrow federal funds from smaller outlying banks.

Several major developments help to explain the expansion of federal funds transactions.[29] Initially some large banks sought to pare their nonearning excess reserves at their Federal Reserve Bank, and so they were willing to lend funds to other large banks that temporarily needed to add to their reserves. Most of these initial interbank transactions were in multiples of $1 million. As interest rates rose during the 1960s, more banks sought to convert excess reserves to earning assets. To serve this growing market, some nonbank firms became brokers in federal funds. Also, partly to provide an additional service to smaller outlying banks, most large money-center banks became dealers in federal funds. As dealers, they stand ready to buy and/or sell federal funds. If, for example, to accommodate its smaller correspondents a dealer bank purchases more federal funds than it wants at that time, then this bank in turn lends some of its excess federal funds to other large banks. Thus at many times a dealer bank simultaneously reports both federal funds purchased and sold, the total amounts of which are not equal. As correspondent banks have extended federal funds transactions to banks of all sizes, transactions of less than $1 million have become common and transaction costs are virtually zero. Thus all banks now have convenient access to the federal funds market.

Nonmember banks, even though they have no balances at a Federal Reserve Bank, can participate in the federal funds market through their city correspondents. To illustrate, a nonmember bank concludes that its demand balances at its correspondent bank exceed what it currently needs to meet its state reserve requirements and to compensate its correspondent for services received. Therefore it calls its city correspondent and arranges to lend it federal funds. The lending bank converts a noninterest-earning asset (part of its correspondent balance) to an earning asset (federal funds sold), and the correspondent bank converts a noninterest-paying liability (part of the outlying bank's correspondent balance) into an interest-paying liability (federal funds purchased). The city correspondent agrees to this transaction partly as a service to the outlying bank, but also because it knows that if it does not do so then some rival money-center bank will likely do so.

Money-market analysts monitor fluctuations in the federal funds rate as a sensitive indicator of monetary policy and conditions in the banking system. Until 1965 most observers assumed that no member bank would

29. Robert E. Knight, "An Alternative Approach to Liquidity," Part III, *Monthly Review* (Federal Reserve Bank of Kansas City), April 1970, pp. 3-12. "The Federal Funds Market Revisited," *Economic Review* (Federal Reserve Bank of Cleveland), February 1970, pp. 3-13.

borrow federal funds at a rate above the Federal Reserve discount rate. When a member bank can temporarily borrow at the discount window at the discount rate, why would it pay a higher rate to borrow federal funds from another bank? This assumption was refuted in 1965 when some major money-center banks began to bid for federal funds at rates slightly above the discount rate. These banks concluded that, even at the premium rate, they could profitably lend and invest the borrowed funds and that it was more convenient to borrow from other banks than from their Federal Reserve Bank. Since then the federal funds rate often has exceeded the discount rate.

One study observes that the federal funds rate tends to be high early in a reserve period (beginning Thursday) and then to decline as the week progresses. It hypothesizes that early in the reserve period, "the reserve positions of individual banks and the banking system as a whole are still relatively unclear and subject to change as the week progresses, so that the interest rate on interbank [federal funds] loans tends to hover near the banking system's expected rate for the week." As the period progresses, reserve needs and probable deposit flows become clearer for each bank. Some banks will have accumulated excess reserves that will provide no explicit returns after the period closes, and so they want to lend these excess reserves at some positive rate, even if it is lower than it was earlier in the period. Thus "a bank waiting until the end of the settlement week to make up a reserve deficiency will, on average, get funds at a lower rate, but will be risking greater variance from the longer-run average rate."[30] A bank can review such general patterns as it plans its own strategy of when to engage in federal funds transactions.

### Federal Reserve Discount Window

The FRS uses its discount window as one way to provide reserves to individual banks and to the banking system. It provides three principal types of credits through its discount window:

- *adjustment credit* by which member banks can make short-term adjustments (usually up to thirty days) in their reserve balances
- *seasonal credit* by which qualifying member banks can prearrange credit lines against which they can borrow for at least four weeks
- *emergency credit* by which member and/or nonmember banks, and even nonbanking firms, can apply to borrow from the FRS in order to withstand severe financial crises

While it often extends adjustment and seasonal credits, the FRS seldom provides emergency credit.

**Adjustment Credit**   Federal Reserve officials emphasize that member bank access to the discount window is a privilege, not a right. They thus

30. Robert D. Laurent, "Interbank Lending: An Essential Function," *Business Conditions* (Federal Reserve Bank of Chicago), November 1974, pp. 3-7.

encourage member banks to view the discount window as an occasional source of temporary funds, and they administer the window so that member banks are reluctant to rely on it.[31] To illustrate, when a member bank applies to use the window, Federal Reserve officers review the applicant's past and proposed use of the window. If the applicant has been a frequent borrower, the officers may invite the applicant's senior officials to explain how they expect to reduce their bank's use of the discount window; and they may also invite them to the Federal Reserve Bank for a detailed review of the bank's loan policies and recent loans. Most member banks understand the subtle process by which Federal Reserve officials administer the discount window, and so they choose not to use the discount window as a repeated source of short-term reserve balances.

A member bank can offer to *discount,* or sell, some of its loans to its Federal Reserve Bank. These loans must be *eligible paper,* which the Federal Reserve Act defines as "notes, drafts, and bills of exchange arising out of actual commercial transactions. . . ." If the Federal Reserve Bank agrees to buy the eligible paper, then the selling bank has an increase in one asset, its reserve balance, and a decrease in a second asset, its loan portfolio. In practice, most banks choose not to discount loans with their Federal Reserve Bank. When a bank discounts a loan then, because of the administrative procedures, the bank's borrower may learn that its loan has been discounted. Many bankers reportedly believe that such a borrower may view the discounting of its loan to a third party as a breach of the two-party (borrower and bank) relationship and/or as a sign of poor financial planning—and possible weakness—within the bank.

As an alternative to direct discounting of some eligible paper, a bank can apply to *borrow* at the discount window, in which case it pledges some collateral with its Federal Reserve Bank. It can pledge various types of collateral, such as U.S. Treasury securities, some federal agency securities, eligible paper, home mortgage loans, and any other collateral that is satisfactory to its Federal Reserve Bank. The Federal Reserve Bank reviews the borrowing request and the proposed collateral, and, if it agrees to the request, then the borrowing bank receives an increase in its assets (its reserve balance) and a corresponding increase in its liabilities (borrowings from Federal Reserve Bank). Although it can pledge various types of collateral, a bank usually pledges long-term U.S. Treasury securities. This way it avoids the transaction costs and uncertainties of selling such securities and then later repurchasing similar securities.

To facilitate borrowings at the discount window, a member bank files a borrowing resolution and a continuing lending agreement with its Federal Reserve Bank.[32] Then its authorized officers can promptly arrange a specific adjustment credit from the discount window. Also, an outlying bank often

31. Elijah Brewer, "Some Insights on Member Bank Borrowing," *Economic Perspectives* (Federal Reserve Bank of Chicago), November-December 1978, pp. 16-21.

32. Carol C. Madeley, "Through 'the Window' at the Fed," *Voice* (Federal Reserve Bank of Dallas), November 1978, pp. 16-18.

leaves its investment securities in safekeeping with its Federal Reserve Bank or with a large correspondent bank. It then instructs the custodial institution to deliver suitable securities to the discount window to serve as collateral for a proposed borrowing. Thus, as it manages its investment portfolio, a bank must explicitly plan to hold suitable types and amounts of securities to meet its various probable collateral requirements.

Whether it uses the discounting or borrowing procedures, a borrowing member bank pays annual interest at the current discount rate. If the discount rate changes while the bank is in debt to the FRS, then the borrowing bank has to start paying the new rate until the loan is repaid or the discount rate again changes. Also, if it borrows with nonstandard collateral that is satisfactory to its Federal Reserve Bank, a member bank pays an interest rate that is 0.50 percentage points above the current discount rate.

At any time, a member bank evaluates the costs and convenience of its using the discount window compared to its using other cash adjustment procedures. Although each bank thus makes a series of decisions over time, surveys provide some insights into this decision process. One study seeks to identify factors that explain differential borrowing behavior of member banks in the Tenth (Kansas City) Federal Reserve District. It concludes that bank size is an important factor. "Most of the smaller District banks do not borrow, while a large majority of the larger banks do borrow."[33] Among the borrowing banks, smaller banks borrow more (relative to their required reserves) but less frequently than do large banks. The study also reports that, compared to nonborrowing banks, borrowing banks tend to have higher ratios of loans to deposits and of farm loans to total loans. Another survey reports that, instead of buying federal funds, country banks often prefer to use the discount window of their Federal Reserve Bank.[34] These banks cite how their use of the discount window has various advantages: convenience, dependability, timing within a day, and possibly lower costs. While various member banks at times borrow from their Federal Reserve Bank, another study notes the persistence of a "reluctance to borrow" factor that limits the magnitude and frequency of member-bank borrowing. "This factor, which depends in part on the way that Federal Reserve officials administer the extension of credits, appears to limit borrowings, regardless of the interest rate-discount rate spread."[35]

While it usually responds to borrowing requests from its member banks, at times the FRS actively encourages its member banks to use the discount window. To illustrate, in September 1966 the FRS sent its member banks a letter asking them to curtail expansion of business loans. The letter

33. J. A. Cacy, "Determinants of Member Bank Borrowing," *Monthly Review* (Federal Reserve Bank of Kansas City), February 1971, pp. 11-20. Also R. Alton Gilbert, "Benefits of Borrowing from the Federal Reserve when the Discount Rate Is Below Market Interest Rates," *Review* (Federal Reserve Bank of St. Louis), March 1979, pp. 25-32.

34. Parker B. Willis, *A Study of the Market for Federal Funds,* a paper prepared for the Committee for the Fundamental Reappraisal of the Discount Mechanism, Board of Governors of the Federal Reserve System, March 28, 1967.

35. Cacy, "Reserve Adjustment Behavior of Tenth District Banks," p. 9.

further requested the banks not to sell municipal bonds (in a market that was approaching disarray), but instead to come to the discount window for special accommodation. Although the FRS thus has broad powers to provide emergency credit to various banks and nonbank firms, an individual bank has to rely on its own cash-flow management as its principal first-line defense against financial emergencies.

**Seasonal Credit** While the discount window traditionally has been for short-term adjustment credits, in 1973 the FRS began to offer a seasonal borrowing privilege to its member banks. This privilege, which is available to member banks with total deposits below $500 million, is to "assist a member bank that lacks reasonably reliable access to national money markets in meeting seasonal needs for funds arising from a combination of expected patterns of movements in its deposits and loans" (Regulation A).

The FRS invites member banks to apply for credit assistance prior to their seasonal needs. Federal Reserve employees use a statistical computer program to project a bank's seasonal need for funds, based on the bank's loans and deposits during the preceding five years. The FRS then applies policy guidelines as to what part of the projected seasonal needs can be met by borrowing from the discount window. To qualify for this seasonal credit, a bank is to have a projected seasonal need that persists for at least four consecutive weeks; and it is not to engage in unusually high levels of federal funds sales during periods when it uses its seasonal borrowing privilege. (Federal Reserve officials judge what constitutes unusually high levels of federal funds sales.)

One study reviews initial use of the seasonal borrowing privilege, and it estimates that "the number of banks actually using the privilege and the volume of credit extended was considerably smaller than it might have been." It concludes that large nonagricultural banks initially received most of the total credit extended under this seasonal privilege and that "as knowledge and familiarity with the privilege spreads, more funds should flow to banks in need of seasonal funds."[36] Another study reports that less than one-fourth of eligible banks in the Ninth (Minneapolis) Federal Reserve District used the seasonal borrowing privilege in 1974, and that most of these users were affiliates of multibank holding companies "which—it can be argued—have greater access to nonlocal sources of funds than do nonaffiliate banks."[37]

### Other Short-term Borrowings

America's large banks have developed other types of short-term nondeposit transactions by which they can rapidly adjust their cash flows. To illustrate,

---

36. Margaret E. Bedford, "The Seasonal Borrowing Privilege," *Monthly Review* (Federal Reserve Bank of Kansas City), June 1974, pp. 10-16.

37. John Rosine, "District Seasonal Borrowing in 1974," *Ninth District Quarterly* (Federal Reserve Bank of Minneapolis), July 1975, pp. 10-17.

a large bank in particular, if it is faced with unexpected net cash outflows, can examine whether to borrow short-term in the Eurodollar market as an alternative to its selling short-term investments, buying federal funds, and/or borrowing at the discount window.

Large banks developed new sources of short-term borrowings in response to constraints on, and comparative disadvantages of, previous sources of funds.[38] The general pattern has been: banks develop new sources, the FRS impedes these sources, the banks develop new sources, and so on.

Negotiable CDs were a major banking innovation of the early 1960s. As deposits, negotiable CDs are subject to reserve requirements, and until 1969 they were subject to interest-rate ceilings.

In 1964 several large banks began to issue short-term promissory notes, which, as nondeposits, were not subject to reserve requirements or interest-rate ceilings. In 1966 the FRS amended its Regulations D and Q so that bank promissory notes would be treated similarly to deposits—thus removing the previous advantages of bank promissory notes.

In 1966 and 1969 large banks experienced potential disintermediation as other money-market interest rates exceeded the maximum rates that banks could pay on their CDs. To help offset their net deposit outflows, large banks began to borrow from their foreign branches, which had access to the Eurodollar market. Initially these borrowings were not subject to reserve requirements or interest-rate ceilings, and they had other technical advantages (see Chapter 21). In 1969, however, the FRS subjected foreign-branch borrowings to reserve requirements.

Large banks also have developed other direct and contingent liabilities, such as federal funds transactions and repurchase agreements with nonbank customers, and in turn the FRS has been quick to monitor, and usually to seek to regulate, these new types of potential cash-adjustment transactions.

Even the preceding summary demonstrates why, if it develops a major new type of short-term borrowing, a bank has to anticipate that the FRS will move to subject the unconventional procedure to its moral suasion and/or regulatory powers. Yet while it cannot rely on unconventional short-term borrowings as part of its cash-adjustment procedures, a bank can factor such borrowings into its broader strategies of liabilities management.

## LIABILITIES MANAGEMENT AND SPREAD MANAGEMENT

Liabilities management is the process by which a bank manages its interest-sensitive liabilities in order to adjust its cash flows and/or to manage

---

38. Donald M. DePamphilis, "The Short-term Commercial Bank Adjustment Process and Federal Reserve Regulation," *New England Economic Review* (Federal Reserve Bank of Boston), May-June 1974, pp. 14-23. Robert E. Knight, "An Alternative Approach to Liquidity," a four-part series, *Monthly Review* (Federal Reserve Bank of Kansas City), December 1969, pp. 11-21; February 1970, pp. 11-22; April 1970, pp. 3-12; and May 1970, pp. 3-18. Adrian W. Throop, "A New Emphasis in Regulations Affects Liability Management," *Business Review* (Federal Reserve Bank of Dallas), November 1974, pp. 1-14.

its growth and profitability. It is an abrupt departure from traditional bank portfolio practices.

Until the 1960s most banks focused on the asset side of their balance sheet. In summary, they:

- sought deposits, but primarily noninterest-paying demand deposits
- relied on their reserve balances, correspondent balances, and short-term investments as their principal cash-adjustment procedures
- allocated their other assets among traditional bank loans and investments
- viewed their deposit growth rate as a principal constraint on their growth in total assets and profits

While they adhered to these summary portfolio practices, banks were viewed as having stable—but constrained—growth prospects.

## ADVENT OF LIABILITIES MANAGEMENT

By the 1960s some large banks began to focus more on the liabilities side of their balance sheet.[39] They started to offer and to manage negotiable CDs as a way to adjust their cash flows and to attract funds from large investors. For example, to offset an unexpected large outflow from its demand deposits, a large bank could try to sell some of its negotiable CDs at rates similar to or slightly above the current market rate. Not only could it thus manage its negotiable CDs as a cash-adjustment procedure, a large bank could plan to continuously manage its outstanding CDs so that they would provide a major ongoing source of funds. Similarly, it could use net federal funds purchases and other short-term borrowings as cash-adjustment procedures and as ongoing sources of funds. Thus, in contrast to the traditional emphasis on asset management, a bank that practices liabilities management:

- continues to seek core deposits in demand-deposit accounts and consumer time deposits, but it also has interest-sensitive liabilities (such as negotiable CDs, federal funds purchases, and other short-term borrowings) that account for a large proportion of its total liabilities
- manages its cash flows via adjustments in both short-term assets and short-term liabilities
- allocates its funds among loans and investments that cover a broad range of types and maturities

---

39. Jack Beebe, "A Perspective on Liability Management and Bank Risk," *Economic Review* (Federal Reserve Bank of San Francisco), Winter 1977, pp. 12-25. L. G. Gable, "Liability Management: An Indictment," *The Journal of Commercial Bank Lending,* August 1974, pp. 2-10. Stuart A. Schweitzer, "Bank Liability Management: For Better or For Worse?," *Business Review* (Federal Reserve Bank of Philadelphia), December 1974, pp. 3-12. William L. Silber, *Commercial Bank Liability Management,* a study prepared for the Trustees of the Banking Research Fund, Association of Reserve City Bankers, 1977. Jean L. Valerius, "Liabilities that Banks Manage," *Business Conditions* (Federal Reserve Bank of Chicago), June 1975, pp. 3-9.

- tries to match the average maturities of its core deposits and interest-sensitive funds with the average maturities of its loans and investments—or at least has explicit reasons when it mismatches the average maturities
- expects to manage its growth of assets and profits by using interest-sensitive liabilities as a supplement to its growth in core deposits

A large bank, with its issuance of negotiable CDs and its access to diverse short-term borrowings, is most likely to practice liabilities management, but any bank can engage in some features of the practice.

## SPREAD MANAGEMENT

As it actively manages its interest-paying liabilities, a bank also focuses on managing the spread, or difference, between its interest revenues and its interest expenses. A measure of this spread is the *net interest margin* which is defined, in ratio terms, as a bank's:[40]

$$\begin{array}{r} \text{Gross interest earned} \\ \textit{Minus} \quad \underline{\text{Gross interest expense}} \\ \text{Net interest margin} \end{array}$$

The net interest margin can be computed for any time period. If it is computed for a one-year period, then the gross interest earned is a bank's total interest revenues for the year divided by the average interest-earning assets for the year.[41] (The average assets can be an average of daily totals or, less precisely, an average of week-end or month-end totals.) Similarly, the gross interest expense is a bank's total interest expense for the year divided by the average interest-paying liabilities for the year.

As a numerical example, in one year a bank has total interest revenues of $145 million, and it has average interest-earning assets of $1,550 million. Its gross interest earned is thus 9.4 percent. In the same period, the bank has a total interest expense of $80 million, average interest-paying liabilities of $1,100 million, and thus a gross interest expense of 7.3 percent. Its net interest margin for the one-year period is 2.1 percent.

A bank can use its net interest margin (NIM) as a control device to help manage the rate spread between its interest revenues and interest expenses.

---

40. While net interest margin is an accepted concept and management tool, banks differ somewhat in their terms for and computations of their net interest margin. Larry L. McGregor, "Spread Management: A Tool for Improving Bank Profits," *The Magazine of Bank Administration,* March 1977, pp. 16-23. Also "Insured Commercial Bank Income in 1977," *Federal Reserve Bulletin,* June 1978, pp. 441-447.

41. Banks receive tax-exempt and/or tax-sheltered income from some assets such as municipal securities and direct lease financing. Most banks adjust such interest income to a taxable equivalent basis that then can be more directly compared to a bank's taxable income. If, for example, it is in a 40% tax bracket, then to convert its tax-exempt income to a taxable equivalent basis, a bank would multiply its tax-exempt income by 1.67, where 1.67 is before-tax interest revenue divided by the after-tax interest revenue.

To do so, it has to compute regularly its NIM for each week or month. With its series of NIM computations, the bank's senior officials and staff then can:

- compare the bank's NIM to standards such as the bank's targeted NIM and/or the actual NIM for similar banks
- monitor trends in its NIM in order to detect promptly whether the margin is narrowing or widening
- analyze the subcomponents of its NIM in order to pinpoint which categories of interest revenues and/or expenses explain the aggregate changes in its NIM
- analyze the extent to which changes in its NIM reflect explicit management decisions and/or interest-rate developments beyond the bank's short-run control

One banker reports how his bank, after it began to monitor its NIM, increased its NIM and achieved greater consistency in its margin.[42] Banks' use of the NIM follows directly from liabilities management and spread management, and it relates to bank management of investments and loans.

## SUMMARY

Cash flow management is a convergence point for a bank's diverse activities. Its goal is to profitably manage the cash flows while subject to required reserves and the need to meet unexpected net cash outflows.

Although their historical rationale (to protect depositors) is questionable, reserve requirements have become an instrument of monetary policy and a part of the banking system. Subject to legislative limits, themselves subject to revision, the FRS sets reserve requirements for all national and state member banks. In recent years the FRS has implemented policy and procedural changes, such as graduated reserve requirements, marginal reserve requirements, and a revised definition of a reserve city bank. Each state, except Illinois, sets reserve requirements for its state-chartered banks, and most such state requirements apply only to nonmember banks. The principal difference between FRS and state requirements is the form of reserve-eligible assets. A member bank must hold its required reserves in the form of balances at its Federal Reserve Bank and vault cash, neither of which asset earns interest. In contrast, depending on its state's requirements, a nonmember bank usually can hold a wider range of reserve-eligible assets that include vault cash, demand balances with other (correspondent) banks, cash items in collection, and possibly some interest-earning investment securities. Whether it is a member or nonmember, a bank adheres to its required reserves; but it also needs to review its strategic decision whether to be a member of the FRS.

---

42. McGregor, "Spread Management: A Tool for Improving Bank Profits."

Many banks have concluded that the costs—especially those of the reserve requirements—exceed the benefits of FRS membership. As a nonmember, a bank adheres to its state's required reserves; and it receives from its city correspondent bank(s) most of the "free" services (except convenient access to the discount window) that it could receive as a member bank. Various studies document the cost burden of FRS membership, and the FRS has witnessed an erosion in its membership. FRS officials and some analysts assert that the erosion in FRS membership leads to inefficiencies and inequities in the conduct of monetary policy. While not all analysts accept these assertions, the FRS has tried to reduce the burden of membership; it has proposed an explicit pricing system by which it would pay interest on bank reserves and charge explicit fees for its services, and it has supported proposals for some form of uniform required reserves that would apply to all or all large financial institutions that offer transactions (check-like) accounts. It is likely that Congress will legislate some form of uniform required reserves, and so each bank needs to monitor these legislative proposals and prepare for the probable changes in the required-reserve procedures that would then apply to it and its rivals.

To meet its net cash outflows without its having to incur costly portfolio transactions, each bank has to

- identify its principal sources of cash flows
- develop and refine systems by which to predict and monitor the cash flows
- evaluate, and frequently reevaluate, cash-adjustment procedures

Even as it engages in individualized analyses of its cash flows, a bank keeps informed about developments in cash-flow systems and procedures.

As schematically summarized in Exhibit 8-2, a bank's cash flows relate to changes in its principal balance-sheet items. In the short run, a bank has very little control over many of its balance-sheet changes, and so it focuses on those over which it has more short-term control: its short-term noncash assets and its short-term nondeposit liabilities.

Cash-flow managers use cash-planning systems that focus on cash flows within future planning periods. They categorize the future cash flows as scheduled, unscheduled but predictable, or unexpected. Whatever its size, a bank has procedures to help it project its scheduled and unscheduled, but predictable, cash flows. To develop its projections, a medium-sized bank is likely to extrapolate and reevaluate its past cash-flow patterns; a large bank evaluates the extent to which it should develop and refine advanced programming and statistical procedures by which to forecast its cash-flow patterns. By thus projecting its cash flows, a bank has standards against which to compare its actual cash flows. If its actual flows start to depart substantially from its projected flows, then a bank can begin to implement appropriate cash-adjustment procedures.

To accommodate its projected net cash outflows and its unexpected net cash outflows, a bank engages in transactions that involve its: possible excess reserves at its Federal Reserve Bank, correspondent balances, short-term investments, federal funds activities, and possible borrowings from its Federal Reserve Bank. While banks of all sizes engage in these types of cash-adjustment procedures, some large banks have developed imaginative new forms of short-term borrowings that, at times, can also be used to make short-term cash adjustments. Thus each bank has to reevaluate frequently the costs and probable benefits of its using various procedures. This periodic reevaluation also enables a bank to review its broader policies and strategies in areas such as: Federal Reserve membership, use of the various borrowing privileges provided by the FRS, and extent of participation in the federal funds market. As an extension of its cash-flow management, a bank also has to review the expected returns and risks from its engaging in liabilities management and spread management.

# 9

# MANAGING THE INVESTMENTS PORTFOLIO

Investment securities account for about a third of a bank's total assets, and they play a pivotal role in a bank's total portfolio strategies. Thus this chapter focuses on:

- setting investment objectives
- return-risk criteria
- bond portfolio components
- investment policies and strategies
- bond trading tactics
- performance evaluation
- other investment activities, such as dealer activities and underwriting

## SETTING INVESTMENT OBJECTIVES

Senior officials must first specify, or reaffirm, the principal objectives for the investments portfolio. This first step is crucial because a bank's investments portfolio potentially has multiple—and conflicting—objectives.

### PROVIDING BACKSTOP LIQUIDITY

To accommodate net cash outflows, a bank usually reduces its cash balances, reduces its short-term noncash assets, and/or increases its short-term liabilities. Sometimes, however, a bank misestimates its cash flows and so it takes further actions to meet current or pending cash outflows. One such action is for the bank to sell some of its investment securities, which are mostly bonds. A bank can promptly sell some of its bonds in order to replenish its cash balances or its short-term assets.[1] When it sells some bonds, a bank usually incurs more cost and inconvenience than when it reduces its cash balances or sells some short-term noncash assets. Yet even within the investments portfolio, some bonds are more liquid than others. A U.S. Treasury security that matures in two years is almost as liquid as a ninety-day Treasury bill.

## PROVIDING BACKSTOP REVENUES

To service its depositors, a bank seeks to provide them with a safe depository for their funds and to meet their legitimate borrowing needs. Yet, even though it provides for its estimated cash-flow needs to meet these dual responsibilities, a bank's available funds at times exceed its customers' demand for creditworthy loans. Such episodes typically reflect seasonal or cyclical downturns in loan requests. When it thus faces slack loan demand, instead of sharply reducing its lending standards and/or building up substantial short-term assets, a bank seeks alternative earning assets, such as marketable securities. This increase in the investments portfolio can quickly change to a decrease when loan demand again increases, and so an investments manager also tries to structure the portfolio in ways that will accommodate subsequent upturns in loan demand.

## RECONCILING THE DUAL OBJECTIVES

To reduce potential conflicts, a bank's senior officers must explicitly evaluate the objectives of the investments portfolio.[2] If they decide that the primary objective is to provide backstop liquidity, it implies portfolio policies that forego the potential added revenues from less-marketable, more volatile securities. If they decide that the primary objective is to provide backstop revenues, especially during periods of slack loan demand, it implies policies that forego some flexibility to meet a subsequent resurgence of loan demand. Thus each bank has to evaluate how much backstop liquidity and flexibility it is willing to forego in pursuit of somewhat higher revenues. Especially during periods of slack loan demand, a bank has to evaluate explicitly the costs and benefits of its reaching for higher revenues in ways that may limit its flexibility to meet a subsequent resurgence in loan demand by its current and potential customers.

---

1. A bank's investments portfolio includes some money market instruments, such as U.S. Treasury bills, that mature within one year. Yet banks generally view these money market investments as part of their subportfolio of short-term noncash assets. One author provides a framework by which to analyze the liquidity of various bank assets. He points out that, among other variables, "the price that can be obtained by liquidating an asset depends on both the time available prior to its disposal and the number of units to be sold." James L. Pierce, "Commercial Bank Liquidity," *Federal Reserve Bulletin,* August 1966, pp. 1093-1101.

2. David L. Hoffland, "A Model Bank Investment Policy," *Financial Analysts Journal,* May-June 1978, pp. 64-67.

## RETURN-RISK CRITERIA

As they identify the returns and risks associated with an investments portfolio, senior management develops criteria by which to set and monitor portfolio policies and practices.

### RETURNS

Over a specific holding period, the annual *total return* from a bond investment consists of two components: one is the interest income, which reflects explicit cash inflows periodically received from the issuer of the bond; the second is the capital gain or loss on the bond.[3]

To illustrate, a bank buys 100 bonds at their par value of $1000 each. Its total investment is $100,000, plus minor transaction costs. Each bond pays annual interest of $80 until its maturity, many years from now, when it will be redeemed at $1000. If the bank receives the scheduled inflows of interest and the principal repayment at maturity, then its total annual return over the long holding period is 8 percent.[4] (The interest component is 8 percent and the capital gain or loss component is zero.) This total return disregards possible transaction costs and taxes.

During the first year it holds the bonds, the bank receives $8000 ($80 per bond) in total interest. Its one-year interest return is 8 percent. During the year interest rates generally rise, so that the end of the year each bond has a market price of $980. If the bank sells the bonds, its total capital loss is $2000 ($20 per bond), or 2 percent of the purchase prise. The bank's total return for the one-year holding period is 6 percent, consisting of the interest component of 8 percent and the capital-loss component of −2 percent. Even if it decides not to sell the bonds and realize the loss, the bank's total return still is 6 percent if it values its bonds at the market price at which they can be sold. In this case, instead of having a realized loss, the bank has a "paper loss" of $20 per bond. If, instead of falling to $980, the price per bond is $1020 at the end of the one year, then the bank's total return on this investment, whether realized or not, is 10 percent (8 percent interest return plus 2 percent capital gain). These illustrative one-year returns of 6 percent and 10 percent disregard possible transaction costs and taxes.

Although the computations are more complex, annual total returns can be calculated for holding periods of any length. All such total-return calculations incorporate the two components, income and price change. The price-change component arises from changes in market prices, which in turn primarily reflect general changes in interest rates.

Although it reviews past returns in order to evaluate past investment

---

3. For brevity, this chapter uses the word *return* instead of rate of return.

4. More advanced analysis also considers the rate(s) at which the bank can reinvest the interest income over the total holding period.

policies and decisions, a bank makes its current investment decisions based on its expected returns in future holding periods. Yet to evaluate expected returns, a bank also has to evaluate the risks associated with possible future outcomes.

## RISKS

Investors can conveniently compute the expected return from a bond about which they are confident they will receive the scheduled payments of interest and principal and will hold until maturity. The expected return from such a bond consists of the future stream of interest and the capital gain or loss resulting from the difference, if any, between the purchase price and the eventual redemption price. To illustrate, a bank is certain of its expected return when it buys a five-year U.S. Treasury security that it plans to hold until maturity. The "risks" of bond investment arise when one cannot be certain of timely repayment and/or when one has to sell (or value) bonds prior to their redemption.

### Credit Risk

The credit (or default) risk of a bond investment is that the issuer fails to make timely payments of interest and/or principal. An issuer is in *default* if it thus fails to meet its contractual debt obligation.

There is a chance, however slight, that any issuer will default on its scheduled payments of interest and principal. Because the federal government has extensive powers to tax and to create money, the credit risk of a U.S. Treasury security approaches zero. Other domestic issuers do not have the power to create money, and so they must rely on future revenues to service their debt. Thus, there is a chance, however slight, that some of these issuers will default. When buying bonds that may default, investors insist on higher promised returns (a risk premium) to compensate them for bearing higher credit risk.

### Interest-Rate Risk

All bonds, even those with zero credit risk, involve interest rate risk, which arises because interest rates—and asset prices—fluctuate over time. Interest-rate risk has two dimensions: one reflects the fluctuations in interest income over time; the second reflects the fluctuations in the market price of a bond over time.

A bank that buys a bond and holds it to maturity, without its defaulting, will realize the expected return based on the purchase price. If the bank then wants to reinvest the principal, however, the bank is likely to find that interest rates of similar-quality bonds then differ from that which was received on the maturing bond. To illustrate, the maturing bond provided an 8 percent return. At maturity, when it comes time to reinvest the principal in a similar quality asset, the bank can only obtain an expected return of 6 percent, and so the bank faces a substantially lower return from the replacement investment. The bank's stream of income thus can fluctuate over time, even if the bank sequentially holds each bond to maturity and thus incurs no capital losses or gains.

Banks often do not hold bonds to maturity. At times they buy bonds that they specifically plan to sell prior to maturity; at other times they buy bonds that they later decide to sell in order to obtain cash for other uses. When they sell a bond prior to maturity, they find that the sale price usually differs from both the purchase price and the eventual redemption price. The sale thus results in a realized capital gain or loss on the transaction.

Prices of long-term bonds adjust more sharply to changes in interest rates than do prices of short-term bonds. To illustrate, both a three-year bond with a 7 percent coupon and a similar-quality twenty-year bond with an 8 percent coupon currently trade at par ($1000). If both short-term and long-term interest rates suddenly go up 2 percentage points, to 9 percent and 10 percent respectively, then the price of the three-year bond will fall to about $948 and that of the twenty-year bond to about $828. Just as the potential capital loss is greater for the long-term bond, so is the potential capital gain greater if general interest rates were to fall. Thus, as interest rates fluctuate over time, prices of long-term bonds fluctuate more widely than do those of short-term bonds.

Interest risk confronts portfolio managers with a basic choice. If they confine their holdings to bonds of short maturities, they avoid wide price fluctuations and chances of substantial capital losses or gains. While the market value of their bonds is thus stable, they can experience wide fluctuations in their income stream as they reinvest in new short-term bonds whose interest rates can differ sharply from those of the maturing bonds. In contrast, if they confine their holdings to bonds of long maturities, portfolio managers can be confident of stable income streams for long periods but the market value of their bonds will fluctuate widely over time. Banks need not worry about interim fluctuations in bond values if they are certain to hold the bonds to maturity. If, however, they have to sell long-term bonds prior to maturity, banks can sustain substantial capital losses or gains. Moreover, if they have to value their bonds at market prices for reporting and regulatory purposes, then the banks will have to report the widely fluctuating bond values, with their implicit "paper" capital losses or gains. Bankers and other investors have to be aware of this basic trade-off between widely fluctuating income streams and widely fluctuating asset values.

### Marketability Risk

Bonds also involve a marketability risk, which increases gradually from about zero for bonds that are actively traded in competitive markets. U.S. Treasury bonds have virtually no marketability risk. Many dealers and investors actively buy and sell these bonds and so, at any time, transactions of almost any size take place at competitive prices and transaction costs. At the other extreme, if they buy some long-term bonds of a small school district, bankers face the prospect that they will not find many competing buyers if they later decide to sell the bonds. In addition, because of the less competitive market, the bankers will likely have to accept a price that is lower than those of more marketable bonds that have similar coupons, default risk, and maturity. Potential buyers insist on this price concession to help compensate for the marketability risk that they in turn assume by buying these obscure bonds. The marketability risk of other bonds lies between these two illustrative extremes of bonds of the U.S. Treasury and those of a small school district.

## BOND PORTFOLIO COMPONENTS

Although they cannot know extensive details about many individual securities, senior officers and directors have to keep informed about the principal types of securities that constitute their bank's investments portfolio.

Exhibit 9-1 summarizes how the distribution of investment securities held by all insured commercial banks has changed over time. At year-end 1950, U.S. Treasury securities constituted almost all (84 percent) of the banking industry's investment securities. Municipal bonds accounted for 11 percent and federal agency securities accounted for a minor part of bank portfolios. Since then the proportion of U.S. Treasury securities has declined, and the proportion of municipal and federal agency securities has increased. One author summarizes several reasons for the remarkable growth in bank holdings of municipal securities:[5]

- the sharp increase of outstanding municipal debt issues
- improved marketability of many such issues
- the tax-exempt feature of interest from municipals
- the increasing costs of bank funds
- new techniques of bank liquidity management

This historical summary provides perspective for bank officials as they examine current portfolio alternatives.

### U.S. TREASURY SECURITIES

U.S. Treasury securities are backed by the full faith and credit of the national government. Their credit risk approaches zero.

Publicly traded Treasury securities differ in their coupons (contractual interest rates), redemption provisions, and length to maturity. (At year-end 1978, for example, there were about one hundred seventy different issues of

---

5. Thomas E. Davis, "Bank Holdings of Municipal Securities," *Monthly Review* (Federal Reserve Bank of Kansas City), December 1970, pp. 3-12.

**EXHIBIT 9-1**

**Percentage Distribution of Investment Securities Held by All Insured Commercial Banks: Various Years, 1950-77**

| Categorized by Issuer | Year-end | | | |
|---|---|---|---|---|
| | 1950 | 1961† | 1970‡ | 1977‡ |
| U. S. Treasury | 84 | 73 | 42 | 38 |
| Federal agencies | † | 2 | 9 | 14 |
| States and their political sub-divisions | 11 | 22 | 47 | 45 |
| Other* | 5† | 1 | 2 | 2 |
| Total | 100 | 98 | 100 | 99 |

*Includes stock in Federal Reserve Bank until 1976.

†Federal agency securities were first reported as a separate category in 1961. Until then they were included among Other.

‡Excludes Trading Account securities, which were first reported as a separate category in 1970.

Source: Calculated from figures reported in the *Annual Report of the Federal Deposit Insurance Corporation*, Table 107 (1950), Table 109 (1962), Table 109 (1974), Table 109 (1977).

publicly traded Treasury securities.[6]) There are three principal categories of these securities: bills, notes, and bonds. From the date of its issuance, a *bill* has a maturity of 360 days or less, a *note* or a *bond* has a longer initial maturity. As a note or bond approaches maturity, its returns and risks are similar to those of bills having a similar length to maturity. In practice, an original thirty-year bond that will mature 180 days from now is similar to a bill that will mature about the same time. Financial publications, such as *The Wall Street Journal* and bond-dealer newsletters, report daily quotations for outstanding Treasury securities, all of which trade in active markets and have no marketability risk.

Yields differ among the various Treasury securities. A bond's *yield* is its annual rate of return if held to maturity or, in some calculations, if held to the earliest date at which the issuer can *call* the bond for redemption prior to its maturity. All Treasury securities have zero credit and marketability risks, therefore yield differences among these securities reflect current and anticipated interest rates.

A *yield curve* portrays, at a specific time, the yield to maturity (or call date) for various issues of bonds that have similar risk attributes. Exhibit 9-2 is an illustrative yield curve for U.S. Treasury securities. It is an upward sloping yield curve, whereby yields gradually increase as length to maturity increases. Issues maturing in 1979 yield about 7 to 7½ percent, issues maturing in the 1990s yield about 8 percent. Investors know that long-term bonds are subject to greater price fluctuations than are short-term issues, and

6. *Treasury Bulletin*, January 1979, Tables MQ-1 through MQ-3, pp. 79-81.

**EXHIBIT 9-2**

## An Illustrative Yield Curve

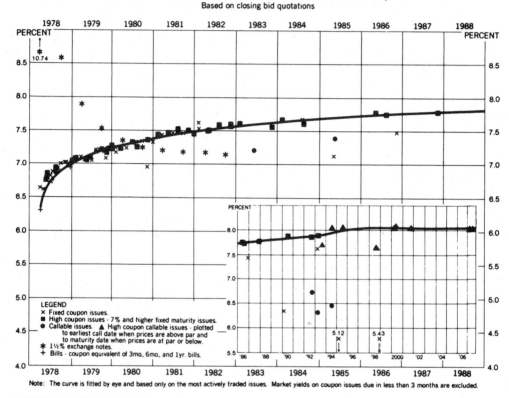

### YIELDS OF TREASURY SECURITIES DECEMBER 30, 1977
Based on closing bid quotations

Note: The curve is fitted by eye and based only on the most actively traded issues. Market yields on coupon issues due in less than 3 months are excluded.

Source: *Treasury Bulletin*, January 1978, p. 85.

so they usually insist on higher promised yields to maturity from long-term bonds.

Sometimes a yield curve slopes downward or has unusual humps in intermediate maturities. A downward-sloping yield curve usually arises when interest rates are historically high and when many borrowers and lenders expect long-term rates to fall. Borrowers with these expectations willingly pay comparatively high short-term rates rather than borrow long-term funds at what they believe to be unusually high rates. Lenders prefer to lend long-term to lock in what they believe to be unusually high yields and some potential capital gains if interest rates fall as expected. Under these conditions lenders insist on yield premiums when meeting short-term borrowing requests or buying short-term investments. A yield curve's shape thus embodies a consensus of expectations about future interest rates.

Current federal tax laws stipulate that a bank's returns from its Treasury securities are ordinary income, subject to corporate tax rates. This is true for both the interest income and the capital gains or losses that a bank realizes from its transactions in these securities. In contrast, interest income from Treasury securities is exempt from state and local taxes.

A bank considers not only the potential risks and returns from Treasury securities; it also considers the role of these securities as collateral that it has to pledge to secure public deposits. Banks also use Treasury securities for other purposes. Member banks can use them as collateral at the Federal Reserve discount window; nonmember banks in some states can use them to meet part of their required reserves; banks with trust powers often use them to qualify for certain fiduciary accounts; and all banks can use them to obtain short-term funds via repurchase agreements. Thus each bank evaluates its holdings of Treasury securities in the broad context of deposit-acquisition strategies, cash flow management, and fiduciary relationships.

The U.S. Treasury engages in an ongoing process of refinancing its maturing debt issues. Almost each week the Treasury invites subscriptions for one or more new issues. Banks often subscribe to new issues for their own investment accounts and, at times, as agents for some of their customers. To encourage bank participation, the Treasury often designates that each subscribing bank can credit its subscribed amounts to its Treasury Tax & Loan (TT&L) account.

## FEDERAL AGENCY SECURITIES

The U.S. government sponsors some privately owned financing agencies, such as the Federal National Mortgage Association, Federal Home Loan Banks, Banks for Cooperatives, Federal Intermediate Credit Banks, and Federal Land Banks. These *federally sponsored agencies* have authority to raise funds in public capital markets. Although the U.S. government does not guarantee the debt issues of these agencies, many investors doubt that the government will permit one of its federally sponsored agencies to default. The absence of an explicit guarantee implies, however, that debt issues of these federally sponsored agencies have somewhat higher credit risk than do U.S. Treasury securities.

Although they trade in active competitive markets, federal agency securities also have somewhat higher marketability risk than do direct Treasury obligations. Because of their (however slightly) higher risk, debt issues of federally sponsored agencies provide higher yields than do Treasury securities that have similar coupons, maturities, and redemption provisions. Financial publications, such as *The Wall Street Journal,* regularly report current prices and yields of publicly traded debt issues of these agencies.

Other federal agencies and corporations, such as the Export-Import Bank and the Tennessee Valley Authority, also have authority to obtain funds in public capital markets. The variety of these borrowers has proliferated in recent years, as exemplified by the Postal Service and various loan-guarantee programs. Unlike those of federally sponsored agencies, the obligations of these agencies and programs are guaranteed by the U.S. government.

## MUNICIPAL SECURITIES

The term "municipal securities" encompasses a vast heterogeneous universe of debt obligations of states and their political subdivisions. Issuers of these securities range from very large states and cities to small fire, school, and sanitary districts. Municipal securities are usually classified as: *warrants* or *short-term bills,* with original maturities of one year or less, or all other obligations, primarily *bonds* with original maturities of more than one year. Most municipal securities are *general obligation* issues, backed by the issuer's full faith and taxing power, or *revenue* issues, backed by a pledge of specific revenues, such as from tolls, electricity fees, or rental income from industrial buildings.

Although they cannot afford to develop expert knowledge of many different municipal securities, bank officials need to have general knowledge of risk-return attributes of principal categories of municipal securities.

Some municipal issuers have defaulted in the past, and some will default in the future. Investors therefore try to assess the default risk for municipal issuers. One way is to evaluate an issuer's past financial history and its probable future patterns of revenues available to service its debt. Even if it does not formally default, there is a possibility that a municipal issuer can legally defer its scheduled payments on some of its debt. Recent publicity about New York City's financial condition reaffirms the need for investors to assess the default risk of municipal bonds.

Few investors can afford independently to evaluate the credit risk of many different municipal bonds. They therefore turn to rating services, such as Moody's Investors Service and Standard and Poor's Corporation. These services commit substantial resources to the financial analysis of various bond issuers, and they summarize their analyses in the form of *bond ratings.* Moody's rates municipal bonds in nine principal categories: Aaa, Aa, A, Baa, Ba, B, Caa, Ca, C. Bonds "rated Aaa are judged to be of the best quality;" bonds "rated C are the lowest rated class of bonds."[7] These ratings summarize the evaluator's assessment of probable default risk; market values of even the highest-rated bonds are subject to interest-rate risk. Standard & Poor's rates municipal bonds in six principal categories: AAA, AA, A, BBB, BB, B. Bonds rated AAA represent bonds of the highest quality; their "capacity to pay interest and repay principal is extremely strong."[8] B-rated municipal bonds are of low grade.

---

7. *Moody's Municipal & Government Manual,* Moody's Investors Service, Inc., New York, Vol. 1, 1979, p. vi.

8. *Bond Guide,* Standard & Poor's Corporation, New York, June 1979, p. 6. For an extensive introduction to bond rating systems, see Hugh C. Sherwood, *How Corporate and Municipal Debt Is Rated: An Inside Look at Standard & Poor's Rating System,* Wiley-Interscience, New York, 1976. For an empirical analysis of bond rating systems, see Thomas F. Pogue and Robert M. Soldofsky, "What's in a Bond Rating," *Journal of Financial and Quantitative Analysis,* June 1969, pp. 201-228.

While they independently evaluate various bonds, the rating services usually assign similar ratings to the same bond issue. In mid-1979, for example, Moody's rated general obligation bonds of the state of California as Aaa, and Standard & Poor's rated them as AAA. At times, however, the services assign slightly different ratings to the same issue, with Moody's, for example, rating an issue Aa and Standard & Poor's rating it A. Notably rare are instances such as the one during 1976 when Moody's reduced its rating of some bonds issued by the Municipal Assistance Corporation for the City of New York from A to B while Standard & Poor's adhered to its A+ rating.

To develop their ratings, the services evaluate an issuer's debt-servicing capacity under various economic conditions. There are, however, two major categories of municipal bonds for which the rating services also evaluate the debt-servicing capacity of private firms associated with a municipal issue.

Subject to legal guidelines, municipalities can issue *industrial revenue bonds,* which although issued by a municipal authority, are not direct obligations of the issuer. A private firm, which leases a municipally owned building or makes environmental improvements with the proceeds of such a bond, pledges to service this specific bond indebtedness of the issuing municipality. In these cases the rating services analyze the debt-servicing capacity of the guarantor firm.

*Insured municipal bonds* are those in which an insurance association agrees to insure, for a fee, the timely payment of interest and principal on an issue of municipal bonds. Various issuers—usually small ones—thus insure their bonds in order to broaden their marketability and probably reduce their interest costs. In evaluating such bonds, the rating services consider not only the issuer's debt-servicing capacity but also the resources of the insuring organization.

The rating services do not assign ratings to all municipal bonds. Some issuers, or their underwriters, choose not to pay a rating fee to a rating agency, and so their bonds may be *nonrated.* There are other reasons why a bond is nonrated. Moody's, for example, does not assign ratings to issues of small size and of limited marketability after their initial offering.

Most municipal securities have greater marketability risk than do U.S. Treasury and federal agency securities. This risk is lowest for large issues of top-quality municipal issuers whose bonds actively trade in nationwide markets. Toward the other end of the spectrum, marketability risk is comparatively high for inactively traded, long-term bonds of small, obscure issuers. The market for such a bond issue tends to be local, not regional or national.

Returns from municipal securities differ from those from U.S. Treasury and federal agency issues. Interest income from municipal securities is exempt from federal income taxes. If, for example, a bank is in the 40 percent marginal tax bracket, then it receives higher after-tax income from a municipal bond that pays interest of 5 percent than it does from a U.S. Treasury bond that pays interest of 8 percent, but subject to the 40 percent tax. A bank's capital gains or losses from sales of its municipal securities, the second component of total return, are subject to tax as ordinary corporate income.

In addition to evaluating the comparative risks and returns from municipal securities, bank officials also consider how investments in these securities relate to other bank policies and strategies. Many public agencies permit banks to include at least some municipal securities among the collateral they pledge against public deposits. Therefore before they decide to buy or sell a specific municipal security, bank investment officers usually review its eligibility for various pledging requirements. Banks try to nurture long-run customer relationships. A bank that has, or is trying to get, deposits of various municipal units usually sees itself as obligated to meet legitimate borrowing needs of these public depositors. Thus a medium-sized rural bank often is a principal buyer of municipal securities issued by its local depositors; and money-center banks frequently invest in, and underwrite, municipal issues of their public depositors. Not only do banks often invest in municipal issues of their depositors, one researcher provides initial evidence that these banks often will accept a lower return from their depositors' debt issues than will competing bidders.[9] If it thus accepts a lower return, a bidding bank can pay implicit interest on a demand deposit that the municipal issuer keeps with the bank.

## OTHER SECURITIES

As summarized in Exhibit 9-1, "other securities" account for a small proportion of total bank investments. Member banks include in this category the dollar amount of their required stockholdings in their Federal Reserve Bank. Under unusual circumstances, such as collateral from a foreclosed loan, a bank can temporarily own corporate stock of nonaffiliate firms. Although banking laws and regulations permit most banks to own corporate bonds, few banks do so. They prefer the return-risk attributes of various government bonds to those of most corporate bonds, and they choose to service corporate customers via direct loans instead of indirectly via purchase of corporate bonds.

## INVESTMENT POLICIES AND STRATEGIES

To control default and marketability risks, a bank sets quality standards for securities in its portfolio; and it sets diversification guidelines for the total portfolio. To control—or at least adapt to—interest-rate risk, a bank uses interest-rate forecasts; and/or it systematically structures the maturities of bonds in its investments portfolio.

A bank's investment policies guide the portfolio managers who make daily investment decisions, and they provide standards by which senior

9. Neil B. Murphy, "A Test of the Deposit Relationship Hypothesis," *Journal of Financial and Quantitative Analysis,* March 1967, pp. 53-59.

officials then review the outcomes of these daily decisions. Therefore, to avoid misunderstandings, it is vital that the senior officers and directors, in consultation with the investment managers, write and periodically review a bank's investment policies.

## QUALITY OF INDIVIDUAL SECURITIES

Bank regulations restrict bank investments to high-quality securities, usually defined as those among the four highest bond ratings. A national bank or a state member bank is not to hold a bond rated below Baa by Moody's or BBB by Standard & Poor's. If it holds a bond rated below these ratings, a bank can expect its examiners soon to request the bank to sell the bond. The FDIC and state banking agencies set similar quality standards for investments by banks they examine.

Although it can hold only high-quality securities, a bank often chooses to establish stricter internal policies concerning the ratings of bonds in its portfolio. Toward one extreme, a bank can set a policy that it will hold mostly triple-A bonds. If so, it will hold Treasury notes and bonds, federal agency issues, and some municipals. Toward the other end of the spectrum, a bank can have a policy that, once it holds what it judges to be enough Treasury bonds to meet its pledging requirements, it will hold many lower-rated bonds among those eligible for bank investments. A bank that does so accepts somewhat higher default and marketability risks in anticipation of higher promised returns. If bond markets are efficient, however, then a higher promised return incorporates a risk premium to help offset the higher risks, and so a bank that follows this higher-risk policy may not generate significantly higher realized returns over time.

While it cannot hold low-rated securities, a bank can own nonrated securities, in which case it has to be prepared to convince its examiners that the default risk of its nonrated securities is not greater than those of eligible rated securities. The FDIC, for example, has a Securities Unit, the staff of which reviews rated bonds and evaluates the investment quality of nonrated bonds. Bank regulatory agencies have been experimenting with statistical classification procedures as a way to aid their evaluation of bank investments.[10]

Most banks have some nonrated bonds in their investments portfolio. Often these nonrated obligations are of local governmental units that have deposits at the bank. In addition, a bank can try to boost its returns by buying nonrated bonds of other nearby governmental units, the financial condition of which it can conveniently evaluate. If it is convinced that their default risk is low, then, because of the higher marketability risk, the bank is likely to receive a higher return from these nonrated issues than from rated issues with similar default risk.

---

10. Joseph J. Horton, Jr., "Statistical Classification of Municipal Bonds," *Journal of Bank Research,* Autumn 1970, pp. 29-40. Willard T. Carleton and Eugene M. Lerner, "Statistical Credit Scoring of Municipal Bonds," *Journal of Money, Credit, and Banking,* November 1969, pp. 750-764.

## DIVERSIFICATION BY ISSUERS

The OCC requires national and state member banks to diversify their investments among various issuers, and it specifies three classifications for marketable instruments eligible for bank investment.[11]

*Type I securities* are those issued by the U.S. Treasury, most federal agencies, and if general obligations, by states and their political subdivisions. Subject only to its prudent judgment, a bank can freely invest in Type I securities.

*Type II* and *Type III securities* include others in which banks can invest, the distinction being that banks cannot underwrite or deal in Type III securities. A bank can invest no more than 10 percent of its capital and surplus in the Type II and III securities of any one issuer. (This percentage limitation applies to the par value of the securities.) The bank also must exercise its prudent judgment about the default and marketability risks of such purchases. Instead of focusing on an issuer's past and current resources, a bank can base its judgment on reliable estimates of future outcomes. In such cases, however, a bank is not to invest more than five percent of its capital and surplus in obligations of any one issuer. In addition to its general guidelines about Type II and III securities, the OCC can issue rulings concerning the eligibility of and limitations on purchases of specific securities. To demonstrate that it exercises prudent judgment, each national and state member bank is to maintain credit files about the investment securities it owns.

Most states also limit the amount that a state nonmember bank can invest in eligible securities of any one issuer.

Few banks can afford to incur large losses on an investment that accounts for ten percent of their capital and surplus. Therefore a bank is likely to have an internal policy that requires broader diversification than that imposed by its supervisory agencies. To illustrate, a bank can specify that, other than for Treasury securities or federally guaranteed securities, no more than two percent of its investments portfolio will represent obligations of any one issuer. When it diversifies among many issuers, a bank limits the adverse impact if one or several issues should default and/or encounter limited marketability. Yet a broad-diversification policy has its costs. Securities eligible for bank investment usually have minimum face amounts of $5000, and they customarily trade in blocks of $25,000. Thus a bank usually holds at least $25,000, and often multiples of $100,000, in any one issue. Its administrative costs will likely increase if a bank tries to hold comparatively small amounts of many different issues. Any bank therefore must evaluate whether the incremental costs of unusually broad diversification start to exceed the risk-reduction benefits of such a policy.

Geographical location of issuers is an additional criterion for portfolio diversification, especially by a medium-sized or small bank that faces a

---

11. The U.S. Code empowers the Comptroller of the Currency to regulate investment securities activities of national banks *and* state member banks.

nondiversified loan demand. An illustrative rural bank lends mostly to local farmers and to nearby residents and businesses. Unless it participates in some out-of-town loans originated by its city correspondent(s), this illustrative bank's loan portfolio is sensitive to local economic conditions. Therefore, to diversify explicitly its total asset portfolio, this bank can purchase bonds of issuers in geographical regions where the economies are somewhat independent of the bank's local economy. Even large banks, with their more diversified loan portfolios, often have criteria for some geographical diversification of their investments. Conversely, at times banks use geographical criteria to specify debtors whose issues they do not want in their investments portfolio. In the mid-1970s, reportedly some regional money-center banks revised their investment policies to avoid municipal securities issued by some large Eastern cities.

Portfolio theory demonstrates that investors develop efficiently diversified portfolios by focusing on returns and risks from various combinations of individual securities. Although by law it has to diversify by issuer, a bank can also use computer programs to identify efficient portfolios. These programs require analysts to specify the expected return and expected risk (distribution of returns) of each individual security, and the interrelationships among expected returns from various securities. Given these inputs, the program will identify efficient combinations (portfolios) of the securities. When the analysts revise their estimates, then the bank reruns the program based on the new information. However, the administrative and transaction costs of frequent portfolio revision can exceed the possible benefits of this diversification procedure. Some researchers outline how banks can apply modern portfolio theory to their investments portfolio, but there is little evidence that banks yet do so.[12] Instead, most banks continue to diversify their bank portfolios among issuers and maturities.

## AGGRESSIVE PORTFOLIO MANAGEMENT

Interest-rate fluctuations provide opportunities for banks that aggressively manage part of their investments portfolio. To illustrate, if they confidently forecast that long-term interest rates are about to rise sharply, bond portfolio managers can avoid potential capital losses if they now sell many of their bank's long-term bonds and reinvest the sale proceeds in short-term securities, the prices of which do not fluctuate as widely as do those of long-term issues. Conversely, if they forecast a subsequent fall in long-term rates, the managers can shift funds from short-term securities to long-term issues in order to "lock in" some of the currently high long-term rates and to generate capital gains if rates fall, and bond prices rise, as expected.

Most banks recognize that aggressive portfolio management relies on interest-rate forecasts, which often prove unreliable; and so they limit its

---

12. George H. Hempel and Jess B. Yawitz, "Maximizing Bond Returns," *The Bankers Magazine,* Summer 1974, pp. 103-114. Jess B. Yawitz, George H. Hempel, and William J. Marshall, "A Risk-Return Approach to the Selection of Optimal Government Bond Portfolios," *Financial Management,* Autumn 1976, pp. 36-45.

use. A bank, for example, that substantially increases its short-term investments in anticipation of rising long-term rates may do so when many other investors similarly demand, and accept, comparatively low yields on short-term securities. If long-term rates fail to rise as soon and as far as expected, then the bank has to accept an extended period of low returns on its short-term investments. The cost to the bank of this erroneous forecast is primarily some foregone earnings from its investments portfolio. In contrast, the cost to a bank is potentially high if it substantially increases the proportion of long-term investments based on an incorrect forecast that long-term interest rates are about to fall. If these rates then rise, rather than fall, the bank will find itself with large potential capital losses, possibly during a period of strong loan demand. It can sell some of the long-term bonds, realize the losses from them, and use the sale proceeds to help meet its loan demand. Often, however, a bank is reluctant to realize large losses from its securities. Its stockholders may view large reported losses as a sign of management ineptness. Also, in contrast to its unrealized losses, a bank must immediately charge its realized losses against its income and/or capital accounts. Thus a bank that goes long and is proved wrong can severely limit its ability to accommodate some future loan demands, the meeting of which helps it to retain and/or obtain depositors.

Because aggressive portfolio management involves hazards as well as opportunities, most banks have policies that limit their portfolio managers from making sudden major shifts in the maturity structure of the bank's investments. Also, some banks designate one part of the total investments portfolio as a *trading account* in which a designated supervisor has substantial, but not unlimited, leeway to manage the account actively — subject to performance reviews by senior officials. The bank then views the other part of its total investments portfolio as a separate portfolio that is to provide backstop liquidity and/or backstop revenues.

Before it initiates a policy of aggressive portfolio management, a medium-sized bank will want to assess the financial environment within which it proposes to compete. Banks are only a fraction of the many bond investors, many of which devote full time to analyzing risk-return opportunities among various securities. When many rational well-informed investors, who have access to large amounts of capital, compete in a marketplace, it is improbable that any one of them can have a persistent advantage over the others. In fact, their intense competition contributes toward making an *efficient market,* wherein at any time the prices of almost all publicly traded securities are ''right,'' based on information known to investors at that time. If, as is likely, bank investment decisions involve securities that trade in an efficient market, then the officers and directors of a medium-sized bank will correctly question the value of their committing substantial resources to aggressive management of their bank's investments portfolio. Instead, they may choose to have the bank focus its resources and skills to compete for deposits, loans, and other banking business in its local competitive environment.

## STRUCTURING OF INVESTMENT MATURITIES

Most banks diversify their investment portfolios against fluctuating interest rates.

### Laddered Maturity Structure

A bank can maintain a laddered maturity structure for all or part of its investments portfolio. This policy requires the officers to decide which is the longest maturity judged appropriate for their bank's portfolio and then to instruct the portfolio manager(s) to space the maturities of the investments about equally between the shortest and longest maturity. To illustrate, if it has a total investments portfolio of $30 million and decides that it will hold none with maturities of longer than fifteen years, then a bank will have a perfectly laddered maturity structure if it invests $2 million in securities scheduled to mature within one year, $2 million scheduled to mature between one and two years, and so forth to fifteen years. It is convenient and inexpensive to maintain such a laddered portfolio. One year from now, the current one-year maturities are redeemed and their proceeds are reinvested in bonds with fifteen-year maturities to replace the former fifteen-year bonds that now have fourteen-year maturities.

If it ladders the maturities of its investments, a bank can realize several benefits. It systematically keeps part of the investments portfolio in short-term investments that provide convenient backstop liquidity. Simultaneously it keeps the rest of its investments in intermediate (say five to ten years) and long maturities. If, as historically has been the case, the yield curve is upward sloping, then this longer part of the portfolio will generate higher, more stable, returns over time than will the part invested in short-term securities. A laddered investments portfolio thus provides a compromise adaptation to fluctuating interest rates. It systematically combines short-term securities, the prices of which do not fluctuate widely and thus provide convenient backstop liquidity, with intermediate and long-term securities, the prices of which fluctuate more widely but that are less likely to be sold to meet unexpected cash outflows. Also, a laddered maturity structure systematically diversifies the investments over at least part of the yield curve so that the total portfolio return is a combination of returns from short, intermediate, and long maturities. As a compromise policy, a laddered maturity structure avoids both the risks and potentials of more aggressive portfolio management.

A bank that has a laddered maturity policy allows its investment officers some flexibility to depart from precisely equal spacing between maturities. Based on their interest-rate forecasts, the portfolio managers at times may decide to weight the maturity structure more heavily with long (or short) maturities. Similarly, what if a bank sells some investments in order to meet unusual loan demands? Should it sell only some short-term maturities that involve small, if any, capital losses? If these securities are sold, then the investments portfolio is no longer laddered across all maturities. Alternatively, if, to maintain the strict laddered portfolio, it sells some investments from various maturity categories, then the bank will incur higher transaction costs and potential capital losses on the long-term maturities that it sells. Thus the portfolio managers have some flexibility as to how they maintain the laddered-maturity structure. A variant is for a bank to hold short-term Treasury and federal agency securities to provide backstop liquidity and to ladder the maturities of its municipal holdings across all maturities or across intermediate and long maturities. While there are many variants, the concept of a strictly laddered maturity structure provides a standard by which to evaluate costs and benefits of other maturity structures.

## Barbell Maturity Structure

As a major alternative to a laddered maturity structure, various researchers suggest a barbell maturity structure in which a bank divides its investments between only short-term securities and the longest maturities judged appropriate for the portfolio. Even though it excludes intermediate maturities, a barbell policy also diversifies a portfolio against fluctuating interest rates. The short-term securities provide backstop liquidity. With this buffer the bank is unlikely to have to sell other investments to meet unusual net cash outflows. Therefore it concentrates its other investments in long-term securities that generally provide higher and more stable returns. The barbell maturity structure excludes the intermediate maturities that do not provide the capital-loss protection of short maturities or the income and capital gains potential of long maturities.

A strict barbell maturity structure implies equal proportions of securities with short or long maturities. In practice, proponents of the barbell maturity structure recognize that the proportions will likely vary based on a bank's need for backstop liquidity and its interest-rate expectations. As with a laddered maturity policy, a barbell maturity policy involves periodic reinvestment of funds from maturing short-term securities. However, it also requires periodic selling of long-term securities as their maturities become shorter and then periodic reinvestment of these sale proceeds in new long-term securities. Because of these extra transactions, the barbell policy involves greater administrative costs than does the laddered policy.

Recent studies report about barbell maturity structures. One study tests the attributes of optimal bond portfolios, and it concludes "that optimal portfolios will frequently consist of short and/or long bonds with no purchases of intermediate issues."[13] A subsequent study extends this initial research and reports that "optimal portfolios in a multiperiod environment with normally shaped yield curves tend to be laddered on both the long and

13. Dwight B. Crane, "A Stochastic Programming Model for Commercial Bank Bond Portfolio Management," *Journal of Financial and Quantitative Analysis*, June 1971, pp. 955-976. Also, Charles R. Wolf, "A Model for Selecting Commercial Bank Government Security Portfolios," *The Review of Economics and Statistics*, February 1969, pp. 40-52.

short ends of the maturity range, with an absence of intermediate maturities."[14] Another study examines return-risk outcomes from various maturity structures under a variety of assumptions concerning management's risk measures and interest-rate expectations. "On the assumption that the management measures risk as variability of net portfolio return (coupon income plus capital gains and losses)," this simulation analysis also provides support for a barbell policy, whereby a portfolio is "split between a spaced group of short maturity bonds and a longer investment security."[15] This study also notes that management's interest-rate expectations are a key factor in allocating the portfolio between short and long maturities.

Two authors explicitly test barbell versus laddered maturity structures, and they use simulation techniques to examine, for various-length investment periods, outcomes from portfolios of municipal securities. These researchers summarize their conclusions as follows:

> . . . barbell maturity structures do offer some significant advantages to banks that wish to manage their portfolios actively. They provide more liquidity and flexibility than laddered portfolios with the same level of expected return. The total return of barbell portfolios may be more volatile, but this may not be an important price to pay for some banks. On the other hand, banks that do not want to actively manage their municipal portfolio may find laddered portfolios very attractive. They can provide a comparable return with less uncertainty that the return will be achieved.[16]

These conclusions reaffirm the need for each bank carefully to examine its own tolerance for various risks associated with fluctuating interest rates.

While it has to evaluate which maturity policy is most appropriate for its corporate goals and constraints, a bank also can look to current banking practices for some guidance. Exhibit 9-3 summarizes the maturity distribution for investments held by all insured banks. Although some banks reportedly use barbell policies, this Exhibit, based on aggregate data, closely approximates a laddered structure for municipal holdings and a clustering of Treasury and federal agency issues among short maturities. On a less aggregate basis, two authors used statistical tests to examine the maturity structure of investments held by a large sample of banks in the southeastern United States. They conclude that differences in deposit size largely explain differences in investment policy. "Small banks hold more short maturities and fewer long bonds, than larger banks do."[17] The larger

---

14. Stephen P. Bradley and Dwight B. Crane, "Management of Commercial Bank Government Security Portfolios: An Optimization Approach Under Uncertainty," *Journal of Bank Research,* Spring 1973, pp. 18-30.

15. Ronald D. Watson, "Tests of Maturity Structures of Commercial Bank Government Securities Portfolios: A Simulation Approach," *Journal of Bank Research,* Spring 1972, pp. 34-46.

16. Stephen P. Bradley and Dwight B. Crane, "Simulation of Bond Portfolio Strategies: Laddered *vs* Barbell Maturity Structure," *Journal of Bank Research,* Summer 1975, pp. 122-134.

17. Robert R. Dince and James C. Fortson, "Maturity Structure of Bank Portfolios," *The Bankers Magazine,* Autumn 1974, pp. 96-102.

**EXHIBIT 9-3**

**Percentage Distribution, by Maturities, of Investment Securities Held by All Insured Commercial Banks: Year-end 1977**

| Years to Maturity | ——————— Categorized by Issuer ——————— | | |
|---|---|---|---|
| | U. S. Treasury | Federal Agencies | States and Their Political Subdivisions |
| 1 or less | 38 | 26 | 16 |
| 1 to 5 | 52 | 42 | 28 |
| 5 to 10 | 9 | 14 | 29 |
| Greater than 10 | 1 | 19 | 26 |
| Total | 100 | 101 | 99 |

*Note:* Column totals may not add to 100 because of rounding.

*Source:* Calculated from figures reported in *Assets and Liabilities, Commercial and Mutual Savings Banks*, December 31, 1977, Federal Deposit Insurance Corporation, Table 1.

sample banks hold their municipal investments in a way that closely resembles a laddered maturity structure. Moreover, the laddered approach seems evident both in a period of high and in a period of comparatively low interest rates.[18]

# BOND TRADING TACTICS

A large bank has bond specialists who use detailed economic forecasts and advanced computer systems to help them evaluate and make major trading decisions about their bank's multimillion—at times multibillion—dollar investments portfolio. While it thus commits substantial specialized resources to its own portfolio analyses and decisions, a large bank provides similar advisory services to its outlying correspondent banks. It reviews a smaller bank's stated investment policies and then uses these guidelines as a basis to review the smaller bank's investments portfolio and to recommend specific transactions. Thus, although they seldom can afford to become full-time investment specialists, the investment officer(s) and directors of a medium-sized bank need to know about some bond trading tactics.

### RIDING THE YIELD CURVE

When the yield curve is upward sloping, bond traders can try to increase their portfolio returns if they:

- purchase bonds with maturities at the upward end of the yield curve
- hold the bonds until their maturities become shorter

---

18. Also see William R. McDonough, "Large Banks Employ Flexible Maturity Structures," *Business Review* (Federal Reserve Bank of Dallas), February 1975, pp. 10-14.

- sell the bonds when their maturities are at the lower end of the yield curve
- reinvest the sale proceeds in bonds with maturities that have maturities at the upward end of the yield curve. (This assumes that the yield curve usually slopes upward.)

When they thus ride the yield curve, bond traders do not expect to hold the bonds until maturity.

To illustrate, a bank's investment department observes that, for U.S. Treasury securities:

- one will mature in three years with a yield to maturity of 7 percent
- a second one will mature in five years with a yield to maturity of 7.5 percent

These two bonds have the same (zero) default risk and marketability risk, yet because of the current interest-rate structure the bond with the five-year maturity provides a yield to maturity that is 0.5 percentage points, or 50 basis points, higher than that of the bond with the three-year maturity. (A *basis point* is 1/100 of one percent.) To ride the yield curve, the bank buys the five-year bond, but not with the expectation of holding it until maturity. It plans to sell the bond as it approaches maturity and then reinvest the sale proceeds in another bond that perhaps again has a five-year maturity. While it thus can use this tactic to try to increase the returns from the bond portfolio, the bank also exposes itself to greater interest-rate risk. The bank's investment officers must evaluate whether the potentially higher returns warrant the acceptance of additional interest-rate risk and the transaction costs of selling bonds in order to reinvest the proceeds in other bonds.

## ARBITRAGE

Perfect arbitrage is buying a marketable asset (or a call on such an asset) in one market and simultaneously selling it at a profit in another market. For example, a professional trader with access to rapid communications and large sums of money suddenly learns that the British pound can currently be bought for $2.02 in London and sold for $2.04 in New York. The simultaneous purchase in London and sale in New York "locks in" a profit of $.02 per pound, minus transaction and administrative costs. The trader's actions, and those of others who similarly note the rate discrepancy, will help remove the discrepancy as the competing traders buy pounds in London and sell them in New York. The rate in the two markets soon will become almost the same. At times a large money-center bank may identify and profit from a pure-arbitrage situation. In view of time delays and transaction costs, it is unlikely that medium-sized banks should commit resources to search for perfect-arbitrage opportunities.

Imperfect arbitrage is when investors try to profit from what they believe to be temporary discrepancies among prices of approximately similar marketable assets. One opportunity for imperfect arbitrage occurs when an investor observes that the yield curve for a category of securities, such as U.S. Treasury bonds, is basically smooth, but that one issue offers a higher yield to maturity than do other issues that have similar maturities. The investor further examines the reported yield to see whether it reflects unusual redemption or tax provisions. If the investor concludes that the issue is similar to issues in the only slightly shorter or longer maturities, then the investor will likely buy the higher-yielding issue to try to benefit from what seems to be a temporary discrepancy in market prices. In contrast to riding an upward-sloping yield curve, the investor buying this bond is relying on benefitting from a departure from the yield curve.

Other imperfect-arbitrage opportunities arise because of changing risk premiums among otherwise approximately similar bonds. Assume that single-A municipal bonds usually trade at prices that provide yields to maturity of 10-15 basis points higher than those from double-A bonds with similar coupons, redemption provisions, and marketability risk. The higher yield from the lower-rated bonds provides a risk premium for their higher default risk. An investor notes that this risk premium for most single-A bonds currently is 20 basis points and that for some issues it is 25 basis points. If the investor judges that this wide spread is a temporary departure from the typical spread, then the investor will likely try to boost his or her portfolio returns by switching from some double-A bonds to some approximately similar single-A bonds. Before he or she engages in this switching tactic, the investor also analyzes the probable transaction costs and tax implications.

There are numerous possibilities to arbitrage within the universe of publicly traded investment securities. No individual or team of people can hope to screen the changing risk-return relationships among so many potential pairs of securities. Therefore some major bond investors use computerized procedures to search for arbitrage opportunities.

One author reports on how a large money-center bank uses a computer program to help identify arbitrage opportunities in Treasury bonds.[19] He summarizes the derivation and structure of the program, which is run each evening based on the day's closing prices. When the investment officers arrive the next morning, they use this updated information, along with other tables, charts, and market experience, to help them decide whether or not to arbitrage and, if so, in which issues. The program thus provides specific recommendations; it does not make policies or implement decisions. Reportedly the bank's arbitrage profits increased substantially after installation of the program. Ironically, when they use these types of modern systems to aid in their arbitrage decisions, competing investors reduce the

---

19. Robert L. Kramer, "Arbitrage in U.S. Government Bonds: A Management Science Approach," *Journal of Bank Research,* Summer 1970, pp. 30-43.

probability that many arbitrage opportunities can persist in financial markets.

## TAX SWAPS

Interest income from municipal securities is not subject to federal income tax. In contrast, because they are defined as ordinary income that is customary to banking, a bank's capital gains and losses from sales of municipal securities are subject to federal income tax. This tax environment provides opportunities for a bank to boost its after-tax returns from municipal securities.

An illustrative bank owns some bonds for which it paid $25,000 and which today are worth $20,000. It can now sell the bonds, realize a $5,000 capital loss, use this loss to help offset other income, and thus lower its tax bill. It cannot, however, immediately repurchase these, or substantially equivalent bonds, without having the Internal Revenue Service disallow the tax benefits of such a "wash-sale" transaction. Therefore the bank identifies some somewhat dissimilar bonds, the purchase of which helps fulfill basic portfolio objectives and also happens to provide tax benefits.

Investment officers of a bank of any size can seek to identify potential tax swaps. The investments team of a large bank often uses specialized computer programs to review potential returns, risks, and tax consequences of various tax swaps. This team also uses such programs to make tax-swap recommendations to outlying correspondent banks.

There are limits to the number of tax swaps in which a bank will engage. A bank's senior officials often are reluctant to have their bank report substantial realized losses in any one reporting period. The realized losses have to be charged against the bank's income and/or capital, and some investors may disapprove of a bank's realizing large securities losses, even if the bank transforms much of the loss into tax savings. Also, if it has incurred substantial operating losses or if it uses other tax shelter strategies, than a bank may choose not to realize securities losses in order to offset other taxable income.

Until 1969 the tax laws were such that many banks concentrated their net realized capital gains in one year and their net realized capital losses in a separate year. The Tax Reform Act of 1969 removes the incentive for banks to make such decisions about net gain or loss years. In the current tax environment, it is generally advantageous to defer tax payments by delaying realization of capital gains as long as possible. Yet, based on his analysis, one researcher hypothesizes that, during years of slack loan demand and potentially low profits, many banks will "sell securities in order to realize capital gains for the purpose of enhancing the level of reported profits even though such action results in tax payment at an earlier date than is absolutely necessary."[20]

---

20. Edward J. Kane, "Banks and Balance-Sheet Cosmetics: Tax Swapping Then and Now," *New England Economic Review* (Federal Reserve Bank of Boston), May-June 1973, pp. 33-38.

## OTHER INVESTMENT ACTIVITIES

Most large banks are dealers in and underwriters of investment securities. In these capacities they own securities that they segregate from their investment and trading-account securities. By law, banks cannot deal in and underwrite municipal revenue bonds and corporate bonds and stocks. They can, however, arrange private placements—in contrast to market distributions—of such issues.

### DEALER ACTIVITIES

At a specific time, a dealer firm makes a market in a security by standing ready to buy it at a specific *bid* price and to sell it at a higher *asked* price. The difference between the dealer's bid and asked price represents the *price spread*.

Seldom does a dealer firm simultaneously buy and sell a security, and so it has an inventory of securities that it has bought and not yet sold and a negative inventory of securities that it does not own but has sold (short) and thus will soon have to purchase. The market prices of securities that a dealer firm owns or is short fluctuate over time, and so the dealer does not always realize its spread on a specific transaction. Over time the dealer firm rapidly adjusts its bid and asked prices to incorporate new information and to adjust its inventory.

In any period, a dealer firm's revenues reflect its realized price spread and the frequency of its transactions. For example, even if it has a small price spread per transaction, a dealer's revenues can be high if it successfully engages in many such transactions. From these revenues the dealer subtracts its administrative and financing costs. Its remaining profit (or loss) provides a rate of return on the capital it has invested in its dealer activities.

National and state member banks can act as dealers in Type I and Type II securities, which are mostly U.S. Treasury, federal-agency, and general-obligation municipal bonds. These banks cannot be dealers in most revenue bonds issued by states and their political subdivisions.

Most dealer banks are large banks that compete against other dealer banks and against nonbank dealers. They stand ready to quote bid and asked prices on U.S. Treasury securities and on many federal-agency and general-obligation municipal securities. They maintain inventories of many of the issues. These banks operate their dealer activities as a separate profit unit within the investments department. (The regulatory agencies require banks to report their dealer inventories at market prices, in contrast to the amortized-cost basis they use to report their investment securities.) Large banks also cite their dealer activities as an additional service they provide for outlying banks and for trust and investment advisory accounts of wealthy individuals and organizations.

The FRS and the U.S. Treasury have embarked on a program to automate the government securities market and to provide for book-entry ownership and transfer of government securities. Instead of having pieces of paper to represent ownership, owners of U.S. Treasury or federal agency securities will have their ownership represented by a computerized book entry, much as a demand deposit is a book-entry form of money. Moreover, owners of book-entry securities, or their agents, will be able to transfer ownership via wire systems and computer terminals that link major participants in the government securities market. This automated, book-entry program "is intended to reduce the time, money, personnel, and space required to handle the increasing volume and velocity of transactions in Government securities and, at the same time, to ensure adequate controls and reduce to a minimum the risk of loss or theft of such securities." An initial step in this program was taken in 1968, when member banks could have their Federal Reserve Bank hold in safekeeping their U.S. Treasury securities in book-entry, instead of physical form. A second step was to arrange for bank and nonbank dealers to have their government securities in book-entry form. Subsequent steps are to extend the system to member banks for their customer securities and trust accounts. This latest phase of the conversion process is a gradual one, impeded in part by state laws that limit the form in which securities in trust accounts can be held. The objective of the automation program will be achieved—when most transactions in government securities "can be effected by means of wire messages among the major participants in the market, without the need for physical securities. In the light of the experience to date, that time does not seem too far distant." [21]

## UNDERWRITING ACTIVITIES

A securities *underwriter* (or underwriting syndicate) agrees to buy an entire new issue of marketable securities from an issuing firm or public body, and the underwriter plans to sell the issue to the public at a slightly higher price. The underwriter accepts the task of publicly marketing the securities and the risk of some losses if it has to reduce the public offering price in order to sell the entire issue. While such a loss occasionally occurs, an underwriter usually earns a profit from the total underwriting revenues that it receives over time.

Until 1933 many large banks, or their investment banking affiliates, were major underwriters of diverse debt securities. Depression conditions of the early 1930s triggered a series of Congressional Hearings concerning banking and financial markets. Many participants in these Hearings concluded that bank underwriting activities contributed importantly to speculative financial markets, financial conflicts of interest, and bank failures. As a result, Congress passed the Banking Act of 1933, which often is called the Glass-Steagall Act. This Act required banks to terminate or divest themselves of many traditional underwriting activities. The Act, as amended, permits banks to underwrite only Type I and Type II securities.

---

21. Richard A. Debs, "The Program for the Automation of the Government Securities Market," *Monthly Review* (Federal Reserve Bank of New York), July 1972, pp. 178-182.

In recent years some large banks and other proponents have sought changes in the Glass-Steagall Act so that banks can underwrite revenue, as well as general obligation, municipal bonds. Revenue bonds account for a growing proportion of municipal financing since World War II.

One author identifies three main issues in the controversy as to whether banks should be permitted to underwrite and deal in municipal revenue bonds.

- "Will the infusion of bank underwriters lead to interest cost savings for states and municipalities?
- "Will permitting banks to underwrite revenue issues ultimately tend toward undesirable concentration in the hands of a few large banks?
- "Are there inherent conflicts of interest involved in further combining commercial and investment banking activities?" [Those who oppose the broadening of bank underwriting powers because of potential conflicts of interest customarily allege that a bank, as underwriter, at times will be tempted to place its slow-moving offerings with its trust clients and outlying correspondent banks].[22]

The reviewer observes how participants in the controversy offer their answers to these questions, but they provide limited supporting evidence. He then concludes that: "for more than 30 years many people, some of them congressmen and senators, have been brought up believing that such conflicts [of interest] were intimately associated with the financial excesses that preceded the Great Depression. And this factor, more than any other, makes somewhat remote the prospects for relaxing restrictions on bank underwriting of municipal revenue bonds."

Large banks compete to participate in permissible underwritings. Usually a new issue is sold not by a single underwriter, but by an *underwriting syndicate* that consists of some banks and investment banking firms that temporarily unite to underwrite a specific bond issue. When a state, for example, proposes to offer a large issue of general-obligation bonds, it solicits bids. One or more large underwriting firms then tries to organize an underwriting syndicate of which it is manager or comanager. It invites other firms to participate in the syndicate's pricing decision, marketing effort, underwriting risk, and potential profits. Almost daily *The Wall Street Journal* and other financial newspapers contain underwriting notices that include the names of participating underwriters, many of which are large money-center banks.

As with its dealer activities, a bank usually has separate internal

---

22. Richard R. West, "Should Commercial Banks Be Allowed to Underwrite Municipal Revenue Bonds?" *The National Banking Review,* September 1965, pp. 35-44. Also, Larry R. Mote, "Banks and the Securities Markets: The Controversy," *Economic Perspectives* (Federal Reserve Bank of Chicago), March-April 1979, pp. 14-20; and Lewis T. Preston, "The Glass-Steagall Act: Barrier to Competition," *The Morgan Guaranty Survey,* April 1979, pp. 6-11.

accounts for its underwriting unit; and it then evaluates the returns, and any additional benefits, that it derives from its underwriting activities.

## PRIVATE PLACEMENTS

The Glass-Steagall Act prevents banks from dealing in and underwriting corporate bonds and stocks, but it does not prevent them from arranging private placements of such issues. A *private placement* is when an issuer bypasses a public offering and directly sells new securities to one or several large institutional investors, such as insurance companies and pension funds. An issuing firm usually finds that a private placement involves fewer legal and regulatory restrictions that does a publicly offered issue. Its proponents also claim that, compared to a public offering, a private placement often results in lower costs, for example, by avoiding underwriting fees and by enabling the issuer and potential purchasers bilaterally to negotiate the issue's terms.

Some large banks arrange private placements by their corporate clients. A bank that does so has specialists who help a client tailor a private placement to offer to large investors. The bank receives a fee for this specialized service. As a related service, some large banks also alert their corporate clients to merger opportunities, and they advise them in merger strategies and negotiations.

## SUMMARY

A bank's senior officers and directors, together with the investments officers, periodically review the objectives of and policies for the investments portfolio. The bank's investments managers then implement these policies through a series of specialized investment decisions.

Participants at the policy and procedural levels each benefit if their bank has a written statement of investment policies. The senior officials periodically review and occasionally revise this internal document in the context of the bank's changing resources and environment; meanwhile, the investments officers have a formal set of standards by which they can implement—and be held accountable for—their specific decisions.

There are many interrelationships among a bank's investment policies and its policies in areas such as cash flow management, loans, and tax planning. Thus as they review the investment policies, the senior officials have to decide the:

- extent to which the investments portfolio is to provide backstop liquidity and/or backstop revenues
- amount and frequency of capital losses that the bank is willing to incur in its investments transactions
- extent to which the bank should try to obtain investment income that is exempt from federal and/or state and local taxes

- extent to which the bank should build an internal investments staff in contrast to using external investment services available from large correspondent banks and nonbank advisory services
- amount of authority to delegate to the bank's investments specialists and the criteria by which to monitor and evaluate the performance of the specialists

Over time these investment policies are subject to review and possible revision.

All those who set and review the investment policies cannot be experts in bank investments, but they need to have basic knowledge about:

- laws and regulations that limit a bank's investments, such as pledging requirements and classification of securities as Type I, II, or III
- return and risk dimensions of the principal investment securities issued by the U.S. Treasury, federal agencies, and states and their political subdivisions
- risk-control procedures, such as bond-rating systems, diversification strategies, and structuring of investment maturities
- the principal interest-rate and cash-flow projections that underlie the bank's current investment strategies
- bond trading tactics, such as riding the yield curve, arbitrage, and tax swaps
- and, especially for large banks, investment-related opportunities in areas such as dealer activities, underwriting, and negotiations of private placements

A bank has in-house specialists in these matters, and/or it draws on the specialized investment skills and information that are available from large correspondent banks and other outside sources. Also, either directly or indirectly through outside specialist organizations, a bank can use computers to help it analyze many of its investment decisions.

# 10
# LOAN PORTFOLIO POLICIES

Its loan portfolio typically accounts for over half of a bank's total assets and generates over two-thirds of its total revenues. A bank uses its loan policies and loan decisions to strengthen its relationships with current and potential depositors. Also, it often considers how its loan decisions can benefit its community, for example by helping to finance employment opportunities and new residences. While it expects its loan portfolio to provide revenues and associated benefits, a bank also expects occasional loan losses.

This chapter demonstrates how a bank can evaluate various loan opportunities, organize its lending personnel, and establish policies for its total loan portfolio. The next chapter introduces how a bank uses loan decision and review systems to implement its policies, and the subsequent three chapters focus on business loans, consumer loans, and real estate loans.

## EVALUATING LOAN OPPORTUNITIES

A bank uses a three-step process to evaluate its loan opportunities. It:

- reviews laws and regulations that prohibit or restrict certain loans and loan terms
- assesses its own limitations that relate to its location, size, competitive environment, and internal resources (although it can modify some of its limitations over time, in the short run a bank has to have loan policies that are consistent with its environment and resources)
- estimates the expected net returns from various types of loans that it can make

This is a dynamic process in which a bank frequently reevaluates its loan opportunities in view of new developments that affect any or all of the three basic steps.

## LEGAL AND REGULATORY CONSTRAINTS

Whether it has a national or state charter, a bank has to identify specific lending practices forbidden to it by applicable laws and regulations. By law, for example, no national bank "shall make any loan or discount on the security of the shares of its own capital stock, nor be the purchaser or holder of any such shares, unless such security or purchase shall be necessary to prevent loss upon a debt previously contracted in good faith . . ." (12 U.S.C. 83). Also, a national bank is not to make loans secured by its own subordinated debentures, nor is it to lend to its bank examiners.

A national bank also encounters diverse restrictions on its loan policies and procedures. These restrictions are extensive, detailed, and subject to change. A bank's senior officers and directors usually can only acquaint themselves with these lending limitations, about which the loan officers and legal staff need precise current knowledge.

National banks face a *10% lending limit,* whereby: "the total obligations to any national banking association of any person, copartnership, association, or corporation shall at no time exceed 10 per centum of the amount of the capital stock of such association actually paid in and unimpaired and 10 per centum of its unimpaired surplus fund" (12 U.S.C. 84). This 10% lending limit thus sets a maximum amount that a national bank can lend to any one customer, and this maximum relates to a bank's size, as measured by its capital and surplus. Over time a bank can try to increase its lending limit by increasing its capital and surplus. In the short run, however, if it encounters a loan request that exceeds its legal limit, then a bank either has to deny the request or else try to meet it by inviting other banks or nonbank firms to participate in the loan. The 10% limit is subject to extensive detailed exceptions, such as for loans secured by: goods or commodities in shipment, shipping documents or warehouse receipts covering readily marketable staples, or United States obligations. There are about fourteen exceptions to the 10% lending limit, and some of these exceptions in turn involve other restrictions.

When it wants to make real estate loans, a national bank also encounters restrictions. In general, a national bank cannot make an additional real estate loan if, at the time, its aggregate outstanding real estate loans exceed its unimpaired capital plus surplus, or 70 percent of its time and savings deposits, whichever is greater. If it satisfies this aggregate constraint, a bank still has to comply with many detailed limitations. It must, for example, generally require a borrower to amortize any real estate loan that exceeds 50 percent of the appraised value of the property that secures the loan, or that has a length to maturity of more than five years. Moreover, the OCC requires specific minimum amortization rates that relate to a loan's maturity terms and its percentage of appraised value.

To reduce the potential for conflicts of interest, there are strict laws and regulatory guidelines that govern loan transactions between a national bank and its executive officers. The guidelines are less explicit about transactions between a bank and its directors and their associates; but, to protect themselves from potential entanglements, most banks have internal guidelines for such "insider" transactions that are scrutinized by bank examiners.

The FRS administers Regulation U, which sets a maximum percentage that a bank can lend against collateral consisting of most publicly traded common stocks and convertible securities. To illustrate, when the FRS margin requirement is 60 percent, then a bank is not to grant a new loan that exceeds 40 percent of the dollar amount of eligible securities that a borrower proposes to pledge as collateral. The FRS changes its margin requirements over time; occasionally it sets them as high as 100 percent. It also specifies detailed procedures to direct and monitor lender compliance with Regulation U. The FRS also administers Regulation B, which implements the Equal Credit Opportunity Act, and Regulation Z, which provides for truth in lending.

Although not subject to the lending constraints imposed by the OCC, a state bank is subject to similar restrictions imposed by state laws and regulations. Some states, for example, have *usury laws* that specify a maximum interest rate that a lender can charge on certain loans, especially loans to individuals. Also, a state bank is subject to many lending regulations administered by the FRS and to federal laws that prohibit loans to federal bank examiners. Its compliance is monitored by its state and federal bank examiners.

## DEMAND AND RESOURCE ANALYSIS

After it filters out those that fail to meet legal and regulatory constraints, a bank has to analyze further the comparative merits of its remaining loan opportunities.

There are six principal categories of loans: business, agricultural, consumer, real estate, international, and other (which consists primarily of loans to banks and other financial institutions). Few banks can develop specialized loan portfolios that encompass all these categories. Instead each bank identifies its principal loan demands and evaluates its abilities to service the demands.

Its location and size limit a bank's loan opportunities. A bank of almost any size or location can service the loan demands of nearby small businesses, consumers, and potential home buyers. In contrast, a bank seldom makes agricultural loans unless it is located in a rural area or it is a large city bank that participates in agricultural loans with its rural correspondents. It is primarily large money-center banks that have specialized units that lend to medium-sized and large firms, large real-estate developers, international borrowers, and to other banks and financial institutions.

Branching restrictions impose geographical constraints on a bank's loan portfolio, but these constraints are seldom binding. Many states specify that a bank can operate branches only in the vicinity of its head office. Whether it has a national or state charter, a bank must adhere to the branching restrictions, if any, of the state in which it is located. In Illinois, for example, where branching is severely limited, large Chicago banks find it difficult to make consumer loans directly to residents of outlying suburbs. These large banks make consumer loans indirectly, however, via their credit card systems and their financing of the accounts receivable of some suburban retailers.

Banks cannot branch across state lines. Most large banks, however, have the resources to send loan officers to call on distant potential clients and to establish loan production offices in other states. A *loan production office* is not a branch that accepts deposits; it is a physical office that a bank staffs with some full-time loan officers who solicit and help service loans for their bank. Even if it lacks the resources to build and staff an extensive network of branches or loan production offices, a medium-sized bank can broaden its loan opportunities by purchasing home mortgage loans on properties outside its immediate geographical area and by participating in large loans arranged by its money-center correspondent bank(s).

Its competitive environment also affects how a bank evaluates its loan opportunities. Each bank compares its strengths to those of its principal competitors. If faced, for example, by aggressive competition from entrenched S&Ls and mutual savings banks, a bank will likely decide not to commit substantial resources to compete directly against such rival firms. Instead it will develop a passive policy of accommodating the mortgage loan requests of its good customers. Similarly, after it examines its competitive opportunities, such a bank may decide not to compete actively against nearby credit unions and small loan companies, but instead to focus its resources on specialized loan opportunities for which it does not face such intensive competition, for example in loans to small businesses. Its wide variety of lending powers thus enables each bank to identify those lending areas in which its own current and potential resources give it a comparative advantage over rival firms.

Its human resources also affect how a bank evaluates its loan opportunities. Unless it is very large, a bank seldom has loan officers who specialize in the many types of loans that their bank can potentially make. For example, a medium-sized rural bank has several officers who are skilled in making seasonal loans to nearby farmers, whose borrowing records and crop practices are well known to the lending officers. These officers thus structure and monitor a portfolio of short-term agricultural loans that involve infrequent losses. If, however, this bank now wants aggressively to increase its home mortgage loans, the bank's agricultural lending specialists are unlikely to be as skilled in reviewing property appraisals and evaluating a potential homeowner's long-run repayment capacity. The officers similarly whould have to undergo a major shift in their decision processes if they were to become involved in the detailed credit reporting and associated administrative details that accompany a large portfolio of consumer loans. Therefore, if it wants to build up its home mortgage loans or consumer loans, this illustrative rural bank will likely have to go outside its present organization to hire some loan officers who have experience with these specialized types of loans.

The federal government, through its agencies, offers diverse loan-participation and loan-guarantee programs. Before it becomes involved in such programs, a bank has to judge whether its potential benefits from such participation are likely to exceed the costs of training or hiring a person to administer the details of such loan programs.

In summary, each bank is likely to specialize in certain categories of loans. Its specialization partly reflects past policies and historical happenstance. Therefore a bank's senior officials have to review periodically whether their bank faces major changes in its loan demands and competition and, if so, whether it has appropriate resources to meet those changing conditions.

A bank's size is a key factor affecting the composition of its loan portfolio. (Most large banks are based in large cities, and so there is a close association between a bank's size and its location.) Exhibit 10-1 summarizes the loan-portfolio composition of all insured banks, grouped by asset-size categories. In contrast to those of smaller banks, the loan portfolios of big banks contain large proportions of business loans and small proportions of agricultural loans. Large banks also have large proportions of loans categorized as "other," which primarily include loans to financial institutions and loans for purchasing and carrying securities. Medium-sized banks, many of which are located in suburbs, have notably high proportions of real estate loans and consumer loans. A survey of the loan portfolio composition of banks in one Federal Reserve District reports results that are consistent with the aggregate information summarized in Exhibit 10-1.[1]

## EXHIBIT 10-1

### Loan-Portfolio Composition of All Insured Banks: Year-end 1977
#### (Percentage of Total Loans)

| Loan Category | All Banks | Under 5 | 5-10 | 10-25 | 25-100 | 100-300 | 300 or More |
|---|---|---|---|---|---|---|---|
| Business (commercial and industrial) | 20 | 15 | 16 | 18 | 22 | 28 | 33 |
| Agricultural | 16 | 31 | 26 | 17 | 8 | 2 | 2 |
| Real estate | 33 | 24 | 29 | 34 | 37 | 37 | 30 |
| Consumer (to individuals) | 29 | 27 | 27 | 29 | 31 | 29 | 25 |
| Other | 3 | 2 | 2 | 2 | 2 | 4 | 10 |
| Total | 101 | 99 | 100 | 100 | 100 | 100 | 100 |
| Total loans as a percentage of total assets | 55 | 51 | 55 | 56 | 56 | 55 | 52 |

*Note:* Column totals may not add to 100 because of rounding.

*Source:* Table C (Nation), *Bank Operating Statistics*, 1977, Federal Deposit Insurance Corporation.

1. "Loan Portfolio Composition," *Business Conditions* (Federal Reserve Bank of Chicago), November 1973, pp. 14-15.

## RETURN-RISK ANALYSIS

After it screens out infeasible loan opportunities (because of legal and regulatory constraints) or impractical ones (because of its competitive environment and resource limitations), a bank has to allocate its portfolio among the remaining feasible loans. How should, for example, a medium-sized suburban bank divide its total loan portfolio among loans to businesses, home buyers, and consumers? If its objective is to maximize its long-run returns, then the bank should frequently adjust its loan portfolio toward those loans that provide the highest net returns. To illustrate, if it has limited funds to lend and has to choose between some business loans that provide an expected net return of 8 percent and some consumer loans that provide an expected net return of 11 percent, then the bank is likely to make the consumer loans.

A bank estimates its *net return* from a loan as follows:

Expected gross return

*Minus*   Operating expenses +
          Adjustments for risks

*Equals*   Expected net return

The expected gross return consists of the contractual interest return plus associated benefits that the bank expects to derive from the loan. For example, a bank generally expects its borrowers to keep deposits and to use other of its banking services. Although it is difficult to measure all the associated benefits from making specific loans, a bank generally obtains or retains larger deposit balances when it lends to business firms rather than to homeowners and consumers. Before it refuses a loan request from a long-time customer, a bank has to consider whether it will lose associated revenues if the dissatisfied applicant takes his or her account(s) elsewhere.

Each loan involves operating expenses that fall into two principal categories:

- initial administrative costs
- subsequent processing costs

The initial costs of making a home mortgage loan or consumer loan are often similar to those of a large business or agricultural loan. Yet the subsequent costs of processing installment repayments from a home mortgage loan or consumer loan can substantially exceed those of processing a large loan that has a similar duration but has infrequent repayments. To try to reduce, or at least control, their operating expenses on small consumer loans, some banks use statistical systems to screen applications; and many banks use computer-based systems to process routine repayments and reviews of their consumer loans.

A loan's default risk is that the borrower fails to repay the loan (or repays all or some of it only after the lender incurs substantial delays and/or collection costs). To control the default risk of its loans, each bank develops procedures to analyze loan applications and to monitor its loans outstanding..

A loan's interest-rate risk centers on unexpected interest-rate fluctuations that occur after the loan is made. This risk is most evident when a bank makes long-term loans with fixed interest rates that do not correctly anticipate subsequent fluctuations in market interest rates. For example, when it makes a twenty-year mortgage loan at a fixed interest rate, a bank commits funds for a long period during which interest rates can unexpectedly change sharply. If rates go up more sharply than anticipated, then the bank will regularly receive the contractual payments of interest and principal; but it will have to forego the opportunity to obtain higher interest income from the loan. If, instead, rates go down more sharply than anticipated, then the borrower will likely refinance the loan at lower rates and fully repay the mortgage loan. In this case the bank then has to reinvest the funds at the lower rates that are then prevalent in financial markets.

A bank can hedge against unexpectedly large changes in market interest rates. It can make many of its loans for short periods, at the end of which the bank renews the loan or relends the funds at the then-prevalent rates. It can offer long-term loans in which the contractual interest rate varies with subsequent market rates. Then if rates unexpectedly rise sharply the bank will automatically receive a higher interest rate from such floating-rate loans. In this way the bank transfers much of the interest-rate risk to the borrower. (If market interest rates decline, then the rate on the floating-rate loan will also decline.) Even with fixed-rate, long-term loans a bank can protect itself from falling interest rates by insisting on prepayment clauses, whereby a borrower pays a contractual penalty fee if it prepays a loan.

To test whether banks use net returns as a criterion for portfolio allocation decisions, one study examines the aggregate portfolio behavior of 71 member banks over a six-year period.[2] The banks are all in the Seventh (Chicago) Federal Reserve District, and they all have deposits of under $50 million. The author uses standardized cost accounting data to estimate the gross annualized yields from three categories of loans as follows:

| | |
|---|---|
| Commercial and agricultural | 7.5% |
| Real estate | 7.0% |
| Installment | 10.8% |

The author then adjusts the gross yields for estimated: associated benefits from deposit relationships, operating expenses, and default risk. After these adjustments, he estimates the net annualized returns as follows:

2. David Updegraff, "Small Bank Portfolio Behavior," *Business Conditions,* (Federal Reserve Bank of Chicago), March 1973, pp. 3-10. This study's reported *levels* of returns, which reflect the time period of the study (1966-1971), are less important than is the study's demonstration of how the *range* of adjusted net annual returns is less wide than that of the gross annual yields. These range relationships are likely to hold in periods of other interest-rate levels.

| Commercial and agricultural | 6.8% |
| Real estate | 6.2% |
| Installment | 7.0% |

Thus the estimated net returns for the loan categories range between 6.2 and 7.0 percent, which is a narrower range than that of the gross yields (7.0 to 10.8 percent). Based on his analysis, the author concludes that, ''although it is not possible to prove rigorously, . . . it appears quite possible that small banks approach a profit-maximizing allocation of assets.'' He further observes that the sample banks have a long-run profit perspective because during periods of intense loan demand they apparently forego temporarily high yields in order to accommodate the loan demands of their long-established business and agricultural customers.

Return-risk analysis provides a framework for most loan decisions. A bank's directors and senior officers establish policies to control the risks of the diverse loans made by their bank. To implement these policies, the loan officers and supporting staff analyze and review the return-risk attributes of specific loan applications and of loans currently outstanding.

## STRUCTURING FOR LOAN DECISIONS

Loan decisions are made at two principal levels: policy and review, and specific implementation. Bank directors and senior officers focus on policy and periodic review. They delegate to loan officers, their assistants and staff, the authority to initiate and implement many loan decisions that meet the policy guidelines.

Exhibit 10-2 summarizes the principal participants in bank loan decisions. Policy and review decisions are primarily made by a bank's:

- board of directors
- directors' loan committee
- executive loan committee, which consists of senior loan officers and some other senior officers of the bank

In contrast, decisions to recommend and, if approved, to implement specific loans are made by a bank's:

- senior loan officers, who supervise and work with
- other members of their loan group, and
- associated personnel, such as credit analysts and problem-loan specialists

The organizational structure of Exhibit 10-2 applies to most medium-sized and large banks. In a medium-sized bank, the same officers often set and implement loan policies, subject to review by the board of directors. In contrast, a large bank—especially if it specializes in many types of loans and

**EXHIBIT 10-2**

**Structuring for Loan Decisions**

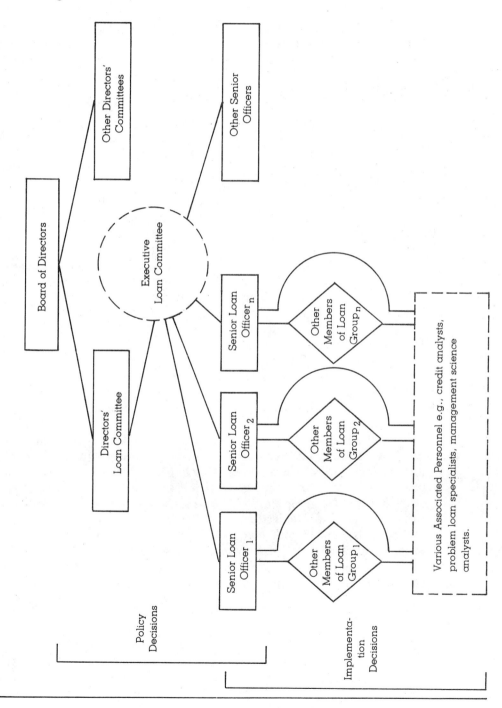

operates an extensive branch network—has a detailed hierarchy of loan officials. Although it contains more components, the large bank's organization chart is a logical extension of the one summarized in Exhibit 10-2.

The board of directors is at the apex of the loan-decision structure. The directors are ultimately accountable for their bank's loans. If they permit loan officers to make loans that violate bank laws or regulations, the directors face legal penalties. The directors also are responsible to stockholders for their bank's overall operations, of which loan returns and risks constitute a major part.

Because loan decisions are a major part of its responsibilities, the board of directors usually has a *directors' loan committee,* comprised of directors who focus on loan policies and outcomes. The directors' loan committee has periodic meetings for which the agenda focuses on the bank's loan policies, current and projected loan-portfolio composition, and possible problem loans. The loan committee regularly reports its analyses, projections, and recommendations to the board of directors. Because of its size, a full board seldom can meet on short notice, and so it empowers its loan committee to make interim decisions that require prompt action. These committee decisions are then subject to review by the full board of directors.

Members of the directors' loan committee maintain close and continuous association with the *executive loan committee,* which meets frequently (at least weekly) to review loan policies, trends, and major loan decisions. In addition to senior loan officers, other members of this committee include the bank's president and other senior nonloan officers, such as the head of a large bank's resource-planning department.

Almost all medium-sized and large banks have *senior loan officers,* each of whom heads a loan group that also contains junior officers and some associated loan personnel. Loan groups reflect geographical specialization, borrower specialization, or a combination of these two basic categories. A large money-center bank, for example, has one or more groups that specialize in loans to borrowers in its metropolitan area and/or state, and it has other groups that specialize in loans to borrowers grouped by other regions or countries. A medium-sized or large bank also has various groups that specialize in home mortgage loans or consumer loans; and a large bank also has additional groups for loans to financial institutions, large real-estate firms, and specific industries, such as agribusiness, petroleum, and transportation. In addition, a large bank usually has a group that specializes in loan participations with correspondent banks and in loans secured by controlling stock of some smaller correspondent banks. There are many possible configurations of loan groups. Each bank develops a grouping system that seems appropriate for its specific size, location, and areas of specialization. Because these factors change over time, a bank's senior officers and directors occasionally review and revise the loan groupings within their bank.

Members of a bank's loan groups immerse themselves in the daily activities of analyzing, negotiating, monitoring, and reviewing specific loan agreements. These loan specialists make their decisions and recommendations in the context of loan policies set by the bank's directors and senior officers.

## SETTING AND REVIEWING LOAN POLICIES

Officers and directors have to define and regularly review their bank's loan policies. This process alerts them to *changes* in:

- laws and regulations that affect bank loan decisions
- bank loan markets
- relationships between bank loans and other components of a bank's balance sheet and income statement

A written loan-policy statement provides a control system by which senior officials can delegate many decisions to junior loan officers, who then have guidelines as to the loans they: can make, cannot make, and cannot make without prior approval from a superior officer or committee.[3] Over time the senior officials systematically review the junior officers' loan decisions to confirm that they adhere to the bank's policy statement. This review process provides the senior officers with new information that they can use to review and possibly revise the loan-policy statement.

A bank's policy statement has to be consistent with the bank's objectives and circumstances. Yet as it develops and reviews its individualized statement, a bank can compare it to guidelines that most banks incorporate into their loan policies.

### CUSTOMER RELATIONSHIP

As a matter of policy, most banks make loans only to customers who use or are likely to use other of the bank's services. A bank thus seeks to solidify or develop a long-term comprehensive relationship with its principal borrowers. It especially expects a borrower to maintain deposit balances with it. At times this deposit relationship is an explicit part of the loan agreement.

### LOCATION OF BORROWER

Most banks have a stated policy of making loans primarily to borrowers who reside or have operations near the bank. These are four principal reasons for such a policy.

- A distant borrower is not likely to find it convenient to use other of the bank's services. (Thus the geographical criterion relates to the customer-relationship criterion.)

---

3. Robert B. Maloane, "Written Loan Policies," *The Journal of Commercial Bank Lending,* June 1976, pp. 18-24.

- Compared to a nearby customer, it is more difficult to evaluate and monitor the financial activities of a similar but distant customer.
- A loan to a distant borrower is less likely to provide associated benefits to a bank's community than is, for example, a similar-risk loan to a nearby business firm or consumer.
- Bank examiners are aware of the first three reasons, and so they closely question a bank about its loans to distant borrowers. The examiners often pointedly inquire as to the specific benefits a bank expects from such a loan.

Its size and structure affect how a bank specifies geographical criteria for its loan policies. A medium-sized bank generally has a policy of servicing nearby borrowers. A large bank with a statewide branching network has a policy to service small and medium-sized customers throughout its state, and it also views itself as a regional bank that competes for large borrowers—and customers—throughout nearby states. Similarly, a large money-center bank usually has a loan policy that focuses on consumer and small-business loans within its metropolitan area or state, while it simultaneously specifies broader geographical guidelines for loans to large regional, national, and even international borrowers.

## SIZE OF TOTAL LOAN PORTFOLIO

A bank needs a policy concerning the size of its total loan portfolio. Usually a bank specifies a guideline such that, at any time, its total loans will be close to a specific proportion of its total assets or total deposits. For example, after they estimate the stability of the bank's sources of funds and other balance-sheet relationships, a bank's officials decide that their bank will generally maintain a loan-to-deposit ratio of 65 percent. This target ratio provides a policy norm. As the deposits expand, so can the bank's total loans. During periods of slack loan demand, the actual ratio will likely be less than the target, but the senior officials will likely accept this departure rather than have the loan officers sharply reduce their lending standards. The loan-to-deposit guideline becomes more restrictive when loan demand is unusually strong. Then, to stay at or near the norm, the loan officials have to allocate loans among the many potential borrowers. This policy constraint forces the loan officers to make difficult decisions, but it also enables the bank to maintain some target relationships among the components of its total balance sheet. The senior officials will periodically review this loan-to-deposit constraint and occasionally revise it, but this revision process involves careful policy review—not an ad hoc response to unusually strong loan demand.

## PORTFOLIO COMPOSITION

A bank needs specific diversification policies for its loan portfolio. It may also choose to state policies whereby it commits itself to try to make certain types of loans and to avoid specific types of loans. To illustrate, after careful review of its competitive environment, its current and potential loan demands, and its various resources, a bank specifies some target proportions of its total loan portfolio that will be accounted for by loans to: businesses, consumers, home buyers, and other categories of borrowers. In this way it seeks to maintain a portfolio that is systematically diversified among various categories of loans. Over time there will likely be occasional departures from the target proportions, but these deviations alert senior officers to review and either reaffirm or revise the target proportions.

In its loan policies, a bank may specifically state its commitment to try to make certain types of loans, such as to minority businesspeople and for community improvements. The bank may also state its policy of avoiding specific loans, such as loans for "speculative" purposes.

## INTERNAL LENDING AUTHORITY

A bank's policy statement also stipulates an internal loan-authority system so that senior officers and loan committees do not have to make decisions as to whether to grant or deny each loan application. Senior officials cannot afford the time to make many routine loan decisions, each of which involves small amounts of their bank's funds. Also, a bank's long-term customers expect a prompt response to a loan request; and potential new borrowers, once they have completed a detailed application, similarly expect a prompt decision. Therefore, to expedite loan decisions and to direct senior management resources primarily to complex decisions involving large and/or unusual loan requests, most banks have policy guidelines that require a system of lending authority. A bank's policy statement can require that the senior loan officers design and implement a loan-authority system, subject to review by the directors; or it can specify in some detail the basic components of such a system.

A *loan-authority system* builds on the principle of management by exception, whereby junior officers make routine, noncritical decisions, subject to subsequent review; and they refer nonroutine, potentially critical decisions to a superior officer or committee. Consider an illustrative large bank. It has an extensive network of branches at which it receives many requests for consumer loans. It places junior loan officers, who specialize in consumer loans, in those branches that receive most of the applications. It authorizes these loan officers to receive and quickly evaluate such applications. If a loan applicant meets specific criteria, such as having a satisfactory employment record, financial statement, and credit record, then the junior loan officer can directly approve the request up to a maximum dollar amount, say $5,000. If the application basically looks acceptable but fails to meet one of the specific loan criteria or exceeds the authorized loan limit, then the junior officer is to refer it to a higher officer who has more authority to make nonroutine loans and to make larger loans, say up to $20,000. This superior officer, in turn, reviews the nonroutine request. If it is within his or her lending authority, the officer will deny the request or offer to make the loan, subject to a more complete loan agreement that involves, for example, pledged collateral. If the loan request also exceeds this loan officer's authority or contains unusual elements, the officer will in turn refer it to a superior officer, who will make a decision or refer it to a loan committee for its decision. Thus in a loan-authority system the senior officers receive only the exceptional loan applications for their decision. However, these senior officers do receive periodic reports of all loans made at lower levels and subsequent reports of the bank's collection experience with these loans.

Although the basic features of a loan-decision system are similar throughout its loan operations, a bank generally specifies more flexible criteria and higher limits for its officers who make loans to business firms, farmers, and other major borrowers. Senior loan officers often view it as a symbol of achievement when they can tell their major customers that they, the loan officers, have the authority to commit their bank up to its legal lending limit. However the bank's executive loan committee and its directors' loan committee will quickly review any such large loan.

A loan-authority system also designates certain loan requests as specific exceptions that must be referred to senior officers and/or to the directors' loan committee for their scrutiny and decision. These exceptional loan requests usually include any from a bank's major stockholders, directors, or their close associates. Some of these applicants can apply—or be thought to apply—pressures on loan officers. Also, if granted, such a loan request is subject to subsequent scrutiny by examiners and reporters, especially if the loan becomes a problem. Therefore a bank usually has a firm policy that only its senior officers and directors can make final decisions about these types of sensitive loan requests.

## LOAN TERMS

Often a bank sets policies governing the terms of specific loans. For example, it sets an internal policy that its maximum loan to any one borrower will not exceed 5 percent of its capital and surplus. (This internal policy thus is more restrictive than the 10%-rule that affects most loans by national banks.) Other loan policies that it can set include a:

- maximum length for any loan
- requirement that no loan will be made without the borrower and bank each signing a written repayment schedule
- requirement that certain types of loans cannot exceed a maximum proportion of the appraised value of pledged collateral or a maximum proportion of a borrower's net worth

As with most policies, these are guidelines to which exceptions can be made if approved by senior officials. Although they can set many specific policies concerning loan terms, a bank's senior officials usually choose to specify only several basic policies and then have the senior loan officers develop more specific policies, the results of which will be regularly reviewed by directors and senior officers.

## CREDIT FILES

As a matter of policy, most banks require that their loan departments maintain a credit file on each borrower. A *credit file* contains all the credit information submitted by or about a borrower and also a record of the internal decisions and reviews concerning the borrower. A complete credit file typically contains the following items:

- past and current financial statements and financial projections submitted by the borrower (ideally the statements contain audited figures)
- any outside credit reports about the borrower
- a copy of each loan application, and a copy of the internal analyses and decisions about each application
- a historical record of the borrower's repayment patterns and the profitability of the borrower's overall association with the bank
- a summary of periodic internal reviews of the credit file

Complete credit files are a basic source of management information. They are valuable to loan officers who make subsequent loan decisions about past borrowers, and they are useful to senior officers and directors who monitor and review loan policies and specific decisions.

## SYSTEMATIC LOAN REVIEW

Another policy area is for a bank to specify general procedures to identify and manage potential problem loans. One way is to have a policy requiring systematic monitoring and review of all loans. Any loans, for example, on which scheduled payments are delinquent more than five or ten days are flagged for more complete review by loan officers and loan committees. These officers and committees also are to review any loans in which the borrower violates the loan agreement, for example by not providing timely audited financial statements or by not maintaining the agreed level of collateral or deposits.

A systematic review process sorts out those loans about which the loan officers have little immediate concern and those about which they decide to initiate prompt follow-up action. The senior officers can extend this procedure and require a periodic listing of past-due loans categorized, for example, as those that are past due: less than thirty days, between thirty and sixty days, and over sixty days. For those that are long overdue the bank also needs policy guidelines as to when to initiate legal action and when to charge off specific loans as losses.

## SUMMARY

A bank's loan policies guide the officers who make numerous loan decisions, and they provide standards by which senior officials evaluate specific decisions and portfolio outcomes. Over time senior officials frequently review—and sometimes revise—their bank's loan policies.

Bank loan policies must comply with laws and regulations that prohibit some loans and restrict the terms of many loans. One basic constraint is the 10% lending limit that, despite some exceptions, sets a maximum amount that a national bank can legally lend to any one borrower. This maximum loan limit relates to a bank's size, as measured by its capital and surplus.

A bank's loan policies also have to incorporate a realistic evaluation of the bank's: loan demands, competitive environment, and financial and human resources. Because it can seldom modify these constraints in the short run, a bank has to develop a feasible set of policies consistent with these constraints. Over time, however, it can try to modify some of its constraints, for example, by expanding its size and revising its roster of skilled personnel.

Return-risk analysis provides a framework by which a bank can develop policies concerning the principal components of its loan portfolio. This analytical framework requires a bank to focus on net returns (adjusted for expenses and risks) from various categories of loans and from specific loan proposals.

Each bank develops an organizational structure within which loan decisions are made and reviewed. Directors and senior officers focus on decisions at the policy and review level; and they become involved in loan requests that are classified as "exceptional" because of their size, purpose, or departure from bank policies. The senior officials delegate to loan officers extensive loan authority—subject to bank policies and review procedures.

Each bank's loan policies have to be appropriate for the bank's goals, opportunities, and resources. A bank can compare its individualized policies to a list of general guidelines that include:

- customer relationship
- location of borrower
- size of total loan portfolio
- portfolio composition
- internal lending authority
- loan terms
- credit files
- systematic loan review

Although it identifies the principal areas of a bank's loan policies, this listing does not specify procedures by which each bank can develop its specific numerical policies, such as the size of its total loan portfolio or the diversification guidelines for the portfolio. To set these types of policies, a bank has to conduct individualized analyses and internal discussions, which in turn provide new insights to the participants in the process of stating or revising a specific set of loan policies.

Even with its individualized policies, a bank retains the flexibility to permit carefully documented exceptions, and it periodically reviews and possibly revises some of its policies. It is within this policy framework that the loan officers make their many loan decisions each day.

# 11
# LOAN DECISION
# AND REVIEW SYSTEMS

To implement its loan policies, a bank uses a loan decision and review system that has four principal parts:

- obtain applications
- analyze and negotiate the applications
- monitor and review current and past loans
- revise loan policies and procedures

Exhibit 11-1 schematically summarizes these sequential steps, each of which contains subparts. This flow chart provides the framework for this chapter and for the subsequent chapters about loans to businesses, consumers, and owners of real estate.

## OBTAIN LOAN APPLICATIONS

Most banks do not wait to respond to specific loan requests; instead they market their loan services among two principal categories of borrowers:

- those with comparatively large, specialized loan needs
- those with comparatively small, standardized loan needs

Many business and agricultural borrowers are in the first category; and many householders who want installment loans and bank credit cards are in the second category.

### CROSS SELLING TO CURRENT CUSTOMERS

A bank engages in cross selling when it tries to sell additional banking services to its customers who use only some of its services. Bank officers

**EXHIBIT 11-1**

## Loan Decision and Review Systems: A Single-Loan Framework

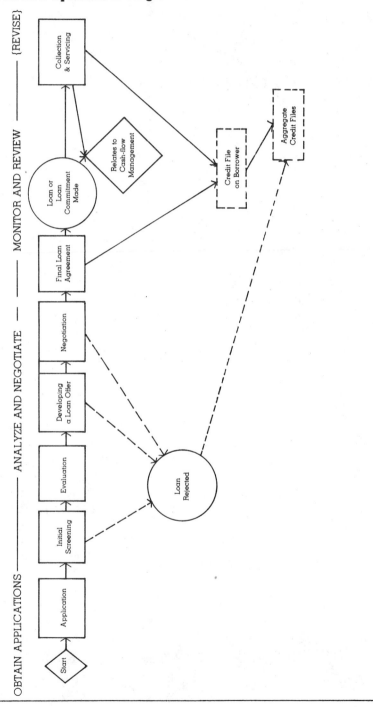

thus engage in cross selling when they tell customers with large deposit balances that the bank would also like to service these customers' loan requests. The officers use such cross selling to develop profitable loan accounts and to strengthen long-run relationships with major depositors.

A bank similarly cross sells various services to its household customers, but in this case it relies more on marketing strategies rather than personal cross selling by bank officers. One procedure is for a bank's marketing personnel to prepare descriptive brochures about the bank's loan services. (Medium-sized and small banks can conveniently choose from among various advertising brochures provided by bank trade associations and by some marketing firms.) The bank places these brochures in its lobby, where depositors are likely to pick up a copy; and it occasionally encloses such brochures with periodic statements mailed to all household depositors. A second procedure is for the marketing personnel to try to identify key characteristics of potentially profitable borrowers and then to direct a cross-sale campaign to these targeted subgroups of depositors.

## SOLICITING LOAN APPLICATIONS FROM NEW CUSTOMERS

To encourage loan applications from people who do not already use some of its services, a bank engages in direct-call programs and advertising.

### Direct-Call Programs

Some of a bank's senior officers personally call on financial officers of large firms that are potential customers of the bank. Although studies indicate that it is difficult to persuade a large firm to switch banks, bank calling officers try to obtain an initial part of a large firm's banking business. One way is for the calling officers to indicate that their bank would like to help service a firm's total loan demand. Once it establishes a foothold relationship, then the bank tries to cross sell additional services to the firm.

Each bank has to evaluate its expected net benefits from direct-call programs. Large money-center banks have specialized officers who call on large firms throughout a wide geographical area. In contrast, small and medium-sized banks focus their direct-call activities on nearby firms, which are large relative to these banks but which are too small to warrant direct calls by large money-center banks. All banks thus focus their direct-call programs on what to them are major potential customers. Seldom do banks use direct call programs to solicit loan applications or other business from potential household accounts.

### Advertising

A bank directs its advertising toward groups of potential customers, some of whom are probable loan applicants.

Toward business firms, a bank portrays its ability and willingness to provide diverse corporate banking services, of which loans are implicitly a major component. In its institutional advertising a bank seldom emphasizes specific loan programs; instead it emphasizes its capacity to develop creative financing packages for most large borrowers.

In contrast, in its retail advertising a bank often cites some of its loan programs, such as installment loans, bank credit cards, and home mortgage loans. A bank can conveniently mass market these types of loans involving standardized terms and procedures.

## INITIAL LOAN APPLICATIONS

An initial loan application comes in one of three principal forms:

- an oral request
- a brief written request
- a detailed written request, perhaps on a standardized application form, that is accompanied by supporting documents.

Bank loan officers are likely to receive oral loan applications from customers who have prior loan relationships with the bank. If they know that such an applicant has an excellent credit record and if the initial application easily meets bank policies, then the loan officers may quickly respond with an oral commitment to make the loan. Even then, however, the loan officers will likely request the applicant to follow up with a written application ''for the record.'' In some cases the loan officers defer making a decision until the applicant submits a written application, possibly with supporting documents.

While oral loan applications and agreements thus are feasible, a bank usually requires written loan applications. For applicants who have previous borrowing records with the bank, the loan officers request the applicants to report any major recent changes in their legal and economic status and to provide some recent financial statements. In contrast, for applicants who have no previous borrowing record with the bank, the loan officers request the applicants to provide detailed supporting information, such as, for corporate borrowers: copies of corporate borrowing resolutions, past financial statements, financial projections, and details about the firm's officers, directors, principal stockholders, banking relationships, and past borrowings from other lenders.

However it is initially submitted, a loan application is for one of three types of loan agreements:

- a specific loan
- a loan commitment that can be either formal or informal
- a loan take-down against a previous loan commitment

When they request a specific loan, applicants soon want to borrow the total amount in order to pay for an item like a car, house, or vacation.

In contrast, some applicants do not immediately need a loan, but they plan to borrow funds in the near future—or at least they want to be confident that they can borrow funds in the near future. Therefore they apply for a *loan commitment,* whereby, a bank agrees to stand ready to meet a borrower's subsequent loan requests, usually up to an agreed maximum amount and only if the borrower continues to meet agreed conditions. A loan commitment can be an informal, moral commitment by a bank; or it can be a written, legally binding commitment, in which case the potential borrower usually has to pay a commitment fee to the bank. Although loan commitments are more prevalent among major borrowers, individuals similarly apply for a loan commitment when they request their bank to provide standby credit, up to an agreed maximum amount, for times when they write checks that exceed the balance in their checking account.

When a major borrower subsequently applies to *take down* (borrow funds under) a prior loan commitment, a loan officer may quickly review and grant the request. As long as the applicant adheres to the terms of the commitment, a loan officer cannot readily deny a takedown that conforms to a prior commitment. In some cases, such as when individuals overdraw their checking account for which they have prearranged for standby credit, a bank automatically honors take-downs that do not exceed the preagreed maximum amount of standby credit.

## ANALYZE AND NEGOTIATE THE LOAN APPLICATIONS

A member of a bank's loan department initially screens each loan application to check whether it is complete, and at times this person has the authority to make or deny some loan requests. If it passes this initial screening, then an application is subject to further evaluation before a loan officer decides either to deny the requested loan or to develop a loan offer that may be subject to negotiation with the applicant. If both the applicant and loan officer agree to terms, then the bank prepares a final loan agreement to be signed by its representative and by the borrower.

When they analyze and negotiate a loan, bank loan officers develop answers to a sequence of questions:

- Does the loan request meet policy guidelines?
- What are the expected returns from this loan?
- What is the default risk of this loan?
- How can the risks be controlled?
- What loan terms, if any, shall we offer?

While these questions are common to all loans, a bank does not commit similar amounts of resources to analyze and negotiate each loan application that it receives. While it commits substantial resources to analyze and negotiate applications for large, unusual loans, a bank often has computer-based systems that help its loan officers to evaluate quickly many applications for small routine loans. When they decide to grant such loans, the loan officers usually offer a standard loan agreement. They seldom negotiate terms with an applicant, who then decides whether or not to accept the standardized loan offer. When it thus standardizes some procedural steps, a bank expedites—but does not omit—answering the five basic questions that underlie a loan offer.

## DOES THE LOAN REQUEST MEET POLICY GUIDELINES?

A loan officer, or an assistant, quickly reviews each loan application to check whether it complies with applicable laws and regulations. As summarized in the previous chapter, a bank cannot make certain loans, such as to its bank examiners; and it faces restrictions as to the maximum amounts and the terms that it can legally offer on some categories of loans, such as those that are subject to FRS margin requirements. To expedite this initial review process, bank loan personnel have to know the applicable laws and regulations, as summarized by their bank's supervisory agencies and/or legal counsel. A loan officer, or an assistant, also checks whether each loan application meets the bank's internal loan policies.

If a requested loan violates either external constraints or internal policies, then a loan officer may promptly decide to reject the request. At times, however, a loan officer decides that a loan request warrants further evaluation. Then, instead of rejecting the proposal, the officer proceeds to analyze the loan's potential returns and risks. If this subsequent analysis indicates that the bank probably should grant the loan, then the officer examines various ways to make it acceptable. For example, if the original proposal violates legal or regulatory constraints, then the loan officer can try to redesign the loan request so that it becomes suitable for the bank. If the original proposal violates internal policies, then the loan officer can similarly try to redesign the loan or recommend that the bank grant the requested loan as an explicit exception to its loan policies.

## WHAT ARE THE EXPECTED RETURNS FROM THIS LOAN?

Most loans involve a specific amount of money that a borrower is to repay, together with a specific rate of interest, according to an agreed schedule. If he or she assumes that such a loan will be repaid as agreed, a loan officer, or an assistant, can quickly compute the expected interest return from the loan and also expected returns for alternative interest rates and repayment schedules. If a proposed loan involves a floating interest rate, then a loan officer has to estimate the expected interest return based on various assumptions concerning future interest rates. Even in these cases, the loan officer can develop probability estimates of the return from a specific loan.

The expected interest return from a specific loan is only one part of a bank's total expected return from granting a loan. A loan officer also tries to estimate the expected benefits from maintaining and/or solidifying a customer relationship. Has the applicant been, or is he or she likely to be, a profitable customer? Does the applicant maintain, or is he or she expected to maintain, large inactive deposits? Is the applicant likely to use other services—such as trust, international banking, or corporate financial services—that generate profits for the bank? Does the applicant have close family, social, or corporate ties with other current or potential customers of the bank? At least implicitly a loan officer tries to weigh the consequences of granting or denying a loan request by a major customer or potential customer. The interest return from such a loan can be a small part of the total return that the bank stands to gain if it makes the loan or forego if it denies the loan request. To thus help their loan officers who service major accounts, some large banks have internal information systems that record the various services used by each major customer and contain numerical estimates of how much each such customer contributes to the bank's profitability over time.

Especially on large loans to major customers, a bank loan officer will sometimes negotiate items that contribute to the estimated total return. To illustrate, a loan officer may offer a major customer at least two choices: the bank will make the requested loan at a 7 percent interest rate if the customer agrees to maintain average demand deposits amounting to 15 percent of the outstanding loan, or the bank will make the requested loan at a 9 percent interest rate if the customer decides not to commit itself to the deposit requirement. The first offer involves a lower explicit interest rate, but it incorporates an implicit return to the bank from the borrower's agreeing to maintain the required deposit balance.

## WHAT IS THE DEFAULT RISK OF THIS LOAN?

When a borrower defaults, a bank collects little, if any, of its money; or it eventually collects most or all of its funds, but usually after long delays and associated administrative and legal costs. Sometimes, to avoid ill will and to protect its creditor position, a bank commits additional resources to help a borrower avoid probable default. It can, for example, negotiate a restructuring of the borrower's debts, and it can agree to accept a reduced interest rate and/or longer repayment period on its outstanding loan. Even among its loans that do not default, a bank incurs some unexpectedly high administrative costs monitoring loans by borrowers who are persistently delinquent in their payments.

A bank knows that any loan involves a probability of default and/or unexpected administrative costs. Therefore it commits substantial resources to try to estimate the default risk of individual loans and of categories of loans.[1]

---

1. In contrast, control of interest-rate risk is primarily a policy decision at the portfolio level. A bank's senior officials regularly review forecasts of interest rates and costs of funds, and they use this information to decide whether to revise the bank's policies concerning its lowest interest rates for various loans. Loan officers then incorporate their bank's interest-rate policies when they evaluate and negotiate specific loans.

Bank loan officers and staff use *credit analysis* to estimate the probability that a proposed loan will become a subsequent collection problem. In medium-sized banks the loan officers do much of the credit analysis associated with their total evaluation of a loan request. In contrast, large banks employ and train people who specialize in credit analysis. These large banks either assign some analysts to each loan group, where they specialize in the group's loans; or else they combine the analysts as a resource pool that is available to each loan group. Potential loan officers of large banks often receive their initial training as analysts.

A credit analyst tries to estimate an applicant's willingness and ability to repay a requested loan. To estimate willingness to repay, an analyst tries to judge the applicant's character. Is the applicant, whether an individual or firm, one whose record is replete with past-due payments and defaults? If the applicant has previously borrowed from the bank, then the analyst reviews the past payment patterns as recorded in the bank's credit files. If the bank has no credit file for the applicant, then the analyst obtains information about the applicant's repayment record with other creditors. As part of the loan application, the potential borrower has to report the names of current and recent creditors; and so the credit analyst calls or writes some of these creditors to verify the applicant's information and to inquire about the creditors' experience with the applicant. In addition, the credit analyst will check the applicant's credit rating, as reported by credit-information services such as local credit bureaus (for individuals) and Dun & Bradstreet (for firms). This reviewing of past credit records helps the analyst to estimate the applicant's apparent commitment to timely repayment of debts.

To estimate an applicant's ability to repay a proposed loan, a credit analyst needs skills as a financial analyst. To evaluate a business or agricultural loan, a credit analyst examines the projected financial statements provided by the applicant. These projections usually include cash budgets and pro forma balance sheets, income statements, and sources and uses of funds statements. First, based on these projections, what is a realistic repayment pattern for possible amounts of bank borrowing? Second, are the projections realistic? Here the analyst has to examine the principal assumptions used by those who prepared the projections. Do relationships assumed in the projections seem valid, especially when compared to relationships calculated from the applicant's past financial statements?

To illustrate, a loan applicant projects substantially higher profits and cash inflows during a coming period. The credit analyst notes that this projection assumes a profit margin (ratio of profit to sales) that is notably higher than the firm's historic profit margin. The analyst also calculates that if the firm maintains its historic margin and does not achieve the higher margin, then the firm's cash inflows will likely be insufficient to repay the loan within the time period proposed by the applicant. The analyst alerts the loan officer to this discrepancy. The loan officer, in turn, raises the question with the applicant, who may have persuasive reasons to support the projected increase in the profit margin. Alternatively, the applicant may revise the projections and request a loan that has a longer repayment period, and the loan officer and credit analyst then evaluate this revised application.

Credit analysts use past and projected financial relationships to estimate whether and how loan applicants can repay their requested loans on schedule. It is tedious and costly for analysts to have to calculate many financial relationships, and so some large banks now have computer programs that their credit analysts use to calculate quickly past relationships and various projected relationships. This way the analysts can focus their attention on the computed relationships.

One official reports how his bank's loan officers and credit analysts use computer programs to analyze rapidly credit proposals and financial statements. One of the programs calculates key financial ratios derived from a firm's last six financial statements. Another program uses an analyst's assumptions to "produce a complete financial forecast for the next five months, quarters or years. The print-out includes a detailed ratio analysis, income statement, sources and application of funds statement and proforma balance sheet. The program focuses on *how much money* is needed, *when* it is required, and how it can best be financed." This program is flexible so that credit analysts also can evaluate what happens to the computations if they vary some key assumptions. The banker also summarizes related programs used by the bank's credit analysts and loan officers, and he emphasizes that it is the loan officers—not the computer—that make final credit decisions. The "computer programs provide the accounting and analytical framework through which the loan officer quantifies his judgments about the components of the borrower's cash flow."[2]

When a loan applicant has previously borrowed from a bank, a credit analyst often reviews the credit file to examine the accuracy of the applicant's past financial projections. If past performance usually corresponds with an applicant's projected performance for the periods, then the analyst attaches greater confidence to the applicant's current projections. In contrast, if the past projections have seldom been achieved, then the analyst will closely scrutinize the applicant's current projections.

While they apply detailed credit analysis to an application for a large specialized loan, banks do not devote similar resources to an application for a consumer loan or home mortgage loan. For these smaller, more standardized loans, banks try to identify some key criteria that they believe will help predict the probable repayment patterns of various applicants. They then incorporate these criteria into informal decision rules (such as, a borrower's monthly mortgage payments should not exceed 25 percent of his or her net monthly income) or into formal credit scoring systems, in which if an applicant scores above a specific numerical cut-off point then he or she is classified as a prime applicant for a consumer loan. Bank loan officers seldom rely on specific decision rules or credit scoring systems; they use

---

2. Leonard N. Druger, "Financial Engineering," *Bankers Monthly Magazine,* May 15, 1969, pp. 24-27.

these tools to expedite their evaluation of applications for small standardized loans.

## HOW CAN THE RISKS BE CONTROLLED?

To control its loan risks, a bank uses risk-control procedures that include:

- covenants
- collateral
- cosigners
- insurance and participation

It applies such procedures to large nonstandardized loans and to many real estate and consumer loans.

Loan officers evaluate and negotiate risk-control procedures for those loan applications that they judge, after initial analysis, to have minor risk. They seldom use these procedures to control the risks of what they judge to be a high-risk loan. While it wants the extra protection of risk controls, a bank prefers not to have to invoke some of these procedures. For example, a bank views a home mortgage as added protection for a basically sound loan. It does not want to incur the costs, including ill will, of having to foreclose on a home mortgage loan.

### Covenants

A written loan agreement contains convenants whereby a borrower commits itself to do or not do specific future actions. Covenants enable a lender to strengthen its position *vis a vis* a borrower and possibly a borrower's other creditors.

**Updated Financial Statements**   A basic covenant is when a borrower agrees to provide specific financial statements at specific intervals during the life of the loan. For large borrowers these periodic statements include audited balance sheets and income statements and also updated pro forma statements and cash budgets. For individuals the statements may involve occasional updates of a financial profile that was required when they applied for the loan. A related covenant is that, in addition to the regular statements, the borrower agrees to inform the bank promptly of any significant changes in its financial position or outlook. These covenants help provide credit analysts and loan officers with timely information about events that can jeopardize their bank's creditor position.

**Adherence to a Written Repayment Schedule**   This covenent has a borrower agree to adhere to a written schedule of repayment dates. If a borrower persistently makes late payments and, especially, does not alert the loan officer to this probable tardiness, then the lender gains new insights about the borrower's willingness or ability to make timely payments. The lender can review the loan relationship and insist that the borrower adhere to the repayment agreement, and/or it can use this information when it next evaluates a loan request by the borrower.

**Compensating Balances**   Under this covenant a borrower agrees to maintain specific levels of deposits at the lending bank. A borrower, for example, agrees to maintain average demand deposits amounting to 15 percent of the outstanding loan. If this borrower would not customarily maintain this level of deposits, then the bank obtains a higher total return from this arrangement than it would if the loan were made at the same interest rate but without the deposit requirement. Compensating balances also are a risk-control procedure. If a borrower defaults, then the lending bank uses its right of *offset*, whereby it uses the borrower's deposit(s) at the bank to offset the borrower's loan from the bank. If, for example, a defaulting borrower owes a bank $100,000 and has a deposit of $15,000 with the bank, then, after offsetting these two items the bank's net remaining claim is $85,000. The bank thus protects at least part of its loan against claims by other creditors of the defaulting borrower.

**Constraints on Subsequent Financial Transactions**   Especially in a large loan to a corporate borrower, a loan officer may request that the final loan agreement contain covenants whereby, for example, during the life of the loan the borrowing firm agrees to:

- not pay dividends that exceed its future earnings and some dollar amount of its retained earnings
- not increase salaries and bonuses of its senior officers
- not sell or pledge major assets of the firm or merge the firm
- not incur total debt in excess of a specific proportion of the firm's net worth
- maintain a specific minimum ratio of short-term assets to short-term liabilities
- maintain adequate amounts of insurance

There are many variants of these covenants, a principal objective of which is to protect the bank's claim against the firm's assets and future cash flows and to reduce the chances that the firm will become illiquid or insolvent. The bank can, however, waive such covenants for a specific loan agreement.

**Acceleration Clause**   So that it can enforce the other covenants in a loan agreement, a bank often insists on an acceleration clause whereby, if a borrower violates other covenants, then the bank can insist that the entire loan amount become immediately due and payable. This powerful clause enables a bank to take strong action. If a violation occurs, a bank retains the right to decide whether and when to invoke the acceleration clause. Because of the potency of this sanction, most borrowers plan their affairs to avoid triggering such an acceleration clause.

## Collateral

To secure a loan, a loan officer can request a borrower to pledge collateral such as marketable securities, accounts receivable, inventories, and/or buildings. Collateral helps a lender to control its risk in two ways. One, a borrower knows that if it defaults then it forfeits its claim to the pledged assets—except to the extent that the realizable dollar amount of the pledged assets exceeds the debt to the lender. If the lender sells the pledged assets and does not receive enough money to pay off the defaulted loan, then the borrower continues to owe the lender for the remainder of the unpaid loan. Two, the lender has a secured claim against the pledged assets. Without this specific security, if a borrower defaults, then a lender is likely to be one of many general creditors who share in the final settlement of the defaulter's financial affairs.

A bank seeks to maintain the value of collateral that secures its loans. The dollar value of marketable securities fluctuates over time, and so a bank insists that a borrower who pledges such collateral must agree to maintain a minimum dollar amount of such collateral as a multiple of the loan. If the value of the collateral subsequently falls below this minimum multiple (such as 1.5 times), the bank will call on the borrower to provide additional collateral and/or reduce the amount of the loan. Similarly, if it accepts a house as collateral for a mortgage loan, a bank has the borrower agree to maintain adequate insurance and to pay the property taxes when due.[3]

## Cosigners

Sometimes a loan officer suggests that an applicant have its proposed loan cosigned by another party who then is also responsible for timely repayment of the loan. The cosigner should be a firm or person with an impeccable credit record.

To illustrate, a loan officer receives a loan application from a corporate affiliate of a large holding company that has an excellent credit record. The loan officer evaluates the affiliate's financial record and projections and concludes that the proposed loan involves little risk and promises an acceptable return. Yet, if for some reason the affiliate fails to repay its proposed loan, the bank will have no recourse against the parent holding company, which is a separate legal entity. Therefore the loan officer asks the affiliate whether it will have its parent firm cosign the loan agreement. As an inducement, the loan officer may offer to have the bank accept a lower total return if the parent firm cosigns the loan. Similarly, when they evaluate loan applications from individuals, loan officers note some cases where they will: make a loan *only if* it is cosigned (to minors, for example, who are related to good customers of the bank), or negotiate other terms *if* a loan is cosigned.

---

3. As additional protection, a lending bank may request or insist that the borrower enter into an escrow arrangement whereby the borrower's monthly loan repayments include amounts that will service the insurance payments and/or taxes on the property. The bank then holds these supplemental amounts in an escrow account, from which it then has the responsibility to pay, as the homeowner's agent, the periodic insurance and tax bills.

Most banks are reluctant to use cosignatures as a risk-control procedure, especially for loans to individuals. Even if a loan officer carefully explains a cosigner's responsibilities, a person may quickly cosign a loan agreement of a relative or friend. Subsequently, if the borrower does not meet the terms of the loan agreement, the bank can turn to the cosigner. However, the bank may be reluctant to do so if such action is likely to alienate a cosigner who is a valued customer who may have misunderstood his or her potential liability to repay the loan.

## Insurance and Participations

As another risk-control procedure, a bank can arrange to have some loans fully or partly insured by government agencies or private firms. If a borrower defaults on an insured loan, the lending bank has recourse against the insurer, who then has to honor its contractual commitment to pay the insured portion of the loan.

In contrast to insured loans, loan participations involve no recourse to a third party if a borrower fails to meet the terms of its loan. Banks arrange loan participations among themselves, as part of their correspondent relationships, as well as with governmental and other nonbank organizations.

**Loan Insurance Programs** To encourage loans that in its judgment serve national interests, Congress has created federal agencies that lend funds and that often insure loans or participate in loans by private lenders. For example, to promote foreign trade, Congress established the Export-Import (Ex-Im) Bank of Washington; and to promote small businesses, Congress established the Small Business Administration (SBA). These two federal agencies are representative of many that directly lend funds, insure, or participate in private loans to qualifying borrowers. As direct lenders, these federal agencies somewhat compete with private lenders; but as insurers and participants they also cooperate with private lenders. A more recent financing program is the Federal Student Loan Program, which insures some student loans made by private lenders.

Federal agencies also help to finance home ownership. Among their other activities, the Federal Housing Administration (FHA) and the Veterans Administration (VA) have mortgage insurance programs. Also some private firms, such as Mortgage Guaranty Insurance Corporation, have programs to insure home mortgage loans.

Most insured loans carry a lower promised return than do similar noninsured loans. At times, the stated interest rate is less. Even when the stated interest rate is nominally similar, the lender may have less discretion to request other terms, such as compensating balances, that can boost its expected total return. Also, other things equal, if the lender has to pay the insurance premium, this cost reduces the net return that can be expected from an insured loan.

To participate in loan-insurance programs, a bank incurs costs to have some employees keep informed about new programs and about changing details of existing programs. In a medium-sized bank, several loan officers likely focus on programs that relate to their bank's real estate, small business, and, possibly, student loans. A large bank may also assign several specialists the task to keep specifically informed about the variety and content of numerous loan-insurance programs.

Also, a bank often incurs incremental costs to process insured loans. To satisfy the requirements of a potential insurer, a lending bank has to obtain detailed information from and about applicants; and it has to provide multiple copies of special forms to the insurer. Also, the lender usually has to warrant that an applicant meets all the qualifications for certain federally insured loans. If a borrower falls behind in its payments, then the lender has to coordinate its subsequent collection activities with those of the insurer. Although federal agencies presumably try not to impose burdensome processing costs on private lenders, private loan insurers emphasize their abilities to expedite loan decisions and control processing costs.

In summary, a bank has to evaluate whether loan-insurance programs provide risk reduction benefits that exceed their associated costs. Unless it can spread the specialized administrative and processing costs over enough insured loans, it is questionable whether a bank should have its loan officers make occasional insured loans. Therefore, at the policy level, a bank should periodically reevaluate whether to continue and/or initiate its participation in specific loan-insurance programs, and if so, what resources it will commit to such programs.

**Loan Participations**   Banks of all sizes use loan participation agreements as a way to share the risks and returns of specific loans. If such a participated loan defaults, then each participant limits its potential loss to its agreed share of the total loan. In theory, each participant is to receive, independently evaluate, and periodically review, all the credit information applicable to a loan in which it participates. In practice, each participant seldom does all these things. When it participates in a large corporate loan originated by its major correspondent bank, a small or medium-sized bank often defers to the lead bank's judgment, supplemented by some cursory review of the loan. Similarly, to some extent a large city bank may rely on the record and judgment of outlying smaller banks in whose loans it participates.

A bank that originates a loan participation seeks to avoid possibly tarnishing its reputation and jeopardizing future relationships with its correspondent banks. Therefore, although it seldom has any legal liability to its coparticipants, a large bank will often go to great lengths to try to salvage a problem loan that it has previously originated. Although there is no recourse agreement, sometimes it will buy back the loan participations—especially those held by its smaller correspondent banks.[4]

---

4. Robert Morris Associates, the national association of bank loan and credit officers, interprets applicable national banking laws and regulations to provide "that any suggestion of a 'recourse provision,' that is, a provision suggesting that the purchasing bank could subsequently 'sell back' its portion of a participated loan to the originating bank, would cause the interbank transaction to be regarded by the regulators as a 'borrowing/lending' transaction between the two banks subject to the debt restrictions of 12 U.S.C. 82 and the lending limits restrictions of 12 U.S.C. 84." "Guidelines for Upstream Downstream Correspondent Bank Loan Participations," Robert Morris Associates, 1975.

## WHAT LOAN TERMS, IF ANY, SHALL WE OFFER?

Once he or she has analyzed a proposed loan's returns and risks, a loan officer has to develop a negotiating strategy and anticipate how the bank's senior officials will evaluate the final loan decision.

### Preparing to Negotiate

Loan officers have to prepare to negotiate some terms of major loan offers that they develop for valued customers or potential customers.

As one strategy, a loan officer can develop an initial offer and also some contingency offers that incorporate different loan terms. If the applicant accepts the initial offer, then the loan officer does not have to fall back on the contingency offers. If, instead, the applicant objects to some terms of the initial offer, then the loan officer is prepared to introduce and negotiate some alternative loan terms.

As a second strategy, a loan officer can include some alternative terms as part of the initial offer so that the applicant and the bank can then negotiate these proposed alternatives. Even in this case, a loan officer will want to have some contingency plans by which to plan a response to alternative terms that the applicant may request. In particular, the loan officer needs to plan ahead as to which terms are negotiable and which, if any, are nonnegotiable.

To determine the extent to which they should develop contingency loan terms, loan officers try to estimate the probability that an applicant will accept an initial loan offer. If an applicant is a valued customer with a past record of negotiating loan terms, then a loan officer carefully prepares some contingency offers. Moreover, the officer designs an attractive initial offer, so that the applicant has little incentive to seek better terms from a competing bank.

Loan officers also stand ready to negotiate the terms of some home mortgage loans and consumer loans. To illustrate, a bank stands ready to make some home mortgage loans, subject to the following guidelines:

- applicant must be a current customer or a potentially profitable customer
- interest rate of 9%
- minimum downpayment of 20%
- maximum maturity of 25 years

This bank, however, allows its loan officers some flexibility to modify these terms, especially in response to an application by a highly valued customer. In such a case a loan officer will prepare to offer a lower rate, especially if the applicant agrees to a comparatively large downpayment and/or short maturity. The loan officer will immediately alert the applicant to these negotiable terms if, in the officer's judgment, the applicant will reject the initial standardized terms and promptly apply to a competing firm that offers more flexible terms on such loans.

### Negotiating a Final Loan Agreement

Loan officers also try to anticipate how their senior officials will evaluate specific loan offers and outcomes. These senior officials often oversee and participate in negotiations that involve major customers and/or in decisions that potentially depart from the bank's policies. Over time these officials also review each loan officer's record of loan decisions. Loan officers therefore try to understand the criteria by which these senior officials monitor and review loan decisions.

If a bank's directors and senior officers emphasize avoidance of loan losses, the loan officers will focus their evaluations and negotiations on potential risks and risk-control procedures. If they have even minor doubt about a specific loan, the loan officers will probably reject it. Given their perception of how their performance will be reviewed, these loan officers will choose not to make even some potentially high-return loans that involve only a slight chance of loss.

Within limits senior officials can use the granting of loans as a strategy to build their bank. While no bank emphasizes loan volume regardless of the consequences, some banks reportedly have had decision rules whereby their loan officers must justify why they propose to reject—or have rejected— specific loans. In such a decision environment, loan officers are likely to design initial and contingency offers that loan applicants will find difficult to refuse.

Instead of emphasizing either loss avoidance or the granting of loans, a third approach is for senior officials to use risk-return criteria to evaluate a loan officer's performance. They then try to assess whether a loan officer's loans are likely to result in high total returns when adjusted for risk. To estimate future results, they are likely to measure, over time, the total returns from an officer's past loans—after appropriate adjustments for realized and potential loan losses.

When it makes a loan or formal loan commitment, a bank has its staff prepare a final loan agreement for signing by the borrower(s) and by appropriate bank officers. One copy of this agreement goes into the credit file for this loan account and another copy, or summary, goes to the bank's loan servicing and collection unit(s).

## LOAN MONITORING AND REVIEW SYSTEMS

A loan application—after possible negotiations—has one of the three basic outcomes:

- loan granted
- loan rejected by the bank
- loan offer rejected by applicant

Whichever the outcome, the loan officer summarizes it for the bank's records, which provide the information base for subsequent review of the bank's loan policies and procedures.

In order to alert senior officials to potential problem loans, a bank has monitoring systems for its outstanding loans. Bank examiners and outside auditors also periodically review a bank's loan portfolio and make estimates as to the likelihood that specific loans will default.

## MONITORING LOAN PAYMENTS AND COLLATERAL

Most banks have systematic procedures for collecting loan payments. One procedure is to have especially designated note windows, at which tellers receive and record note payments and also regularly review their ledgers in order to identify past-due loans. In addition, many banks have automated part of their loan collection activities.

Many banks, when they make a consumer installment loan, provide the borrower with a booklet of encoded coupons, each of which states the amount of loan payment that is due by a specific date. For example, if a loan is to be repaid in monthly installments of $100 each over a two-year period, the bank gives to the borrower a booklet that contains 24 coupons, each of which is sequentially dated in one-month intervals, beginning with the first installment. Each month the borrower then mails to the bank, or gives to any teller, the appropriate coupon together with the scheduled payment. Each coupon is encoded in machine-readable symbols so that the bank's data-processing system can automatically record receipt of the scheduled payment.

Some banks have further automated their collection procedures, especially for loans created when household depositors write checks against a line of credit associated with their checking account. Often these check-credit loan agreements provide for repayment procedures whereby the borrowers authorize their bank to debit their account directly for an agreed minimum monthly repayment on the outstanding balance of the loan. In addition, the borrowers usually have the flexibility to pay more than this minimum preauthorized repayment.

Automation not only helps control costs of collecting and processing loan payments, it also expedites the monitoring of loan payments and the preparation of reports for senior officials. In banks where the loan records are on computer files, staff specialists can program the dates when loan payments are due from each borrower. Then, each day or so, the bank runs a computer program that matches the list of payments due by that day against a list of loan payments actually received. (For installment loans, a list of payments received can be readily derived from the encoded coupons.) Such a program thus identifies borrowers who have not made their scheduled payments on time, and this list of past-due borrowers is sent to senior officers for their review and action. If it does not have in-bank computer capability, a medium-sized bank has access to such automated monitoring systems from large correspondent banks or other firms that provide data-processing services. If it decides not to automate at least part of this monitoring activity, then a bank assigns an employee the regular task of manually updating a list of past-due loans.

Banks have been slower to automate their large loans, many of which involve nonstandardized repayment provisions. Yet a survey of automated commercial loan systems reports that their major functions center on loan accounting and servicing. These automated loan accounting systems perform functions such as:

- "posting transactions to loan and borrower records
- accruing interest
- billing principal and interest due
- providing information on loan and borrower status and history
- reporting maturities, past-due loans and other exceptions
- preparing basic operating, accounting, and auditing reports
- and facilitating preparation of various loan portfolio breakdowns (by rate and industry, for example)"[5]

These automated systems promptly alert loan officers to their borrowers whose repayments depart from the agreed schedule, and they also alert senior officers and directors to broader developments in the total loan portfolio.

Banks also use systematic procedures to monitor the market value of securities they hold as collateral for loans. One way is to prepare a list of the specific securities associated with each collateralized loan. An assigned employee periodically checks the market value of each pledged security and calculates whether the dollar amount of pledged collateral has declined to a point below that specified in the loan agreement. The employee then prepares a report listing all undercollateralized loans. (While its procedures require periodic updates of the market prices of its pledged collateral, a bank will require more frequent updates during periods when market prices are falling rapidly.)

A bank can use computer technology to automate its monitoring of loan collateral. It can design a system in which it stores a list of each loan's collateral, if any. Then the system matches these lists against a frequently updated master file of recent market prices for many securities and automatically flags those loan accounts in which the value of collateral has fallen below some minimum programmed level. Large banks, especially, can examine the net benefits of using such an automated system to monitor their collateralized loans.

## USING CREDIT FILES

Bank credit files, if complete, contain the following types of information about each borrower:

5. A. Van R. Halsey, "An Automated System for Commercial Loans," *The Magazine of Bank Administration,* November 1971, pp. 22-25, 81.

- financial statements and projections submitted by the borrower
- credit reports, if any, from external sources
- copies of each loan application
- internal summaries of analyses, contingency plans, negotiations, and outcomes for each application
- historical records of a borrower's repayment patterns, adherence to terms of loan agreements, and total profitability for the bank
- summaries of internal reviews of the credit file

Before they respond to a previous borrower's current credit request, loan officers and members of loan committees refer to the borrower's credit file, which is continually updated for an active loan account. Senior officers and directors also use reports derived from credit files to review past loan decisions, strategies, and policies.

Some parts of credit files can be stored in computer systems and then retrieved in the form of summary reports about specific loan accounts and about categories of loans. Some automated systems, for example, summarize key attributes of a customer's relationship with the bank, such as its: loan balances over time; repayment delinquencies, if any; average deposit balances and volatility; and estimated overall profitability. Some automated systems reportedly are also able to:

- forecast cash flows for the loan portfolio and its subcomponents
- summarize unused loan commitments
- report the "profitability of deposit and loan relationships by borrower, related borrowers, loan officers and division"[6]

In banks where credit files are not as automated, senior officers request their staff members to prepare manually similar reports and forecasts based on information from noncomputer-based credit files.

## BANK EXAMINER LOAN REVIEW SYSTEMS

Each bank is subject to unscheduled visits by federal and/or state field examiners. During their visit these examiners review a bank's loan policies and procedures, and they also scrutinize many of the specific loans.

### Reviewing Loan Policies and Procedures

Because they cannot afford the time to scrutinize each loan, field examiners initially divide a bank's loan portfolio into at least four basic categories:

- installment
- home mortgage
- collateralized
- other, primarily commercial and industrial

---

6. Halsey, "An Automated System for Commercial Loans," p. 24.

For each category, the examiners review the bank's general loan policies and procedures.

Within each category, the examiners then review:

- all past-due loans
- all previously criticized loans
- all large loans, relative to a bank's capital
- a sample of the remaining loans[7]

The examiners check whether these selected loans comply with applicable laws and regulations, and they estimate the likelihood that the loans will result in losses for the bank. In this review process, the examiners use information contained in the bank's credit files. While they thus partly rely on the quality of the credit files, the examiners have no direct knowledge of the borrowers; and they use their analytical experience from examining various banks over time. From these perspectives, the examiners give a semiautonomous evaluation of a bank's loans.

Most banks have granted many small standardized loans to consumers and homeowners, and so examiners focus their evaluation on a bank's policies and procedures for such loans. For example, what is the maximum amount that a bank will lend as a proportion of a borrower's income and/or net worth? Also, what have been the trends in delinquencies and repossessions among these loans of a bank? If they are satisfied with the procedures and trends, the examiners then review small samples of these loans.

When they review collateralized loans, field examiners also focus on a bank's policies and procedures, such as: what types of collateral it accepts, how much it will lend as a proportion of various forms of pledged collateral, and how it monitors and enforces its collateral requirements. Then the examiners focus on a sample of collateralized loans to check for possible violations of laws and regulations (such as FRS margin requirements) and to verify whether the bank adheres to its collateral policies and procedures.

Field examiners focus their detailed attention on the other loans, especially those to businesses, farmers, and major real-estate owners and developers. Many of these loans are large relative to a bank's total loan portfolio and its capital accounts, so that possible losses from these loans can jeopardize a bank's solvency. Therefore examiners take large samples of these loans and carefully scrutinize them for signs of pending problems. For each sampled loan, the examiners check whether the bank has a complete

---

7. Some bank supervisory agencies are experimenting with the use of management-science techniques to help guide allocation of examiner time among banks and within banks. One researcher reports his design and testing of an analytical system by which to select loans for examiner evaluation, and he concludes that "a test of two simple versions of the model indicates that the model provides a significant improvement over current selection methods." Also, he points out that "the combination of a linear programming model and a sampling plan can also be used for bank auditing and other financial audits, where, for practical purposes, only a stratified sample of all the accounts can be verified." Yair E. Orgler, "Selection of Bank Loans for Evaluation: An Analytical Approach," *The Journal of Finance,* March 1969, pp. 75-80.

and timely credit file on the borrower. They then review this file to check for possible violations of a loan agreement, such as when a borrower fails to provide audited financial statements according to schedule. The examiners use the information in the credit files to help them evaluate the likelihood of problems and eventual losses from specific loans.

### Classifying Sampled Loans

The examiners judge the default risk of each sampled loan. If, in their judgment, a loan's default risk is high, the examiners classify the loan as:

- substandard
- doubtful
- loss

A *substandard* loan involves high default risk and so should be carefully monitored to avoid possible, eventual loss. A *doubtful* loan has a higher probability of some loss, the exact amount of which cannot be confidently estimated. (Examiners use this classification sparingly.) A *loss* loan is one that the examiners judge to involve imminent, measurable loss; and so the examiners expect the bank to write off promptly such a loan loss.

To measure the accuracy of loan criticisms by bank examiners, a researcher focuses on large business loans made by a sample of national banks in New England. As one test, the researcher traces the subsequent outcomes for a sample of criticized loans. Only about 40 percent of these criticized loans result in subsequent losses or criticisms. Yet this outcome is not surprising, because "examiner criticisms may reduce the probability of default since, as a rule, the management of the bank is expected to take remedial actions with regard to these criticized loans." The author cites some evidence that is consistent with this view. As a second test, the researcher reverses the time sequence and investigates whether a sample of loans that actually defaulted had been previously criticized by examiners. Among these sample loans, the examiners had previously classified 64 percent as "substandard" and/or "doubtful." (In contrast, for a separate sample of loans paid in full, only 1 percent had been previously criticized.) The researcher concludes that his "study, though not definitive, suggests that bank examiner criticisms on business loans are reasonably accurate."[8]

In discussions with a bank's senior officers, the field examiners cite the loans that they propose to criticize. The examiners thus give the officers an opportunity to respond to the initial criticisms. If the officers then

---

8. Hsiu-Kwang Wu, "Bank Examiner Criticisms, Bank Loan Defaults, and Bank Loan Quality," *The Journal of Finance,* September 1969, pp. 697-705. Another study reports similar results for a sample of banks in the Tenth (Kansas City) Federal Reserve District. It concludes that bank examiners "appear to catch a large portion of the problem loans in the pool of loans that they examine" and that they also succeed "in categorizing bank loans according to their relative risk of default." Kenneth Spong and Thomas Hoenig, "Bank Examination Classifications and Loan Risk," *Economic Review* (Federal Reserve Bank of Kansas City), June 1979, pp. 15-25.

demonstrate why some of the initially criticized loans should not be so classified, the field examiners are likely to revise or withdraw their initial criticism of these specific loans.

After its examiners thus visit a bank, the supervisory agency sends its examination report—which contains lists of classified loans—to the bank's board of directors; and it may also schedule a meeting between the directors and the examiners who evaluated the bank. A supervisory agency expects the bank to respond constructively to its examination report. Therefore the directors initially review the report and ask the senior officers to comment on its specific criticisms and suggestions. Concerning the classified loans, the directors ask the loan officers whether they agree with the examiners' evaluations; and, if the answer is yes, the directors expect follow-up actions to reduce the likelihood of eventual losses from the loans classified as "substandard" or "doubtful." Also, they ask the senior officers whether they propose to have the bank charge off the loans classified as "loss." In cases where they conclude that, in their judgment, a loan should not have been so classified, the officers and directors prepare a rebuttal of the examiners' criticism. Thus a bank's loan review process incorporates the semiautonomous reviews by bank examiners.

## MANAGING PROBLEM LOANS AND LOAN LOSSES

No matter how carefully its loan officers evaluate and try to control a loan's default risk, a bank expects some of its loans to become problems, of which some, in turn, will result in losses. Therefore, once a loan is identified as a problem or as a potential problem, bank officials face two basic decisions:

- How shall the bank try to avoid or limit possible loss?
- When shall the bank charge off the loan, and how?

Exhibit 11-2 summarizes the principal elements of these sequential decisions.

Each bank monitors its outstanding loans in order to identify promptly loans in which a borrower fails, for example, to make scheduled payments, provide timely financial statements, or maintain agreed financial ratios. Instead of waiting until such adverse events occur, some banks monitor their major borrower's financial statements in order to detect pending problems; and some researchers report their experiments with statistical early warning systems that help alert a lender to significant deterioration in a borrower's financial condition. In addition, its examiners' listing of classified loans provides a bank with additional—or at least confirming—information about its problem loans.

Once they identify a loan as a problem, bank loan officers act promptly to try to prevent loss or at least to mitigate the possible loss. Often they have to decide whether to attempt a work-out solution or to enforce their bank's position, for example by invoking an acceleration clause. The loan officers

**EXHIBIT 11-2**

**Loan Charge-Offs and Loan Losses: A Framework**

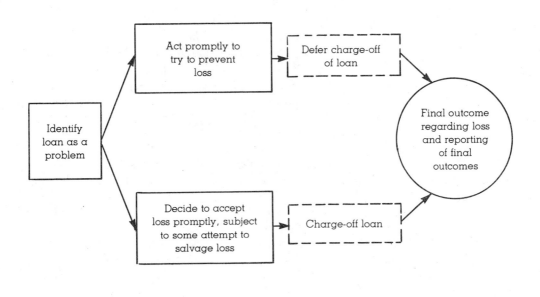

try to predict which course of action is more likely to avoid loss and how each course of action is likely to affect the borrower and the borrower's employees, community, and other creditors. Often the officers opt for a work-out approach, and some large banks have teams of specialists who develop and implement work-out solutions for problem loans. Yet if it attempts a work-out solution, a bank will likely have to allocate costs of work-out specialists and lawyers; and, as part of the eventual solution, it may have to accept a lower return and/or lend additional money to the problem borrower. Unless it is confident that the expected benefits from attempting a work-out solution will exceed its potential additional costs, a bank will likely decide to promptly accept the loss to date and then try to salvage the loss, probably through legal actions.[9]

---

9. An official of a large money-center bank emphasizes "that the normal desire of banks is to work things out with problem customers short of bankruptcy proceedings. This requires a great deal of cooperation between people with different interests, and it has to be recognized that reasonable accommodation between creditors and security holders cannot always be achieved. Distasteful though it is, recourse to the bankruptcy courts is sometimes the only way of equitably apportioning loss." Ellmore C. Patterson, "Credit Quality: Lessons of Recent Experience," *The Morgan Guaranty Survey,* June 1976, pp. 11-14.

Most banks have a balance-sheet account, *reserve for loan losses,* against which they charge off loans and to which they credit recoveries from previously charged-off loans. This procedure assumes that a bank is certain to incur occasional loan losses but that the timing of such losses is uncertain. Therefore, by using reserve accounting a bank can systematically recognize its expected losses as an ongoing business expense instead of having to recognize them only when they occur, often at irregular intervals and in irregular amounts.

Since 1921 federal tax laws and regulations have permitted a bank to deduct from its before-tax income an expense item, *provision for loan losses,* and to transfer this amount to its reserve for loan losses. Unless its actual losses exceed this accounting deduction, a bank thus shields some income from federal taxes. To control possible losses of revenue, the Internal Revenue Service (IRS) for many years has set guidelines as to the maximum loan-loss reserve that a bank can create via deductions of before-tax income, and the maximum and minimum amounts that a bank can transfer to its reserve in any one year. A bank is free to use its after-tax income to build up a larger loan-loss reserve, but few banks choose to do so.

The Tax Reform Act of 1969 contains new loan-loss reserve guidelines that are to be sequentially implemented until 1988. Beginning in 1988, "banks will be limited to a tax-free reserve no larger, as a fraction of their eligible loans, than the ratio of uncollected loans to eligible loans on an average basis over the prior six years."[10] *Eligible loans* in this computation are a bank's total loans minus:

- "loans to banks
- certain loans secured by deposits
- loans guaranteed by the United States and instrumentalities thereof
- loans evidenced by securities
- loans of Federal funds
- commercial paper including short-term notes which may be purchased on the open market."[11]

Until this six-year average procedure becomes effective in 1988, a bank's maximum loan-loss reserve is 1.2 percent of eligible loans until 1982, at which time this maximum becomes 0.6 percent.

Changes incorporated in the Tax Reform Act of 1969 will likely affect the banking system and individual banks. One study reviews various functions that loan-loss reserves can perform, and concludes that "the reserve level to be provided by the 1969 legislation will not serve to protect the public against banking difficulties arising from unexpectedly large loan

---

10. Stuart A. Schweitzer, "Bank Loan Losses: A Fresh Perspective," *Business Review* (Federal Reserve Bank of Philadelphia), September 1975, pp. 18-29.

11. *The Adequacy of Bad Debt Reserves for Banks: A Preliminary Study,* a study by Carter H. Golembe Associates, Inc., prepared for the Trustees of the Banking Research Fund, Association of Reserve City Bankers, 1972.

losses, nor would it serve to encourage banks to adopt the kind of innovative lending policies which adequacy of capital and reserves should make possible."[12] From the viewpoint of an individual bank, its future transfers to loan-loss reserves will be constrained, especially if its loan-loss reserve already is at its currently permissible maximum. To illustrate, under the previous guidelines a bank built up its loss reserve to about 2.4 percent of its loans. Its new maximum is 1.2 percent. Therefore it cannot transfer funds to build up its reserve until—because of loan expansion and/or loan losses charged against the reserve—its current percentage declines to the new (lower) permissible maximum.

Within the applicable legal and regulatory guidelines, a bank can adopt a "conservative" or "aggressive" approach to provide for possible loan losses.[13] Under the conservative approach, a bank builds up and maintains a large reserve against which it can charge large, even if unlikely, losses. This bank deducts large amounts for its provision for loan losses (a pretax expense) and transfers these amounts to its reserve.[14] Other items equal, this higher expense reduces its tax bill during the period when it builds up the reserve. If this annual expense item exceeds the bank's probable loss experience, then the bank indefinitely defers some taxes; and it has a large reserve against which it can charge off subsequent realized losses without directly charging these losses against its earnings or, possibly, capital accounts. Over time, this approach is likely to dampen possible fluctuations in the bank's reported earnings. In contrast, under the aggressive approach, a bank deducts comparatively small amounts of pretax earnings and thus reports lower expenses and higher earnings during these periods. It foregoes some potential tax deferrals, and it builds up a comparatively small loan-loss reserve. This bank may then face occasional years in which its loan losses exceed its reserves, in which case it will have to charge this excess amount directly against its reported earnings for that year.[15] Other things equal, this bank's reported earnings will be more volatile than those of a conservative

---

12. *The Adequacy of Bad Debt Reserves for Banks: A Preliminary Study,* p. 20. A sequel study provides a detailed analysis of the loan-loss provisions of the Tax Reform Act of 1969, examines initial bank experience with the new provisions, and recommends changes in the Act. *The Tax Treatment of Loan Losses of Banks: The View from 1977,* a study by Golembe Associates, Inc., prepared for the Trustees of the Banking Research Fund, Association of Reserve City Bankers, 1977.

13. This conservative-aggressive dichotomy follows that used by John M. Godfrey, "Accounting for Loan Charge-Offs," *Monthly Review* (Federal Reserve Bank of Atlanta), August 1975, pp. 118-123. As an appendix to this article, the author provides a numerical example of how a "conservative" and an "aggressive" bank each provides for loan losses. Also Howard B. Silverman, "Judgment Considerations in Determining the Adequacy of the Loan Loss Reserve: A Banker's Point of View," *The Magazine of Bank Administration,* April 1978, pp. 26-29.

14. A bank's loan-loss reserve technically has three components: valuation portion, deferred income tax portion, and contingency portion. Schweitzer provides a brief summary and illustration of these components.

15. Godfrey reports (p. 122) that "at 116 [Sixth Federal Reserve] District banks, 1974 loan losses exceeded the amount of reserves held at the beginning of the year. . . . As a result, these banks had to make large provisions during the year in order to maintain some reserves for future losses. In many respects, these banks more closely approximated the behavior of the 'aggressive bank' because their reserves were not sufficient to cover their bad loans."

bank that has systematically built up a large reserve against which it can charge unusual loan losses.

In addition to its basic decisions as to the level of loan-loss reserves it wants to maintain over time, within limits a bank can control the timing and magnitude of loan losses and recoveries that it enters against the reserve. A bank has to have a strong case not to promptly charge off a loan classified as "loss" by its examiners, but it has more leeway on loans classified as "doubtful" or "substandard" and on loans that the bank itself views as problems. A "conservative" bank, especially one with a large loan-loss reserve, may decide to charge off immediately any loan that it views as a problem. If and when it receives payment on the loan or no longer views it as a problem, the bank then treats this amount as a recovery. In contrast, a bank without a large reserve is likely to try to defer some large charge-offs if it believes that it has a reasonable probability of working out these loans. At some point, however, a bank's supervisory agencies will insist that the bank no longer defer some of these charge-offs.

In contrast to a bank's senior officials and examiners, stockholders and interested citizens have little information about the magnitude of a bank's problem loans. These people can review a bank's periodic statements that report the amounts of: loan-loss reserves, provisions for loan losses (expense item), and charge-offs and recoveries from the loan-loss reserves. These figures—which reflect a bank's tax environment, risk aversion, and policy decisions—seldom provide direct insight into a bank's problem loans, many of which the bank is trying to work out with the borrowers and other creditors.

The Financial Accounting Standards Board proposed guidelines by which a bank would have to reduce the reported value of loans and investments that have been significantly restructured, for example, work-out loans in which a bank forgives past interest and/or lowers the interest rate for future payments. This proposal stirred much discussion within the accounting and financial community. Some bankers stated that, if adopted, such guidelines would substantially limit their flexibility to restructure some problem loans in ways that, in the long run, could benefit banks, borrowers, and other participants in the economy.

In summary, Exhibit 11-2 identifies the sequential decisions between (1) a bank's identifying a loan as a problem and (2) the final loss, if any, from the loan and the final accounting entry associated with the bank's loan-loss reserve. To decide about loan work-outs and charge-offs, a bank considers its tax environment and reporting requirements as well as its views as to the probable final outcomes from specific loans.

## REVISION OF LOAN POLICIES AND SYSTEMS

Senior officials regularly read about economic trends and major events in industries and regions in which their bank is a major lender. Through selective reading and industry seminars, they keep informed as to how their bank's loan activities will likely be affected by changes in laws, regulations, government loan programs, accounting procedures, and competition for various loans. Also, they expect the loan officers to monitor and analyze events that relate to specialized loan areas and to alert the senior officials as to why and how the bank should revise its loan policies and systems in response to, or in anticipation of, major external changes.

A second level of information flow centers on internal reports and analyses of the loan portfolio. The senior officials receive regular and special reports from the personnel who implement the loan policies and from examiners and auditors. If they believe that the reporting system is incomplete, the senior officials can request supplementary reports and analyses. Thus an internal reporting system, if effective, enables senior officials to identify apparent deficiencies in past policies and procedures. A bank's officials, for example, observe an uptrend in problem loans. After further analysis, they conclude that the bank has to revise some of its policies, such as the types of loans it makes, and/or some of its procedures, such as how it controls loan risks and how it monitors loans in order to detect pending problems. Thus if it is carefully constructed and used, a bank's internal reporting system provides a feedback mechanism for top-level review—and possible revision—of loan policies and systems.

## SUMMARY

Loan decision and review systems contain four sequential components:

- obtain applications
- analyze and negotiate the applications
- monitor and review current and past loans
- revise loan policies and procedures

Within this common framework, each bank structures and modifies the details of its specific loan decision and review system.

Loan applications range from a brief oral request to a lengthy document that is accompanied by detailed financial information about the applicant. An application is for a specific loan, loan commitment, or loan take-down against a prior commitment. Most applications are from people who have previously borrowed from the bank, or they are from people whose loan accounts the bank has solicited by its cross-selling strategies, direct-call programs, or targeted advertising campaigns. Each bank views its loan activities as integral parts of its long-term relationships with current and potential customers.

For applications that pass an initial screening, the loan officers proceed to develop answers to five basic questions:

- Does the loan request meet policy guidelines?
- What are the expected returns from this loan?

- What is the default risk of this loan?
- How can the risks be controlled?
- What loan terms, if any, shall we offer?

In many banks the loan officers use computerized analytical systems to expedite their analyses of these questions—especially as they relate to applications for small standardized loans.

The loan officers check whether a loan request meets the bank's policies. If they conclude that a specific request would violate the policies, the loan officers may promptly decide to disapprove it. Sometimes, however, the officers decide to evaluate further the requested loan's potential returns and risks in order to determine whether to recommend that the bank grant the loan as a policy exception or that the bank propose a restructuring of the request so that it can meet the policy guidelines.

The expected return from a loan includes more than that implied by the stated interest rate; it includes the expected returns that the lender will likely receive by providing other services to the borrower—and possibly to the borrower's associates. Bank loan officers also have to try to predict the probable consequences if they were to disapprove a loan to a customer who then decides to move all of his or her banking business to a rival bank.

Loan officers use credit analysis to estimate the default risk of a requested loan. Although they sometimes perform diverse financial computations, most loan officers focus on interpreting the initial credit analyses prepared by specialists or by special computer programs.

To further reduce the risk of low-risk loans, bank loan officers use diverse risk-control procedures that include: covenants, collateral, co-signers, and insurance and participations.

After they thus evaluate a proposed loan, the loan officers develop a loan offer; and they identify which terms, if any, they are willing to negotiate. One strategy, especially for large loans, is for a loan officer to prepare some contingency plans to which he or she can turn if an applicant rejects the initial loan offer.

If a loan officer and applicant negotiate a final agreement, this is signed and recorded in the credit file on the borrower. Moreover, if at this or an earlier point the two parties do not reach a loan agreement, then this negative outcome is recorded in the credit files.

A bank systematically monitors and reviews its total loan portfolio and the loans that comprise the portfolio. To expedite this process and to help control costs, most banks have automated some of their loan collection and servicing functions.

Credit files are the heart of a bank's loan decision and review system. A loan officer reviews the appropriate file before deciding whether to grant a new loan request from an established customer. Bank examiners use these credit files to expedite their review of a bank's loan policies, procedures, and portfolio components. If, in their judgment, a loan's default risk is too high, then the examiners classify the loan as: substandard, doubtful, or loss.

The examining agency submits its lists of classified loans to the bank's directors for their review and remedial action.

Subject to legal, regulatory, and accounting guidelines, a bank has leeway as to how it manages and reports its loan losses. A bank can create a loan-loss reserve, and most banks do so. Within limits a bank can decide on the magnitude of this reserve and on the timing of some of its charge-offs to and recoveries from this reserve. While they have long been able to monitor reported changes in a bank's loss reserves, stockholders and interested outsiders have had virtually no access to information about a bank's problem loans. Recent proposals by the SEC and by some members of the accounting profession are likely to require banks to provide more information about their problem loans.

A complete loan decision and review system channels relevant information to senior officials who then review, and at times revise, various parts of their bank's loan policies and decision system(s).

# 12
# BUSINESS LOANS

The following summary categorization suggests the variety of business loans:

- *short-term*, with an original maturity of one year or less, or *term*, with an original maturity that exceeds one year
- *unsecured*, or *secured* by specific collateral
- principal activity of borrower, such as manufacturing, trade, or services

Yet even this initial summary obscures the diversity of business loans and procedures that include:

- direct-call programs
- prime-rate, and floating-rate, loans
- compensating balance requirements
- loan pricing systems
- loan commitments
- loan participations
- specialized lending to small businesses and agricultural firms
- equipment leasing

Bankers, and in some cases bank supervisory agencies, are reexamining how banks apply these specialized procedures to business loans.

## CULTIVATING BUSINESS BORROWERS

Banks emphasize a long-run relationship between themselves and their business borrowers. They provide depository, lending, and associated services to their business clients; and they expect their clients to maintain bank deposits for transactions purposes and to apply to their bank(s) for diverse loan needs.

Personal associations reinforce the long-term relationships between banks and their business clients. Bank officers and businesspeople often serve on the same boards of directors, and they participate in similar civic and social activities. A bank's senior officers thus develop personal ties with various businesspeople whose firms are current or potential clients of the bank.

## STRUCTURING DIRECT-CALL PROGRAMS

Banks use direct-call programs to reinforce relationships with current business customers and to develop new customer relationships. Loan officers of a medium-sized bank periodically call on the bank's major business clients. During such a call, an officer inquires about a firm's recent activities and its projected financing needs. The calling officer reaffirms the bank's willingness to provide various services, including loans. Similarly, when he or she calls on a nearby business firm that is a potential customer, a loan officer alerts the firm's officers to the bank's loan capabilities and other services.

Large banks have direct-call programs that are more comprehensive than are those of most medium-sized banks. A large bank's loan officers call on their borrowing customers, but in addition a large bank often has some specialists who are experts in the financing needs of certain industries, and these specialists focus their calls on current and potential clients in these industries. One team of callers may specialize in textiles, a second team in petroleum, and other teams in industries where their bank has decided to focus its call programs and its perceived lending skills.

A large bank bases its callers at its headquarters and at its outlying loan production offices, if any. These callers visit current and potential borrowers within a broad radius of their bank's headquarters.[1] When he or she visits a firm, a caller outlines the bank's current loan terms for the types of loans in which the firm may be interested. The caller defers discussion of specific terms until after the bank receives and evaluates a written, or possibly oral, loan application. When loan demand is slack, however, a caller more promptly emphasizes the bank's willingness to provide competitive loan terms.

---

1. A researcher analyzes geographical markets for business loans and reports that banks primarily confine their small loans to small firms located near the bank. "On average, the greater proportion of these transactions (87.5%) were loans in amounts less than $100,000 to firms with total assets less than $1 million" (based on 1955 survey data). He also reports that there is a national market for large loans to large firms; most of these transactions involve "loans in excess of $100,000 to firms with more than $5 million in assets." The author also suggests "that once a firm can go outside of its local area to obtain a loan, it is for all practical purposes borrowing in the national market." Robert A. Eisenbeis, "Local Banking Markets for Business Loans," *Journal of Bank Research,* Summer 1971, pp. 30-39, and "Nonlocal Bank Markets for Business Loans," *Journal of Bank Research,* Winter 1972, pp. 41-47.

## CYCLICAL DIMENSIONS OF DIRECT-CALL PROGRAMS

Most banks increase their call programs when loan demand is slack, and they deemphasize their calls when loan demand is strong. This cyclical approach to call programs can be counterproductive.

When business loan demand is slack, bank loan officers have fewer applications to process. They have more time to call on current and potential borrowers who, at the same time, also receive calls from other banks. In such periods, when many banks call on potential borrowers, most businesses can readily negotiate loans from their current banks.

Conversely, when loan demand is strong, bank loan officers have to analyze and negotiate diverse loan applications; and senior loan officers have to make difficult decisions as to how to accommodate the many loan requests from current business customers. In such periods many banks conclude that they have neither the officer time nor the loanable funds to warrant active call programs. Therefore they reduce their direct calls, especially on noncustomers; and the calls they do make tend to be courtesy visits in which the callers do not actively solicit new borrowing requests that may be difficult for the bank to accommodate.

Ironically, it is during periods of strong loan demand that some business firms, disappointed in their loan relationships with their current banks, seek to add banking relationships. However, when they then turn to banks whose callers visited them during previous periods, these firms learn that many of the banks have had to focus on meeting the loan demands of their current customers and so they no longer actively seek new borrowers. Loan callers also must find it discouraging to have called often on a potential borrower and then to have their bank rebuff the firm when it finally applies for a loan.

A bank can examine the benefits and costs of initiating countercyclical call programs. Such a program requires a bank to project future periods of strong loan demand. The bank then has to structure its expected cash flows in order to accommodate the anticipated loan requests of its business customers and also the loan requests of other firms that will likely be searching for new sources of bank loans. A bank thus positions itself to call on targeted new borrowers during periods when they are willing to add banks or switch banks. Before it initiates a countercyclical call strategy, a bank has to evaluate whether, in its case, the long-run benefits from its being able to accommodate new business borrowers will likely exceed the short-run costs (such as foregone interest income) of its building potentially excess liquidity during periods prior to projected upsurges in loan demand. Also, if many large banks adopt it, this countercyclical strategy will be less effective for any one bank that uses it.

## EVALUATING BUSINESS LOAN APPLICATIONS

Most banks have commercial loan officers who specialize in the evaluation and negotiation of business loans. Often these officers supplement their basic lending procedures with specialized procedures such as prime rate, compensating balances, account profitability analysis, detailed cash flow forecasting, and tailored protective covenants.

## PRIME RATE

Prime rate is the rate that a large money-center bank charges on short-term loans to its largest, most creditworthy business customers. Seldom will a bank lend funds at a rate below its current prime rate. From this base rate the bank scales upward the interest rates that it charges on loans to smaller and/or less creditworthy borrowers. A medium-sized bank similarly has a base rate, sometimes called a local prime rate, that it charges its most creditworthy local or regional borrowers.

### Origins of Prime Rate

The prime-rate convention began in the 1930s. During the Depression, banks faced slack loan demand; and so, to avoid competitive rate cutting, some large banks "agreed to charge not less than 1½ percent for loans to business borrowers of high credit standing. This would, in turn, guide lending policies on non-prime borrowers as well."[2] This industry practice of setting a base price was consistent with national economic policies of that time.

For decades the prime rate was an administered price. In response to recent or expected changes in credit conditions, one of the nation's largest banks would sometimes announce a change in its prime rate after which other money-center banks soon announced similar changes in their prime rate. Although one of the large New York banks usually initiated the change, sometimes a large regional bank took the initiative. Between 1934 and 1965, there were infrequent changes in the prime rate (on average about once every 1½ years), and most of the changes were in increments of one-quarter or one-half of a percentage point. These infrequent changes usually lagged behind changes in yields on money-market instruments. In contrast, between 1966 and 1971 there were more frequent changes in the prime rate (on average, about once every 2½ months), and most changes were in increments of one-quarter of a percentage point.

The news media publicized the announced changes in the prime rate, especially when the changes occurred during periods of high, and rising, interest rates. Thus critics began to question the procedure whereby a large money-center bank announced a change in its prime rate and other banks followed with similar changes. Two coauthors note "there had long been a history of Congressional antagonism which viewed prime pricing policy as a collusive arrangement among a handful of the largest banks. In more recent times, Congressional hostility to the action of many of the nation's

---

2. Murray E. Polakoff and Morris Budin, *The Prime Rate*, a study prepared for the Trustees of the Banking Research Fund, Association of Reserve City Bankers, 1973, p. 6.

commercial banks in raising the prime rate by a full percentage point in July, 1969, is a matter of historical record."[3] The Justice Department threatened to investigate pricing policies by banks. In view of such hostility, banks were reluctant to increase their prime rate beyond the 8½ percent rate that they instituted in July 1969; and they focused on ways to make smaller, more frequent, and less newsworthy changes in their prime rate.

### Formula Prime Rates

In 1971, First National City Bank (Citibank) announced its introduction of a formula prime rate. The bank proposed to keep its prime rate about one-half a percentage point (50 basis points) above the average rate on 90-day commercial paper placed through dealers. Each week the bank would recalculate its prime rate; and if the formula warranted it, it would change its rate in increments of ⅛ of a percentage point. "The choice of the commercial paper rate reflected the high degree of substitutability between bank loans and commercial paper. Moreover, because of its relatively large volume, commercial paper was considered fairly well insulated from unusual disruptive influences on both domestic and foreign credit markets, resulting in a reliable indicator of the 'free market rate' for short-term business credit."[4] Some other large money-center banks subsequently introduced their versions of formula prime rates. Although similar in principle to that of Citibank's formula, in some cases these formulas: use other money-market indexes, schedule longer intervals between rate adjustments, or adjust in increments of other than ⅛ of a percentage point.

Selection of an appropriate prime-rate formula is a basic decision for a bank's senior management. A formula specifies a mathematical relationship between a bank's prime rate and a specific index or set of indexes. All such indexes have limitations, primarily because they reflect past interrelationships in financial markets. Even after it chooses one—or a combination—of these indexes, a bank's management has to decide on the formula's spread between the prime rate and the index. For example, what should be the size of the spread; and should it be a constant amount in percentage points or should it vary depending on the level of money-market interest rates? Two coauthors analyze these basic issues, test various indexes, and conclude that use of such indexes, perhaps *"modified to include specific market conditions of particular banks, opens a variety of possible alternatives to bankers in setting their own prime rates."*[5]

A bank with a formula prime rate reserves the right to revise its formula and to depart from its formula. To illustrate, in 1979 Citibank revised its

---

3. Polakoff and Budin, *The Prime Rate*, p. 24.

4. Randall C. Merris, "The Prime Rate," *Business Conditions* (Federal Reserve Bank of Chicago), April 1975, pp. 3-12. Also by Randall C. Merris, "The Prime Rate Revisited," *Economic Perspectives* (Federal Reserve Bank of Chicago), July-August 1977, pp. 17-20; and "Prime Rate Update," *Economic Perspectives* (Federal Reserve Bank of Chicago), May-June 1978, pp. 14-16. In the latter two articles Merris examines why and how a bank may willingly make some loans at rates below its stated prime rate.

5. Polakoff and Budin, *The Prime Rate*, p. 32.

initial formula in order to link its prime rate to the average rate that large banks pay on 90-day negotiable certificates of deposit. Also, while its initial formula called for a half percentage point spread above the specified commercial paper rate, Citibank later sequentially increased the spread to 1½ percentage points. During 1973, because of actions by the Committee on Interest and Dividends (CID), banks briefly abandoned their formula prime rates. Subsequently, some banks returned to formula prime rates, but CID guidelines prevented them from precisely implementing their formulas, especially when rates on commercial paper were rapidly rising. Therefore some banks that were leading proponents of formula prime rates announced that, while retaining the formula concept, "they would use it as an indicator of the direction of prime rate changes rather than as a precision instrument."[6]

A formula prime rate enables a bank to defuse critics of the prime-rate convention. Compared to the traditional prime rate, a formula provides for frequent small changes that become less newsworthy. Also, if it has a formula prime rate, a bank can use this procedure to rebut criticism of its increases in its prime rate. Its spokespeople point out that the prime rate changes are in response to changes in the money market rates that serve as the formula's index and that therefore the bank is simply adjusting its rates to competitive market rates.

Many large banks do not use formula prime rates. Senior officers of these nonformula banks regularly meet to decide whether or not to change their bank's prime rate and, if so, by what amount. They base their decisions on various analyses and judgments of current and expected credit conditions. While they may seem complex, in practice these decisions incorporate much of the information that is also reflected in the money market indexes used by formula banks. Also, because they compete for prime borrowers in regional and national markets, both nonformula and formula banks closely monitor the prime rates posted by their rivals; and the senior officials of formula banks retain administrative flexibility to interpret and implement their formula prime rates. Under these conditions there have not been—nor are there likely to be—wide discrepancies between the prime rates posted by formula and nonformula banks.

### Applying the Prime Rate

Whichever way their bank sets its prime rate, loan officers have to decide which firms qualify for this rate. Their decision is easy in the case of very large, creditworthy firms that have convenient access to other banks and to nonbank sources of funds, such as the commercial paper market.

Once they identify the obvious prime borrowers, the loan officers begin to face more difficult decisions. Other of their bank's business customers are only slightly smaller, more risky firms with fewer borrowing alternatives.

---

6. Merris, "The Prime Rate," p. 12.

Yet some of these firms want the prestige—and lower interest rate—associated with prime borrowers. If their current bank refuses to classify them as prime, some of these firms may begin to search for a bank that is willing to classify them as prime; and to qualify for a prime classification they may willingly accept a loan agreement that contains conditions by which a bank reduces its risks and/or boosts its total return. To retain or attract such firms, the loan officers may decide to classify them as prime; but before they do they need to evaluate the probable consequences if they subsequently try to retract the prime designation. A bank may generate greater ill will if it subsequently tries to retract a marginal prime classification than if it initially explains why it cannot classify a firm as prime.

For firms that clearly do not qualify as prime, loan officers and committees develop and negotiate loan offers that contain diverse provisions, one of which is the explicit interest rate that has been scaled upward from the bank's prime rate.

## COMPENSATING BALANCES

As a condition for its granting a loan, a bank often requires a business borrower to maintain compensating balances which are demand, or possibly time, deposits that account for an agreed percentage of the total loan. To illustrate, a bank and a business borrower agree that the firm's demand deposits at the lending bank will, on average, be at least 20 percent of a total loan. Similarly, a bank may request compensating balances as one of the terms of a loan commitment.

### Rationality of Compensating Balance Requirements

There is a long tradition of compensating balance (CB) requirements for bank loans to business. Some bankers initially saw this device as a way to gain additional pricing flexibility. If, for example, it faces a situation where higher explicit interest rates will likely encounter usury ceilings or borrower resistance, a bank can decide not to raise the explicit interest rate but instead to insist on a CB that effectively increases the implicit interest rate. For example, for whatever its reasons a bank is reluctant to post an interest rate above 10 percent for a specific business loan of $1,000,000. It offers to lend the amount at 10 percent *if* the borrower agrees to maintain an average CB of 20 percent. If the borrower would not otherwise maintain this amount ($200,000) of deposits, then the bank gains some demand deposits part of which—after meeting the associated reserve requirements—it can lend or invest and thus increase its total return from the 10 percent loan. The borrower, maintaining a higher level of demand deposits than it would without the requirement, in effect pays a rate higher than 10 percent. The bank may even agree to lend $1,200,000 at 10 percent so that the borrower has its requested loan of $1,000,000 as well as the $200,000 to meet its CB requirement. In such a case the business borrower pays interest on the total

$1,200,000; but it only has use of $1,000,000. Its effective interest cost therefore exceeds 10 percent.

Some critics cite instances in which CB requirements are suboptimal for both lending banks and business borrowers. When it has to borrow more than it wants to in order to satisfy a CB requirement, a business borrower pays an effective interest rate that exceeds the stated rate for the funds it needs. The lending bank gains an additional deposit, against which it must maintain required reserves. Because of these reserve requirements, the bank cannot fully lend or invest these additional deposits in earning assets. Under these circumstances, one author demonstrates how, "by eliminating compensatory balance requirements, a bank can enlarge its own earnings while at the same time reducing the effective rate of interest paid by the borrower."[7] A similar approach is for a bank to negotiate an explicit compensating fee instead of insisting on a compensating balance that is subject to reserve requirements.[8]

From the viewpoint of a business borrower, CB requirements are not irrational in cases where the borrower would voluntarily maintain at the lending bank a working balance that is at least as large as the CB requirement. If it agrees to the CB requirement, the firm may get a lower stated interest rate than it would without the requirement. Also, because a CB requirement usually stipulates an average—not minimum—balance, the firm retains its flexibility to draw its deposit balances below the average if it offsets this temporary short-fall with above-average deposits during other times while the CB requirement is in effect.

A bank realizes that often it does not gain additional deposits via its CB requirements. Many of its business borrowers use their working balances at the bank to meet their CB requirements. Yet a bank can use CB requirements to gain flexibility in pricing its business loans. If a customer has maintained, or agrees to maintain, a large deposit balance, a loan officer can offer such a borrower a lower stated interest rate to reward the deposit relationship.[9] If it makes such a price concession, the lender then uses a CB requirement to guarantee that the borrower does not shortly transfer some of its balances to other banks also to gain price concessions or other services from them. Also, even if they generally apply to working balances already on deposit, a bank's CB requirements can mitigate the volatility—and associated liquidity management costs—of these business deposits. Two coauthors note that it is not accidental that CB arrangements are prevalent "on loans to that type of borrower ordinarily holding large working balances

7. Douglas Hellweg, "A Note on Compensatory Balance Requirements," *The Journal of Finance,* March 1961, pp. 80-84.

8. Christian T. L. Janssen, "The Case for the Compensating Fee," *The Bankers Magazine,* Summer 1969, pp. 43-46. Also in the same issue, Omer L. Carey, "Compensating Fees and Time Deposits: Changes in Bank Attitudes," pp. 47-50.

9. One study demonstrates how banks apparently use CB agreements to circumvent the prohibition of interest payments on demand deposits. R. Alton Gilbert, "Effects of Interest on Demand Deposits: Implications of Compensating Balances," *Review* (Federal Reserve Bank of St. Louis), November 1977, pp. 8-15.

(business firms) and are virtually non-existent on other types of loans, such as mortgage loans, consumer loans, or farm loans.''[10] The usual CB requirement for business loans is 20 percent, the most common requirement on unused loan commitments is 10 percent. Most banks that use CB requirements indicate their willingness to negotiate specific terms, but they maintain guidelines to serve as a departure point for such negotiations.[11] ''During periods of rising interest rates and generally tight credit conditions, banks usually raise their compensating balance requirements, apply these requirements to a larger proportion of their loans, and enforce the requirements more rigorously. During periods of falling interest rates and increased credit availability, the reverse is generally true.''

Each bank has to evaluate its use or potential use of CB requirements. Many small banks believe that CB requirements unnecessarily complicate a loan agreement, and so they choose not to use them. A medium-sized or large bank however recognizes that many rival banks use CB requirements for their business loans. Therefore it has to evaluate whether it, too, should use CB requirements to gain additional pricing flexibility and to forestall deposit outflows.

### Variants of Compensating Balance Requirements

Instead of having business borrowers use demand deposits to meet their CB requirements, some banks encourage their borrowers to use—at least in part—a noninterest-paying time deposit, which has a lower reserve requirement than does a similar-sized demand deposit.

If it does not have adequate working balances to meet CB requirements, a business borrower sometimes negotiates a *link financing* arrangement with a third party. To illustrate, a firm wants to borrow $1,000,000 and its average working balance at its bank is $100,000. The bank wants a 20 percent compensating balance. Therefore the borrower seeks a third party, such as an insurance company, that agrees to keep a deposit of $100,000 at the lending bank in return for an interest payment by the borrowing firm. The borrower thus arranges for a total loan of $1,000,000; the bank gets its $200,000 compensating balance ($100,000 of which is an additional deposit *if* the third party transferred the amount from another bank); and the third party receives a negotiated rate of interest on its bank deposit.

To avoid possible multiple counting of business deposits with it, a bank needs effective account-analysis systems.[12] For example, a business firm maintains an average balance of $200,000 with a bank, which, in turn,

10. Richard G. Davis and Jack M. Guttentag, ''Are Compensating Balance Requirements Irrational?'' *The Journal of Finance*, March 1962, pp. 121-126.

11. Joseph E. Burns, ''Compensating Balance Requirements Integral to Bank Lending,'' *Business Review* (Federal Reserve Bank of Dallas), February 1972, pp. 1-8.

12. Paul S. Nadler, ''Compensating Balances and the Prime at Twilight,'' *Harvard Business Review*, January-February 1972, pp. 112-120.

provides many services to this depositor. Because of the processing costs associated with it, this illustrative deposit relationship contributes only a small amount to bank profits. In this case, the bank has to be cautious about then also counting this deposit as a compensating balance, in return for which the bank offers a lower stated interest rate on a loan.

## ESTIMATING ACCOUNT PROFITABILITY

When they evaluate business-loan applications, loan officers try to estimate the profitability of an applicant's relationship with the bank. In many banks this estimation procedure rests on informal judgments; in some large banks the loan officers have access to computerized account-analysis systems. Whether it is informal or computerized, the estimation procedure focuses on a business account's past relationship as a guide to the expected future profitability of that relationship.[13] If the analysis is of a new account, then a loan officer has to explicitly focus on the expected future profitability of the account relationship.

While they use extensive judgment to try to estimate the expected benefits, where possible the loan officers also try to control the future outcomes, for example by requesting a compensating balance that helps cement the association between the applicant and the bank. Often, however, the long-run relationship rests on a tacit agreement whereby a bank stands ready to accommodate its business customer's loan requests; and it in turn expects the borrower to use the bank's other services. From its view, a business firm relies on one or several banks for most banking services; and it in turn expects its bank(s) to meet its reasonable borrowing requests.

Loan officers look beyond the direct relationship between their bank and a major business customer. They also try to estimate whether and how this corporate relationship may bring additional business to the bank. Especially in cases where a bank also has various customer relationships with a firm's officers and principal stockholders, a loan officer tries to estimate the value of this associated business to the bank.

As they try to estimate the future benefits if their bank makes a loan, loan officers and loan committees know that their rejection of some loan requests can lead to the loss of a corporate client and also possible loss of associated accounts. Therefore these loan officials strive to accommodate loan requests, especially those by long-time business customers. Even if it faces strong loan demand, a bank seeks to accommodate its established customers, whose loan requests usually receive higher priority than those of noncustomer firms. Consistent with this pattern of a bank's accommodating its valued business customers, a study of business loan behavior by New York City banks concludes that these banks are willing, even eager, "to satisfy the rising financial needs of their regular customers . . . who are predominantly large corporations. These corporations maintain sizable

---

13. Daniel L. White, "The Present Value Approach of Selecting Bank Customers," *Journal of Bank Research,* Summer 1974, pp. 96-101.

deposits with NYC banks and thus provide them with funds for lending. The banks feel, therefore, that they have to satisfy their customers when a case of need arises. Otherwise customers may shift their deposits to other banks."[14]

## RISK ANALYSIS AND CONTROL

Once they receive a loan application, the loan officers proceed to evaluate whether it complies with the bank's policies and, if it does not, whether to analyze it further as a possible exception to bank policy.

To evaluate the default risk of a loan proposal, a commercial loan officer focuses on the question: How probable is it that the borrower will be able to repay the loan according to its proposed repayment schedule? In cases where he or she is certain that it will be repaid as proposed, the loan officer classifies the proposed loan as having zero default risk. In most cases, however, a loan officer is not so confident and has to estimate the likelihood that the loan, if made, will be repaid on schedule. The officer also tries to identify and control key factors that will affect the borrower's ability to repay the loan on schedule.

### Cash Flow Forecasting

Cash flow forecasting is at the heart of procedures by which loan officers try to estimate the likelihood that a proposed loan will be repaid on schedule. Most commercial loan officers have had previous training as credit analysts who dissect a proposed borrower's past and projected financial statements. *Spread sheet analysis* is the procedure by which credit analysts focus on a series of interrelated financial statements. The analysts calculate key ratios from the financial statements, and they then evaluate trends in and interrelationships among such ratios. In this way a trained analyst evaluates the credibility of a firm's projected cash flows, especially if these flows are the proposed bases for repayment of a loan.

Credit analysts search for inconsistencies in a firm's financial projections. To illustrate, a firm projects rapid sales growth; and yet, based on its past performance and industry standards, its projections do not provide for associated increases in accounts receivable and inventories. In such a case, sales and profits may well increase; but the firm is likely to face cash flow problems as it has to increase its accounts receivable and inventories while it also has to repay its bank loan according to the proposed schedule.

Instead of having a credit analyst compute the ratios from an applicant's financial statements, many large banks have computer programs that compute the ratios. This process gives the analysts more time to interpret the ratios and to test which relationships will likely occur if one varies the assumptions underlying the projections.

At a more advanced level, some banks have on-line programs that

---

14. George Budzeika, "A Model of Business Loan Behavior of Large New York City Banks," *Journal of Bank Research*, Winter 1971, pp. 58-72.

enable an analyst or loan officer to "talk" with the computer that calculates various ratios and other financial relationships. The banker has a computer terminal through which he or she submits the applicant's financial statements to a computer system that is programmed to provide rapid analyses of the figures. The computer is also programmed to recalculate the figures under alternative assumptions. For example, on the first run, the computer provides a projected sources and uses of funds statement based on the applicant's pro forma balance sheet and income statements. The bank analyst then asks the computer for another calculation based on the assumption that the firm achieves only half its estimated sales. Based on this recalculation, the analyst tries to estimate whether the firm can repay its bank debt on schedule. Similarly, the analyst can examine likely outcomes associated with changes in other key assumptions, such as the firm's future levels of inventories, accounts receivable, and capital expenditures. As summarized by one banker, "the ability to tie into a central computer through any telephone, at nominal cost, has provided the loan officer with analytical capabilities that were not possible before." This banker also notes how his bank "developed a simple computer program to forecast the cash flows of its corporate customers. This program has since evolved into a comprehensive computer system for statement spreading, credit analysis, new business development and financial planning."[15]

With their initial training as credit analysts, loan officers develop long-run skills in financial statement analysis. Even in a large bank where specialists do much of the detailed credit analysis, a loan officer's training enables him or her to quickly comprehend and question an analyst's interpretation of an applicant's financial statements.

Although loan officers and credit analysts will not be supplanted by computers, some researchers are experimenting with statistical procedures that may help banks screen among commercial loan applicants. One study analyzes the repayment performance of a large sample of French textile firms. It uses 41 financial ratios and various tests to try to discriminate statistically between "problem firms" (nonpayments or bankruptcies) and nonproblem firms. The study reports that "the actual discrimination of firms through the use of financial ratio analysis interpreted through modern statistical procedures proved to be only moderately successful. With the entire 41-ratio profile, a rather effective accuracy of classification was achieved. But when we attempt to reduce the number of analytical measures to a manageable number (e.g., ten), the accuracy of discrimination falls and only certain enterprises can be classified as good or bad credit risks with any confidence." Despite these inclusive results, the coauthors encourage further testing of statistical analyses of default risks of commercial loans.[16]

15. Leonard N. Druger, "Financial Engineering," *Bankers Monthly Magazine,* May 15, 1969, pp. 24-27.

16. Edward I. Altman, Michel Margaine, Michel Schlosser, and Pierre Vernimmen, "Financial and Statistical Analysis for Commercial Loan Evaluation: A French Experience," *Journal of Financial and Quantitative Analysis,* March 1974, pp. 195-211. Gunter Dufey constructively critiques this study in the same journal, pp. 213-214.

## Covenants

Covenants are a principal risk-control procedure, especially for business loans. While there are many standard covenants, loan officers try to tailor a set of covenants which they believe will protect the bank and also be acceptable to a specific borrower.

A basic covenant is that a business borrower agrees to provide the bank with periodic audited financial statements. Sometimes a bank also wants a covenant that requires the borrower to pay for some surprise audits, the results of which are given to the bank. These types of covenants enable the lender to keep punctually informed about a borrower's subsequent financial activities.

Compensating balances, which are part of most business loans, provide some protection to a bank. If one of its business borrowers subsequently defaults, the lending bank offsets the firm's deposit against its remaining loan balance. This procedure reduces the bank's creditor claim to the amount of the loan that remains after the offset. Although this procedure theoretically helps a bank control its default risk, in practice a problem borrower that has to meet an average CB requirement is likely to reduce its bank deposit to a low level prior to default.

Commercial loan officers and a bank's legal staff imaginatively design other covenants to propose to an applicant, who may then accept all or some of them during the process of negotiating a final loan agreement. Although they are tailored to meet the preference of a lender and a specific borrower, most of these covenants constrain the borrower's financial flexibility throughout the life of the loan. Examples are:

- maximum amounts that can be paid as dividends, salaries, and bonuses
- maximum amounts of new indebtedness
- limits on the selling or pledging of a firm's assets
- minimum levels of insurance

The usual procedure is for such covenants to specify relationships among a firm's financial figures, such as a maximum dividend payout relative to future earnings and past retained earnings.

An acceleration clause is an integral part of most loan agreements between banks and business firms. This clause permits a bank to demand immediate full repayment if a borrower fails to meet other terms of the loan agreement. This sanction is so powerful that a borrowing firm has a strong incentive to comply with the other terms of the loan agreement.

## Other Risk-Control Procedures

A commercial loan officer also can try to control a loan's default risk through use of such procedures as: pledged collateral, cosigners (especially among affiliated firms or closely held firms), and loan insurance programs (such as with the Small Business Administration).

# DEVELOPING MULTIDIMENSIONAL LOAN OFFERS

Exhibit 12-1 summarizes the complex process by which a banker prepares a loan offer and possible contingency offers. Such a schematic summary cannot, however, include all the subtle dimensions of loan-offer strategies:

- There are gradations within and between categories like ''prime'' and ''nonprime.''
- There are interrelationships among the principal components. For example, a loan officer may offer to a nonprime borrower an interest rate only slightly above prime *if* the borrower agrees to a high CB requirement.
- The interrelationships among the decision variables change over time. To illustrate, when it faces strong loan demand, a bank will likely increase its prime rate, its CB requirements, *and* its qualifying standards for the prime rate.
- Components such as processing costs and estimated account profitability are sensitive to a bank's cost accounting procedures. In most cases a loan officer has to accept the figures derived from the bank's cost accounting system.

Some banks have formal procedures that help the loan officers to evaluate systematically the various components of a loan offer. Even in banks with informal procedures, the loan officers implicitly go through a similar process to prepare and negotiate business-loan offers.

In cases where they conclude that a requested loan is unsuitable for the bank's portfolio, loan officers promptly communicate this decision to the applicant firm. They may also cite why, based on their analysis, the applicant should examine other sources of financing, such as leasing, a securities offering, or a loan from a nonbank lender that specializes in high-risk commercial financing.

## PRIME LOANS

In cases where they conclude that a loan request complies with bank policies and has virutally zero default risk, loan officers proceed to investigate whether the loan should be classified as ''prime.'' They check whether the applicant is a large firm whose account relationship has been—and/or is expected to be—profitable for the bank. (Also for a large, virtually zero-risk loan, the processing costs account for a small percentage of the total amount of the loan.) If they conclude that the loan qualifies as prime, the loan officers develop an offer that incorporates the bank's current prime rate and associated CB requirements. They may also incorporate some customary risk-control procedures into a proposed loan agreement; but, on a prime loan, they seldom insist on extensive protective covenants. In summary, once they classify a proposed loan as prime, the loan officers proceed to offer the applicant their bank's current standardized terms for its prime customers. They know that their prime customers have convenient access to

**EXHIBIT 12-1**

**Negotiating a Multidimensional Loan Offer:
A Decision Table**

| Estimated Default Risk of Requested Loan | Decision Variables (Usually Subject to Negotiation) | | | | |
|---|---|---|---|---|---|
| | Risk Control Procedures | Components of Estimated Return | | | |
| | | Interest Rate | Compensating Balance (CB) Requirements | Estimated Profitability of Total Account Relationship | Per-unit Processing Costs |
| Virtually zero<br>↓<br><br>Greater than zero, but acceptable | Few, primarily standard ones<br>↓<br><br>More, and more specifically tailored to borrower | Prime rate at time<br>↓<br><br>Scaled above prime | Minimum CB requirement at time<br>↓<br><br>Probably higher than minimum CB requirement at time | ↑<br>↓<br>Account analysis and projections<br>↓<br>↓ | Low<br>↓<br><br>Higher |

other bank and nonbank sources of funds, and so the loan officers have limited flexibility to negotiate nonstandard loan offers with prime firms.

## NONPRIME LOANS

Loan officers devote most of their analytical and negotiating skills to the many loan requests that are neither obvious rejects nor obvious prime loans.

As they evaluate an applicant's financial history and prospects, loan officers mentally rank the default risk of the requested loan. As one loan officer summarizes the process, "We all mentally risk rate our loans, charging higher rates for riskier credits and lower rates for better loans. However, better results can probably be obtained from a more formal risk rating procedure where various categories of financial risk are described. This will permit loans to be graded by different officers at different times with a degree of uniformity."[17] This banker categorizes business loans rated by default risk, ranging from those with minimum risk (such as "lowest risk working capital loans" and "secured short-term loans to top-grade

---

17. Lawrence T. Jilk, Jr., "The Risk Factors in Commercial Lending," *The Journal of Commercial Bank Lending,* May 1972, pp. 18-28.

investment houses'') to those with higher risk that then require continual detailed supervision (such as ''loans involving unusual risks because of industry conditions, political or economic problems, etc.'') Some banks use this type of formalized risk-classification procedure.

Once they initially rate a requested loan's risk, loan officers proceed to structure a possible loan offer. If the requested loan is small and involves even a slight chance of delayed payments and associated collection costs, then this loan's per-dollar processing costs will likely exceed that of a large prime loan. Has the total account relationship been profitable and/or is it expected to be profitable? A loan officer also examines how the bank, if it makes the loan, can control its risks via procedures like protective covenants, collateral, and, possibly, cosigners. The officer develops a tentative combination of risk-control procedures that the applicant is likely to accept. The loan officer then determines an appropriate interest rate and CB requirements for the initial multidimensional loan proposal, and he or she also prepares—either formally or implicitly—some contingency proposals. In this way, if the applicant refuses to accept all the proposed covenants, the officer is prepared to offer an alternate package in which, for example, the borrower pays a higher interest rate and/or agrees to a higher CB requirement.

Commercial loans are very heterogeneous, and so most banks expect their commercial loan officers to develop and refine their loan-offer skills primarily through their years of experience. Some banks, however, have more formal loan-pricing systems. One such system is when a bank has standardized worksheets on which its loan officers quantify the various dimensions of revenues, risks, and expenses of a proposed loan.[18] While they help structure the analysis, such worksheets still require extensive judgment by the loan officers who use them.

Banks often assign their experienced officers to prime (low-risk) loan accounts, and they assign their less experienced officers to smaller accounts that often involve greater risk and more complex loan agreements. Ironically, if they were to have their more experienced officers service the nonprime accounts, then banks could probably increase their risk-adjusted returns from these accounts. Therefore two coauthors suggest that ''fundamental changes are needed regarding future man-power policy, allocating greater skills to the higher-risk credit both to raise levels of profitability and to reduce loan losses.''[19]

## MONITORING AND REVIEW SYSTEMS

Each bank systematically monitors and reviews the aggregate performance of its business loans and also the performance of specific loans within the portfolio.

18. James A. Hoeven and Jerome S. Oldham, ''Commercial Loan Profitability-Pricing Analysis,'' *The Journal of Commercial Bank Lending,* June 1976, pp. 44-57.

19. John T. Ponting and George Robert Sanderson, ''Profitable Loans, Risk, and the Loan Officer,'' *The Bankers Magazine,* Spring 1976, pp. 68-72.

## MONITORING PORTFOLIO DEVELOPMENTS

To monitor the composition of their bank's business-loan portfolio, senior officers and directors focus on the principal subcategories, such as loans classified by: types of borrowers, amounts, maturities, fixed or floating rate, and secured or unsecured. When they detect major changes among these categories, the officials determine whether the changes are consistent with the bank's policies and portfolio strategies or whether they reflect a cumulative outcome from a series of specific loan decisions. This review process enables the senior officials to direct the general composition of the business-loan portfolio over time.[20]

A bank's senior officials also monitor the returns from subcategories of business loans. Especially if the realized returns are lower than had been expected, the senior officials request further analyses of the unexpected outcomes. These analyses help the officials to decide whether to revise their future expectations and/or whether and how to revise the pricing and risk-categorization procedures for future business loans.

The senior officials regularly receive internal listings of delinquent loans and/or problem loans. Once they have been alerted to new delinquent loans, the senior officials ask the responsible loan officers how they plan to prevent the loans from becoming problems. Concerning problem loans, the senior officials also monitor what the responsible operating officers are doing to protect or salvage the bank's loan position. In addition to their receiving internal listings of delinquent and/or problem loans, the senior officials receive similar, although not necessarily identical, listings in their reports from outside auditors and bank examiners.[21]

## MONITORING SPECIFIC LOAN ACCOUNTS

Commercial loan officers monitor their outstanding loans in order to check whether each borrower is adhering to the terms of its loan agreement with the bank. Is the borrower making its loan payments according to the agreed schedule; is it providing timely, audited, financial statements; and is it

---

20. Some large banks are experimenting with computer models to help them analyze the sensitivity of their business-loan portfolio to probable future events, such as changes in the prime rate. For example see Wolfgang P. Hoehenwarter, "Method for Evaluation of the Economic Characteristics of Loan Portfolios," *Journal of Bank Research,* Winter 1976, pp. 257-267. As part of this article, a planning officer of a large bank describes his firm's application of the model. He concludes: "The results of the program appear to be accurate to an acceptable variance level from the actual results over the test period. Therefore, predictions of rate changes (available through either research institutions or in-house economic research departments) and forecast of loan volumes (available from conscientious planning endeavors) enable the program to provide excellent insight into the income contributions of isolated loan categories and the sensitivity of those loan categories to changes in the key rates."

21. To help bank officers and bank examiners more effectively allocate their time when they review loan portfolios, a researcher develops and tests a model that analytically discriminates between "good" and "bad" loans. "In a large bank the computation can be performed by a computer; and if the loan portfolio is maintained on auxiliary storage, the credit score can be computed periodically. . . . But even if the scoring model is not automated, its main advantage is in releasing loan officers and bank examiners from routine evaluations of all loans and allocating their time to a small proportion of riskier borrowers." Yair E. Orgler, "A Credit Scoring Model for Commercial Loans," *Journal of Money, Credit, and Banking,* November 1970, pp. 435-445.

adhering to its CB requirements? To answer such questions, loan officers and their immediate supervisors monitor the credit files of the outstanding loans that they have made. Also, most banks have monitoring systems that promptly alert loan officers when a loan account fails to meet its scheduled deadlines.

There are additional ways by which loan officers try to anticipate and prevent problem loans. They regularly visit with their borrowing customers in order to learn more about a borrower's recent progress and future plans, and they scrutinize a borrowing firm's recent financial statements to gain new insights into its recent and projected financial performance. When they visit a borrowing firm, loan officers directly observe and judge the firm's operating facilities; and sometimes they thus detect performance clues that are not apparent in financial statements. Similarly, when they discuss a firm's plans with its principal officers, the loan officers develop insights into the managers' capabilities and plans.

Most business loans are repaid according to schedule, and so the officers focus on loans where a borrower requests permission to delay a scheduled payment, or, without prior warning, fails to make a scheduled payment.

Loan officers often try to accommodate a borrower that requests a minor extension of a payment deadline. They ask the reason for the requested delay and try to determine whether the request reflects the borrower's having temporarily adverse cash-flow patterns or more complex financial problems. The requested delay alerts the lender to the need to reexamine the borrower's financial condition and prospects.

In contrast, loan officers critically review their bank's relationship with a borrower that, without warning, fails to make a scheduled payment. In such a case, depending on the customer relationship, a loan officer may allow several days' grace before calling the borrower to inquire about the reason for nonpayment. Unless the borrower provides a satisfactory explanation, the loan officer will ask the borrower to come to the bank for a detailed reexamination of the loan relationship. This invitation puts the borrower on notice that the bank may declare the loan in default and take steps to protect its creditor position, possibly by invoking the acceleration clause.

When it believes that a borrower cannot repay a loan according to schedule but is acting in good faith, a bank usually tries to accommodate the borrower. The loan officers often conclude that, if their bank accepts delayed repayments and possibly restructures the loan's terms, then the loan is likely to work out over time. In contrast, if it were to insist on prompt repayment, the bank, by its action, would likely encourage other of the firm's creditors to rush to protect their positions—thus potentially triggering the failure of the borrowing client. A lending bank incurs various legal costs to recover its funds from a failed firm; and, unless its creditor position is well protected, it will probably recover only a portion of its loan. Thus one banker summarizes, "Banks have a strong aversion to bankruptcy, because they feel that restructuring usually affords a better chance of recovery of their loans. Although there may be a tendency to apply it too uncritically, this is generally a correct analysis; and the result is that the banks frequently find themselves committed to long-term work-outs rather than demanding payment on loans they recognize as problems.''[22]

Most large banks have problem-loan specialists who develop plans to restructure problem loans in ways that will be acceptable not only to the bank but also to a borrower and to the borrower'a other creditors. Proposals for debt restructuring seldom are standardized; they involve specialized financial and legal analyses and extensive negotiations among a problem borrower and its various creditors.[23] To help train their new loan officers, some banks have the trainees review cases based on past problem loans and even work for awhile with current problem loans. With this training perhaps some of these future loan officers will avoid making some problem loans.

## LOAN COMMITMENTS

Banks often commit themselves to meet some customers' future loan requests. To learn more about this practice, the Federal Reserve System conducted several surveys from which it concluded that the definition of commitments varies among banks, and the degree of formalization of individual commitments varies among banks.[24] In view of such variations, the FRS defines loan commitments as "official promises to lend that are expressly conveyed, orally or in writing, to the bank's customers. Such commitments are usually in the form of a formally executed agreement or a letter signed by one of the bank's officers."

Loan commitments, as defined by the FRS, encompass a variety of arrangements, one of which is a confirmed *credit line* in which a bank offers to lend up to a maximum amount of funds to a customer anytime during a specific period, usually within one year. A credit line seldom specifies the terms and conditions under which the loan will be made. Although it can cancel some credit lines for cause, in practice a bank views itself as morally bound to meet most credit lines that it grants.

In contrast to credit lines, *formalized loan commitments* involve detailed agreements that specify the terms and conditions under which subsequent loans will be made. For example, a bank and a business customer sign a written agreement containing the following illustrative conditions:

---

22. Ellmore C. Patterson, "Credit Quality: Lessons of Recent Experience," *The Morgan Guaranty Survey,* June 1976, pp. 11-14.

23. Robert H. Behrens, "Salvaging the Problem Loan," *The Bankers Magazine,* Spring 1975, pp. 74-78. Paul H. Hunn, "Big Trouble: Managing Major Problem Loans," *The Bankers Magazine,* Autumn 1975, pp. 22-32.

24. "Loan Commitments at Selected Large Commercial Banks: New Statistical Series," *Federal Reserve Bulletin,* April 1975, pp. 226-229.

- the customer may borrow up to $10 million during the coming two-year period
- the interest rate will float at one percentage point above the bank's prime rate
- any outstanding borrowing at the end of the period can be converted to a five-year loan having agreed repayment provisions
- the borrower will maintain an agreed level of compensating balances and will comply with the covenants included in the agreement

A formalized loan agreement is a legally binding contract between the two parties. Even if its financial condition starts to deteriorate, a business customer can still borrow funds according to the agreed terms. Most formalized loan commitments are for term loans that have an original maturity of more than one year, or they are *revolving credits* that permit a borrower to draw down and repay loans at will (with no repayment penalty) and that provide for the commitment to rebound after a borrower repays a takedown.

## BUSINESS USE OF LOAN COMMITMENTS

Corporate treasurers use loan commitments to assist their cash-flow management. When its cash-flow needs are predictable, such as seasonal, a firm can use a loan commitment to help meet these foreseeable needs. In addition, a corporate treasurer sometimes wants a loan commitment that will help assure the firm's access to funds during uncertain periods of cash flows. One illustrative firm plans to sell additional securities in order to finance an expansion of its production facilities. It negotiates a formalized commitment with its bank so that it can initially borrow funds to start its new construction. If it subsequently concludes that it is disadvantageous to sell additional securities, then the firm can take down the rest of the commitment and convert it to a term loan subject to the conditions of the formalized agreement. A second illustrative firm issues commercial paper, and so it negotiates revolving credit lines against which it can conveniently draw if for some unexpected reason it were to find that it has to redeem net amounts of its commercial paper.

Business firms willingly pay a price to confirm their access to bank loans. A firm with a credit line may agree to maintain a compensating balance (CB) amounting to 10 percent of the unused portion of the credit line plus 20 percent of the used portion of the credit line. To obtain a formalized loan commitment, with its more specific provisions, a firm may have to pay a *commitment fee,* say half a percent, on the unused portion of the commitment. A bank's policies concerning its CB requirements and commitment fees vary over time, and they are subject to negotiation with specific customers. As credit conditions tighten, a bank generally raises its requirements and fees; and, as credit conditions ease, it lowers and sometimes eliminates its requirements and fees—at least for some of its prime business customers.

## BANK MANAGEMENT OF LOAN COMMITMENTS

When it offers loan commitments, a bank expects to benefit by solidifying its customer relationships and by obtaining the compensating balances and possible fees associated with its commitments. Yet to be able to honor its commitments during their effective periods, a bank has to manage its cash flows so that it can meet both predictable and unpredictable takedowns of its outstanding commitments.

To manage its loan commitments, a bank first has to compile regularly information about the amounts and types of its commitments. Then it has to develop some predictions as to the probable usage pattern of the commitments. For example, a bank determines that it has outstanding loan commitments of $300 million. The commitments are broadly diversified among various business customers, and so it is unlikely that most of the customers will simultaneously take down their commitments. Members of the bank's staff therefore review past usage patterns and conclude that their best estimate is that 50 percent of the amount of outstanding commitments will be taken down in the coming year. The staff members may go further and estimate the probable usage rates; if credit markets suddenly become tighter, or if there is an unexpected economic slowdown. Once it thus determines its volume and composition of commitments and estimates probable usage rates under various economic conditions, the bank can reexamine how it will meet its various commitments; for example, will it plan to reduce other of its assets and/or increase its deposit and nondeposit liabilities? As they thus examine the future cash-flow implications of their bank's commitments, a bank's senior officers may make a policy decision to change the rate at which the bank makes new commitments. Although it can thus somewhat control the rate of change in its commitments, a bank has little control over the usage patterns of its current and future commitments.

One researcher provides a detailed study of how some large banks use reporting systems and forecasting procedures to manage their loan commitments. "Several large banks use pro forma financial statements . . . to help assess and plan for future trends. Some have developed computer programs to help prepare such statements on a regular basis."[25] The author further notes, however, that a bank does not necessarily need to develop an automated system in order to have better information about its loan commitments. Some banks, even with many borrowing customers, use manual systems for their loan commitment reports and analyses.

One bank officer reports how his large bank, to track its loan commitments, uses a set of charts that summarize historical relationships between loan commitments and borrowings against these commitments. This bank finds that "the usage rate of aggregate firm commitments during periods of tight money reaches peaks that can be anticipated within a tolerable margin of error. . . . Thus without bothering with an analysis of

---

25. Dwight B. Crane, *Managing Credit Lines and Commitments,* a study prepared for the Trustees of the Banking Research Fund, Association of Reserve City Bankers, 1973, p. 27.

the various subcategories of firm commitments or lines of credit, we have a means of estimating total borrowings under commitments in periods of tight money."[26]

Even as it projects aggregate usage rates, a bank can also use other procedures to help control the risks associated with its loan commitments:

- To control their default risk, subject proposed commitments to a credit-approval process similar to the one used for business-loan applications.
- Seldom make formalized loan commitments for periods that exceed three years nor credit lines for periods beyond one year. If they thus limit the time period of each commitment, the loan officers can periodically review each firm's financial developments and propose possible revisions in the commitments.
- To control interest-rate risk, use floating interest rates on loans taken down from the commitments and peg the floating rate to the bank's cost of funds or to a market rate, such as that for commercial paper.

One banker states that many banks, by focusing on CB requirements, have underpriced their loan commitments and that "corporations have been able to purchase insurance lines of credit, in excess of their immediate needs, at a nominal cost."[27] He therefore proposes that banks "charge substantial fees for access to credit." These fees, he believes, will:

- generate major revenues for banks
- provide a more precise pricing system than do CB requirements
- reduce demand for lines of credit

While it has not been widely adopted, this type of proposed fee is consistent with the recent trend toward more explicit pricing of banking services.

Officials of the FRS at times question the loan commitment practices of large banks. These officials reportedly believe that "banks' aggressive efforts to fulfill these obligations to corporate customers hinder the Federal Reserve's attempt to control inflation and lead to an undesirable differentiation in the impact of tightening credit conditions."[28] To monitor bank loan commitments, in 1975 the FRS inaugurated a monthly survey of loan commitments by about 150 large banks that must submit a completed questionnaire (Exhibit 12-2) that summarizes the used and unused portions of various categories of commitments. This reporting requirement presumably builds on the internal information systems that large banks use to monitor and control their loan commitments.

---

26. James H. Higgins, "Loan Commitments," *The Journal of Commercial Bank Lending*, July 1972, pp. 2-9.

27. Lowell W. Bryan, "Put a Price on Credit Lines," *The Bankers Magazine*, Summer 1974, pp. 44-49.

28. Crane, *Managing Credit Lines and Commitments*, p. 43.

## EXHIBIT 12-2

FR 2039
Approved by Federal Reserve Board — January 1978
Approval expires January 1980

# MONTHLY SURVEY OF LOAN COMMITMENTS

As of last day, _____

Month/Year

This report is authorized by law [12 U.S.C. §248(a) and 12 U.S.C. §248(i)]. Your voluntary cooperation in submitting this report is needed to make the results comprehensive, accurate and timely.

The Federal Reserve System regards the individual bank information provided by each respondent as confidential. If it should be determined subsequently that any information collected on this form must be released, respondents will be notified.

In order to reduce reporting burden, banks may elect to include only those single commitments that are greater than $100,000. Otherwise, commitments should be reported without any limitation as to individual size. The $100,000 cut-off, if adopted, should apply uniformly to all offices of the bank. Please check which option characterizes reporting at your bank.

1. Single commitments only over $100,000 ☐

2. No size limitation ☐

### PLEASE SEE INSTRUCTIONS ON REVERSE BEFORE COMPLETING THIS FORM

| COMMITMENTS AND OUTSTANDING LOANS MADE UNDER COMMITMENTS | Unused Commitments | | Outstanding Loans Made Under Commitments | | Total | |
|---|---|---|---|---|---|---|
| | Mil. | Thou. | Mil. | Thou. | Mil. | Thou. |
| 1. FOR COMMERCIAL AND INDUSTRIAL LOANS (exclude mortgages and loans for purchasing and carrying securities) | | | | | | |
| a. Commitments for term loans . . . . . . . . . . . . . . . . . . . . . | | | | | | |
| b. Commitments for revolving credits . . . . . . . . . . . . . . . . | | | | | | |
| c. Confirmed lines of credit. . . . . . . . . . . . . . . . . . . . . . . | | | | | | |
| d. Other commitments for commercial and industrial loans . . . . | | | | | | |
| e. Total. . . . . . . . . . . . . . . . . . . . . . . . . . . . . . . . . | | | | | | |
| 2. FOR LOANS TO NONBANK FINANCIAL INSTITUTIONS (exclude loans for purchasing and carrying securities and mortgages; include loans for mortgage warehousing). . . . . . . . . | | | | | | |

_____       _____

Person to be contacted concerning this report (PLEASE PRINT)           Area code/Telephone number

_____

Name and Location of Bank

PLEASE RETURN THE COMPLETED QUESTIONNAIRE TO THE
FEDERAL RESERVE BANK NOT LATER THAN TEN BUSINESS
DAYS AFTER THE LAST DAY OF MONTH

FORM 601-050 A

Source: Federal Reserve System

## LOAN PARTICIPATIONS

At times a creditworthy customer requests a loan that exceeds the amount that its bank can legally or prudently lend. Such a request may exceed a bank's legal lending limit or may result in the bank's violating its diversification policies for its loan portfolio. In such cases a bank can invite one or more of its correspondent banks to participate in the loan. An upstream loan participation is one in which a bank arranges to place part of a loan with a larger correspondent bank. Conversely, a downstream loan participation is one in which a bank participates in part of a large loan originated by a larger bank. Downstream participations are a service that large correspondent banks provide to smaller banks that face slack loan demand.

Because of inconsistencies among bank participation procedures, a committee of Robert Morris Associates (the national association of bank commercial loan and credit officers) developed a set of 11 guidelines for bank loan participations. These guidelines include:

- "The originating bank should provide the prospective participant with full information on the borrower to enable it to make an independent credit decision. Moreover, it is the continuing obligation of the originating bank to provide the participant current information as it becomes available and to inform the participant of adverse changes in the status of the borrower for the duration of the loan.
- "Each participant should arrive at its own credit decision independently.
- "A loan participation is a non-recourse transaction. (A bank should not participate in a loan anticipating that the originating bank will repurchase the participation.)
- "The responsibilities for administration, documentation, collateral servicing and collection should be fixed at the inception of the participation. Such duties should be performed in a manner which preserves the interests of each bank."[29]

Other of the guidelines cite the need for: respect for confidential information, prompt decisions and payments, and clear understandings concerning a loan's terms. In total these guidelines help structure the responsibilities of banks that participate in loans with their correspondents.

There are other procedures by which a bank can participate in loan transactions. A *syndicated loan* is one in which a group of large banks lend to a large borrower, such as a major business firm or a foreign country. Usually one large bank develops and manages a specific syndicated loan, and it receives a fee for its services. An interbank *loan pool participation* is one in which a bank participates in a pool of loans created and managed by

---

29. "Guidelines for Upstream Downstream Correspondent Bank Loan Participations," Robert Morris Associates, November 1975.

another, usually larger, bank. Although it may change the specific pooled loans over time, the managing bank adheres to agreed guidelines concerning the amount, quality, and variety of pooled loans. Banks also participate in various loan transactions with public and private nonbank lenders, and participants in these transactions will reduce the chance of subsequent misunderstandings if—as with bank loan participations—each understands its responsibilities and if the participated loan is carefully structured.

## LENDING TO SMALL BUSINESSES

Whatever its size, a bank receives loan applications from nearby small business firms, most of which are more geographically limited in their choice of banks than are large, publicly held firms. When they review a loan application from a small business, loan officers often have to rely on unaudited financial statements that crudely summarize the firm's brief operating history; and they seldom receive carefully prepared financial projections by the applicant. Based on such limited supporting information, the loan officers cannot conveniently analyze the credit risk of the proposed loan; and, especially if the application is for a small amount of funds, the per-unit costs to analyze and administer the requested loan are likely to exceed those for a large loan to a prime borrower. Also, the loan officers may conclude that it is unrealistic to expect a small firm to maintain sufficient compensating balances to help boost the total return from the loan. Thus, in view of the probable risks and costs, the loan officers are likely to deny a request for a small-business loan *unless* they can:

- negotiate an interest rate that is high enough to compensate for the costs and risks of the loan and/or
- be reasonably confident that the firm, if successful, will develop a future account relationship that will be profitable to the bank, and/or
- conveniently control the loan's risk, primarily via personal endorsements, collateral, or insurance programs

Even if it has a policy to help small local businesses, a bank is unlikely to have this policy supersede the need for prudent return-risk analyses of applications for small business loans.

Various studies examine the financing needs and problems of small businesses, and they generally conclude that potentially profitable small businesses face handicaps in obtaining medium-term and long-term capital. An official of the Small Business Administration reports about a study, the results of which, "together with first-hand observations of the financial problems of many small business concerns, have confirmed the Agency's belief that a small business capital gap does exist, especially with respect to intermediate and long-term credit."[30] This official, in his article, also

---

30. W. J. Garvin, "The Small Business Capital Gap: The Special Case of Minority Enterprise," *The Journal of Finance,* May 1971, pp. 445-457.

summarizes the results of other studies that examine the financing problems of small businesses.

Legislators and other government officials frequently express their concern about whether small firms have reasonable access to funds, and at times they take specific actions to try to facilitate small-business access to funds.

In 1973 the Committee on Interest and Dividends (CID) set guidelines calling for a system of *dual prime rates*: a "large-business prime rate," and a "small-business prime rate." The large-business prime rate is an extension of the traditional prime rate practice. The small-business prime rate is for a bank's most creditworthy small borrowers. Compared to the large-business prime, the CID expected banks especially to restrain the frequency and magnitude of increases in their small-business prime rates. Although it is not clear how many small businesses were able to borrow at the posted small-business prime rate, this rate remained below the large-business rate until the dual-prime system lost its official status in 1974. Some banks, however, voluntarily report and promote a small-business prime rate.

The Congress created the Small Business Administration (SBA) in 1953, and since then it has steadily expanded the SBA's resources and authority. The SBA makes direct loans, and it lends in cooperation with banks and other institutions. It has power to make direct loans, however, only to firms that demonstrate their inability to obtain "financing at a 'reasonable' (undefined) rate of interest from a bank or other financial institution" and for which a loan participation is not available.[31] The SBA also adheres to congressional guidelines concerning collateral requirements and maximum amounts, maturities, and interest rates for various types of loans that it makes.

Banks and other institutions participate in most SBA loans.[32] These participations are of three principal types:

- *immediate* participation, in which both the SBA and a private lender immediately share a loan
- *deferred* participation, in which a private lender first makes the total loan, but this lender can subsequently request the SBA to purchase up to an agreed part of the loan
- *guaranteed* loan, in which a private lender can sell up to an agreed part (not to exceed 90%) of the loan to the SBA only if the borrower defaults in loan payments for 60 days.

In loans in which it participates with the SBA, a bank can set its interest rate above that charged by the SBA. A bank pays a fee to the SBA for its deferred or guaranteed participation. A bank also has to adhere to specific

---

31. Carolyn N. Hooper, "SBA's Business Loan Program: Retrospect and Prospect," *Journal of Bank Research,* Autumn 1971, pp. 39-49.

32. Hooper, "SBA's Business Loan Program: Retrospect and Prospect," p. 42.

administrative procedures for its loan participations with the SBA. To try to reduce administrative costs, a bank and the SBA can execute a "master guaranty agreement against which all subsequent transactions are written."

A senior officer of a large metropolitan bank reports about his bank's long, substantial working relationship with the SBA; and he encourages smaller banks to examine the benefits of working with the SBA.[33] Among the benefits he cites are:

- Bank examiners do not classify the SBA-guaranteed portion of a bank loan as a risk asset in their computations of a bank's capital adequacy.
- The SBA-guaranteed portion of a loan is usually eligible collateral to pledge against public deposits.
- For clients whose loans it participates in with the SBA, a bank can draw on the managerial and technical resources of the SBA, examples of which are SCORE (the Service Corps of Retired Executives) and task forces of students supervised by faculty and SBA representatives.

Each bank has to evaluate whether, in its case, the benefits of loan participations with the SBA are likely to exceed the administrative costs of such participations. Apparently many banks conclude that the benefits exceed the costs, because about sixty percent of U.S. banks participate in SBA loan programs.[34]

## AGRIBUSINESS LOANS

During recent decades, as their operations have become larger and more capital-intensive, farm operators have had to request larger loans to help finance their seasonal plantings, capital investments, and transfers of ownership. These farm loans have many similarities to loans made to nonagricultural firms.

In the aggregate, agricultural loans account for about five percent of total bank loans, and this ratio is similar to that of a decade earlier. Among banks, however, this ratio varies widely. In about fifteen percent of the nation's banks, primarily those with deposits under $25 million, farm loans account for over fifty percent of their total loans. Most of these smaller banks, which "supply a major share of total bank lending to agriculture," are located in agricultural states that restrict branch banking.[35]

---

33. George J. McClaran, "Cutting Your Risks in Small-Business Loans," *Banking,* March 1976, pp. 40, 52.

34. SBA programs focus on loans to small businesses. The Congress also passed legislation providing for creation of Small Business Investment Companies (SBICs) which help channel equity types of funds to small firms. Some banks, or their parent holding companies, own an interest in an SBIC; and various banks cooperate with SBICs to develop financing packages for small firms. Dale S. Hanson, "Creative Financing in Today's Economy," *Banking,* January 1971, pp. 58-60.

35. Mary Hamblin, "Bank Lending to Agriculture: An Overview," *Monthly Review* (Federal Reserve Bank of Kansas City), November 1975, pp. 11-16.

When it receives a loan request that exceeds its legal lending limit, a rural bank usually tries to enter into a loan participation with its city correspondent. If it is part of a multibank holding company, then the rural bank will likely try to enter into a loan participation with one or more of its coaffiliate banks. If it is part of a branch system, then, subject to its system's internal policies and control procedures, a rural branch can extend a loan up to the amount of the total system's legal lending limit. In these ways large banks, although not headquartered in agricultural areas, often hold some agricultural loans in their portfolio.

Banks categorize their agricultural loans by whether or not they are secured by farm real estate. About seventy-five percent of bank agricultural loans are short-term loans not secured by farm real estate. Most of these are seasonal loans, whereby a bank lends funds to a farmer during planting time and plans to be repaid after the harvest.

When they analyze an application for a farm loan, rural loan officers, even if informally, evaluate various aspects of returns, risks, and risk-control procedures. A rural bank often has a standard rate that it charges on farm loans, and it infrequently changes this rate over time. It is especially likely to have such a pricing policy if it operates in a state that has a usury ceiling that specifies a maximum interest rate on certain types of loans, such as farm loans below a maximum dollar amount, and/or if it views its costs of funds as insulated from money-market fluctuations. A rural bank, especially a small one, seldom requires compensating balances or complex loan agreements; and it seldom engages in prolonged negotiations with a loan applicant. In rural communities a bank loan officer already knows much about the character and resources of nearby loan applicants. To monitor outstanding agricultural loans, a bank officer frequently chats about crop prospects with borrowers when they visit the bank or when they participate in community activities that the banker also attends.

Most rural banks operate within a competitive system that contains nearby components of the Farm Credit Administration and the Farmers Home Administration. The *Farm Credit Administration* (FCA) supervises and coordinates various agencies that lend to farmers. These agencies include the:

- Federal Land Banks, which, through local Federal Land Bank Associations, make long-term loans secured by farm and rural real estate
- Federal Intermediate Credit Banks (FICBs), which lend funds to local Production Credit Associations (PCAs), which in turn make short- and intermediate-term loans to finance agricultural production
- Banks for Cooperatives, which lend to rural cooperatives (these loans are generally classified as business loans, not as farm loans)

The *Farmers Home Administration* (FHA), which is part of the Department of Agriculture, makes short- and long-term loans to farmers who cannot obtain loans through conventional lenders.

Between 1964 and 1974, the FCA increased its share of total agricultural lending from 17 percent to 29 percent.[36] Much of this gain was triggered by the Farm Credit Act of 1971, which permitted the Federal Land Banks and PCAs to make larger loans to a wider variety of rural borrowers.

Federal Land Bank Associations and PCAs offer an expending set of services to rural borrowers, who must first become members by investing in the stock of a local association. In addition to loans, the agencies offer data processing services that help their members' financial planning and record-keeping. Their members can invest in Farm Credit Investment Bonds, which have $1000 denominations and pay a floating interest rate that reflects money-market interest rates. Although they compete with rural banks in various ways, FCA agencies can also cooperate with rural banks, for example by entering into loan participations with them.

## SETTING LOAN PRIORITIES

If they seek to maximize their long-run profits, banks will develop policies that encourage their loan officers to make high-return (risk adjusted) loans. For example, an illustrative bank places high priority on loans to prime borrowers. Even if such loans involve low stated interest rates, the bank expects that its total returns from prime loans (when adjusted for compensating balances, total customer profitability, and processing costs) will generally exceed those from many smaller, riskier loans.

In addition, during periods when credit is tight, most banks reportedly implement *differential priorities* by which they strive to accommodate the borrowing requests of their major business and agricultural borrowers; but they deemphasize making new loans to small businesses, financial institutions, individuals, and real-estate borrowers.[37] From the viewpoint of a profit-maximizing bank, these differential priorities are rational, especially if it faces ceiling rates that it can charge on some types of nonbusiness loans.

Some critics object to a system in which banks, acting in their own long-run interests, set priorities for loans within their portfolios, especially during periods of tight money. They argue that such priorities are often unfair to small businesses, home buyers, and consumer borrowers. Often these critics carry their cases to the Congress and to federal bank supervisory agencies, and they advocate public policies that would channel the loan priorities of banks and other lending institutions.

Governmental units can institute *selective credit policies* (or controls) that encourage "socially desirable" (a value judgment) loans and discourage, for example by quotas or penalties, "socially undesirable" loans. The

---

36. Hamblin, "Bank Lending to Agriculture: An Overview," p. 12.

37. Various policy proposals and actions assume that differential lending practices exist, but there has not been extensive confirmation of such practices. For a summary of previous studies and some additional evidence, see Duane G. Harris, "Some Evidence on Differential Lending Practices at Commercial Banks," *The Journal of Finance,* December 1973, pp. 1303-1310.

United States already has some selective credit policies, and various constituents and Congressmen advocate the expansion of such policies.

Congress has created various federal programs and agencies that are designed to channel loans to special categories of borrowers, such as home buyers, small businesses, rural firms and cooperatives, and students. Some of these programs involve subsidies and tax preferences. Congress has passed other laws designed to restrict certain types of loans. For example, Congress authorizes the FRS to regulate the maximum percentages that institutions can lend to borrowers planning to purchase or carry marketable securities (Regulation U).

The FRS at times explicitly communicates its view about suitable priorities for bank loans.[38] In 1929 and 1966 the various Federal Reserve Banks wrote to their members asking them to discriminate against certain categories of loans (''speculative'' collateral loans in 1929 and business loans in 1966). In 1973 the Chairman of the Board of Governors wrote to a senior official of each member bank to invite his or her ''personal cooperation '' in seeing that the bank appropriately disciplined its rate of credit expansion. Member banks that were unresponsive to these FRS letters at least tacitly understood that their access to the discount window would be jeopardized; and, especially in 1966, cooperative banks that made certain priority loans were assured of courteous consideration at the discount window.

In September 1974, during a period of historically high inflation and interest rates, the Board of Governors sent to member banks a statement by its Federal Advisory Council (FAC) a statutory board composed of 12 prominent bankers. In part, this letter contained the following priority statements.

> The basic credit needs for normal operations of all established business customers should, of course, be met to assure the production and distribution of goods and services. . . .
>
> Loans for purely financial activities, such as acquisitions or the purchase of a company's own shares, would normally not be appropriate uses of limited bank funds.
>
> Loans for speculative purposes, such as purchasing securities or commodities other than in the ordinary course of business, excessive inventory accumulation, or investing in land without well-defined plans for its useful development, are not generally suitable.
>
> A regrettable aspect of restrictive monetary policy is that it tends to produce an uneven impact, bearing more heavily on some sectors of the economy than others. Therefore, banks should make an effort to utilize their limited funds equitably, giving consideration, for instance, to the special vulnerability of the homebuilding industry.

---

38. Edward J. Kane, ''The Central Bank as Big Brother'' (A Comment), *Journal of Money, Credit, and Banking,* November 1973, pp. 979-981.

Similarly, consumer credit should receive its share of bank funds. The basic requirements of individuals for household needs and automobiles should be accommodated, but discretionary spending that might be deferred should not be encouraged.[39]

To determine how banks adapted their lending policies to the FAC statement, the Board of Governors conducted two subsequent surveys focusing on questions of credit allocation by money-center banks. These banks generally reported that they were disapproving large proportions of applications for loans "for purely financial activities" and "for speculative purposes."[40] There may have been some "biases" in these reporting procedures.

Proponents of selective credit policies suggest additional techniques to channel funds toward "priority" borrowers or to restrict loans to "nonpriority" borrowers. A bank's reserve requirements currently relate to its deposit structure. One proposed procedure would set *asset reserve requirements,* with priority categories of assets (for example, home loans) having lower reserve requirements than nonpriority categories of assets. A variant would be to permit a bank to count some of its high-priority loans to meet its reserves required against liabilities. Another variant would be to require supplemental reserves for certain types of nonpriority loans or loan commitments.

Congress regularly receives proposals to expand selective credit policies. Despite the many proposals, the Federal Reserve Bank of Philadelphia noted the lack of research that evaluates various credit-allocation techniques; and so it sponsored such a set of studies. A summary of these studies concludes that "the case now for a larger role for selective credit controls is less than convincing. The benefits are elusive and, even if defined, difficult to achieve, and the costs of implementation may be sizeable. Therefore, the justification for additional selective credit controls, given the current state of knowlege, must rest more on 'hunch' than any systematic analysis."[41]

A bank's senior officers thus have to set and monitor loan priorities that comply with current selective credit policies, and they have to engage constructively in the ongoing debate as to whether and how the government should change its set of selective credit policies.

---

39. *Federal Reserve Bulletin,* September 1974, pp. 679-680.

40. *Federal Reserve Bulletin,* July 1975, pp. 405-406.

41. Ira Kaminow and James M. O'Brien, "Selective Credit Policies: Should Their Role Be Expanded?" *Business Review* (Federal Reserve Bank of Philadelphia), November 1975, pp. 3-22. Another article that summarizes the issues, evidence, and alternatives related to selective credit policies is by Randall C. Merris, "Credit Allocation and Commercial Banks," *Business Conditions* (Federal Reserve Bank of Chicago), August 1975, pp. 13-19. For a survey of selective credit controls used in other nations, see Donald R. Hodgman, *Selective Credit Controls in Western Europe,* a study prepared for the Trustees of the Banking Research Fund, Association of Reserve City Bankers, 1976.

# EQUIPMENT LEASING

A business firm sometimes chooses to lease equipment, rather than to borrow funds to buy it. In some cases a firm thus can: obtain 100 percent financing of its equipment, avoid incurring explicit debt, avoid compensating balance requirements, and/or reduce its risk of owning equipment that unexpectedly becomes obsolete. Even prime corporate customers have some financing decisions whereby, perhaps for tax reasons, they find it advantageous to lease equipment.

Many large banks lend to unaffiliated equipment leasing firms, and thereby they finance equipment leasing. These loans often are secured by specific leases, and thus the lending banks have to analyze the quality of various lease agreements.

The OCC has ruled that national banks can own or lease "personal property acquired upon the specific request and for the use of a customer and may incur such additional obligations as may be incident to becoming an owner and lessor of such property." Although it can thus own personal property as part of specific leasing agreements, a national bank cannot buy such property to hold in inventory pending possible future leasing contracts. The OCC further rules that lease financing agreements are not loans, and therefore not subject to legal lending limits and usury ceilings. Many states also permit state-chartered banks to engage in some leasing activities; and the FRS permits bank holding companies to have nonbank affiliates that lease personal property.

Direct leasing activities are most prevalent among large banks that strive to provide a full set of corporate financial services. These banks offer leasing services as an additional source of profits and also as a way to retain current customers and to attract new customers away from nonbank leasing firms and from other banks that do not offer leasing services. Although it can directly provide many leasing services, a large bank typically has a nonbank coaffiliate that specializes in leasing activities. This coaffiliate faces few of the barriers, such as branching restrictions, that impede a bank's direct geographical expansion into other states.

A *lease agreement* often is a complex document that specifies "the number, size and time sequence of lease payments" and that "usually includes clauses covering cancellation rights and conditions, renewal or purchase options, treatment of tax benefits, prepayment requirements, and particular legal, financial and servicing obligations of the lessor, lessee and third parties. Since leases can be tailored to meet special needs of the parties involved, there is in fact an almost limitless variety of actual lease contracts."[42]

Banking organizations primarily write *financial leases,* whereby a client (lessee) leases the equipment for most of its estimated useful life and

---

42. Steven J. Weiss and Vincent John McGugan, "The Equipment Leasing Industry and the Emerging Role of Banking Organizations," *New England Economic Review* (Federal Reserve Bank of Boston), November-December 1973, pp. 3-30.

assumes responsibility to pay for the equipment's taxes, maintenance, and insurance. Financial leases are noncancellable, especially during their early years; and they usually are *full-payout leases,* whereby the "income realized over the basic term of the lease is calculated to compensate the lessor for the full cost of the equipment plus a net rate of return. The 'payout' to the lessor may include tax benefits and realization of 'residual value' (the anticipated net value of the equipment at the end of the lease) of the equipment, in addition to scheduled payments." Because it wants to limit bank leasing to "the functional equivalent of an extension of credit," the FRS insists that holding company affiliates write only full-payout leases, wherein "the estimated residual value of the property at the expiration of the initial term of the lease . . . *in no case shall exceed 10 percent of the acquisition cost of the property to the lessor.*"[43]

The principal alternative to a full-payout lease is an *operating lease,* which is usually short term and subject to cancellation after due notice. In operating leases, a lessor usually assumes greater risk as to the equipment's obsolescence and residual value. National banks, in contrast to affiliates of bank holding companies, have more flexibility to write operating leases. Some bank holding companies therefore urge the FRS to permit holding-company leasing affiliates to write operating leases so that they can better compete against national banks and especially against nonbank lessors.

Calculation of returns from lease agreements often is a complex, at time controversial, process. A specific calculation depends on such factors as the timing of payments, possible early termination, projected residual value, and tax implications.[44] Tax considerations are an especially important part of leasing. If it carefully structures the transaction, a lessor can obtain tax benefits that arise from the investment tax credits and depreciation associated with the equipment. In some cases, a lessor can use these credits to reduce its tax liabilities whereas the user of the equipment, such as a railroad or airline, has a low level of taxable income and so cannot fully use the tax benefits. With as little as 20 percent equity, a lessor (or lessor group) can structure a *leveraged lease,* whereby the lessor gains the full tax benefits and also deducts interest paid to third-party lenders, such as insurance companies and pension funds, that provide loan funds for much of the leveraged-lease transaction. Specialists in some large banking organizations package complex leasing deals in ways that enable their participants to share the tax benefits.[45] Thus if they engage in imaginative leasing transactions, large banking organizations can somewhat control their levels of taxable income.

43. Weiss and McGugan, "The Equipment Leasing Industry and the Emerging Role of Banking Organizations," pp. 6, 21.

44. Peter K. Nevitt and Thomas C. Heagy, "Economics of Direct Lease Investment," and Richard B. Stebbins, "Early Termination in Leveraged Lease Financing," both in *The Bankers Magazine,* Summer 1975, pp. 43-49 and 34-37, respectively.

45. John W. James and Alan I. Goldman, "Innovative Bank Leasing," *The Bankers Magazine,* Summer 1975, pp. 39-42.

Some large banks package leasing transactions in which they invite smaller banks to participate. In these participations, as with loan participations, a smaller bank has to analyze carefully a proposed transaction from the viewpoint of the bank's return-risk objectives and its current and projected tax status. It is questionable whether most medium-sized and small banks should try to develop the in-bank skills necessary to evaluate participations in complex leasing transactions.

## SUMMARY

Each bank tailors diverse business loans for clients with whom it seeks to develop and cement long-run relationships.

Some of a bank's officers call on current and potential business customers. These officers thus keep informed about a firm's recent developments and its prospects, and they personally communicate their bank's readiness to provide diverse services to the firm and its principal officers. Many banks increase their schedule of direct calls during periods of slack loan demand, and they reduce their schedule when they face strong loan demand from current customers. Therefore, a bank can examine whether to adopt a countercyclical calling strategy whereby it plans ahead so that it can lend to potential clients during future periods when loan demand is strong and other banks are reducing their call programs.

The prime rate is the lowest interest rate that a bank will offer on short-term loans to its largest, most creditworthy business borrowers. A bank announces its prime, or base, rate; it seldom cuts its prime rate for a specific borrower; and it scales its other interest rates upward from its prime rate. Traditionally, the prime rate has been an administered price that a bank infrequently changes in response to actual and/or expected changes in credit conditions—including prime rate changes by rival banks. Some banks, however, use formulas to help their senior management set their bank's prime rate and to help defuse criticism of their changes in prime rate.

Most banks expect and/or require their business borrowers to maintain compensating balances (CBs) that are associated with the size of a loan, or loan commitment. Because most CBs are in the form of demand deposits that have associated reserve requirements, some commentators contend that CBs are irrational; and they propose alternatives such as compensating fees or CBs in the form of noninterest-paying time deposits, with their lower required reserves. Yet in many cases CBs are not irrational, either from the viewpoint of a lending bank or a business borrower. Therefore each bank has to evaluate its current or potential use of CB requirements as a way to gain additional pricing flexibility and to forestall deposit outflows.

Loan officers evaluate how a specific loan request relates to a long-run relationship between the bank, the applicant firm, and associates of the applicant. They try to determine whether their disapproval of a requested loan will likely jeopardize a complex set of long-run customer relationships.

Commercial loan officers use specialized procedures to analyze and control the risk of requested business loans. They use cash flow forecasting to estimate the applicant's ability to service its proposed debt on schedule. Whether they use computer-based programs or manual procedures, the analysts test what can happen to the projected cash flows if one varies some key assumptions about the applicant's future operations. The loan officers then evaluate various covenants that can help the bank control its lending risk, and they may examine other risk-control procedures such as collateral, cosigners, and loan insurance.

After they evaluate a requested loan, the loan officers develop a multidimensional loan offer, the terms of which are likely to meet the bank's objectives and be acceptable to the applicant firm. A loan offer to a prime business borrower, with its alternative sources of funds, is more standardized than is an offer to a nonprime borrower that poses greater credit risk. For any loan offer, the loan officers prepare some contingency plans as to terms that they are willing to negotiate with the applicant.

Each bank has systems by which its senior officials monitor the composition of the business-loan portfolio and the specific loans within this portfolio. When they detect that a loan or group of loans may pose problems, the officials focus on strategies to mitigate and/or to salvage the potential problems. One way is for the bank to agree to restructure a loan in ways that will ease the borrower's debt-servicing burden and yet protect the bank's creditor position.

Banks often make specific oral or written commitments to lend to their business clients. These loan commitments range from credit lines, which a bank views as morally binding, to formalized loan commitments that involve specific agreed terms and are legally binding. Business firms use loan commitments to help buffer their future cash flows, and banks offer such commitments in order to solidify customer relationships and to obtain CBs and possible revenues from commitment fees. To service their commitments, banks use computer-based or manual systems to monitor and forecast their commitment levels and usage rates. The FRS also monitors loan commitment practices, especially those of large banks.

When it receives a creditworthy loan request that exceeds its lending limit, a bank is likely to arrange an upstream loan participation with one of its large correspondent banks. Sometimes it may also enter into a downstream loan participation with a correspondent bank. A committee of Robert Morris Associates provides guidelines for banks that engage in loan participations. Some banks also participate in syndicated loans and/or loan pools.

Any bank receives loan applications from nearby small businesses. In contrast to large firms, many of these small-business applicants have primitive financial control systems, small loan requirements and CBs, and few financing alternatives. To help control the risks of its small-business loans, a bank can examine whether to enter into participation or insure some of these loans with the Small Business Administration.

Rural banks service the financing needs of nearby agribusiness firms. They make agricultural loans to farm operators; and, when they encounter such loan requests that exceed their lending limits, the banks often arrange upstream loan participations with their city correspondents. Yet as they try to service their agribusiness clients, rural banks face competition from federal agencies like the Farmers Home Administration and components of the Farm Credit Administration. In some cases rural banks can arrange loan participations with such agencies.

Each bank has internal loan priorities by which it seeks to achieve its long-run corporate objectives. It sets and administers its internal priorities within the context of governmental priorities that are embedded in tax, subsidy, and regulatory programs. Some people advocate an increase in government-administered selective credit policies that would seek to promote ''socially desirable'' loans and deter ''socially undesirable'' loans. Although these proponents have not presented a convincing case for more controls, bankers who oppose such controls need to document and present their views in appropriate public-policy forums.

To provide a broad set of corporate banking services, many large banks offer to purchase and lease equipment to their business clients. They do so directly and/or through a coaffiliate firm that specializes in equipment leasing, and they primarily write full-payout financial leases. While it can gain major tax benefits from its leasing activities, a bank needs to have specialists who negotiate the complex leases and effective systems to monitor and control its leasing activities. Most medium-sized and small banks choose not to engage in direct lease financing.

# 13

## CONSUMER LOANS

Historically, many banks chose not to engage in consumer lending but instead to service their traditional clients: businesses, governmental units, and wealthy individuals. Also, many bankers disapproved in principle of consumers' borrowing to purchase such items as automobiles and household appliances. In their view, consumers who insisted on such borrowing should turn to finance companies that specialized in consumer credit.

By the 1950s most banks began to reexamine their antipathy toward consumer lending:

- To broaden their sources of funds, many banks began to seek household deposits. Once it began to develop such depository relationships with consumers, it was logical for a bank to examine what additional services, such as loans, it could provide to these new customers.
- There was increasing acceptance of the fact that consumers would use credit to purchase such durables as automobiles and household appliances.
- Many large banks were indirectly financing consumer credit by lending to specialized consumer-credit firms that in turn made consumer loans. Why should not these banks reexamine the returns and risks from directly engaging in consumer loans?
- As they reviewed the profitability and growth of firms that lent to consumers, additional banks concluded that they could control the risks of consumer lending and could obtain net returns that compared favorably with those from other bank loans and investments.

Thus by the late 1960s virtually all banks engaged in some consumer lending.

## PRINCIPAL TYPES OF CONSUMER LOANS

Most banks now offer consumer loans that differ in their terms, purposes, and flexibility.

### SINGLE-PAYMENT LOANS

A single-payment loan is one in which the entire principal, and its accumulated interest, is to be repaid at one time. A single-payment loan can be in the form of a *demand note,* in which the borrower agrees to repay promptly the entire loan on demand from the lending bank. Usually, however, a single-payment loan has an agreed repayment date that can be extended subject to mutual agreement between the borrower and the lending bank.

Although it can be granted for almost any purpose, a single-payment loan is especially appropriate when a borrower plans to repay the total loan from a cash inflow that he or she confidently anticipates, for example from the sale of an asset or from a bonus or tax refund. A bank is most likely to agree to such a single-payment loan if the applicant has already established a satisfactory deposit and/or borrowing relationship. In such a case the bank may ask for no collateral, or it may offer a lower interest rate if the customer agrees to collateralize the loan, for example with high-quality marketable securities.

Single-payment loans account for about twenty percent of all consumer loans, and installment loans account for the other eighty percent.

### INSTALLMENT LOANS

An installment loan is one in which a borrower and lender agree to a schedule by which the borrower systematically repays the principal, and the associated interest, in two or more repayments. From a lender's viewpoint, one benefit of an installment loan is that a lender can protect itself by setting the repayment schedule so that the remaining loan balance always is less than the depreciated value of a pledged asset, such as an automobile. Also, in many installment loans, a lender further protects itself by restricting the purchaser's title to the asset until the loan is fully repaid. With an installment loan, a borrower can conveniently plan his or her future cash flows in order to service the debt; and the lender can plan its series of cash inflows from the scheduled repayments. With its systematic debt-servicing features, an installment loan enables a consumer to finance diverse purchases.

#### Automobile Loans

Loans to finance the purchase of new or used automobiles account for about half of bank installment loans to individuals. Banks account for a majority of automobile installment financing in the United States; financing subsidiaries of automobile manufacturers and credit unions account for most of the remainder.

To finance automobile purchases, banks either lend directly to a borrower; or they *purchase installment contracts* from nearby automobile dealers. A bank can control its volume and terms of direct loans better than it can control those of contracts purchased from dealers. To illustrate, to deter direct installment loans during a period of strong loan demand, a bank can curtail its advertising of such loans; and it can raise its credit standards and/or loan terms. When it later decides to increase its direct automobile loans, a bank reverses these actions. In contrast, a bank has less flexibility to change the volume and/or terms of automobile financing contracts that it purchases from dealers. During a period of strong loan demand, a bank generally continues its purchases of dealer contracts in order to honor explicit prior commitments and/or to maintain long-run relationships with dealers from which it gets automobile loans, deposit balances, and possibly other business.

When it finances the purchase of an automobile, a bank usually retains title to the automobile until the loan is fully repaid. For many years banks were reluctant to offer maturities beyond 36 months on new-car loans. Recently, however, as new-car prices have increased, some banks have begun to make automobile loans with maturities of 42 to 48 months. From a borrower's viewpoint, a longer payment period reduces the monthly payments.

### Loans to Finance Purchases of Other Consumer Goods

Most banks also stand ready to finance purchases of other consumer goods, such as boats, furniture, household appliances, mobile homes, and recreational vehicles. An installment loan for such a purchase takes one of three following forms:

- a direct loan to a borrower to finance a specific purchase
- purchase of an installment contract from a dealer
- credit extended on a bank credit card used for a specific purchase or series of purchases

While most banks engage in these types of loans, so do credit unions, finance companies, credit card companies, and credit departments of large retail organizations.

### Other Installment Loans

This residual category encompasses installment loans for other household or personal purposes such as unexpected medical bills, vacations, and home improvements. Although they make direct installment loans for such purposes (especially for home improvements), many banks now offer a *check-reserve plan* whereby a depositor can overdraw his or her checking account up to a preagreed maximum amount; and the bank will honor the "overdraft" by crediting the account—usually by a rounded larger figure, such as multiples of $100—and then will treat this advance as an installment loan.

## LOANS TO INDIVIDUALS TO PURCHASE AND CARRY SECURITIES

Although the FRS does not classify them as consumer loans, securities loans to individuals are closely related to consumer loans. A bank often is more willing to lend to and/or charge a lower rate from an individual who agrees to pledge marketable securities as collateral for a loan. Also, if he or she wants to borrow temporarily, a bank customer who has a margin account with a brokerage firm is likely to compare the terms of borrowing against the margin account with the terms offered by the bank or by other nonbank lenders.

The Securities Exchange Act of 1934, as amended, empowers the FRS Board of Governors to set *initial margin requirements* by which the Board specifies the minimum proportion of cash that a person has to use to pay for a securities purchase. The person can use credit to finance the rest of the purchase. FRS margin requirements:

- apply to all stocks and convertible securities listed on registered stock exchanges and to a subset of widely held, actively traded securities (primarily of large firms) that are traded in over-the-counter (OTC) markets
- apply to all banks, brokerage firms, and to most other lenders
- may be raised (to a maximum of 100 percent) or lowered by the Board of Governors of the FRS

To illustrate, if a person wants to buy $10,000 worth of stock that is subject to margin requirements, and if the current margin requirement is 60 percent, then this person has to pay at least $6,000 in cash and can finance the remainder with a loan from a bank, brokerage firm, or other lender that is subject to margin rules.[1]

Before it makes a loan, a bank is supposed to inquire about the purpose of the loan. If the purpose is to purchase or carry securities, then the loan is subject to FRS margin requirements. There is, however, a grey area in cases in which an applicant states that the loan's purpose is, for example, to buy an automobile or do some remodelling, but then offers to collateralize the loan with securities that are subject to margin requirements. Even though such a loan enables the applicant to carry—not to have to sell—the

---

1. In a more complete analysis, a person who has additional unpledged eligible securities could pledge $15,000 of these securities and the $10,000 of newly purchased securities and thus fully finance the new purchase by borrowing 40% (or $10,000) against this total eligible collateral of $25,000.

securities, a loan officer may agree to the loan and have the borrower describe the special purpose of the loan on a FRS form. (As part of their examination procedures, federal bank examiners review a bank's credit files for possible violations of FRS margin requirements.)

Although FRS margin requirements apply only to new loans, a bank also needs internal procedures to monitor subsequent fluctuations in the market value of pledged collateral. To monitor these values, a bank usually codes its loans secured by marketable securities and then has some of its personnel recompute the current value of the collateral:

- at regular intervals
- whenever there is a general decline in securities prices
- whenever such a loan comes up for possible renewal

When it negotiates a loan to a person who pledges securities as collateral, a bank can offer to set up the loan as a: demand note, single-payment note with a specified maturity (possibly subject to renewal), or as an installment loan.

## CONSUMER CREDIT REGULATIONS

Until the late 1960s, diverse state laws governed most consumer credit transactions. Since 1968, however, Congress has rapidly passed a series of consumer credit laws, and it has delegated the administration of these laws to the FRS and other federal agencies. These new federal laws and regulations, while still in flux, have dramatically altered the ground rules by which banks and other lenders engage in consumer credit transactions.

### STATE LAWS

Each state has its own laws that affect consumer credit transactions. Therefore, whether it has a state or national charter, a bank needs legal counsel to determine the extent to which its consumer loans are subject to the laws of the state within which it operates.

#### Usury Laws

Most states have a *usury law* which sets the maximum interest rate that a lender can charge on specific categories of loans. Although they differ among states, usury ceilings generally:[2]

---

2. For a summary table of each state's usury laws, see Norman N. Bowsher, "Usury Laws: Harmful When Effective," *Review* (Federal Reserve Bank of St. Louis), August 1974, pp. 16-23. The author notes that "due to the complex nature of this area of the law, the table may not be completely accurate with respect to certain specific technical provisions."

- apply to small loans to individuals and not to large loans to corporate borrowers
- apply to most bank and nonbank lenders
- exempt certain types of consumer loans

A state bank is subject to the usury laws, if any, of its state. Under federal law, a national bank can charge rates that do not exceed its state's usury ceilings or it can charge up to one percentage point more than its Federal Reserve Bank's discount rate. For example, if its Federal Reserve Bank's discount rate currently is 8 percent, then a national bank can charge 9 percent, even if it is located in a state that has a usury rate of 8 percent.

Usury laws have a long history traceable to Biblical times. Their proponents assert that usury laws help prevent powerful lenders from charging exhorbitant interest rates, especially to unwary individual borrowers. Opponents of usury laws usually reject the dichotomy of powerful lenders who can exploit powerless individual borrowers, and they cite why and how:[3]

- Market competition among lenders removes opportunities for excessive interest rates.
- A small loan involves high administrative costs per dollar lent.[4]
- In practice, lenders and borrowers often can structure a specific loan to circumvent restrictive usury ceilings.
- When they cannot be readily circumvented, usury ceilings lead lenders to redirect their loans to areas not subject to ceilings and lead at least some borrowers to unregulated loan sharks.

Despite such opposition, usury laws remain embedded in the constitution and/or laws of some states.

## Uniform Commercial Code

Because of the variety of state laws and court decisions, the National Conference of Commissioners on Uniform State Laws and the American Law Institute developed the *Uniform Commercial Code* (UCC), which is a model set of laws to govern modern business transactions. The UCC's Article 9 (Secured Transactions, Sales of Accounts, and Chattel Paper) covers virtually all installment credit transactions in which a lender or seller maintains a security interest in a borrower's and/or purchaser's personal property. Virtually all state legislatures have adopted the principal provi-

3. For example, Bowsher; George A. LeMaistre, "The Consequences of Usury Ceilings," *Issues in Bank Regulation,* Autumn 1977, pp. 16-19; Robert E. Keleher and B. Frank King, "Usury: The Recent Tennessee Experience," *Economic Review* (Federal Reserve Bank of Atlanta), July-August 1978, pp. 69-80.

4. Thomas A. Durkin, "Consumer Loan Costs and the Regulatory Basis of Loan Sharking," *Journal of Bank Research,* Summer 1977, pp. 108-117.

sions of Article 9, but many have altered the standardized text. Thus a bank's loan officers have to learn the details of their state's laws that apply to installment credit transactions.

Recent state laws and federal regulations are eroding the *holder-in-due-course doctrine,* which prevents a purchaser from asserting claims or defenses against a party that acquires its debt instrument from a preceding seller or lender. To illustrate, a merchant purchases a shipment of grain and signs a note by which it agrees to pay the seller at a future date. The seller in turn discounts the note at a bank. If it subsequently concludes that the grain shipment does not meet its expectations, the purchaser cannot withhold payment from the bank that now holds the note. The bank is a holder in due course, and so has an enforceable claim against the purchaser and has no obligation to satisfy the purchaser's complaint against the seller.

While it facilitates the flow of commercial transactions, the due-course doctrine has been abused in some consumer credit transactions. For example, a high-pressure salesperson could persuade an unwary consumer to sign an installment contract to buy costly merchandise and then promptly discount the contract with a lender that is protected by the due-course doctrine. If he or she subsequently wanted to rescind the purchase or found defects in the merchandise, the purchaser had little recourse against a recalcitrant seller or against the lender protected by the due-course doctrine. Such actual and potential abuses have led to recent revisions of the applicability of the due-course doctrine to consumer transactions:

- about 30 states now restrict application of the doctrine
- proposed recodification of the UCC effectively eliminates the doctrine
- the Federal Trade Commission, in 1975, issued a Trade Regulation Rule ''Preservation of Consumers' Claims and Defenses,'' that limits the application of the doctrine

These developments have led many banks to carefully reevaluate the reputations of merchants from whom they purchase installment paper, and, in some cases, insist on *recourse agreements* whereby the merchant agrees to repurchase contracts in which a purchaser is exercising his or her rights covered by the FTC's new Trade Regulation Rule.

## FEDERAL LAWS AND REGULATIONS

Since 1968 Congress has passed a rapid series of laws designed to govern consumer credit transactions, and it has assigned the administration of these laws to the FRS and other federal agencies.

### Truth in Lending Act

The Federal Consumer Credit Protection Act, as amended, contains a principal section that is commonly called the Truth in Lending Act. Its principal objective is to require lenders to disclose their credit terms in standardized ways so that borrowers can compare terms offered by various lenders.

Prior to this act, some lenders quoted their loans on an add-on basis by which, for example, they might quote a 6 percent add-on rate for a four-year loan of $5,000. The total interest charge would be $1,200 ($5,000 x .06 per year x 4 years), and this amount would be added to the loan so that the borrower would repay the total of $6,200 in monthly installments spread over the four-year period. When the borrower thus systematically repays the loan, the average outstanding amount of principal is only about half of the $5,000 borrowed, or $2,500. On this basis the effective "annual percentage rate" of interest is almost 11 percent—or almost twice the quoted add-on rate of 6 percent. In addition, a lender might add other charges, such as investigative costs or premiums for required insurance, to its quoted add-on rate.

The Truth in Lending law applies to virtually all parties that extend consumer credit, such as merchants and lenders. They must clearly and conspicuously disclose in writing their credit terms prior to the signing of a credit agreement. The law requires the creditors to disclose the:

- *finance charge,* which includes almost all the costs that the customer will have to pay as a condition for receiving the credit
- *annual percentage rate* (APR), which uses a standardized actuarial method to compute the annual total cost of the finance charge, so that a borrower can compare APRs among lenders
- various terms and conditions associated with their credit offering, *if* they choose to advertise any one term, such as "no down payment"

The law also grants a borrower the right to rescind a credit contract within three business days if the contract is secured by the borrower's residence.

When the credit agreement involves an open-end credit account—such as revolving charge accounts, credit cards, or checking-reserve privileges—the lender has to disclose: when a finance charge may be imposed, how the lender computes the balance against which the finance charge is levied, and how the charge is computed. For example, by which date must a specific balance be paid to avoid any finance charge, and is the finance charge computed on the ending balance for a billing period or on the average daily balance?

The Consumer Credit Protection Act, of which Truth in Lending is a major part, stipulates procedures for promptly resolving billing errors or disputes (so-called Fair Credit Billing), and it contains special provisons that apply to credit cards:

- Except for renewal, credit cards can be issued only in response to an application.
- A cardholder has a maximum liability of $50 for unauthorized use of his or her credit card, and a cardholder discharges even this maximum liability if he or she notifies the issuer before any unauthorized use of the card.

These conditions thus constrain the procedures by which banks and other issuers market their credit cards, and they encourage issuers to implement effective control systems that impede unauthorized use of their credit cards.

The Federal Reserve System has primary administrative responsibility for enforcing the Truth in Lending law, and it does so via its lengthy *Regulation Z*. To help lenders comply with Truth in Lending, the FRS makes available sets of tables that help creditors determine annual percentage rates for various types of installment loans.

### Equal Credit Opportunity Act[5]

The Equal Credit Opportunity Act (ECOA), as amended, prohibits discrimination in the granting of credit based on an applicant's:

- race
- color
- religion
- national origin
- age
- receipt of public assistance benefits
- good faith exercise of rights under the Consumer Credit Protection Act

The ECOA is a hybrid law that bans discrimination in the granting of credit and that contains specific consumer-protection provisions that require creditors (1) to notify credit applicants as to the action taken on their application, and (2), if credit is denied, to inform an applicant as to the reason for the denial.

Regulation B, by which the FRS primarily administers the ECOA, broadly prohibits credit discrimination and contains technical provisions that apply to consumer credit. If, in response to a credit application, a merchant or lender takes *adverse action,* by which it refuses "to grant credit in substantially the amount or on substantially the terms requested," then the merchant or lender must, within 30 days, notify the applicant of:

- the adverse decision
- the ECOA's prohibition of credit discrimination
- *either* the specific reasons for the adverse action *or* a disclosure of the applicant's right to a statement of reasons, in writing if so requested

The ECOA statute requires that the notice contain the "specific reasons for the adverse action taken," but it does not define "specific." Therefore Regulation B contains a model credit-denial form whereby a lender can check as the principal reason(s) items such as: credit application incomplete, insufficient credit references, and insufficient income.

The ECOA, as administered through Regulation B, contains three other major consumer credit provisions:

---

5. "Equal Credit Opportunity," *Federal Reserve Bulletin,* February 1977, pp. 101-107.

- If both a husband and wife use a revolving-credit account, then the creditor has to maintain the account in each name and report the account's credit experience in a way that creates a credit history in each spouse's name. The intention of this provision is to provide married women with a credit history in their own names.
- If it uses a numerical credit-scoring system to evaluate applications, a creditor must stand ready to demonstrate that it is a "statistically sound, empirically derived credit system."
- So that the federal agencies can monitor compliance with the ECOA, a creditor is to request its applicants to give their age and marital status; and the creditor is to record the information that is thus voluntarily supplied. (If a credit application involves a lien on residential property, then the potential creditor is also to request and record the applicant's race and/or national origin.) To help creditors comply with this provision, Regulation B contains model application forms. Although it is not required to use them, a creditor that uses these model forms is deemed to comply with this provision of Regulation B.

Even the preceding summary suggests the complexity of the ECOA and Regulation B. To help banks comply with these new rules, the American Bankers Association (ABA) has developed a *Comprehensive Compliance Manual* that is almost two hundred pages long. The ABA also has prepared a summary "Consumer Loan Checklist on ECOA Regulation," but notes that it is important for loan officers "to understand in considerably more detail the entire provisions of Regulation B" and also "applicable state law."[6]

### Other Applicable Federal Laws

Although Truth in Lending and the ECOA are the principal federal consumer-credit laws, Congress has passed additional laws that affect consumer credit transactions. In 1976, for example, Congress passed the Consumer Leasing Act, which requires lessors to disclose additional information to potential consumer lessees. A bank's consumer credit department—and its legal counsel—thus has to keep informed about recent and proposed changes in consumer credit legislation and regulations; and within this complex and rapidly changing environment, bank officers have to develop and review consumer-loan decision systems.

## CONSUMER-CREDIT PROCESSING SYSTEMS

At the policy level, a bank's senior officials evaluate their bank's competitive environment and alternative opportunities in order to decide on, and review, the extent to which their bank will engage in consumer lending.

---

6. "ABA's Help on Equal-Credit Compliance," *Banking,* March 1977, pp. 54 ff.

Subject to policy guidelines and review, a specialized department (or set of departments) administers a bank's consumer loan activities. The consumer loan department follows the basic steps of a loan decision and review system:

- obtain applications
- analyze and negotiate
- monitor and review
- revise

Throughout this sequence the department uses systems that standardize and expedite its processing of consumer loans. This standardized, batch-processing of consumer loans contrasts to the more individualized steps by which bank loan officers process business and real-estate loans, most of which involve large dollar amounts and complex customer relationships.

## OBTAIN APPLICATIONS

A bank uses cross selling and advertising to solicit consumer loan applications. In addition, it receives some unsolicited applications.

To cross sell its consumer loan services, a bank can publicize them via:

- inserts in the periodic statements that it mails to its depositors
- lobby advertising
- special mailings to targeted subgroups of current customers

To broaden its base of consumer-loan applicants, a bank has to evaluate various advertising media, ranging from neighborhood newspapers and programs to billboards, broadcasting, and large-circulation newspapers.

Under Truth in Lending regulations, a bank cannot selectively advertise some of its loan terms. If it chooses to advertise some terms, then it must advertise all its applicable terms and conditions. Faced with these constraints and if it is reluctant to engage in explicit price competition, a bank will use its cross selling and advertising to alert potential borrowers to its consumer credit activities.

When a person specifically inquires about a consumer loan, then, under the ECOA, the banker who receives the inquiry has to alert the person to his or her consumer credit rights and record the inquiry as an initial credit application. (The federal bank regulatory agencies have developed standardized forms to service such initial applications.) Also, to adhere to Truth in Lending guidelines, the banker promptly discloses the bank's credit terms for the category of credit that is the subject of the consumer inquiry.

After the initial discussion with the banker, the inquirer may decide not to proceed with a written loan application, in which case the banker is to record this outcome. If, however, the person wishes to proceed, then the banker asks the person to complete a written credit application. The application form is likely to be one of the model forms that the FRS has developed to facilitate compliance with the ECOA (Exhibit 13-1). These

## EXHIBIT 13-1

## Model Credit Application Form

[Open end, unsecured credit]

### CREDIT APPLICATION

**IMPORTANT: Read these Directions before completing this Application.**

Check
Appropriate
Box

☐ If you are applying for an individual account in your own name and are relying on your own income or assets and not the income or assets of another person as the basis for repayment of the credit requested, complete only Sections A and D.

☐ If you are applying for a joint account or an account that you and another person will use, complete all Sections, providing information in B about the joint applicant or user.

☐ If you are applying for an individual account, but are relying on income from alimony, child support, or separate maintenance or on the income or assets of another person as the basis for repayment of the credit requested, complete all Sections to the extent possible, providing information in B about the person on whose alimony, support, or maintenance payments or income or assets you are relying.

**SECTION A—INFORMATION REGARDING APPLICANT**

Full Name (Last, First, Middle): ..................................................................... Birthdate: / /

Present Street Address: ..................................................................... Years there: ............

City: .................................. State: .................. Zip: .............. Telephone: ....................

Social Security No.: ..................................... Driver's License No.: ...........................

Previous Street Address: ..................................................................... Years there: ...........

City: .................................. State: .................. Zip: ..............

Present Employer: ..................................... Years there: ............... Telephone: ...........

Position or title: ..................................... Name of supervisor: .............................

Employer's Address: .....................................................................

Previous Employer: ..................................................................... Years there: ...........

Previous Employer's Address: .....................................................................

Present net salary or commission: $.............. per ............. No. Dependents: ........... Ages: ...........

**Alimony, child support, or separate maintenance income need not be revealed if you do not wish to have it considered as a basis for repaying this obligation.**

Alimony, child support, separate maintenance received under: court order ☐ written agreement ☐ oral understanding ☐

Other income: $............. per ............. Source(s) of other income: ...........................

Is any income listed in this Section likely to be reduced in the next two years?
☐ Yes (Explain in detail on a separate sheet.) No ☐

Have you ever received credit from us? ............. When? ............. Office: ...........................

Checking Account No.: ..................................... Institution and Branch: ...........................

Savings Account No.: ..................................... Institution and Branch: ...........................

Name of nearest relative
not living with you: ..................................................................... Telephone: ...........

Relationship: ................. Address: ...........................

**SECTION B—INFORMATION REGARDING JOINT APPLICANT, USER, OR OTHER PARTY (Use separate sheets if necessary.)**

Full Name (Last, First, Middle): ..................................................................... Birthdate: / /

Relationship to Applicant (if any): .....................................................................

Present Street Address: ..................................................................... Years there: ...........

City: .................................. State: .................. Zip: .............. Telephone: ....................

Social Security No.: ..................................... Driver's License No.: ...........................

Present Employer: ..................................... Years there: ............... Telephone: ...........

Position or title: ..................................... Name of supervisor: .............................

Employer's Address: .....................................................................

Previous Employer: ..................................................................... Years there: ...........

Previous Employer's Address: .....................................................................

Present net salary or commission: $.............. per ............. No. Dependents: ........... Ages: ...........

**Alimony, child support, or separate maintenance income need not be revealed if you do not wish to have it considered as a basis for repaying this obligation.**

Alimony, child support, separate maintenance received under: court order ☐ written agreement ☐ oral understanding ☐

Other income: $............. per ............. Source(s) of other income: ...........................

Is any income listed in this Section likely to be reduced in the next two years?
☐ Yes (Explain in detail on a separate sheet.) ☐ No

Checking Account No.: ..................................... Institution and Branch: ...........................

Savings Account No.: ..................................... Institution and Branch: ...........................

Name of nearest relative not living
with Joint Applicant, User, or Other Party: ................. Telephone: ...........

Relationship: ................. Address: ...........................

**SECTION C—MARITAL STATUS**
(Do not complete if this is an application for an individual account.)

Applicant: ☐ Married  ☐ Separated  ☐ Unmarried (including single, divorced, and widowed)
Other Party: ☐ Married  ☐ Separated  ☐ Unmarried (including single, divorced, and widowed)

*Note:* This is one of five model application forms that the Board of Governors of the Federal Reserve System provides in its Regulation B.

## EXHIBIT 13-1 (Concluded)

## Model Credit Application Form

**ION D—ASSET AND DEBT INFORMATION** (If Section B has been completed, this Section should be completed giving information about both the Applicant and Joint Applicant, User, or Other Person. Please mark Applicant-related information with an "A." If Section B was not completed, only give information about the Applicant in this Section.)

*ASSETS OWNED* (Use separate sheet if necessary.)

| Description of Assets | Value | Subject to Debt? Yes/No | Name(s) of Owner(s) |
|---|---|---|---|
| Cash | $ | | |
| Automobiles (Make, Model, Year) | | | |
| Cash Value of Life Insurance (Issuer, Face Value) | | | |
| Real Estate (Location, Date Acquired) | | | |
| Marketable Securities (Issuer, Type, No. of Shares) | | | |
| Other (List) | | | |
| Total Assets | $ | | |

*OUTSTANDING DEBTS* (Include charge accounts, instalment contracts, credit cards, rent, mortgages, etc. Use separate sheet if necessary.)

| Creditor | Type of Debt or Acct. No. | Name in Which Acct. Carried | Original Debt | Present Balance | Monthly Payments | Past Due? Yes/No |
|---|---|---|---|---|---|---|
| 1. (Landlord or Mortgage Holder) | ☐ Rent Payment ☐ Mortgage | | $ (Omit rent) | $ (Omit rent) | $ | |
| 2. | | | | | | |
| 3. | | | | | | |
| 4. | | | | | | |
| 5. | | | | | | |
| 6. | | | | | | |
| Total Debts | | | $ | $ | $ | |

*(Credit References)*                                                                          Date Paid

1. _____ $ _____

2. _____

| | | | |
|---|---|---|---|
| Are you a co-maker, endorser, or guarantor on any loan or contract? | Yes ☐   No ☐ | If "yes" for whom? | To whom? |
| Are there any unsatisfied judgments against you? | Yes ☐ No ☐ | Amount $ | If "yes" to whom owed? |
| Have you been declared bankrupt in the last 14 years? | Yes ☐ No ☐ | If "yes" where? | Year |

Other Obligations—(E.g., liability to pay alimony, child support, separate maintenance. Use separate sheet if necessary.)

Everything that I have stated in this application is correct to the best of my knowledge. I understand that you will retain this application whether or not it is approved. You are authorized to check my credit and employment history and to answer questions about your credit experience with me.

_____    _____    _____    _____
Applicant's Signature                    Date                     Other Signature                            Date
                                                                 (Where Applicable)

model forms, while optional for creditors, have become the accepted standard.

To comply with the ECOA, a loan officer avoids asking questions that are not on the bank's standardized application form. The loan officer does, however, encourage the applicant to provide all information required by the form because an incomplete credit application can result in adverse action on the request.

## ANALYZE AND NEGOTIATE

Banks of various sizes use standardized procedures to analyze consumer loan applications and to develop initial loan offers. In addition, large consumer-credit departments often use special computer-based systems to help their personnel analyze the applications.

A first step is to check that a written loan application is complete. If an application is received in person, the recipient loan officer quickly reviews it with the applicant. If the application arrives by mail, then a bank employee checks for possible omissions that the applicant will be asked to complete. The complete application serves as the source document for subsequent analysis.

Next, the credit department verifies some information contained in the application, especially if the applicant has no previous relationship with the bank. For example, a bank employee is likely to verify the applicant's statements about employment history and banking relationships.

If the applicant has previously borrowed from the bank, then the credit department reviews the applicant's credit history as summarized in the credit files. If the applicant is new to the bank, an employee of the credit department checks the applicant's credit history as recorded by a consumer reporting agency and/or by creditors of the applicant. (If it subsequently takes adverse action on the application, then under the ECOA the bank has to disclose whether it obtained information from an outside source and offer to disclose the nature of any such adverse information.)

By this point, a credit-department employee acting within policy guidelines may decide to deny the credit request for reasons such as: incomplete application, inability to verify applicant's statement(s), and/or adverse credit history. Otherwise the application flows on to specialized personnel for more complete analysis.

### Judgmental Credit-Evaluation Systems

In these systems a specialized analyst relies primarily on judgment to estimate an applicant's creditworthiness and debt-servicing capacity. Operating within bank policies and guidelines, the analyst focuses on the *3 Cs of credit,* the applicant's character, capacity, and collateral.

Under the ECOA an analyst cannot use personal value judgments to evaluate an applicant's *character.* The analyst has to rely on objective criteria such as the stability of the applicant's employment and residency and the applicant's past record of servicing debts.

To judge a person's *capacity* to repay additional debt, an analyst evaluates how an applicant's assets and levels and sources of income relate to the applicant's various outstanding debts. The analyst thus estimates whether the applicant can comfortably repay the requested loan and, if not, whether a smaller loan would be appropriate.

If the applicant offers to pledge *collateral,* such as an automobile or marketable securities, the analyst evaluates the probable value of the collateral throughout the anticipated life of the loan.

The ECOA bans age discrimination in granting credit, but it permits a creditor that uses judgmental systems to ask an applicant's age and to use age to determine a "pertinent element of creditworthiness." This standard is vague. Its basic intent is to prohibit arbitrary rules, such as denying credit to anyone over 68. Yet it permits a judgmental credit denial to an elderly person if the creditor evaluates the facts and determines that the "particular applicant does not meet the creditor's usual standards."

One does not readily become an analyst capable of applying judgmental credit-evaluation systems. Most banks have programs to help train potential analysts in the 3 Cs of credit. These training programs require a trainee to evaluate past loan applications, form judgments, and then review their judgment process with experienced loan personnel. An analyst then begins to evaluate new applications and prepare initial recommendations for review by a senior employee. Such a training process helps a person acquire the skills of judgmental consumer-credit analysis.

## Credit-Scoring Systems

Some consumer credit departments, especially large ones, use statistically derived credit-scoring (CS) systems that predict the probability of subsequent repayment problems. These CS systems are an aid to the consumer-lending personnel who make the final credit decisions.

To develop a CS system, a research team first reviews a large sample of a bank's past loans and classifies each loan as either a "good" one, which was repaid promptly, or a "bad" one, which involved overdue payments, follow-up procedures, and/or possible defaults. Then the team hypothesizes attributes that would have helped predict the subsequent classification of "good" or "bad," and it uses statistical techniques to develop and test a model to predict the classifications.

Assume, for example, that the researchers develop a model that "best" classifies loans as "good" or "bad" based on three attributes of an applicant: credit rating, months at current employer, and years at current residence. Each attribute can have a score of 1 to 5. A score of one represents the lowest of five credit ratings and the briefest periods of current employment and residency; a score of five represents the highest of five credit ratings and the longest periods of current employment and residency. In this illustrative CS system, an applicant who scored 15 points (a maximum of five points on each of the three attributes) would be classified as a "good" risk, and an applicant who scored the minimum of 3 points would be classified as a "bad" risk. Not everyone who scores 15 points will turn out to be a "good" risk, but, on average, the lender expects to encounter substantially fewer repayment problems from applicants who score 15 points in contrast to those who score 3 points. Within the range of 3 to 15 points, the researchers try to estimate appropriate cut-off criteria whereby, for example, scores of 11 to 15 are "good," scores of 3 to 7 are "bad," and intermediate scores of 8 to 10 warrant closer scrutiny by credit analysts.

Proponents of CS systems assert that they:

- are more objective than individualized credit analysis
- expedite credit evaluation by screening out clearly good and clearly bad risks so that credit analysts can focus their attention on the grey area of intermediate scores
- can help train new loan officers concerning attributes that best predict "good" and "bad" credit risks
- are flexible so that a lender that decides to increase its consumer lending, and is willing to accept more risks, merely has to lower its cut-off criteria—but not beyond the point where expected incremental returns turn negative (conversely the lender can stem the growth in consumer loans by raising its cut-off scores)

CS systems have potential weaknesses, one of which is how does a lender get a valid sample of "poor" credit risks?[7] If, as is usually done, a lender samples only from among loans it has made in the past, then the sample contains only loans that were originally evaluated and approved by loan officers who screened out what they believed to be the "bad" risks. A lender can remove this potential sampling "bias" only if it uncritically approves all loan applications for a period long enough to develop an adequate record of good and bad loans. Few, if any, lenders will accept the losses associated with this broadened sampling procedure.

The ECOA and Regulation B set strict standards for the use of CS systems in consumer credit applications. A lender is to use only "a demonstrably and statistically sound, empirically derived credit system." This standard sounds vague and/or complex, but the FRS proceeds to define this standard to mean a CS system that fundamentally is "based on the creditor's recent experience with credit applications, and generally accepted statistical techniques must be used for sampling and validation."[8] Only a CS system that meets this standard can use an applicant's age as a predictive variable. Even then, however, the user must adjust its system if "any category of applicants aged 62 or older currently is being assigned fewer

---

7. Thomas R. Harter, "Potentials of Credit Scoring: Myth or Fact," *Credit and Financial Management*, April 1974, pp. 27-28.

8. "Equal Credit Opportunity," p. 105, and Regulation B, 202.2 (p).

points than any category of applicants younger than 62.'' The user either has to increase the scores for the older category or lower those for the younger categories.

Despite various constraints on the derivation and application of CS systems, some banks and other consumer lenders continue to refine and use such systems to help expedite the processing of credit applications.[9]

### Loan Offer

Once he or she decides to make a loan offer, a consumer loan officer seldom departs from the terms and conditions that, as required by Truth in Lending, were disclosed prior to receiving the loan application. Evaluation of the application then focused on whether or not to approve a standardized loan; it did not try to tailor a nonstandardized loan. To illustrate, assume that for loans on new automobiles a bank's current guidelines are: 20 percent downpayment, 12 percent APR, and a 48-month repayment period. When making a loan offer, an officer is unlikely to depart from these guidelines except for a valued customer. Even then, instead of relaxing the terms for an automobile loan, the officer may agree to reclassify the loan into a category that offers a lower rate, such as a single-payment loan or an installment loan collateralized by marketable securities. Thus, despite occasional exceptions, to expedite loan processing and to maintain equity among applicants for similar loans, consumer loan officers usually adhere to internal policy guidelines for categories of consumer loans.

An applicant who accepts the loan offer then signs a loan contract and associated forms, especially if the lender is to have a security interest or collateral. The bank uses standardized forms that financial printers have designed to comply with applicable laws and regulations. Traditionally, at least from a borrower's view, these forms are a labyrinth of legal terms. Recently some banks have introduced new consumer credit forms that contain simpler and clearer language that is understandable to the average borrower. Another innovation is to offer loan contracts that provide a borrower with greater repayment flexibility. To illustrate, a lender may offer a contract in which there are to be 22 monthly payments spaced over a 24-month period. The borrower, if subsequently faced with a temporary cash-flow problem, can then choose in which of two months he or she will omit a payment without violating the contract.

If after evaluation a loan officer decides not to make a loan offer ''in substantially the amount or on substantially the terms requested by an applicant,'' then under the ECOA this is an adverse action. Within 30 days the lender has to inform the applicant about this adverse action and about the applicant's rights under the ECOA. Exhibit 13-2 displays a standardized form that a bank can use to comply with these ECOA provisions.

---

9. Credit-scoring techniques also can be used to classify delinquent installment borrowers into groupings of those who are likely eventually to repay and those who are unlikely to repay their debt. A lender can then concentrate its resources on trying to collect from those who will likely repay and not on those for whom collection efforts will likely prove futile. For example, see Sylvia Lane, ''Submarginal Credit Risk Classification,'' *Journal of Financial and Quantitative Analysis*, January 1972, pp. 1379-1384.

**EXHIBIT 13-2**

Illustrative Statement of Credit Denial, Termination or Change

**STATEMENT OF CREDIT DENIAL, TERMINATION OR CHANGE**

DATE _____ 19 _____

No. _____

> The Federal Equal Credit Opportunity Act pro-
> hibits creditors from discriminating against credit
> applicants on the basis of race, color, religion, national
> origin, sex, marital status, age (provided that the
> applicant has the capacity to enter into a binding
> contract); because all or part of the applicant's income
> derives from any public assistance program; or because
> the applicant has in good faith exercised any right
> under the Consumer Credit Protection Act. The
> Federal Agency that administers compliance with this
> law concerning this creditor is:

Dear _____

Your Application for (Description of account, transaction or requested credit): _____

_____

has been acted upon (Description of adverse action taken): _____

_____

| PRINCIPAL REASON(S) FOR ADVERSE ACTION CONCERNING CREDIT: | | DISCLOSURE OF USE OF INFORMATION OBTAINED FROM AN OUTSIDE SOURCE |
|---|---|---|
| ☐ Credit application incomplete. | ☐ Too short a period of residence. | ☐ Disclosure inapplicable. |
| ☐ Insufficient credit references. | ☐ Temporary residence. | ☐ Information obtained in a report from a consumer reporting agency. |
| ☐ Unable to verify credit references. | ☐ Unable to verify residence. | Name: _____ |
| ☐ Temporary or irregular employment. | ☐ No credit file. | Street Address: _____ |
| ☐ Unable to verify employment. | ☐ Insufficient credit file. | |
| ☐ Length of employment. | ☐ Delinquent credit obligations. | Phone: _____ |
| ☐ Insufficient income. | ☐ Garnishment, attachment, foreclosure, repossession, or suit. | ☐ Information obtained from an outside source other than a consumer reporting agency. Under the Fair Credit Report-ing Act, you have the right to make a written request, within 60 days of receipt of this notice, for disclosure of the nature of the adverse information. |
| ☐ Excessive obligations. | ☐ Bankruptcy. | |
| ☐ Unable to verify income. | | |
| ☐ Inadequate collateral. | | |
| ☐ We do not grant credit to any applicant on the terms and conditions you request. | | |
| ☐ Other, specify:_____ | | By_____ |

BANKERS SYSTEMS, INC., ST. CLOUD, MINN., FORM DN-1R REVISED 3/77                    Telephone No._____

Source: Bankers Systems, Inc., St. Cloud, Minnesota

## MONITOR AND REVIEW

At the policy level, a bank, especially a large one, uses a portfolio perspective to monitor and review its consumer loans. To illustrate, the senior officials generally set a target whereby consumer loans will account for a specific percentage of the bank's total loans. Over time the officials revise the target proportion to reflect changing credit conditions and loan opportunities. Within this context, the senior officials receive frequent reports summarizing the aggregate amount of, and recent changes in, the consumer loan portfolio and its principal subcomponents such as: direct installment loans, purchased dealer paper, and credit card commitments and usage. Similarly, these officials receive frequent reports that summarize the amounts of—and changes in—the total past-due loans and of such loans classified, for example, as past due: 10 to 30 days, 31 to 60 days, and 61 days or longer.[10] In summary, the senior officials focus on levels and changes in dollar measures of their bank's consumer loan portfolio. In contrast to large business loans, they seldom focus on specific consumer loans. They delegate this detailed review to the consumer loan officers and auditors.

A consumer loan department closely monitors the repayment patterns of categories of loans and specific loans. When it makes an installment loan, a bank typically gives the borrower a book of machine-readable encoded coupons. By each scheduled repayment date, the borrower is to mail or hand in a payment along with an encoded coupon. The bank then machine-processes these repayments. It has computer programs that alert loan officers to installment accounts for which a scheduled coupon has not been received by the repayment date or within a brief grace period. If, after a brief interval, the repayment still has not arrived, the bank sends standardized reminder notices, after which it uses other follow-up procedures, such as subsequent form letters, telephone calls, possible repossession, and legal action.

### Legal-Regulatory Compliance

Despite the complexities of modern consumer-credit regulations, a bank that fails to comply with them is vulnerable to regulatory rebuke, penalties, and possible lawsuits. For example, the federal banking agencies require a noncomplying bank to reimburse its customers who have been ''overcharged'' via violations of Regulation Z (Truth in Lending). A bank that violates the ECOA is vulnerable to an individual or class-action lawsuit by an aggrieved applicant. The bank faces high legal costs to defend itself; and, if the bank loses, the court, in determining what amount of punitive damages to award, is to consider among other factors ''the frequency and persistence of failures of compliance by the creditor.'' Thus, in addition to wanting to comply with the law, a bank has economic incentives to adopt a compliance program.

An effective consumer-credit compliance program has to start at the senior level, whereby a bank's directors:

- inform themselves about the need for compliance
- adopt a written policy that the bank intends to comply with all applicable consumer credit laws and regulations
- designate a consumer-credit compliance officer
- institute and periodically review a comprehensive compliance program

As summarized by one author, a comprehensive compliance program in turn has six basic parts:

---

10. To help it evaluate its delinquency rates on installment loans, a bank can get detailed industry data, nationwide and by state, for various types of installment loans from a quarterly bulletin published by The American Bankers Association.

- "the education of bank personnel
- "the establishment of nondiscriminatory lending criteria
- "the establishment of loan application procedures
- "checking note, application, security agreement, disclosure statement and adverse action forms and, if necessary, ordering new ones
- "the establishment of an audit program
- "The establishment of a procedure to handle consumer complaints."[11]

When it has a consumer-credit compliance policy and program, a bank positions itself to prevent noncompliance and to demonstrate that its possible violations inadvertently occurred despite the program.

## REVISE POLICIES AND PROCEDURES

As it analyzes changing conditions and actual versus expected outcomes, a bank revises some of its consumer credit practices over time.

As they observe the rapid expansion of consumer credit regulations and consumerism, a bank's senior officials will institute policy reviews of the costs and benefits associated with their bank's consumer credit activities. As a result, they are likely to decide to reduce their bank's involvement in some types of consumer credit transactions. To illustrate, some banks already report how they have reduced their purchase of dealer installment contracts because of recent revisions in the due-course doctrine. As part of their review and revision process, the senior officers also monitor competitive developments and changing opportunities in banking activities that are less regulated than are consumer credit transactions. Some banks reportedly have decided to refocus their resources on expansion of their wholesale—not retail—activities.

A bank's consumer credit department continually has to review, and at times revise, its processing systems. In response to changing regulations, at times it has to revise its forms, computer programs, and/or procedures by which its employees process the transactions. With computers it can automate many processing functions, and so a bank often encourages its consumer borrowers to establish a line of revolving credit via checking-reserve plans and/or bank credit cards. This way the bank has to process only the initial application for a revolving-credit line and, if it approves it, then use its computer programs to process subsequent loans against the approved credit line. The costs of this procedure are generally less than those of a series of consumer loans to the borrower.

---

11. Joyce M. Saxon, "Implementing a Program for Consumer Regulation Compliance," *The Magazine of Bank Administration,* November 1977, pp. 18-21. (This article is the first of a detailed seven-part series that, with the exception of its April 1978 issue, was published by *The Magazine of Bank Administration* from November 1977 through June 1978. Also see William R. Hearn, "Why Have a Compliance Officer?" *The Journal of Commercial Bank Lending,* August 1978, pp. 29-39.

# CONSUMER CREDIT REGULATIONS: COSTS AND BENEFITS

Congress, before deciding to pass a rapid sequence of consumer credit legislation, relied on anecdotal testimony of alleged abuses in consumer loan practices. Congress seldom evaluated the frequency of these alleged abuses and their impact on individuals and groups, nor did it estimate the costs of trying to prevent such abuses.

Various bankers, bank regulators, and legislators have begun to advocate a reexamination of the costs and benefits of myriad consumer credit regulations. Although it is in its early stages, this reexamination process will affect banks, bank regulators, and consumers.

## COSTS

Although it is impossible to measure them all, one can identify some categories of costs associated with recent consumer credit regulations.

### Interpretation of Laws and Regulations

Congress passes the laws and then usually delegates their interpretation to the FRS. Because of the amount and rapidity of new legislation, the FRS created and staffed a special Division of Consumer Affairs (DCA), which is to write regulations and to ensure compliance with the laws and regulations. As part of these responsibilities, the DCA also: prepares model forms, issues "official staff interpretations" on which creditors can rely without potential civil liability, answers inquiries, and conducts special seminars to acquaint and update member banks concerning consumer credit regulations.

Bankers and other consumer lenders incur costs in having their legal counsel, specialized consumer compliance officer(s), and lending personnel interpret and apply the changing regulations.

Even though regulators and lenders try diligently to interpret the laws, there will be differing interpretations that will have to be resolved by them or by the courts, which already have made hundreds of decisions related only to Truth in Lending legislation. As summarized by an FRS official before a congressional committee, "We now have a system that layers State laws, State regulations, Federal laws and regulations, staff interpretations, and State and Federal Court decisions." He cites various examples of conflicting federal and state consumer credit laws and questions whether and when: a state law should be preempted by a federal law, and/or an intrastate transaction should be exempted from a federal law. In summary, the official observes:

> . . . given the sheer quantity of State and Federal statutes, regulations, interpretations, and judicial decisions, and given the fact that they fit together so badly, it is not surprising that the loan officer of a small bank—charged

with the varied responsibilities of making instalment loans, buying dealer paper, overseeing a credit-card operation, making home mortgage loans, extending construction credit, arranging for credit insurance, and so forth—is hard pressed to comply.[12]

But comply he or she must.

### Compliance Costs

The FRS, in cooperation with other supervisory agencies, has to develop systems to encourage and, where necessary, enforce compliance. The FRS tries to encourage compliance via its model forms, official staff interpretations, and training sessions. Also, it invites industry comments on proposed changes in consumer credit regulations; it has established a Consumer Advisory Council and study groups to evaluate the impact of consumer credit laws; it processes consumer inquiries and complaints under its Regulation AA; and it participates in interagency task forces that focus on consumer affairs.

To monitor compliance, the FRS has trained specialized personnel to conduct consumer compliance examinations of State member banks.[13] These examiners scientifically sample a bank's loan files to check for compliance with Truth in Lending, and they scrutinize accepted and rejected credit applications for possible violation of the ECOA. If a bank has unusually few rejected applications, the examiners are instructed to suspect possible prescreening of applications, a practice that can violate the ECOA. The examiners use a special report form that encompasses each consumer law and regulation covered by the compliance examination program. In coordination with the FRS, the other federal banking agencies have developed similar examination procedures.

A bank incurs costs to comply with the regulations and to document its compliance. Its senior officials, legal counsel, consumer compliance officer(s) and auditors spend time having to develop compliance procedures that they then have to monitor and review. A bank similarly incurs costs to purchase and process authorized forms that it then has to, by law, retain for periods of about two years so that the examiners can review them. Some of the costs are transitional costs in response to new regulatory requirements; other costs are incremental continuing costs associated with the new requirements.

If it is found to have violated some consumer credit regulations, a bank faces regulatory criticism and possible sanctions, such as having to reimburse overcharges in violation of Truth in Lending. A key issue is whether a regulator concludes that a violation was intentional or whether it

---

12. *Federal Reserve Bulletin*, February 1977, pp. 125-128.

13. "Complying with Consumer Credit Regulations: A Challenge," *Federal Reserve Bulletin*, September 1977, pp. 769-773.

was an unintentional episode that occurred despite a bank's compliance program.[14]

What especially concerns lenders are their potential liabilities under civil class-action lawsuits permitted under the ECOA. Even if it successfully defends itself, a bank faces the attendant publicity and the defense costs.

An author has tried to quantify many of the costs associated with Regulation B and the ECOA. He estimates a total cost "for Regulation B of $293.3 million or a little more than $4.04 per household." This breaks down into "$127.5 million or $1.76 per household in recurring costs every year and $165.8 million or $2.28 per household in one time costs."[15] Even as approximations, these cost estimates lead to questions concerning:

- Who eventually bears the costs?
- Who benefits from the consumer credit regulations?
- Do the benefits warrant the costs?

In answer to the first question, it is likely that most of the costs eventually are borne by consumers, to whom they are shifted by the creditors, and/or by citizens whose tax dollars directly or indirectly finance the regulatory apparatus.

## BENEFITS

Consumer credit regulations are to provide at least two major benefits. They are to enable potential borrowers to do informed comparison shopping among lenders, and they are to forestall human indignities whereby some people encounter discrimination and/or shabby treatment in their credit transactions.

Several studies evaluate whether Truth in Lending regulations have increased consumer awareness of their actual borrowing costs.

One survey reviews the experience in Massachusetts, in which state truth-in-lending legislation predates similar federal legislation. It finds that "annual rate disclosure has not stimulated active consumer shopping for credit and has had no appreciable effect on competition," and it notes that, although part of their apathy arises from lack of understanding, at least some consumers are insensitive to rate differences because of their lack of alternative credit sources and/or their preference for convenient credit despite its cost. Even though the benefits were not immediately evident, the survey also reports that lenders and retailers found that they could "operate under the law without substantial difficulty."[16]

---

14. Joyce Saxon and Alonzo Sibert, "Proposed Guidelines for Truth in Lending Compliance," *Issues in Bank Regulation*, Autumn 1977, pp. 20-25.

15. James F. Smith, "The Equal Credit Opportunity Act of 1974: A Cost/Benefit Analysis," *The Journal of Finance*, May 1977, pp. 609-622.

16. Robert W. Pullen, "The Impact of Truth-in-Lending Legislation: The Massachusetts Experience," *New England Business Review* (Federal Reserve Bank of Boston), October 1968, pp. 2-8.

Another study uses nationwide samples to evaluate whether people who received automobile loans after Truth-in-Lending legislation had more accurate perceptions of their actual interest costs than did people who received similar loans prior to the legislation. It concludes that the later borrowers "are more aware of the true rate of interest that they are paying than were consumers who borrowed before the law was enacted." Yet despite this improvement, "borrowers are still largely unaware of the rate of interest they are paying, even though this rate has, by law, been imparted to them." Also, "personal characteristics of borrowers [such as income and age] make very little difference in whether they know the interest rate they are paying."[17] A subsequent study further analyzes personal attributes that best explain different gains in APR awareness. It finds that "differences in the educational level of installment borrowers and in their knowlege of the existence of the federal Truth-in-Lending law have been most closely associated with differences in the beginning levels of APR awareness and in gains in awareness of APR's for each of the three types of credit investigated." It concludes with the possibility that "such interest rate awareness differentials will lessen over time as awareness levels rise generally or as public policy attempts to correct these differences."[18]

In 1977 the FRS conducted a survey to estimate the:

- extent to which consumers were exercising their rights under the ECOA and the Fair Credit Billing Act
- compliance costs borne by the creditors

The surveyed firms consisted of three large banks and also some large retailers. The principal survey results are as follows:

- The firms notified almost 50 million customers of their right, under the ECOA, to separate credit histories for married persons. About 11 percent of the customers exercised this right. The firms estimate their costs of maintaining dual reporting, once established, range from "negligible" to about $90,000 per year.
- When they notify their consumer credit applicants about an adverse action, some firms include the reasons for denial as part of the notice; others provide reasons only on request. The estimated costs of supplying the reasons vary widely among the firms. "Many of the rejected credit applicants who were initially given reasons for credit denial supplied additional information, and a high proportion of these were then granted credit."
- The proportion of credit customers who inquire about their billing

---

17. Lewis Mandell, "Consumer Perception of Incurred Interest Rates: An Empirical Test of the Efficacy of the Truth-in-Lending Law," *The Journal of Finance,* December 1971, pp. 1143-1153.

18. George G. C. Parker and Robert P. Shay, "Some Factors Affecting Awareness of Annual Percentage Rates in Consumer Installment Credit Transactions," *The Journal of Finance,* March 1974, pp. 217-225.

statements also varies among the firms. Only a small proportion of these questions follow the formal procedures of Regulation Z, but most of the firms treat all their inquiries, whether formal or informal, alike.[19]

## REEVALUATING COSTS AND BENEFITS

It is difficult to compare directly the costs and benefits of current consumer credit regulations. One can identify and try to measure many of the costs, and identify who eventually bears them. The benefits, however, go beyond economic benefits such as the ability of consumers to do informed comparison shopping among sources of credit. They include personal and social benefits for some consumers who otherwise might not receive courteous equitable treatment by creditors. Yet, as summarized by one observer, "While individual consumers may find the changes helpful, there are ample reasons to wonder if the total benefits to the total consuming body are worth the total price."[20] Other bankers, regulatory officials, and Congressmen have begun to raise similar questions. If they conclude that the total costs exceed the total benefits, they may want to explore ways to achieve similar benefits at lower costs. Some principal cost-reduction possibilities include reducing the:

- number of—and rapidity of changes in—the regulations
- overlap among federal and state regulations
- potential civil liabilities except in cases of willful violations

Such changes, if adopted, could revise the cost-benefit equation and create a more stable environment for consumer lending activities.

## BANK CREDIT CARD SYSTEMS

Many department stores and oil companies have long encouraged their customers to apply for a card by which to charge purchases at the issuer's retail outlet(s). These cards are to provide customer convenience and to help build sales within the issuing organization.

*Travel and entertainment (T&E) cards* began when Diners Club developed a system whereby its cardholders could charge purchases at various participating establishments such as restaurants, retailers, and transportation companies. The American Express card and Carte Blanche similarly are worldwide T&E cards.

Bank credit cards subsequently began when an issuing bank would enroll cardholders who could use their bank card to charge purchases at

---

19. "Exercise of Consumer Rights Under the Equal Credit Opportunity and Fair Credit Billing Acts," *Federal Reserve Bulletin*, May 1978, pp. 363-366.

20. Thom McCord, "Coping with Consumer Credit Regulations," *Issues in Bank Regulation*, Winter 1978, pp. 3-5.

nearby participating merchants. (An initial survey reported that in 1967 about 200 banks offered credit card plans, which had about $0.6 billion in outstanding balances.) From this base, bank credit cards have evolved into nationwide—and even worldwide—systems, such that by 1977 the two largest bank credit card associations report about 17,000 participating financial institutions (primarily banks) and almost $11.5 billion in outstanding balances.[21] This expansion process affects consumer credit practices and funds transfer systems.

## BANK CREDIT CARD PROCESSES

Bank credit cards initially were designed to service retail transactions within the metropolitan area or state of the issuing bank. An issuing bank would enroll nearby merchants and cardholders in its system. Soon, however, problems arose when several local banks each offered a different credit card and when a cardholder wished to use the card outside the area. Many merchants were reluctant to enroll in various systems, and cardholders would at times encounter a merchant who did not participate in the same system as did the cardholder. Therefore, to gain wider acceptance and usage of their cards, issuing banks began to participate in regional—and then nationwide—credit-card interchange systems.[22]

Today most card issuing banks participate in one or both of two nationwide *bank card associations:* Master Charge (the Interbank Card Association) and VISA (formerly Bankamericard). These bank card associations develop systems to expedite processing of their cards; and they promote acceptance of their card by banks, potential cardholders, and merchants.

An issuing bank seeks to expand its cardholder base both directly and often indirectly via smaller agent banks. A participating merchant enrolls with a bank that issues Master Charge and/or VISA, and it agrees to accept all such cards, whether issued by nearby or distant banks. Exhibit 13-3 summarizes how these participants relate to each other in credit card processing systems.

When presented with a Master Charge or VISA card, an employee of a participating merchant confirms the card's validity and, if the purchase exceeds a prespecified amount, calls a nearby interchange system for a credit authorization. The employee then completes the standard forms associated with the credit card transaction, gives a copy to the cardholder, and retains several copies for subsequent processing.

Later in the day the participating merchant assembles copies of all the credit card transactions and then transmits these forms in a batch to its local processing center. The merchant's local bank promptly gives it credit for the credit card sales invoices, except that it discounts the total amount by a

21. *Banking,* September 1977, p. 112.

22. For a summary of the early evolution of credit card systems, see Robert Johnston, "Nation-Spanning Credit Cards," *Monthly Review* (Federal Reserve Bank of San Francisco), March 1972, pp. 13-19.

**EXHIBIT 13-3**

**Bank Credit Card Systems**

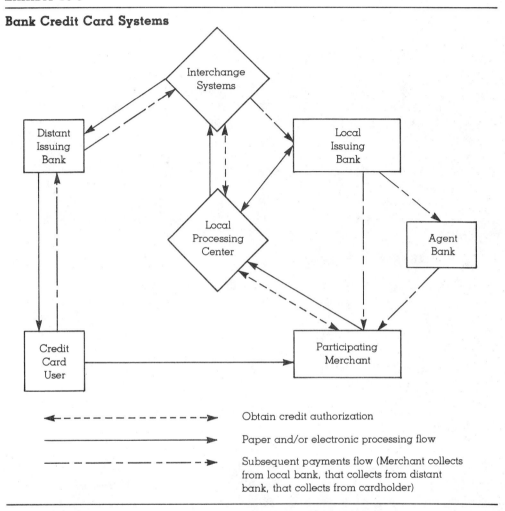

preagreed percentage and then credits the merchant's account with the remaining amount. The bank assumes the collection costs and credit risks for these credit card sales; it has no recourse against the merchant.

Unlike a check, a credit card form seldom flows back to the cardholder who signed it. When it receives credit card forms deposited by local merchants, a processing center encodes the basic information about each credit card transaction and then transmits this summary information, via computerized interchange systems, to the issuing bank that thus promptly:

- receives information about a specific transaction
- reimburses, through a clearing system, the local bank that credited the recipient merchant's account
- adds the transaction to the cardholder's monthly bill

To illustrate, the New England Bankcard Association (NEBA) has 134 member institutions, the assets of which range from $10 million to $2 billion.[23] NEBA uses on-line systems to process authorization calls and associated transactions for its members. It has a direct line to a switch in New York that in turn links NEBA to other Master Charge and VISA data bases throughout the country. NEBA electronically transmits 25,000 items each day, and it retains the actual credit card transaction forms in its vault from which it can automatically retrieve photocopies in response to customer inquiries. An official of a large bank similarly reports how every out-of-state—but domestic—credit card transaction by one of his bank's cardholders now "comes back as electronic tape and, in many cases, comes back the same day that it is negotiated, or perhaps only one day later."[24] His bank is preparing to extend this EFT mode to overseas transactions by its cardholders. No wonder that many observers see credit card clearing systems as the vanguard of comprehensive EFT systems.

## PARTICIPANTS IN BANK CREDIT CARD SYSTEMS

This section examines why various parties choose to participate in bank credit card systems.

### Credit Card Users

Almost 75 million people have a Master Charge and/or VISA card, and almost half of these represent active accounts that have outstanding balances.

A cardholder often finds the card to be a convenient way to execute some transactions:

- Some merchants will promptly accept an approved credit card, but they will not accept a personal check, except possibly after a lengthy verification process.
- Through the billing process a user gets a systematic record of all expenses charged against the account.
- The user need not immediately pay for the transaction for which he or she will be billed at a later date.
- A cardholder can conveniently arrange to get a modest cash advance from a participating bank.

For a cardholder, the card's convenience benefits are likely to exceed its costs.

---

23. "New England Bankcard Association Helps Community Banks Streamline Credit Card Service," *The Magazine of Bank Administration,* April 1978, pp. 14, 18.

24. "Special Report: Bank Cards," *Banking*, September 1977, pp. 42-45 ff.

- Most issuing banks do not charge an annual fee for a bank card. In contrast most T&E cards involve an annual fee of about $25.
- Most banks do not levy any service charges on their credit card accounts.
- A cardholder with an active account receives a monthly bill from the issuing bank. If the total account is paid by a specific due date, usually 25 days later, then there is no finance charge. (A cardholder who charges an item shortly after one billing date will not be billed for it until the next billing date 30 days later, from which time the cardholder has another 25 days within which to pay without incurring any finance charge.)
- If a cardholder does not fully pay the monthly bill within the prescribed time limit, then the unpaid balance becomes a revolving credit for which the APR usually is 18%. In states that have usury ceilings below 18%, a cardholder is likely to face an annual fee for the card or have to get a card from an out-of-state bank that is not subject to the usury ceiling.

In summary, cardholders who pay their bill by the due date pay nothing for the convenience of their cards. Cardholders who cannot or choose not to pay all their bill by the due date have convenient access to a revolving line of credit.

Several studies profile the principal users of bank credit cards. One study analyzes samples of active and inactive cardholders. It reports that "active cardholders possess a significantly higher educational attainment, a higher level of income, a higher socioeconomic standing, and a lower age as compared with the inactive cardholders." The researchers also find that "the active cardholders have more favorable attitudes toward both credit in general and bank charge-cards in particular than do the inactive card-holders," who "fear that charge-cards may induce them to rely on credit excessively" and who believe that "bank charge-card utilization should be confined to emergency needs." This attitudinal finding should alert banks to reevaluate their advertising emphasis on bank credit card "convenience" — "which a majority of the inactive cardholders may preclude as an acceptable reason for activating their accounts."[25] Another study seeks to explain interstate differences in customer use of credit cards and check-credit plans. Among its conclusions it reports that "credit cards are used more intensively where a large proportion of the population is between 18 and 45 and less intensively in states which derive a large proportion of their income from farming."[26]

25. R. Y. Awh and D. Waters, "A Discriminant Analysis of Economic, Demographic, and Attitudinal Characteristics of Bank Charge-Card Holders: A Case Study," *The Journal of Finance,* June 1974, pp. 973-980.

26. Richard L. Peterson, "Factors Affecting the Growth of Bank Credit Card and Check Credit," *The Journal of Finance,* May 1977, pp. 553-564.

**Participating Merchants**

Almost 1.5 million merchant outlets accept Master Charge, 1.5 million accept VISA, and many of these accept both cards:

- Many merchants accept bank credit cards as a service to people who prefer to use a card. Acceptance thus helps a merchant build sales or at least not lose some potential sales to rival merchants who accept the card(s).
- Instead of administering and financing their own credit plans for qualified customers, some merchants conclude that it is more cost-effective to accept bank credit cards.

Each merchant has to analyze whether its profits from incremental sales and its possibly reduced costs of administering and financing open-book credit warrant its having its credit card sales discounted by its local issuing bank. Although the average discount is about 3.5 percent, the discounts range from 2 to 5 percent, with high volume and/or high sales ticket retailers usually having the smaller discounts.

Bank credit cards have not been widely accepted by large department stores and other retailers that have their own extensive revolving-credit plans. These retailers often conclude that the net benefits of maintaining their own plans exceed those of switching to acceptance of bank credit cards. By operating their own plans, these firms:

- avoid paying discounts to issuing banks
- retain their own files of credit card customers with whom they regularly communicate via statements and advertisements
- receive the finance charges paid by customers who use extended repayment terms

Yet with growing consumer use of bank credit cards, some major chains of department stores have decided to accept bank cards while maintaining their own revolving-credit plans; other holdouts will likely adopt this strategy.

**Issuing Banks**

Issuing banks usually are large banks that issue and process credit cards throughout a state or multistate region. These large banks, which issue cards directly and through smaller agent banks, project various benefits from their credit card programs:

- expand the package of services provided to current and potential retail customers
- broaden their consumer loan portfolios by extending revolving credit to cardholders who do not pay their bills by the due date (many of these consumer borrowers may reside outside the issuing bank's market area for traditional installment loans)

- obtain commissions and associated business from participating merchants
- have its credit card system contribute to the bank's total profits
- develop experience and processing systems that the bank can extend into other funds-transfer developments

After they absorbed extensive development costs, most issuing banks reportedly now have profitable credit card programs.

**Credit Card Revenues**  An issuing bank's credit card system generates two principal revenue streams:

- discounts from participating merchants
- interest from card users who do not pay their total bills by the due date

In addition many merchants and cardholders maintain account relationships from which an issuing bank can generate incremental revenues. An issuing bank has some control over these revenues, and it can seek to develop supplementary revenues.

Discounts from participating merchants account for about thirty percent of aggregate bank revenues from credit card plans, and finance charges paid by cardholders account for virtually all the remaining revenues.[27]

Cardholders who use the revolving credit and/or cash advance features of their credit cards contribute the majority of revenues. In contrast, many cardholders pay their total bills prior to the due date and thus incur no finance charge for the convenience of the credit card. One large bank briefly levied a 50-cent service charge on its accounts that were active and then fully paid by the due date. In response to customer protests and competition, the bank withdrew this service charge. Experiments with explicit service charges and/or annual membership fees are likely to recur, especially if state usury ceilings constrain issuing banks from increasing their finance charges during extended periods of high interest rates.

**Credit Card Costs**  An issuing bank can identify and try to measure several principal cost categories associated with its credit card operations.

A bank incurs *carrying costs* because it promptly reimburses a participating merchant for a credit card transaction and yet does not receive payment from the credit card user until after a subsequent billing date. To reduce its carrying costs, subject to competition and other cost constraints a bank can try to:

- expedite processing of credit card transactions in order to include them in a cardholder's next bill
- shorten the period between the billing date and due date

---

27. *Functional Cost Analysis*, 1977 Average Banks, as reported by the Federal Reserve System.

- promptly process cardholder payments via lock boxes and other accelerated collection systems
- eliminate inactive accounts

A bank's staff has to analyze the extent to which reduced carrying costs warrant increased processing costs.

A bank also incurs *losses* from some of its credit cards. As with other consumer loan transactions, a bank screens applicants, establishes maximum credit lines, and uses monitoring and collection procedures to control its losses due to defaults. Fraud constitutes a second area of potential losses. By law, if a holder's lost or stolen credit card is used by unauthorized persons, the cardholder's maximum loss exposure is $50. The issuing bank bears the additional loss exposure. To control losses due to fraud, issuing banks and interchange systems have developed elaborate on-line authorization systems to prevent use of known stolen or lost cards and to detect suspicious card-usage patterns. Issuing banks also have had to develop intricate systems to control the distribution of their cards, and some banks provide credit cards that incorporate a photograph of the cardholder.[28]

An issuing bank incurs diverse *processing costs* associated with its credit card program. To the extent warranted, it can use automated internal systems to try to control these costs. It also has to evaluate its net costs of having some processing done externally by interchange systems, specialist banks, and/or nonbank specialists.

An issuing bank in effect provides credit lines to its cardholders, who can charge items and then pay by the due date or use extended repayment terms. A bank thus has to manage these commitments and its total portfolio in ways that enable it to honor its various credit lines, most of which can be activated at the discretion of the user.

## Agent Banks

Most medium-sized and small banks also participate in credit card systems, usually as agents of larger banks or of the card associations. An agent bank accepts this role primarily so it can service its current and potential depositors who want to participate in a credit card system.

An agent bank publicizes its ability to provide a Master Charge and/or VISA card. It accepts cardholder applications and forwards them for approval by the large bank with which it works. In most cases, an agent bank acts as a conduit between local cardholders and merchants and the large bank. It agrees to have the large bank obtain most of the revenues from finance charges and merchant discounts and bear the various costs associated with the program. By acting as an agent, a smaller bank can thus:

- broaden its customer service package

---

28. Lawrence F. Linden, "Bank Card Fraud and How to Prevent It," *The Bankers Magazine,* Spring 1976, pp. 103-107.

- build, or at least obtain, account relationships with local merchants who wish to be part of bank credit card systems
- usually obtain some incremental profits.[29]

### Interchange Systems

Many large banks initially offered their own credit card, but they soon concluded that it was advantageous to become part of the Master Charge or VISA system. To do so a bank has to belong to Interbank Card Association (ICA), which licenses Master Charge, or to VISA U.S.A. Inc.[30]

As a member of ICA or VISA, an issuing or agent bank can offer a customer a standardized, widely accepted card that also contains the bank's name. Either directly or indirectly via regional interchange systems, a member bank has access to ICA's or VISA's credit authorization and processing systems. A member bank sets its credit screening standards and billing practices, but all its credit card transactions flow through its association's central accounting system.

Initially, the bylaws of VISA precluded its member banks from also offering Master Charge. In response to objections raised by banks that wanted to offer both cards and to antitrust questions raised by the Department of Justice, VISA abandoned the bylaw in 1976. Since then many banks engage in *duality* whereby they offer both cards to their customers.

Widespread duality is likely to lead to major changes in bank credit card systems:

- To expedite the verification and processing of both cards they offer, banks will want them to be compatible, but then why have two cards and not just one? Many regional interchange systems already process transactions involving both cards. VISA has offered to use its network to process its members' Master Charge transactions, but ICA has responded by prohibiting the processing of Master Charge transactions through any system maintained by a rival nationwide bank card association.
- Yet the Department of Justice will likely scrutinize the situation if one of the two systems becomes dominant or if there is either a legal or *de facto* merger of the two systems.

Meanwhile, the two bank card associations have stepped up their rivalry, for example by promoting national and multinational acceptance of their cards

---

29. Although it is possibly outdated, a study provides insights into the marketing of credit card systems, via agents, in small outlying cities. J. Van Fenstermaker and Donald Perry, "An Examination of a Charge Card System Operating in a Smaller Community Through Correspondent Banks," *Journal of Bank Research,* Spring 1971, pp. 9-13.

30. VISA U.S.A. Inc. was called National BankAmericard Inc. between 1971 and 1976. For brevity this book consistently uses the current VISA name.

and by developing new services such as nationwide check-verification systems and travelers checks.

## EXTENSIONS OF BANK CREDIT CARDS

Banks are no longer the exclusive issuers or agents for bank credit cards. Recently a large S&L association, a nationwide brokerage firm, and a regional supermarket chain began to offer bank credit cards to their customers. These developments portend increasing acceptance of bank credit cards and also increasing rivalry among bank and nonbank issuers of these cards.

With a credit card, a user later pays for the transaction; in contrast, with a *debit card* a cardholder's account is immediately debited and the funds transferred to the recipient's account. Most banks and interchange systems can readily extend their credit card technology to debit card transactions— thus placing themselves at the vanguard of EFT developments.

## SUMMARY

Within the past twenty to thirty years most banks have sharply increased their consumer loan activities. Modern banks make single-payment loans, they make installment loans to finance purchases of automobiles and other goods and services, and they lend to individual investors who purchase or carry securities that are subject to the initial margin requirements of the FRS.

Consumer lending is subject to extensive laws and regulations. It has to comply with applicable state usury laws, which set maximum interest rates on most consumer loans, and with other state laws, such as those based on the model Uniform Commercial Code and those related to the holder-in-due-course doctrine. A bank also has to comply with recent federal laws and regulations that include the Truth in Lending Act and Equal Credit Opportunity Act.

Senior officials set and review their bank's consumer lending policies. The consumer loan personnel use standardized processing systems to:

- facilitate compliance with applicable regulations and bank policies
- expedite loan decisions
- control the costs associated with analyzing loan applications and servicing loans

As part of its consumer-loan processing systems, a bank uses judgmental credit-evaluation systems; and in some cases it uses empirically derived credit-scoring systems. To protect itself from regulatory rebukes and possible lawsuits, each bank needs a consumer-credit compliance program that is overseen by a designated officer and by the board of directors.

Some observers have begun to question the costs and benefits associated with recent consumer credit regulations. The total costs include compliance costs (borne by lenders, regulators, and—indirectly—by consumers) and also possible litigation costs and penalties imposed for noncompliance. The total benefits of consumer credit regulations are less tangible. They go beyond economic benefits; they include social and personal benefits for some consumers who might otherwise find it infeasible, and possibly humiliating, to engage in consumer credit transactions. The question is whether such benefits can be achieved at lower cost.

From their modest fragmented origins, bank credit card systems have developed into two nationwide—almost worldwide—systems. Most banks now participate in one or both of the bank card associations, Master Charge and VISA. These participant banks, either directly or indirectly through a large issuing bank, are linked to card processing centers and interchange systems. Each bank has to evaluate the revenues and costs associated with the bank credit cards that it processes, and it can examine new ways to boost the revenues and control the costs. Some observers view bank credit cards and their processing systems as the forerunners of debit cards and advanced electronic funds transfer (EFT) systems.

# 14
# REAL ESTATE LOANS

Each bank lends to customers who use the funds to buy property and/or who pledge property as loan collateral. These real estate loans range from standardized residential mortgage loans to complex financing packages for large-scale property developers. This chapter focuses on the principal:

- types of real estate loans
- legal and regulatory constraints on residential mortgage loans (RMLs)
- management strategies for a portfolio of RMLs
- innovations in RML instruments and markets
- management strategies for large-scale real estate loans

## RESIDENTIAL MORTGAGE LOANS

Bankers and bank supervisory officials subclassify residential mortgage loans (RMLs) in several ways:

- those secured by *one- to four-family residences,* or those secured by *multifamily* (more than four families) *residences*
- *conventional* loans that are not insured by a government agency, or *government-insured loans* that are insured by the Federal Housing Administration (FHA) or guaranteed by the Veterans Administration (VA). (There are private firms that insure some conventional loans.)
- *first mortgage loans* that have a first lien on a property; or *junior mortgage loans,* the claim of which is subordinated to that of the first mortgage

These subcategories can overlap; for example, most bank real estate loans are conventional loans that are secured by first mortgages on one- to four-family residences.

## LEGAL AND REGULATORY GUIDELINES

A bank's RML policies and procedures have to comply with complex, and changing, laws and regulations.

### Usury Ceilings

All but four states impose rate ceilings on conventional loans, and the federal government puts ceiling rates on FHA-insured and VA-guaranteed loans. As with usury laws on consumer loans, these ceiling rates are supposed to protect small, unwary borrowers from paying exhorbitant interest rates to powerful lenders.

Most states have *fixed ceiling rates* on RMLs.[1] These rates range from 8 to 21 percent and under most credit conditions the higher ceilings do not deter lenders from making RMLs. Some state laws authorize a state agency to use its judgment or a specified formula to establish, review, and revise a *floating ceiling rate* on RMLs. (To illustrate, by law the Pennsylvania Banking Commission computes its state's ceiling each month "by adding 2.5 percentage points to the long-term U.S. government bond rate for the second preceding month and rounding to the nearest one-quarter of a percent.") State usury ceilings also differ in how they apply to RMLs of various sizes and to fees associated with RMLs.

A federal rate committee sets and monitors the ceiling rate(s) on FHA and VA loans, and over time it adjusts the rate(s) to reflect changes in market rates on similar instruments. While it formally adheres to these ceiling rates, a lender can try to increase its effective return by charging additional fees (discount points) from a home seller, who in turn can try to add this cost to the asking price for the house.

Various studies analyze the benefits and costs of usury ceilings on RMLs. One study reviews why it is difficult to justify such ceilings, especially for conventional RMLs, unless local markets lack competition and/or borrowers lack comparative information on rates for RMLs.[2] Even if these conditions hold in some markets, usury ceilings benefit some borrowers to the detriment of other borrowers; and they disrupt the availability and flows of funds for RMLs. A study empirically tests (1970) "the relation between 'unduly low' usury ceilings and the level of single family homebuilding" in various metropolitan areas, and reports that "when usury ceilings are low relative to market interest rates, they have the dual effect of both widening the regional variation in mortgage rates (by up to one-half) and of reducing the level of home building (by approximately one-fourth)."[3] Another study analyzes the terms and flows of conventional

1. Helen Frame Peters, "The Mortgage Market: A Place for Ceilings?," *Business Review* (Federal Reserve Bank of Philadelphia), July-August 1977, pp. 13-21. This source has a summary table (1977) of state usury ceilings that apply to RMLs, but it notes the "many exceptions and other provisions associated with state ceilings."

2. Peters, "The Mortgage Market: A Place for Ceilings?" pp. 15-17

3. Philip K. Robins, "The Effects of State Usury Ceilings on Single Family Homebuilding," *The Journal of Finance,* March 1974, pp. 227-235.

RMLs in 15 large metropolitan areas between 1965 and 1970. It concludes "that the legal restrictions on contract interest rates resulted in the noninterest rationing of borrowers through (1) the requiring of higher loan fees, (2) the requiring of higher downpayments, and (3) the requiring of shorter loan maturities" and "that contract interest rate restrictions reduced the incentive of lenders to make mortgage loans, with loan volume being reduced and new construction concommitantly curtailed."[4]

Even as usury ceilings undergo reexamination from a public-policy perspective, a bank has to keep informed about, and adhere to, the usury ceilings that apply to its RMLs.

### Restrictions on Residential Mortgage Loans

Throughout the 1960s and 1970s Congress eased restrictions on RMLs made by national banks, so that now these banks can offer terms similar to those offered by nonbank lenders. A national bank has to comply with these principal restrictions:[5]

- Its *total real estate loans* secured by first liens cannot exceed (1) 100 percent of its paid-in, unimpaired capital plus 100 percent of its unimpaired surplus *or* (2) 100 percent of its time and savings deposits, whichever amount is greater.
- The *maximum maturity* of conventional, fully amortized real estate loans is thirty years, and for such loans the *maximum loan-to-appraised-value ratio* is 90 percent.
- *FHA and VA RMLs* are *exempt* from the preceding restrictions on aggregate amounts and terms.
- It can, without restriction, deal in, underwrite, and invest in specific *housing-related securities* such as those issued by the Federal Home Loan Bank Board, the Federal National Mortgage Association, and the Government National Mortgage Association.
- It can make *junior-mortgage real estate loans* (secured by other than first liens), but in total these cannot exceed 20 percent of its unimpaired capital plus surplus. (This amount is in addition to the 100 percent limit on first-lien RMLs.)

A state bank similarly has to identify and adhere to detailed laws and regulations that constrain its RMLs. To illustrate, in most states a state bank can make second mortgages; but in many of these states it can do so only if it holds the first mortgage or if the second mortgage is to enable a borrower to repay his or her other loans at the bank.

---

4. James R. Ostas, "Effects of Usury Ceilings in the Mortgage Market," *The Journal of Finance,* June 1976, pp. 821-834.

5. The following summary of the principal restrictions does not encompass the many exceptions and details that are included in 12 U.S.C. 371.

### Consumer Protection and Community Reinvestment Laws

As they have done for consumer loans, Congress and various state legislatures have passed new laws that are supposed to protect individual borrowers and/or to promote RMLs within communities. They have delegated the administration of these laws to bank supervisory agencies and other agencies.

**Real Estate Settlement Procedures Act (RESPA)**   This law, which is administered by the Department of Housing and Urban Development (HUD), applies to most RMLs. It requires a lending institution, such as a bank, to provide an applicant with a:

- special information booklet that describes settlement costs and borrowers' rights
- written good faith estimate of the loan's settlement costs
- copy of a uniform settlement statement that meets the disclosure requirements of the Truth in Lending Act and Regulation

The lender has to retain the uniform settlement statement; and, to protect itself, can retain signed receipts whereby a borrower acknowledges receipt of the special information booklet and good faith estimate.

**Fair Housing Act, Equal Credit Opportunity Act, and Regulation B**   The Fair Housing Act applies to most housing-related loans, and it prohibits lender discrimination on the basis of an applicant's age, sex, race, national origin, religion, or marital status. The Act's antidiscrimination objectives are similar to those of the Equal Credit Opportunity Act (ECOA), which is implemented by Regulation B. These laws and regulations overlap such that a violation of the Fair Housing Act is also likely to violate the ECOA, but a violation of Regulation B does not necessarily violate the Fair Housing Act.[6] As in consumer loans, a lender, within thrity days of receiving a completed application, has to inform the applicant whether or not the loan is approved, and if not approved inform the applicant of his or her right to receive a statement of specific reasons for the denial.

**"Redlining" Controversies**   Some citizen-action groups claim that some banks and other lenders practice *redlining,* whereby they draw a figurative line around blighted or declining city neighborhoods and then refuse to lend to neighborhood residents or to people who want to buy properties in the redlined neighborhoods. Although they contend that it can apply to any type

---

6. Joyce M. Saxon, "Implementing a Program for Consumer Regulation Compliance: Part IV," *The Magazine of Bank Administration,* February 1978, pp. 25-27. Two coauthors report about a pilot program used by the OCC, in cooperation with the FDIC, that uses computer-based statistical procedures to monitor and evaluate whether a bank seems to violate antidiscrimination laws in its housing-related loans. Lewis Mandell and Harold Black, "Monitoring Discrimination in Lending," *The Bankers Magazine,* Winter 1977, pp. 80-82.

of loan, the critics focus on the redlining of RMLs and home improvement loans, especially of applicants from inner-city neighborhoods. They point out that the practice contributes to and perpetuates blighted neighborhoods because even financially qualified borrowers cannot obtain the necessary mortgage financing to purchase older residences to restore and inhabit. The critics further allege that redlining is inequitable because a redlined neighborhood's long-time residents, many of whom are depositors at redlining financial institutions, face curtailed demand for their homes when potential purchasers cannot obtain mortgage financing.

Bankers and officials of other lending institutions usually deny that redlining exists, and/or they contend that their institutional obligations to depositors and stockholders require them to avoid making risky loans. They point out that property values in declining neighborhoods provide less secure collateral than do property values in stable, prosperous neighborhoods. Thus these officials acknowledge that their institutions, while they do not redline, may appear to do so because they make few RMLs in areas with low or potentially declining property values. Also, bankers in some cities can point to positive programs in which local financial institutions pool resources to encourage loans that will help revitalize inner-city neighborhoods.

Critics have found it difficult to prove that specific institutions practice redlining. They rely primarily on testimonial statements by loan applicants who believe that they have been victims of redlining. Yet even this limited evidence has led some state legislatures and city councils to pass laws and ordinances designed to prevent redlining. It also has led to congressional passage of the Home Mortgage Disclosure Act.

**Home Mortgage Disclosure Act**   The Home Mortgage Disclosure Act (HMDA) requires lenders to disclose their mortgage loans by geographical area. With their access to this information, citizens and public officials can try to determine whether lenders practice redlining.

The HMDA applies to most banks, S&Ls, credit unions, and other firms that make federally related mortgage loans. The FRS writes the regulations (Regulation C) to administer the Act, but various federal agencies enforce the Act as it applies to the financial institutions they regulate.

Regulation C applies to federally insured and/or federally regulated depository institutions that have $10 million or more in assets and that have offices in major metropolitan areas ("standard metropolitan statistical areas" or SMSAs).[7] These institutions must compile information on the number and total dollar amount of RMLs and home improvement loans that they originate or purchase. They have to classify this information by census tracts (or in some cases by ZIP codes) within an SMSA, and they have to make this information publicly available at their office(s). To facilitate

---

7. The FRS can exempt from its Regulation C any lending institution that complies with similar state or local disclosure laws.

compilation and disclosure of the required information, the FRS provides lenders with a standardized Home Mortgage Disclosure Form.

In late 1976, when lending institutions first disclosed information required by Regulation C, there was an initial flurry of interest by citizens' groups and news media. Since then, surveyed lending institutions report limited public requests for the disclosure statements. (One survey of S&Ls reports that of almost 2,800 respondents, 60 percent had no requests and 21 percent had one or two requests.[8]) Currently, various federal agencies are engaged in studies to evaluate the usefulness of the HMDA. An apparent limitation of the Act is that, while it discloses infomation about loans made, it discloses nothing about the demand for loans in various geographical areas.

**Community Reinvestment Act**  The Community Reinvestment Act (1977) requires the federal bank regulatory agencies (FDIC, FRS, OCC) and the Federal Home Loan Bank Board to encourage banks and thrift institutions "to help meet the credit needs of the local communities in which they are chartered." The Act requires each agency, when it examines an institution, to assess "the institution's record of meeting the credit needs of its entire community, including low- and moderate-income neighborhoods, consistent with the safe and sound operation of the institution," and to "take that record into account in its evaluation of any application by the institution for a charter, deposit insurance, branch or other deposit facility, office relocation, merger, or acquisition of bank or savings institution shares." This Act, with its criteria and enforcement powers, thus goes beyond the disclosure requirements of the HMDA.

The Community Reinvestment Act (CRA) does not define key terms such as "credit needs," "entire community," "neighborhoods," and "take that record into account." Therefore, before writing regulations to implement the CRA, the four agencies held joint public hearings and invited written public comments. Among those testifying or submitting comments, many people expressed concern that the CRA: was vague in some areas, might lead to some form of mandatory credit allocation, and might result in costly record-keeping and reporting requirements for lending institutions.

To implement the CRA, the four federal agencies have regulations in which they list factors that they consider when they assess a financial institution's performance in meeting its community credit needs. The factors are:

- "Activities undertaken by the bank to determine the credit needs of its local community, including the extent of the bank's efforts to communicate with members of the community regarding credit services offered by the bank.
- "Marketing and credit-related programs to make the community aware of the credit services offered.

---

8. *Federal Reserve Bulletin,* August 1978, pp. 631-636.

- "The extent of participation of the bank's board of directors in formulating policies and reviewing performance.
- "Evidence that the bank actually encourages applications for the types of credit it has listed in its CRA Statement. Any efforts by the bank to discourage applicants from applying for any of the types of credit it is claiming to provide to the community will be considered a negative factor.
- "Geographic distribution of a bank's credit extensions, credit applications, and denials.
- "Evidence of discrimination or other illegal credit practices, including any violations of either the Equal Credit Opportunity Act or the Fair Housing Act.
- "The bank's record of opening and closing offices and providing services at these offices, in order to determine whether each office is providing appropriate credit services to its local community.
- "Participation in local community development and redevelopment programs.
- "Origination or purchase of residential mortgage loans, home improvement loans, and small business or small farm loans within the community.
- "Participation in Government-insured, -guaranteed, or -subsidized loan programs for housing, small businesses, or small farms.
- "The ability of the bank to meet the community credit needs, given the bank's size, financial condition, various legal restrictions, local economic factors, and other variables.
- "Any other factors that bear on whether the bank is meeting the credit needs of the entire community, including low- and moderate-income neighborhoods."[9]

The CRA is recent and potentially far-reaching in its consequences, and so bankers have to keep informed about how the federal agencies proceed to interpret and enforce the Act.

## MANAGING THE PORTFOLIO OF RESIDENTIAL MORTGAGE LOANS

Subject to applicable legal and regulatory constraints, a bank's senior officials set, and at times revise, policy guidelines for the portfolio of RMLs. Specialized officers and staff in turn implement the policies.

### Bank Policies

As part of its written loan policy, a bank usually limits its RMLs to current or potential customers who reside in the bank's trade area. With the advent

---

9. Richard B. West, "The Community Reinvestment Act and Regulation BB," *Voice* (Federal Reserve Bank of Dallas), December 1978, pp. 25-28. These factors are from the FRS's Regulation BB; reportedly the other agencies use identical factors.

of the HMDA and the CRA, a bank is likely also to have a policy that encourages its loan officers to make prudent RMLs to qualified borrowers in low- and moderate-income neighborhoods in which the bank has offices.

Either as a policy or as a strategic decision, a bank has to decide the extent to which it wants to divide its portfolio between conventional and government-insured RMLs. It also has to decide on the extent to which it wants to engage in *primary lending,* in which it originates and holds RMLs, in contrast to *secondary lending,* in which it either buys insured RMLs originated by others or it originates RMLs and sells them to other investors. Most banks focus on primary lending.

## Obtain Applications

A bank cross sells and at times advertises its willingness to make RMLs. It thus invites potential borrowers to inquire about its current terms for RMLs.

To comply with the Fair Housing Act and the ECOA, bank advertising must prominently indicate that the bank makes housing loans without regard to race, color, religion, sex, or national origin. In its written and oral advertisements, a bank can satisfy this requirement by publicizing that it is an "equal housing lender."

Bank loan officers have to be wary that they do not prescreen—or seem to prescreen—applications in ways that violate the equal housing laws. A general inquiry about a bank's current terms for its RMLs does not constitute an "application" under the ECOA and Regulation B. If, however, a loan officer asks the inquirer for credit information on which to recommend whether the person should proceed with a written application, then the process may constitute an application under the ECOA. Therefore, to protect their institution from regulatory criticism and possible lawsuits, bank loan officers should limit themselves to answering general inquiries and to inviting inquirers to submit a written application that can be recorded and processed according to regulatory guidelines.

Many lenders require that potential borrowers pay a fee of about $100 when they submit a written application for an RML. This fee helps pay for the property appraisal and the credit report(s) about the applicant. An applicant is reluctant to pay such a fee without assurance that the lender will likely make the loan if basic conditions are met. Yet to give this assurance, the lender has to engage in some preapplication screening that it has to structure carefully so as not to violate the ECOA. To deal with this dilemma, one author recommends that banks use a written preapplication form that contains questions that "loan officers normally ask in the preapplication interview such as income, debts, and net worth."[10] A bank that uses and retains such written preapplications, which are applications under Regulation B, can document how it accepts and evaluates RML applications in compliance with the ECOA.

10. Joyce M. Saxon, "Implementing a Program for Consumer Regulation Compliance: Part V," *The Magazine of Bank Administration,* March 1978, pp. 32-35.

### Analyze and Negotiate

A bank has standardized terms for most of its RMLs. Over time it changes these terms, and at any time it may grant exceptions.

**Interest Rates and Fees**    At any time a bank has standard interest rates for its principal categories of RMLs. It bases these rates on:

- legal ceilings, if applicable
- local competition
- its cost of funds
- the extent to which it wants to make RMLs

It usually has current rates for conventional RMLs and for government-insured RMLs. It permits loan officers to depart from these rates in special cases involving valued customers and/or unusually low-risk loans.

A bank also has a standardized set of fees to which it alerts potential applicants. These fees include possible: application fees, estimated settlement costs (as required by the RESPA), and penalty fees for prepayment of an RML, especially if such prepayment results from the borrower's refinancing the property at a lower rate.

**Maximum Maturity**    Subject to laws and local competition, a bank sets a maximum maturity for its principal categories of RMLs. Under current law, a national bank cannot exceed a maximum maturity of thirty years on its conventional, fully amortized, real estate loans. A state bank is subject to the applicable laws, if any, of its state. The maximum maturity for most government-insured RMLs is thirty-five years.

**Maximum Loan-to-Appraised-Value Ratio**    To comply with the law and to help control its default risk, a bank has a maximum loan-to-appraised-value ratio for its principal categories of RMLs. A bank can set its maximum ratio below the legal maximum, in which case it increases the purchaser's required equity in a property and/or reduces its RMLs to potential purchasers who cannot meet the equity requirements.

A property's appraised value affects the maximum dollar amount that a bank will lend on the property. For example, if a bank's maximum loan-to-appraised-value ratio is 80 percent and the appraised value of a property is $50,000, then, unless there is an exception, the bank will not lend more than $40,000 against the property. If a prospective borrower agrees to buy the property for $50,000, then he or she has to finance the difference ($10,000) with cash and/or subordinate financing. If a prospective borrower agrees to buy the property at a price that exceeds the appraised value, then he or she has to finance the total difference between the purchase price and the maximum amount that the bank will lend based on the property's appraised value.

Critics of redlining contend that appraisal procedures can contribute to neighborhood decline. They charge that some appraisers lower their appraised value of properties in neighborhoods where the residential mix is undergoing changes—or is expected to change—in its race, national origin, and/or income levels. This appraisal process leads to lower maximum loans which may result in lower property values that then attract lower-income families. Thus the critics contend that appraisal procedures can themselves contribute to changing neighborhoods.

When they examine whether a bank complies with equal housing laws, examiners review the appraisal standards used by the bank. Whether the appraisals are done by outsiders or by bank employees, the examiners evaluate whether the standards seem to:[11]

- assign a lower value to a property in an integrated neighborhood
- equate an integrated neighborhood to a deteriorating neighborhood
- conclude that inner-city neighborhoods inevitably will deteriorate

Thus to avoid possible criticism and/or litigation, a bank needs to have internal procedures to assure that its use of appraisals complies with equal housing laws. Also, it needs to review periodically its files of loan applications and decisions to check whether there are local census tracts or ZIP code areas in which the bank has made disproportionately few RMLs and, if so, why.

**RML Insurance Programs**   If it participates in government mortgage-insurance programs, a bank can limit its risks and yet offer higher loan-to-appraised-value ratios and/or longer maturities than it offers on conventional RMLs. These terms enable some people to obtain RMLs, who otherwise could not meet the down-payment and/or monthly-payment requirements of conventional RMLs.

The Federal Housing Administration (FHA) and the Veterans Administration (VA) are the principal administrators of federal HML insurance programs. These programs require lenders to use standardized forms and procedures to qualify an RML for FHA insurance or a VA guarantee. Under these programs if a borrower defaults on the scheduled repayments, then the insuring agency assumes the loan and reimburses the lender for most of its foreclosure expense.

Because they involve standardized documentation and no default risk, FHA and VA loans trade in more active secondary markets than do conventional RMLs. Thus a bank may choose to hold some FHA and VA loans knowing that it can conveniently sell them if it subsequently wants to readjust its loan portfolio. From a bank's view, government mortgage-insurance programs provide risk-control benefits, but they also involve incremental processing costs compared to most conventional and privately insured RMLs.

Private firms, such as Mortgage Guaranty Insurance Company

11. Saxon, "Implementing a Program for Consumer Regulation Compliance: Part IV," p. 27.

(MGIC), also offer mortgage-insurance programs. A bank can forward an RML application to a private mortgage insurer, which has its underwriting staff evaluate the applicant's repayment capacity and the value of the property that would be mortgaged. The private insurer then responds whether or not it will insure the loan and what its insurance fee would be. To compete against government-insurance programs, the private insurers emphasize their financial capacity, expeditious processing, and willingness to insure types of loans, such as large loans and vacation-home loans, that are ineligible for government insurance. If it subsequently wants to readjust its loan portfolio, a bank will find a broader secondary market in which to sell its privately insured RMLs than it will for its noninsured RMLs.

**RML Evaluation and Decision Systems**    Each bank has specialists who evaluate every written application for an RML loan. If their bank receives few RML applications, these specialists are likely to be loan officers who evaluate various types of loans and who use basic guidelines to evaluate the RML applications. In contrast, if their bank originates many RMLs, the specialists will focus on the RMLs, and evaluate them by using standardized analytical systems.

The specialists estimate an RML applicant's ability and willingness to service the debt. They use information provided by the applicant and supplemental information, such as credit files and credit reports, in order to analyze an applicant's:

- level and stability of income, especially as they relate to the applicant's projected living expenses and aggregate debt-servicing requirements
- total assets and net worth
- history of saving and of servicing debts
- proposed equity in the property to be purchased

If he or she concludes that an applicant's repayment capacity meets the bank's standards, a loan officer proceeds to prepare a loan offer that adheres to the bank's current terms concerning rates, maturities, and loan-to-appraised-value ratios. The loan officer usually has leeway to depart from the current terms either in the loan offer or in negotiations with an applicant.

When an application fails to meet the bank's standards, a loan officer prepares to reject the loan in a way that complies with the notification requirements of the ECOA.

In cases where initial analysis of an application places it in a grey area between "accept" and "reject," a loan officer more fully reviews the risk-return dimensions of the proposed loan. (To aid in the decision, the loan officer may choose to forward the application to a mortgage insurer for an independent evaluation by its underwriters.) Under terms of the ECOA, the loan officer has to proceed to make a decision so that the bank can communicate its final decision to the applicant within thirty days of having received the completed application.

## RESIDENTIAL MORTGAGE LOANS AND INTEREST RATE FLUCTUATIONS

Because of laws and custom, a bank's RMLs traditionally have been fixed-rate contracts in which a borrower gradually repays the loan through a lengthy series of equal monthly payments. This type of long-term, fixed-rate contract is suitable during periods when interest rates are low and financial-market participants confidently anticipate stable future interest rates. In contrast, such a contract leads to severe problems when interest rates approach historic highs and financial-market participants expect rates to fluctuate widely—but unpredictably.

During periods of high, uncertain interest rates and substantial loan demands, a bank quickly reviews its overall lending priorities, especially its priorities for long-term, fixed-rate RMLs, that in many cases are subject to usury ceilings.

If it cannot or chooses not to raise sharply its RML rates to curtail its dollar volume of RML applications, a bank uses an internal priority system to "ration" its mortgage loans. One study interviewed diverse mortgage lenders to learn how they ration mortgage loans, and it reports the following priorities:[12]

- first honor prior loan commitments
- reject all out-of-area applicants
- generally refuse to finance purchases of vacation homes

After this initial set of priorities, a mortgage lender usually ranks applicants by groups:

1. "long-established depositors
2. "buyers of houses on which lenders already have mortgages (refinancing loans)
3. "borrowers referred by brokers and builders who have a long-established association with lender
4. "commercial mortgage borrowers
5. "applicants 'off the street' with no ties to lender"

Beyond this ranking, to further ration mortgage loans among applicants, a lender usually raises its downpayment requirements (lowers its loan-to-appraised-value ratio) and/or it reduces the maximum maturity for which it is willing to make RMLs. By thus tightening its RML loan terms, a bank screens out some applicants who cannot meet the terms, generally reduces an RML's credit risk, and increases the monthly amount and shortens the future period of cash inflows from an RML.

This rationing process of RMLs has recurred throughout recent decades

12. Paul S. Anderson and James R. Ostas, "Private Credit Rationing," *New England Economic Review* (Federal Reserve Bank of Boston), May-June 1977, pp. 24-37.

as interest rates have generally risen and fluctuated widely and unpredictably. Public officials, financial leaders, and other interested parties have expressed concern over how such rationing of RMLs can contribute to:

- unavailability of mortgage funds for potential homeowners who do not have substantial resources or established credit with mortgage lenders
- homebuilding cycles
- liquidity and solvency problems for specialized financial intermediaries (such as S&Ls) that are "locked into" older, low-rate, fixed-rate mortgages

To mitigate these effects of interest-rate fluctuations on RMLs, the public and private sectors have been developing new markets for, and new types of, RMLs.

## THE SECONDARY MARKET FOR RESIDENTIAL MORTGAGE LOANS

The secondary market for RMLs is one in which various participants buy and sell previously originated RMLs.[13] This market developed rapidly during the 1970s, so that now a participant bank can:

- originate loans and/or loan participations to sell to other lenders or investors
- purchase loans and/or loan participations originated by others
- buy and sell futures contracts that are based on standardized RML contracts

A bank can use these new market opportunities to help it manage its portfolio returns, risks, and cash flows. From a public-policy view, an active secondary market for RMLs facilitates interregional funds flows between lenders and home buyers; and it thus contributes to efficient allocation of credit within the national economy.

### Federal Participants and Programs

A set of federal agencies participates in the secondary market for RMLs, facilitating participation by others.

The FHA and VA triggered the development of the secondary market, in which even distant participants can buy and sell standardized, government-insured loan contracts. Prior to these federal insurance programs, most RMLs were nonstandardized, noninsured contracts that their originators held or possibly placed with local investors.

The Federal National Mortgage Association (FNMA, or Fannie Mae) is a federally sponsored institution that is owned by public stockholders and

---

13. This section draws on Peggy Brockschmidt, "The Secondary Market for Home Mortgages," *Monthly Review* (Federal Reserve Bank of Kansas City), September-October 1977, pp. 11-20.

that has public responsibilities. The President of the United States appoints five of the FNMA's fifteen directors, and the Secretary of Housing and Urban Development (HUD) has some regulatory powers over the FNMA. Although it originally purchased only government-insured mortgages, the FNMA now also purchases conventional mortgages. The FNMA maintains an ongoing program in which it buys and sells RMLs in the secondary market. It especially buys mortgages when private lenders such as banks tighten their funds available for RMLs. It restricts the types of RMLs that it buys by setting limits on their size, length to maturity, and loan-to-appraised-value ratio. It also requires the use of uniform mortgage documents.

Throughout most of the 1970s, the FNMA was a net buyer of RMLs. It finances its purchases primarily by selling debentures and mortgage-backed bonds, which are federal agency issues that trade in public capital markets. The FNMA plans new programs in which it buys RMLs, packages them into a pool, and then sells participations to investors.

The Government National Mortgage Association (GNMA, or Ginnie Mae) began in 1968 as part of the Department of HUD. Among its functions, the GNMA buys RMLs to help finance low-income housing and to help provide housing credit during tight-credit periods. The GNMA sells most of the RMLs that it buys. One of its procedures is to buy RMLs from originators at premiums above current-market prices and then sell them to the FNMA or other investors at market prices, absorbing the difference as a housing subsidy. Another procedure is to transfer RMLs back to their originator, which then uses them for mortgage-backed securities that it sells, forwarding the proceeds to the GNMA. The GNMA also has authority to guarantee the payment of interest and principal on mortgage-backed bonds issued by the FNMA and the Federal Home Loan Mortgage Corporation.

In 1970 the GNMA initiated a *pass-through program* by which it sponsors approved private originators of RMLs to pool (package) sets of RMLs and to issue securities that participate in the pools. The GNMA requires that a pool contain at least $1 million of FHA and/or VA RMLs that were made within the last twelve months. The GNMA guarantees the timely payment of interest and principal on the securities that participate in such a pool. The private firm that creates a pool and issues its securities retains responsibility for servicing the RMLs. It collects all payments, including prepayments, from the pool's RMLs, and each month it "passes through" these receipts (minus servicing and guarantee fees) to the holders of the participation certificates, who are the legal owners of the pool's RMLs.

Some large banks are approved originators of GNMA pass-through securities. They sell the securities directly or through securities dealers. A GNMA pass-through security has a minimum denomination of $25,000, and its usual denomination is much larger. Its stated maturity represents those of its underlying RMLs (usually thirty years); but because of prepayments of the underlying RMLs its actual maturity will usually be shorter. Since their origins in 1970, GNMA pass-through securities have expanded rapidly as measured by their total dollar amount outstanding and their weekly trading volume on the secondary market. Banks and bank trust departments are among the institutional holders of these pass-through securities.

The Federal Home Loan Mortgage Corporation (FHLMC, or Freddie Mac) began in 1970, and it provides support primarily for conventional RMLs. It buys such RMLs, primarily from S&Ls, and then pools them, selling participations in the pools. In one such program the FHLMC sponsors pools of Guaranteed Mortgage Certificates (GMCs). GMCs are similar to Ginnie Mae pass-through securities in that their holders periodically receive all interest and principal payments and prepayments (minus expenses) from the underlying pool of RMLs. They differ in that GMC holders receive their participation payments semiannually instead of monthly, and the FHLMC guarantees a minimum amount of principal repayment each year and agrees to redeem GMCs at par on specific dates fifteen to twenty years after their issue. In addition to its sponsorship of pools, the FHLMC buys some FHA and VA loans that it then uses to collateralize mortgage-backed bonds that it issues.

## Private Participants and Programs

Partly in response to recent federal programs, private firms have increased their participation in the secondary market for RMLs.[14] Private mortgage insurers, with their standardized procedures and contracts, reduce the credit risk and contribute to the marketability of the conventional RMLs that they insure.

Banks of various sizes interface with federal agencies and programs. They originate FHA and VA RMLs, and they buy and sell these instruments in the secondary market. (When it originates and sells an RML, a bank usually continues to service it on behalf of the new holder.) Banks can buy and sell such securities as the GNMA-backed pass-through certificates, and large banks can evaluate the net benefits of being an approved originator of pass-through certificates.

In 1977, Bank of America became the first large money-center bank to sell, via a public offering, *private pass-through certificates*. These certificates are not debt obligations of the sponsoring bank; they offer participation in a pool of conventional mortgages originated and serviced by the bank. The mortgage pool consists of almost 3,000 RMLs, most of which have thirty-year maturities and loan-to-appraised-value ratios of 80 percent or less. A private mortgage insurer reviewed all the RMLs and fully insured the component loans up to 5 percent of the original unpaid balance of all the RMLs in the pool. As with GNMA pass-through securities, the sponsoring bank collects all receipts from the pool; and each month it passes through the net receipts to the holders of the participation certificates.

While no bank has yet done so, some large S&Ls have issued marketable securities that they collateralize with either government-insured

---

14. The Federal National Mortgage Association (FNMA), with its publicly appointed directors and public responsibilities is an anomalous "private" participant in the secondary market for RMLs.

or privately insured RMLs. Unlike participation certificates, these mortgage-backed bonds do not represent ownership of a pool of RMLs; they provide specific interest payments, have specific maturities, and are direct obligations of the issuer.

## Mortgage Futures Markets

A bank can examine whether, and to what extent, it can use mortgage futures contracts to hedge the interest-rate risk associated with RMLs. These futures contracts are a recent innovation in financial markets, and bank supervisory agencies closely monitor bank proposals to participate in this new market.

Mortgage futures markets began in 1975 when the Chicago Board of Trade initiated a futures contract that is negotiable and standardized to represent a GNMA pass-through certificate with a principal amount of $100,000 and a stated interest rate of 8 percent. Board rules permit delivery of a GNMA pass-through certificate with another yield, provided the certificate yields an equivalent 8 percent when calculated at par and when it is assumed that a thirty-year certificate will, because of prepayments of the underlying RMLs, actually mature twelve years after its issue date. The price of a GNMA futures contract is quoted as a percentage of its par value; and so when market interest rates rise, the price of a contract falls, and vice versa. Market prices of these futures contracts are reported daily in financial newspapers such as *The Wall Street Journal*.

A bank or other financial institution can use mortgage futures contracts to hedge against interest-rate fluctuations that can affect its RML holdings and/or commitments. To illustrate, assume that a large bank commits itself to make a set of RMLs at a specific rate and then to pool these RMLs and sell GNMA-approved participation certificates in the pool.[15] If market interest rates rise between the time it first commits itself to the RMLs and later sells the participation certificates, the bank will have to sell the certificates at a discount and thus sustain some financial loss. To hedge itself, the bank can sell an equivalent dollar amount of GNMA futures contracts at the time it makes the RML commitments. The contracts extend over the period until the bank plans to issue the pass-through certificates. If interest rates rise during the interval, then the price of the contracts will fall, and the bank can conclude the hedge by then buying offsetting contracts at the lower price. The gain from these contracts will about offset the loss that the bank incurs in assembling a pool of RMLs at one rate and then having to sell the participation certificates at a lower price to yield the higher prevailing rate. In contrast, if interest rates fall during the interval, then the price of the contracts will rise such that the bank will incur a loss when it

---

15. This illustration is adapted from one by Neil A. Stevens, "A Mortgage Futures Market: Its Development, Uses, Benefits, and Costs," *Review* (Federal Reserve Bank of St. Louis), April 1976, pp. 12-19. Stevens provides a more detailed numerical example, and he points out some associated costs and risks of this illustrative hedging strategy.

buys offsetting contracts to conclude the hedge. The loss on the futures contracts will about offset the bank's gain from its selling the participation certificates at a lower effective interest rate (higher price) than the interest rate on the underlying RMLs. There are also procedures by which a bank or other financial institution can use mortgage futures contracts to hedge inventories of RMLs, commitments to sell RMLs, and forward cash flows.[16] By so doing it manages its interest-rate risk and maintains its potential profits from originating and servicing RMLs.

## ALTERNATIVE MORTGAGE INSTRUMENTS

Senior officials of lending institutions and public-policy officials have begun to question the traditional form of long-term, fixed-rate RMLs that schedule equal monthly payments to cover interest and to fully amortize the loan by its maturity. These officials raise their questions because of the following types of observations:

- Because of their alternative lending opportunities and their concern about becoming "locked" into long-term, fixed-rate RMLs, financial institutions ration their RMLs when interest rates are high and potentially unstable. This process cuts off some potential borrowers and disrupts the housing industry.
- As home costs and interest rates have climbed, many Americans find it difficult to accumulate a down payment for their first house and/or to service the monthly repayment of a traditional RML.
- Other types of mortgage-loan contracts are used—apparently successfully—by lenders and borrowers in other industrialized nations.

Although they encounter legal and regulatory barriers, some banks and other financial institutions have begun to examine, and in some cases offer, alternative mortgage instruments (AMIs) that depart from the traditional long-term, fixed-rate RML. Bankers need to keep informed about proposed and experimental AMIs.

### Alternative Fixed-Rate Mortgage Instruments

Alternative fixed-rate mortgage instruments center around a fixed-rate contract; but, in contrast to traditional amortized RMLs, they involve unequal monthly payments.

**Graduated-Payment Mortgages**   A graduated-payment mortgage (GPM) has a fixed interest rate and maturity and a specified schedule of monthly payments, whereby the early payments are less than the amount needed to fully amortize the loan, but subsequent payments increase gradually until,

---

16. Stevens, "A Mortgage Futures Market: Its Development, Uses, Benefits, and Costs."

by about the tenth year, they level off at an amount that will fully amortize the remainder of the loan by its maturity. A GPM, with its lower initial monthly payments and higher later payments, is intended to benefit young home buyers who find it difficult to meet initial payments on a traditional RML but who expect their incomes and debt-servicing capacity to increase over time.[17]

**Flexible-Payment Mortgages**   A flexible-payment mortgage is a variant of a GPM. It, too, involves a fixed rate and maturity; but its scheduled early monthly payments cover only the interest and its scheduled later payments (after about five years) reach a fixed level to cover remaining interest and to amortize the loan's principal by maturity.

**Reverse-Annuity Mortgages**   A reverse-annuity mortgage (RAM) also involves a fixed rate, but it enables a person who has a substantial equity in a home to use the home as collateral for a line of credit against which the homeowner can borrow in scheduled monthly increments. A RAM is intended to benefit elderly homeowners, who in many cases own their property and now want to borrow against it gradually as a way to supplement their retirement income. Borrowers under RAMs thus systematically increase their debt secured by their home. A usual expectation is that this increased debt (representing the cash advances and the accumulating interest) will be repaid out of a borrower's estate. Both borrowers and lenders would have to plan carefully their use of RAMs so that a borrower is unlikely to outlive the scheduled incremental borrowings and so that a lender schedules its future cash flows to meet the contractual incremental borrowings against the RAMs it made.

**Roll-Over Mortgages**   A roll-over mortgage loan is written with a fixed rate for a fixed period, such as five years; but its monthly payments are based on an assumed amortization period of, say, twenty-five years. At the end of each five-year period, the borrower has to repay the unamortized principal or refinance the remainder (roll it over) at the current interest rate. Thus, at the end of the first five years the borrower can roll over the loan at the current rate, and his or her monthly payments then are based on the new rate and on an assumed amortization period of the remaining twenty years. In Canada such roll-over mortgages have been used for conventional single-family RMLs for over forty years, and the practice reportedly is well accepted by borrowers and lenders.

### Variable-Rate Mortgages

A variable-rate mortgage (VRM) is one in which the interest rate can vary, both upward and downward, over time, and this variable rate usually

---

17. To facilitate computation of annual percentage rates (APRs) for GPMs, the FRS amended its Regulation Z to permit GPM lenders to use some standardized APR computation tables prepared by the FHA.

fluctuates in association with a specific reference rate or index. A VRM is a more complex instrument than a traditional fixed-rate mortgage. Like a fixed-rate mortgage, a VRM agreement must specify the initial interest rate, the initial length to maturity, and the initial monthly payment. In addition, a VRM must specify whether and to what extent these loan terms can subsequently change.

A VRM has to specify the reference rate or index to which its rate will be linked. For example, the rate can be a market index, such as the market rate on three- to five-year U.S. Treasury securities; an index of aggregate funds costs for lending institutions that make VRMs; or an index of a specific lender's cost of funds. A VRM also has to specify:

- the frequency of rate changes
- the maximum and minimum rate changes from one period to another
- notification requirements concerning each rate change
- prepayment opportunities and/or penalties
- the maximum amount by which, during the VRM's life, the rate can change from the initial rate

In addition, a VRM contract has to stipulate how future rate changes, both upward and downward, will affect the future schedule of payments. To illustrate, if interest rates were to rise, the principal alternatives would be to:

- maintain the same monthly payment but extend the maturity
- increase the monthly payment and retain the initial maturity
- combine increasing the monthly payment and lengthening the maturity

The complexities of a VRM are such that both borrowers and lenders need to understand its contractual intricacies and implications.

Their proponents cite how VRMs, compared to fixed-rate mortgages, have net benefits for lenders, borrowers, mortgage markets, and housing markets. Yet opponents cite various disadvantages of VRMs; and, in some cases, opponents have blocked experimentation with VRMs at both the state and federal level.[18] In California some large S&Ls and banks have been offering VRMs since the mid-1970s. One analyst reviews the initial experience with VRMs in California, notes many of the actual and potential problems, and concludes that "the California experience to date suggests that it may not be easy to realize the full potential of this mortgage instrument."[19]

18. For recent reviews of the procedural and public-policy issues associated with VRMs, see Eleanor Erdevig, "Is There a Future for Variable Rate Mortgages?," *Business Conditions* (Federal Reserve Bank of Chicago), November 1975, pp. 3-11; William R. McDonough, "Advantages of Innovations in Variable-Rate Mortgages," *Business Review* (Federal Reserve Bank of Dallas), December 1976, pp. 1-8; and George G. Kaufman, "Variable Rate Residential Mortgages: The Early Experience from California," *Economic Review* (Federal Reserve Bank of San Francisco), Summer 1976, pp. 5-16. Usury laws, with their upper ceilings on interest rates, can impede experimentation with VRMs.

19. Kaufman, "Variable Rate Residential Mortgages: The Early Experience from California," p. 15.

### Banks and Alternative Mortgate Instruments

In view of the ongoing discussion about AMIs and the expanding experimentation with AMIs, especially by S&Ls, a bank needs to plan its offerings of AMIs. For example, as regulations permit VRMs and as other lenders offer them, a bank has to evaluate whether to offer VRMs and, if so, how to structure the specific terms of its VRMs in comparison to those of its traditional fixed-rate, long-term RMLs.

## LARGE-SCALE REAL ESTATE LOANS

Many banks also make loans that help finance major real estate developments (such as office buildings and shopping centers), and/or are secured by nonresidential properties.[20] These large-scale real estate loans involve nonstandardized terms and specialized processing; and so they are more similar to business loans than to RMLs.

## CONSTRUCTION LOANS

In a construction loan a bank provides interim, or bridge, financing to a developer of a project such as a housing tract, commercial building, or industrial structure. As a condition for a construction loan, a bank usually requires the borrower to have obtained from a *take-down lender,* such as a major insurance company, a prior commitment to provide long-term mortgage financing for the completed project. The bank expects the borrower to use this long-term financing to repay the construction loan.

The preceding functional definition of a construction loan encompasses some loans that banks carry as business (commercial and industrial) loans. For example, a national bank classifies as a commercial loan:

- a construction loan on an industrial or commercial building if the loan's maturity does not exceed five years and if it involves a binding commitment by "a financially responsible lender to advance the full amount of the bank's loans upon completion of the buildings" (12 U.S.C. 371)
- a construction loan for residential or farm buildings if its maturity does not exceed five years—even if there is no take-down commitment
- a construction loan, whether or not secured by a mortgage, that is based primarily on the borrower's general credit standing and/or debt-servicing capacity

These "business" construction loans are exempt from legal limits that constrain a national bank's mortgage loans and loan-to-appraised-value ratios.

---

20. Agricultural loans, which would fall within this category, are discussed in Chapter 12.

In 1971 the FRS conducted a special survey of bank construction loans.[21] This survey, the first in over twenty years, includes "business" construction loans. The survey reports that:

- Banks in total make more construction loans than does any other category of lender.
- Almost two-thirds of all surveyed banks make construction loans; large banks account for the largest dollar amount of such loans.
- Large banks focus on construction loans for multifamily units and nonresidential properties; small banks focus on construction loans for one- to four-family residences.
- Because many construction loans are classified as business loans, traditional measures, which include only mortgage loans, understate bank involvement in real estate finance.

These survey results demonstrate that most banks engage in construction lending.

One author reports on construction lending by large commercial banks.[22] These banks, which focus on construction loans for large-scale real estate projects, gradually disburse the funds as construction progresses; and they expect total repayment when the take-down lender provides the long-term financing for the completed project.

A lending bank faces various risks that may delay timely and/or full repayment of its construction loans. These risks include:

- delays due to adverse weather and/or strikes
- engineering and/or construction errors
- cost overruns
- legal steps by developers and/or take-down lenders to withdraw from unfinished projects that no longer seem financially viable

To control its construction-loan risks, a large bank can: employ specialists to evaluate and oversee construction projects, concentrate on loans to borrowers with strong credit ratings, and diversify among projects.[23]

The author reports that "gross yields on high-quality construction loans were 3 to 4½ percentage points higher than those on prime commercial loans." When asked to account for this yield difference, the interviewed bankers offered three typical explanations:

- "The deposit relationship offered by construction borrowers was not as attractive as that offered by commercial borrowers.

---

21. "Construction Loans at Commercial Banks," *Federal Reserve Bulletin,* June 1972, pp. 533-544.

22. Peter A. Schulkin, "Construction Lending at Large Commercial Banks," *New England Economic Review* (Federal Reserve Bank of Boston), July-August 1970, pp. 2-11.

23. Diversification among projects can be a frail risk-control strategy if financial results of many of the projects are subject to similar events, such as unanticipated high interest rates or short-run excesses in rental units.

- "The expenses to the bank of construction lending were greater than those of commercial lending.
- "The risks in construction lending were greater than in commercial lending."[24]

At the time of the study, lenders reported low losses from their recent construction loans, but some lenders cautioned against extrapolating this recent experience. Their warnings were generally disregarded—and subsequently proved correct.

## REAL ESTATE INVESTMENT TRUSTS AND BANKS

A real estate investment trust (REIT) is a nondeposit financial intermediary that obtains funds from various sources and channels the funds into real estate loans and/or ownership. Under federal legislation passed in 1960, if it meets certain conditions, an REIT can operate much like an investment company that: invests in a portfolio of assets, pays no corporate income taxes, and passes through its income to its stockholders who are subject to personal income taxes.[25] As can other investment companies, an REIT can choose to be open-end, in which it continually stands ready to redeem or sell its shares, or closed-end, with a fixed common-stock capitalization. Virtually all REITs are closed-end. Unlike most registered investment companies, which by law and choice seldom use borrowed funds to leverage their portfolios, REITs have willingly leveraged their real estate portfolios.

There are two basic types of REITs: *construction and development (C&D) REITs* focus on construction lending; *long-term investment REITs* primarily hold long-term mortgage loans or ownership interests in income properties.

The REIT industry expanded rapidly in the late 1960s and early 1970s, and many large banks helped fuel this expansion:

- Various large banks were affiliates of bank holding companies (BHCs) that decided to sponsor an REIT, and in many cases the BHC gave its sponsored REIT a name similar to that of the affiliate bank.[26]
- Many large money-center banks lent substantial sums to bank-sponsored REITs and to REITs that had the sponsorship of nonbanking firms or independent sponsorship. (By the mid-1970s, the REITs owed $11 billion to banks, and this sum equaled about half of aggregate REIT assets.)

24. Schulkin, "Construction Lending at Large Commercial Banks," p. 5.

25. Peter A. Schulkin, "Real Estate Investment Trusts: A New Financial Intermediary," *New England Economic Review* (Federal Reserve Bank of Boston), November-December 1970, pp. 2-14.

26. Shulkin identifies reasons why a BHC would want to sponsor a REIT; and he outlines how a bank-sponsored REIT can lead to conflicts of interest among parties associated with a BHC, its lead bank, and its REIT.

- To build their portfolios, especially of construction loans, the REITs had to compete aggressively against large money-center banks that made similar loans.

Having fueled REIT expansion, many large banks soon faced an REIT financing debacle.

By 1975 some large REITs were on the brink of collapse; and, with hindsight, one can summarize key factors that led to this situation:[27]

- Many REITs were highly leveraged.
- Many REITs were poorly hedged; they relied on short-term, interest-sensitive borrowings to help finance longer-term, often fixed-rate, assets.
- As observed by a senior supervisory official, "In financing REITs initially, it appears that banks made little financial and credit analysis of these loans."
- By 1974 the REITs began to face higher interest costs and difficulties of rolling over some short-term borrowings, and they found that their returns from real estate assets—because of cost overruns and high vacancy rates—were falling below expectations. Many REITs had left themselves with little margin for such adverse outcomes.

As troubles loomed for many REITs and their creditors, the FRS signalled the large banks to take actions to avert—or at least try to limit—a financial disaster among REITs. Some REITs subsequently entered bankruptcy, and the large banks slowly continue to unwind their costly involvement with them.

## SALVAGING PROBLEM REAL ESTATE LOANS

By the mid-1970s large banks took steps to identify and salvage their problem real estate loans, many of which were to REITs.[28] From a bank's view, a problem loan can be in one of several stages:

- a loan from which the bank currently receives interest, but, by agreement, at a rate below the initial contractual rate
- a nonearning loan
- a loan for which the probability of repayment is so low that the bank needs to increase its provision for loan losses
- a loan that warrants a charge-off against reserves

When faced with an early-stage problem loan, a bank has to decide whether to try to salvage something by foreclosing on the loan or whether to

---

27. Wyndham Robertson, "How the Bankers Got Trapped in the REIT Disaster," *Fortune,* March 1975, pp. 113-115 ff.

28. For reporting purposes, bank loans to REITs are included among loans to financial institutions. From an operating viewpoint, such loans to REITs are intertwined with real estate loans.

try to "work out" the loan with the borrower and the other creditors. Often a bank is reluctant to foreclose on a loan, especially if this action might trigger associated lawsuits by the borrower and its other creditors. Therefore, when it faces a set of problem loans such as those to REITs, a bank is likely to assemble a team of specialists to work out the problem loans. These work-out specialists come from within the bank; and they draw on outside consultants, such as specialists in real estate financial transactions.

A work-out team faces a lengthy assignment. Once it identifies a problem loan, it has to evaluate the net benefits of using one of several work-out strategies:

- lend additional funds so that the original borrower can complete and carry its real estate projects until they generate cash flows to service the total debt
- negotiate with the original borrower to have it sell its projects to other parties that have the capacity, perhaps supplemented by additional loans, to increase the projects' cash flows
- negotiate to have the borrower *swap* one or more properties to the bank in exchange for debt reduction or cancellation, and possibly a cash payment by the bank

Swap arrangements are a principal way by which some large banks try to work out of their problem real estate loans. A swapping bank exchanges its creditor position, in which it has to coordinate its claims with those of other creditors, for that of an owner of a project received in a swap. A swapping bank faces legal limits as to how long it can own a nonbanking property, and so it has to have or retain property managers who proceed to increase a property's cash flows and market valuation. As stated by one senior banking officer, "As lenders, our objective is recovery of principal. Swaps are part of that strategy." Swapping procedures and salvage operations require a long-run commitment. As one banker said in 1976, "Nobody will know how things come out in this game for 10 years."[29]

## SUMMARY

All banks make residential mortgage loans (RMLs); most large banks also make specialized loans to developers of large-scale real estate properties.

Most of a bank's RMLs are conventional loans that are secured by first mortgages on one- to four-family residences. Each bank has to monitor that its RML policies and procedures conform to state usury ceilings, regulatory restrictions on amounts and types of RMLs, and recent consumer protection laws and regulations. These guidelines are complex and in flux. A bank has

---

29. "Are Swaps the Way Out for Banks?" *Business Week,* October 11, 1976, pp. 53, 55-56. Also, John M. Hamstra and S. Michael Edgar, "Evaluating that REIT Swap Proposal," *The Journal of Commercial Bank Lending,* April 1978, pp. 26-39.

to be sensitive to how its RML practices appear to critics of "redlining" and to citizens' groups that have new power under the Community Reinvestment Act.

Specialized loan officers administer a bank's portfolio of RMLs subject to their bank's policies and strategies concerning:

- geographical and/or customer priorities for RMLs
- standardized terms for RMLs
- level of involvement in RML insurance programs
- risk analysis of RML applicants

The loan officers process the RML applications in ways that comply with equal housing laws and associated procedural regulations.

Traditional RML markets and instruments have undergone reexamination and some changes in recent years. Federal policy has fostered development of a secondary market for RMLs. Specialized federal agencies, private insurers, banks, and other financial institutions are current and/or potential participants in this secondary market and its offshoots, mortgage futures markets. Banks, as issuers and/or as investors, will likely focus increased attention on pass-through certificates, which represent participations in portfolios of RMLs. Banks, other RML lenders, and public officials also are evaluating—and in some cases experimenting with—alternative mortgage instruments that include: graduated-payment mortgages, flexible-payment mortgages, reverse-annuity mortgages, roll-over mortgages, and variable-rate mortgages.

Large banks in particular also engage in large, complex loans to help finance major real estate projects. These banks have specialized units that focus on construction loans and loans to real estate investment trusts (REITs). In many cases these banks also have and/or retain specialists who work to salvage problem real estate loans. These problem-loan specialists and senior officials use swap arrangements as one way to try to extricate their bank from problem real estate loans.

# 15

# MANAGING BANK CAPITAL

Bank stockholders, creditors, and regulators have different perspectives concerning the function(s) of bank capital. Not surprisingly then, they also have differing views about the appropriate types and amounts of bank capital. A bank's senior officials have to understand and try to reconcile these differences so that they can effectively manage their bank's capital over time.

## ANALYZING THE BANK CAPITAL QUESTION(S)

The topic of bank capital involves a set of interrelated questions to which different parties, depending partly on their views of risk and possible economic events, can offer different answers. Exhibit 15-1 schematically summarizes these interrelated questions.

### FUNCTIONS OF BANK CAPITAL

A bank's capital, which consists primarily of stockholders' equity, provides a buffer to absorb unusual losses sustained by a bank. This buffer helps protect a bank's creditors, and it can help a bank to weather temporary adversity and thus continue as a going concern. Emphasis is on capital's *helping* role as a buffer. The extent to which a bank's capital actually protects creditors and the bank's ongoing operations in turn relates to risks associated with the bank's total portfolio and possible changes in its economic environment.

#### Portfolio and Operating Risks

A bank willingly accepts some risks as part of its ongoing banking activities. Although it attempts to limit and control its risks, a bank anticipates that at times it will have, or could have, losses in some of its activities.

**EXHIBIT 15-1**

**Analyzing the Bank Capital Question(s)**

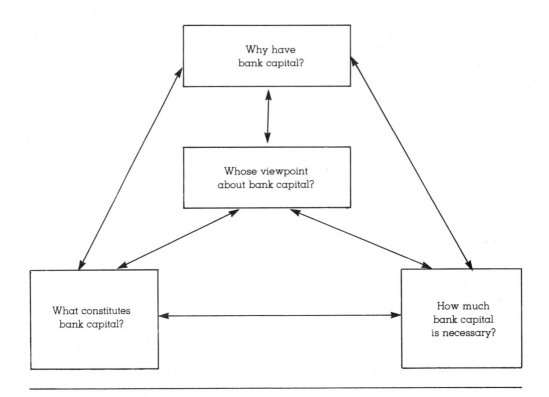

**Bonds**   Even if it confines itself to securities with low default risk and
diversifies widely among issuers and among maturities, a bank expects to
incur occasional losses primarily because of the interest-rate risk associated
with long-term securities. Trading account securities especially involve risks
of losses associated with unanticipated upswings in interest rates.

**Loans**   Even if it has a restrictive loan policy and strict control and
collection procedures, a bank expects to lose on some of its loans. (If its loan
losses were to approach zero, then critics would contend that such a bank
does not perform the lending functions expected of a publicly chartered
bank.) Anticipating that it will have to charge-off some loans over time, a
bank builds up and uses its loan-loss reserve accounts.

**Fixed Assets**   A bank's premises and equipment are part of its total assets,
and they provide the operating base for the bank's total portfolio. Bank
buildings often involve specialized construction, and much banking equipment is both specialized and subject to obsolescence. While the issue is not
conclusive, many bankers and bank regulators assert that a bank ought to
finance its fixed assets primarily with long-term capital funds provided by its

stockholders. On this basis a bank does not finance long-term, virtually nonmarketable, operating assets with funds provided by depositors and other short-term creditors.

**Unanticipated Liquidity Demands**   Even if it has diversified sources of deposits and other short-term liabilities, a bank anticipates some periods of net cash outflows. One way to meet net outflows is to reduce short-term assets that involve little risk of capital loss. If, however, the outflows are large, unanticipated, and expected to continue, then the bank will likely start to replenish short-term assets by selling some longer-term securities on which it will likely realize capital losses if interest rates have risen. These liquidity demands—and their associated losses from unanticipated sales of longer-term securities—will be magnified if the bank simultaneously has to meet loan commitments that it previously extended to potential borrowers.

**International Transactions**   Large banks with multinational banking operations are vulnerable to possible losses in foreign exchange operations and international lending. Although they have ways to control these risks, multinational banks have to anticipate occasional—perhaps substantial—losses in some of their international activities.

**Trust Activities**   If it has a trust department, a bank is vulnerable to possible lawsuits charging that the department violated its fiduciary responsibilities to some accounts under its supervision. Whether charged with intentional violations or errors of judgment, a bank incurs costs to defend itself; and it may incur additional large costs if it loses the case or settles out of court. It is difficult for a bank or a bank regulatory agency to predict the extent of possible losses a bank's trust department might incur.

**Losses Due to Dishonesty**   Not only are banks subject to portfolio risks associated with judgmental errors, but they are vulnerable to losses due to criminal actions by employees and/or outsiders. Most banks have elaborate control systems to forestall and detect cash shortages and fraudulent schemes by bank insiders. Bank audits and examinations also try to curtail such criminal activities; and banks can, at a cost, insure themselves against employee dishonesty. Despite strict policies and elaborate controls, a bank also remains vulnerable to unanticipated losses associated with criminal fraud by bank customers and other outsiders. Almost by definition a bank cannot predict the extent of possible losses due to dishonesty. Only when it detects such a scheme does a bank start to learn the possible magnitude of its eventual losses.

**Summary**   A bank faces risks in many of its portfolio and operating activities. Despite its efforts to control such risks, a bank knows that at times it will likely incur large, unanticipated losses in some of its banking activities. Therefore it positions itself to sustain such losses and still continue as a going firm.

## Risks of Economic Instability

A bank faces portfolio and operating risks even if there are no major shocks to the economic system(s) within which it operates. Yet within this century various economic systems have experienced financial panics, deep depression, and high inflation. If such economic events can recur in the future, what can or should a bank do to prepare for such contingencies?

The United States and most industrialized nations have national policies and institutions that seek to forestall, or at least temper, adverse economic events. At the policy level, the United States has the Employment Act with its goals of low unemployment, stable prices, and stable growth. Commentators assert that many tools of fiscal policy (such as Social Security, unemployment benefits, and graduated taxes) provide a cushion against destabilizing economic events. As the nation's central bank, the Federal Reserve System seeks to conduct monetary policy consistent with the objectives of the Employment Act, and it acknowledges its role as lender of the last resort to provide liquidity to the financial system in periods of unusual stress. The Federal Deposit Insurance Corporation insures bank deposits up to $40,000 and thus reduces the probability that insured depositors will participate in possible runs on banks. Yet to what extent can such policies and institutions successfully temper adverse economic events that arise in interdependent economic systems, many of which have substantial fixed commitments to groups of citizens? For example, the oil embargo and quadrupling of oil prices by the Organization of Petroleum Exporting Countries sent major shockwaves throughout the economies of most industrialized nations. Some of the world's largest banks have incurred large publicized losses in their multinational transactions, and while many of them survived such losses some did not. In the late 1960s and early 1970s several large American banks failed or came close to failure.

Few banks, if any, can insulate themselves against major shocks within interdependent economic systems. If it were to try to be self-sufficient, a bank would have to maintain prime short-term assets well in excess of its needs under normal operating conditions. Moreover, for planning purposes, many banks assume that the federal government and the central bank have the responsibility and power to avert widespread destabilization of the nation's banking and financial systems. Using this planning assumption, a bank tries to reduce its vulnerability to initial shocks so that it can continue as a going concern until the government stabilizes the situation.

## Absorbing Temporary Set-backs

A bank can develop several lines of defense by which to meet unanticipated net cash outflows and/or losses.

**Liquidity**   Liquidity management, which involves cash flow planning and careful structuring of short-term assets and liabilities, is a bank's first line of defense. To illustrate, if two similar-sized banks suddenly face similar temporary adversity, then, other items equal, a bank with substantial liquidity but with less capital is likely to withstand such adversity better than an illiquid bank that has more capital. To some extent liquidity thus can substitute for capital but capital seldom can substitute for liquidity.

**Earnings**   Compared to a similar-sized bank that has low and erratic earnings, a bank that has high and stable earnings has more flexibility, subject to accepted accounting procedures, to absorb some losses within its current earnings stream. Also, if a bank has a record of comparatively high, stable earnings, then its supervisors and creditors are likely to infer that the bank's management has the demonstrated skills and flexibility to absorb setbacks better than other banks with less successful records.

**Reserves**   Knowing that at times it will encounter losses in its portfolio activities, a bank establishes and manages specific reserve accounts, such as loan-loss reserves, against which it enters specific charge-offs and recoveries. Subject to IRS and accounting guidelines, a bank thus can use transactions within reserve accounts to absorb some types of temporary setbacks from its operations.

**Capital Accounts**   Its capital accounts are a bank's last line of defense against temporary setbacks. From a cash-flow viewpoint, neither capital nor reserves provides a cash buffer to help a bank meet temporary setbacks. From an accounting viewpoint, however, if its losses exceed the amounts that it can absorb in its current earnings stream or applicable reserve accounts, then a bank can charge the excess losses against its equity capital accounts. This equity capital buffer itself has limits. Although it can charge losses against its retained earnings and surplus accounts, by law a bank would *impair its capital* if it were to charge losses against its account designated as paid-in common stock; and the law prohibits a bank from thus impairing its capital. In practice, if a bank's major losses would sharply reduce its reserves and equity cushion, then the bank's supervisors require the bank to raise additional capital if it intends to continue in business. If the bank is unlikely to be able to raise the additional capital, then the supervisors will explore ways to have the bank acquired by a well-capitalized, nonproblem bank; or they will declare the bank insolvent and request the FDIC to pay off insured depositors and to liquidate the bank.

**Summary**   To buffer itself against temporary setbacks, a bank has a series of positions that include its: liquidity, current earnings, reserves, and—as a last resort—capital. Yet a bank is not the only party interested in its having an effective defensive strategy to withstand temporary adversity.

## DIFFERING VIEWS ABOUT BANK CAPITAL

Five principal parties have direct interests in how a bank manages its capital over time. These parties are a bank's:

- stockholders
- creditors
- borrowers
- supervisory agencies
- management

Because their interests in a bank's capital are not identical, these parties can differ as to the appropriate form(s) and amount(s) of bank capital.

### Stockholders' Viewpoint

Stockholders' equity accounts for most, if not all, of a bank's capital. Before a new bank can begin operations, its organizers have to sell all of its initial stock to subscribing stockholders. As it expands over time, a bank increases its stockholders' equity via retention of earnings and/or by occasional offerings of additional stock. Bank stockholders thus have a direct interest in the risks and returns (including dividends) associated with their ownership interest in a bank.

As do most corporate stockholders, bank stockholders expect their firm to continue as a going concern that earns an acceptable rate of return on its stockholders' equity. On this basis they expect a bank's management to avoid risky strategies that may jeopardize the bank's survival and their investment in the bank. If their bank needs additional capital to support its profitable expansion, these stockholders will likely support their bank's increasing its equity capital via retained earnings and/or sales of additional stock. Yet within these general principles, bank stockholders, and their elected directors, engage in more complex assessments of risks and returns associated with bank stock ownership.

**Investor Portfolios**   An investor for whom a specific bank stock accounts for only a small part of a broadly diversified portfolio may prefer to have the bank engage in "risky" strategies that may lead to higher returns. If the bank succeeds, the investor expects to benefit from superior returns. If the bank's risky strategies prove unsuccessful, then the adverse returns will account for only a small part of the total returns from the investor's portfolio. In contrast, stockholders who have invested much of their personal and family wealth in a specific bank will likely want the bank to avoid risky strategies that may jeopardize their long-term returns from the bank.

**Proportion of Equity Capital**   Bank stockholders also can differ as to their bank's proportion of equity capital to total assets. They realize that a base of equity capital is needed to attract and retain funds from depositors and other creditors and to help absorb unusual losses. Yet they also know that *if* their bank successfully leverages its assets, then the expected returns (and variability of returns) on stockholders' equity will generally increase as the proportion of equity capital decreases. From their viewpoint, at least some bank stockholders will question whether more bank capital (especially stockholders' equity) serves their long-run interests as stockholders.

### Creditors' Viewpoint

All banks have depositors as creditors. Especially if it is large, a bank also has creditors who hold the bank's short-term and/or long-term nondeposit liabilities.

Both as an ongoing firm and in the event of liquidation, creditor claims precede the residual claims of stockholders. Thus while they too look to a bank's capital as a buffer to help it withstand temporary adversity, bank creditors focus on the question: If the bank fails and has to be liquidated, will it have sufficient capital to absorb all realized losses so that the creditors will fully recover their funds? From the creditors' viewpoint, as a bank's proportion of equity capital to total assets increases, then—for a given asset structure—the bank's creditors have a more secure position if the firm were to fail. Yet not all bank creditors concern themselves with possible bank failure.

**Insured Depositors**   Depositors of most banks have their accounts insured up to $40,000 by the FDIC, an agency of the federal government. In view of this protection, insured depositors have little reason to concern themselves with a bank's capital cushion.

**Noninsured Creditors**   FDIC insurance does not apply to most account balances that exceed $40,000. Holders of balances above $40,000 thus have part of their deposits at risk, giving them an incentive to investigate the risk (one measure of which is the equity cushion) of their bank(s). A bank's other noninsured creditors include those who lend it federal funds and/or invest in its other nondeposit liabilities not covered by FDIC insurance. The holders of a bank's nondeposit liabilities thus have to evaluate both the expected risks and returns from these holdings. In summary, while insured depositors can be indifferent, noninsured creditors prefer, other things equal, that their bank(s) have a large capital cushion.

### Borrowers' Viewpoint

A major borrower knows that its maximum loan from one bank usually cannot exceed 10 percent of the bank's capital stock and surplus. Thus when it evaluates with which bank to develop a new long-run relationship, a firm considers whether the bank's current and potential capital resources are large enough to accommodate the firm's loan requests.

Large borrowers also consider whether a bank has sufficient capital to withstand adversity. Major borrowers, as a condition of their loans, often maintain deposits that are not covered by FDIC insurance, and so, as depositors, they want their bank to withstand adversity. In addition, these borrowers prefer not to have to have their borrowing relationships disrupted because their bank encounters serious financial problems and/or fails.

Overall, most major borrowers probably prefer to have their bank(s) have a comparatively high and fast-growing capital position.

### Supervisory Viewpoint

Bank supervisory agencies closely monitor a bank's capital. The OCC, the FRS, the FDIC review the capital of a national bank. The FRS, the FDIC, and the state banking agency review the capital of a state member bank. The FDIC and the state banking agency review the capital of a nonmember insured bank.

For several reasons, banking agencies prefer not to have publicized problems and/or failures among banks that they supervise.

**Legislative Accountability**   A bank supervisory agency, whether federal or state, is accountable to a legislative unit. If banks under its supervision encounter publicized problems and/or fail, then agency officials have to defend their agency before the legislators. One or more failures can undo a banking agency's rapport with its legislature.

**Public Inconvenience**   Even if it is an isolated episode involving an insured bank, a bank failure temporarily inconveniences the bank's depositors, borrowers, and community. Although it has been rare, uninsured creditors may not recover their funds. As a government agency, a bank supervisory agency prefers to avoid, or at least mitigate, such public inconvenience.

**Public Confidence**   If one bank has publicized problems and/or fails, then at least some citizens, especially uninsured creditors of banks, may start to question the safety of other banks. While it is difficult to measure this public-confidence element, bank supervisory agencies generally prefer to prevent a bank's failure and, if one fails, to try to demonstrate that the failure is an isolated episode that will not spread throughout the banking system.

**FDIC Insurance Fund**   If a large bank fails or if there is a series of bank failures, then the FDIC faces some depletion, at least temporarily, of its insurance fund. If the FDIC thus has to reduce its fund, then this may reduce the confidence of some depositors who look to the fund and to the FDIC's contingency sources of funds for protection.

**Summary**   From the viewpoint of bank supervisory agencies, banks should try to prevent major problems; and they should also have the resources and skills to withstand temporary adversity. On this basis, whether considering a bank or the banking system, other things equal, bank supervisory agencies prefer banks to have more capital than the banks themselves might choose to have.

### Management Viewpoint

Bank directors and senior officers find themselves at the center of the bank capital question. In many small and medium-sized banks, the directors and senior officers are also the principal stockholders. While they thus identify closely with the stockholders' viewpoint, these officials also are sensitive to the views of the bank's principal creditors and borrowers and to the views of its supervisory agencies. In most of the nation's large banks, the directors and senior officers own a small proportion of the bank's stock. Yet these professional managers similarly have to be sensitive to the different viewpoints of their bank's stockholders, creditors, major borrowers, and supervisors.

Bank officials realize that there is not—and in practice probably cannot be—unanimity concerning the amount and form of a bank's capital. Basically, many bank stockholders, while they accept the need for bank capital prefer their bank to have less capital than would many of the bank's creditors, borrowers, and supervisory agencies. Aware of this basic bank-capital dilemma, a bank's directors and senior officers have to try to satisfy the various viewpoints and to make practical decisions concerning how much capital their bank should have in the near future, the form(s) it should take, and how it should be raised.

## PRINCIPAL FORMS OF BANK CAPITAL

Observers agree that equity serves as a bank's capital base, and, for analytical purposes, they usually include a bank's loss reserves as part of this equity base. In contrast, observers differ as to the extent to which long-term debt instruments, even when subordinated to claims of other creditors, constitute bank capital.

### Equity Capital

A bank's equity capital is the total of several balance sheet categories.

**Common Stock**  This account represents the par value of a bank's common stock times the number of shares outstanding.

**Preferred Stock**  This account represents the par value of a bank's preferred stock, if any, times the number of shares outstanding. Although its contractual rights precede those of common stock concerning a firm's dividends and assets, preferred stock is owners' equity that is subordinate to the legal rights of a firm's creditors. Most banks have no preferred stock.

**Surplus**   A new bank sells its common stock at a price above par value, and it designates part of the difference (between the total amount received and the total par value) to a surplus account. The surplus account is a permanent part of a bank's equity. A bank cannot reduce its surplus, for example by paying dividends that would have to be charged against its surplus account, nor can it—except in liquidation—charge losses against its surplus account. By law a bank cannot lend any one borrower an amount that exceeds a proportion (usually 10 percent) of its common stock plus preferred stock (if any) plus surplus; and so over time, to increase its loan limit, a bank increases its surplus account. To do so, a bank usually redesignates some of its undivided profits as surplus and/or it sells additional stock at a premium over the par value.

**Undivided Profits**   A new bank sells its initial stock at a price above par value, designates part of the total difference to surplus, and the remainder to undivided profits. Compared to its surplus account, a bank has more flexibility with its undivided profits account. Subject to supervisory review, a bank can pay dividends in excess of its current earnings and charge them against undivided profits. Also, if its loss reserves are inadequate, it can charge losses against its undivided profits account. To increase its undivided profits account over time, a bank retains part of its annual earnings and designates them as additions to its undivided profits account.

**Reserves for Contingencies and Other Capital Reserves**   Subject to tax, accounting, and regulatory guidelines, a bank can establish capital-reserve accounts and add to or subtract from these accounts. In the aggregate, these capital reserves account for a small proportion (about two percent) of equity capital in the banking system.

### Loss Reserves

Anticipating that it will incur losses from some of its loans and securities, a bank usually establishes reserves to absorb such losses and reports these reserve accounts as offsets to its loan portfolio and its investments portfolio. Although these reserves are not explicitly reported as part of a bank's balance-sheet capital, most observers consider such reserves as buffers against unforeseen setbacks and so view them as part of a bank's capital.

### Subordinated Notes and Debentures

A bank's subordinated notes and debentures are intermediate- or long-term debt instruments that are contractually subordinate to the claims of the bank's depositors and other creditors.[1] Although it is a legal liability,

---

1. For brevity this book uses the term debentures to encompass both capital notes and debentures. Apparently there is no practical distinction between the two terms, which the supervisory agencies use in tandem or interchangeably. The original intention may have been to classify short-term instruments as notes and long-term ones as debentures. However, current federal banking regulations require that, to

because it is subordinated to other liabilities, a debenture has attributes of bank capital. Reflecting those hybrid characteristics, until 1977 such debentures were termed capital debentures and classified as part of a bank's total capital accounts, but now they are termed subordinated debentures and they are classified as a separate balance-sheet item—neither part of a bank's total liabilities nor part of its equity capital.

**Uses of Subordinated Debentures**   Many nonbanking corporations use long-term debt instruments as part of their financial structure. These firms analyze their expected returns from assets, costs and risks of other sources of funds, and probable benefits to their stockholders. A bank similarly can evaluate potential benefits and costs from issuing subordinated debentures.

*Protection of other Creditors:*   Because they are subordinated to claims of other creditors, a bank's debentures can provide an extra margin of safety to noninsured creditors—and to the FDIC insurance fund—*in the event* that the bank is liquidated. Thus, other things equal, noninsured creditors will prefer to do business with a bank that provides them with this extra protection.

*Cost:*   In contrast to dividends on common and preferred stock, which are paid from after-tax income, interest on debentures is paid before taxes. As a simplified example, if its tax rate is 50 percent and if it issues 8 percent debentures, then a bank has an after-tax cost of 4 percent on these debentures. This percentage may be less than the current dividend yield (paid with after-tax dollars) on its common stock. In practice many banks have marginal tax rates below 50 percent, and for them the tax advantages are less than those of the example.

The flotation costs (primarily marketing and possibly underwriting costs) for a debenture issue usually are less than those to sell a similar dollar amount of common stock or preferred stock.

As a hybrid instrument, a debenture is not a deposit and so not subject to reserve requirements or FDIC insurance assessments. Also, it is not equity, and so member banks do not have to count it as part of their equity that serves as a basis for their required subscription to stock in their Federal Reserve Bank.

*Control:*   Debenture holders have no voting rights in a bank. Therefore, especially if it is closely held and wants to avoid dilution of this control, a bank may prefer to sell debentures instead of common stock with its attendant voting rights.

*Leveraging:*   If they are confident that their bank can earn a return that exceeds what it pays for debenture funds, at least some of a bank's stockholders will welcome this additional leveraging of their equity capital.

---

avoid interest-rate ceilings and reserve requirements, capital notes and debentures must have an average maturity of seven years, with a minimum maturity of five years. Also, the minimum denomination has to be $500.

This leveraging, while it thus may magnify stockholder returns, involves the bank in legally binding obligations to service the debt. If it fails to service its debentures, the bank will likely fail or be salvaged by the supervisory agencies in ways that will result in losses to its stockholders and, probably, to holders of its debentures.

*Reduced Flexibility:*   While it involves potential benefits, debenture financing potentially constrains a bank's financial flexibility. To avoid defaulting on its debentures, a bank has to meet the periodic interest payments and to repay the principal as scheduled. When its debentures reach their maturity date(s), a bank has to refinance them or otherwise have the resources to retire them. Thus, because they mature, debentures are a less permanent source of financing than is equity capital.

Not only do they constrain a bank's cash flows, but as balance-sheet items, debentures restrict a bank's flexibility to charge-off losses. While charging losses against undivided profits is an acceptable accounting practice, a bank cannot charge losses against its liability accounts, including subordinated debentures, except in bankruptcy.

As it analyzes specific benefits and costs of using subordinated debentures, a bank has to consider supervisory views about debenture financing.

**Supervisory Views of Bank Debentures**   Issuance of bank debentures was rare until the 1930s, when some banks began to sell debentures to the Reconstruction Finance Corporation, a federal agency that provided emergency financing during that period of economic stress. Banks that issued these debentures usually faced supervisory mandates to increase their capital in a period when it was difficult to sell additional stock. Bank debt capital thus had an aura of bank weakness, and issuing banks, with supervisory encouragement, moved rapidly to repay their indebtedness and thus eliminate it from their balance sheets.

Although some bankers and scholars subsequently encouraged banks to reevaluate possible use of debenture financing, the historic stigma continued until 1962 when the OCC ruled that national banks could consider debentures as capital for many supervisory purposes. The FRS was less willing to view subordinated debentures as capital, but many states soon modified their laws and regulations to permit state banks to issue debentures and to treat them as capital for supervisory purposes. As a result, for the nation's banks, subordinated debentures now total $6 billion, compared to total equity capital for $79 billion (year-end 1977).

Supervisory agencies differ among themselves and with some bankers concerning how to weigh the benefits and costs of debenture financing. The supervisory agencies acknowledge that, in the event of liquidation, subordinated debentures provide an additional buffer to protect noninsured creditors and the FDIC. They also understand the possible cost advantages and leveraging opportunities associated with debenture financing. What concerns some supervisors, however, is how, especially during volatile economic periods, the debt-servicing obligations of debentures can constrain individual banks and possibly the banking system.

Because they view debentures as an imperfect substitute for equity capital, the supervisory agencies specify guidelines to limit the issuance and servicing of bank debentures. The OCC stipulates that a national bank's principal amount of outstanding debentures generally "shall not exceed an amount equal to 100 percent of the bank's unimpaired paid-in capital stock plus 50 percent of the amount of its unimpaired surplus fund."[2] Subject to this guideline, the OCC still has the power to approve or disapprove a specific proposed debenture issue. Many states similarly set issuance guidelines for their state-chartered banks. When it evaluates a state-member bank's proposed issuance of debentures, the FRS reviews items such as:[3]

- debt-to-equity ratio
- earnings coverage of fixed charges
- retained income
- debt repayment concentrations
- interbank debt transactions
- covenants that could conflict with sound banking practices

Some of these FRS guidelines are quantitative, such as a maximum debt-to-equity ratio of 50 percent; others are qualitative, such as the need to "avoid excessive concentration of debt repayment in any one year." Within these guidelines the FRS retains administrative flexibility to "consider a full range of financial and other data."

In summary, subject to supervisory guidelines and approval, a bank now can evaluate the specific benefits and costs of its issuing subordinated debentures even if it cannot treat these funds as part of its capital.

## MEASURES OF BANK CAPITAL NEEDS

In principle a bank's capital needs relate to the various risks that it takes, the probable economic scenarios that it foresees, and the risk aversion (or preferences) of its principal stockholders and senior officials. By trying to conceptualize and measure these complex factors, a bank develops insights into its capital needs over time.

In practice, at least as a first approximation, bank officials compare their bank's capital resources to those of "similar" banks that presumably face similar risks. These officials also realize that bank stockholders, creditors, borrowers, and supervisory agencies similarly find it difficult to estimate a bank's capital needs and so they also compare capital ratios among "similar" banks.

---

2. 12 C.F.R. 14.5.

3. *Federal Reserve Bulletin*, July 1976, pp. 602-604.

### Bank Capital Ratios

Bank supervisory agencies and other interested parties use capital ratios to compare banks and to identify trends within banks and the banking system. These ratios use different definitions of bank capital. *Equity capital* encompasses the total stock accounts (which include paid-in surplus and undivided profits), and it usually includes reserves for losses on loans and securities. *Total capital* is equity capital plus any subordinated debentures.

**Total Capital to Total Assets**   This ratio summarizes the relationship between two major balance-sheet items: total capital and total assets. The ratio indicates to what extent a bank uses its capital to finance its total assets; the higher the ratio, the higher the proportion of total assets financed with owners' equity and subordinated debt.

**Total Capital to Risk Assets**   Although a bank's assets involve a spectrum of risks, this ratio classifies bank assets as either "riskless" or "risk;" and it defines risk assets as a bank's total assets *minus* its (1) cash, (2) due from banks, (3) U.S. Treasury securities, and (4) federal agency securities.[4] This ratio, sometimes called the *risk-asset ratio,* assumes that most bank losses will arise from risk assets, which are only part of total assets. Mathematically, a bank's ratio of total capital to risk assets always exceeds its ratio of total capital to total assets, the extent of the difference depending on how a bank's assets are split between the riskless and risk categories.

**Equity Capital to Total Assets**   Some observers view debentures as an imperfect substitute for equity capital, and so this ratio focuses on the relationship between a bank's equity capital and its total assets. This ratio indicates to what extent a bank uses its equity capital (its owners' investment) to finance its total assets; the higher the ratio, the higher the proportion of total assets financed with owners' equity. Mathematically, this ratio has to be less than the ratio of total capital to total assets for any bank that has debentures among its total capital.

**Equity Capital to Risk Assets**   This ratio follows directly from the preceding definitions of "equity capital" and "risk assets." This ratio excludes debt capital, and so for any bank that has debentures its ratio of equity capital to risk assets has to be less than its ratio of total capital to risk assets.

### Applying Bank Capital Ratios

No one capital ratio fully summarizes a bank's capital position in relation to its specific risks or to that of other banks. Yet, taken together, these

---

4. If they have convenient access to the information, some analysts extend the definition of riskless assets to include federally guaranteed loans and federal funds sold.

ratios—and further refinements of them—provide initial insights into bank capital trends and comparisons.

**Trends in Bank Capital Ratios**   Exhibit 15-2 summarizes the average capital ratios for all banks between 1960 and 1975. This exhibit indicates that since 1960 the ratios of capital (whether total capital or equity) to total assets have declined from 9 percent to about 7 percent. Also, since 1960, the risk-asset ratios have generally declined from 16 percent to about 9 to 10 percent. Since the capital numerators are the same in both sets of ratios, these relationships suggest that during the period banks' risk assets grew more rapidly than did their total assets. The declines in these capital ratios were widespread among banks of various size categories.

Even though bank capital ratios have declined over recent years, it is possible that the initial ratios, in retrospect, were too high, and/or banking conditions have changed over time so that banks can confidently operate with lower capital ratios than they could in earlier decades. To test these possibilities, one study uses data from 224 large banks during the two subperiods 1965 to 1969 and 1970 to 1973, and it reports that for these banks "capital account variability has increased, using the median figures, by less than 1% of the increased capital levels. The mean figures tell a similar story." Thus, he concludes, that "while variability may have increased, on average, capital growth has been high enough that overall risk in the banking system has declined over the period 1965 to 1973."[5]

In contrast, some bank supervisory officials have publicly expressed concerns about declines in bank capital ratios—especially since, in their judgment, some banks have begun to engage in "riskier" portfolio strategies. To illustrate, a former Chairman of the Board of Governors of the FRS notes how since 1960 the "enormous upsurge in banking assets has far outstripped the growth of bank capital. . . . Thus, the capital cushion that plays such a large role in maintaining confidence in banks has become thinner, particularly in some of our largest banking organizations."[6] Beyond expressing their concerns, the bank supervisory agencies have sought to stem the decline of—and to encourage increases in—capital ratios among banks that they supervise.

**Supervisory Use of Capital Ratios**   When they evaluate a bank's capital, the supervisory agencies consider such factors as a bank's: quality of management, earnings history and prospects, portfolio structure and potential volatility, expense structure, and future financial needs. Within this context, the agencies also use ratio analysis as part of their evaluation. As a rule of thumb, for example, the FDIC considers a bank's capital to be "inadequate" if its capital-asset ratios are below the mean ratio for the

---

5. Anthony M. Santomero, "Bank Capital: A Regulation Perspective," *Financial Management,* Winter 1976, pp. 56-64. This analysis includes debentures as part of total capital accounts.

6. Arthur F. Burns, "Maintaining the Soundness of Our Banking System," *Monthly Review* (Federal Reserve Bank of New York), November 1974, pp. 263-267.

**EXHIBIT 15-2**

## Trends in Bank Capital Ratios: 1960-75

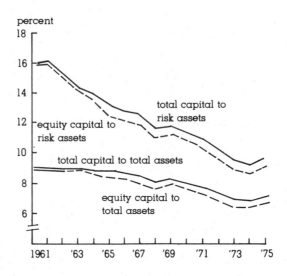

*Note:* Equity capital is defined to include the reserve for losses on loans and securities. Total capital equals equity capital as defined above, plus subordinated notes and debentures. Total assets includes consolidated foreign and domestic assets. Risk assets equals total assets less cash and due from banks, less U.S. Treasury and Government agency securities. Ratios are based on aggregate data for all commercial banks.

*Source:* Harvey Rosenblum, "Bank Capital Adequacy," *Business Conditions* (Federal Reserve Bank of Chicago), September 1976, p. 3.

industry.[7] The FRS pays close attention to a member bank in which the ratio of total capital to total assets is less than 8 percent and/or its risk-asset ratio is below 12.5 percent. The OCC also focuses on the risk-asset ratio. The agencies do not report how they develop their capital-ratio guidelines, and they emphasize that any such guidelines are basically aids to supervisory judgment.[8] Yet a bank knows that if its capital ratio(s) fall below its

---

7. John J. Mingo, "Regulatory Influence on Bank Capital Investment," *The Journal of Finance,* September 1975, pp. 1111-1121. Mathematically, some banks will have capital ratios below the industry mean.

8. One study examines a sample of 722 banks between 1962 and 1968 and concludes,

Although the evidence is somewhat mixed, it does not appear to support the hypothesis that there exist *significant* differences in the amount of capital funds held by national, state F.R.S. member, and nonmember banks, when the influence of other factors is held constant. The differences that are evident are rarely of such magnitude as to be important either in a statistical or economic sense. However, this is not prima-facie evidence of similarity in the applied capital standards of the supervisory agencies. It is conceivable that systematic differences among the bank classes in management conservatism, or responsiveness to bank examiners' suggestions for additional capital, may offset differing agency standards thus negating supervisory impact on capital.

Lucille S. Mayne, "Supervisory Influence on Bank Capital" *The Journal of Finance,* June 1972, pp. 637-651.

agency's current standards, then it had better prepare to justify such exceptions to the agency.

Bank supervisory agencies have various powers to encourage banks to meet an agency's capital standards. Among extreme sanctions, the OCC or a state can revoke a bank's charter, the FRS can terminate a bank's membership, and the FDIC can terminate a bank's FDIC insurance. As a less extreme sanction, an agency may cite a bank's "inadequate" capital as a basis for denying a bank's application to expand its branches or to merge. Also, the Bank Holding Company Act gives the FRS broad powers to approve or deny bank holding company applications to expand their activities, and the FRS has used these powers to encourage bank holding companies to increase the capital of their affiliate banks.

Aware of the powers available to its supervisory agencies, a bank is likely to accommodate supervisory views about its capital position. One study explicitly tests whether supervisors have been able to encourage increases in capital by banks, which, in their judgment, have inadequate capital. The study uses a random sample of 323 banks, and it reports that

> . . . the lower is the ratio of actual capital to capital desired by the regulators the more likely is the banker to add to capital over the next period, *ceteris paribus,* to satisfy the demands of the bank examiner. Moreover, the effect of regulatory demands on capital is nonlinear in nature; regulators place the greatest "pressure" on banks with the most "inadequate" capital, such that these banks experience the greatest capital investment rates, *ceteris paribus.*[9]

The study also concludes that its results, coupled with those of a prior study, indicate that "the level of bank capital is now greater than it would be in the absence of bank capital regulation."

**Capital Ratios and Asset Growth**   Via their official statements and policy actions, various bank supervisory agencies express their reluctance to allow bank capital ratios to fall below their levels of 1974. On this basis the banking industry's ratio, for example, of total capital to total assets should not fall below about 8 percent. Such a standard, if adhered to, will preclude repetition of the 1960s and early 1970s, during which time bank asset growth exceeded bank capital growth, thus leading to declines in bank capital ratios (see Exhibit 15-2).

Various researchers have developed projections of bank capital needs based on alternative assumptions about bank asset growth and bank capital ratios. One long-range study focuses on the time period between 1975 and 1985.[10] This study summarizes the projected levels of bank assets in 1980 and 1985 *if* bank assets were to grow at annual compounded rates ranging

9. Mingo, "Regulatory Influence on Bank Capital Investment," p. 1119.

10. George H. Hempel, *Bank Capital: Determining and Meeting Your Bank's Needs,* Bankers Publishing Company, Boston, 1976. Other analysts used similar procedures to project bank capital needs in the 1970s. For example, Warren R. Marcus, "Financing Tomorrow's Bank Growth," *Journal of Bank Research,* Autumn 1974, pp. 156-160.

from 2 to 16 percent. If, for example, one assumes that bank assets were to grow at an annual rate of 10 percent (similar to that of the early 1970s) and that the ratio of total capital to total assets has to stay at 8 percent, this implies that total capital in the banking system would have to expand to $125 billion by 1980. If one extends the same set of assumptions to 1985, by then the capital base will have to be about $200 billion. These capital estimates are substantially higher than the system's total equity capital of $79 billion at year-end 1977, and the implied increases in bank capital substantially exceed those of recent decades. Thus if the supervisory agencies adhere to an 8 percent standard for the ratio of total capital to total assets, then the banking system will have to decelerate its recent rate of asset expansion and/or accelerate its rate of capital growth.

**Capital Ratios and Bank Size**  The preceding discussion focuses on average and normative capital ratios of the banking industry.[11] Yet when comparing a bank's capital ratios to those of "similar" banks, one is likely to compare ratios among banks of "similar" size and possibly among banks in similar geographical areas and subject to similar federal supervision.

Exhibit 15-3 summarizes that, on average, the ratio of equity capital to total assets declines as bank size increases. Although not reported in the Exhibit, the ratio of total capital to total assets similarly is inversely related to bank size.

Average capital ratios summarize underlying distributions of such ratios. To illustrate, for all banks, the distribution (year-end 1977) of the ratio of equity capital to total assets is:[12]

| Ratio (percent) | Percent of all banks |
|---|---|
| under 5 | 3.0 |
| 5 to 8 | 52.3 |
| 8 to 11 | 33.7 |
| 11 to 15 | 7.9 |
| 15 or more | 3.2 |
| Total | 100.1 |

This distribution itself summarizes a more detailed distribution of the ratio for banks categorized by asset size.

The fact that capital ratios vary among banks suggests that bank supervisory agencies perceive differences in risks and capital needs among banks and so they choose not to, or cannot, enforce uniform ratios among

---

11. The question of bank capital becomes more complex when one extends the topic to encompass bank holding companies, as is done in Chapters 19-20.

12. Summarized from the *Annual Report of the Federal Deposit Insurance Corporation: 1977,* Table 114, p. 174. (Percentage figures do not total 100.0 because of rounding.) The same table also provides a detailed distribution of the ratio of equity capital to risk assets.

**EXHIBIT 15-3**

**Capital Ratios Distributed by Bank Size**

| Ratio | All Banks | Banks with Total Assets (in Millions) | | | | | |
|---|---|---|---|---|---|---|---|
| | | Under 5 | 5-10 | 10-25 | 25-100 | 100-300 | 300 or More |
| Equity capital to total assets | 8.2 | 10.0 | 9.0 | 8.2 | 7.6 | 6.9 | 6.3 |
| Equity capital to net loans* | 16.1 | 20.9 | 18.0 | 16.1 | 14.7 | 13.7 | 12.7 |

*In contrast to a risk-asset ratio, this ratio focuses on the net loans component of risk assets.

Source: Table C (Nation), *Banking Operating Statistics*, 1977.

banks. Also, by choice some banks may have capital ratios that depart from the norm(s). If, however, a bank's capital ratios fall well below the norms, its management had better be prepared to explain the variance to the supervisory agencies and noninsured creditors. In contrast, if its capital ratios substantially exceed the norms, a bank's management had better confirm that this reflects the preferences of the bank's stockholders.

## MARKETS FOR BANK CAPITAL

Although earnings retention is a principal way for a bank to increase its capital, bank officials also examine the markets in which their bank's capital securities currently trade and may be sold.

With some exceptions, the common stock of most large money-center banks—or of their parent holding company—is widely held and regularly traded in national or regional securities markets. This market breadth contrasts to the limited markets for shares of most small and medium-sized banks that are not affiliates of large multibank holding companies. Although they are sometimes traded in public markets, debentures of large banking organizations, and especially of smaller banks, usually are closely held and inactively traded.

### EQUITY MARKETS FOR LARGE MONEY-CENTER BANKS

National reporting of bank share prices has increased in recent decades. From 1950 to 1973 the number of banks having their stock prices reported in a national newspaper more than doubled to about two hundred.[13] In the

---

13. Paul F. Jessup, ''New Markets for Bank Stocks,'' *The Bankers Magazine,* Winter 1974, pp. 29-34. This article serves as the basis for much of this section.

earlier part of the period, the reported prices primarily were of shares of banks in eastern financial centers; the later coverage encompasses a more geographically diverse set of banking organizations.

Shares of most large money-center banks trade in the over-the-counter (OTC) market, and they are included in the NASDAQ system which is a computerized communications network that links together a large part of the OTC market.[14] For its stock to be eligible for inclusion in the NASDAQ system, a company must have *at least*:

- $1,000,000 in assets
- 100,000 shares outstanding
- 300 stockholders
- two broker-dealers registered as market makers who continually quote the stock in the system

Also, a firm must agree to meet specific reporting and disclosure standards. Most large money-center banks meet these eligibility requirements, except, in some cases, for the minimum number of stockholders. Even if a bank meets these initial requirements, its stock will receive nationwide financial coverage (for example in *The Wall Street Journal*) only if its dollar volume of trading activity also meets NASDAQ standards. Therefore a large banking organization that wants nationwide reporting of its stock price will welcome buying and selling activity in its shares.

With minor exceptions, it was not until the late 1960s that banking organizations began to apply to have their stock listed on the New York Stock Exchange (NYSE) and/or other national or foreign stock exchanges. For its stock to be listed on a registered stock exchange, such as the NYSE, a bank has to meet the exchange's listing criteria. Some money-center banks, whose shares could qualify for listing, choose not to have their shares listed on the NYSE. Apparently these banks conclude that the net benefits of an NYSE listing do not exceed those associated with inclusion in the OTC NASDAQ system.

A large money-center bank, especially if its stock is widely held and actively traded, is likely to have a formal shareholder relations program. At one level, such a program actively communicates a bank's plans and progress to professional bank-stock analysts and portfolio managers.[15] At another level, such a program seeks to develop and strengthen relations with nonprofessional investors. For example, some banks offer *dividend reinvestment plans* whereby a stockholder can elect to have his or her periodic cash dividends reinvested, at a nominal charge, in additional shares of the bank's stock. Additionally, some dividend reinvestment plans permit a

---

14. NASDAQ system is the acronym for the National Association of Securities Dealers Automated Quotation System.

15. Robert M. Baylis, "Stockholder Communications for Banks," *The Bankers Magazine*, Spring 1974, pp. 74-78.

stockholder to invest, again at a nominal charge, additional cash in the bank's stock.

Because they are accountable to their stockholders and they may at some point want their bank to sell additional stock, bankers have reasons to be concerned about how the market values their bank's stock over time. One study seeks to identify the characteristics of banks whose stocks have high price-earnings (P-E) ratios in contrast to those with low P-E ratios.[16] The study examines 41 return-risk attributes associated with a sample of 80 banks between 1963 and 1972. It reports that distinctions between banks with high and low P-E ratios are best explained not by traditional asset-liability ratios or income-expense ratios but by "variables measuring growth of the firm and its market along with the stability of that growth." Another study tests the efficiency of the market for shares of large banks. This study uses a sample of 85 large banks whose shares traded in the OTC market during December 1961 through February 1968 and concludes that, "the market for bank stocks is operationally efficient given the over-the-counter market structure" but that it "is less allocatively efficient than the New York Stock Exchange."[17]

## DEBENTURE MARKETS FOR LARGE MONEY-CENTER BANKS

When selling debentures, large banks have two principal alternatives: a public offering or a direct placement.

In a *public offering*, a bank uses a syndicate of investment banking firms to underwrite and market the issue to institutional and individual investors. The offering has to be registered with the Securities & Exchange Commission (SEC), and it has to meet the SEC's disclosure requirements, concerning which a bank will want to rely heavily on advice from its legal counsel, accountants, and investment advisors.

Until 1974 the major rating services such as Moody's and Standard & Poor's did not rate bank debentures or stock. (The services apparently adopted this policy because of concern that if it were to reduce or withdraw a bank's rating, a rating service might be violating state statutes that were designed to prevent rumormongering about a bank's financial condition.) Now these services do rate senior capital offerings of many parent bank holding companies, but their ratings criteria differ from those that they apply to nonbanking firms.[18] One banker reports how his organization learned from one agency that "short of having one of the five or ten best

---

16. Richard A. Shick and James A. Verbrugge, "An Analysis of Bank Price-Earnings Ratios," *Journal of Bank Research*, Summer 1975, pp. 140-149.

17. Robert L. Hagerman, "The Efficiency of the Market for Bank Stocks: An Empirical Test" (Comment), *Journal of Money, Credit, and Banking*, August 1973, pp. 846-855. Briefly, allocative efficiency refers to allocation of resources to their highest-valued use, and operational efficiency refers to minimization of transaction costs.

18. Paul F. Jessup and Mary Bochnak, "Why Not Deregulate Bank Debt Capital?" *Financial Management*, Winter 1976, pp. 65-67.

performance records for the past five years, it is extremely difficult to obtain an Aa rating if total assets of the holding company do not exceed $2 billion. Another agency uses a minimum of $150 million of equity as a basis for Aa qualification."[19] With this advent of ratings, a large bank, especially if it plans to make a public offering of debentures, will want to investigate current applicable ratings criteria and examine how its actions may lead to an upgrading or downgrading of its rating(s).

In a *direct placement,* a large bank negotiates, either directly or through an investment banking firm, to sell an issue directly to one or more institutional investors, such as large insurance companies and pension funds. If it thus limits its sale to several large knowledgeable investors, a bank can obtain exemption from SEC registration and disclosure requirements. In some cases a bank concludes that a direct placement is more expeditious and/or involves lower total costs than does a public offering. An institutional purchaser of a direct placement is likely to hold the issue until it matures or is called. In contrast, purchasers of publicly offered debentures anticipate that these instruments will continue to have a public market until their redemption.

## EQUITY MARKETS FOR MEDIUM-SIZED AND SMALL BANKS

Among medium-sized and small banks one pattern of ownership is where a bank was formed and has continued as a "community bank" with perhaps hundreds of stockholders, no subset of which controls the bank. To preserve this stockholder distribution, the bank usually has an officer who introduces potential selling stockholders to local people who have expressed interest in buying some noncontrolling shares in their community bank. These bank-stock transactions involve no dealer, and they are infrequent and nonpublicized.

The more prevalent ownership pattern is where a group of stockholders controls a bank that also has some minority stockholders. There are several principal variants of this control pattern:

- A control group can consist of several individuals, for example a family, who in total own 50 percent or more of a bank's stock and who coordinate their control position.[20]
- *Chain banking* arises when members of such a control group, as individuals, control more than one bank.
- There are financial and tax reasons why a control group may decide to control a corporation (a one-bank holding company, or OBHC) that in turn controls a bank (see Chapter 20). Because of tax laws, an OBHC usually owns at least 80 percent of a bank's stock, and so minority

---

19. Richard A. Gallant, "Approaches to Capital Planning," *Journal of Bank Research,* Autumn 1975, pp. 173-176.

20. If the other shares are widely distributed, then a group with less than 50 percent of a bank's stock may effectively control the bank's policies.

stockholders generally account for a small proportion of the stock of a
bank controlled by an OBHC. (In some cases a group of individuals
controls a chain of such OBHCs).

- Where permitted by state law and subject to FRS regulation, a
corporation can become a multibank holding company (MBHC) that
controls more than one bank. An MBHC generally tries to have no
minority stockholders in banks that it controls. While they thus control
banks, most MBHCs and some OBHCs are themselves large organizations, the shares of which are widely held and not split between a
control group and a set of minority stockholders.

Exhibit 15-4 schematically summarizes these principal patterns of bank
stock ownership.

Especially among banks not controlled by bank holding companies, a
principal issue is the split, and possible conflicting interests, between a
bank's controlling block of stock and its minority shares. (Potential conflicts
are less likely to involve bank holding companies that try to have no
minority stockholders of banks that they control.)

A new bank seldom begins with a split between control shares and
minority shares. To discourage initial control blocks, a chartering authority
encourages a bank's organizers to sell the stock widely among community
residents who are potential customers of the bank, and it often limits the
maximum subscription by any one purchaser of the new shares. While most
banks thus begin as a "community bank," often a group of individuals
gradually purchases additional shares as they become available in the
inactive local market; and thus the group accumulates a control block of the
bank's stock.[21]

The market for the controlling stock of a medium-sized or small bank
differs from the inactive local market for its minority shares. Regional
banking magazines and national financial publications, such as *The Wall
Street Journal,* regularly contain classified advertisements in which control
of a bank (or of a small OBHC) is offered or sought. These advertisements
are placed by offering and bidding groups and by firms that, for a
commission, specialize in bringing together prospective sellers and buyers
of control blocks of bank stock. Although they do not usually operate on a
commission basis, correspondent departments of large banks also keep
informed about and at times introduce prospective sellers and purchasers of
control blocks of banks.

After some failures of small banks in which control had recently
changed, in 1964 Congress passed Public Law 88-593, which provides that
when "control" of any insured bank changes, a chief executive officer of
the bank must promptly report the change to the appropriate federal banking

---

21. Instead of gradually accumulating a control block, a group can extend a *tender offer* in which it bids
for enough shares to perfect a control block. While it can expedite development of a control block, a
tender offer requires a bidding group to disclose more information concerning its financial resources and
objectives; and it may evoke counteroffers from competing groups.

**EXHIBIT 15-4**

## Principal Patterns of Bank Ownership: A Schematic Summary

OWNERSHIP PATTERN I: "COMMUNITY BANK," NO CONTROL GROUP

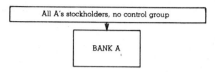

OWNERSHIP PATTERN II: BANKS CONTROLLED BY A GROUP OR COMPANY

1. Individuals who directly control one bank

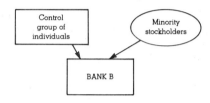

2. Chain Banking

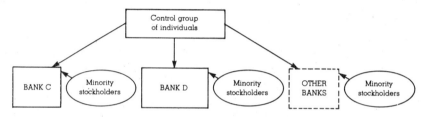

3. One-Bank Holding Company*†

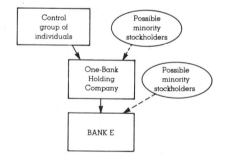

4. Multibank Holding Company†

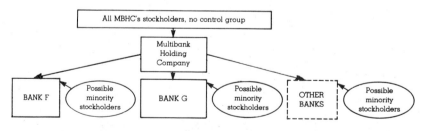

*This diagram summarizes an OBHC that itself is controlled by a group. This situation is prevalent amoung medium-sized and small banks. As explained in the text, many large money-center banks are controlled by an OBHC, the shares of which are widely held and not controlled by a group.

†As explained in the text, compared to cases II 1 and II 2 the likelihood and extent of minority stockholders is less in cases II 3 and II 4.

agency. (Also, with minor exceptions, insured banks must report their loans that are secured by 25 percent or more of the voting stock of an insured bank.) Thus when a person or group now acquires control of a bank, the bank's federal supervisory agency is alerted to the change. The agency then can try to evaluate the new control group's resources, skills, and intentions; and it can closely monitor how the new control group operates the bank. The agency can request detailed reports, send its examiners into the bank, and issue *cease-and-desist orders* to prohibit what it judges to be unsound banking practices. These powers enable a federal banking agency to dissuade retention of control by new stockholders who, in the agency's judgment, are not suitable thus to control a bank.

To finance the purchase of a control block of a bank's stock, a group (or individual) typically uses a *bank-stock loan* in which it pledges the controlling stock as collateral for a loan from a large correspondent bank. Compared to other business loans, terms of most bank-stock loans seem generous:

- The rate is usually set to float close to the lender's prime rate, and there are reported instances of loans below prime.
- Bank-stock loans usually are not subject to the FRS' Regulation U, and lenders often agree to lend an amount that is close to the book value of the collateral.
- Lenders generally do not press for rapid repayment of the principal.

Lending banks justify such terms based on the low risk of bank-stock loans.

Some observers note, however, that a lender may receive additional compensation in the form of "excess" compensating balances held by (or fees paid by) the bank that is controlled by the recipient(s) of the bank-stock loan. If it thus redirects some of its bank's resources to a lender in return for preferential loan terms, a controlling group benefits itself to the detriment of the bank's minority stockholders who do not share in the preferential loan terms. In 1970 the Department of Justice announced that it may prosecute controlling stockholders who borrow at preferential rates by having their bank maintain excessive nonearning correspondent balances at the lending bank. The federal bank supervisory agencies also have begun to scrutinize and criticize bank-stock loans that may involve preferential rates.

To test the possible conflicts of interest associated with bank-stock loans, one study analyzes 326 Texas banks in 1972, and it compares a sample of banks in which control is financed with bank-stock loans to a sample of banks without bank-stock loans. The study observes the potential for conflicts of interest because many of the loans were at rates of 3 percent or 4 percent (well below the market interest rate) and "there are cases where correspondent accounts were transferred to the lending bank just after a stock loan was made." Yet based on more complete analysis, the study concludes that possible abuses or conflicts of interest are not, on the average, "evident in observable measures of bank profit, public service or stockholder compensation."[22]

Diversion of credit life insurance commissions is another area of potential conflicting interests between a bank's control group and its minority stockholders. Many banks offer to sell *credit life insurance* to their installment loan borrowers so that, if a borrower were to die or become disabled, the insurance proceeds would repay the loan. In most banks the commission income becomes part of the bank's total revenues, but some banks divert at least some of this commission income to specific officials or major shareholders of the bank. Such diversion has long been an accepted practice among bankers who justify it as a way to provide additional compensation to key personnel, some of whom may happen to be controlling stockholders. In early 1976 about 28 percent of the national banks thus diverted at least some commission income from sales of credit life insurance.

One study uses a sample of 277 national banks in five southern states to examine some economic effects of diversion of credit life commissions by bankers. The study reports that "diversion of credit life commissions to bank officials leads to the selling of more credit life insurance than would be true if such diversion were not allowed," and that among banks where diversion occurs "there is substantial incentive for those officers to promote sales of credit life insurance in order to achieve compensation comparable to the salary they would make in a similar, but non-diverting bank."[23]

Concerned that diversion of credit life commissions may involve misapplications of bank funds, in 1976 the OCC adopted new regulations to stem such diversions among national banks. State banks are not yet subject to such regulations.

Potential conflicting interests between controlling and minority stockholders arise not only in banking but in any corporation in which the shares are split between a control group and minority stockholders. Yet banking is one of few businesses in which: a new firm has to be chartered as a corporation (or national association) with stockholders, and the chartering authorities encourage broad community distribution of the initial share offering. From this initial base, the shares of many banks subsequently become split between a control block and the remaining minority shares. In contrast, organizers of most nonbanking firms can choose to operate as a sole proprietorship, a partnership, or a corporation; and, if they decide to operate as a corporation, they can also decide to restrict the distribution of shares among the major organizers and thus not have to create minority stockholders.

22. Manferd O. Peterson and Hugh S. McLaughlin, "Conflict of Interest and the Financing of Commercial Bank Stock Ownership," *Journal of Bank Research,* Spring 1974, pp. 7-12. In a subsequent article, one of these authors examines the broader benefits, costs, and proposed regulatory changes associated with bank-stock loans. Manferd O. Peterson, "Bank Stock Loans and Correspondent Banking," *Issues in Bank Regulation,* Winter 1978, pp. 12-19.

23. Lewis Mandell and Lorman L. Lundsten, "Diversion of Credit Life Insurance Commissions by Bankers," *Journal of Bank Research,* Summer 1977, pp. 72-76.

## DEBENTURE MARKETS FOR MEDIUM-SIZED AND SMALL BANKS

Because it is too small to warrant the costs of an underwritten public offering, a medium-sized or small bank's debenture issue usually is directly placed with an institutional investor; or it is sold locally to residents of the bank's community. In either case there is virtually no secondary market for the debentures.

Even with direct placements, a medium-sized or small bank finds that its proposed issue often is too small to interest large institutional investors that buy debentures of large banking organizations. Therefore the bank has to place its issue with a smaller institutional investor or, more likely, with a large money-center bank that, as part of its correspondent services, buys debentures of smaller banks. For example, one study reports that it informally surveyed more than thirty small-bank debenture issues in 1975 and found that about half were directly placed with another bank and that in each case "the purchasing bank was a city correspondent of the small bank."[24]

*Interbank term lending* describes the practice by which large banks buy debentures of smaller banks or otherwise lend them funds for extended periods. Proponents of the practice cite how such interbank term loans enable large banking organizations, with their more extensive access to long-term funds, to channel capital to smaller banks. In contrast, others observe how the practice can result in double-counting of capital in the banking system. This potential for double-counting arises when a large bank raises capital and lends part of it to smaller banks that in turn count it as part of their capital.[25] Concern about such double-counting has contributed to the recent regulatory decisions to sharpen the distinction between subordinated debentures and other forms of capital and to monitor interbank term loans.

As an alternative to a direct placement, a medium-sized or small bank can try directly to sell debentures, usually in minimum denominations of $500, to its customers and community residents. An issuing bank may conclude that local potential purchasers, with their limited investment alternatives, will accept a lower interest rate on the debentures than would an institutional investor or correspondent bank. Yet there are also potential "costs" to a local offering of bank debentures. One "cost" is that purchasers may withdraw funds from lower-yielding time deposits at the bank and use these funds to buy the higher-yielding debentures. A second "cost" relates to possible misunderstanding and potential ill will among some buyers of the debentures. Federal banking regulations require an offering bank to give to a potential purchaser an *offering circular* that describes the principal terms and conditions of the debenture issue. The

---

24. Donald G. Simonson and Edmond E. Pace, "Getting Capital: What Community Banks Can Do," *The Bankers Magazine*, Winter 1976, pp. 89-96.

25. Instead of lending term funds directly to a smaller bank, a large bank can lend funds to a control group and/or to a bank holding company that in turn purchases shares and/or debentures of a smaller bank. In these cases the supervisory agencies also express concern about potential "double-counting" of capital and about the debt-servicing capacity of the borrower(s).

offering circular advises the potential purchaser that the debentures: are subordinated to the claims of the bank's general creditors, cannot be used as collateral for a loan from the issuing bank, cannot be redeemed prior to maturity, and are unlikely to have a continuous secondary market. Even though alerted to these terms, some buyers may still view their debentures as analogous to the time deposits that they customarily own, and so feel misled if and when they subsequently try to redeem the debentures prior to their maturity.

In view of the impediments to their marketing of debentures, and perhaps because of tax factors and risk aversion of their major stockholders, most medium-sized and small banks do not issue debentures. In the aggregate, among banks with total assets of $10-500 million, debentures account for less than 0.5 percent of their total liabilities and equity capital. For smaller banks the ratio is miniscule.[26]

## BANK CAPITAL PLANNING

Whether a bank's procedures are informal or highly structured, at times each bank's senior officials have to reexamine the interrelated components of the capital planning process, as summarized in Exhibit 15-5.

## CAPITAL STRUCTURE POLICY

As a first step, a bank's senior officers have to establish and periodically reexamine policies concerning:

- What should be the bank's norms concerning its capital ratios?
- Of a bank's "total capital," what proportion should be equity and what proportion should be near-capital, such as subordinated debentures?
- By how much should the bank's actual ratios be permitted temporarily to depart from the preceding target ratios?

### Target Capital Ratios

As a minimum a bank will want to maintain its capital ratios at levels that avoid repeated supervisory criticism. If it chooses to operate with low ratios, a bank can anticipate occasional examiner criticism indicating that the bank's ratios fall below the supervisor's acceptable bounds. To avoid repeated criticism and more stringent suasion or sanctions by its supervisory agency, the bank then will act to increase its capital ratios to levels acceptable to the agency.

---

26. For a detailed trend analysis of debenture issues by banks of various size categories, see Douglas V. Austin, "Senior Debt and Equity Securities," *The Bankers Magazine,* Winter 1974, pp. 73-84.

**EXHIBIT 15-5**

**Bank Capital Planning:
A Schematic Model**

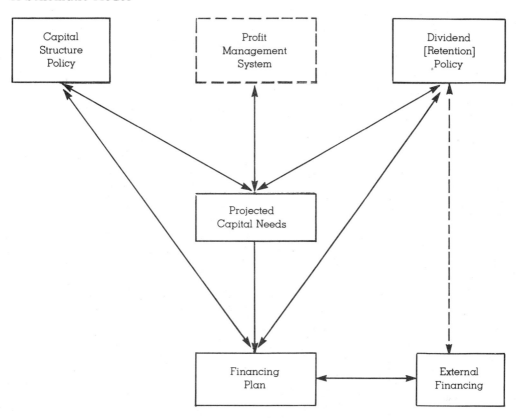

Not only its supervisors, but also its creditors, borrowers, and stockholders monitor a bank's capital ratios. Knowing this, a bank may have a policy whereby its capital ratios remain below the average for similar banks but never so low that its ratios are outliers that rank it, for example, among the lowest 10 percent or 25 percent of similar banks. That some banks have such a policy is suggested by the frequency distributions of bank capital ratios between 1960 and 1975. One study shows that "the proportion of banks with low capital ratios has increased while the fraction with high ratios has fallen" and thus "the distribution of ratios has become more bunched at the low end."[27]

As an explicit policy, a bank may decide to maintain capital ratios that exceed those of similar banks. This policy can be part of a broader management policy to maintain—and possibly project an image of—a

27. Robert A. Taggart, Jr., "Regulatory Influences on Bank Capital," *New England Economic Review* (Federal Reserve Bank of Boston), September-October 1977, pp. 37-46.

conservative bank. Alternatively, this policy of maintaining an extra margin of capital can help a bank support greater risks in its portfolio and in its costly development of facilities and systems in areas such as electronic funds transfer systems. As summarized by one banking official, "if we err in the area of capital adequacy, it would seem that we should take our chances on being overcapitalized rather than allow ourselves to be exposed to the risks inherent in being undercapitalized."[28]

### Target Proportions of Equity and Debentures

While they unequivocably view a bank's various capital stock accounts as capital, bank supervisory agencies continue to have an ambivalent view about subordinated debentures as capital. Therefore, for planning purposes, a bank's senior officials have to keep abreast of evolving supervisory interpretations of the role of subordinated debentures in banking. Among banks that it supervises, the FRS sets a maximum debenture-to-equity ratio of 50 percent. Reportedly the OCC has a similar guideline for national banks. Thus within these constraints a bank's total capital, defined as equity plus subordinated debentures, can range from all equity to about 67 percent equity and 33 percent debentures.

A bank may decide to maintain an all-equity capital structure, especially if it is skeptical about the net benefits from using leverage and/or if in practice the supervisory agencies exclude debentures from many of their capital-adequacy computations.

Most large banks, and many smaller ones, have issued subordinated debentures either directly or indirectly through a parent holding company. Presumably each of these banks analyzed its alternatives and concluded that a debenture issue provided specific benefits (such as low cost of funds, retention of control, improved capital ratios, and/or potentially higher returns to stockholders) that exceeded the "costs" of increased volatility of stockholder returns and reduced future financial flexibility.

One study uses a sample of about 175 banks, with deposits ranging from $300 million to $1 billion, to "examine the effect of leverage on the rate of return on equity." It reports that "there is no evidence that banks with higher leverage have higher returns on equity" and, secondly, that "banks with higher leverage tend to earn lower returns on assets." Thus the authors conclude that, in their opinion, "a deliberate policy to achieve high financial leverage is misguided; its effect is to subject the stockholders to higher risk without compensation."[29] Subsequently, another set of authors reexamined and extended this analysis of bank leverage. These authors analyzed a sample of 104 large banks and concluded that, while not all banks have favorable financial leverage, most banks do, and so "bank leverage *can* pay." Thus, "in an era when equity capital is becoming either

---

28. Gallant, "Approaches to Capital Planning," p. 174.

29. T. Carter Hagaman and Philip K. Chamberlain, "Bank Leverage Doesn't Pay," *The Bankers Magazine*, Spring 1975, pp. 25-30.

desparately scarce or exceedingly expensive, it makes sense to consider in a prudent manner levering residual returns to common stock investors."[30]

In conclusion, each bank needs to analyze the extent to which it will use debentures as part of its total capital. To retain some financial flexibility, however, it should set a policy whereby its proportion of debentures to equity remains below the maximum permitted by its supervisory agency.

### Permitted Variance from Targets

Over time a bank's actual ratios will depart from the target ratios. For example, if its rate of capital growth is below its rate of asset growth, then a bank's ratio of capital to total assets will decline over time. Issuance costs, especially for external capital, make it uneconomic to raise new capital whenever a key ratio departs from its target. Therefore a bank is likely to have guidelines that permit the capital ratio to fall below the target until it becomes economic to raise a block of capital that will then bring the ratio back to the target or, more likely, above the target. While it thus permits some variance between actual ratios and target ratios, an effective capital planning system uses periodic projections of capital needs as a tool to predict pending ratio changes and to identify financing plans that will prevent unexpected variances between actual and targeted ratios.

## DIVIDEND [RETENTION] POLICY

A bank's dividend policy basically determines how, over time, it divides its annual earnings between dividends paid to its stockholders and earnings retained to increase the bank's equity capital. Thus a bank's dividend policy and its retention policy are inexorably intertwined.

As with most nonbanking firms, a bank's directors and senior officers generally use a payout ratio to guide their interim dividend decisions. A *payout ratio* is the amount of a firm's dividends paid to common stockholders divided by the earnings available to common stockholders, or, on a per-share basis, dividends per share divided by earnings per share.

A bank generally develops a target payout ratio that it plans to use over time. When they set and occasionally reexamine this target ratio, a bank's officials evaluate the following items.

### Shareholder Expectations

If a bank is closely held, what magnitude of dividends do the principal stockholders expect from their investment? In some banks, because of their alternative cash flows and their tax status, the principal stockholders prefer the bank to retain most of its earnings and distribute only a small part as

---

30. John D. Martin, Arthur J. Keown, and David F. Scott, Jr., "Bank Leverage Really Does Pay," *The Bankers Magazine,* Spring 1977, pp. 70-76.

dividends. In other banks, the principal stockholders may need and want the bank to have a high dividend-payout ratio.

If it is large and has its shares traded in national markets, a bank should consider some evidence that, other things equal, investors will pay a higher price relative to expected earnings for shares of banks that have higher payout ratios.[31]

## Payout Ratios of Similar Banks

As a comparative standard, a bank will want to consider the payout ratios of similar banks. Thus, for banks of various size categories the average dividend payout ratio is as follows:[32]

| Asset Size ($ million) | Dividend Payout Ratio(%) |
|---|---|
| under 25 | 25 |
| 25-100 | 28 |
| 100-300 | 34 |
| 300 or more | 41 |

A bank can compare its target or actual payout ratio to these standards or to the ratios of other banks that it considers more similar to it.

## Projected Capital Needs

If it expects its assets to grow rapidly and/or if because of increased risks it wants to increase its capital ratios, a bank will specify a lower payout ratio than will another bank that projects less growth in its capital needs.

## Alternative Sources of Capital

If, either directly or through a parent holding company, it has convenient access to external capital, then a bank will generally have a higher payout ratio than will a bank that has fewer viable options for raising additional capital. Large banks generally have more financing alternatives than do small banks, and so when dividend payout ratios are categorized by bank size, one observes that the average ratio increases as bank size increases.

## Administering Payout Ratios

Once it selects a target payout ratio, a bank uses this as a guide for its actual dividend decisions. If a bank were to adhere strictly to a constant payout

---

31. Richard H. Pettway, "Market Tests of Capital Adequacy of Large Commercial Banks," *The Journal of Finance,* June 1976, pp. 865-875. Also, two senior officials of a large bank state why they believe that "the trend among banking institutions to lower dividend payouts is counter-productive. Dividend policy should reinforce investment interest in a stock by appealing to the broadest possible market." T. Carter Hagaman and Herbert J. Marks, "Earnings Stability: Key to the Equity Market," *Journal of Bank Research,* Autumn 1975, pp. 183-186.

32. Table D (Nation), *Bank Operating Statistics,* 1977.

ratio, then whenever earnings fell, it would have to reduce its dividend. Banks, like most corporations, are reluctant to cut dividends. Therefore, in practice, if a bank's earnings increase, the board of directors is likely to increase the dividend toward that implied by the target payout ratio only if it is confident that the bank's earnings will stay near or above the new, higher level. Then, if earnings fall, the board will try to avoid cutting the dividend even if this means that the bank's actual dividend payout ratio temporarily exceeds the target ratio. In practice, a bank's actual dividend payout ratio can exceed 100 percent if the bank's current dividends exceed its current earnings and the bank makes up the difference by charging its retained earnings account.

A bank's *retention ratio* is the proportion of interim earnings that the bank retains in the firm—and thus does not pay out as dividends. More formally, the retention ratio is one minus the dividend payout ratio.

## PROJECTED CAPITAL NEEDS

A bank can develop a comprehensive projection of its capital needs based on various assumptions and forecasts about its supervisory environment, total portfolio structure, earnings, cash flows, and risk aversion. As a first approximation, however, a bank can use a simplified model to project its capital needs and then use more comprehensive analyses to refine these initial projections.

### A Simplified Model to Project Bank Capital Needs

If it focuses on three interrelated decision variables, a bank can initially project its capital needs under alternative sets of assumptions.

**Model Specification** The model's three basic variables, expressed as ratios, are:

- A/C, which is Total Assets divided by Total Capital
  This *leverage ratio* is the reciprocal of a basic capital ratio: total
- capital divided by total assets. It indicates how many dollars of total assets a bank is financing with each dollar of its capital.[33]
- NI/A, which is Net After-tax Income divided by Total Assets
  This is a basic *return-on-assets ratio.*
- RE/NI, which is the amount of Retained Earnings for a period divided by Net Income.
  This is the *retention ratio,* which as previously shown is one minus the payout ratio.

---

33. This simplified model focuses on total assets and total capital. One can decompose total capital into (1) debentures and (2) equity. If, however, it decides to maintain a constant ratio of debentures to equity, then as implied in this simplified model, a bank's leverage ratio (A/C) is a determinant of both its equity growth and its total capital growth over time.

These three ratios thus involve:

two balance-sheet items—

A, total assets
C, total capital

and two flow items related to the income statement—

NI, net after-tax income
RE, retained earnings

For simplicity, the balance-sheet items are as of the end of the preceding year and the flow items are for a one-year period.

The simplified capital-projection model incorporates the three basic variables as follows:

$$A/C \times NI/A \times RE/NI = RE/C = g,$$

Where RE/C (the Retained Earnings for the period divided by the Capital at the beginning of the period) is the maximum internally financed growth rate of capital which, for brevity, is also denoted as $g$.

If one specifies a value for A/C (the leverage ratio), NI/A (the return-on-assets ratio), and RE/NI (the retention ratio), then one can compute $g$ (the maximum internally financed growth rate of capital).

**Examining the Model's Implications** The model implies that, other things being equal, a bank's $g$ will increase if the bank's: (1) leverage ratio (A/C) increases, (2) return-on-assets ratio (NI/A) increases, (3) retention ratio (RE/NI) increases, or (4) the total increase in one or more of these ratios exceeds total declines in the remaining ratios. Thus if it wants to increase its bank's $g$, management has to evaluate whether and how it can change the three basic variables that, in this simplified model, determine $g$.

Exhibit 15-6 uses the model to quantify a bank's $g$ under some alternative assumptions. Assumption 1 sets A/C (the leverage ratio) at 10.0, which is the reciprocal of a capital-to-assets ratio of 0.10 (or 10%). Under this assumption, $g$ increases as the return on assets (NI/A) increases and/or as the retention ratio (RE/NI) increases. Assumption 2 sets the leverage ratio at 12.5, a higher level than that set under assumption 1. With A/C set at 12.5, $g$ increases as NI/A increases and/or as RE/NI increases; but in all cases, for the same NI/A and RE/NI, $g$ under assumption 2 is greater than that under assumption 1.

**Controlling the Decision Variables** How can a bank's management use the simplified model and the illustrative relationships of Exhibit 15-6 to help plan its capital needs?

First, a bank can examine its implied $g$ based on the bank's recent ratios for A/C, NI/A, and RE/NI. For example, if its A/C is 10.0, its NI/A is 1.0, and its RE/NI is 0.6, then, from Exhibit 15-6, its implied maximum

## EXHIBIT 15-6

## Projecting a Bank's Internally Financed Rate of Capital Growth

Assumption 1: Bank maintains a capital-to-assets ratio of .10 (or 10%). This implies a leverage ratio (A/C) of 10.0.

| Rate-of-return-on-assets Ratio (NI/A) | Retention Ratio (RE/NI) | | | | |
|---|---|---|---|---|---|
| | 0.2 | 0.4 | 0.6 | 0.8 | 1.0 |
| 0.6 | 1.2 | 2.4 | 3.6 | 4.8 | 6.0 |
| 0.8 | 1.6 | 3.2 | 4.8 | 6.4 | 8.0 |
| 1.0 | 2.0 | 4.0 | 6.0 | 8.0 | 10.0 |
| 1.2 | 2.4 | 4.8 | 7.2 | 9.6 | 12.0 |
| 1.4 | 2.8 | 5.6 | 8.4 | 11.2 | 14.0 |

Assumption 2: Bank maintains a capital-to-assets ratio of .08 (or 8%). This implies a leverage ratio (A/C) of 12.5.

| Rate-of-return-on-assets Ratio (NI/A) | Retention Ratio (RE/NI) | | | | |
|---|---|---|---|---|---|
| | 0.2 | 0.4 | 0.6 | 0.8 | 1.0 |
| 0.6 | 1.5 | 3.0 | 4.5 | 6.0 | 7.5 |
| 0.8 | 2.0 | 4.0 | 6.0 | 8.0 | 10.0 |
| 1.0 | 2.5 | 5.0 | 7.5 | 10.0 | 12.5 |
| 1.2 | 3.0 | 6.0 | 9.0 | 12.0 | 15.0 |
| 1.4 | 3.5 | 7.0 | 10.5 | 14.0 | 17.5 |

As discussed in the text, this exhibit illustrates financial relationships based on the following equation:

$$g = A/C \times NI/A \times RE/NI,$$

where:

$g$ is the maximum internally financed rate of capital growth

A/C is Total Assets divided by Total Capital

NI/A is Net After-tax Income divided by Total Assets

RE/NI is Retained Earnings for a period divided by Net Income

To illustrate, under Assumption 1, the leverage ratio (A/C) is 10.0. Then if NI/A is 0.6 and RE/NI is 0.2, the total equation is $10.0 \times 0.6 \times 0.2 = 1.2$, which is $g$, the maximum internally financed rate of capital growth, as reported in the table.

---

internally financed growth rate of capital ($g$) is 6% per year. Its capital and its total assets will not grow more rapidly than 6% annually as long as these ratios hold and the bank does not use external financing.

Second, a bank can set a target rate of growth ($g$) and then examine what its ratios would have to be to achieve such growth. To extend the preceding example, assume that the bank would like to have its capital and assets grow at 8% per year. If it chooses to keep its leverage ratio at 10.0, then this bank can increase its growth rate to 8% *if* it increases its retention ratio to 0.8, or its return-on-assets ratio to 1.33, or achieves some combinations of net increases in these two ratios.[34] At this point, the bank has to evaluate the feasibility of increasing its retention rate (and thus reducing its dividend payout ratio) and/or increasing its return on assets. Moreover, if it chooses to do so and anticipates that supervisory agencies will permit it to do so, the bank can increase its internally financed growth to 7.5% by—other things being equal—increasing its leverage ratio to 12.5 (see Exhibit 15-6).

Third, a bank can extend the simplified model to project the extent to which it would have to raise external capital to sustain a target growth rate. To continue the preceding example, assume that the bank wants to grow at an annual compound rate of 8% but concludes that it cannot change its basic ratios. Further assume that its current capital is $50 million and its planning period is 5 years. At the projected maximum internally financed growth rate of 6%, the $50 million will grow to about $66.9 million in 5 years [$50 million $(1 \times .06)^5 =$ $50 million $(1.338)$]. If it wants its capital and assets to grow at an annual compound rate of 8%, then at the end of 5 years the bank will need about $73.5 million in total capital [$50 million $(1 \times .08)^5 =$ $50 million $(1.469)$]. Thus, under these conditions the bank will have to use external sources to meet the implied capital shortfall that builds to $6.6 million [$73.5 million minus $66.9 million] over the 5-year period.

Banks use this type of capital planning model to help project their capital needs. An official of a large banking organization reports that his firm, having "reached a more highly leveraged position in the industry," has initiated a strategy to increase its return on assets to a rate that will allow retained earnings "to grow fast enough to provide flexibility in support of asset growth. Generally this means that retained earnings should increase at least at the same rate at which assets increase. Thus the internal rate of growth becomes self-supporting of the balance sheet, not an easy order, but certainly a worthy planning objective."[35]

Bank supervisors also use this type of capital planning model to help project the capital needs of the banking industry and/or categories of banks. To illustrate, a senior official of the OCC notes that, in 1974, for the 58 largest national banks the average: leverage ratio is 16.0, return-on-assets ratio is 0.53, and dividend [retention] ratio is 0.5. "If we assume that levels of capital adequacy in these banks are bottoming out, then in order to maintain the same capital to asset ratio these banks could only expand 4.3% on an annual basis. Any growth beyond this figure without an increased return on assets would result in further capital deterioration apart from an equity capital injection by the shareholders or the sale of debt securities."

---

34. The necessary rate-of-return-on-assets ratio of 1.33 can be interpolated from Exhibit 15-6 or it can be directly computed from the general equation: $10.0 \times NI/A \times 0.6 = 8.0$, which when solved for $NI/A = 1.33$.

35. William C. Langley, Jr., "Strategies in Today's Capital Environment," *Journal of Bank Research,* Autumn 1975, pp. 177-179.

The official then extends his analysis to develop a 5-year projection of these banks' capital needs.[36]

As summarized in the capital planning model of Exhibit 15-5, to project its capital needs a bank has to specify its capital structure policy and its dividend [retention] policy. Yet there is also a "feedback" process in which a bank uses its initial projections of capital needs to reexamine, and possibly revise, its initial policy inputs and its profit-management system. By going through this iterative process of projecting its capital needs, a bank also positions itself to evaluate alternative financing plans.

## EVALUATING ALTERNATIVE FINANCING PLANS

To develop a specific financing plan, a bank's officials project the bank's capital needs for a coming period (for example, for five years) and then evaluate how and when the capital needs should be met, for example by retained earnings and/or by a series of offerings of additional capital securities. In principle, a bank has many possible financing plans available to it. In practice, a bank's feasible set of financing plans depends on factors such as its supervisory environment, capital structure policy, dividend [retention] policy, and markets for its capital instruments.

### Reliance on Common Stock

If its policy is to rely on common stock for capital and to maintain a specific capital-to-assets ratio, then an expanding bank has to build its equity via retained earnings and/or occasional sales of additional stock.

If it concludes that most of its stockholders will accept a low payout ratio, then a bank can conveniently build its capital base via retained earnings. Alternatively, if it concludes that its payout ratio has to approximate or exceed that of similar banks, then the bank and its stockholders have to accept a lower rate of internally financed growth or the bank occasionally has to sell additional equity.

When it sells additional equity, a bank is likely to use a *preemptive rights procedure,* in which its current stockholders have the right to subscribe, on a pro rata basis, to the firm's new offering of common stock. Common law doctrine has viewed preemptive rights as a way by which a stockholder can maintain his or her proportionate ownership interest in a firm, and this doctrine has been codified in various statutes. For example, shareholders of a national bank were presumed to have preemptive rights until 1962, when the OCC ruled that shareholders of a national bank could adopt or amend their association's articles "in order to modify or eliminate preemptive rights." A state bank is subject to its state statutes, some of which require preemption while others presume preemption unless otherwise authorized by a bank's stockholders. Because the statutes vary among

---

36. Justin T. Watson, "A Regulatory View of Capital Adequacy," *Journal of Bank Research,* Autumn 1975, pp. 170-172. (The derivation is as follows: $16.0 \times 0.53 \times 0.5 = 4.24 \cong 4.3$)

states and can change over time, a state bank has to determine whether or not it can sell additional shares other than by a preemptive rights offering.

Since 1962, national banks and some state banks have gained flexibility to choose between preemptive offerings and public offerings. Yet a survey of over 100 stock offerings by banks between 1966 and 1969 reports that only 3 percent of these offerings were sold other than by preemptive rights. The author concludes that "use of preemption—as one possible financing procedure—is not rejected. What must be rejected are traditional provisions requiring preemption, and unexamined decisions to use preemption, without analysis of alternative financing procedures that may better serve the interests of a bank and its shareholders."[37]

One policy is for a bank to maintain a high dividend payout ratio and then frequently offer its stockholders the right to subscribe to additional shares. This policy is generally suboptimal for the bank's stockholders, who receive cash dividends—on which they pay income taxes—and then use after-tax dollars to purchase the additional shares. In contrast to this indirect reinvestment procedure, the bank's stockholders, especially those in high tax brackets, will prefer a policy whereby the bank maintains a low payout ratio and then relies on retained earnings, instead of frequent stock sales, to increase its equity capital over time.

### Expanding the Set of Possible Financing Plans

If it does not limit itself to common stock financing, a bank can evaluate the benefits and costs of various procedures to raise additional capital.

A large banking organization, partly because of broad market recognition of its securities, can examine financing options that include preemptive offerings, and public offerings or private placements of common stock, preferred stock, and debentures. To identify and evaluate its set of options, a large bank's capital planning staff examines what other banks have done and also draws on the expertise of investment bankers and financial consultants. One innovation is the use of convertible debentures, convertible preferred stock, and debt offerings that use such "sweeteners" as *warrants,* which enable their holder to purchase the issuer's stock at a specified price within a specified period. Another innovation has been the use of *sale-and-leaseback agreements* by which a banking organization sells some of its buildings or expensive equipment to an institutional investor and then leases the building or equipment for a specific minimum period on the basis of an agreed schedule of lease payments.[38] These innovations are illustrative of options that a capital planning staff needs to evaluate for possible inclusion in a total

37. Paul F. Jessup, "Why Preemptive Rights in Banking?" *The Bankers Magazine,* Summer 1970, pp. 85-90. This article also summarizes how a bank holding company has flexibility to avoid statutory preemptive requirements by choosing to be chartered by a state that does not require preemption, and it demonstrates why bankers apparently "see elimination of preemptive rights as among the benefits of establishing a one-bank holding company."

38. Robert L. Nessen, "Bank Premises: When To Own, When To Lease," *Banking,* June 1977, pp. 49-51 ff.

financing plan. If, as is likely, the supervisory agencies constrain bank use of subordinated debentures, then one can anticipate an upsurge of public equity offerings—both of common and preferred stocks—by large banking organizations that conclude that they cannot rely exclusively on retained earnings to support their growth goals.

In contrast to most large banks, a medium-sized or small bank has a narrower set of financing alternatives. In the usual case, a group of individuals control a smaller bank, and these people are reluctant to use financing techniques that will dilute their control. While they are not the only factors, control considerations help explain why smaller banks rely on retained earnings, occasional preemptive rights offerings of common stock, and occasional private placements or local offerings of subordinated debentures that carry no voting rights. Although not widely done, sale-and-leaseback arrangements open another financing possibility for smaller banks. When raising additional capital, a smaller bank may conclude that it is at a disadvantage compared to large banking organizations and so include this consideration when and if it is invited to become part of a large branch system or multibank holding company.

The general case involves a bank that needs to increase its capital over time in order to support its actual and anticipated asset growth. In some cases, however, a bank's senior officials conclude that the bank is overcapitalized relative to its foreseeable needs. Such a capital surplus can arise, for example, because a bank projects a decline in its assets or because a new management team concludes that prior management has built too large a capital cushion. In these cases, a bank can try to reduce its capital—in absolute terms—by repurchasing some of its shares or, in the case of an affiliate bank, by paying dividends in excess of earnings to the parent holding company. While these steps are possible, bank supervisory agencies are reluctant to approve such contraction of a bank's capital. Therefore, if it proposes to reduce its capital, a bank needs to present a persuasive supporting case to its supervisory agency.

## SUMMARY

A bank's senior officials intermittently have to decide whether and how their bank should increase its capital. Thus these bankers specifically address a set of interrelated questions, the answers to which depend partly on whether one is a bank stockholder, creditor, borrower, supervisor, or manager.

What are the functions of bank capital? One function is to provide a buffer to help a bank continue as a going concern despite temporary setbacks that occur in its portfolio, operating systems, and/or economic environment. Along with its liquidity, current earnings, and reserves, a bank's capital is one buffer to absorb such temporary setbacks. A second function is to help protect a bank's creditors and the FDIC *if* a bank fails. To the extent that it is seen thus to provide an effective buffer against adversity, bank capital helps sustain confidence in a specific bank and the banking system. How well bank capital fulfills its functions in turn relates to its form and amount.

What are the principal forms of bank capital and how do they differ in fulfilling the bank-capital functions? The principal form of bank capital is equity, which itself consists of a bank's common stock, preferred stock (if any), surplus, undivided profits, and possible capital reserves. To the extent that it does not impair its capital, a bank can charge-off losses against its equity accounts. A bank's loss reserves help fulfill the buffer and confidence functions, and so most analysts include a bank's loss reserves as part of its capital.

In contrast, there is not substantial agreement as to whether, and to what extent, subordinated debentures fulfill the functions of bank capital. Although they help protect general creditors and the FDIC *if* a bank fails, when compared to equity capital, subordinated debentures provide less flexibility to absorb losses, and they require periodic servicing of their interest and principal. Concerned with these hybrid characteristics, the bank supervisory agencies never fully equated subordinated debentures with equity capital. Now the agencies require a bank to report its subordinated debentures, if any, as a special balance-sheet category that is distinct from, yet close to, its capital accounts. Thus, subject to various supervisory guidelines, a bank can continue to evaluate the benefits and costs of debentures as one possible form of long-term nondeposit funds.

How much capital does a bank need? To develop a detailed answer to this question, one has to estimate: the probable risks that a bank faces, its probable ability to manage such risks, and the willingness of its stockholders and other concerned parties to accept risks by their bank(s). While they thus evaluate such complex risks, a bank and its concerned parties can use ratio analysis to develop initial estimates of a bank's capital needs. Ratio analysts focus on how a bank's various capital ratios compare to those of "similar" banks and how they have changed and are likely to change over time. Thus, as one analytical tool, ratio analysis can provide tentative answers to questions about how much capital a specific bank—and the banking system—currently needs and is likely to need within a planning period.

Bank managers, stockholders, and supervisors all concern themselves with the market(s) in which a bank's capital securities trade and in which a bank occasionally sells additional stock and/or subordinated debentures.

The shares of most large money-center banks (or of their parent holding companies) are bought and sold in national securities markets such as the NASDAQ system and the NYSE. Transactions in these shares, none of which constitute a controlling block, potentially receive widespread investor attention. In contrast, the large banking organizations use either public offerings or direct placements to sell debentures, for which the secondary market generally is less active than is that for the bank's shares.

Shares of most medium-sized and small banks trade inactively in local markets, and, even then, there are differences in the markets for the control shares and minority shares of these smaller banks. Bank-stock loans provide the principal vehicle to finance the purchase of control of a bank. In recent years the bank supervisory agencies have adopted new policies to monitor when control of a bank changes, the financing of such control changes, and possible inappropriate diversion of bank resources by its controlling stockholders. Because of the limited marketability of their shares, most smaller banks build their capital over time via retained earnings, occasional preemptive stock offerings, and possible long-term borrowings from correspondent banks or local residents who buy the bank's subordinated debentures. Advocates of multioffice banking assert that smaller banks can improve their access to capital by becoming part of a large multioffice banking organization.

To avert supervisory criticism and to maintain flexibility, a bank engages in capital planning, a process that involves interrelated components.

Senior officials establish, and at times reexamine, policies concerning their bank's capital structure. To illustrate, they specify the bank's norms concerning its capital ratios, the proportion of "total capital" that will be equity and the proportion that will be near-capital such as subordinated debentures, and the temporary variances that will be permitted from these target ratios.

Dividend [retention] policy is a second major component of the capital planning process. The senior officials generally administer this policy by specifying a target payout [retention] ratio that is subject to review and occasional exceptions. They set the target ratio based on their evaluation of shareholder expectations, payout ratios of similar banks, projected capital needs, and alternative sources of capital.

To project its capital needs for future planning periods, a bank can use a simplified model to develop initial projections under alternative assumptions. On this basis, a bank will want to focus on how its capacity for internally financed growth depends on its leverage ratio, return-on-assets ratio, and retention ratio. Then the bank can use more complex models and analyses to refine its initial assumptions and projections.

As another integral part of its capital-planning process, a bank has to evaluate the benefits and costs of alternative financing plans that use various mixes of internal and external financing. Many banks no longer have to use preemptive rights offerings when selling additional common stock, and so they can evaluate alternative ways to increase their equity capital. Moreover, they can explore the net benefits to them of using such recent innovations as convertible debentures and sale-and-leaseback agreements. At least for large banking organizations, the range of possible financing plans is limited only by the creativity of their capital-planning staffs and advisors, and by the probable response of their supervisory agencies that retain extensive veto power over a bank's plans for its long-term financing.

As demonstrated in the Appendix to this chapter, as an extension of their long-range capital planning, a bank's senior officials need to keep informed about recent and pending developments in the area of bank supervision and public policy.

# APPENDIX
## BANK CAPITAL, BANK RISKS, AND PUBLIC POLICY

As part of their capital-planning process, bankers need to stay abreast of public-policy discussions concerning bank supervision and the safety of the banking system. These discussions may lead to revised supervisory rules by which banks will have to operate.

## SUPERVISORY OBJECTIVES AND PROCEDURES

By statute, bank supervisory agencies pursue dual objectives: to maintain a sound banking system, and to foster a competitive banking system that serves the public interest. Each objective focuses on the banking system, and the two objectives can conflict. To illustrate, if the bank supervisory agencies foster intensive competition within the banking system, then at least some banks that adopt innovative strategies will miscalculate the risks and so encounter severe financial problems that can lead to failure. Conversely, if they focus on maintaining a sound banking system that involves few, if any, bank failures, the supervisory agencies can stifle competition and innovation that serve the public interest. Even if they cannot perfectly reconcile these two potentially conflicting goals, bank supervisory agencies, and bankers, need to evaluate public policy alternatives that work toward simultaneous achievement of the two goals.

### SOCIAL COSTS OF BANK FAILURES

A bank *fails* when its chartering agency determines that the bank's equity accounts have become, or are about to become, zero or negative. Once it makes this determination, the chartering agency usually works closely with the FDIC and exercises one of three principal options:[1]

- close the bank permanently
- close the bank but arrange to have its deposit liabilities and assets assumed by another bank

---

1. Chayim Herzig-Marx, "Bank Failures," *Economic Perspectives* (Federal Reserve Bank of Chicago), March-April 1978, pp. 22-31. R. Alton Gilbert, "Bank Failures and Public Policy," *Review* (Federal Reserve Bank of St. Louis), November 1975, pp. 7-15.

- without officially declaring it to have failed, arrange to have the bank acquired by another bank.

If the supervisory agencies close a bank permanently, the FDIC promptly pays off the insured depositors. Yet because permanent closure removes a local bank and thus may inconvenience community residents, the supervisory agencies generally exercise the second or third option, in which another bank assumes a failing bank's deposit liabilities and assets. To expedite these *deposit-assumption* options that involve a successor bank, the FDIC usually agrees to assume the doubtful assets of the failing bank.

Although FDIC insurance protects depositors and deposit-assumption procedures provide continuity of local bank facilities, there are additional costs of bank failures. Stockholders and holders of subordinated claims (such as debentures) are likely to lose much of their investment in a failed bank. In principle these investors knowingly accept this risk when making such uninsured investments; in practice some of these investors—especially local residents who buy a bank's subordinated debentures—probably are unaware of and unprepared for the risk of loss. Even in deposit-assumption procedures, a failed bank's borrowers incur disruption "costs" involving their credit lines and long-term banking relationships.

Bank supervisory agencies express concern that a publicized bank failure may undermine public confidence in other banks and in the banking system. Although it is difficult to quantify this public-confidence "cost," one concern is that a major failure could so deplete the FDIC insurance fund that public confidence would be further undermined, and other banks, and indirectly their customers, would face higher future assessments in order to rebuild the FDIC insurance fund.

Because they are accountable to elected legislatures and because publicized bank failures are more tangible than are the outcomes of a competitive, innovative, banking system, bank supervisory agencies are likely to emphasize their goal of a sound banking system that involves few bank failures.

## LESSONS FROM PAST BANK FAILURES

A study reviews bank failures from 1890 through 1973 to develop a set of lessons that are applicable to the present and probable future:[2]

- Widespread bank failures (as in the 1930s) result from the central bank's permitting or causing precipitous declines in the money supply.
- FDIC insurance is likely to forestall runs on banks and banking panics.
- Adverse local conditions may still contribute to failures of localized banks that cannot, or choose not to, diversify their portfolios.

---

2. George J. Benston, "How We Can Learn from Past Bank Failures," *The Bankers Magazine,* Winter 1975, pp. 19-24. Also George J. Benston, "Bank Examination," *The Bulletin* (New York University), May 1973.

● Inadequate diversification continues to cause bank failures.
● Fraud continues to be a major cause of bank failures.
● Poor management causes some bank failures.

The first two lessons highlight the role of public policy to forestall economic conditions that trigger and/or spread bank failures. The second two lessons stress the need for public policies that permit—even require—adequate diversification within bank portfolios. The last two lessons indicate the need for supervisory agencies to refine their procedures in order to prevent and/or promptly detect fraud and mismanagement.

## PREVENTING BANK FAILURES

The supervisory agencies have a large and expanding array of powers and procedures by which they can try to prevent bank failures.

### Laws and Regulations to Constrain Bank Risks

Bank supervisory agencies develop and support legislation designed to help prevent bank failures. If enacted, then the supervisory agencies use their supervisory powers to administer the legislation. Illustrative of this process are laws and regulations that:

● prohibit or limit the interest rates that banks can pay on deposits
● limit, in most cases, a bank's maximum loan to one borrower to 10 percent of the bank's capital stock and surplus
● prohibit risky loans and investments involving, for example, speculative real estate and common stocks
● limit a bank's bond investments to those with top ratings or to nonrated bonds with similar high-quality attributes

### Examination Practices

The supervisory agencies use bank examinations to monitor developments and to detect potential problems within a bank and the banking system. As part of a bank examination, the supervisory authorities attempt to calculate the adequacy of a bank's capital. For a while the Federal Reserve System experimented with a *Form for Analyzing Bank Capital* (or ABC Form), in which its examiners tried to quantify the risks associated with various components of a bank's total portfolio. Even then the form explicitly warned that "the complexity of the [capital adequacy] problem requires a considerable exercise of judgment." The FRS ended its use of this form in the mid 1970s, and now the various supervisory agencies compute a bank's capital adequacy based on comparative ratios and ad hoc supervisory judgments about such factors as a bank's portfolio, earnings history and prospects, and management.[3] The federal supervisory agencies rate a bank based on a *Uniform Interagency Rating System,* by which an examination team evaluates a bank's capital adequacy, asset quality, management ability, earnings level and quality, and liquidity. The team then combines these factors to assign a composite, or overall, rating to the bank. The ratings range from 1 to 5, wherein the banks judged to be soundest are rated 1 and those least sound are rated 5. Prior to the inauguration of this uniform rating system in 1978, each agency had its own system to rate banks that it supervised, thus complicating interagency comparisons of ratings.

In cooperation with the FRS and the OCC, the FDIC maintains a problem-bank list by which it monitors its insurance exposure. As part of the examination process, a bank is identified as a *problem bank* if it has "violated a law or regulation or engaged in an 'unsafe and unsound' banking practice to such an extent that the present or future solvency of the bank is in question."[4] The FDIC further subclassifies these problem banks:

- *Serious Problem-Potential Payoff:* a bank in this category represents a 50 percent probability of soon needing FDIC financial assistance.
- *Serious Problem:* when in this category a bank involves a likely ultimate FDIC payoff unless drastic changes occur.
- *Other Problem:* although it is less precarious than in the prior categories, a bank in this category warrants close supervisory attention.

A study analyzes banks on the FDIC's problem list as of January 1973, and reports that the most frequent problem description is " 'poor asset condition due to present and/or prior management.' Basically, this means that capital is 'inadequate' with respect to the asset and managerial quality of the bank."[5] The study also compares various performance ratios of a sample of problem banks and of "similar" nonproblem banks between 1969 and 1971. Its results indicate that as early as "two years prior to recognition of the problem status, there were statistically significant differences between the groups." The evolving financial difficulties were reflected in ratios measuring the pending problem group's "loan portfolio, capital adequacy, efficiency, profitability and liquidity." The authors conclude that these

---

3. For more detail concerning which factors are considered by the OCC to determine the adequacy of a national bank's capital, see Robert R. Dince and James C. Fortson, "The Use of Discriminant Analysis to Predict the Capital Adequacy of Commercial Banks," *Journal of Bank Research,* Spring 1972, pp. 54-62. This study uses a statistical model to try to replicate, with public data, a two-way classification of banks, the capital of which is either adequate or inadequate by OCC standards. Although their model correctly replicates many of the classifications, the authors also verify that the actual OCC classifications encompass "dynamic and subjective factors" as required by the OCC's standards for capital adequacy.

4. Joseph F. Sinkey, Jr., and David A. Walker, "Problem Banks: Identification and Characteristics," *Journal of Bank Research,* Winter 1975, pp. 208-217.

5. Sinkey and Walker, "Problem Banks: Identification and Characteristics," pp. 211, 217.

results warrant pursuit of a goal to develop early warning systems to identify future problem banks.[6]

## Early Warning Systems

Between World War II and 1973, most bank failures were among banks with deposits under $50 million. In view of this experience, the supervisory agencies focused their traditional examination procedures on smaller banks. During 1973 and 1974, however, two exceptionally large banks failed, and there were news reports that other large banks were on the FDIC problem list. These events led federal supervisory agencies to review their examination practices and to explore whether they could develop computer-based "early warning" systems to help them promptly detect deterioration in a bank's financial condition.

An early warning system (EWS) can complement traditional bank examination procedures. To do so, it uses financial information, as reported by banks, to which it applies statistical tests to separate the set of financially strong banks from those that seem to be developing financial difficulties. With this initial classification, a bank supervisory agency can promptly allocate a larger portion of its examination resources to the potential problem banks. (This EWS procedure thus is similar to the credit-scoring procedures that banks use to help them allocate their loan-officer resources.)

There are two basic generations of early warning systems.[7] Illustrative first-generation systems are the OCC's National Bank Surveillance System (NBSS) and the FDIC's Financial Trend Analysis and its Just a Warning System (JAWS). These first-generation systems compute a bank's key financial ratios and trends, and they then flag any measure that departs significantly from a predetermined norm.

Second-generation systems seek to rank banks by using statistically derived models that simultaneously evaluate a set of performance measures. The Federal Reserve Bank of New York has been developing and testing such a second-generation EWS System. In a recent progress report, researchers from the Bank observe that results from some nationwide tests indicate "a remarkable degree of consistency in the extent to which bank vulnerability can be detected through statistical techniques that employ regularly reported financial data." The authors conclude how their methodology can be extended to screen banks for vulnerability in selected

---

6. Three other studies similarly detect statistically significant changes in financial variables of pending problem and/or failed banks: Paul A. Meyer and Howard W. Pifer, "Prediction of Bank Failures," *The Journal of Finance*, September 1970, pp. 853-868; Joseph F. Sinkey, Jr., "The Failure of United States National Bank of San Diego: A Portfolio and Performance Analysis," *Journal of Bank Research*, Spring 1975, pp. 8-24; and Joseph F. Sinkey, Jr., "Identifying Large Problem/Failed Banks: The Case of Franklin National Bank of New York," *Journal of Financial and Quantitative Analysis*, December 1977, pp. 779-800.

7. Robert A. Eisenbeis, "Financial Early Warning Systems: Status and Future Directions," *Issues in Bank Regulation*, Summer 1977, pp. 8-12.

areas such as foreign operations, bank holding companies, and internal control and audit systems.[8]

### Audit Requirements

Bank supervisory agencies traditionally assert that their examinations are not audits and so a bank needs to have effective programs of internal and/or external audits. Yet fraud, embezzlement, and other financial irregularities have been principal causes of bank failures since World War II. These are the types of problems that an effective audit program should prevent or promptly detect.

A potential weakness of early warning systems is their reliance on data provided by a bank. If some of a bank's personnel are participants in a scheme to defraud it, then the bank's records and internal documents are likely to be falsified in ways that will escape early detection by an EWS.

Aware that traditional examination practices and early warning systems may fail to detect some of a bank's risk exposure, the supervisory agencies have stiffened their audit requirements, and, in some cases, they have expanded their examinations to include some audit functions. Also, in addition to stressing the need for effective audit procedures, at times a supervisory agency insists that a bank improve its internal audit systems and/or commission an outside audit.

## PUBLIC POLICY ALTERNATIVES

Public officials and bankers can evaluate proposals that are designed to reconcile the dual goals of a sound banking system and a competitive, innovative banking system.

### NO BANK FAILURES

For practical purposes, a policy goal of no bank failures is infeasible. To try to achieve such a goal, public policy would have to restrict severely the risks that each bank could take; and it would likely insist on high capital ratios to absorb temporary setbacks. Also, the supervisory agencies would have to monitor closely each bank, and, even then, it is not clear that a monitoring system can promptly detect risks associated with fraud and embezzlement. At the extreme, this policy alternative would impose high costs on bank

---

8. Leon Korobow, David P. Stuhr, and Daniel Martin, "A Nationwide Test of Early Warning Research in Banking," *FRBNY Quarterly Review,* Autumn 1977, pp. 37-52. Earlier progress reports include: David P. Stuhr and Robert Van Wicklen, "Rating the Financial Condition of Banks: A Statistical Approach to Aid Bank Supervision," *Monthly Review* (Federal Reserve Bank of New York), September 1974, pp. 233-238; and Leon Korobow and David P. Stuhr, "Toward Early Warning of Changes in Banks' Financial Condition: A Progress Report," *Monthly Review* (Federal Reserve Bank of New York), July 1975, pp. 157-165.

supervisors, the banking industry, and the public. Also, if banks were so constrained, one could anticipate the rapid development of "nonbank" institutions that do not fall within the policy constraints and so can profitably undertake risks that are prohibited to banks.

## OCCASIONAL CONTAINED FAILURES

Current public policy accepts occasional bank failures but tries to restrict their effects from rippling through the banking system. Even if they cannot prevent all failures, current laws and supervisory procedures limit bank risk-taking to the extent that the failure rate has been low since the 1930s. FDIC insurance coverage stems runs on nonfailing banks, and FDIC pay-off and deposit-assumption procedures mitigate even the local impact of a bank failure. Moreover, some commentators cite therapeutic benefits associated with an occasional bank failure. An official of the FRS observes that "an occasional failure eliminates the inefficient and is a signal to other firms to exercise caution. Relatively free entry and exit are indicators that an industry is competitive. Regulation that is sufficient to prevent new firms from entering and prevent failure is sufficient to inhibit growth and vitality in a competitive economy."[9]

## NO FAILURES OF LARGE MONEY-CENTER BANKS

Even if one concludes that a no-failure policy is infeasible and/or inefficient, one can advocate a policy of no failures among large money-center banks. Compared to a small localized bank failure, a failure of a large money-center bank involves substantial social costs because of the:

- large amount of deposits that exceed the FDIC insurance maximum
- diverse uninsured creditors whose claims involve noninsured transactions in areas such as federal funds and foreign exchange
- widespread holders of the bank's (or its parent holding company's) debentures and stock
- extensive disruption of established customer relationships and loan commitments
- substantial outlays by the FDIC to administer a pay-off or deposit-assumption procedure
- widespread publicity that could unsettle the confidence of uninsured creditors and investors in other banks

Although a large-bank failure thus involves substantial costs and widespread effects, the social costs of avoiding any such failure also are high. The supervisory agencies would first have to differentiate between the

---

9. Darryl R. Francis, "Economic Forces Facing the Bank Holding Company Movement," *Review* (Federal Reserve Bank of St. Louis), September 1974, pp. 8-12. Also see, A. Dale Tussing, "The Case for Bank Failure," *The Journal of Law and Economics,* October 1967, pp. 129-147.

fail-safe banks and the other banks. If they knew which banks were fail-safe, uninsured creditors and investors would prefer to deal with these banks if they offered returns similar to those of the non-fail-safe banks. Thus the fail-safe banks would have an advantage in competing for funds. Yet to keep the large banks fail-safe and to protect the FDIC insurance fund, the supervisory agencies would have to limit and monitor the risks borne by the fail-safe banks. These specialized costs of supervision and compliance would be paid by the supervisory agencies, the fail-safe banks, and indirectly by other banks and the public.

In summary, a no-fail policy for large money-center banks involves other ''costs'' that can exceed the benefits of such a policy. The policy removes the fail-safe banks and their clients from the discipline of possible failure. In the 1970s, bank supervisory officials both in the United States and in some other nations decided not to prevent some large-bank failures. Their decisions reinforced market discipline and caution among other banks and among bank creditors and investors.

## 100 PERCENT DEPOSIT INSURANCE

As an alternative to its present policy of insuring a bank deposit up to a maximum amount (currently \$40,000), the FDIC could fully insure all bank deposits.[10]

Its advocates point out that, compared to the present policy, 100 percent deposit insurance is more equitable because it would:

- protect all depositors, not just a qualifying subset of depositors
- treat all banks more equitably than does the current policy, by which large money-center banks and smaller banks pay a similar FDIC assessment schedule related to their total deposits, yet the larger money-center banks have larger proportions of deposits that exceed the FDIC insurance maximum
- remove the inequity of current policies, by which, if a bank fails, its uninsured depositors in effect receive 100 percent coverage if the FDIC uses a deposit-assumption procedure, but they become general creditors for amounts above the insurance maximum if the FDIC uses the pay-off procedure

Views differ concerning the economic efficiency of 100 percent deposit insurance. Its proponents cite how the policy will reduce costs to uninsured depositors who have to evaluate their bank's risks and/or who choose to diversify their risks by having accounts to the insured maximum at various

10. Gary Leff, ''Should Federal Deposit Insurance be 100 Percent?'' *The Bankers Magazine,* Summer 1976, pp. 23-30. Instead of 100 percent deposit insurance, one variant is 100 percent insurance of demand deposits and savings deposits—but not of large CDs. Stanley C. Silverberg and Theodore G. Flechsig, ''The Case for 100% Insurance of Demand Deposits,'' *Issues in Bank Regulation,* Winter 1978, pp. 37-44.

banks. Proponents also note that 100 percent insurance reduces the probability of runs on banks by uninsured depositors. In contrast, its opponents point out that, compared to the current policy, 100 percent deposit insurance:

- removes the competitive market discipline of uninsured depositors who try to control their risks by evaluating a bank's soundness
- implies higher FDIC pay-offs, which will likely lead to higher FDIC assessments that will be borne by banks and indirectly by bank customers
- leads to higher supervisory costs (to limit FDIC losses) and higher compliance costs by banks faced with the additional supervision
- involves administrative costs of deciding just which of a bank's liabilities qualify as "deposits" eligible for the 100 percent coverage

To measure some of these costs, a study uses different assumptions to estimate "what a system of 100% deposit insurance could directly cost banks." Between 1934 (when the FDIC began) until 1974, uninsured depositors lost a total of $21.8 million due to bank failures. Assuming that the FDIC maintains its past trend in its ratio of its insurance fund to total bank deposits, to cover the estimated stream of losses to uninsured depositors the FDIC assessment rate would have to rise by less than 1 percent of its 1974 rate. Using the same ratio assumption, to cover a "worst case" situation "the assessment rate need only rise by 10% over that existing in 1974." The author concludes that "100% deposit insurance would most likely cost banks between 1% and 10% more than they paid for the $40,000 coverage level in 1974."[11] These estimates, while helpful, focus only on some of the total costs of 100 percent deposit insurance.

## RISK-ADJUSTED DEPOSIT INSURANCE

Under the current policy, a bank's FDIC assessment depends only on the bank's total deposits. It does not distinguish between a bank's proportions of insured and uninsured deposits, and it takes no account of differences in risks among banks. A conservative bank pays the same assessment as a risky bank of the same deposit size.

As an alternative to the present policy, why not introduce an FDIC assessment system that explicitly prices for differences in risk to the FDIC fund?[12] (This system could provide for 100 percent deposit coverage.) Other things equal, a conservative bank would be a preferred risk and would pay a lower FDIC assessment than would a similar-sized bank that pursues riskier

11. David Burras Humphrey, "100% Deposit Insurance: What Would It Cost?" *Journal of Bank Research,* Autumn 1976, pp. 192-198.

12. Clifton H. Kreps, Jr. and Richard F. Wacht, "A More Constructive Role for Deposit Insurance," *The Journal of Finance,* May 1971, pp. 605-613. Thomas Mayer, "A Graduated Deposit Insurance Plan," *The Review of Economics and Statistics,* February 1965, pp. 114-116.

policies. Its proponents observe that, compared to the current policy, a risk-adjusted system is more equitable and it is efficient because it allows banks, within limits, to choose and pay for their own risk preferences and it reduces the supervisory costs of controlling risks among all banks. As concluded by one observer, "The important change is the substitution of a pricing mechanism for the 'adequacy versus inadequate' capital rules. This will provide greater flexibility for bankers willing to pay the full cost of stretching their capital."[13] In contrast, its opponents enumerate how difficult it would be for the FDIC to quantify, price, and monitor the various risks.

## 100 PERCENT REQUIRED RESERVES

Another policy proposal is to require banks to maintain 100 percent reserves against their demand deposits.[14] These reserves would be risk-free assets such as vault cash, balances at the Federal Reserve Bank, or short-term U.S. Treasury securities. With this protection of demand deposits (a principal component of the money supply), there would be little need for extensive government involvement in banking and for FDIC insurance.

Its advocates summarize various benefits for a policy of 100 percent required reserves:

- In contrast to the current fractional-reserve system, this policy would facilitate FRS control of the money supply, and this money supply would be fail-safe.
- It would permit dismantling of extensive government intervention in bank loan and investment decisions.
- It would allow each bank to select its portfolio risks to the extent that is acceptable to its stockholders and its creditors whose accounts are not fully backed by required reserves.

Because it involves such a radical change from established practices, a policy of 100 percent required reserves is unlikely to receive rapid acceptance and implementation.

## MONITORING MARKET RISK-PREMIUMS

To detect possible changes in the risks of a bank and/or the banking system, why not have bank supervisory agencies monitor the risk premiums that banks pay to their investors and uninsured creditors? This policy proposal rests on two key assumptions:

---

13. Ronald D. Watson, "Insuring Some Progress in the Bank Capital Hassle," *Business Review* (Federal Reserve Bank of Philadelphia), July-August 1974, pp. 3-18.

14. Arthur J. Rolnick, "Bank Regulation: Strengthening Friedman's Case for Reform," *Quarterly Review* (Federal Reserve Bank of Minneapolis), Summer 1977, pp. 11-14. The author points out how his proposal is an extension of earlier proposals by Milton Friedman, *A Program of Monetary Stability* (Fordham University Press: New York), 1959.

- Noninsured investors and creditors are rational, risk-averse market participants who have access to—and can promptly evaluate—new information that can affect their expected returns and risks associated with their claims on banks.
- These investors correctly analyze and act on perceived changes in risk either as soon as or sooner than can the supervisory agencies.

If these assumptions hold, then the supervisory agencies can use market changes in risk premiums as part of an EWS and thereby reduce the amount of resources used to supervise banks. Also, they can look toward the discipline of a competitive marketplace to enforce capital adequacy standards on individual banks and the banking system.[15]

One must question how closely the market for bank shares and uninsured liabilities approaches the conditions necessary for a competitive market.

- Although shares and marketable liabilities of large banking organizations trade in active public markets, this is not the case for most banks, the shares of which are closely held and inactively traded.
- If they believe that the supervisory agencies cannot or will not allow a large bank to fail, then shareholders and uninsured creditors have little motivation to evaluate the risks borne by such banks.
- Financial disclosure, even by large money-center banks, has been limited until recent years. Investors still do not have access to all information available to examiners nor to examination reports, and they do not know which banks are on the FDIC problem list.
- Until recently, the rating services did not rate the default risk of bank securities. The current rating criteria for banking firms differ from those applied to nonbanking firms.

Several studies try to evaluate the market's role in evaluating capital conditions and/or changing risks in large banks. One study examines whether "the market for unsecured obligations of large banks can provide an 'early warning' system to alert bank investors and regulators about the capital adequacy levels of these banks." It concludes that "the tests employed did not find investors very sensitive to the presence of unacceptable levels of risk due to thin capital ratios in these larger banks and holding companies."[16] In another study the same author examines the effects that two large bank failures had on "the returns required by investors in large bank common securities." He concludes that "the market for bank equities

15. George S. Oldfield, "The Free Market Regulation of Bank Capital," *Financial Management,* Winter 1976, pp. 56-58. George J. Vojta, "Capital Adequacy: A Look at the Issues," *The Magazine of Bank Administration,* September 1973, pp. 22-25.

16. Richard H. Pettway, "Market Tests of Capital Adequacy of Large Commercial Banks," *The Journal of Finance,* June 1976, pp. 865-875.

exhibited only a transitory structural change in the perceived risk of bank investments to holders of nondiversified portfolios of bank securities.''[17] In 1976 a major newspaper reported the names of thirty-five banks on the FDIC problem list. A study analyzes what impact, if any, this public disclosure had on the share prices of the named banks, and it finds no evidence that the disclosure "was anticipated (or deemed relevant if it was) or perceived as significant detrimental news at the time of the release or for the following ten weeks.''[18] In total, these studies provide inconclusive evidence about the efficiency of the market for unsecured obligations of large banks. Until there is more conclusive evidence concerning the market's efficiency or inefficiency, bank supervisory agencies will likely monitor market risk premiums as one signal about changes in banking risks, but they are unlikely to revamp their traditional procedures to evaluate banking risks and capital adequacy.

## SUMMARY

Bank capital questions are part of a broader set of issues concerning bank risks and public policy. These issues face bankers, their customers, and—importantly—the supervisory agencies charged with the dilemma of maintaining both a sound banking system and a competitive, innovative banking system that serves the public.

Despite procedures to defuse its impact, a bank failure imposes costs on various people and institutions and may weaken public confidence in other banks and the banking system. Therefore the supervisory agencies try to avert failures and to contain any failures that do occur.

The supervisory agencies have extensive and expanding capabilities to avert failures. They enforce diverse laws and regulations that limit bank risks. To monitor bank compliance, the supervisory agencies use traditional examination practices by which they have access to virtually any of a bank's records; and they now augment their examination procedures with early warning systems and stiffer audit routines and requirements.

Various commentators question current supervisory objectives and procedures, and they suggest public policy alternatives. One subset of policy goals involves no failures, occasional failures, or no large-bank failures. To achieve one of these goals, society has to accept substantial supervisory and compliance costs and extensive restrictions on bank risk-taking and innovation. Alternative proposals include 100 percent deposit insurance, risk-adjusted deposit insurance, 100 percent required reserves, and increased monitoring of market risk-premiums. Although each of these

---

17. Richard H. Pettway, "The Effects of Large Bank Failures Upon Investors' Risk Cognizance in the Commercial Banking Industry," *Journal of Financial and Quantitative Analysis,* September 1976, pp. 465-477.

18. James M. Johnson and Paul G. Weber, "The Impact of the Problem Bank Disclosure on Bank Share Prices," *Journal of Bank Research,* Autumn 1977, pp. 179-182.

proposals can provide some comparative benefits based on equity and economic efficiency, viewed in total no one proposal promises net benefits that dominate those of the other proposals or of the present system of occasional contained failures. Therefore it is most probable that the present system will continue, with gradual increments in the extent of deposit insurance coverage (but probably not to 100 percent) and with some experiments to incorporate risk-premiums into the FDIC assessment schedule and/or into early warning systems by which the supervisory agencies monitor large banks.

# 16
# TRUST SERVICES AND STRATEGIES

A trust department provides specialized services for individuals and organizations, many of which use—or potentially use—other bank services. While it thus complements other services, a trust department can also be a profit center that directly and/or indirectly contributes to a bank's total profits. This chapter introduces bank trust departments from the viewpoints of their:

- principal services
- management strategies
- expansion strategies

It concludes by surveying recent public-policy debates concerning the power and accountability of bank trust departments.

## TRUST SERVICES: A PRIMER

A trust department has legal powers to act as a fiduciary to hold and/or service assets for the benefit of others. By law and custom this fiduciary, or trust, responsibility involves high standards of integrity.

A bank first has to apply for and receive trust powers from its chartering agency. Once it has these powers, a trust department has to adhere to strict standards established by statute and common law. Thus when not in contradiction with state or local law, a national bank can apply to the OCC for the power:

> to act as trustee, executor, administrator, registrar of stocks and bonds, guardian of estates, assignee, receiver, committee of estates of lunatics, or in any other fiduciary capacity in which State banks, trust companies, or other corporations which come into competition with national banks are permitted to act under the laws of the State in which the national bank is located. (12 U.S.C. 92a)

If it engages in any of these powers, a national bank has to segregate all assets that it holds in any fiduciary capacity from the bank's general assets; it has to keep detailed, separate records of all fiduciary transactions; and its trust department is subject to OCC regulations and examinations.

In its fiduciary capacity, a trust department can serve as a *trustee,* in which it has legal title to the assets involved, or as an *agent,* in which it does not have legal title to the assets. This distinction between trustee and agent applies to both personal and corporate trust services.

## PERSONAL TRUST SERVICES

As a fiduciary, a bank trust department provides specialized services for various individuals.[1]

### Trustee

A trust department usually acts as a trustee for individuals under terms of a person's will that provides for a trust (a *testamentary trust*) or through agreement with a living person who establishes a *living* (or *inter vivos*) *trust.* A living trust typically is established by busy and/or elderly people who choose not to involve themselves in the daily management of their substantial assets and so designate themselves as living beneficiaries of an account managed by a trust department.

A trust department administers and distributes a trust's assets subject to legal guidelines and a written trust agreement. As trustee, it decides how a trust's funds should be invested and distributed in order equitably to serve the differing interests of that trust's living beneficiaries and/or its *remaindermen* who share in the final distribution of the trust's assets. (By law, a personal trust has to have a limited life, and seldom does such a trust last beyond forty years.) For example, if one of a trust's living beneficiaries wants and needs high current income, the trustee has to weigh how meeting this objective (perhaps through high-yielding, fixed-income securities and partial distribution of capital) will likely affect the rights of other beneficiaries and/or remaindermen. At times a creator of a trust stipulates that a trust department share these investment and distribution responsibilities with cotrustees or others, such as a lawyer or a relative of the trust's creator.

Once appointed, a trust department usually remains trustee of a testamentary trust throughout its duration. In contrast, a trust department is subject to displacement by a living trust's creator, who, for example, can shift the trust to another trustee.

---

1. This section draws on Edna E. Ehrlich, ''The Functions and Investment Policies of Personal Trust Departments,'' *Monthly Review* (Federal Reserve Bank of New York), October 1972, pp. 255-270.

### Executor or Administrator

A trust department becomes an *executor* of an estate if it has been so named in a will and subsequently appointed by a court. It becomes a court-appointed *administrator* of an estate if a person dies without leaving a valid will or if a will names an executor who is unable or unwilling to serve.

As executor or administrator, a trust department administers the settlement of an estate. In this process it conserves the estate's assets; sells real property that is not to be transmitted as such to beneficiaries; settles debts, taxes, and other claims; and promptly distributes the net assets to beneficiaries unless it is then to serve as the estate's trustee. The settlement process takes from two to four years unless an estate is very large and/or complicated.

### Guardian or Conservator

At times a court appoints a bank trust department to act as a *guardian* of a minor's estate or as a *conservator* (or "committee") of an estate held for a mentally incompetent person. In those capacities a trust department administers an estate on behalf of the beneficiary. Although the trust fees from such an estate may not exceed its associated administrative costs, a trust department often accepts such an appointment as a social responsibility.

### Personal Agency Account

In a personal agency account a bank provides investment, custodial, and/or managerial services; but it does not hold title to the account's assets even though the assets may be registered in the name of the bank and/or one of its nominees. An agency account terminates when the client dies.

There are two principal types of personal agency accounts. In a *managing agency account,* subject to preagreed guidelines and periodic review, a bank fully manages the client's portfolio. It has discretionary powers to make changes within the portfolio without first obtaining the client's specific approval. In an *advisory agency account,* a trust department does not have similar discretionary powers; it reviews the portfolio and submits specific investment recommendations to the client for acceptance or nonacceptance. If the client accepts the recommendation, then the trust department executes the portfolio transaction(s) on behalf of the client. In both managing agency and advisory agency accounts, a trust department provides custodial services for the assets, collects income received from the assets, and informs clients of such events as bond calls and tender offers that affect securities in a client's agency portfolio.

## CORPORATE TRUST SERVICES

Bank trust departments also provide various services to corporations and to nonprofit institutions such as churches, unions, and universities.

## Employee Benefit Accounts

Employee benefit accounts primarily encompass pension and/or profit sharing plans that a trust department administers for sponsoring organizations and the plans' beneficiaries. Depending on the terms agreed to with an account's sponsoring organization, a trust department can:

- have sole investment responsibility for an account
- serve as an agent that provides portfolio advice to an account's administrators, at whose direction the department then executes specific transactions
- serve only as an agent that executes specific transactions as directed by an account's administrators

Trust departments of large money-center banks administer most employee benefit accounts, for which business they compete with other bank trust departments and also with nonbank firms such as life insurance companies and investment counselors.

## Registrar or Transfer Agent

A publicly traded corporation usually has a bank trust department serve as its *registrar,* maintaining the official corporate record of each holder of the firm's outstanding stock certificates and recording each transfer of stock from one holder to another. A trust department also may serve as a company's *transfer agent,* processing the transfer of registered stock certificates among holders. As a double-check system, a corporation usually has one trust department serve as its registrar and a separate trust department serve as its transfer agent. Also, a corporation can have a trust department serve as its registrar and/or transfer agent for its outstanding registered bonds, if any.

## Dividend Disbursement Agent

As a company's *dividend disbursement agent* (DDA), a bank trust department prepares the dividend checks and mails them to registered stockholders who, by owning the stock on the record date, are eligible to receive the dividend.[2] A DDA earns revenues on the funds during the interval from when the dividend-paying company deposits the funds until the DDA has to honor the checks deposited by laggard recipients. (A bank trust department has a similar role and can achieve similar benefits if it is the payment agent for a corporate or governmental bond issue.)

To broaden its DDA services, a trust department can offer to administer

---

2. Some large banks perform such functions as dividend disbursement agent and transfer agent within a corporate services department that is separate from the bank's trust department.

a dividend reinvestment plan for a corporate client.[3] Under such a plan, a company's stockholders can authorize the trust department, as agent, to:

- open an account for a participating stockholder
- briefly hold a stockholder's dividend amount, pool it with that of other participants, and use the total amount to purchase the company's shares in public markets or to purchase authorized but unissued shares from the company
- hold the full and fractional purchased shares on behalf of the participant who can later instruct the agent to sell any or all of the full shares or have a stock certificate issued to the participant

Some dividend reinvestment plans have additional features by which a participant also can contribute cash (up to a maximum amount per period) for the pooled purchase and/or can use the reinvested dividends to purchase shares at a discount from their current market price.

From a client company's viewpoint, its dividend reinvestment plan helps solidify stockholder relations and, when it involves authorized but unissued shares, serves as a convenient source of additional equity capital. As an administrator of a dividend reinvestment plan, a trust department gets service fees from the participants and/or client firm, and it has a brief use of the funds prior to their being used to pay for purchases of the company's stock.

## Trustee of Bond Issues

Most publicly traded bond issues contain an indenture agreement that seeks to protect the claims of the bondholders by constraining the actions of the issuing firm. For example an indenture agreement may limit a firm's flexibility to incur additional debt and to pay cash dividends. Because it is impractical for each bondholder to monitor the issuer's adherence to the agreement, a bank trust department can accept this monitoring role as agent for the bondholders. If it detects a violation of the agreement, then the trustee is to act promptly to protect the interests of the bondholders.

## CONCLUSION

About thirty percent of insured banks in the U.S. exercise trust powers. Of these, the smaller banks primarily engage in personal trust and estate services. The large money-center banks offer more comprehensive services that include agency accounts and various corporate trust services. While many of their services have long histories, bank trust departments have been

---

3. Paul F. Jessup and Thomas W. Von Kuster, Jr., "Banking on Dividend Reinvestment," *The Magazine of Bank Administration*, February 1974, pp. 45-48.

innovative developers of new services and new ways to deliver traditional services.

## MANAGING TRUST OPERATIONS

Exhibit 16-1 provides a schematic model of the principal components of a bank's trust operations. Any bank with trust powers has these basic components, although it may obtain some of its support services from outside sources. This organizational model provides a framework by which to examine a trust department's principal:

- internal operations
- interface with its support services and its bank's nontrust activities
- expansion opportunities

The model also can provide insights into recent public-policy debates concerning the power and accountability of bank trust departments.

### OBJECTIVES AND CONSTRAINTS

If it has no trust department, a bank has to expect that some of its wealthy customers and corporate clients will obtain services from trust departments of other banks. Some of these customers, if pleased with the trust services, will also shift part of their nontrust business to the banks with trust services. A small bank has to evaluate whether this potential loss of some business warrants the probable net costs of having a trust department, especially if there is little demand for its services. In contrast, a medium-sized or large bank, with its broader range of current and potential customers, usually has a trust department, an objective of which is to retain and attract customers for the bank's trust and nontrust services. A bank with a trust department thus views it as part of its full-service capabilities to develop and solidify long-run customer relationships.

As they focus on profit management and profit-center concepts throughout the organization, a bank's senior officials extend these concepts to trust operations. They have their staff develop systems to try to measure the extent to which the trust operations directly and/or indirectly contribute to the bank's total profits. Also, within the trust department, senior officers evaluate how to boost profits from specific activities, usually by raising fees, controlling costs, and/or focusing on current and potential trust accounts that will likely be profitable over time. Yet as they try to develop and refine their profit-management systems, trust departments face constraints on their prices and costs.

Statutes, regulations, and judicial review procedures limit the fees that a trust department can charge its noncorporate accounts. Some states have statutory ceilings on fees that trust departments can charge for administering testamentary trusts and estates. (To illustrate, in 1969 New York's statutory

**EXHIBIT 16-1**

**Bank Trust Operations:
An Organizational Model**

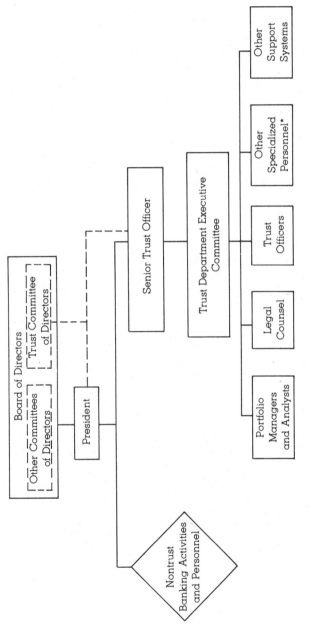

*Depending on a trust department's size and specialization, this category can include specialists in such areas as accounting, auditing, business development and marketing, computer systems, farm management, and tax planning.

ceilings were raised for the first time in fourteen years.) In cases where a trust department is a court-appointed fiduciary, its fees are subject to applicable local law, if any, and to approval by the court. In cases where its fees are not subject to local law and/or court approval, a trust department usually is subject to supervisory mandates that its fees be reasonable compensation for services rendered and to possible judicial review in cases where trust beneficiaries protest what they view to be unreasonable fees.

Corporate trust services are seldom subject to statutory ceilings, but a bank that offers such services finds itself competing against large trust departments and various nontrust financial institutions. Competition thus limits a bank's flexibility to price its corporate trust services.

Law and custom set high performance standards for people or firms that accept fiduciary responsibilities. To meet such standards, a trust department has or retains trained trust officers, legal counsel, and specialized support personnel.

When it invests a client's funds, a trust department operates within the context of two principal constraints. As accepted by the trust department, a specific will, trust instrument, or agency agreement constrains how the account is managed. If, for example, a will specifies that all of an estate's assets are to be held in U.S. Treasury securities, then, unless overturned by a court, this constraint is binding. Secondly, most states set fiduciary guidelines based on the *prudent man rule*, which in essence requires that a trustee invest "only in such securities as would be acquired by prudent men of discretion and intelligence in such matters who are seeking a reasonable income and the preservation of their capital."[4] The prudent man rule also is part of the common law that governs fiduciary relationships.

Both in statutes and in common law, the prudent man rule is a general guideline that is subject to interpretation and specific judicial decisions. A trust department operates within this guideline even in cases where a specific trust agreement gives extensive investment discretion to the trustee. As it applies the guideline to a specific case, a trustee evaluates how—especially in an inflationary environment—to achieve simultaneously the twin objectives of reasonable income and preservation of capital.

Thus, as it seeks ways to increase profits from its trust operations, a bank faces constraints on both its pricing policies and the costs necessary to meet fiduciary performance standards. Within these constraints, a trust department has room to innovate in its pricing policies, operating procedures and costs, and mix of services.

## STRUCTURE AND OPERATIONS

A bank's board of directors is at the apex of the trust operations. The directors are responsible for the "proper exercise" of a bank's fiduciary

---

4. Cited by Ehrlich (p. 259) as the wording of the rule used in many state statutes. Ehrlich reports that 45 states have this type of statutory guideline; 3 states have no guidelines for fiduciary investments; and 2 states limit fiduciary investments to fixed-income instruments.

powers. In national banks the board of directors is responsible for "all matters pertinent" to the exercise of the bank's fiduciary powers such as:

- setting policies
- investing and disposing of fiduciary assets
- directing and reviewing the actions of all personnel who conduct the bank's fiduciary procedures

While it thus bears final responsibility, a board of directors assigns the administration of the fiduciary powers to committees, officers, and employees.

Along with its audit committee and loan committee, a board of directors usually has a trust committee of several directors who focus on the trust operations. This committee actively works with the bank's president and its senior trust officer(s) to establish and review trust policies and procedures.

A trust department has a senior trust officer who works closely with the bank's president, trust committee of directors, and, to a lesser extent, board of directors. In coordination with these other parties, the senior trust officer manages the trust operations. In a medium-sized trust department, the senior officer directly administers the department's trust officers, legal counsel, and other operating personnel. In a large trust department, the senior trust officer(s) work closely with senior members of the trust department's specialist groupings, both directly and through meetings of a trust department executive committee in which these senior people participate.

## Trust Officers

Trust officers are a trust department's principal interface with its clients. In a small department, a trust officer often has additional duties in such areas as legal matters, new business development, operations, and portfolio decisions. In a large trust department, a trust officer specializes in account administration and draws on the back-up resources of other specialists who are employed or retained by the department.

A trust officer first meets with a potential client, who typically has been referred to the trust department by a lawyer or another client. The trust officer reviews with the potential client his or her current financial situation and probable future needs in areas such as estate planning and living trusts. The officer demonstrates how certain of the department's services can benefit the potential client, his or her family, and heirs. If the person becomes a client of the trust department, then the trust officer, through occasional meetings or correspondence, keeps informed about major changes in the client's financial and/or family situation. This updating process enables the trust officer to suggest appropriate changes in the client's trust program and to understand the probable financial needs of family members who become beneficiaries of a testamentary trust. The fiduciary relationship between a trust officer and an individual client thus is similar to a long-term professional relationship between a family doctor or lawyer and a client.

Many wealthy families use trust accounts to preserve the family fortune from taxes and wastrel heirs. These families, at times through succeeding generations, are among the principal clients of an established trust department. Yet established trust departments and especially newer trust departments develop ways to broaden their base of individual clients.

In addition to referrals from current clients and lawyers, a trust department encourages the banking officers to alert their clients to available services within the bank's trust department. It also may place some directed advertising in media (such as concert programs and theatre playbills) that it associates with potential clients.

To broaden its range of clients beyond established wealthy families, a trust department examines the potential profitability of new services and more efficient ways of delivering traditional services. To illustrate, some trust departments offer:

- *Common trust funds,* similar to mutual funds, that invest in diversified portfolios of securities that are judged consistent with a fund's goals. A trust department can have several common trust funds, with different return-risk objectives and portfolios. If agreed to by a trust client, the department places the client's funds in one or more of the common trust funds that are appropriate for the client. In this way a trust department can pass through some diversification benefits and scale economies to clients whose accounts are not large enough to warrant the minimum fees associated with a portfolio that is directly managed by the trust department.
- *Minitrusts* for accounts below a certain amount, such as $100,000, that: use standardized legal documents, place assets in common trust funds, restrict account activity and services, and charge an annual minimum fee of several hundred dollars. Some trust departments view their minitrust packages as a way to initiate client relationships that will build over time.
- *Financial planning services* for high-income executives, professionals, and others who wish to build their estates by using the services of professional estate planners and tax experts.
- *Tax-deferred retirement plans,* such as federally authorized Keogh or H.R. 10 plans for self-employed individuals and Individual Retirement Accounts for people who are not otherwise covered by a retirement plan.

As it broadens the services it offers to a wider range of clients, a trust department has to develop appropriate systems to support its trust officers who service these clients.

### Legal Counsel

Legal counsel is an integral part of trust operations. To illustrate, the OCC requires that if it exercises trust powers a national bank has to ''employ or retain legal counsel who shall be readily available to pass upon fiduciary matters and to advise the bank and its trust department.'' (12 C.F.R. 9.7) A state bank similarly employs or retains legal counsel.

A small trust department usually retains outside legal counsel to provide support for the senior trust officer(s), some of whom have legal training. A large trust department that engages in complex fiduciary responsibilities has in-house, full-time, legal counsel that in turn receives support from specialized law firms retained by the bank.

A trust department's legal counsel reviews fiduciary matters from the department's and bank's viewpoint. It cooperates with—but does not try to supersede—the legal counsel that a client employs to represent his or her position in fiduciary matters.

### Portfolio Managers and Analysts

Subject to legal guidelines and internal policies, a portfolio manager structures and revises an assigned set of portfolios.

The principal legal guidelines are the prudent man rule and the trust agreement that applies to a specific fiduciary portfolio. In addition, some states have officials who prepare a *legal list* of investment securities that are judged suitable for fiduciary accounts. These securities usually are of companies that have lengthy histories of earnings and dividends.

In 1974, Congress passed the Employment Retirement Income Security Act (ERISA), which sets extensive new guidelines for the administration of pension funds, many of which are trust-department clients. Although some of its rules remain subject to legal interpretation, the ERISA contains a version of the prudent man rule whereby a fiduciary is to act in a way that ''a prudent man acting in a like capacity and familiar with such matters would use.''

Within the legal guidelines, a trust department's senior officials set internal policies to guide and monitor portfolio managers. A large trust department, for example, usually has an investment policy committee comprised of senior officials. This committee develops an internal list of approved securities from among which the portfolio managers select specific securities to add to the portfolios that they manage. The committee also draws on in-house economists and/or economic consultants to help it develop investment scenarios and associated strategies to help guide portfolio managers in their specific decisions. Over time the committee revises its approved list, scenarios, and associated strategies; and it considers proposed exceptions to its guidelines.

Within the guidelines a portfolio manager structures and revises individual portfolios to try to meet their goals. Some portfolios have general goals such as the generation of reasonable income consistent with the preservation of capital; but, increasingly, trust departments and clients seek to establish quantitative return-risk objectives by which to guide portfolio management and evaluate its performance. Thus, for example, a trust agreement may specify how a portfolio's total returns and its volatility of returns over time should compare to those of standardized measures of total market returns. In such ways investment strategy committees and portfolio managers have begun to use elements of modern portfolio theory.[5] As an extension of this theory, some large bank trust departments offer to use the *index fund* concept, by which a portfolio manager constructs a portfolio that, with a high degree of confidence and at low cost, replicates the return-risk performance of a standardized market measure, such as the Standard & Poor's Index of 500 stocks.

To implement modern portfolio theory, a portfolio manager uses computer models developed and/or leased by the bank. One large bank, which has fiduciary trust accounts exceeding $1 billion, reports how it applies computer analysis to various portfolios that it manages. When considering changes in a major portfolio, the portfolio manager uses a remote terminal to feed a listing of the account's current holdings into a central computer system, which then reports "current numerical ratings of the portfolio's diversification, market value, market related risk (beta coefficient) and standard error factor of the estimate." The portfolio manager then has the computer analyze how proposed changes in the portfolio's holdings will affect the portfolio's diversification and risk measures. An officer of the bank states that this computer-assisted system enables the bank to "maintain portfolio performance with fewer holdings and transactions, which cuts costs both for the bank and the customer." The officer also reports how his bank uses computerized stock valuation programs, model portfolios, and performance evaluation systems; and he concludes how "in approaching potential clients that have definite constraints on return, yield and other factors, we can diagram realistic objectives according to loss probabilities, and this capability is proving to be an important factor in attracting new business."[6]

To evaluate whether and how to change a portfolio's holdings, a portfolio manager has to obtain and review reports prepared by securities analysts. A small trust department draws primarily on outside research; a large trust department has its own staff of analysts supplemented by outside research provided by brokerage firms and other firms that specialize in institutional research. With the end of fixed minimum commission rates on the New York Stock Exchange and a reduction in institutional research that was based on such a rate structure, large trust departments have built their in-house investment research capabilities and, in some cases, they sell their

5. For a brief introduction to modern portfolio theory, see J. A. McQuown, "Technical and Fundamental Analysis and Capital Market Theory," *Journal of Bank Research,* Spring 1973, pp. 8-17.

6. "How One Bank Fine-Tunes Its Investment Decisions," *Banking*, July 1976, pp. 92, 94.

investment services to smaller trust departments and other clients. One large bank pioneered the selling of *stepped research,* whereby it prices its investment-advisory letters based on various levels of frequency and detail.[7] A client can then choose a service level and price that is most appropriate for its requirements.

Even as he or she draws on modern portfolio theory and extensive back-up resources, a portfolio manager has to evaluate special factors that affect specific fiduciary portfolios. Some accounts, for example, contain a disproportionately large amount of a stock purchased years ago at a low cost basis. Before revising the diversification of such a portfolio, the portfolio manager—in consultation with the trust officer(s), legal counsel, tax experts, and beneficiaries—has to evaluate and review the after-tax consequences of reducing the large, low-tax-basis, holding.

## Other Specialized Personnel and Systems

A large trust department has additional specialized personnel who develop and administer special trust services. These personnel use computer-based systems to assist their decision-making and their processing of special services.

**Business Managers and Farm Managers**   At times a trust department has to administer an estate that contains a family-owned business. The department has or retains personnel who oversee the management of this firm on behalf of the estate's beneficiaries. Usually this is an interim process, after which control of the firm passes directly to the beneficiaries and/or is sold for their benefit.

A trust department similarly can serve as an interim overseer for a farm or ranch that is part of an estate. Some trust departments, however, offer ongoing farm management services for estates and living trusts. Among trust departments offering these services, several manage over 500,000 acres and many others, of various sizes, manage up to 100,000 acres. The large trust-department managers operate through regional offices, and they employ and/or retain experienced specialists who have degrees in agricultural sciences.

**Stock Purchase Plans**   Through their trust departments, several large banks offer such stock investment plans as Automatic Investment Service (AIS), under which a bank customer selects stocks from a list of about twenty-five well-known companies and authorizes the bank, as agent, to make monthly purchases of the selected stocks. The bank debits the authorized amount from the client's checking account and commingles the funds with those of other small investors in order to pay lower per-unit transaction costs on the aggregate purchases. Although various banks

---

7. Joe Asher, ''To Build Profits: Which Way Trust?'' *Banking,* February 1977, pp. 37 ff.

developed or contracted for the computer software to offer them, the stock purchase plans have not won a wide following among individual investors. Nevertheless, the plans illustrate how bank trust departments are willing to develop new "retail" services, some of which compete against services offered by retail-oriented brokerage firms.

**Master Trustee Services**  A master trustee serves as custodian for a pension plan; it holds securities and processes the records even when the fund's actual management is split among various portfolio managers. In response to the Employment Retirement Income Security Act (ERISA), which mandates additional responsibilities and reporting requirements for pension plans and their managers, many large companies discontinued direct detailed supervision of their pension plans. They now contract with a large trust department, as master trustee, to monitor the plan's various portfolio managers and to develop centralized, standardized performance reports.

To perform an expanded master-trustee role, a trust department develops computer systems and data bases by which to evaluate the performance of a plan's portfolio managers. As it builds its analytical capabilities, a master trustee offers additional services, usually on a fee basis. One large bank has extended its performance review systems to include subprograms that analyze portfolio risk, execution of orders, and market timing. In some cases a master trustee assumes total fiduciary responsibility, whereby a corporate client gives it the power to replace—not just evaluate—the pension plan's portfolio managers.

**Special Corporate Services**  The Banking Act of 1933 bars banks from either underwriting or acting as dealers in most types of securities.[8] The principal exceptions involve U.S. government securities and general-obligation municipal securities. Despite this barrier, banks, primarily through their trust departments, have creatively extended their services into some traditional investment-banking activities.

A large trust department has a staff of specialists who engage in corporate services that generate fee revenues for the department. Although their bank cannot underwrite corporate securities, these specialists arrange private placements whereby a corporate client sells additional securities directly to a small number of institutional investors. The seller thus bypasses a public offering, and it pays a fee to the trust department as the agent that arranged the placement. These specialists, also as agents, advise corporate clients about possible acquisition opportunities and associated merger or tender-offer strategies. These specialists also have access to back-up systems that will process the transfer of securities and/or funds that are associated with a corporate client's acquisition(s).

---

8. William E. Whitesell, "Glass-Steagall: Resurrection for Interment?" *Business Review* (Federal Reserve Bank of Philadelphia), June 1970, pp. 3-9.

### Other Support Systems

Behind the scenes, a trust department has clerical personnel and related support systems to process its specialized trust services. Therefore it has at least one operations officer who focuses on ways to control, and possibly reduce, the costs of these support services while still maintaining their fiduciary quality and security. In addition to trying to improve the performance of current support systems, the officer evaluates the net benefits of automating additional clerical activities and/or of subcontracting some labor-intensive activities.

A large trust department uses its in-house computer capabilities to automate parts of its specialized systems that involve record-keeping and reporting, portfolio analysis, and dividend disbursements. In turn, it can sell some of its computer capabilities to smaller trust departments.

In addition to its possibly buying computer capabilities from a large trust department, a smaller trust department can evaluate whether to:

- buy, from nonbank vendors, software packages that go on a bank's own computer
- lease time-sharing facilities from a service bureau that specializes in serving trust departments
- lease or buy minicomputers that have suitable software packages

When evaluating such alternatives, an operations officer has to analyze not only their probable dollar costs but also their longer-run flexibility, quality, security, and implications for client relationships.

A trust operations officer similarly can evaluate the net benefits of subcontracting some back-office, labor-intensive functions to specialist nonbank firms. To illustrate, some of the nation's largest trust departments subcontract the processing of their stock transfer and registrar services to a nonbank firm that offers diverse accounting, custodial, record-keeping, and transfer services to bank trust departments.

## MANAGING TRUST DEPARTMENT PROFITABILITY

A trust department faces internal and external pressures to improve and standardize its profit measurement systems. Of 99 large banks that responded to a questionnaire, 95 reported that "they attempt to measure trust department profitability at least to some degree."[9] Yet when interviewed "many trust officers expressed doubt that a meaningful and comparable measure of trust department profitability is possible." An ABA task force, charged with developing a uniform method of cost reporting for

---

9. Keith V. Smith and Maurice B. Goudzwaard, "The Profitability of Commercial Bank Trust Management," *Journal of Bank Research,* Autumn 1972, pp. 166-177.

trust departments, has encountered delays in achieving its goal because of "deep differences in theoretical approaches taken by different trust departments."[10] Nevertheless, trust departments have to prepare to meet detailed reporting requirements that are pending from the OCC and, potentially, from the SEC.

Exhibit 16-2 provides a framework by which to examine the principal components of a trust-department profit equation. The exhibit identifies two cost categories ("direct" and "allocated overhead") which a trust department must cover before it contributes to bank "profits." Even within this categorization people can differ as to what constitutes a trust department's "costs" and how to allocate them. To cover its costs and contribute to profits, a trust department generates fees, credit balances, and other benefits.

## FEES

Subject to applicable statutes, regulations, and competition, a trust department develops fee schedules for various services. It usually scales its fees so that the incremental percentage fee declines as the account size exceeds specified amounts. To illustrate, for basic personal trust accounts, a trust department specifies the following fee schedule:

| Account-size Bracket ($000) | Percentage Rate Applicable to Bracket |
|:---:|:---:|
| 0-100 | 1.0 |
| 100-500 | 0.5 |
| 500 & over | 0.3 |

Minimum fee: $500

Under such a schedule, an account with $70,000 of assets pays an annual fee of $700; an account with $700,000 of assets pays an annual fee of $3,600, which amounts to 0.51 percent of the total assets.[11] For multimillion dollar accounts, such as those of employee benefit plans, the percentage fee falls below 0.50 percent. When it serves as a master trustee for a large corporate account, a department's basic percentage fee may be about 0.10 percent— supplemented by additional fees for additional services.

If many of its fees are a function of an account's total assets, then a trust department finds its fee revenues sensitive to changes in asset values. Especially if equities constitute large proportions of its accounts, then, other things equal, the department's fee revenues increase as the stock prices generally rise; and its revenues decrease as stock prices decline. To buffer such a decline in its revenues, the department can try to increase its

---

10. "Can Trust Officers Solve the Cost Accounting Puzzle?" *Banking,* March 1978, pp. 54, 57.

11. $0.01(\$100,000) + 0.005(\$400,000) + 0.003(\$200,000) = \$3,600$

**EXHIBIT 16-2**

**Measuring Trust Department Profitability:**
**A Framework**

*Costs and*
*Contribution to*
*Bank Profits*                    ————————— *Revenues and Other Benefits* —————————

```
┌ ─ ─ ─ ─ ─ ─ ─ ┐
│               │
│   "Profits"   │
│               │                                                  ┌ ─ ─ ─ ─ ─ ─ ┐
├ ─ ─ ─ ─ ─ ─ ─ ┤                                                  │   "Other     │
│               │                                                  │  Benefits"   │
│  Allocated    │                                   ┌ ─ ─ ─ ─ ─ ┐  ├ ─ ─ ─ ─ ─ ─ ┤
│  Overhead     │                                   │  Credit   │  │   Credit     │
│  Costs        │                                   │  Balances │  │   Balances   │
├ ─ ─ ─ ─ ─ ─ ─ ┤              ┌ ─ ─ ─ ─ ─ ┐          ├ ─ ─ ─ ─ ─ ┤  ├ ─ ─ ─ ─ ─ ─ ┤
│               │              │           │          │           │  │              │
│               │              │           │          │           │  │              │
│  Direct Costs │              │   Fees    │          │   Fees    │  │    Fees      │
│               │              │           │          │           │  │              │
└───────────────┘              └───────────┘          └───────────┘  └──────────────┘
```

percentage fees, but it must anticipate critical questioning by trust beneficiaries who also observe the reduced values of their trust accounts.

To reduce the sensitivity of its fee revenues to stock-market fluctuations, a trust department can take various steps to diversify its revenue base:

- Add accounts in which equities do not constitute large proportions of total assets. (Although the values of other assets will fluctuate over time, their fluctuations are not likely to be as wide as—nor perfectly positively correlated with—the general fluctuations in stock prices.)
- Add additional services that involve fixed fees or that in other ways are less directly linked to fluctuations in stock prices. For example, a trust department can evalute its adding new master-trustee services and/or corporate services such as dividend reinvestment plans and private placements.

A proposal, which does not necessarily reduce the sensitivity of fee revenues to fluctuations in stock prices, is for a trust department to offer a two-part fee schedule for managing pension funds. One part would be a basic fee "for covering costs related to safekeeping of the assets and to achieving what might be termed standard investment results;" a second, supplemental part would "provide both rewards and penalties for short term investment results different from the agreed upon standard; long term, the plan should provide rewards for consistent above average investment results."[12] Another author uses simulation techniques to test this basic proposal and several modifications of it; and he concludes that such an incentive plan "seems to be sound when applied to pension fund performance of the 1960s."[13] Yet questions remain. At what rate should the advisor participate in a fund's superior returns? Will incentive fees improve performance?

## CREDIT BALANCES

At any time some of a trust department's accounts have cash that the trust department deposits in the bank. These cash balances arise from:

- estate accounts in which there are pending payments or distributions
- trust and agency accounts that have received cash inflows that await reinvestment or distribution
- other accounts, such as those for corporate funds temporarily held prior to distribution as dividends and/or held for reinvestment via dividend reinvestment plans.

Many of these temporary cash balances thus reflect cash-flow patterns within separate trust accounts. At any time, however, the sum of these cash balances deposited with the bank can be large. "At many banks, the trust department deposits are larger than those of the bank's biggest outside depositor."[14]

Many large banks allocate to their trust department a *credit balance* that reflects the profit to the banking operation from having cash balances deposited by the trust department. However, at least one large bank gives its trust department no credit balances "on the ground that such balances might tempt the department to keep assets in cash longer than is proper, and that the practice 'distorts the performance' of the trust department."[15] Whether or not it receives credit-balance allocations to include in its "revenues," a trust department contributes to its bank's total profits when it deposits cash balances within the bank.

Although it generates some cash balances for its bank, a trust department has policies and procedures by which its portfolio managers

---

12. George P. Williams, Jr., "An Incentive Plan for Bank Managed Pension Funds," *Journal of Bank Research,* Spring 1971, pp. 25-30.

13. James D. McWilliams, "A Closer Look at Incentive Fees for Bank Managed Pension Funds," *Journal of Bank Research,* Winter 1973, pp. 238-246.

14. Edna E. Ehrlich, "The Functions and Investment Policies of Personal Trust Departments: Part II," *Monthly Review* (Federal Reserve Bank of New York), January 1973, pp. 12-19. This source quotes a retired senior bank officer who, in a speech to trust officials, commented that "one of the most important reasons for a bank to have a trust department is to benefit by its inevitable cash balance" (*American Banker,* July 3, 1972).

15. "Can Trust Officers Solve the Cost Accounting Puzzle?" p. 54.

invest an account's temporarily excess cash. The principal investment vehicles are:

- Daily-interest savings accounts, especially for small sums of money
- Externally managed money market mutual funds or an internally managed common trust fund that holds only prime money-market instruments
- Money-market instruments such as Treasury bills, CDs, and commercial paper
- Participations in a *master note,* which is a large loan that a trust department negotiates with a prime customer of the bank. A master note has: an agreed maximum amount, a short maturity that often is renewable on a daily basis, and an interest rate close to that which the borrower currently pays on its 180-day commercial paper. A trust department has various of its accounts participate in one or more of these master notes, which it sometimes calls variable-rate notes or demand notes.

By thus keeping its accounts' temporarily excess cash invested in interest-earning assets, a trust department meets its fiduciary responsibilities and defuses potential criticism by trust beneficiaries and public officials.

## OTHER BENEFITS

A trust department's activities provide other benefits to its bank. These benefits, although difficult to measure, include:

- services, such as dividend disbursement and stock transfer, for the bank and its stockholders
- community goodwill from services such as court-appointed guardianships
- retention and/or attraction of customers who use other of the bank's services

If it has an appropriate accounting system, a bank can try to "credit" its trust department for such services. To illustrate:

> some banks allow credit for loan and deposit relationships developed by the bank with trust department customers, for services performed for the bank by the trust department, for unprofitable trust accounts kept by the department for various reasons for customers of the bank, and for investments that the department makes in certificates of deposit issued by the bank.[16]

Even without such a system, a bank's senior officials recognize that a trust department's other benefits contribute to the bank's total profits.

---

16. Ehrlich, January 1973, p. 14.

## DIRECT COSTS

Even without an advanced accounting system, a bank identifies some costs that are directly associated with its trust operations. These costs include: salaries and benefits paid to full-time trust employees; legal fees paid for outside counsel; and fees paid for investment research, computer software and time-sharing, and other outside services that are used exclusively by the trust department. A bank's senior officials, cost accountant(s), and senior trust officer(s) agree not only on most of these direct costs but on the assumption that the department's revenues should at least cover its direct costs.

## ALLOCATED OVERHEAD COSTS

Cost accountants face conceptual and practical difficulties when they try to allocate overhead costs to a department (cost center), especially when some departmental activities overlap with those of other departments. To illustrate, in a small trust department, unless one requires detailed time records, it is difficult to allocate the cost of time of a senior officer who performs both trust and nontrust activities. Similarly, it is difficult to allocate precise costs for the trust department's occupancy and its shared use of computers with nonbank departments. (Some of these allocated costs become more readily identifiable as direct costs if a trust department buys services, such as computer services, from outside sources rather than shares facilities with nontrust departments.) Despite such difficulties, a bank's cost accountant(s) and officials try to identify the trust department's share of overhead costs; and they usually expect the department's revenues and other benefits to contribute toward these overhead costs.

## PROFITS

If their bank has, or is contemplating, a trust department, senior officials have to grapple with the basic issues of trust revenues, benefits, costs, and profits. A first step is to understand both the various ways in which a trust department generates revenues, cash balances, and other benefits and the various costs associated with a trust department.

Despite difficulties in computing and comparing trust-department profits, there is evidence that trust department profitability varies widely. A pair of authors reports that within their sample of 680 trust departments, "profit as a percentage of department revenue ranged as high as 20% for some banks," but only 17% of the sample trust departments were profitable when profits were unadjusted for credit balances. (Even when they try to adjust for credit balances, the authors estimate that only 35% of the sample trust departments are profitable.) The authors further report that "average profitability appears to improve as the size of the department increases" and that "certain types of trust business, notably employee benefit accounts, tend to be more profitable than other business types as size increases."[17]

---

17. Smith and Goudzwaard, "The Profitability of Commercial Bank Trust Management," p. 171.

To bolster their department's contribution to bank profits, senior trust officials can seek improvements in their cost accounting systems. If their bank is a member of the FRS, then they can have their department participate in the Functional Cost Analysis program. They can also evaluate whether to buy or lease analytical systems from other sources. To illustrate, the data processing affiliate of one bank holding company offers a tested Profitability Analysis/Cost Accounting System for trust departments.[18] Its affiliate bank reports that, by using this system, it has:

- trimmed direct expenses by almost 20 percent
- eliminated one unprofitable trust service
- adjusted some of its fee schedules based on factual analysis
- refocused its business-development efforts to build use of its high-return trust services

Even without such a system a trust department can internally evaluate ways to prune low-profit or unprofitable accounts and to build its high-return services.

While a trust department thus tries to increase its contribution as a profit center, the bank's senior officials still have to evaluate complex ways in which a trust department contributes to the bank's total profits. Even if, based on the bank's accounting system, the trust department only breaks even or contributes modest profits, the senior officials have to estimate whether or not the bank's total profits would be higher without the trust operation, and whether or not the trust department's profit contribution helps stabilize the bank's pattern of total profits over time.[19]

## EXPANDING TRUST OPERATIONS

A trust department expands internally when it builds its resources and capabilities at one location; it expands externally when it thus increases its capacity and operates from additional locations.[20] Although it faces few constraints on its gradual internal expansion, a trust department can encounter legal and resource constraints on its external expansion.

---

18. C. Colburn Hardy, "How One Bank Improved Trust Department Profits," *Banking,* January 1975, pp. 102-103.

19. As a department within a bank, a trust department does not have a capital base on which to compute its rate of return on capital. If, at an extreme, a trust department has no assigned capital costs (they approach zero), then its return on capital is potentially limitless. Alternatively, to try to allocate a capital base (and cost) to the department just compounds the difficulties of measuring its "profitability."

20. This section focuses on how to expand an existing trust department. Also, it defines external expansion to include the adding of new locations, whether acquired via mergers or established *de novo.* (An alternative viewpoint is that internal expansion should include *de novo* expansion.) For information about whether and how a bank should start a trust department, see James B. Bexley, "Establishing a Trust Department in a Small Bank," *The Magazine of Bank Administration,* August 1973, pp. 34-36; and Richard B. Evans, "Starting a Trust Department in a Community Bank," *The Magazine of Bank Administration,* June 1976, pp. 28-31.

## INTERNAL EXPANSION

To guide its internal expansion, a trust department's senior officials have to develop a long-range plan that has the support of the bank's directors and senior officers. The plan specifies a set of objectives for the trust department, and it identifies strategies by which the department expects to add profitable services for individuals and corporations.[21] It also estimates the additional resources that the department needs to build its cadre of managers, specialists, and support personnel; and it projects how the department will build its computer capabilities and related analytical systems. In summary, by planning and controlling its expansion, a trust department systematically builds its capabilities, revenue base, and potential profits.

## EXTERNAL EXPANSION VIA MULTIPLE LOCATIONS

Instead of operating from only one location, a trust department can examine the feasibility and net benefits of its operating from additional locations.

### Intrabank Locations

If it is part of the head office of a branch system and/or of the lead affiliate of a multibank holding company, then a trust department can implement a long-range plan to place trust officers in some of the outlying branches and/or affiliates. These outlying officers are mostly generalists who develop and service new trust accounts and who draw on detailed support from specialists and back-up systems located in the principal trust office.[22]

### Interbank Locations

At least two states, Florida and Michigan, have laws that permit banks with trust powers to open and operate trust locations in other banks within the state. In summary, the Michigan law:

- "permits banks with trust departments to contract for trust services with state or national banks that have no trust departments
- "permits contracts between banks having trust departments
- "authorizes the state's FIB [Financial Institutions Bureau] commis-

---

21. A study analyzes various characteristics of individual users of trust services, and it reports that "both customer attitude toward bank services and income-related variables are important delineators of this market." Terrence F. Martell and Robert L. Fitts, "Determinants of Bank Trust Department Usage," *Journal of Bank Research,* Spring 1978, pp. 8-14.

22. As a variant of this satellite strategy, some merging banks and multibank holding companies choose to consolidate their trust operations in one principal location and then maintain satellite trust personnel in selected outlying branches and/or affiliate banks.

sioner to set regulations and approve contracts where at least one of the parties is a state bank.''[23]

A bank with a trust department (a provider bank) and a smaller (host) bank negotiate a trust service contract that includes provisions about: naming the provider bank for all trust accounts, supplying staff and office space, sharing (if any) of revenues and costs, and protecting customer relationships. The Michigan FIB has approved over twenty such trust service contracts. Where feasible, a bank with a trust department can evaluate this contractual avenue for adding locations, and a bank without a trust department can evaluate the net benefits of thus indirectly providing trust services without having to build its own trust department.

## Interstate and International Locations

With minor exceptions, federal and state laws prevent a bank or a bank holding company from expanding its full-service banking offices across state lines. Yet a banking organization located in one state can seek to:

- establish full-service trust affiliates in other states
- open limited-service offices in other states
- expand abroad

Some bank holding companies located in northern states have received state and federal approval to open full-service affiliate trust companies in such sun-belt states as Arizona and Florida. Although they service some of the lead bank's trust clients who have retired to such locations, these affiliate trust companies also seek to build their local clientele. (The Florida legislature subsequently passed a law that in effect prevents additional out-of-state banking organizations from establishing trust affiliates in Florida, but this law is being contested in the courts.) An expansionary trust department thus has to have its legal counsel carefully review the legal feasibility of opening full-service affiliates in other states.

A trust department also can evaluate the feasibility and expected net benefits of opening out-of-state limited-service offices, of which there are three principal types:

- *Representative offices* which, to the extent permitted by state law, act as an outpost to develop and service clients locally whose accounts are primarily serviced by the home office
- *Investment management offices* that provide portfolio-management services for pension funds, corporations, other large organizations, and affluent individuals

---

23. Henry J. Schaberg, " 'Provider' Banks and 'Host' Banks: The New Interbank Trust System in Michigan," *Banking*, February 1977, pp. 44 ff.

● *Farm management offices* that provide a local base for the specialists who service agricultural properties managed by the parent trust company

Also, some large banking organizations have begun to build their international trust capabilities via offshore offices and affiliates that focus on providing investment management services to their clients.

## TRUST DEPARTMENTS AND PUBLIC-POLICY ISSUES

After passage of the Banking Act of 1933 (the Glass-Steagall Act), bank trust departments maintained a low profile until the 1960s, when some critics began to question, and propose changes in, trust practices. To defuse such criticisms, many trust departments have reevaluated, and in some cases revised, their practices, and they seek to increase public understanding of their activities.

### PUBLIC-POLICY DEBATES

This section summarizes the principal issues debated by critics and defenders of trust practices. Both sides have relied more on broad assertions than careful analysis.

### Economic Power

Critics suggest various ways by which trust departments, especially large ones, either have or can have excessive economic power. Industry spokespeople deny the practical extent of such power.

**Aggregate Size and Concentration**   Some critics object to the sheer size and concentration of trust assets. They point out that trust departments administer over $500 billion in total assets and that a small number of large departments accounts for most of these assets.[24] One source notes that, among their assets, "trust departments held $224 billion of common stocks in 1971, a much greater volume than any other type of institutional investor. . . . The bank holdings accounted, moreover, for 21.7 percent of total stocks outstanding (common and preferred), compared with the 8.0 percent held by other major institutional groups combined, namely, the mutual funds, the life insurance companies (including separate accounts), and the property and liability insurance companies."[25] Critics point to and criticize

---

24. These aggregate figures are from *Trust Assets of Insured Commercial Banks–1977*, a joint publication of the Board of Governors of the Federal Reserve System, the Federal Deposit Insurance Corporation, and the Office of the Comptroller of the Currency. This periodical publication is a useful source of numerical information about the trust industry and about the largest bank trust departments.

25. Ehrlich, January 1973, pp. 15-16.

such concentration figures; trust industry spokespeople usually reply that such figures reflect votes of confidence in the types and quality of services provided by bank trust departments.

**Voting Power** Critics also point out that large bank trust departments hold large percentages of the voting shares of some American firms, including other banks.[26] They assert that the large trust departments thus have unacceptable amounts of voting power by which to control American industry.

Trust spokespeople respond that in many cases, although the stock is registered in its name, a trust department is an agent that votes the proxies as directed by trust beneficiaries; and/or it shares voting decisions with cotrustees or coexecutors. Even in cases where several trust departments in total own a large percentage of a firm's voting shares, these spokespeople question why one should assume that the departments all vote the same way on proxy matters.

Some critics contend that bank trust departments generally support existing managements and do not use their voting power to promote the social accountability of firms in which they own stock. Respondents note that this criticism basically contradicts the criticism that trust departments have excessive voting power, and they point out that some trust committees have developed guidelines on how the department should vote its shares on proxy issues that involve corporate social responsibility.

**Impact on Securities Markets** Critics point out various ways in which trust department securities transactions can adversely affect securities markets.

One criticism is that large trust departments concentrate their holdings in shares of large companies that are currently fashionable in securities markets. The critics contend that this selectivity benefits these companies to the detriment of smaller, newer firms that need investment capital.

Trust spokespeople respond that trust departments have fiduciary responsibilities to buy stocks of companies that they judge most attractive and that, because of the size of their portfolios, large trust departments have to focus on shares of firms that have large capitalizations. Sensitive to this criticism, however, some large trust departments have developed common trust funds that diversify among shares of smaller, emerging companies.

A second criticism is that trust-department turnover practices can adversely affect stock prices. (Turnover is a measure of the average frequency at which an investor buys or sells shares; a high turnover rate means that, on average, an investor holds shares for a brief period.)

The SEC conducted a detailed survey of transactions by 50 large trust departments between 1965 and 1969, and it reported that during that period

---

26. For example see "Commercial Banks and Their Trust Activities: Emerging Influence on the American Economy," Staff Report for the Subcommittee on Domestic Finance, House Committee on Banking and Currency, 90th Congress, 2d Session, July 8, 1968.

trust departments about doubled their equities turnover rates for employee benefit trusts. The SEC study also analyzed a sample of stock trading by institutional investors and "found that a stock position change by trust departments, like that by mutual funds, 'sometimes does have a significant price impact' but that 'situations in which the trading of an institution may create or accentuate price movements are more or less matched in number and importance by situations in which the trading behavior of an institution reduces the magnitude of the price impacts of trading by others.' "[27] These mixed results provide inconclusive support for the position(s) of critics or defenders of trust department turnover practices.

### Public Disclosure

As fiduciaries, bank trust departments have always been accountable to clients about their accounts. Trust spokespeople emphasize this confidential fiduciary relationship between a trust department and a client.

In contrast, until the 1970s bank trust departments faced few, if any, requirements to disclose their aggregate activities either to bank supervisory agencies or to the public. Only gradually did supervisory officials, Congressmen, and members of the public become aware of trust departments as "quiet giants" in financial markets.

In 1968 the federal bank supervisory agencies began their periodic surveys of *Trust Assets of Insured Commercial Banks.* Congressional subcommittees began to conduct and publish studies that provided more detailed information about trust activities. In 1974 the OCC announced new disclosure requirements for national banks, the trust departments of which held stocks valued at over $75 million. These banks had to start submitting annual reports about their investment and voting policies and their securities holdings and transactions, and quarterly reports on stock transactions exceeding 10,000 shares or $500,000. The OCC also reevaluated examination practices for trust departments under its supervision. Other federal and state bank supervisory agencies similarly have increased their disclosure requirements for bank trust departments.

Faced with increased disclosure requirements and as a way to help increase public understanding of their activities, trust departments of some major banks now prepare and distribute reports, much like corporate annual reports, that summarize their policies and operations and disclose their principal stockholdings and transactions. While they have thus increased their public disclosure, trust departments face proposals that would require them to disclose more detailed information about their activities, costs, and profits.

### Potential Conflicts of Interest

Observers point out potential conflicts of interest that face officials of trust departments within a bank. Defenders of trust practices reply that banks

---

27. *Institutional Investor Study Report of the Securities and Exchange Commission,* as cited by Ehrlich, January 1973, pp. 17-18.

have systems to prevent such conflicts, and that there have been few, if any, documented abuses.

**Cash Balances**  Critics cite how a bank can benefit if trust officers deposit a trust account's cash balances as a nonearning or low-earning deposit with the bank. Defenders reply that most trust departments, as fiduciaries, have policies and procedures by which a trust account manager deposits temporarily excess cash in money-market instruments.

A related criticism is that trust departments, as part of a bank, have incentives to execute transactions through brokerage firms that hold large deposits with the bank. Some of these linked transactions may fail to give the best executions and transaction costs to the client(s) on whose behalf they are made. Acknowledging that there have been such linkages in the past, trust defenders assert that the practice has ceased and that trust departments have a fiduciary obligation to use the best available execution procedure.

**Privileged Information**  Critics point out possible ways that trust officials can obtain and use "inside information" to the detriment of public participants in securities markets. For example, when he or she negotiates or reviews a loan agreement with a publicly traded corporate client, a bank loan officer may learn of some unusually positive or negative corporate development that is not generally known to investors. The loan officer might relay this information to some trust officers who evaluate its potential market impact and decide whether and how to engage in transactions in the stock on behalf of their clients.

Defenders of trust practices point out that most trust departments have policies that establish an ethical barrier (a "Chinese Wall") between their trust and nontrust activities. The policies prohibit loan officers and trust officers from exchanging privileged information, and, in some cases, they involve a physical separation of a bank's trust and nontrust departments.

## PUBLIC-POLICY PROPOSALS

Critics of trust practices have proposed several major changes:

- increased disclosure requirements
- required separation of trust business from banks (The degree of proposed separation ranges from total separation to having trust companies as coaffiliates within bank holding companies.)
- limitations on a trust department's holdings of a company's voting securities

Although they accept the likelihood, and possible benefits, of increased disclosure, defenders of trust practices generally reject proposals for required separation and investment limitations. They view such proposals as infeasible and/or inappropriate. Yet in view of the continuing debate and proposals, banks and their trust departments may benefit from some contingency planning to adjust to such proposals, if adopted.[28]

## SUMMARY

Compared to most other banking activities, a bank trust department is a low-profile operation that:

- is not reported as part of a bank's consolidated report of condition
- is largely autonomous (the "Chinese Wall") from a bank's nontrust operations
- discreetly conducts its specialized fiduciary services on behalf of wealthy families, large firms, and other select clients

Yet many bankers and nonbanker citizens can benefit from knowing more about a bank trust department's: services, structure, strategies, and susceptibility to public-policy debates.

A trust department acts as a fiduciary that holds and/or services a client's assets. There are many variants of this fiduciary responsibility. As a trustee or as an agent, a trust department services beneficiaries of estates and beneficiaries of living trusts that have been established with it. To service its corporate clients, a trust department also serves in such capacities as: administrator of employee benefit accounts, registrar, transfer agent, dividend disbursement agent, and/or trustee of bond issues.

If it has—or evaluates whether to have—a trust department, a bank views its trust activities as part of the full set of services that it offers to attract and retain select customers. It realizes that among its fiduciary services:

- all require high standards of integrity and professionalism, as codified, for example, in the prudent man rule
- some are subject to price ceilings as set by statutes, regulations, and/or court rulings
- some, such as corporate trust services, are subject to intense competition from other large banks and nonbank firms

While it recognizes such constraints, a bank examines ways by which its trust department can contribute to the size and stability of the total bank's stream of profits.

A trust department is a pyramidal structure, at the top of which is the bank's board of directors. These officials direct and oversee the trust

28. For more information about the public-policy issues and proposals, see Donald S. Green and Mary Schuelke, *The Trust Activities of the Banking Industry,* a study prepared for the Trustees of the Banking Research Fund, Association of Reserve City Bankers, 1975, especially Section VI and Appendix B. Also, "Trust Separation from the Bank," *Banking,* February 1974, pp. 26-29 ff.

operations, which are administered by trust officers, who in turn have the support of legal counsel, portfolio managers and analysts, and computer systems personnel. Some large trust departments also have specialists who manage businesses, farms, and ranches and/or corporate-finance specialists who provide advisory and private-placement services for corporate clients.

Banks face conceptual and measurement problems when they try to evaluate and manage their trust department profitability. While it recognizes these problems, as a basic framework a trust department tries to estimate the extent to which its fees, credit balances, and associated benefits cover the department's direct costs and allocated overhead costs. A trust department also analyzes how it can increase and/or decrease these components of its profit equation. Some departments use computer-based systems to help them in their profitability analysis and management.

A trust department can expand internally by adding personnel, services, and systems; and it can expand externally by adding new locations from which it provides its services. Within a multioffice banking organization, the head-office or lead-bank trust department can expand its service locations to include selected branches and/or coaffiliate banks. A trust department also can evaluate the legal feasibility and expected net benefits of its expanding intrastate, via service contracts with outlying banks, and/or interstate via affiliate trust companies, representative offices, investment management offices, and farm management offices. A large trust department also can evaluate whether to add international offices and/or trust affiliates.

Despite—or perhaps because of—their low profile, bank trust departments are the center of a public-policy debate. Critics charge that trust departments have, or can have: excessive economic power, distortional effects on securities markets, inadequate public accountability, and potential conflicts of interest. Trust department spokespeople try to rebut and/or defuse such criticisms. One outcome has been that bank trust departments have begun to disclose and explain more about their activities and about their internal procedures to avoid potential misuses of trust powers. Over time this disclosure process will increase citizen awareness of trust services and practices.

# 17

# EXPANSIONARY BANKING SYSTEMS: AN INTRODUCTION

The preceding chapters focus on a bank as a complex portfolio of assets, liabilities, and capital. This portfolio perspective helps one to develop a comprehensive view of bank management and bank operations.

This chapter and the subsequent four chapters focus on strategies by which banking organizations expand into new domestic and international markets. When it plans to expand, a banking organization has to evaluate the principal constraints associated with each expansion strategy. This chapter introduces why most banks face statutory and regulatory restrictions on multioffice expansion. The subsequent four chapters then focus on how banking organizations expand, subject to constraints, and how, over time, they work toward gradual removal of the constraints.

## FOUR PRINCIPAL EXPANSION STRATEGIES

A banking organization can expand:

- internally
- by branching
- by using a bank holding company
- by building its international operations

These principal expansion strategies are not equally feasible for all banks.

### INTERNAL EXPANSION

A bank expands internally when it increases its total deposits and assets over time without adding or acquiring new offices or affiliates. In this process, a bank competes primarily for deposits and other sources of funds, increases its loan portfolio, and develops and markets new services. As it expands internally, a bank faces such constraints as:

- the size of the market(s) that it can realistically serve
- laws and regulations that limit which services it can offer and how it offers them (for example, the prohibition of interest on demand deposits)
- competition from banks and from nonbank financial institutions
- its available resources, especially its capital and its managerial resources

Subject to such constraints, virtually any bank, no matter what its size or location, develops and executes plans to expand internally.

## EXPANSIONARY BRANCHING

Expansionary branching occurs when a bank adds physical locations from which it conducts its banking operations.[1] Traditionally, these branches have been "brick-and-mortar-type" buildings that sometimes are called facilities, offices, or stations. Because of recent technological developments, banks and their customers can conduct many banking transactions through networks of computer terminals, and so there is extensive debate as to whether or not to classify such terminals as branches.

If it adds branches, a bank can enter new geographical areas and/or increase the number of physical locations in a community that it already serves. By branching into new areas an expansionary bank finds itself less constrained by the size and growth rate of the geographical area(s) that it already serves. Other constraints, however, face a bank that wants to expand via new branches:

- laws, especially state laws, that typically limit: the areas in which a bank can branch, the types of services that a branch can offer, and, at times, the procedures by which a bank can add branches
- legal and regulatory criteria whereby a bank has to demonstrate the financial, competitive, and public merits of a proposed new branch
- probable opposition from banks and other financial institutions located near where a new branch is proposed
- financial and personnel resources needed to establish and operate additional physical locations

Subject to such constraints, virtually any bank can branch if its state law permits branching. Large banks, however, with their financial, managerial, and technical resources, generally can more readily expand their branch systems than can most small or medium-sized banks. One basic

---

1. An alternative view is that a bank expands internally if it builds new (*de novo*) branches and that it expands externally if it acquires other banks that it then converts to branches. An expansionary banking system, however, typically uses both branching methods as parts of a comprehensive branching strategy, and so this book includes both methods in its discussion of expansionary branching.

way by which a large bank can add branches is to acquire—to the extent permitted by law—smaller banks and convert them to branches.

## USING A BANK HOLDING COMPANY

By using a bank holding company (BHC), an expansionary banking organization can enter geographical and product markets that are not conveniently open to a bank. Some states prohibit or restrict a bank's branching opportunities, but they permit a company to own banks in markets throughout the state. In such states a parent BHC can develop a *de facto* branch system. Also, to the extent permitted by federal law and regulation, a BHC can expand into nonbanking activities; and its nonbanking affiliates can operate offices in various states even though a bank, by law, can operate full-service branches in, at most, one state.[2]

Constraints face a banking organization that wants to expand indirectly via a BHC:

- some states prohibit a company from controlling more than one bank and thereby prevent a BHC from expanding by adding new affiliate banks to its system
- a BHC is subject to a federal law, the Bank Holding Company Act, as administered by the FRS
- by statute, the FRS defines the permissible nonbanking activities in which a BHC can engage, and it controls a BHC's formation or acquisition of banks and of firms engaged in permissible nonbanking activities
- probable opposition from banks and bank-related firms that would face competition from new affiliates of an expansionary BHC
- financial and personnel resources needed to establish and operate additional banking and permissible nonbanking affiliates

If its state prohibits or restricts branching but permits a BHC to control more than one bank, then an expansionary banking organization—especially a large one—is likely to develop and expand a BHC that controls various banking and permissible nonbanking affiliates. If, because of state law, it cannot use the BHC vehicle to acquire additional banks, a large expansionary banking organization will likely be part of a one-bank holding company that can expand into permissible nonbanking activities. Also, even in states where it can branch state-wide, a large branch system typically is part of a one-bank holding company that can expand its permissible nonbanking activities. (Although it is primarily large banking organizations that thus use a BHC vehicle to expand into new geographical and product markets, many controlling stockholders of small and medium-sized banks gain tax

---

2. There are minor exceptions to this general prohibition of interstate branching.

advantages by indirectly controlling the bank via a nonexpansionary one-bank holding company.)

## INTERNATIONAL EXPANSION

International expansion occurs when a banking organization expands its international operations into new services and new geographical areas. If it adds new services and staff to its head-office international banking department, then a bank can be said to be expanding internally. Usually, however, such head-office expansion is part of a broader strategy by which a bank expands into additional markets by adding overseas offices and investing in overseas affiliate banks and bank-related firms.

If it wants to expand abroad, a banking organization faces the following types of constraints:

- requisite governmental permission from the host country to operate within its political boundaries
- federal laws and regulations that control foreign expansion by American banking organizations
- probable competition, and at times opposition, from banks that already operate in a potential host country
- extensive financial resources, specialized personnel, and stringent control systems in order to accept and control the additional risks of multinational operations

Only large banking organizations—and especially those that want directly to serve multinational clients—have the resources and incentives to expand into foreign banking markets. Most other American banks use the correspondent banking system to service their customers' occasional international banking transactions. Yet even as some large American banks expand abroad, large foreign banks expand into various metropolitan markets in the United States and thereby present new competition for banks already in these markets.

## SUMMARY

Exhibit 17-1 summarizes how an expansionary organization can expand via one or more of four principal paths (internal, branching, BHC, and international) and also indicates that such expansion generally poses new competition for nonexpansionary banks. In two of the domestic expansion paths, however, an expansionary bank may acquire another bank and convert it to a branch or to a BHC affiliate.

Previous chapters discuss how a bank can expand internally. Therefore this chapter and the subsequent four chapters focus on expansionary banking via branching, BHCs, and international operations.

**EXHIBIT 17-1**

**Principal Banking Expansion Strategies**

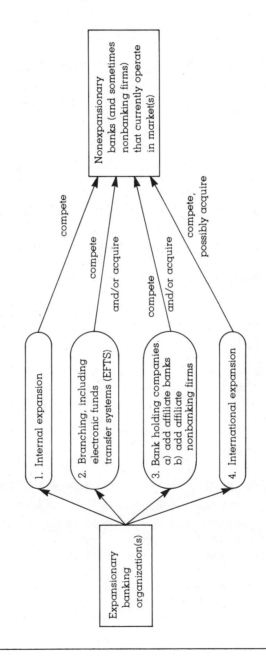

*Note:* This schematic framework summarizes the dynamics of expansionary banking organizations, the theme of Chapters 17-21.

## EXPANSIONARY OR NONEXPANSIONARY BANKING ORGANIZATIONS

At the risk of oversimplifying some complex issues, it is helpful initially to classify banks as either expansionary or nonexpansionary.

### EXPANSIONARY BANKING ORGANIZATIONS

An expansionary banking organization typically is: large, based in a major metropolitan area, and anxious to expand both internally and—to the extent feasible—externally via branches, a BHC, and, in some cases, international operations.

Often—but with notable exceptions—a large metropolitan bank has traditionally focused on wholesale banking (the servicing of major firms, other banks, governmental units, and wealthy individuals), and it has not actively developed retail services or branches by which to serve many small firms and individual customers. In many cases a metropolitan bank thus developed its wholesale services not only by choice but also because of state laws that prohibited or severely restricted its opportunities to expand into new markets via branches and/or coaffiliate banks. If as a wholesale bank it could meet its growth objectives, a large metropolitan bank lacked strong motives to expand into outlying areas. However, by the 1950s and 1960s a large metropolitan bank typically foresaw slower expansion opportunities for its traditional wholesale services; and, at the same time, it observed that many current and potential retail customers were locating in outlying suburbs and smaller, outlying cities. Therefore it concluded that, to maintain its growth, it would have to follow its current customers who migrated to outlying areas and to compete for new customers in these areas. Often, however, it found its new expansion plans blocked by state laws that restricted the extent to which a bank could add branches and/or coaffiliate banks via a BHC. Among the supporters of such laws were, and are, nonexpansionary banks.

### NONEXPANSIONARY BANKING ORGANIZATIONS

A nonexpansionary banking organization typically is a small or medium-sized bank that is located outside the center of a major city. Whether it is located in a city neighborhood or, more generally, in an outlying suburban or rural community, a nonexpansionary bank primarily serves retail customers in its immediate area. Although, over time, a nonexpansionary bank expands via internal growth and, where permitted, by adding some branches, it still is helpful to contrast such a bank to most large money-center banks that have the motivations and resources rapidly to expand into new markets.

While it has some of the world's largest banks, the United States also has thousands of small and medium-sized nonexpansionary banks scattered throughout most states. This deposit-size distribution and localized banking contrasts to that of most nations, which have a comparatively small number of large banks tht operate regional or nationwide networks of branches.

Within the United States there has been a long tradition of fostering and preserving many small and medium-sized banks, each of which primarily serves nearby customers. Historically, many states set low entry barriers (such as the initial capital requirements) so that groups of qualified people could readily obtain a charter for a new bank in their community. Many states, in their original Constitution or by subsequent legislation, restricted multioffice banking. These laws impeded the physical expansion of large banks into new areas, helped preserve the independence of outlying banks, and made formation of a new bank the principal way by which a growing community could gain a banking office. Federal policy also has helped foster and preserve many nonexpansionary banks. Chartering procedures for national banks have required less capital for new banks in small communities. The FRS, with its discount window and services, provides benefits to small and medium-sized member banks; and the FDIC insures most deposits (up to $40,000) in a bank of any size. Federal laws prohibit interstate branching, restrict bank mergers, and control BHC acquisitions of banks. This heritage of public policy, laws, and regulations thus contributes to the present banking structure in which there are: (1) large, usually urban-based, expansionary banking organizations and (2) many more smaller, outlying, nonexpansionary banking organizations.

## RESTRICTING MULTIOFFICE EXPANSION: AN ONGOING DEBATE

Spokespersons for expansionary banking organizations present reasons why public policy should reduce barriers to multioffice expansion by banks. In opposition, spokespersons for many nonexpansionary organizations present their reasons why public policy should continue to restrict such expansion, especially by large money-center banks. Other parties, such as legislators, bank regulatory officials, study commissions, and academic researchers, have professional responsibilities to evaluate whether—and, if so, how—to modify public policy that restricts bank expansion.

Although the issues are complex and the evidence basically inconclusive, here is a composite summary of the cases for and against reducing the restrictions on external expansion, especially by large banking organizations. The objective of this summary is to present the principal issues of a major, prolonged debate. Subsequent chapters more fully develop the specific issues and evidence cited in this summary of opposing cases.[3]

3. Five recent, comprehensive summaries of the principal issues and evidence associated with multioffice banking are the following. Norman N. Bowsher, "Have Multibank Holding Companies Affected Commercial Bank Performance?" *Review* (Federal Reserve Bank of St. Louis), April 1978, pp. 8-15. Dale S. Drum, "MBHCs: Evidence after Two Decades of Regulation," *Business Conditions* (Federal Reserve Bank of Chicago), December 1976, pp. 3-15. Gary G. Gilbert and William A. Longbrake, "The Effects of Branching by Financial Institutions on Competition, Productive Efficiency and Stability: An Examination of the Evidence," *Journal of Bank Research,* (Part I) Autumn 1973, pp. 154-167, (Part II) Winter 1974, pp. 298-307. Robert J. Lawrence and Samuel H. Talley, "An Assessment of Bank Holding Companies," *Federal Reserve Bulletin,* January 1976, pp. 15-21. Larry R. Mote, "The Perennial Issue: Branch Banking," *Business Conditions* (Federal Reserve Bank of Chicago), February 1974, pp. 3-23.

## A CASE FOR REDUCING RESTRICTIONS ON MULTIOFFICE EXPANSION

As an initial question, why restrict banks from adding new locations from which they can transact banking services? A nonbanking firm, subject to basic antitrust laws and to financial and managerial constraints, usually is free to place service units in any market that it believes will contribute to its long-run profitability. Therefore why should not a bank have similar freedom to decide whether and how to enter a new geographical market? On this basis, the burden of proof should be on those who favor restrictions on multioffice expansion.

Its proponents cite various ways in which multioffice expansion can produce public benefits.

### Bank Size

First, a bank that can readily expand into new areas has an opportunity quickly to increase its size, especially if it acquires other, usually smaller, banks. This larger size should enable a banking organization to:

- develop more depth of management and specialized personnel
- develop and offer more specialized services for various customers
- achieve economies of scale, whereby its per-unit production costs will be less than those of a smaller firm that produces similar services
- have a larger capital base, and thus a larger lending limit for any one borrower
- compete more effectively against other large banking organizations that operate in regional and national markets

Thus, primarily because of its size, a large multioffice banking organization can effectively serve its various current and potential customers.

### Diversification

A large banking organization, especially if it operates in various geographical markets, can broadly diversify its sources and uses of funds among various customers that differ in size, location, and sensitivity to economic conditions. If other factors such as capital base are similar, then a large bank with a broadly diversified portfolio should be able to accept greater credit and interest-rate risks within its portfolio than can a bank with a small, less diversified portfolio. Alternatively, if other factors such as the credit and interest-rate risks are similar, then a large bank with a broadly diversified portfolio should be able to operate with lower capital ratios than can a bank with a small, less diversified portfolio. In the first case the bank with the broadly diversified portfolio should be able to increase the risk level of its loans without significantly increasing its total risk; in the second case it can operate with a lower cost of capital funds. In either case it may pass on some of the diversification benefits to its customers.

## Funds Flows

Especially if its branches or affiliate banks operate across a broadly diversified economic area, a large banking organization can conveniently transfer funds from surplus areas to deficit areas. To illustrate, some branches (or affiliates) in mature economic communities will generate more deposits than they can lend in their communities. Within a branch system, these fund-gathering branches can transfer funds to other branches in which the loan demand exceeds the local deposits. If viewed as separate entities rather than as part of a consolidated system, some of these latter branches can show loan-to-deposit ratios that exceed 100 percent. This internal transfer process may help finance economic development of emerging areas within a state.

## Safety

A large, geographically dispersed banking organization, with its financial and managerial resources and its diversification opportunities, is less likely to fail than is a small bank that has limited resources and is dependent on local economic conditions. Proponents of this position note that many small local banks failed in the 1920s and 1930s, during which time there were fewer failures among large banking systems in the United States and in major industrialized nations.

## Services

A large multioffice system can conveniently offer a wide range of banking services throughout its network of physical locations. For example, at its various locations a large organization can conveniently offer specialized lending programs, trust services, and international banking transactions. Also, by strategically placing its branches and computer banking terminals throughout the area it serves, a large banking organization can have facilities near where its current and potential customers live and work and can service these customers as they travel throughout the area.

## Competition

Its advocates assert that benefits of competition will follow from reducing restrictions against multioffice banking. To illustrate, if it knows that other banking offices cannot conveniently enter its area because of restrictions on multioffice banking, then in some cases a nonexpansionary bank may fail to meet the banking needs of its customers and community. In contrast, if such restrictions are eased, then such a bank will behave more competitively because it anticipates that otherwise an expansionary system may acquire it or apply to place a new branch or affiliate bank in the community. Also, because of their size, diversification, and total-system perspective, multioffice systems are likely to have more offices competing in some local geographical areas that otherwise would warrant fewer, separately chartered, separately capitalized, nonaffiliate banks.

### Summary

Proponents of multioffice banking usually cite how, in contrast to a diffused structure with many small banks, multioffice systems will likely achieve private and public benefits because of their:

- typically large size
- diversification benefits
- convenient intrasystem funds flows
- lower probability of failure
- convenient networks of offices that provide a wide range of banking services
- procompetitive expansionary behavior

As with many prolonged public-policy debates, opposing parties can persuasively present their case and point out weaknesses in their opponent's case.

## A CASE AGAINST REDUCING RESTRICTIONS ON MULTIOFFICE EXPANSION

Opponents of liberalized multioffice banking stress how banks differ from most nonbanking firms. A bank is to meet prudently the depository and borrowing needs of its customers and community. Because its basic functions thus differ from those, for example, of a chain of retail stores, a bank is subject to many legal and regulatory constraints, such as: interest-rate ceilings, reserve requirements, investment restrictions, loan restrictions, capital requirements, and periodic examinations. These constraints all reflect a public-policy view that banking differs substantially from most other businesses. From this viewpoint, one cannot urge removal of multioffice restrictions merely because many nonbanking firms do not face similar restrictions.

Opponents of multioffice expansion usually rebut each point of the case for such expansion.

### Bank Size

Multioffice banking systems on average are larger than most small nonexpansionary organizations, but many of the presumed size benefits are available through the correspondent banking system. A nonexpansionary bank, for example, can offer such customer services as credit cards and international transactions, and it can refer its customers to the trust services of its correspondent bank(s). By means of loan participations with its correspondent bank(s) or possibly with nonbank institutions, a nonexpansionary bank can conveniently meet appropriate loan requests that exceed its legal lending limit. A nonexpansionary bank can send its key personnel to development programs at its major correspondent bank or at schools of banking that often are staffed by experienced officers from large banks. Concerning key personnel, opponents of multioffice expansion often assert that the owner-managers of a nonexpansionary bank typically have a deeper understanding of and commitment to their community than do transitory managers of multioffice banking organizations.

### Diversification

Although it cannot diversify its sources of funds as broadly as can most large multioffice banking systems, a nonexpansionary bank can diversify its assets by types, maturities, and geographical locations of borrowers. It can be a net seller of federal funds, invest in a variety of investment securities, and participate in large loans originated by its principal correspondent(s).

### Funds Flows

As parts of an integrated financial system, nonexpansionary banks can transfer funds from surplus areas to deficit areas. One principal way is for a bank to be a net seller of federal funds to other, usually larger, banks. Another way is for a bank to engage in upstream or downstream loan participations.

Although both the correspondent banking system and multioffice systems provide mechanisms for interregional transfers, a basic normative issue is *to what extent should there be such interregional funds flows?* Opponents of multioffice banking assert that such a system is likely to transfer funds from outlying locations to its major office(s) so that the system can service its large corporate customers. These opponents further assert that, in contrast, a local nonexpansionary bank is likely to focus on the legitimate credit needs of its local community.

### Safety

Even if the proportion of failures is lower among large expansionary banks than among smaller nonexpansionary banks, this is not a sufficient reason to reduce restrictions on multioffice banking.

Inappropriate economic policies contributed, at least in part, to the many failures among small banks during the 1920s and 1930s. Subsequent national economic policies seek to avoid a repetition of Depression conditions. Also, the advent of FDIC insurance reduces the likelihood that a bank will face a run in which depositors rush to withdraw their funds from a bank rumored to be in financial difficulties.

Some large banks survived the Great Depression not by their own resources but because they received financial support from the federally funded Reconstruction Finance Corporation.

Even if large banks are less likely to fail than smaller ones, the total social cost of an occasional large-bank failure can exceed that of more frequent failures of small banks. Compared to some failures among dispersed smaller banks, an occasional large-bank failure potentially involves more depositors whose accounts are not fully insured by the FDIC, more borrowers whose credit lines are disrupted, extensive interbanking relationships (for example, in federal funds transactions), and widespread publicity that leads people to have less confidence in other banks. Some large banks failed in the 1960s and 1970s. To reduce the probabilities of such publicized failures in the future, the regulatory agencies incur costs to regulate and closely monitor large banks.

At least partly because they tried to expand rapidly, some large banks encountered serious control problems that jeopardized their survival. Multioffice banking restrictions reduce opportunities for some banks thus to expand beyond their planning and control capabilities.

### Services

Customer conveniences of large multioffice systems do not clearly surpass those provided by nonexpansionary banks.

A customer technically has access to a wide variety of specialized services, such as trust and international banking services, at any office of a multioffice system. Realistically, however, each office in a multioffice system cannot afford to have resident specialists in areas such as trusts and international banking. Therefore a system's small outlying offices refer their customers' nonroutine transactions to specialists at the major office(s). This intrasystem specialization is similar to that by which nonexpansionary banks use their large correspondent banks to service their customers' infrequent specialized transactions.

The offices of some systems are autonomous to the extent that a regular customer of one office (branch or affiliate) cannot conveniently transact business at another office. Although some multioffice systems have developed customer identification procedures and centralized customer information files to expedite such intrasystem transactions, retail customers can achieve similar convenience by using a major bank credit card at any bank that participates in this broader interbank system.

Various studies document that, on average, there are more banking offices per capita in major population areas where branching is permitted than there are in similar areas in which branching is prohibited or very restricted. The statistics are less conclusive that multioffice banking systems provide more offices per capita in small rural towns. Thus, in states that ease multioffice restrictions, city dwellers will likely gain the convenience of more banking offices per capita, but rural residents cannot count on similar convenience benefits.

### Competition

The lifting of multioffice restrictions may lead to various anticompetitive outcomes, especially in the long run. Studies report that, compared to similar states that prohibit or curtail multioffice banking, states that permit extensive multioffice systems: (1) generally contain fewer banking organizations—but often more banking offices, and (2) the largest three to five banks usually account for a larger proportion of total bank deposits within a state. These facts indicate that multioffice banking generally leads to a more concentrated banking structure at the state level.

To what extent will several large banking organizations compete aggressively when their offices face each other in most major markets within a state, especially if other banking organizations cannot readily enter these markets? One such barrier exists when a state restricts entry by out-of-state banking organizations. Another barrier occurs if the large organizations use a *preemptive strategy* of trying to open offices in promising sites before newly chartered banking organizations can justify entry into such locations. A third barrier occurs when, because of managerial and/or capital constraints, a state's smaller banking organizations cannot mobilize the resources to compete effectively against large, embedded, multioffice systems.

Value judgments also enter the debate about expanded multioffice banking. Some people object to the potential economic and political power of large multioffice systems, especially those based in distant cities. These people contrast such concentrated power centers to the diffused centers that exist in a system of local, nonexpansionary banks. They also note how, in many countries, the dominant multioffice banking systems have been nationalized or are vulnerable to nationalization.

### Summary

Opponents of expanded multioffice banking either reject or rebut many of the benefits claimed for such multioffice systems. They note how many nonexpansionary banks can:

- share in the size benefits achieved by their large correspondent bank(s) and also retain their commitment to their local communities
- diversify their portfolios of assets
- transfer funds among geographical areas, to the extent that there should be such interregional funds flows
- avoid imposing substantial social costs of failure on their customers and society
- provide convenient services as needed by their customers
- serve their local markets without becoming part of systems that have offices in local markets throughout a broader region such as a state
- be part of a diffused system of economic and political power

Although it, too, contains many valid points, the case against reducing restrictions on multioffice banking is no more conclusive then the one for reducing such restrictions. Aware of these opposing, basically inconclusive, positions concerning multioffice restrictions, various bankers and public officials have to make decisions about whether and how to revise such restrictions.

## MULTIOFFICE EXPANSION AND PUBLIC POLICY

The debate about multioffice expansion spans many decades of American banking, and it is unlikely soon to be resolved. In practice, both expansionary and nonexpansionary bankers have to operate subject to the current, and slowly changing, restrictions on multioffice operations.

With its resources and motivations to add new offices (or affiliates), an expansionary banking organization continually explores ways to expand within its current framework of multioffice restrictions. For example, if it faces branching restrictions, an expansionary organization can try to develop networks of computer terminals that perform many retail banking functions and yet may not be subject to applicable branching restrictions. Over time, the expansionary organization also can support legislation or regulations that would liberalize current multioffice restrictions. The next four chapters focus on how expansionary banking organizations thus can expand subject to current multioffice constraints and how they can develop and support proposals that would liberalize current constraints.

The officers and principal stockholders of a nonexpansionary banking organization often oppose multioffice expansion on principle and/or because they want to shield their bank from entry of new, nearby offices of large expansionary systems. Yet these opponents eventually may find it advantageous to sell their nonexpansionary bank to an expansionary banking organization that has the resources and willingness to pay a premium for the acquisition. Thus, over time, some bankers who oppose multioffice expansion will willingly accept *controlled* expansion by large multioffice systems. The next two chapters more fully examine the processes by which a nonexpansionary bank may decide to become a branch or affiliate of an expansionary banking organization.

Legislators and bank regulators have to evaluate public-policy issues associated with multioffice restrictions. One issue is the extent to which multioffice expansion will likely benefit various categories of bank customers. A second, and interrelated issue, is the extent to which multioffice expansion will likely affect concentration and competition in various banking markets. To try to answer such complex questions, these public officials can review position papers by interested banking organizations and professional studies by researchers associated with academic institutions, bank regulatory agencies, legislative staffs, and special study commissions.

## SUMMARY

An expansionary bank can evaluate whether and how it can:

- expand internally
- add branches, at times via mergers
- use a bank holding company
- expand internationally

If it concludes that its resource base and/or the current legal and regulatory restrictions preclude it from some of the strategies, a bank then selects from among its feasible strategies, and plans how to modify its current constraints over time.

Many large money-center banks have the motivations and resources to try to expand into new geographical and product markets. Often, however, these markets contain smaller nonexpansionary banks that oppose such entry. Many of these nonexpansionary banks support laws and regulations that impede multioffice expansion. Thus, while there is a gradual consolidation trend within banking, the United States contains (1) large, usually urban-based, expansionary banking organizations and (2) many more smaller, outlying, nonexpansionary banking organizations.

American banking has engaged in a lengthy, sometimes emotional, debate concerning whether, and, if so, how to reduce barriers to multioffice expansion. Proponents of reduced multioffice restrictions present a persuasive case why such liberalization favors competition and how it will benefit banking customers. Those who oppose reduced restrictions similarly present a persuasive case why such liberalization can reduce competition, especially in the long run, and why it is unlikely to provide net benefits to banking customers. Most bank officers are not disinterested participants in the debate, and some levels of the debate involve value judgments.

Legislators and bank regulators have to evaluate the public-policy dimensions of multioffice restrictions. When they deliberate about possible changes in such restrictions, these officials can review extensive published research that tries to measure various benefits and costs associated with the restrictions and with changes in them. While multioffice restrictions will likely change over time, expansionary banking organizations have to operate imaginatively within the context of current and probable future restrictions. Subsequent chapters examine how they can thus try to expand via branching, bank holding companies, and international operations.

# 18

# BRANCH SYSTEMS

If it adds physical locations from which it conducts banking activites, a bank can expand into new geographical areas and add to its customer roster. To implement such an expansionary strategy, a bank has to analyze a series of issues:

- laws and regulations that restrict branching activities
- whether and how to add new (*de novo*) branches
- whether and how to acquire banks to convert into branches
- probable changes in branching restrictions
- principal alternatives to expansionary branching

This chapter examines this sequence of topics.

## BRANCHING RESTRICTIONS

Each bank faces laws and regulations that restrict its flexibility to conduct banking activities at locations away from its head office. These restrictions reflect a legacy of opposing views and interests.

### A CAPSULE HISTORY OF BRANCHING RESTRICTIONS

Early in American history, some banks, such as the first and second Banks of the United States, operated branches in cities away from their head office.[1] Residents of some outlying regions objected to distant banks operating branches in their local areas, and opponents also objected to the perceived centralization of financial power in distant big-city banks.

---

1. This section draws on Larry R. Mote, "The Perennial Issue: Branch Banking," *Business Conditions* (Federal Reserve Bank of Chicago), February 1974, pp. 3-23

Meanwhile, even branching proponents noted how difficult it was for a head office to supervise the activities of geographically distant branches. Alexander Hamilton expressed concern that problems in distant branches could jeopardize a total branch system. Thus, for logistical reasons most banks chose not to develop branch networks and so branching critics initially had little to oppose.

In 1863 Congress passed the National Bank Act that provides for the chartering and supervision of national banks. The Congressmen did not discuss branching in their debates preceding this new law. Yet the law contained a statement that required the organizers of a national bank to specify: "the *place* where its operations of discount and deposits were to be carried on, designating the state, territory, or district, and also the particular county and city, town, or village"(italics added). If one strictly interprets the singular noun *place*, this statement precludes a national bank from operating at more than one location. From 1865 until 1922, the Comptrollers of the Currency applied this strict interpretation of *place*. Thus national banks did not have branches, except for national banks that had converted from state charters and, under an amendment to the National Bank Act, were permitted to retain any existing branches.

Until about 1916 the issue of branching restrictions was comparatively quiet. Some banking officials and study commissions advocated that national banks receive permission to branch, especially into small towns that might not otherwise have a separate bank. These advocates cited the prevalence of branches throughout other nations.

While a national bank could not add branches, a state-chartered bank could do so if its state law did not expressly prohibit branching. Thus in states where branching was feasible, some state banks began to develop branch networks. Although advances in communications and transportation enabled them more effectively to supervise their branches, most of these expansionary banks chose to limit their branching networks to the head-office city. A major exception was California, where statewide branching was permitted in 1909. There several large state banks began to develop extensive branching systems.

As branch systems began to emerge, many local bankers began to oppose the spread of multioffice banking. These local bankers emphasized how, in their judgment, a system of independent community banks was preferable to large multioffice systems. Also, these local bankers must have had some concerns as to how expansionary branching systems might affect the future profitability and valuation of their local banks.

The topic of branch banking erupted in acrimonious debate at the 1916 convention of The American Bankers Association (ABA). Although there was sharp division among them, the attending bankers passed a resolution opposing "branch banking in any form." Later, in 1922, the participants at the ABA convention passed a resolution stating that "branch banking is contrary to public policy, violates the basic principles of our Government and concentrates the credit of the nation and the power of money in the hands of a few."

In 1922 the Comptroller of the Currency, concerned that national banks were at a competitive disadvantage in states where state banks could branch, reversed his predecessors' interpretation of *place*. He ruled that, in a state where a state bank could branch, a national bank could open limited-service branches within its home-office city.

In 1927 Congress passed the McFadden Act, which authorizes national banks to establish full-service branches in states where state banks can branch. Initially, the Act restricted these new branches to a national bank's head-office city. The House sponsor of this Act saw it as "an anti-branch-banking measure severely restricting the further spread of branch banking in the United States." Shortly after passage of the McFadden Act, six states passed laws to prohibit branch banking. The McFadden Act was modified in 1933 when Congress passed legislation allowing national banks to add branches outside their home-office city "*subject to* the restrictions as to location imposed by the law of the State on state banks" (italics added).

As one observer graphically summarizes the situation: "The political struggle between pro- and anti-branching forces has settled into a continuing trench warfare, with attrition on both sides but no victory in sight for either. . . ." Each side develops its persuasive case and tries to rebut its opponents' case. Each side works hard to present its case to public officials and interested citizens. Over time, various federal and state officials and study commissions have developed position statements on the issue of branching restrictions. Although the gradual trend is toward reduction of such restrictions, senior bank officials have to develop and implement branching strategies within the context of current and probable future branching restrictions.

## APPLICABLE BRANCHING RESTRICTIONS

The McFadden Act subjects a national bank to the branching restrictions of the state in which it is located. No state has legislation that permits interstate branching by state banks, and in effect the McFadden Act disallows interstate branching by national banks.[2]

Although they vary widely, state branching restrictions fall into three principal categories:

- permissible services
- geographical constraints
- procedural requirements

Each state's branching restrictions reflect some combination of these basic constraints.

---

2. There are isolated cases of interstate branching. For example, special legislation permits the Bank of California, which is headquartered in California, to retain some full-service branches in Oregon and Washington.

## Permissible Services

Some states have laws that permit a bank to operate *full-service branches* (FSBs), whereby a bank can offer any permissible banking service at any of its branches. This is permissive legislation; it allows a bank to operate FSBs; it does not require or expect a branch system to operate each branch as an FSB.

Other states permit a bank to offer a full set of banking services at its home office, but they restrict the services that a bank can offer at other locations. These states permit a bank to have *limited-service facilities* (LSFs) at which customers typically can make deposits and withdrawals but cannot open accounts or apply for loans. States that permit LSFs use various names for them, such as branch, facility, detached facility, and paying and receiving station. Whatever the technical name used in their state, a bank's officials focus on interpreting the range of services that their bank can offer at its LSFs. In some cases they have to rely on legal counsel and court tests to determine whether their bank can offer a new banking service at its LSFs.

While state laws thus differ in their service constraints on—and names for—"branches," for convenience most banking people use the term *branch* for any banking facility (FSB or LSF) that is detached from its bank's head office.

## Geographical Constraints

States also vary in their laws restricting the geographical area within which a bank can operate branches. There are three principal categories of geographical constraints on branching:

*Unit (non-branch) banking,* where a bank has to conduct all of its banking business from one location; it can have no branches. (Seldom is the restriction total; most unit-banking states permit a bank to operate one or two LSFs within a close range of its principal location.)

*Limited branching*, where a bank can operate branches within a defined subarea of the state. Depending on its state's limited-branching law, a bank typically can operate branches within one of the following subareas—its head office:

- city
- county
- county plus adjacent counties
- county plus adjacent counties and additional counties that in total comprise a statutory banking "region" within the state

While most use political boundary constraints, some limited-branching states permit a bank to operate branches within a specific mileage radius of its head office.

*Statewide branching,* where a bank can operate branches throughout its state.

Some state laws have additional variants on the basic three-way geographical classification of unit banking, limited branching, and statewide branching. For example, Virginia laws permit a bank to add branches in counties contiguous to its head-office county and to add branches in any other city or county only if it acquires existing banks and converts them to branches.

### Procedural Requirements

A state that permits branching sets procedural constraints on how a bank can branch.

**Approval Criteria**   Each state requires that a bank apply for approval before it adds a branch, and it establishes some conditions and criteria that govern approval of branch applications. Some states will not permit a bank to add a branch unless the bank meets specific capital requirements and/or demonstrates that there is a public need for the branch. A state requires an applicant bank to file public notices of its branch application. This way other parties, such as local citizens and representatives of nearby financial institutions, have an opportunity to submit their views about the proposed branch.

**Home Office Protection Laws**   Many states have home office protection (HOP) laws by which an out-of-town bank cannot establish a new branch in a community that contains the home office of one or more banks. To enter such a protected community, an expansionary bank has to acquire an existing bank and then convert it to a branch.

Exhibit 18-1 schematically portrays a community that contains the head offices of two banks, A and B. In a state with an HOP law, an out-of-town bank cannot build a new branch in this community. It can, however, negotiate to acquire one of the two banks and convert it to a branch. (The acquired bank may itself have branches that also become branches of the out-of-town bank.) Even if one bank thus becomes part of an out-of-town branch system, no other out-of-town bank can build a new branch in the community so long as it contains a home office of a bank. This protection continues until when, and if, both banks (A and B) merge into out-of-town banks. Only then can other out-of-town banks apply to build new branches in the community.

From a public-policy perspective, it is difficult to justify an HOP law that limits entry into protected communities. The residents of such communities cannot benefit from the competitive spur of entry by an *additional* banking organization; they can only anticipate possible policy changes if an out-of-town banking system enters their community by acquiring an existing bank.[3] An HOP law strengthens the bargaining

---

3. Home office protection laws do not prevent the possible chartering of a new bank in a protected community or the possible establishment of a new bank or branch just outside the boundaries of the protected community.

**EXHIBIT 18-1**

**Home Office Protection Laws: A Schematic Summary**

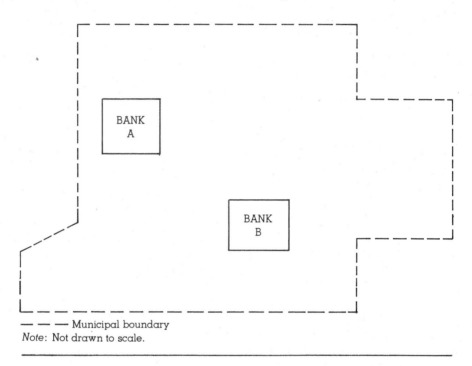

— — — Municipal boundary
*Note:* Not drawn to scale.

position of a bank in a protected community. The bank knows that an
out-of-town bank cannot build a new branch in its community, and so it can
await attractive merger proposals from out-of-town banks that are anxious to
enter its community. Expansionary banks realize that HOP laws thus reduce
their bargaining power with protected banks; but they usually accept an HOP
law as part of compromise legislation that reduces other, usually geographical, barriers to expansionary branching.

State HOP laws are designed primarily to protect small-town banks,
and so they usually apply to communities below a specific population. Also,
some states have HOP laws that are scheduled to phase out over time. In
such a state, a protected bank knows when its protection will end, and it has
to plan its long-run strategies within this context.

### Summary of Current Branching Restrictions

The many variants of branching restrictions make it difficult to neatly
categorize states by their branching laws and/or to summarize each state's
branching laws. With this important caveat, Exhibit 18-2 provides a
summary of each state's geographical constraints on branch expansion. Each
bank, however, has to focus on a detailed interpretation of its state's current
laws, and it has to anticipate, and perhaps participate in, proposed
amendments to current laws.

**EXHIBIT 18-2**

**Geographical Constraints on Full-Service Branching: A Summary**

**(Year-end 1978)**

| Unit Banking*<br>(no branching) | Limited Branching | Statewide Branching |
|---|---|---|
| Colorado | Alabama | Alaska |
| Illinois | Arkansas | Arizona |
| Kansas | Florida | California |
| Minnesota | Georgia | Connecticut |
| Missouri | Indiana | Delaware |
| Montana | Iowa | Hawaii |
| Nebraska | Kentucky | Idaho |
| North Dakota | Louisiana | Maine |
| Oklahoma | Massachusetts | Maryland |
| Texas | Michigan | Nevada |
| West Virginia | Mississippi | New Jersey |
| Wyoming | New Hampshire | New York |
|  | New Mexico | North Carolina |
|  | Ohio | Oregon |
|  | Pennsylvania | Rhode Island |
|  | Tennessee | South Carolina |
|  | Wisconsin | South Dakota |
|  |  | Utah |
|  |  | Vermont |
|  |  | Virginia† |
|  |  | Washington |

*Note*: As discussed in the text, the diversity of state branching restrictions makes it difficult neatly to categorize states by their branching laws. Each bank has to examine the specific branching restrictions of the state within which it operates.

*Most of these states permit banks to have some limited-service facilities.

†Virginia permits banks to branch *de novo* and by acquisition within counties that are contiguous to a bank's head-office county and to branch elsewhere in the state only by acquisitions of banks that are then converted to branches.

The McFadden Act and subsequent court cases uphold the principle that a state's branching laws apply to both state and national banks that operate within the state. Congress has the power to revise this current principle. It could, for example, pass legislation that would allow national banks to branch widely within states that restrict branching and/or to branch across state lines. Although its political likelihood currently is low, such federal legislation would lead to sharply different branching rules for national banks. As a consequence, state legislatures would likely reverse their restrictions so that their state-chartered banks could have branching opportunities similar to those of national banks.

## ADMINISTRATION OF BRANCHING RESTRICTIONS

An expansionary bank has to keep abreast of the rulings and procedures by which bank supervisory agencies interpret and administer branching statutes.

## Defining the Limits of Administrative Rulings

Some OCC rulings have tested the extent to which state branching restrictions apply to national banks.[4]

In the *Walker Bank* case (1966) the Supreme Court rejected a branch approved by the OCC, ruling that "national bank branching is limited to those states the laws of which permit it, and even there only to the extent that state laws permit branch banking." This decision, and subsequent ones, reaffirm that national banks are bound by state laws that restrict bank branches as to locations, numbers, home office protection, and/or cases in which an applicant bank demonstrates a public need for a branch.

In the *Dickinson* case (1969) the Supreme Court reversed an OCC ruling that would have allowed a national bank to operate an off-premise depository and to provide its merchant customers with daily armored-car services, the cost of which would be paid by the bank. The Court held that the OCC could not interpret its powers under the National Bank Act in a way that would "frustrate" congressional intent to provide for "competitive equality" between national and state banks.

In 1974 the OCC ruled that unmanned electronic terminals, detached from a bank's head office, were customer-bank communications terminals (CBCTs); were not branches; and therefore were not subject to state branching restrictions. The OCC further proposed to allow national banks to operate CBCTs within 50 miles of their head offices, even if this involved interstate operations. This ruling was promptly contested in various court cases, and in 1976 the U.S. Supreme Court refused to review a lower court decision that if detached unmanned electronic terminals perform basic banking services, then they are branches and subject to state branching restrictions. The OCC then rescinded its ruling about CBCTs.

## Processing Branch Applications

The OCC processes branch applications by national banks. A state's bank supervisory agency processes branch applications by its state-chartered banks, in addition to which the FDIC and FRS have statutory powers to rule on branch applications by insured nonmember and by state member banks, respectively.

The federal agencies have standardized branch-application forms that, as summarized from the FDIC form, require an applicant bank to provide the following types of information:

---

4. The following rulings and legal decisions are extracted from James F. Bell, "The Current Status of Multi-Office Branching," *The Bankers Magazine,* Summer 1976, pp. 43-49.

- resolution by the board of directors
- summary financial condition of the bank
- location of each current and pending branch
- planned premises for, and investment in, proposed branch
- three-year deposit and earnings projections for proposed branch
- proposed officers of proposed branch
- economic and demographic data that will demonstrate how the proposed branch would meet community convenience and needs

Although their application forms vary, ranging from a one-page questionnaire (Maryland) to almost twenty pages of questions (Pennsylvania), state banking agencies usually require similar information from banks they supervise.[5]

The application form becomes a key document in a supervisory agency's decision as to whether or not to approve a new branch. Therefore an applicant bank needs to research and document the information that it submits in its branch application. If it frequently adds branches, an expansionary bank has specialists who develop and document the case for each proposed branch. A bank that infrequently adds a branch is likely to retain consultants to help prepare its branch application(s).

Most branching statutes require an applicant bank to publicize a proposed branch via a legal notice in a community newspaper. Also, by statute or as a courtesy, the recipient supervisory agency notifies other supervisory agencies and potentially interested banks about the application, which is placed in a public file that is open to inspection by interested parties. If they choose to do so, interested parties can submit written comments and/or request a public hearing about the application. Traditionally, the interested parties to a branch application have been other financial institutions whose business might be affected by the proposed branch, and public hearings have been infrequent. Under the recent Community Reinvestment Act (CRA), local citizens' groups are likely to become more active supporters or opponents of branch applications by banks that operate or propose to operate in their community; and the supervisory agencies will likely have to increase their use of public hearings as a forum for these interested parties. Expansionary banks thus need to analyze and plan their current "community" actions in order to buttress their case for branch expansion into additional communities.

## BRANCH EXPANSION STRATEGIES

Where it can add branches, an expansionary bank needs to have a branch-expansion strategy that includes:

---

5. Carl S. Meyer, "How to Branch Yourself Out of Profits," *The Bankers Magazine,* Winter 1976, pp. 103-108. This article contains a table that summarizes each state's branch-application requirements.

- a total-system perspective to guide the development and integration of current and projected branches
- branch-site locational analyses
- facilities planning that encompasses both "brick-and-mortar" branches and unmanned service facilities
- acquisition programs by which to acquire banks to convert into branches.

Even as it thus expands, a branch system has to develop contingency plans to meet probable changes in branching laws and regulations.

## DEVELOPING AN INTEGRATED BRANCH SYSTEM

If it operates from two or more locations, a bank can be classified as a branch system. This classification thus includes cases where:

- a unit bank decides to alleviate its space congestion by adding a second facility rather than expand or move the principal office
- a local bank decides to add one or several small branches near its head office

Even in such a small-scale branch system, a bank has to analyze the objectives, legal feasibility, location, and cost of a new branch.

In contrast, a large expansionary branch system has to continuously focus on how its various branches, current and potential, fit together as an integrated system.

### Deposit Expansion and Diversification

An expansionary bank looks to branching as a way to retain, build, and diversify its deposits and other sources of funds. Especially when laws and regulations curtail explicit price competition, a bank relies on nonprice competition to compete for deposits—and customer convenience is a key part of nonprice competition. Thus, where branching is permitted, expansionary banks, especially those based in city-center locations, seek to develop branch networks that can conveniently service current outlying depositors and attract additional depositors. Such a network also enables a bank to diversify its sources of deposits among large numbers of geographically dispersed households and small firms. This added diversification may reduce the bank's liquidity-management costs.

### Loan Expansion and Diversification

Over time, a bank's branch depositors use such other services as credit cards, installment loans, and business loans. In this way a large expansionary bank can conveniently develop a diversified portfolio that includes loans to large firms, small businesses, consumers, and real estate owners.

Moreover, if it has branches in various economic regions within a state, a branch system can structure a loan portfolio in which borrowers are not equally sensitive to regional economic events, such as crop losses and employee layoffs.

## Possible Scale Economies

If it develops and manages an integrated branch system, a large bank is likely to achieve some scale economies that are less available to loosely structured banking systems.

In an integrated branch system, each branch does not have·to be a full-service bank, with its attendant costs. An integrated branch system has a head office, some full-service branches, and some limited-service branches that process routine deposit and loan transactions. These limited-service branches refer complex transactions to a nearby full-service branch or to the head office.

An integrated branch system expects each of its branch managers to think in terms of total-system profitability. Thus when he or she receives a large and/or unusual loan request, a manager of an outlying branch quickly screens it and, if it looks promising, forwards it upstream within the system. This way the head office learns about outlying loan opportunities at potentially lower search and information costs than if it has to rely on upstream requests from outlying correspondents and/or from traveling loan officers.[6]

Branching systems and their proponents cite additional ways by which an integrated branch system can achieve scale economies by centralizing such activities as capital management, computer systems, management development, marketing, portfolio management, and purchasing. The net benefits of such centralized activities have not yet been conclusively demonstrated.

## Intrasystem Funds Flows

A large, integrated branch system facilitates funds flows from surplus economic regions to deficit regions. Such a system has some branches in communities where the residents are net savers. Although they service local loan demands, these branches serve principally as *deposit-gathering branches* that, through an intrasystem transfer mechanism, provide funds that can be lent by *loan-generating branches* that face credit-worthy loan demands that exceed their local sources of funds. (In this way some loan-generating branches, if viewed as separate entities, have loan-to-deposit ratios that exceed 100 percent.) As parts of an integrated branch

6. For a more complete analysis of why one can expect lower search and information costs for loans within a branch system in contrast to within the correspondent banking system, see J. Lloyd Blackwell III, "Branch Banking: A Note on a Theory Dilemma," *The Journal of Business,* October 1977, pp. 520-525.

system, however, the loan-generating and deposit-gathering branches partially offset each other; and the branch system has other branches in which the local loan requests and deposits are more evenly matched.

## SELECTING BRANCH LOCATIONS

An expansionary bank engages in an ongoing planning process by which it:

- initially identifies areas where it would like to have additional branches
- has specialists analyze and rank various potential branch sites
- selects those branches that will best contribute to the system's long-run objectives

The bank updates these analyses to incorporate demographic and legal changes.

### Mapping a Site-Selection Strategy

A bank's branch-planning personnel have a large-scale map that identifies the total area in which the bank can branch—or will likely be able to branch. On this map they pinpoint the bank's current and pending branches, and they initially identify locations (such as communities or new shopping areas) that seem to be logical locations for new branches.

Exhibit 18-3 is a schematic mapping of a branch system that has its head office at the center of a major city (A). The bank also has full-service branches and limited-service branches throughout the city and in some nearby cities (B and C). It has no branch in city D, a rapidly growing city. Even this schematic summary suggests some general branching strategies:

- *Defensive branching* whereby the bank seeks to solidify its current deposit base by adding convenience branches (either full-service or limited-service) near its current locations (such as in the head-office city and city B)
- *Market-representation branching* whereby the bank seeks to broaden its branch network in areas in which it has few or no branches (such as in cities C and D)
- *Preemptive branching* whereby the bank seeks to identify specific prime locations in which it then promptly applies to locate branches before other banks and financial intermediaries do so

These general strategies are not mutually exclusive.

### Analyzing Branch Sites

Once they identify areas within which it seems logical to expand, a bank's branch-planning personnel prepare or commission detailed analyses of specific branch sites in or near these areas. These specialists use guidelines

**EXHIBIT 18-3**

## Schematic Mapping of a Branch System

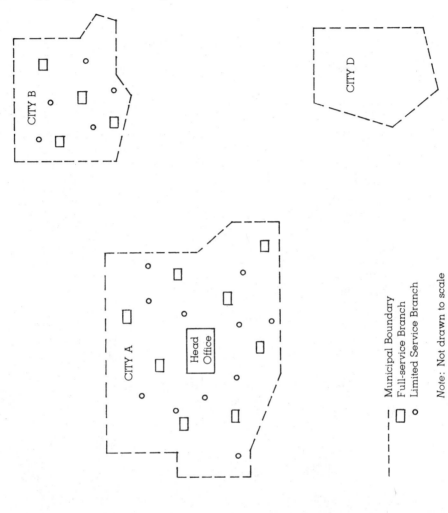

Municipal Boundary
Full-service Branch
Limited Service Branch

*Note:* Not drawn to scale

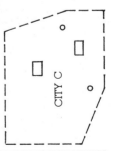

by which to identify and evaluate potential sites. They search, for example, for sites that:

- are in or near high-traffic areas, such as shopping centers
- are near major streets or highways
- provide convenient entry, exit, and parking
- provide flexibility for future expansion of facilities

They also develop some preliminary estimates of the deposit potential near each site.

As they begin to focus on a specific site, the specialists use this point from which to define and analyze the branch's probable market area. One view of its probable market is the entire *trade area* in which the branch will likely service customers. A narrower definition is the *service area* in which a bank expects most—such as 67 percent—of the branch's customers to be located. Even within these categories, a bank's researchers focus on such submarkets as small-business accounts and consumer loans.

Branch-site specialists use various procedures to analyze a market.[7] They use survey techniques to estimate where nearby residents and firms currently bank and shop. They also identify items that delimit a branch's probable market. These items include:

- natural barriers, such as rivers
- constructed barriers, such as limited-access expressways
- alternate trading magnets, such as larger nearby shopping centers

Once they thus estimate the market area, the researchers analyze its demographic and economic attributes. They focus on the area's current and projected:

- population
- housing patterns
- sales
- per capita income
- businesses
- deposits in banks and nonbank intermediaries

They need this type of information in order to project the proposed branch's deposits and profits and to demonstrate to the supervisory agencies how the proposed branch will service the convenience and needs of its community.

As they evaluate its location, probable market, and proximity to other branches, the branch-planning specialists also evaluate whether a proposed branch should be a full-service branch, a limited-service facility, or an

---

7. Joseph Garafolo and Winston M. Miller, "Bank Location and Site-Selection Strategy," *The Bankers Magazine,* Autumn 1977, pp. 50-54. "Locating Bank Offices through Research, Evaluation," *The Bankers Monthly Magazine,* October 15, 1968, pp. 28-30 ff.

unmanned facility. This way they can compute and rank each proposed branch's expected benefits relative to its cost, so that the bank's senior officials can decide which branches to open, and when.

Before it opens a new branch, an expansionary bank needs to select the branch's manager and key personnel. This way the manager can help set the branch's initial goals and agree to have his or her performance judged against these goals. These goals typically include projected numbers of new checking and savings accounts and the totals of such deposits.[8]

## ACQUISITION OF BANKS TO CONVERT TO BRANCHES

To expand its branch network, a bank has two basic choices: (1) add *de novo* branches that are newly built or leased or (2), where practical, acquire existing banks to convert to branches. Where feasible, an expansionary bank often prefers to enter a new area by acquisition rather than *de novo*. In this way it:

- acquires a banking operation that has an established record, physical plant, personnel roster, customer base, and community reputation
- can have more confidence in the branch's future performance than it can if it starts a *de novo* branch
- faces one less nearby competitor—the acquired bank

Sometimes an expansionary bank cannot choose between *de novo* and acquisition procedures. To enter a community that is subject to home-office protection laws, an expansionary bank has to acquire an existing bank. To enter an area devoid of existing banks, it has to open a *de novo* branch. Where at least initially it seems to have a choice as to how to enter a new area, an expansionary bank uses legal and financial analysis to decide the means of entry.

### Bank Merger Policy

Expansionary bankers have to plan their strategies in the context of the Bank Merger Act. This federal law resulted from major public-policy debates and court decisions during the early 1960s, and it governs current bank mergers.

**The Bank Merger Act of 1960: Origins and Initial Applications**   Although their pace accelerated during the 1940s and 1950s, bank mergers were not subject to special statutory guidelines. The National Bank Act and the FDIC Act required merging banks to obtain prior approval from a federal bank supervisory agency, but the laws contained no standards to guide these

---

8. One author reports how his branch system has experimented with growth models to project the patterns by which a new branch's accounts will grow over time. These projections can supplement those prepared by the branch-planning staff and the branch managers. Robert L. Kramer, ''Forecasting Branch Bank Growth Patterns,'' *Journal of Bank Research,* Winter 1971, pp. 17-24.

regulatory decisions. The Sherman Act (1890) and the Clayton Act (1914) are the foundations of federal antitrust policy, but some of their technical provisions made it unclear as to whether these general antitrust laws were applicable to bank mergers.

By 1960 a majority of Congressmen accepted the view that banking was a special, highly regulated industry in which some mergers might provide public benefits that more than offset their possible anticompetitive effects. Congress thus passed the Bank Merger Act of 1960, which established special procedures and criteria to govern bank mergers:

- If two banks propose to merge, then they must obtain prior approval of the federal agency that would primarily supervise the continuing bank. Thus if it is to be a national bank, the continuing bank needs the approval of the OCC; if it is to be a state member bank, it needs the approval of the FRS; and if it is to be a state nonmember bank, it needs the approval of the FDIC.
- The supervisory agency was to evaluate a proposed merger based on three general criteria:
  1. *Banking factors,* such as the banks' financial history and condition, earnings prospects, and management
  2. *Convenience and needs* of the community to be served
  3. *Competitive effects* of the merger
  The Act did not clearly define these three criteria, nor did it indicate how a supervisory agency was to weight each criterion when deciding whether or not to approve a proposed merger.
- The Department of Justice (DOJ) could give its advisory opinion as to the competitive effects of a proposed merger, but the appropriate banking agency could disagree with this opinion and/or conclude that other factors outweighed possible anticompetitive effects and so approve the merger.

From its beginning the Bank Merger Act of 1960 contained unresolved issues that had to be addressed in subsequent administrative decisions and court cases.

One study documents how each federal banking agency evolved its own doctrine by which to administer the Bank Merger Act of 1960.[9] By year-end 1962 the three agencies had approved 424 mergers and had denied 20. The DOJ objected to the effects on competition of about 45 percent of the approved mergers, some of which involved large money-center banks.

In 1960 the Philadelphia National Bank (the second-largest bank in Philadelphia) proposed to merge with the Girard Trust Corn Exchange Bank (the third-largest bank in Philadelphia). The DOJ objected to the anti-competitive effects of the merger, and it went to court to block the Philadelphia-Girard merger. It charged that the merger violated the Bank Merger Act of 1960 and also the Clayton Act, as amended by the

---

9. George R. Hall and Charles F. Phillips, Jr., *Bank Mergers and the Regulatory Agencies: Application of the Bank Merger Act of 1960,* Board of Governors of the Federal Reserve System, 1964.

Celler-Kefauver Act in 1950. The District Court rejected the DOJ's case, and it upheld the merger.

The DOJ appealed the decision to the U.S. Supreme Court, which, in a landmark decision (1963), upheld the DOJ's position and ruled against the proposed Philadelphia-Girard merger. In summary, a majority of the justices concluded that:[10]

- The Bank Merger Act of 1960 did not exempt bank mergers from the Clayton Act, as amended in 1950
- The relevant line of commerce, or product market, is "commercial banking," especially checking accounts. (It is not a broad range of financial services provided by banks and in some cases by nonbank firms.)[11]
- The relevant geographical market is "the four-county Philadelphia metropolitan area, which State law apparently recognizes as a meaningful banking community in allowing Philadelphia banks to branch within it. . . ." (The Court thus rejected the bank's contention that, depending on the services and customers involved, it competed in international, national, regional, and local markets.)
- Based on its market definitions, the majority decision concluded that:

  Specifically, we think that a merger which produces a firm controlling an undue percentage share of the relevant market, and results in a significant increase in the concentration of firms in that market, is so inherently likely to lessen competition substantially that it must be enjoined in the absence of evidence clearly showing that the merger is not likely to have such anticompetitive effects.

  As a guideline, the Court held that there is a threat of "undue concentration" in situations where one firm controls 30 percent or more of a relevant market.

- The Court further reviewed and rejected other defense arguments that might justify a bank merger despite its "inherently anticompetitive tendency."

The Philadelphia National Bank decision threw the banking community into disarray. The decision extended the Clayton Act to bank mergers, and it set new guidelines for defining markets and measuring concentration within markets. The DOJ planned to use these guidelines to challenge some past bank mergers that had been consummated with regulatory approval. For example, it challenged a previous merger of two large Kentucky banks. The

10. Hall and Phillips, *Bank Mergers and the Regulatory Agencies: Application of the Bank Merger Act of 1960,* pp. 107-117.

11. Economists and lawyers continue to analyze what is the relevant product market in banking. For example, Alan E. Grunewald, "Commercial Banking as a Distinct Line of Commerce," *Wayne Law Review,* March 1977, pp. 1057-1072; Richard W. Stolz, "Philadelphia National Bank Case Revisited," *Ninth District Quarterly* (Federal Reserve Bank of Minneapolis), Winter 1977, pp. 5-11; and Joel M. Yesley, "Defining the Product Market in Commercial Banking," *Economic Review* (Federal Reserve Bank of Cleveland), June-July 1972, pp. 17-31.

DOJ won this case (the Lexington Bank Case) in which the U.S. Supreme Court reaffirmed its product-market definition of commercial banking and further ruled that bank mergers were also subject to the Sherman Act.

Various bankers claimed that the DOJ's recent victories and pending cases imposed new, unfair, burdens on merging banks. Banks that had already merged especially claimed that they had done so under good-faith interpretations of the Bank Merger Act of 1960, and now some of them faced new challenges by the DOJ, which was using new judicial guidelines. At least some members of Congress were sympathetic to the bankers' viewpoint, and so, in 1966, Congress amended the Bank Merger Act.

**The Bank Merger Act of 1960, as Amended**   The Bank Merger Act (BMA) as amended in 1966 contains these principal provisions:[12]

- Each bank merger has to receive prior approval from the federal banking agency that has primary supervisory jurisdiction over the continuing bank.
- The supervisory agency cannot approve any proposed merger that will result in a monopoly. It may however approve a nonmonopolistic merger that has substantial anticompetitive effects if such effects are "*clearly outweighed* in the public interest by the probable effect of the transaction in meeting the convenience and needs of the community to be served" (italics added). The agency also is to take into account traditional banking factors (such as financial condition, earnings, and management) "of the existing and proposed institutions."
- With minor exception, all mergers consummated prior to June 17, 1963 (the date of the U.S. Supreme Court's Philadelphia National Bank decision) were excused from further prosecution under antitrust laws.
- Any mergers after June 16, 1963, have to be tried under the amended BMA; the DOJ cannot challenge them under other antitrust laws.
- If it decides to challenge a bank merger that has been approved by the appropriate federal banking agency, the DOJ must do so within thirty days of approval or the matter is closed. During this thirty-day interim the merger cannot be consummated—except under unusual circumstances.

In summary, the amended BMA places more weight on the competitive-effects criterion. Also, when the DOJ opposes a bank merger, the Act requires the DOJ to act promptly and to prosecute the case using only the criteria of the BMA. Even so, this amended Act required subsequent judicial interpretation.

In a series of judicial decisions, the courts have ruled that:[13]

---

12. William E. Whitesell, "The Bank Merger Act of 1966: Past, Present, and Prospects," *Business Review* (Federal Reserve Bank of Philadelphia), November 1968, pp. 3-9.

13. Whitesell, "The Bank Merger Act of 1966: Past, Present, and Prospects." Also, "Federal Laws Regulating Bank Mergers and the Acquisition of Banks by Registered Bank Holding Companies," *Economic Review* (Federal Reserve Bank of Cleveland), January 1971, pp. 18-27.

- They are not bound by regulatory opinions; they will separately review all the facts in a contested merger.
- Commercial banking is generally viewed to be the relevant line of commerce, or product market.
- The relevant geographical market is determined on a case-by-case basis.
- In a contested case, the *defendant banks bear the burden* of showing how the proposed merger will likely service community convenience and needs in ways that outweigh any anticompetitive effects. (In most such cases the banks have been unable to convince the courts that their proposed merger will provide convenience-and-needs benefits that outweigh its anticompetitive effects.)
- The BMA also applies to proposed mergers among small, nearby banks.[14]
- In a contested case, the merger cannot be consummated until the courts reach a final decision.

Thus to reduce the likelihood of costly legal defenses and delays, expansionary banks need to select and structure their merger proposals in ways that will likely comply with judicial interpretation of the BMA.

An expansionary bank has to plan its merger proposals in the context of the DOJ's published guidelines about its enforcement of the Clayton Act. The guidelines, while they apply to firms other than just banks, provide insights into how the DOJ is likely to view bank merger proposals.

The DOJ guidelines require initial specification of the relevant product and geographical market(s). The guidelines then view a firm's market share as a proxy measure of its market power. On this basis the guidelines indicate that the DOJ will likely challenge mergers when:

- "The market shares of the first four companies amount to approximately 75% or more and if the merging firms account for approximately the following percentages of the market

| *Acquiring Firm* | *Acquired Firm* |
|---|---|
| 4% | 4% or more |
| 10% | 2% or more |
| 15% or more | 1% or more |

- "The market shares of the first four companies amount to less than 75% and the merging firms account for approximately the following market percentages

---

14. Jerome C. Darnell, "Merger Guidelines from the Phillipsburg National Bank Case," *The Magazine of Bank Administration*, June 1971, pp. 30-33.

| Acquiring Firm | Acquired Firm |
|:---:|:---:|
| 5% | 5% or more |
| 10% | 4% or more |
| 15% | 3% or more |
| 20% | 2% or more |
| 25% or more | 1% or more |

- "The acquiring or acquired firm is among the eight largest and one of them has 2% or more of the market and any set of the largest firms (from the two to the eight largest) has increased by about 7% or more over any period of five to ten years prior to the merger."[15]

The DOJ supplements these numerical guidelines with judgmental factors, and in some cases it may decide to depart from the numerical guidelines. Nevertheless, the guidelines alert expansionary bankers to the types of mergers that will likely face DOJ opposition. Thus, if it chooses to pursue such a merger, an expansionary bank must be especially prepared to document a defensible merger proposal.

## Financial Analysis of Merger Candidates

To develop a specific merger offer, an acquiring bank first enumerates how it expects to benefit by acquiring a bank instead of establishing a *de novo* branch in the area. The expected benefits usually include:

- convenient and prompt entry into the targeted area
- continuation of a "going concern" within its community
- opportunities to restructure profitably the acquired bank's portfolio
- opportunities to achieve system economies by integrating the acquired bank into the branch system

Once it identifies its expected benefits, an acquiring bank uses various valuation procedures, each of which requires judgments, to develop a range of possible prices for the smaller bank. It uses these figures as a basis for its initial offer and its possible contingency offers.[16]

**Market Values of Common Stock**   One valuation method is to analyze the price at which investors currently value the stock of the bank to be acquired. In principle, an efficient market is one in which many informed investors own and/or monitor a company's stock, the market price of which

15. William E. Whitesell and Janet F. Kelly, "Evaluating Bank Mergers: Some Regulatory Considerations," *The Magazine of Bank Administration,* April 1971, pp. 38-41.

16. Stanley E. Shirk, "Evaluating Bank Mergers: Some Financial Considerations," *The Magazine of Bank Administration,* March 1971, pp. 16-21. Ronald Terry and Merrill C. Sexton, "Valuation of Banks in Acquisitions," *The Bankers Magazine,* Summer 1975, pp. 86-89.

thus provides a "best estimate" of the discounted stream of expected cash flows from the stock. If it concludes that the market thus is efficient for the bank it wants to acquire, an acquiring bank can use recent stock transaction prices as a best estimate of the bank's per-share value to investors.

Most acquisitions are of smaller banks, the stock of which is closely held and inactively traded. In these cases an acquiring bank does not heavily weight such recent market prices in its valuation process. It views these recent prices as a lower limit that selling stockholders will likely accept as an offer for their stock.

**Book Value Computations**   Book value is a summary measure of the stockholders' residual claim against their firm's assets. A bank's assets are primarily financial claims, many of which are cash or convertible into cash. Even loans that cannot easily be sold will likely be repaid at maturity. Thus a bank's stockholders and potential owners use the book value (the difference between total assets and total liabilities) to develop initial estimates of the bank's probable value in liquidation and, to a lesser estent, as a going concern.

To evaluate a bank that it may acquire, an expansionary bank has its analysts scrutinize the smaller bank's balance-sheet figures to adjust the book value for items such as:

- substandard loans and other assets
- assets that have fixed interest rates that differ substantially from current market rates
- buildings and equipment for which the depreciated historic cost figures differ substantially from replacement costs, and possibly from liquidation costs
- contingent liabilities, such as loan commitments, possible lawsuits, and noncancellable leases
- reserve accounting practices
- potential tax liabilities

An acquiring bank uses this adjusted book-value computation to estimate a lower limit to its valuation of a smaller bank.

**Earnings Potential**   An acquiring bank focuses on the potential earnings it expects from acquiring a bank that it then will operate as a branch. It uses specialists who:

- analyze the recent earnings history of the smaller bank and, if necessary, adjust the reported earnings for unusual revenue and expense items
- estimate how, by changing its mix of assets and/or liabilities, the smaller bank could increase its future earnings
- further estimate the extent to which the acquired bank, as a branch, can

achieve operating economies in areas such as investment management and data-processing systems

Especially when it thus foresees opportunities to increase a smaller bank's future earnings, an acquiring bank will offer a premium that exceeds the smaller bank's recent transaction prices and adjusted book value.[17]

**Merger Premiums**   An acquiring bank expects to pay a premium price to stockholders of a bank that it wants to acquire. It willingly offers a premium that, in its judgment, will:

- expedite acceptance of the offer by the smaller bank's senior officials and major stockholders
- discourage higher offers by rival expansionary banks
- enable it, and its stockholders, also to achieve financial benefits from the merger

How much of a premium to offer thus involves judgments about future outcomes that differ among proposed acquisitions. Even so, an expansionary bank monitors the types of premiums paid for bank acquisitions in its region. One study, for example, summarizes the average premiums paid by acquiring banks in the Third (Philadelphia) Federal Reserve District between 1968 and 1972.[18] It reports that, depending on which of three premium measures is used, the average premium ranged from 1.8 times (pro rata book value of acquiring bank to that of acquired bank) to 2.2 times (pro rata market value of acquiring bank to book value of acquired bank). The study further reports, and to some extent explains, the variability among such average merger premiums.

**Other Terms of Merger Offers**   In addition to a premium price, an acquiring bank can include other attractions in its merger offer. It typically offers:

- a nontaxable share exchange between its stock and that of the acquired bank (this way the smaller bank's stockholders generally receive stock that has greater marketability and a higher dividend yield than their former stock; and, in contrast to selling for cash, they can defer realizing their capital gains on the merger transaction)
- its system-wide benefit program(s) to qualifying employees of the acquired bank

---

17. One study compares the operating performance of merging and nonmerging banks in the Fourth (Cleveland) Federal Reserve District. It reports that "although banks may merge because of the *expectation* of higher profits," the evidence of the study "indicates that merging banks in the Fourth District did not realize these expectations during the period under review." David L. Smith, "The Performance of Merging Banks," *The Journal of Business,* April 1971, pp. 184-192.

18. Jerome C. Darnell, "Bank Mergers: Prices Paid to Marriage Partners," *Business Review* (Federal Reserve Bank of Philadelphia), July 1973, pp. 16-25.

- management contracts to selected key officers of the acquired bank
- to create a local advisory board in which the acquired bank's directors can participate

These types of terms, while often important, do not readily appear in computations of premiums that acquiring banks offer to potential merger partners.

## MODIFYING A BRANCH SYSTEM OVER TIME

An expansionary branch system engages in a continuing process of building and restructuring its branch network. Even as it adds branches that complement its current branches, it examines ways to increase the profit contribution of its current branches.

### RESTRUCTURING CURRENT BRANCHES

A branch system uses performance evaluation systems to monitor the actual versus targeted performance of its branches and their managers.[19] If over time a branch's performance—such as its profit contribution or deposit growth—falls below its targets, then the bank's senior officials will likely replace the branch manager and then track the branch's performance under its new manager.

A branch system has and/or retains physical planning specialists who review the branches' current structural facilities and propose remodeling projects. Other specialists then analyze these proposals and rank them based on which projects are likely, over time, to generate the greatest dollar benefits (derived, for example, from increased customer convenience and/or more efficient use of space) compared to their estimated remodeling costs. Once they decide how much their bank should allocate to branch remodeling in a coming period, the bank's senior officials then authorize those projects that in general have the highest benefit-cost ratios.

### RELOCATING BRANCHES

At times a branch system moves a branch to a new site. It usually does so if it has observed one or more of the following conditions:

- A growing branch cannot obtain adjacent property on which to expand.
- Recent developments, such as a limited-access expressway, impede access to a branch.

---

19. William H. Ryan and John C. Donaker, Jr., "How Good Is Branch Bank Performance?" *The Bankers Magazine,* Autumn 1975, pp. 102-108.

- Many long-time customers have moved from the declining area in which a branch now finds itself located.
- Because of branching restrictions, a branch system cannot add a branch in a promising new area but can apply to move one of its current branches into the area.

Even when it concludes that one of its branches faces such conditions, a bank has to analyze whether the growth opportunities at a proposed new location will more than offset the business lost because of customers who choose not to bank at the new location.

## CLOSING BRANCHES

Many nonbanking firms divest themselves of facilities that, in their judgment, no longer adequately contribute to the firm's total profitability. In contrast, branch banks traditionally have not focused on how, by closing selected branches, they might boost total-system profitability. In cases where they have examined whether to close an uneconomic branch, they apparently have justified its retention based on:

- its economic role in its local community
- its symbolic role as part of a large bank that wants representation in most communities where it can branch
- its possible eventual contribution to total-system profitability

Large branch systems are likely to reevaluate their traditional reluctance to close uneconomic branches. They will do so because of:

- increasing emphasis on profit-measurement systems and total-system profitability
- reduced profit margins from retail deposit and loan accounts for which they increasingly have to compete against nonbanking firms
- opportunities to substitute unmanned computer-based systems for some brick-and-mortar branches that have high operating costs relative to their revenues
- opportunities to redeploy resources to other areas of the bank or within the parent bank holding company
- recent patterns of branch closings in some countries that have nationwide branch-banking systems

Large branch systems are not likely to publicize their new focus on the economics of branch closings. Yet, among early signs of this new trend, several large banks have closed some of their metropolitan retail branches; and one of the nation's largest banks has announced a plan to sell almost all of its retail branches to a foreign banking organization and to redeploy these sales proceeds in its wholesale banking activities.

# PREPARING FOR NEW BRANCHING OPPORTUNITIES

To prepare for new branching opportunities, an expansionary bank has to:

- monitor, forecast, and support changes in branching restrictions
- position itself to act quickly when it gets new powers to expand its branch network

## PROBABLE EASING OF BRANCHING RESTRICTIONS

During recent decades many states have eased their branching restrictions.[20]

An early clue of pending change is when state officials create a study commission to review their state's banking laws. A commission reviews diverse studies of branch banking, holds hearings, and typically submits a public report that supports some easing of branching (and/or bank holding company) restrictions.

When it eases its branching restrictions, a state usually widens the geographical area within which banks can branch. For example, if it has restricted branches to within a county, then a state is likely to permit branching within adjacent counties; and if it has restricted branches to within adjacent counties, then it is likely to permit branching throughout most or all of the state. A state also can ease its branching restrictions in other ways, such as to: remove unmanned banking terminals from most branching restrictions, permit limited-service facilities (LSFs), increase the permissible number of LSFs, and expand the permissible services of LSFs. When it thus eases its branching restrictions, a state often provides for some home office protection.

Some study commissions and state banking commissioners have proposed *branching* (or holding company) *reciprocity agreements* between states. Under such a proposal two states would each enact a law that permits state banks from the other state to branch in it in return for the right of its state-chartered banks to branch in the other state. Each state's banking commission would, however, retain the right to review and approve or disapprove specific branching applications. (Under the McFadden Act, national banks in the two states presumably could benefit from such a bistate reciprocity agreement.) No such reciprocity agreement has yet been enacted, but these proposals recur and may soon win initial acceptance.

---

20. Benjamin J. Klebaner summarizes the recent history of branching changes and observes that "the dominant tendency in state law has been toward easing restrictions. . . ." "Recent Changes in United States' Commercial Banking Structure in Perspective," *The Antitrust Bulletin*, Winter 1973, pp. 759-786. Also, various articles summarize changes in state branching laws, for example, "Bank Expansion in New York State: The 1971 Statewide Branching Law," *Monthly Review* (Federal Reserve Bank of New York), November 1971, pp. 266-274; "Competition and the Changing Banking Structure in New Jersey," *Monthly Review* (Federal Reserve Bank of New York), August 1973, pp. 203-210; and Ruth Goeller, "Response to Countywide Branching: The New Chapter in Florida Banking," *Economic Review* (Federal Reserve Bank of Atlanta), November-December 1977, pp. 144-146.

At the federal level, various Presidential study commissions have endorsed the easing of branching restrictions within states and, in some cases, across state lines.[21] Congressional committees at times authorize staff studies and/or commission outside studies of state and federal branching restrictions.[22] Congress is unlikely to pass general legislation that permits interstate branching or that permits branching within states that restrict it. It is likely, however, that at some point a situation will arise that will trigger Congressional passage of proposed legislation that would permit, under special circumstances, an out-of-state banking organization to acquire a distressed bank in another state.

Expansionary bankers can participate in the deliberative processes that precede changes in branching restrictions. They can submit specific proposals and offer to present their views at hearings. Also, they can authorize their bank's support of trade groups and specialists that represent their views. In such ways expansionary bankers try to help shape probable changes in branching restrictions.

## POSITIONING FOR POTENTIAL BRANCHES

When it anticipates a pending easing of branching restrictions, an expansionary bank develops and implements plans so that it can quickly add strategic branches.

If it anticipates a widening of geographical boundaries within which it will be able to branch, an expansionary bank has its branch-planning specialists analyze the new area in order to identify acquisition candidates and prime sites for *de novo* branches. If it thus does preliminary market and financial analyses, the bank can promptly apply for strategic branches in the new area.

Some state statutes provide for scheduled expiration of home office protection laws. In such a state, an expansionary bank has its staff monitor the pending expiration date(s) and research promising areas in which the bank soon will be able to place *de novo* branches.

If it anticipates state, or possibly federal, laws that would remove unmanned banking terminals from many branching restrictions, an expansionary bank has and retains specialists who design strategic systems of unmanned terminals. Even while such terminals remain defined as branches, the bank operates some initial terminals in order to test its prototype systems and position itself to expand the systems rapidly in response to reduced legal impediments and increased customer acceptance.

To help position itself for eventual interstate branching, a large money-center bank can, if warranted, open special-purpose offices in other

---

21. Most recently, *The Report of the President's Commission on Financial Structure and Regulation* (The Hunt Commission), 1971.

22. For example, "Compendium of Issues Relating to Branching by Financial Institutions," prepared by the Subcommittee on Financial Institutions of the Committee on Banking, Housing, and Urban Affairs, U.S. Senate, 94th Congress: 2d Session, October 1976.

states. One tactic is to open loan-production offices (LPOs) in strategic cities; another tactic is to open Edge Act offices in selected cities.[23] Although, by law, it cannot offer a full set of banking—especially depository—services at them, an expansionary bank can use these offices currently to provide special corporate banking services and to position itself for when it becomes possible to offer additional banking services at these distant locations.

An expansionary bank can continually examine ways to use a parent bank holding company in order to expand, via coaffiliate banks, within its state and to expand, via bank-related coaffiliate firms, into other states. The next two chapters focus on the dynamics of expansion by bank holding companies.

## SUMMARY

An expansionary bank evaluates strategies by which it can use branches to build its customer base and enter new geographical areas. It faces, however, diverse branching restrictions that reflect a legacy of divisive debate and opposing interests.

Federal legislation (the McFadden Act) subjects each national bank to the branching restrictions of the state in which it is located, and court decisions have upheld a strict interpretation of the McFadden Act. Therefore, whether it has a national or state charter, a bank has to scrutinize the laws of the state within which it has its head office. (Interstate branching is not permitted.)

State branching restrictions fall into three principal categories: permissible services, geographical constraints, and procedural requirements. Some states have a home office protection law.

Where branching is legally feasible or is likely to be feasible, an expansionary bank develops a long-run branching strategy that includes:

- a total-system perspective to guide the development and integration of current and projected branches
- branch-site locational analyses
- facilities planning that encompasses both "brick-and-mortar" branches and unmanned service facilities
- acquisition programs by which to acquire banks to convert into branches

An expansionary bank has to evaluate how its current and proposed branches, in combination, enable the total system to achieve benefits in such

---

23. Chapter 21 provides more information about domestic expansion opportunities available under the Edge Act amendment to the Federal Reserve Act. Also, James C. Baker, "Nationwide Branch Banking: The Edge Act Corporation and Other Methods," *Issues in Bank Regulation,* Summer 1977, pp. 31-36; and Donald E. Pearson and Roger Borgen, "The Great Interstate Banking Debate: It's Already Here," *The Bankers Magazine,* Winter 1975, pp. 79-83.

areas as: deposit and loan expansion, portfolio diversification, possible scale economies, intrasystem funds flows, and bottom-line profitability.

An expansionary bank has and/or retains specialists who identify, evaluate, and rank sites for potential branches. The bank also uses specialists to plan the physical facilities of proposed branches and to prepare branch applications that have to be submitted to bank supervisory agencies.

In some cases, instead of its building new (*de novo*) branches, an expansionary bank examines the feasibility and net benefits of its merging with an existing bank that it then converts to a branch. An expansionary bank has to evaluate whether its proposed bank merger will receive approval from its federal banking agency that administers the Bank Merger Act. To estimate the probability of such approval, a bank has and/or retains lawyers and economists who specialize in bank-merger cases and procedures. In addition, an expansionary bank uses financial analysis to estimate what merger terms it will offer to, and negotiate with, the bank that it wants to acquire. Often an acquiring bank offers terms that include a share exchange and a merger premium for the shares of a smaller, established bank.

Even as it focuses on expansion, a branch system evaluates the performance of its current branches. With these performance appraisals, it can plan how to improve the performance of its current branches, and, in some cases, whether and how to move or close some of its branches.

While it operates within the context of its current branching restrictions, an expansionary bank monitors and tries to influence changes in the applicable branching laws and regulations. It also examines procedures by which it can position itself for a possible reduction of branching restrictions. It identifies geographical areas and specific sites that it wants to enter; it evaluates potential merger candidates; it analyzes whether to open specialized loan-production offices and domestic Edge Act offices; and it examines how to use a bank holding company as a vehicle by which to expand, indirectly, its banking and nonbanking operations.

# 19
# BANK HOLDING COMPANIES

Every banker encounters holding company activities. This is a recent phenomenon. At year-end 1965, bank holding companies accounted for 9 percent of bank assets and they controlled 3 percent of the nation's banks. At year-end 1977, the percentages had increased to 73 percent of total assets and 26 percent of total banks.

Today many banks are affiliates of bank holding companies. Officials of an affiliate bank make their major decisions subject to the objectives and resources of the parent holding company, and they know that the parent firm evaluates the bank's performance.

Officials of nonaffiliate banks also encounter holding companies. A nonaffiliate bank has a correspondent relationship with at least one money-center, affiliate bank; and it likely competes against banks and bank-related firms that are owned by holding companies. Over time a nonaffiliate bank may receive acquisition offers from bank holding companies or their affiliate banks. Even if they reject such offers, the principal stockholders of a nonaffiliate bank may benefit by placing control of their bank in a holding company that the stockholders, or their successors, in turn control.

While it considers public-policy issues, this chapter examines bank holding companies primarily from the viewpoint of their managers and stockholders.

## PRINCIPAL TYPES OF BANK HOLDING COMPANIES

By law, a bank holding company (BHC) is "any company which has control over any bank or over any company that is or becomes a bank holding company. . . ." This definition includes organizations such as associations and partnerships.

In a state that prohibits or restricts branching but that does not prohibit BHCs, a large bank typically organizes a BHC that acquires the bank and subsequently acquires additional affiliate banks in other parts of the state. Such a banking organization that controls two or more banks is a *multibank holding company* (MBHC). It can thus expand into new geographical markets and operate like a *de facto* branch system.

In addition to its affiliate banks, an MBHC usually controls some nonbanking affiliates that specialize in such areas as consumer finance, mortgage banking, and portfolio advisory services. Even if it is based in a state that prohibits MBHCs, a large bank usually is an affiliate of a *one-bank holding company* (OBHC) that also engages in nonbanking activities. With minor exceptions a BHC cannot control banks with offices in more than one state, but its nonbanking affiliates can have offices in various states.

Even when they cannot, or choose not to, acquire other banks or enter nonbanking areas, a bank's controlling stockholders may decide that the tax structure warrants their using a BHC—in this case an OBHC—through which to control the bank.

## DEVELOPMENT OF BANK HOLDING COMPANIES AND THEIR REGULATION

The BHC movement is one of the most important, if not the most important, banking developments in recent decades. By reviewing these BHC developments, one can better understand the current limitations and opportunities available to expansionary BHCs and banks.

### INITIAL DEVELOPMENT OF BANK HOLDING COMPANIES

From a small base, the bank holding company movement rapidly accelerated during the late 1920s. Some large banks saw how they could use a holding company to expand into new markets.[1]

- Although the McFadden Act constrained branching by national banks, there was no federal legislation to limit expansion by BHCs. Therefore, unless explicitly blocked by state law, a BHC could acquire affiliate banks throughout a state—even if the affiliate banks themselves faced branching restrictions or prohibitions.
- While a bank could not branch across state lines, a BHC could acquire affiliate banks in various states. In practice, an expansionary BHC thus could create a *de facto* multistate banking system.
- A BHC was free to acquire nonbank affiliates.

Illustrative of the expansion opportunities available to BHCs, one group announced that its goal was:

1. This section draws on William F. Upshaw, ''Bank Affiliates and Their Regulation,'' *Monthly Review* (Federal Reserve Bank of Richmond), Part I, March 1973, pp. 14-20; Part II, April 1973, pp. 3-9; Part III, May 1973, pp. 3-10.

to establish a nationwide system of branch banks and operate these banks in conjunction with nonbank enterprises. The vehicle to achieve this goal was to be Transamerica Corporation, formed in October 1928, to bring under common ownership several large banks in California and New York. . . . Other subsidiaries of the holding company included a securities and realty corporation that reportedly owned stock in at least 70 domestic and 59 foreign banks, a security underwriting firm, a mortgage company, a fire insurance company, and two farm loan companies.[2]

Most other groups had less ambitious objectives. While using the BHC vehicle to enter new markets, organizers of some regional holding companies claimed that their BHCs also would make defensive acquisitions of outlying correspondent banks that might otherwise be acquired by distant BHCs that seemed poised to enter their region. Most of these regional BHCs apparently did not intend to expand nationwide nor to acquire nonbanking affiliates. Investor optimism of the late 1920s also provided financial incentives to create and expand BHCs.

Opposition to BHCs arose almost as quickly as did the BHCs. Opponents observed how BHCs could circumvent intrastate and interstate branching restrictions. Opponents of BHCs cited some failures of BHCs and their affiliates, and they claimed that the federal banking agencies had inadequate statutory powers to identify and prevent potential abuses within BHCs. Opponents also asserted that the unbridled expansion of BHCs would lead to increased concentration of resources within banking and also among banks and their nonbank coaffiliates.

Triggered by increasing failures of banks and BHCs and by disclosures of abuses by banks and their securities affiliates, Congress passed the Banking Act of 1933. This Act affected BHCs because it:[3]

- required separation of banking from investment banking
- placed limits on financial relationships between banks and their affiliates
- authorized federal banking agencies to obtain and examine reports from banks and their affiliates

The 1933 Act also defined a "holding company affiliate" and prohibited such a firm from voting any stock that it owned or controlled in any *member* bank without first obtaining a voting permit from the FRS. In retrospect, this voting-permit requirement had many exceptions, especially after a 1935 amendment that practically exempted holding companies that controlled only one bank.

From 1931 through 1936 the number of BHCs declined from about one hundred to fifty, and these remaining ones accounted for 8 to 10 percent of

---

2. Upshaw, "Bank Affiliates and Their Regulation," Part I, p. 18.
3. Upshaw, "Bank Affiliates and Their Regulation," Part II, p. 3.

the nation's total bank deposits. Yet in 1938 President Roosevelt asked Congress to conduct "a thorough study of the concentration of economic power in American industry and the effect of that concentration upon the decline of competition."[4] In this context, the President called for special attention to BHCs.

Although it did not move quickly to pass new legislation affecting BHCs, Congress subsequently received a report in which the FRS summarized its experience in regulating BHCs. The Board of Governors noted that it had generally satisfactory relationships with most BHCs. It then summarized an "exceptional case" in which the Board "found that the corporate device of the holding company has not been used solely as a mechanism for the efficient operation of controlled banks but as a device to accomplish by indirection objectives which could not be accomplished directly." The Board specifically criticized how the BHC could: in effect operate a *de facto* branch system despite congressional intent concerning branch expansion, and combine, within one organization, extensive control of banking and nonbanking businesses. The Board concluded its report by affirming its belief "that it is necessary in the public interest and in keeping with sound banking principles that the activities of bank holding companies be restricted solely to the banking business and that their activities be regulated, as are the activities of the banks themselves."[5]

In subsequent congressional testimony, the Chairman of the Board of Governors identified Transamerica Corporation as "the exceptional case where a holding company management has openly defied the Board in its attempt to halt an unbridled bank expansion program." The Chairman pointed out that at year-end 1946, Transamerica operated "619 banking offices having aggregate deposits in excess of 6 ½ billion dollars." Since 1934 the group acquired 126 banks, and at year-end 1946 the group accounted for almost 40 percent of all the banking offices and deposits in its five-state area.

> In addition, (Transamerica) owns and operates many other types of businesses with aggregate resources of more than $275,000,000. . . . There is real estate, iron and brass foundaries, another real estate outfit, buying, processing, and selling fish and seafood, a very big fishing outfit; the manufacture of diesel engines and other products; holding real estate and acting under trusts. . . . Then there is Occidental Corp., Occidental Life Insurance. That is a large life, health and accident company. And so forth.[6]

The FRS, in 1945, proposed new federal legislation to regulate BHCs, but Congress was slow to act on the FRS proposal. Meanwhile the FRS decided to challenge, in court, Transamerica's acquisitions of various

---

4. Cited in Upshaw, "Bank Affiliates and Their Regulation," Part II, p. 7.

5. *Annual Report of the Board of Governors of the Federal Reserve System*, 1943, p. 36. Cited in Upshaw, "Bank Affiliates and Their Regulation, Part II, p. 7.

6. Hearings on S. 829, 80th Congress, 1st Session, (1947), pp. 22, 24, as cited in Upshaw, "Bank Affiliates and Their Regulation," Part II, p. 8.

banks. Although lost by the FRS, this case set major precedents for application of antitrust laws to subsequent banking cases and legislation. The Transamerica decision removed any doubt that, under the Constitution's "interstate commerce" clause, Congress had the power to regulate all BHCs. Also, although it lost this specific case on the ground of failure of proof, the FRS gained support for new legislation to control expansion by BHCs.

## THE BANK HOLDING COMPANY ACT OF 1956

The Bank Holding Company Act of 1956 seeks to control the process by which a BHC acquires additional banks and engages in nonbanking activities.

Initially, the Bank Holding Company Act applied to firms that controlled *two or more* banks. A firm generally was judged to control a bank if it owned or otherwise controlled 25 percent or more of the voting shares of the bank or in other ways controlled a bank's management or policies. The Act excluded individuals and some partnerships and trusts that controlled two or more banks. Congress noted the existence of small one-bank holding companies, but it concluded that such firms did not warrant inclusion in the Bank Holding Company Act. This specific exemption of OBHCs continued until 1970.

Any organization that meets the definition of a "bank holding company" has to register with the FRS, and any firm that proposes to become a BHC must obtain prior approval from the FRS. A BHC must obtain prior approval from the FRS before it:

- acquires control of over 5 percent of the voting shares of any bank
- acquires substantially all of a bank's assets
- merges or consolidates with another BHC.

The FRS has extensive powers to issue orders and regulations by which to administer the Bank Holding Company Act.

The Bank Holding Company Act limits the extent to which a BHC can acquire affiliate banks. Under a grandfather clause, BHCs that controlled affiliate banks in more than one state prior to the Act are permitted to continue such control. But the Act prohibits a BHC from now acquiring control of a bank located in a state other than the one in which the BHC's banking subsidiaries principally operated on July 1, 1956, or when the firm became a BHC, whichever date is later. The only exception to this ban on interstate expansion is if a state's statutes specifically authorize out-of-state BHCs to acquire banks in the state. Affirmative statutes of this type are rare.

When a proposed bank acquisition conforms to the geographical constraint, a BHC must also apply to the FRS for approval of the acquisition. The FRS then evaluates the proposed acquisition based on the:[7]

---

7. Amendments (1966) to the Bank Holding Company Act revised its original criteria so that these current criteria correspond to those used in the Bank Merger Act.

- financial and managerial resources and future prospects of the BHC, its affiliates, and the proposed affiliate
- convenience and needs of the community to be served
- possible anticompetitive effects of the proposed transaction

If it judges that a proposed transaction involves anticompetitive effects, then the FRS can approve the transaction only if the probable convenience-and-needs benefits clearly outweigh the possible anticompetitive effects.

The Bank Holding Company Act of 1956 curtailed nonbank activities by BHCs. Subject to some specific exceptions stated in the Act, BHCs could only have nonbanking subsidiaries "of a financial, fiduciary, or insurance nature and which the Board [of Governors] . . . by order has determined to be so closely related to the business of banking or of managing and controlling banks as to be a proper incident thereto. . . ." This provision gave broad interpretive powers to the FRS, which adopted a narrow view of activities that were "closely related" to banking. There was no grandfather clause by which BHCs could retain nonbanking affiliates that they controlled prior to passage of the Act. Therefore, BHCs that had nonbank affiliates generally divested them. For example, Transamerica Corporation divided itself into two autonomous firms, one of which continued as a registered BHC and the second of which continued to own extensive nonbanking operations.

Shortly before enactment of the Bank Holding Company Act, there was a brief flurry of bank acquisitions by BHCs. After the enactment, BHCs reexamined their status under the new rules; and, subject to the Act, some of the BHCs acquired additional affiliate banks. As summarized in the following figures, however, throughout the decade 1956-65 there was no rapid expansion by BHCs that had to register under the Bank Holding Company Act:[8]

|                                               | 1956 | 1965  |
|-----------------------------------------------|------|-------|
| Number of registered bank holding companies   | 53   | 53    |
| Banks                                         | 428  | 468   |
| Branches                                      | 783  | 1,486 |
| Deposits as a percentage of all bank deposits | 7.5  | 8.3   |

While the registered BHCs slowly expanded, by the mid-1960s banking circles were astir with the rapid emergence of large one-bank holding companies that were not subject to the Bank Holding Company Act or FRS supervision.

---

8. From Table I in Upshaw, "Bank Affiliates and Their Regulation," Part III, p. 7.

## RAPID EXPANSION OF ONE-BANK HOLDING COMPANIES

Congress specifically exempted one-bank holding companies (OBHCs) from the Bank Holding Company Act of 1956. At that time, and in the subsequent decade, most OBHCs were firms that controlled a small or medium-sized bank.

### Bank-Originated One-Bank Holding Companies

Starting about 1967, some large, nonaffiliate, money-center banks began to form OBHCs, of which the bank became the principal affiliate. Senior management of such a bank would ask the bank's stockholders to approve a series of legal moves whereby:[9]

- a new holding company would be chartered
- the bank's stockholders would exchange their bank shares for those of the new firm
- the bank's stockholders would thus become stockholders of an OBHC that would then own the bank

For example, if the share-exchange were on a one-for-one basis, a person owning 100 shares of the bank would exchange these shares for 100 shares of the new bank-originated OBHC. Why did many large banks go through these legal steps to form a parent OBHC?

Large money-center banks in particular saw ways by which, as part of a bank-originated OBHC, they could sidestep hurdles to their expansion:

- The Philadelphia National Bank decision (1963), the Bank Merger Act, and subsequent tests of this Act placed new hurdles before large banks that tried to expand via major bank mergers.
- The Bank Holding Company Act, as administered by the FRS, made it difficult for MBHCs to expand aggressively in either banking or nonbanking areas.
- Beginning in 1962 the OCC issued a series of rulings that liberalized the scope of activities permitted to national banks under the "incidental powers" clause of the National Bank Act. Often, however, national banks that used these broader powers (in areas such as data processing and travel agencies) found themselves facing lawsuits from nonbank firms and trade associations that opposed bank entry into their industries.[10]
- Money-center banks that sought to expand by practicing liabilities

---

9. This summary omits some intermediate steps whereby the new company acquires a charter for a wholly-owned subsidiary bank (a "phantom" bank) into which is merged the original bank. Under applicable merger statutes, this legal step enables the bank-originated OBHC to avoid minority stockholders in the affiliate bank.

10. Robert P. Mayo, "The 1970 Amendments to the Bank Holding Company Act: One Year Later," *Business Conditions* (Federal Reserve Bank of Chicago), December 1971, pp. 2-11.

management faced FRS constraints, especially in the form of the Regulation Q ceilings that applied to all time deposits prior to 1973.

By using the OBHC vehicle, a large expansionary bank could sidestep each of four hurdles.

Instead of acquiring other banks via the merger route, the parent OBHC could negotiate acquisitions of nonbank firms. Ironically, the Department of Justice could not easily block such mergers because, in the Philadelphia National Bank case, it had successfully argued that banking was a "unique line of commerce." Thus, by definition, if a bank-originated OBHC acquired a large nonbank firm, such a firm was not engaged in the bank's line of commerce and so the merger could not increase the bank's share of its product market.

As long as it controlled no more than one bank, an OBHC was exempt from all constraints of the Bank Holding Company Act.

Instead of facing legal challenges to its direct entry into areas such as data processing and travel agencies, a national bank that was part of an OBHC could indirectly enter such areas via coaffiliate nonbanking firms.

The parent OBHC was exempt from the bank supervision and regulations (such as Regulation Q) that applied to its affiliate bank. Thus the OBHC could, for example, issue short-term nondeposit liabilities that were not subject to Regulation Q ceilings and channel these funds to its affiliate bank that was subject to the ceilings. Similarly, the parent firm might choose to issue debentures and then invest these funds in additional common stock issued by its affiliate bank. In this way the affiliate bank could report favorable equity ratios but, viewed in total, the OBHC had increased its use of long-term debt financing.[11]

Proponents of OBHCs suggested additional benefits that could arise from a large bank's using an OBHC conveniently to expand into related financial areas:[12]

- An OBHC could become a convenient one-stop financial center for its customers. Although it could not expand its traditional banking offices into additional states, its nonbank affiliates could operate in broader geographical markets.
- An OBHC would provide an additional competitive spur in the new product and geographical markets it enters.
- The OBHC could enter activities that promised higher returns than those in traditional banking.
- By diversifying into various activities, the OBHC could try to reduce the risk of the total firm.
- If an OBHC thus increased its returns and/or reduced its risks, its securities would likely achieve a higher market valuation.

11. Eugene M. Lerner, "Three Financial Problems Facing Bank Holding Companies" (Comment), *Journal of Money, Credit, and Banking*, May 1972, pp. 445-455.

12. An illustrative case for OBHCs is made by John R. Bunting, Jr., "One-Bank Holding Companies: A Banker's View," *Harvard Business Review*, May-June 1969, pp. 99-106.

- The OBHC could restructure itself so that some affiliates could attract and retain talented people by paying them salaries and bonuses well above those paid by other affiliates. For example, a bank would likely encounter morale problems if it tried to compensate its outstanding portfolio managers at levels well above those of senior loan officers. If, however, they were in an investment-advisory affiliate instead of in the bank, the OBHC could more readily compensate such portfolio managers at higher levels prevailing for their specialized skills.
- Also, by shifting some of the bank's operations into coaffiliate firms, an OBHC could try to improve its understanding of their functional costs and its use of profit centers.

Whether or not the potential benefits were so great, the number of OBHCs, and the assets they controlled, rapidly increased during the late 1960s:[13]

| Date | Number of Banks in OBHCs | Total Deposits (in billions) | Total Deposits as a Percentage of Deposits of All Banks |
|---|---|---|---|
| Year-end 1965 | 548 | $ 13.9 | 4.5 |
| Year-end 1968 | 783 | 108.2 | 27.5 |
| April 1, 1970 | 1,116 | 138.8 | 32.6 |

At year-end 1965, none of the OBHCs controlled a bank having deposits of $1 billion or more. By year-end 1968, 28 OBHCs controlled banks having deposits of $1 billion or more, and most of the nation's largest banks were affiliates of OBHCs.

Most of the large bank-originated OBHCs announced plans to expand into financial services that were a logical extension of traditional banking services, and their initial major expansion was into areas such as real estate financing and insurance. However, some OBHCs announced their intentions to diversify widely among nonbanking activities.

### Opposition to Expansion by One-Bank Holding Companies

Even as large banks rushed to form and expand their OBHCs, various observers began to question, and in some cases oppose, the rapid expansion of OBHCs. These observers raised the following types of questions about OBHCs:[14]

- Even if the bank is sound and supervised, will not depositors, especially uninsured depositors, lose confidence in a bank affiliate of

---

13. From Larry R. Mote, "The One-Bank Holding Company: History, Issues, and Pending Legislation," *Business Conditions* (Federal Reserve Bank of Chicago), July 1970, Table 1, p. 6.

14. For more complete coverage of the issues, see Bunting and Mote. Also, Paul S. Nadler, "One-Bank Holding Companies: The Public Interest," *Harvard Business Review*, May-June 1969, pp. 107-113; and Sanford Rose, "The Case for the One-Bank Holding Company," *Fortune*, May 15, 1969, pp. 163-165 ff.

an OBHC that reports major financial problems in the bank's coaffiliates or in the parent holding company?

- Might not an affiliate bank at times give preferential treatment to its coaffiliate firms?
- Could not the affiliate bank, perhaps tacitly, encourage customers and potential customers to obtain services from its coaffiliate firms as part of a total package of credit? As a hypothetical example, to obtain a loan, a potential borrower may feel obligated to purchase insurance from the bank's insurance coaffiliate. Such conditions are called *tie-in* arrangements.
- When raising funds in capital markets, will not large OBHCs have unfair competitive advantages compared to smaller firms that are not as recognized in the marketplace?
- Will the OBHCs in fact achieve so many of the organizational efficiencies claimed by their proponents?
- Will not the unbridled expansion of OBHCs lead to concentration of economic power? Here some opponents of OBHCs raised the spectre of large Japanese conglomerates, called *Zaibatsu*, that dominate many areas of the Japanese economy.

Not only did some observers pose public-policy questions about OBHCs; but, as they expanded into nonbanking areas, OBHCs evoked growing opposition from established firms that faced this new competition. In 1969, there were introduced in Congress several bills that would restrict activities of OBHCs. Many OBHCs opposed such restrictive legislation, which may not have readily passed except for a milestone financial episode.

While exercising their new freedom to expand into nonbanking areas, the large OBHCs did not fully foresee how a nonbanking firm could become a major OBHC by acquiring a large bank. In 1969, an aggressive firm, in operation for eight years and headed by a 29-year old executive, moved to acquire control of Chemical New York Corporation, an OBHC that controlled the nation's sixth-largest bank and an historic pillar of the banking community. Using diverse tactics, the OBHC successfully repelled the threatened acquisition.[15] This episode alerted senior officers of large banks and OBHCs that their firms, too, were vulnerable to takeover offers by aggressive nonbanking firms. If they were brought under the Bank Holding Company Act, with its restrictions on nonbanking activities, OBHCs would lose some freedoms; but they would gain protection from unwanted takeovers by nonbanking firms.

## AMENDING THE BANK HOLDING COMPANY ACT

At year-end 1970, the Bank Holding Company Act was amended to close the OBHC "loophole" and to preserve the traditional separation between

---

15. John Brooks, "Annals of Finance," *The New Yorker*, August 13, 1973, pp. 34-40 ff.

banking and commerce. The 1970 amendments define a BHC as any company which has control over any bank or over any bank holding company. This new definition ends the exemption for OBHCs, and it includes partnerships and some trusts.

All BHCs have to register with the Board of Governors of the FRS. The registration statement requires detailed information about the holding company, its affiliates, and its various activities.

If it controls, directly or indirectly, more than 25 percent of a bank's voting shares, then a company has to register as a BHC. When a company owns between 5 percent and 25 percent of a bank's voting shares, the FRS has power to determine whether such ownership constitutes control. The Act presumes that a company does not control a bank if it owns less than 5 percent of the bank's voting shares.

The amendments do not change how the Act controls BHC acquisitions of banks. A BHC generally cannot acquire a bank outside the BHC's home state; and it must obtain prior approval from the FRS before it acquires a bank within its home state. In deciding whether to approve or deny a BHC's proposed acquisition of a bank, the FRS evaluates the proposal in relation to banking, community, and competitive factors.

Importantly, the amendments revised the Act's *Section 4(c) (8)*, which limits BHC involvement in nonbanking activities. The revised Section 4 (c) (8) establishes a two-part test to help the FRS determine which nonbanking activities are permissible for BHCs: *first*, is an activity "so closely related to banking or managing or controlling banks as to be a proper incident thereto"? and *second*, if so, whether performance of this activity "by an affiliate of a holding company can reasonably be expected to produce benefits to the public, such as greater convenience, increased competition, or gains in efficiency, that outweigh possible adverse effects, such as undue concentration of resources, decreased or unfair competition, conflicts of interests, or unsound banking practices." Congress delegated to the Board of Governors—subject to judicial review—the power to administer these new criteria.

The amendments provide some "grandfather" relief to OBHCs that engaged in nonbanking activities prior to June 30, 1968. Even so, the grandfather provision prohibits a BHC from expanding its grandfathered activities by acquiring a firm engaged in such activities; and it empowers the Board of Governors to order divestment of grandfathered activities that it finds are contrary to the public interest. The amendments also permit the Board of Governors to exempt from regulation those OBHCs that can demonstrate that regulation of them would result in a definite hardship or detriment to the public interest.

As it amended the Bank Holding Company Act, Congress also passed some related provisions that apply to BHCs. One is an *anti-tie-in provision*, which prohibits banks from packaging their services or in other ways tying their services to those provided by coaffiliates. This provision, however, allows for some exceptions within traditional services of loans, deposits, and trusts. A second provision gives to "banks and businesses, which would become competitors of a holding company as a result of a proposed expansion, the rights to enter proceedings before the Board as interested parties and to obtain a judicial review of an adverse decision.''[16]

In summary, the Bank Holding Company Act, as amended in 1970, sets the general rules by which BHCs have to operate, and it delegates to the FRS extensive power to interpret and implement the general rules.

## ADMINISTERING THE AMENDED BANK HOLDING COMPANY ACT

The FRS foresaw how the 1970 amendments would lead to a surge of expansion proposals by BHCs. First, because they were no longer exempt from the Bank Holding Company Act, OBHCs might as well become MBHCs to the extent permitted by state law. Thus, the FRS faced an upsurge in BHC applications to acquire or establish banks. Second, because the amendments allowed BHCs to engage in activities that are closely related to banking, BHCs quickly developed proposals to expand into these new, as yet undefined, activities.

Congress mandated that once the Board of Governors receives a complete record of a BHC's application, the Board must decide on the application within 91 days. The beginning of this 91-day period, however, depends largely on the Board's decision as to when it has a "complete record," which may require advisory opinions, transcripts of hearings, and any other information that the Board considers necessary to make a final decision. In practice the Board has tried to adhere to a self-imposed 90-day deadline that begins with a BHC's filing of a properly completed application.

The FRS has developed procedures to expedite the processing of applications by BHCs:

- The FRS has gradually developed a list of permissible nonbanking activities in which BHCs can generally engage. If it applies to engage in one of these permissible activities, a BHC can anticipate a more expeditious decision than if it applies to engage in an activity that has not yet been approved by the Board of Governors.
- If it applies to enter *de novo* into one of the permissible nonbanking activities, a BHC can assume that its application is approved unless the FRS disapproves the application within 45 days. (This presumes that *de novo* entry into permissible activities generally is in the public interest.)
- The Board of Governors has developed a system of *delegated authority*, whereby it basically approves "routine" BHC applications that receive unanimous recommendations for approval by a Federal Reserve Bank and by the Board's staff.[17] The Board then focuses its

---

16. Donald L. Kohn and John F. Zoellner, "The Amended Bank Holding Company Act," *Monthly Review* (Federal Reserve Bank of Kansas City), May 1971, pp. 11-20. The preceding summary of the 1970 amendments draws on this detailed article.

17. *Federal Reserve Bulletin*, January 1975, pp. 30-32.

attention on nonroutine applications that, for example, involve nonunanimous recommendations or basic policy issues.

Within this context of the amended Bank Holding Company Act, as administered by the FRS, BHCs plan and implement their expansionary strategies.

## ACQUIRING AFFILIATE BANKS

To expand, a BHC can try to:

- acquire additional banks
- foster expansion by its current affiliates
- acquire premissible nonbanking affiliates

This section focuses on strategies to acquire additional banks.

### APPLICABILITY OF STATE LAWS

The Bank Holding Company Act reserves to each state substantial power to control activities of BHCs within its borders.[18] Therefore, as a first step, a BHC has to determine whether its state has laws that prohibit or restrict its acquisition of banks.

Although their statutes differ in details, the following states prohibit a BHC from controlling more than one bank: Arkansas, Georgia, Illinois, Indiana, Kansas, Kentucky, Louisiana, Mississippi, Nebraska, Oklahoma, Pennsylvania, and West Virginia. BHCs in these states either are OBHCs, or they are MBHCs that operate under a grandfather provision in the state law.

Some states set ceilings whereby a BHC may not exceed a maximum proportion of deposits in the state. If it exceeds the applicable ceiling, then a BHC cannot acquire additional affiliates; it must rely on internal growth of its current affiliates. For example, New Jersey allows a BHC to acquire control of additional banks as long as its aggregate deposits do not exceed 20 percent of total deposits in the state. Iowa sets a deposit maximum of 8 percent; and New Hampshire sets a maximum of 20 percent, or twelve affiliate banks. Such state statutes differ in how they define the ceiling proportion (for example, whether and how they include interbank deposits and foreign deposits), and so a BHC in such states needs to review the specific statute.

Five states require a BHC to apply for state approval before it acquires control of another bank. These states are Connecticut, Florida, Massachusetts, New York, and South Carolina. Some states, such as Michigan

---

18. This section draws on Peter S. Rose and Donald R. Fraser, "State Regulation of Bank Holding Companies," *The Bankers Magazine*, Winter 1974, pp. 42-48.

and Wisconsin, have laws to safeguard minority stockholders in banks sought by BHCs. Wisconsin, for example, prohibits a BHC from acquiring more than 10 percent of a state bank's stock unless at least three-quarters of the voting shares approve the acquisition.

While some states may relax their restrictions on BHCs, additional states reportedly are considering legislation to set deposit ceilings applicable to BHCs. Therefore an expansionary BHC has to evaluate the feasibility of acquisitions in the context of current state laws, and it also will want to participate in the development of possible changes in such laws.

## IMPLEMENTING AN ACQUISITION STRATEGY

If permitted by applicable state laws, a BHC can seek to expand by acquiring

- a *de novo* (newly chartered) bank
- a major bank in a community
- a bank that accounts for a small proportion of banking services in its geographical market, which is called *foothold entry* into a new market

As do branching systems, BHCs generally prefer to acquire existing banks rather than go through the start-up costs, delays, and uncertainties associated with establishing a *de novo* affiliate. Because of a state's home-office protection laws, at times a BHC can enter an area only by acquiring an established bank in the community. Even where it can expand *de novo*, a BHC analyzes its alternatives by evaluating which banks it might acquire and what terms to offer the stockholders of such banks.

### Identifying Acquisition Candidates

At times the principal stockholders of a nonaffiliate bank solicit acquisition offers from BHCs. Over time a BHC thus learns of potential acquisitions that its staff can then evaluate.

In addition, an expansionary BHC maps out an acquisition strategy. It analyzes geographical markets within its state and identifies markets where it would like to add affiliate banks.[19] Knowing that its acquisition proposals will have to be approved by the FRS, a BHC generally tries to expand into areas where its current affiliates account for a minor proportion, if any, of banking services. For example, if it controls large banks in some major metropolitan areas, then a BHC evaluates opportunities to enter other metropolitan areas and county-seat towns within the state.

Several studies document the types of markets in which BHCs acquire banks. One study analyzes MBHC acquisitions of banks in 100 metropolitan markets in ten states; and it concludes that ''MBHCs are more active in

---

19. One banker reports how his BHC uses a research model to help plan its acquisition strategy. George D. Woodward, Jr., ''Analyzing Multi-Bank Holding Company Acquisitions Through Economic Research,'' *The Magazine of Bank Administration*, November 1976, pp. 46-49.

markets characterized by: (1) relatively fast growth in terms of banking offices; (2) relatively favorable conditions as shown by total deposits per bank office; (3) relatively high rates of return; and (4) relatively low concentration."[20] Another study analyzes the geographical markets in which BHCs acquired banks between 1971 and 1974; and it reports that BHCs primarily acquired banks in "urban, manufacturing-oriented, densely populated areas with rapid economic growth and high levels of income."[21]

A BHC then evaluates which banks it might realistically try to acquire in the markets that it seeks to enter. It will be infeasible to acquire banks that are already affiliates of other MBHCs or that have controlling stockholders who set unrealistically high prices. Because the FRS prefers a BHC to enter a new market *de novo* or via a foothold acquisition, it is difficult for a BHC to acquire one of the large banks in a market. Thus an expansionary BHC generally focuses its acquisition search on medium-sized, nonaffiliate banks. One study analyzes MBHC acquisitions of banks in eight states, and it concludes that in seven of the eight states "the median deposit size of acquired banks exceeds, often substantially, the median deposit size of available banks within the states."[22] The study also demonstrates that MBHCs avoid acquisitions of small banks, especially those with deposits below $10 million. A subsequent study examines a larger sample of acquisitions, and it reports similar results: "The large mean size of banks acquired by BHCs stands in sharp contrast to the population of all U.S. banks, three quarters of which have deposits below $25 million." The author notes, however, that in 1974 the mean size of acquired banks dropped almost in half (to $43 million), apparently "a reflection of the Federal Reserve Board's concern with the growing concentration of bank resources in a number of metropolitan areas."[23]

BHCs usually acquire well-managed banks that have typical operating ratios. Occasionally, a BHC acquires a bank that has management problems and/or inadequate capital, and the BHC then injects managerial and/or financial resources into the new affiliate. After reviewing the evidence, however, one analyst concludes that apparently "these alleged benefits of affiliation are somewhat exaggerated."[24]

### Developing Acquisition Offers

A BHC has to develop an offer to submit to a selected bank's management and directors, who then recommend whether the bank's stockholders should

20. Gregory E. Boczar, "Market Characteristics and Multibank Holding Company Acquisitions," *The Journal of Finance*, March 1977, pp. 131-146.

21. Peter S. Rose, "The Pattern of Bank Holding Company Acquisitions" (Research Commentary), *Journal of Bank Research*, Autumn 1976, pp. 236-240.

22. Paul F. Jessup, "Analyzing Acquisitions by Bank Holding Companies" (Research Commentary), *Journal of Bank Research*, Spring 1974, pp. 55-63.

23. Rose, "The Pattern of Bank Holding Company Acquisitions," p. 238.

24. Dale S. Drum, "MBHCs: Evidence after Two Decades of Regulation," *Business Conditions* (Federal Reserve Bank of Chicago), December 1976, pp. 3-15.

accept or reject the offer. Usually a BHC can structure and negotiate an offer in ways that increase the probability of its acceptance.

Instead of offering cash, a BHC usually offers to exchange its stock for that of the selected bank. To illustrate, a BHC may offer three of its shares for each share of the selected bank. If they accept the offer, the selling stockholders thus receive the BHC's shares that generally are more marketable than those of the acquired bank and that may have a higher current-dividend yield. Also, the selling stockholders can defer paying capital gains taxes on the transaction until they or their heirs sell the BHC shares. In contrast, if they accept a cash offer, the selling stockholders immediately realize their gains or losses for tax purposes. Thus, to defer taxes, selling stockholders may prefer a share exchange offer, even if its dollar value is less than an alternative cash offer. A study of BHC acquisitions of 102 banks reports that "31 involved taxable cash purchases and 71 were effected by tax-free exchanges of stock."[25]

Especially when a selected bank's officers and directors also are the bank's major stockholders, a BHC can offer to retain the current officers, at least for a while, so that they will qualify for the BHC's benefit plans. Similarly, the BHC can announce its intention to retain the bank's current directors and policies. While it thus structures its offer to appeal to a bank's management and directors, to expedite acceptance and avoid controversy a BHC seeks to demonstrate that the total offer is fair to all of the bank's stockholders.

A BHC also has to determine the dollar amount, whether in shares or in cash, that it will offer for each share of a bank. To make it attractive to selling stockholders, this dollar amount usually involves a premium over the recent prices at which the bank's stock has been sold. In principle, a BHC should carefully project and discount the various cash flows and other anticipated benefits from a proposed acquisition and then use this valuation procedure to determine what premium, if any, to offer to a bank's stockholders. In practice, the valuation process at times consists of simple decision rules. Two analysts interviewed various BHCs to learn how they determined the purchase premiums that they offered to acquisition candidates, and they report that several BHCs:

> value a bank on the basis of book value plus some percentage of total deposits. This is obviously a poor measure of earning power or cash generation capacity. . . . Other holding companies apparently enter negotiations resigned in the belief that they must pay premiums in line with those exacted by selling stockholders in other recent acquisitions. Negotiations are then little different from the Florence flea market, with the potential buyer responding to the demands of the seller, often without any firm feel for the value of the merchandise. [26]

---

25. Thomas R. Piper and Steven J. Weiss, "The Profitability of Multibank Holding Company Acquisitions," *The Journal of Finance*, March 1974, pp. 163-174.

26. Thomas R. Piper and Steven J. Weiss, "The Profitability of Bank Acquisitions by Multi-Bank Holding Companies," *New England Economic Review* (Federal Reserve Bank of Boston), September-October 1971, pp. 2-12.

A retired chairman of a large BHC reflects that if it wants to buy a bank, a BHC should "be prepared to pay more than a bank is worth, rather than lose it. . . . From an experience of many years in buying banks, my only regrets are for one or two small ones that we missed because of the price, and not for those where perhaps we overpaid."[27] A BHC may willingly pay high premiums if it believes that it has but one chance to buy a specific bank or if it believes that it can use its managerial and financial resources to increase the returns and/or reduce the risk of an acquired bank.

One study analyzes "the profitability of 102 acquisitions by [30 different] multibank holding companies during the period 1946-67."[28] The study uses two tests to evaluate the profitability of these acquisitions, and concludes that, "on average, the acquisitions have been breakeven propositions for the holding companies and have not furthered the interests of their stockholders. . . . Fifty-three percent of the acquisitions were, in fact, unprofitable; their incidence was spread across most of the holding companies. The major reasons for unprofitable acquisitions appear to be overly generous purchase prices and the failure of holding company managements to raise the profitability of the acquired banks, relative to the acquiring holding company." The authors further observe that "the holding companies did not acquire, on average, financially weak or poorly managed banks where dramatic gains could be secured by the infusion of capital or specialized staff. . . . The acquired banks were very similar to other banks in their market areas in terms of portfolio choices, deposit growth and profitability during the five years prior to acquisition."[29] The authors acknowledge possible criticisms of how they measure and interpret the profitability of BHC acquisitions, but their results do alert BHC managements to the need carefully to plan and analyze their acquisitions.

A subsequent study uses a more complex valuation procedure to measure whether stockholders of BHCs benefit from their firms' acquisition programs. The study focuses on how an acquisition program may affect a BHC's subsequent earnings and the valuation of the earnings. The study analyzes 18 BHCs that acquired banks, and it estimates how these acquisitions affected a BHC's subsequent earnings growth and, as a measure of risk, the variability of the earnings growth. Although its results are not statistically powerful, the study concludes that the shareholders of the sample BHCs "experienced improvements in the level of earnings to which they hold claims and, apparently, this improvement grows over time. In addition, to the extent that the owners' conception of risk is accurately measured by the coefficient of variation of income growth rates, risk is reduced through the acquisition program."[30]

27. Baldwin Maull, "Some Observations on Bank Holding Companies," *The Bankers Magazine*, Summer 1972, pp. 19-23.

28. Piper and Weiss. Both articles report on the same basic study.

29. Piper and Weiss, "The Profitability of Multibank Holding Company Acquisitions," pp. 169, 173-174.

30. Walter A. Varvel, "A Valuation Approach to Bank Holding Company Acquisitions," *Economic Review* (Federal Reserve Bank of Richmond), July-August 1975, pp. 9-15.

In conclusion, to best serve their own stockholders and to avoid paying excessive purchase premiums, at least some BHCs need to review and refine the procedures by which they develop their acquisition offers.

### Applying for Acquisition Approval by the Federal Reserve System

A BHC plans its acquisitions and documents its applications in ways that will increase the probability of approval by the FRS. Therefore senior managers of a BHC keep informed about laws and recent regulatory decisions that can affect their acquisition strategy, but they have to rely on staff, legal counsel, and consultants for detailed interpretations and advice.

The Bank Holding Company Act (Section 3) states that: " *In every case*, the Board shall take into consideration the *financial and managerial resources and future prospects* of the company or companies and the banks concerned, and the *convenience and needs of the community* to be served" (italics added).

Moreover, the Act directs the Board not to approve any bank acquisition:

> . . . whose effect in any section of the country may be substantially to lessen competition, or to tend to create a monopoly, or which in any other manner would be in restraint of trade, unless it finds that the anticompetitive effects of the proposed transactions are clearly outweighed in the public interest by the probable effect of the transaction in meeting the convenience and needs of the community to be served.

The FRS (and, in contested cases, the courts) administers these statutory factors that are typically summarized as:

- banking
   financial condition and history
   financial prospects
   management characteristics
- convenience and needs
- competitive

For each application the FRS has to evaluate and weigh these factors. Thus if they review the general pattern of FRS decisions concerning proposed acquisitions, officials of BHCs can develop guidelines as to how to increase the probability of FRS approval of a specific application.

A BHC knows, by statute, that if it proposes an acquisition that probably involves anticompetitive effects, then it will have to demonstrate that the convenience and needs factor *clearly outweighs* the anticompetitive effects. To so demonstrate is a high, although not impossible, hurdle that can involve the costs of expert documentation and probable delays. Therefore, except in special cases, a BHC focuses its resources on acquisitions that do not involve evident anticompetitive effects. It uses its staff and consultants to screen out acquisitions that clearly raise anticompetitive issues; and, if it has some remaining doubt, it is likely informally to solicit the views of the local Federal Reserve Bank before it submits a formal application.

**Preparing an Application to Acquire a Bank**  Once it decides formally to apply to acquire a bank, a BHC submits a detailed application form to the Federal Reserve Bank of the District in which it has its principal banking operations. (Usually the bank to be acquired and the applicant BHC are in the same Federal Reserve District.) The application requires a signed resolution by the applicant's board of directors and the following types of supporting materials:

- description of applicant and proposed transaction
- financial and managerial information
- convenience and needs
- competition among banks
- nonbanking activities—competition

The FRS uses these materials, supplemented by additional information available to it, to analyze and decide on the proposed acquisition.

When it prepares its application, a BHC tries to demonstrate how a proposed acquisition complies with the Bank Holding Company Act. Concerning banking factors, a BHC tries to show how its proposed acquisition will improve the acquired bank's financial and managerial resources, for example by: providing access to the BHC's greater financial resources, having the BHC pledge to invest additional equity capital in the bank, and/or providing management depth. The FRS has cited such benefits as consistent with its approval of some specific applications.

Concerning convenience and needs, the applicant BHC states how its proposed acquisition will likely contribute to the acquired bank's better meeting the current and projected needs of its community. Here the FRS invites a BHC specifically to comment on expected changes in interest rates paid or charged, service charges, loan policies, physical facilities, banking hours, and other available services.

One study surveys the convenience and needs section of 109 applications filed by 21 MBHCs, mostly located in Florida. The study found "few firm commitments, and even these were usually vague as to when and for how long the improvements would be implemented."[31] The applicant BHCs primarily stated that, as a result of a proposed acquisition, an acquired bank would improve its customer services (especially trust and international) and receive from the BHC improved services in such areas as loan participations, data processing, investment advice, and management and personnel.

31. Joseph E. Rossman and B. Frank King, "Multibank Holding Companies: Convenience and Needs," *Economic Review* (Federal Reserve Bank of Atlanta), July-August 1977, pp. 83-91.

The applicant BHCs seldom proposed changes in physical facilities, banking hours, or rates paid to or charged consumers. As a follow-up section, the study concludes that the BHCs usually implemented their proposed convenience and needs benefits. Based on this survey, a conclusion is that BHCs probably can strengthen their applications by more specifically documenting how a proposed bank acquisition will benefit the community.

Another study reviews 44 acquisitions by BHCs in the Seventh (Chicago) Federal Reserve District. It reports that "on average, holding companies made few firm commitments to change or expand services of the banks they acquired. It appears, however, that where changes were proposed, the holding companies carried through with the proposals."[32]

**Evaluating Applications to Acquire Banks** If it finds that a proposed acquisition has anticompetitive effects, then the FRS can approve it *only if* the convenience and needs factor *clearly outweighs* the anticompetitive effects. Thus the competitive effects often are a critical part of an FRS analysis of a proposed acquisition.

When it analyzes an application, the FRS estimates the existing competition between the BHC's affiliates and the bank that the BHC proposes to acquire. To do so, the FRS tries to determine the geographical market served by the bank to be acquired. It then estimates what proportion of this total market is accounted for by the various banks that service it. For example, in a specific rural area, the staff of the FRS may determine that the county boundaries delineate the relevant geographical market and that the banks in the county account for all the existing banking competition within this market. The staff then computes the ratio of each bank's deposits to total bank deposits in the county. It also computes other measures, such as each bank's proportion of total bank loans in the county. If it already has one or more affiliates in the county and these affiliates account for more than a small proportion of banking services in the market, then a BHC knows that the FRS is unlikely to approve the BHC's increasing its share of the market by its acquiring another bank in the county. In practice, especially in metropolitan areas, it is often difficult to determine the relevant geographical market and to enumerate the banks competing in the market. If it proposes to expand in such an area, a BHC can try to delineate the relevant market in a way that suggests minimal existing competition between its current affiliates(s) and the bank it proposes to acquire. Even so, the BHC has to anticipate that its market delineation will receive critical evaluation, and possible rejection if the FRS staff decides on a different specification of the relevant market.

Among its early denials of BHC acquisitions, the Board of Governors often cited adverse effects on existing competition. Therefore BHCs, especially large ones, have revised their strategies and now typically seek to acquire banks in cities distant from those in which they already have affiliate

---

32. David R. Allardice, "Convenience and Needs: a Post-Audit Survey," *Economic Perspectives* (Federal Reserve Bank of Chicago), May-June 1978, pp. 20-23.

banks. Even if it demonstrates that there is no existing competition between its affiliates and a bank it proposes to acquire, a BHC has to anticipate the FRS's reviewing the acquisition's potential anticompetitive effects. The FRS has applied the concept of *potential competition* to at least four different situations:[33]

- As in merger analysis, one situation exists when banks in a market behave competitively because of possible entry by banks outside the immediate market.
- A second situation, sometimes called "probable future competition," takes place when the FRS judges that, if instead of a BHC's acquiring a major bank in a market, it would be more procompetitive if a BHC would enter the market *de novo* (by establishing a new affiliate) or by acquiring a small bank in the market (a foothold acquisition). Thus the FRS may deny a BHC's application to acquire a major bank in a market in which it has no affiliate in the *expectation* that the BHC will subsequently apply for *de novo* or foothold entry.
- A third situation occurs when a BHC applies to acquire a large bank in a market in which the BHC has no affiliate, *if* this acquisition will likely preclude the acquired bank's ever becoming the nucleus of a new BHC that could eventually compete in various markets within the state.
- A fourth situation is when a BHC proposes to enter a new market by acquiring two banks that have some informal affiliation, thereby eliminating the possibility that the two banks may eventually compete with each other in the future.

Since early 1960, the FRS increasingly has cited adverse potential competition as a factor in its denials of BHC acquisitions. One study reviews all of the Board's denial orders between 1957 and 1974. Of the 150 denial orders during this 18-year period, "more than half (76) cited potential competition as either a major or minor factor in the decision to deny the applications," and almost half of these denial orders occurred in 1973 and 1974.[34] As they review these past denials, BHCs gain insights into how the FRS will likely apply its concept of potential competition to future acquisition proposals.

To try to increase the probability of FRS approval, a BHC can emphasize how it believes that a proposed acquisition will be procompetitive. For example, if the proposal involves *de novo* entry, a BHC will point out how this entry will add a new decision maker to the market. As summarized in Exhibit 19-1, some BHCs have successfully emphasized the procompetitive benefits of their acquiring a bank.

33. Harvey Rosenblum, "Bank Holding Companies: Part II," *Business Conditions* (Federal Reserve Bank of Chicago), April 1975, pp. 13-15. A more detailed analysis of the concept of potential competition is by Stephen A. Rhoades, "A Clarification of the Potential Competition Doctrine in Bank Merger Analysis," *Journal of Bank Research*, Spring 1975, pp. 35-42.

34. Rosenblum, "Bank Holding Companies: Part II," p. 14.

## EXHIBIT 19-1

### Types of Benefits Cited by the Board of Governors of the Federal Reserve System in Orders Approving Bank Acquisitions by Bank Holding Companies

BANKING FACTORS

Improved Financial Resources

> Acquiring a financially weak firm
> Improving the debt-to-equity ratio of the acquired firm
> Injecting a specific amount of equity capital into the acquired firm
> Providing "access to the greater financial resources" of the holding company

Improved Managerial Resources

> Alleviating management succession problems
> Providing management depth

Improved Efficiency

> Economies of scale
> Complementary skills

CONVENIENCE AND NEEDS

> Providing an alternative source of services to a market
> Increased lending capacity to support strong economic growth in an area
> Expansion of specialized credit services

INCREASED COMPETITION

> Increased competition through de novo entry
> Reduction of rates charged on loans or other services
> Strengthening the competitive position of a small firm through affiliation with a larger bank holding company
> Increasing competition by changing a limited-service institution into a full-service firm
> Changing a conservative firm into a more aggressive competitor

Source: From Michael A. Jessee and Steven A. Seelig, "An Analysis of the Public Benefits Test of the Bank Holding Company Act," Monthly Review (Federal Reserve Bank of New York), June 1974, Table I, p. 153. The original table and its associated article document specific Board decisions that cite these factors.

One study analyzes the decisions from 1971 through early 1974, when the Board of Governors approved 436 and denied 22 BHC acquisitions of banks. The authors find that the principal reasons for Board denials were: "a lessening of existing or potential competition, a weakening of the financial and/or managerial condition of the bank, and unsound banking practices." The authors conclude their study by observing that:

> . . . public benefits provide the strongest support for an application when the benefits are concrete, when they result in the alleviation of a specific problem,

or when they result in lower prices or increased services to the public. Applicants must recognize that such benefits are essential in cases where even a small amount of competition would be eliminated. Yet the value of substantive benefits is increasingly uncertain the more severe are the anticompetitive or other adverse factors perceived by the Board.[35]

Another pair of authors analyze 86 cases in which the Board of Governors disapproved the formation of a BHC or a BHC's acquisition of a bank. The Board mentioned convenience and needs only in about half of these denials. Three factors that reportedly were most critical in the denials were: "potential competition, the relative size of the bank to be acquired in its own market area, and the financial status of the applicant." Concerning the third factor, in nine of the denials the Board concluded that the applicant would use excessive debt to finance the acquisition. The authors conclude that their review can provide guidelines for expansionary BHCs to:

> Select a bank that is relatively small in its market area, stress the undesirability of entering the market through any other means such as *de novo* entry, be very careful how you finance the acquisition and what fees you plan to charge for management services, and, finally, don't waste much time coming up with new services that might be offered through your new subsidiary unless, in fact, there is a reasonable expectation that they will be offered on an economically viable basis.[36]

Another author suggests similar guidelines to help expansionary banking systems structure their acquisition proposals in ways that will increase the probability of FRS approval.[37]

If the FRS denies its proposed acquisition, a BHC has three options:

- In unusual circumstances, for example if it develops important new information, the BHC can request the FRS to reconsider its decision.
- It can try to appeal the decision in the courts. This can be a costly and prolonged process.
- It can accept the FRS decision and forego the proposed acquisition.

At times rival banking organizations and/or citizens' groups oppose a BHC's proposed acquisition. They can submit written comments to the FRS, and they can request the FRS to hear their views in oral presentations and/or a formal hearing. If the FRS approves the acquisition, these opposing

---

35. Michael A. Jessee and Steven A. Seelig, "An Analysis of the Public Benefits Test of the Bank Holding Company Act," *Monthly Review* (Federal Reserve Bank of New York), June 1974, pp. 151-162.

36. Donald R. Fraser and Peter S. Rose, "Holding Company Expansion: When the Fed Says No," *The Magazine of Bank Administration*, December 1973, pp. 36-40, 44.

37. Douglas V. Austin, "Potential Competition: A Guide for Acquisition-Minded Bankers," *The Bankers Magazine*, Winter 1971, pp. 23-28.

organizations similarly have to decide whether to request reconsideration by the FRS, appeal the decision in the courts, or accept the decision.

The courts have upheld most FRS decisions, and most banking organizations know that there will be times when they will apply for FRS approval of other activities. Therefore banking organizations generally decide not to appeal an acquisition decision by the Board of Governors.

## OPERATING PERFORMANCE OF MULTIBANK HOLDING COMPANIES

Proponents of MBHCs cite how these organizations have various operating advantages compared to most nonaffiliate banks. This section summarizes these presumed benefits and then examines how extensive they are in practice.

### POTENTIAL BENEFITS OF MULTIBANK HOLDING COMPANIES

Banking literature cites various potential benefits that an MBHC, operating as a *de facto* branch system, can provide to its affiliate banks.[38] This literature assumes that the benefits are especially feasible if an MBHC is large, geographically diversified, with some centralized management and a large lead bank. It further assumes that some of the benefits accrue to the customers and stockholders of an MBHC.

#### Human Resources

Compared to most nonaffiliate banks, especially small ones, an MBHC has more depth and internal mobility of its management and personnel. An MBHC recruits people at various entry levels, and it has programs to train and upgrade these people. Its size enables an MBHC to develop depth among its managers and specialists, who can move among the affiliate banks. To attract and retain key personnel, an MBHC develops systemwide employee benefit plans.

#### Convenient Specialized Services

A small or medium-sized affiliate conveniently uses the system's lead bank to offer its customers convenient specialized services such as trusts and international banking. When it has acceptable loan requests that exceed its legal lending limit, the affiliate bank seeks to participate the loan with its

---

38. See, for example, Douglas V. Austin, "Who Needs a Holding Company?" *The Magazine of Bank Administration*, January 1973, pp. 46-48; Robert J. Lawrence, *The Performance of Bank Holding Companies* (a Staff Study), Board of Governors of the Federal Reserve System, 1967; and Steven J. Weiss, "Bank Holding Companies and Public Policy," *New England Economic Review* (Federal Reserve Bank of Boston), January-February 1969, pp. 3-29.

lead bank and/or other coaffiliates. As components of a centralized system, affiliates of an MBHC also try to achieve volume economies in their marketing campaigns and in their purchases of supplies and equipment. Presumably, an MBHC passes some of these operating economies on to its customers.

## Broad Diversification

Its large size and geographical dispersion enable an MBHC to achieve broad diversification compared to a smaller bank that operates in a narrower geographical area. Its size warrants an MBHC's having skilled personnel to analyze and administer its diversification among assets and sources of funds. If it has affiliates throughout its state, an MBHC also can geographically diversify its assets and deposits. For example, it diversifies its assets and deposits among customers in various rural and metropolitan areas that are not all subject to similar economic events. Compared to a less diversified banking organization and other factors being equal, if it uses diversification procedures to control risks, an MBHC should be able to increase other of its risks, for example by having higher loan ratios and/or lower capital ratios. Its geographical diversification also enables an MBHC to transfer funds, via loan participations, from the surplus to deficit areas serviced by its affiliates.

## Access to Capital

While shares of most small nonaffiliate banks trade inactively in local markets, shares of most MBHCs trade actively in regional or national capital markets; and so these MBHCs have more convenient access to additional capital. Moreover, if they believe that MBHCs generally can provide higher and/or more stable returns over time (for example, because of their size, expansion opportunities, and risk-control procedures), then stock investors will value the MBHCs' earnings streams more highly than those of small banks that are not as expansionary or diversified. Similarly, those who purchase bank debt instruments may demand lower risk premiums from widely held debentures of large diversified MBHCs. Thus an MBHC's stockholders, and possibly its customers, may benefit both from their firm's convenient access to capital and its lower cost of capital.

## Summary

Thus, an MBHC's principal potential benefits are:

- depth and internal mobility of its management and personnel
- convenient, specialized services, including large loans, possibly at lower costs
- broad diversification, facilitating risk reduction and intrasystem funds flows
- convenient, and possibly lower-cost, access to capital

These are comparative benefits. Large nonaffiliate banks and branch systems have similar potential benefits, and small nonaffiliate banks can potentially achieve many of these benefits, although perhaps less reliably, through the correspondent banking system. When they raise additional capital, most MBHCs have a comparative advantage over small nonaffiliate banks; but the extent to which an MBHC realizes the other benefits depends in part on whether it operates primarily as a centralized or decentralized system.

## MANAGING A CENTRALIZED OR DECENTRALIZED SYSTEM

An MBHC can operate:

- as a decentralized system in which each affiliate has substantial autonomy
- as a centralized system in which the parent holding company (or its lead bank) closely directs many activities of its affiliate banks
- between these general extremes

While they thus can vary in their degree of centralization, MBHCs also have to decide how far to centralize specific functions within their systems.

Federal and state laws and regulations can limit the degree of centralization within an MBHC. Each bank affiliate of an MBHC has its own charter and its own board of directors, who are legally responsible for its operations. The Federal Reserve Act (Section 23A) restricts some types of loans between a BHC's affiliate banks, and some states prohibit an MBHC from having one trust affiliate to service customers of its various coaffiliate banks.

Even where it can choose to centralize many functions, an MBHC sometimes opts for substantial decentralization in the belief that this autonomy enables each affiliate to respond better to its local market conditions.

Several studies report on the variety of centralization that occurs among and within MBHCs.

Two senior officers of a new MBHC surveyed 12 MBHCs that varied in their locations, sizes, and years of operation. The authors report how the centralization of management control by these MBHCs ranges from " 'loose, with a high degree of autonomy,' to 'moderate, but tightening,' to 'very tight controls—almost like a branch system.' " Most of these MBHCs involve themselves in their affiliates' audits, budgets, capital expenditures, investments, benefit programs, and promotions and salaries of key personnel. Three of the sample MBHCs report substantial centralization in their headquarters, while nine allow each affiliate bank's "chief executive to be fairly independent, although when a bank is not doing well, the full weight of the holding company is brought to bear." These nine MBHCs expect each bank's chief executive to set goals, subject to review; and then they try to measure his or her performance in relation to the goals. "The two most common measurement tools . . . are return on assets and return on equity.'' Most of the MBHCs perform the following services for their affiliate banks: ''investment management, loan participation, auditing, data processing, advertising, market research, and printing and supplies.'' Nearly all of the sample MBHCs recently had raised additional long-term funds (in all cases via debentures), which they then channeled to affiliate banks as equity capital, unless some state law made it advantageous to purchase an affiliate's debentures. Based on their survey results, the executives of the new MBHC developed a set of guidelines that reflected the goals and needs of their specific firm and which, in their judgment, ''represent a minimum of necessary control by the parent company—with a maximum of latitude given to local management.''[39]

Another study surveys 52 MBHCs and uses an index of centralization (centralized, moderately centralized, or decentralized) to measure the extent to which these firms centralize control over ten major policy areas of their affiliate banks. The study's principal conclusions are:

- MBHCs ''differ considerably in the amount of control exercised over their subsidiary banks, but there appears to be no relationship between the degree of centralization and variables such as the size of the holding company, the geographic distribution of its banks, the number of years the company has been in existence, and the size distribution of its banks.'' Therefore a key explanatory factor seems to be the management style of a specific MBHC's senior officers.
- The extent of centralization also differs among the specific policy areas. ''Certain bank investments, specifically securities investments and federal funds transactions, and bank correspondent relationships including loan participations are generally closely controlled by the holding company or the lead bank. On the other hand, pricing policies, decisions on the composition of the loan portfolio, and decisions with respect to individual loan applications are usually made by the individual subsidiary banks.''
- The MBHCs generally participate in their affiliate banks' major decisions concerning bank capital and personnel.[40]

The preceding two studies do not examine whether or how centralization within an MBHC changes over time. At least three factors can contribute toward increasing centralization within some MBHCs:

- In states where liberalized branching is pending or very probable, an MBHC is likely to centralize more functions in the lead bank in anticipation of the other affiliates' becoming branches of the lead bank.

---

39. Edward A. Jesser, Jr., and Kenneth H. Fisher, ''Guidelines for Bank Holding Company Management,'' *The Bankers Magazine*, Summer 1973, pp. 13-20.

40. Robert J. Lawrence, *Operating Policies of Bank Holding Companies: Part I*, Staff Economic Study No. 59, Board of Governors of the Federal Reserve System, 1971. A summary of this study is in the *Federal Reserve Bulletin*, April 1971, pp. 283-284.

- Recent advances in computer-based management systems facilitate further centralization of activities in the MBHC or its lead bank.
- An MBHC's senior officers and their management styles change over time; and, once it begins, a trend toward increased centralization is unlikely to be reversed.

## COMPARING THE PERFORMANCE OF AFFILIATE AND NONAFFILIATE BANKS

Various studies compare the operating performance of affiliate and nonaffiliate banks. Their conclusions provide insights for: managers and stockholders both of MBHCs and of nonaffiliate banks that compete with and may be acquired by MBHCs, and public officials who develop and administer BHC laws and regulations.

Exhibit 19-2 summarizes the principal procedures and results of six studies that analyze the operating performance of MBHC affiliates. All six studies use standard operating ratios, but each study analyzes different samples of banks in different time periods. Four of the studies focus on whether changes occur in the operating performance of banks recently acquired by MBHCs, and, if so, whether these changes differ significantly from those of nonaffiliate banks that are similar in size and location. Two of the studies focus on whether, at a specific time, there are significant operating differences between samples of affiliate and similar nonaffiliate banks.

The six studies, with their different samples and methodologies, report similar conclusions. Although one has to interpret cautiously aggregate ratios, here is a summary of the principal significant differences in the operating ratios of affiliate and similar nonaffiliate banks:

- As a percentage of total assets, affiliate banks have higher ratios of municipal securities and loans and lower ratios of cash and U.S. Treasury securities.
- Two studies report that the affiliate banks have lower ratios of interest on loans to loans, and three studies report that affiliate banks obtain more service charge revenues from their demand deposits.
- Differences are minor in the ratios involving total revenues and total expenses.
- Only one study, the latest and largest, reports significant differences in rates of return and capital ratios, with the affiliate banks having higher rates of return but lower capital. (Several of the other studies report lower, but not significantly lower, capital ratios.)

Overall, there are not many significant or consistent differences between the operating ratios of affiliate and nonaffiliate banks.[41] The principal area of difference is in the composition of their assets.

---

41. Instead of analyzing operating ratios, a recent report tabulates questionnaire responses from large samples of affiliate and nonaffiliate banks. Peter S. Rose, "How the Holding Companies Are Doing," *The Bankers Magazine*, Spring 1977, pp. 88-94.

A staff study, prepared for the Board of Governors of the FRS, reviews and evaluates the available research about BHCs. This study states that "in short, BHC banks exhibit riskier portfolios and more leveraged capital positions than similar unaffiliated banks, but their profitability and growth are no different."[42] Two coauthors review various comparative studies and conclude that "bank holding companies seem to have much less effect on the performance of their affiliated institutions than both the supporters and the critics of the holding company movement would have us believe."[43]

In view of the various benefits postulated for affiliate banks, why do these studies find so few operating differences between affiliate and nonaffiliate banks? If MBHCs gradually change the operating policies of banks they acquire, then the studies need to allow a long interval in which to analyze operating changes after a bank becomes an affiliate. Two of the studies specifically test various postacquisition intervals, and they report some evidence that the postacquisition effects occur gradually over a period of three or four years.[44]

Because they encompass MBHCs that range from highly centralized to highly decentralized, the studies may obscure operating differences that are associated with various degrees of centralization. One study specifically tests "whether the internal organizational structure of a bank holding company significantly affects the performance of its banking affiliates in terms of asset management, deposit structure, capital adequacy, pricing policies, expense control and profitability." The study uses multivariate analysis to examine a large sample (656) of affiliate and nonaffiliate banks, and it finds "few differences between nonaffiliated banks and subsidiaries of decentralized systems" and between affiliates of decentralized and centralized systems.[45] These outcomes do not support the view that centralized MBHCs manage their affiliates more aggressively or efficiently than do decentralized systems.

If MBHCs mostly acquire medium-sized, well-managed banks that operate in competitive markets, then the MBHCs may have limited opportunities to change substantially an acquired bank's operating policies.

The studies focus on the operating performance of the affiliate banks and not on the total performance of the MBHC. Several of the studies report that the affiliate banks have higher ratios of "other" operating expenses to total assets. These other expenses include various fees that an affiliate bank

42. "Bank Holding Company Study Completed," *Voice* (Federal Reserve Bank of Dallas), July 1978, pp. 9-13. Also, see Samuel H. Talley, "Bank Holding Company Operations and Performance," *The Magazine of Bank Administration*, October 1973, pp. 26-29.

43. Peter S. Rose and Donald R. Fraser, "The Impact of Holding Company Acquisitions on Bank Performance," *The Bankers Magazine*, Spring 1973, pp. 85-91.

44. Rodney D. Johnson and David R. Meinster, "The Performance of Bank Holding Company Acquisitions: A Multivariate Analysis," *The Journal of Business*, April 1975, pp. 204-212; and Robert F. Ware, "Performance of Banks Acquired by Multi-bank Holding Companies in Ohio," *Economic Review* (Federal Reserve Bank of Cleveland), March-April 1973, pp. 19-28.

45. Lucille S. Mayne, "Management Policies of Bank Holding Companies and Bank Performance," *Journal of Bank Research*, Spring 1976, pp. 37-48.

## EXHIBIT 19-2

## Principal Operating Differences Between Affiliate and Nonaffiliate Banks

| | Sample Design | | | Rates of Return | | Portfolio Composition | | | |
|---|---|---|---|---|---|---|---|---|---|
| | Number of Affiliate Banks | Principal Location of Banks | Time Period | on Assets | on Capital | Cash | U.S. Government Securities | State and Municipal Securities | Loans |
| **OPERATING CHANGES AFTER ACQUISITION** | | | | | | | | | |
| Lawrence | 43 | Nationwide | 1952-64 | NSD | NSD | ↓ | ↓ | ↑ | ↑ |
| Johnston & Meinster‡ | 27 | Nationwide† | 1952-64 | ..... | ..... | ..... | ..... | ↑ | ↑ |
| Talley | 82 | Nationwide | 1966-69 | NSD | NSD | NSD | ↓ | ↑ | ↑ |
| Ware | 27 | Ohio | 1965-72 | NSD | NSD | NSD | NSD | NSD | NSD |
| **OPERATING COMPARISONS OF AFFILIATE AND NONAFFILIATE BANKS** | | | | | | | | | |
| McLeary | 82 | Sixth (Atlanta) Federal Reserve District | 1966 | NR | NR | NSD | ↓ | ↑ | NSD |
| Mayne | 328 | Nationwide | Yearly Analysis 1969-72 | ↑ | ↑ | ↓** | ↓** | ↑ | NSD |

*Notes:* Arrows, (↑) or (↓), indicate direction of significant difference; NSD is No significant difference; NR is Not reported

*IPC is Individuals, Partnerships and Corporations

†A subset of Lawrence's sample

‡This study uses multiple discriminant analysis (MDA) to rank the performance measures that "best discriminate" between the acquired and nonacquired banks. It reports only five such variables: the four shown in the Exhibit and a fifth, "Interest on Governments to Governments," which increased.

**Mayne combines cash and low risk securities (including U.S. Government securities) as a percentage of total assets and reports that this liquid assets ratio is significantly lower for affiliate banks than for nonaffiliate banks in two of the four years.

pays to its parent MBHC. Thus this "expense item" essentially is a transfer payment that contributes revenues to the parent MBHC.

A recent study specifically tests whether, other things equal, affiliate banks maintain lower proportions of equity capital than do nonaffiliate banks; and it concludes that they do. "The more highly leveraged positions of BHC banks may indicate that capital is being used more efficiently in the holding company form of organization. Alternatively, the lower bank capital may be a natural result of the BHC's desire to channel funds into its nonbank activities—in the attempt to achieve greater earnings at greater risk."[46]

If, as documented by various studies, their affiliate banks do not have significant comparative advantages over nonaffiliate banks, then MBHCs may want to examine some alternative strategies:

46. Arnold A. Heggestad and John J. Mingo, "Capital Management by Holding Company Banks," *The Journal of Business*, October 1975, pp. 500-505. Also, see John J. Mingo, "Capital Management and Profitability of Prospective Holding Company Banks," *Journal of Financial and Quantitative Analysis*, June 1975, pp. 191-203.

| Pricing | | | Total Revenues and Expenses | | | Capital |
|---|---|---|---|---|---|---|
| Interest on Loans to Gross Loans | Service Charges on Demand Deposits to Total IPC Demand Deposits* | Interest on Time Deposits to Total Time Deposits | Total Operating Revenues to Total Assets | Total Operating Expenses to Total Assets | Total Operating Expenses to Total Operating Income | Total Capital to Total Deposits |
| NSD | ↑ | NSD | ↑ | ↑ | NSD | NSD |
| ↓ | ↑ | ..... | ..... | ..... | ..... | ..... |
| NSD | NSD | NSD | NR | NSD | NSD | NSD |
| NSD | NSD | NSD | NR | NSD | NSD | NSD |
| ↓ | NR | NSD | NR | NR | NR | NSD |
| NSD | ↑ | NSD | NR | ↓ | NR | ↓ |

*Sources:* Johnson, Rodney D. and David R. Meinster. "The Performance of Bank Holding Company Acquisitions: A Multivariate Analysis," *The Journal of Business*, April 1975, pp. 204-212; Lawrence, Robert J. *The Performance of Bank Holding Companies*, (a staff study), Board of Governors of the Federal Reserve System, 1967; Mayne, Lucille S. "A Comparative Study of Bank Holding Company Affiliates and Independent Banks, 1969-1972," *The Journal of Finance*, March 1977, pp. 147-158; McLeary, Joe W. "Bank Holding Companies: Their Growth and Performance," *Monthly Review* (Federal Reserve Bank of Atlanta), October 1968, pp. 131-138; Talley, Samuel H. *The Effect of Holding Company Acquisitions on Bank Performance*, Staff Economic Studies (Board of Governors of the Federal Reserve System), 1971, pp. 1-25; Ware, Robert F. "Performance of Banks Acquired by Multibank Holding Companies in Ohio," *Economic Review* (Federal Reserve Bank of Cleveland), March-April 1973, pp. 19-28.

- Focus on acquisitions of small or medium-sized banks that have operating problems and therefore can substantially benefit from affiliation with a well-managed, well-financed MBHC. (Some MBHCs will reject this strategy if they believe that: the administrative cost of such acquisitions approaches that of acquiring a larger, well-managed bank; the managerial costs of improving the operating performance of such banks are uncertain and may be high; and/or even if successful, the profit contribution from such acquisitions will be small in the context of a total MBHC.)
- Lobby for greater branching powers so that their affiliate banks can try to achieve some operating efficiencies as parts of a branch system.
- Continually reexamine the potential returns and risks of selling and spinning-off affiliate banks instead of only trying to acquire them.[47]
- Examine carefully the probable operating benefits of expanding into permissible nonbanking activities.

47. Paul F. Jessup, "Portfolio Strategies for Bank Holding Companies," *The Bankers Magazine*, Spring 1969, pp. 78-85.

## SUMMARY

Expansionary bankers can use a bank holding company (BHC) as a way to expand their banking and/or bank-related activities. Thus BHCs now control over 73 percent of the total assets of U.S. banks; this contrasts with 9 percent at year-end 1965.

By law a BHC is any company that controls any bank or any other BHC. In practice a BHC is either a one-bank holding company (OBHC) that controls only one bank, or it is a multibank holding company (MBHC) that controls two or more banks. In addition to their control of banks, many BHCs own other affiliate firms that engage in permissible nonbanking activities.

BHCs today face extensive legislative and regulatory constraints that reflect an historic legacy of BHC expansion and of attempts to bridle such expansion. Until 1956 BHCs could expand their banking operations across state lines, and they could engage in almost any nonbanking activity. One large BHC, Transamerica Corporation, thus aggressively expanded its operations; and it thereby triggered proposals for federal legislation that would dismantle BHCs or at least would control their expansion.

The Bank Holding Company Act of 1956 is landmark federal legislation that controls how BHCs acquire additional banks and expand into nonbanking activities. This Act, until it was amended in 1970, applied only to MBHCs; and it required them to:

- register with the FRS
- receive FRS approval before they could acquire any additional bank
- forego further acquisitions of banks outside the state in which they had their principal banking operations
- adhere to FRS policies as to permissible nonbanking activities for BHCs

While it thus controlled expansion by MBHCs, the Bank Holding Company Act of 1956 did not apply to OBHCs.

Starting about 1967, some large money-center banks began to originate OBHCs that could then circumvent some regulatory constraints imposed on their affiliate money-center bank and could freely expand into nonbanking activities. Despite growing opposition to its so-called OBHC loophole, the Bank Holding Company Act may not have been amended except that suddenly the large OBHCs recognized their vulnerability to financial takeovers by large nonbanking firms, and so they reduced their opposition to closing the OBHC loophole.

The 1970 amendments to the Bank Holding Company Act:

- extend the legal definition of a BHC to include an OBHC
- tighten the criterion of what constitutes control of a bank
- provide a two-part test by which the FRS is to determine which nonbanking activities are permissible for BHCs
- contain an anti-tie-in provision

To facilitate its administration of the Bank Holding Company Act, the FRS has procedures by which it:

- lists permissible nonbanking activities
- expedites BHC *de novo* entry into permissible nonbanking activities
- delegates authority to the Federal Reserve Banks

Subject to this legal-regulatory framework, a BHC plans and implements its expansion strategies.

An expansionary BHC has to determine the extent to which state laws constrain its acquisition of additional affiliate banks. Then, subject to any such state constraints, it plans a comprehensive strategy by which it identifies acquisition candidates and develops acquisition offers that will likely be accepted by the officials and stockholders of banks that it wants to acquire. In most cases an expansionary BHC proposes a share-exchange offer that includes a purchase premium to the selling stockholders, and several studies suggest that BHCs need to refine the procedures by which they determine their purchase premiums.

BHCs try to select and document their acquisition proposals in ways that will increase the probability of approval by the FRS. Therefore, to reduce probable costs and delays, BHCs focus on selected acquisitions that do not involve evident anticompetitive effects or trigger questions about their effects on potential competition. The BHCs then document how their proposals meet with the banking and the convenience and needs criteria of the Bank Holding Company Act. If the FRS disapproves one of its proposed acquisitions, a BHC can appeal the decision in the courts; but in most cases a BHC decides not to invoke this judicial review.

Various commentators cite how, compared to clusters of nonaffiliate banks, BHCs can achieve benefits from their: management of human resources, specialized services, broad diversification, and access to capital. Yet BHCs differ as to the extent to which they centralize their operations, and even the most centralized systems provide some operating flexibility to managers of their affiliate banks.

Six studies compare the operating performance of affiliate and similar nonaffiliate banks. While they identify some significant differences, when viewed in total these studies indicate that there are not many significant or consistent differences between the affiliate and nonaffiliate banks. These results suggest that BHCs do not have major comparative advantages over clusters of similar nonaffiliate banks. Also, BHCs may want to reexamine whether they can improve their operating performance, for example, by:

- acquiring banks that need substantial improvement in their operations
- where possible, converting to a branch system
- voluntarily selling or spinning-off some affiliate banks

BHCs also need to look beyond their banking operations toward improving and expanding their permissible nonbanking activities.

# 20
# BANK HOLDING COMPANY EXPANSION INTO NONBANKING ACTIVITIES

Bank holding companies can expand into nonbanking activities to the extent permitted by the 1970 amendments to the Bank Holding Company Act. This chapter examines such expansion from the viewpoints of a BHC's motivations, constraints, initial results, and future plans.

## MOTIVATIONS FOR NONBANKING EXPANSION

BHCs expand into nonbanking activities because they have limited opportunities to expand their banking operations and/or they anticipate substantial net benefits from expanding their nonbanking activities. If its state severely restricts branching and MBHCs, then an expansionary banking system has to focus on internal expansion of its affiliate bank and expansion into nonbanking activities. If its state permits branching or MBHCs, a large banking organization may decide to avoid the legal-regulatory hurdles associated with bank acquisitions and instead to expand internally and into nonbanking areas. Even when it can conveniently expand its banking operations, an expansionary system has to compare the net benefits of such expansion against those of expansion into permissible nonbanking activities.

A BHC expects to achieve at least some of the following benefits by expanding into nonbanking areas:[1]

- potentially higher returns by expanding into functional areas that provide higher returns than does traditional banking
- potential risk reduction by diversifying among banking and nonbanking activities whose returns are not equally sensitive to economic events

---

1. These postulated benefits are similar to those used by proponents of OBHC expansion into related financial areas. Also, see Samuel B. Chase, Jr., and John J. Mingo, "The Regulation of Bank Holding Companies." *The Journal of Finance*, May 1975, pp. 281-292.

- also, potential risk reduction by controlling various legally distinct affiliates so that the possible financial problems of one affiliate need not necessarily jeopardize the financial status of the coaffiliates or the parent holding company
- a potentially higher market valuation by investors who believe, other factors equal, that a diversified BHC will achieve higher returns and/or lower risk than will a BHC that limits itself to banking activities
- opportunities to circumvent some constraints that apply to its bank affiliate(s)
- opportunities to provide customers with more convenient services — possibly at lower costs — than those from only a bank or a specialized financial-services firm

Its stockholders and customers will likely benefit if a BHC achieves some of the preceding benefits. Also, there may be broader public benefits.

## INITIAL EXPANSION INTO NONBANKING ACTIVITIES

The 1970 amendments [Section 4(c)(8)] to the Bank Holding Company Act set new guidelines by which the FRS is to determine which nonbanking activities are permissible for BHCs. In summary,

- Is an activity *closely related* to banking?
- And will BHC performance of the activity likely produce *public benefits* that outweigh possible adverse effects?

The FRS has established procedures by which it administers these legislative criteria.

The FRS promptly specified some initial categories of permissible nonbanking activities for BHCs. By the beginning of 1973, the Board of Governors approved sixteen activities which included mortgage banking, finance-company activities, credit cards, factoring, trust services, and some advisory, data processing, and insurance services. The Board specifically *denied* BHC entry into such activities as: underwriting general life insurance, selling combinations of mutual funds and insurance, and various real estate activities.

The Board of Governors interpreted Section 4 (c)(8) to permit BHCs to expand their permissible nonbanking activities across state lines. Thus, while its affiliate bank(s) cannot have interstate banking offices, a BHC can have nonbanking affiliates that can expand nationwide. Moreover, the FRS views it as more procompetitive if a BHC expands its proposed nonbanking activities into geographical areas other than those serviced by the BHC's affiliate bank(s). For example, a large Chicago-based BHC is more likely to receive approval to acquire a mortgage banking firm that operates far from Chicago rather than in or near Chicago.

The 1970 amendments direct the FRS to "differentiate between activities commenced *de novo* and activities commenced by the acquisition, in whole or in part, of a going concern." *De novo* entry introduces a new competitor into a market, and so it generally produces public benefits. Therefore the Board of Governors developed procedures to expedite its processing of *de novo* applications.

When it wants to enter a permissible activity *de novo*, a BHC inserts an official notice in a major newspaper that circulates in the area to be served by the *de novo* operation. Then, within thirty days, the BHC files a copy of the notice with the regional Federal Reserve Bank, which in turn accepts comments on the application for thirty days and processes the application as provided by delegated authority. Only if the application poses potential problems or policy issues will the Bank forward it to the Board of Governors. Unless, within forty-five days, the Bank or the Board notifies it not to do so, the applicant BHC is free to initiate its *de novo* activity. In contrast, if it wants to acquire an established company, a BHC similarly has to file a copy of a newspaper notice and an application with the Federal Reserve Bank. The Bank then publishes the notice in the *Federal Register* so that interested parties can submit comments to the FRS, which then reviews the complete application file in the context of public benefits and possible adverse effects.

Between 1971 and 1973 the Board of Governors approved almost 90 percent of BHC proposals to acquire 259 nonbanking firms.[2] (During the same period the FRS received notification of 720 *de novo* entries.) Most of these acquisitions were of firms engaged in finance (consumer, commercial, general), mortgage banking, insurance, personal-property leasing, and advisory services. During the period the FRS denied 29 proposed acquisitions. In 18 of these denials, the Board's written orders explicitly review the applicant's public-benefit arguments, and in most cases the Board concluded that adverse competitive effects outweighed the possible public benefits. Overall, the denial rate of 10 percent during the initial period was low, probably because most BHCs quickly foresaw FRS opposition if they proposed to acquire major nonbanking firms located close to their affiliate bank(s).

## CURRENT EXPANSION SUBJECT TO A GO SLOW POLICY

By 1974 the FRS had begun to express its concern about the pace of BHC expansion into nonbanking activties and about the decline in capital ratios of many affiliate banks. Therefore it adopted a "go slow" policy that stemmed the initial spurt of BHC expansion into nonbanking areas. This policy continues to limit such BHC expansion.

In 1974 the FRS added four items to its list of sixteen permissible activities: courier service, management consulting to nonaffiliate banks,

---

2. Michael A. Jessee and Steven A. Seelig, "An Analysis of the Public Benefits Test of the Bank Holding Company Act," *Monthly Review* (Federal Reserve Bank of New York), June 1974, pp. 151-162. The authors provide a detailed analysis of the nonbanking acquisitions that were approved or denied by the Board of Governors from 1971 to early 1974.

issuance of travelers checks, and bullion dealer. Also, the FRS extended a previous item, full-payout leasing, to include real property. When it added some of these items, the FRS set restrictive conditions. Concerning courier service, for example, BHCs can "transport materials of limited intrinsic value for which the time element is critical (such as cancelled checks) provided that the services are performed on an explicit fee basis, are profit oriented, are paid for directly by the customer, and are made available to the holding company's competitors at the same rates the holding company charges its other customers."[3] Similarly, the Board stipulated that a BHC can provide management consulting services to nonaffiliate banks, if it is done on a noncontinuing and explicit-fee basis. Between 1976 and 1977 the FRS approved only two additional activities. (Exhibit 20-1 summarizes the complete list of permissible activities at the beginning of 1979.)

While it slowed the rate at which it approved new activities, the FRS increased the number of nonbanking activities denied to BHCs (Exhibit 20-1). In 1974, after lengthy review, the Board of Governors disapproved proposals to permit BHCs to underwrite mortgage guarantee insurance and to operate savings & loan (S&L) associations. Even though it declared that both these activities are closely related to banking, the Board decided to keep these activities on its "pending" list, at least for a while.[4] In its order about the underwriting of mortgage guarantee insurance, the Board stated its view that:

> . . . these are times when it would be desirable for bank holding companies generally to slow their present rate of expansion and to direct their energies principally toward strong and efficient operations within their existing modes, rather than toward expansion into new activities. This is particularly true with regard to expansion into a new area such as private mortgage insurance involving uncertainties which are sufficient in the Board's view to outweigh at the present time the public benefits that might be expected to result from this proposal.[5]

In summary, the Board encouraged managers of BHCs to strengthen their current affiliates—especially the bank affiliate(s)—and to defer proposals to identify new permissible activities.

When it relaxes its go slow policy, the FRS is unlikely soon to add new permissible activities to its list. The FRS has cited a court decision stating that for an activity to be closely related to banking it should meet one of these conditions:

> . . . first, that banks generally have in fact provided the proposed service; second, that banks generally provide services that are operationally or

3. Harvey Rosenblum, "Bank Holding Company Review 1973/74: Part I," *Business Conditions* (Federal Reserve Bank of Chicago), February 1975, pp. 3-10.

4. In 1977 the Board of Governors denied BHC operations of savings & loan associations. BHC underwriting of mortgage guarantee insurance remains on the pending list.

5. *Federal Reserve Bulletin*, October 1974, pp. 727-728.

**EXHIBIT 20-1**

**Summary of Federal Reserve System Rulings about Nonbanking Activities That Are Permissible for, or Denied to, Bank Holding Companies**

**(Mid-1979)**

| Activities Approved by the Board* | Activities Denied by the Board |
|---|---|
| Dealer in bankers' acceptances | Insurance premium funding (combined sale of mutual funds and insurance) |
| Mortgage banking | |
| Finance company operations | Underwriting life insurance that is not sold in connection with a credit transaction by a bank holding company or one of its subsidiaries |
| Credit card operations | |
| Factoring | |
| Industrial loan company or Morris Plan bank | |
| Servicing loans for others | Real estate brokerage |
| Trust activities | Land development |
| Investment or financial advising | Real estate syndication |
| Full payout leasing | Management consulting |
| Community welfare investments | Property management |
| Bookkeeping or data processing services | Operation of S&Ls |
| Insurance agent or broker | |
| Underwriter of credit life insurance and credit accident and health insurance | |
| Courier services | |
| Management consulting advice to nonaffiliated banks | |
| Retail sale of travelers checks, U. S. savings bonds and small-denomination money orders | |

*Many of these approved activities are subject to strict conditions.

*Note:* This is a summary listing that is based on published rulings and interpretations of the Board of Governors. In addition, the Board has used case orders to approve or deny some other activities. For more detail, see Regulation Y, Published Interpretations of the Board of Governors of the Federal Reserve System, and Drum (cited below).

*Sources:* Dale S. Drum, "Nonbanking Activities of Bank Holding Companies," *Economic Perspectives* (Federal Reserve Bank of Chicago), March-April 1977, p. 14; Regulation Y ("Bank Holding Companies"), Board of Governors of the Federal Reserve System; and Published Interpretations of the Board of Governors of the Federal Reserve System.

functionally so similar to the proposed services as to equip them particularly well to provide the proposed services; and third, that banks generally provide services that are so integrally related to the proposed services as to require their provision in a specialized form.[6]

Even if it meets one of these conditions, the activity has to pass the public benefits test.

---

6. *Federal Reserve Bulletin*, February 1976, p. 149.

## INITIAL ANALYSES OF BANK HOLDING COMPANY EXPANSION INTO NONBANKING ACTIVITIES

The FRS go slow policy provides a respite during which the FRS, bankers, and others can assess the initial impact of BHC expansion into bank-related activities.

### DIVERSIFICATION BENEFITS

In principle, a BHC should be able to reduce its total variability of returns by diversifying into activities the returns from which are not perfectly and positively correlated with those from its bank affiliate(s). Can a BHC thus achieve diversification benefits if, by law, it can only expand into activities that are closely related to banking?

One author measures the potential risk of selected nonbanking activities that are, or may in the future be, permitted to BHCs. For these industries the author computes "the annual variability of average industry profits divided by average industry profits" (the coefficient of variation). He also measures the extent to which returns from each industry are correlated with banking returns. If the correlation is not perfect and positive, then there are possible benefits from diversifying into such activities. While he notes the need for caution when interpreting ratios based on aggregate industry data, the author concludes that many of the nonbanking activities "do not necessarily add to the riskiness of the holding company, especially when the benefits of diversification are considered."[7]

Another author uses more complex techniques to determine whether BHCs can and do diversify efficiently into nonbanking activities. The study analyzes risk-return relationships (1961-68) from various industries that BHCs: are permitted to enter, are not permitted to enter, and may eventually be permitted to enter. The study finds that banking is the lowest-risk activity, but it goes further to examine risk-return outcomes from portfolios that combine banking with other activities. The study shows how a BHC that limits itself to banking is likely to suboptimize, because if it were to diversify into selected permissible activities the BHC could increase its expected return without increasing its risk. The study also examines whether, in practice, BHCs diversify efficiently. It concludes that, in general, BHCs "are not doing a very efficient job of diversifying," possibly because many BHCs have been entering mortgage banking and factoring — activities that apparently do not provide efficient diversification benefits to BHCs. Finally, the study concludes that "past Federal Reserve Board decisions with respect to allowable nonbank activities have not seriously limited the ability of bank holding companies to efficiently diversify."[8]

7. Arnold Heggestad, "Riskiness of Investments in Nonbank Activities by Bank Holding Companies," *Journal of Economics and Business*, Spring 1975, pp. 219-223. Also, by the same author, "Diversification, Risk, and the Bank Holding Company." *The Bankers Magazine*, Winter 1976, pp. 109-112.

8. Peter C. Eisemann, "Diversification and the Congeneric Bank Holding Company," *Journal of Bank Research*, Spring 1976, pp. 68-77.

## AUTONOMY OF BANKING AND NONBANKING AFFILIATES

In principle, if it engages in nonbanking activities via specialized affiliates, a BHC will expose the depositors of its affiliate bank(s) to less risk than will a bank that directly engages in similar activities. To illustrate, if its leasing affiliate were to encounter substantial financial problems, then a BHC could let this affiliate solve its own problems—or, as a separate legal entity, possibly even fail—without directly jeopardizing the depositors of the coaffiliate bank(s). In contrast, a bank that directly engages in similar leasing operations and encounters similar problems would have to solve the problems in order to avoid jeopardizing its depositors. In practice, it is doubtful that a BHC can, or will, fully shield its affiliate bank(s) from problems that arise in the nonbanking coaffiliates.

Even if a BHC's banking and nonbanking affiliates operate under separate legal charters, under some state laws a court may *pierce the corporate veil* by ruling that the coaffiliate firms are, in fact, all parts of the same enterprise. In this event, the problems of one nonbanking affiliate could jeopardize the resources of its banking and nonbanking coaffiliates as well as those of the parent BHC.

Even if the courts do not pierce the legal separation of the affiliate firms, BHC officials will likely try to prevent the failure, or even the hint of failure, of one of the BHC's affiliates. This sense of responsibility is especially acute when a BHC's nonbanking affiliates, although legally distinct firms, have names similar to those of the parent BHC and its lead bank. For example, if financial problems at a sponsored REIT become publicized, then some people will likely question the stability of the BHC's affiliate bank(s)—especially if its name is similar to that of the REIT. Such loss of public confidence does happen. In one instance a parent BHC "engaged in imprudent lending and subsequently failed. This failure resulted in runs on the subsidiary bank, which then had to be merged under emergency conditions."[9]

Subject to legal and regulatory constraints, there are various ways that a BHC can use its affiliate bank(s) to try to assist a troubled nonbanking affiliate. It can have its affiliate bank (or banks):

- lend an amount up to 10 percent of its capital to a troubled coaffiliate
- pay special dividends to its parent BHC that in turn channels these funds to the troubled affiliate
- acquire some of the assets of the troubled affiliate

Thus in several cases "mortgage banking affiliates of BHCs encountered serious problems due to risky real estate loans. In an attempt to avoid failure, these mortgage companies sold large amounts of questionable assets to their bank affiliates."[10] These are only some possible ways by which an

9. Robert J. Lawrence and Samuel H. Talley, "An Assessment of Bank Holding Companies," *Federal Reserve Bulletin*, January 1976, pp. 15-21.

10. Lawrence and Talley, "An Assessment of Bank Holding Companies," p. 19.

imaginative BHC can try to assist a troubled affiliate. If they act quickly, supervisory agencies often can prevent, or at least impede, transactions that could jeopardize the affiliate bank and its creditors. Even so, some supervisors express concern about whether they can always shield an affiliate bank from problems that arise in its nonbanking coaffiliates.

In 1978, the Board of Governors began an expanded program by which to monitor large BHCs. When it adopted this new program, the Board said: "The development of numerous complex and diverse bank holding company structures and activities has prompted the expansion of the Board's continuing program for their supervision and regulation."[11] This surveillance program provides for: an annual inspection of most large BHCs, and use by FRB examiners of a standardized "Report of Bank Holding Company Inspection." The program focuses on all BHCs with consolidated assets exceeding $300 million and on other BHCs that control credit-extending subsidiaries, such as finance companies and mortgage companies. The standardized report form has the examiners systematically: prepare a financial analysis of a BHC, review the assets of its nonbanking credit-extending affiliates, and review the procedures by which the BHC supervises its affiliates. Thus this program should provide the FRS with comprehensive, timely information about developments among the various affiliates of large BHCs.

## CAPITAL MANAGEMENT

In principle, because of its diversification, flexibility, management depth, and convenient access to capital markets, a large BHC can accept greater risks than can a small, less-diversified banking organization. To use a simplified example, if the large BHC and the small banking organization have similar capital ratios, then the BHC should be able to accept a greater proportion of default and marketability risks among its assets. Alternatively, if the BHC and the small banking organization have similar risks among their assets, then, other things equal, the large BHC should be able to finance such risks with lower capital ratios.

In practice, even if one accepts that a large BHC can conveniently accept greater risks than can a small banking organization, it is difficult to quantify such risks (many of which are interrelated) and to specify how much more risk a BHC can—or should—accept.

As reported in the previous chapter, various studies demonstrate that MBHCs generally accept greater risks in the portfolios of their affiliate banks, and they do this with similar—or possibly lower—capital ratios.

### Debt-Servicing Capacity

Especially since 1974, the FRS has frequently and explicitly questioned how BHCs propose to finance their expansion into banking and nonbanking

---

11. *Federal Reserve Bulletin*, November 1977, p. 1031.

areas. To illustrate, the Board of Governors unanimously denied a proposal by a large BHC (''Applicant'') to acquire a nuclear leasing firm (''Company''). In its decision the Board stated:

> Even assuming Applicant's favorable projections, it is clear that the acquisition of Company would require Applicant to commit substantial and continuing amounts of funds to support Company's growth.
>
> . . . Company's need for funds, even assuming no growth, will require Applicant to increase its short-term borrowing by a substantial amount, i.e. to the point where Applicant's current liabilities would exceed current assets by a considerable margin if subsidiary banks are not consolidated. . . . Even assuming that there is little growth in nonbanking activities in its system, such [recent banking] growth in the future will require Applicant to supply additional capital to its banks. An application such as the present, which substantially reduces the margin between debt use and debt capacity, would impair the ability to provide such capital.[12]

In this illustrative decision, the Board explicitly questioned how the BHC would finance the simultaneous expansion of its nonbanking and banking activities; and it reaffirmed its view that ''one of the primary purposes of a holding company is to serve as a source of financial strength for its subsidiary banks.''

It is important to distinguish between the capital ratios of a BHC's separate affiliates and those of the consolidated system. A parent BHC often chooses to raise funds by selling its debt instruments and then to use these funds to increase the equity accounts of its banking and/or nonbanking affiliates. While the affiliates thus can show higher equity capital ratios, on a consolidated basis the BHC system has increased the debt it has to service from dividends, interest, and fees from its affiliates, primarily from its lead bank. *Double leveraging* is the term often used to describe this procedure by which a parent BHC issues debt to help finance its purchase of equity, or debt, instruments of its affiliate(s).

In periods of unanticipated adversity, a BHC's debt-servicing requirements can affect various components of the BHC. If, for example, it encounters financial problems, then a large affiliate bank may have to reduce or suspend payments to its parent BHC, which then defaults on its debt and thus jeopardizes confidence in its affiliates(s). Another possibility is that a parent BHC's cash flows become disrupted because one of its nonbanking affiliates encounters serious financial problems. To service its debt, the parent BHC then seeks increased or special dividends from its sound affiliate bank, and thus reduces the bank's retention of capital.

Laws and regulations impede a BHC's suddenly getting additional dividends from its affiliate bank(s). In some cases, the BHC has to request approval from the bank(s)' supervisory agencies. Even so, the supervisors may

---

12. *Federal Reserve Bulletin*, September 1973, pp. 698-700.

face a dilemma. If, to protect the affiliate bank(s), the supervisors refuse the special transfers to the parent BHC, then the parent firm's publicized financial crisis and/or default will probably jeopardize confidence in the affiliate bank(s) that the regulators are trying to protect. Bank supervisors prefer to avoid such a possible real-world dilemma. Thus the FRS, for example, emphasizes that a parent BHC should be "a source of financial strength for its subsidiary banks." Especially in adverse periods the BHC should provide such strength and not have to service its debt by having to draw on the resources of its affiliate banks.

Because it cannot count on suddenly increasing its cash flows from its affiliate bank(s), a BHC remains flexible if it concentrates its financial resources in the parent BHC. To increase this flexibility, a BHC has an incentive to channel funds—to the extent feasible—upstream from its affiliate bank(s). Then, as circumstances warrant it, the BHC can channel funds to its banking and nonbanking affiliates. This behavioral pattern helps explain why affiliates of BHCs are likely, on average, to have lower capital ratios than similar nonaffiliate firms.

## Leveraging of Nonbank Affiliates

Two coauthors analyze BHC leveraging of their nonbanking activities, and they report that "preliminary evidence on holding company participation in two of these [nonbanking] activities—mortgage banking and consumer finance—indicates that BHCs, on average, are leveraging their operations beyond industry standards. Moreover, a few BHCs appear to be leveraging their affiliates in these activities far beyond prudent limits."[13]

A supervisory official states his belief "that for many banks the use of holding companies as a vehicle for obtaining more leverage has become the principal justification for, or 'benefit' from establishing a holding company." He also compares capital ratios for large banks and, on a consolidated basis, for their parent BHCs and concludes that the parent BHCs "in many instances, though not all, have more leverage than their principal subsidiary bank."[14]

Do financial markets deter the extent to which BHCs use leverage? In particular, if a BHC tries to keep increasing its leverage, will investors in the BHC's securities view this policy as increasingly risky and therefore insist on higher compensation (risk premiums) to accept such risk? To date, the answers to these questions are inconclusive.

One author examines the valuation of shares of large BHCs between 1973 and 1975 and finds no "statistical evidence that the market penalizes 'excessive' leverage," or else possibly the market "does not view the levels achieved by banks or bank holding companies to be excessive."[15]

---

13. Lawrence and Talley, "An Assessment of Bank Holding Companies," p. 19.

14. Stanley C. Silverberg, "Bank Holding Companies and Capital Adequacy," *Journal of Bank Research*, Autumn 1975, pp. 202-207.

15. Silverberg, "Bank Holding Companies and Capital Adequacy," p. 206.

In a pair of studies, three researchers use large samples and various statistical tests to examine "the relationship between the financial structure of banking firms [mostly BHCs] and the market values of their equity securities." The authors conclude that "the combined evidence provided by the two studies, covering the period 1970 through 1974, is very strongly suggestive that the market for the equity securities of banking firms is sensitive to leverage."[16] In other words, "once the effects of other share price determinants—such as dividends, earnings growth, firm size and loan loss rate—are accounted for, an increase in leverage will lower share price." However, a subsequent study (1974-75), finds "no statistically significant relationship between financial leverage and share valuation."[17]

Until there is conclusive evidence that financial market participants effectively deter possible excessive leveraging by BHCs, the FRS and other bank supervisors will continue to monitor and try to deter changes—especially declines— in the capital ratios of most BHCs and their affiliates. Therefore expansionary BHCs especially will have to plan how to finance their expansion without substantially reducing their capital ratios. Although this financial constraint will likely slow their rate of expansion, many BHCs thus will have time carefully to evaluate and select from among their expansion opportunities.

## COMPETITION, CONCENTRATION, AND PUBLIC BENEFITS

By law the FRS has to evaluate whether BHC entry into a nonbanking activity "can reasonably be expected to produce benefits to the public . . . that outweigh possible adverse effects, such as undue concentration of resources, decreased or unfair competition. . . ." The FRS evaluates these factors as part of its two-part test to determine which nonbanking activities will be generally permissible for BHCs. Then, on a case-by-case basis the FRS evaluates these factors and applies the balancing test when a BHC applies to acquire a specific firm in a permissible nonbanking activity. As summarized by the Board of Governors: "This balancing test necessitates a positive showing of public benefits, outweighing the 'possible' adverse effects of any proposed acquisition, before an application may be approved. *Applicant must bear this burden*"[18] [italics added]. In principle, these criteria should guide BHCs in planning their nonbanking expansion and should guide the FRS in controlling such expansion. In practice, guidelines pose interpretation and implementation problems for expansionary BHCs and for the FRS.

---

16. Donald P. Jacobs, H. Prescott Beighley, and John H. Boyd, *The Financial Structure of Bank Holding Companies*, a study prepared for the Trustees of the Banking Research Fund, Association of Reserve City Bankers, 1975. Also by Beighley, Boyd, and Jacobs, "Bank Equities and Investor Risk Perceptions: Some Entailments for Capital Adequacy Regulation," *Journal of Bank Research*, Autumn 1975, pp. 190-201. (The quotations are from the second source.)

17. Donald R. Fraser, "Further Evidence on Bank Equities and Investor Risk Perceptions" (Feedback), *Journal of Bank Research*, Autumn 1977, pp. 189-191.

18. *Federal Reserve Bulletin*, February 1974, p. 143.

The FRS consistently has encouraged expansionary BHCs to focus on *de novo* or foothold entry into permissible nonbanking areas. Also, the FRS consistently has discouraged expansionary BHCs from trying to expand, especially by acquisition, into nonbanking activities that are geographically nearby the principal operations of a BHC's banking affiliate(s). Thus when it evaluates the possible adverse effects of a BHC's proposed acquisition of a nonbanking firm, the FRS focuses on whether, and to what extent, the two firms currently compete and potentially compete. In some cases the FRS also specifically focuses on whether a BHC's proposed acquisition will possibly result in "undue concentration of resources." Even if it determines that a proposed acquisition involves possible adverse effects, the FRS has to determine whether likely public benefits will outweigh the possible adverse effects.

Between 1973 and 1974 the nation's three largest BHCs applied to acquire, or retain, firms that were engaged in permissible nonbanking activities. The issue was not whether a specific activity was permissible, but whether, and how, the FRS should allow these large BHCs to acquire firms engaged in permissible activities. These three cases illustrate how the Board's members try to evaluate and weight the possible adverse effects and public benefits associated with specific proposals to expand into nonbanking areas. In only one case was the decision unanimous.

### BankAmerica Corporation and GAC Finance, Inc.

In 1973 the Board of Governors, by a 4-to-3 vote, denied an application by BankAmerica Corporation, a BHC that controls the nation's largest bank, to acquire GAC Finance, Inc., which, as measured by total assets, was the nation's eleventh-largest independent finance company.

Before the Board issued a statement summarizing its reason for the denial, BankAmerica requested the Board to reconsider its denial.[19] When it thus petitioned for reconsideration, BankAmerica provided the Board with new information and with a proposed plan by which BankAmerica would divest additional assets of GAC Finance "within stated time periods if the application, on reconsideration, was approved by the Board." The Board of Governors agreed to reconsider BankAmerica's proposed acquisition of GAC Finance.

Concerning existing competition, the Board concluded that direct competition between the two firms occurred primarily within California. Anticipating this conclusion, the two firms originally had offered that, if the acquisition were approved, they would promptly divest the finance company's thirty-six offices in California.

Concerning potential competition, the Board concluded that, if the initial application were denied, then BankAmerica would likely "commence an expansion into other States in the consumer lending field, either through

---

19. *Federal Reserve Bulletin*, September 1973, pp. 687-694.

establishment of consumer finance offices *de novo* or through means of foothold entry.'' Moreover, this expansion was most likely in states close to California, the base of BankAmerica's large affiliate bank. In its request for reconsideration, BankAmerica proposed to sell within one year all of GAC Finance's consumer loan offices in ten western states, including California, and half of the offices in Colorado and Texas. The Board concluded that this revised proposal ''in large measure eliminates the Board's earlier expressed concern over the question of probable future competition'' between the two firms.

The Board was ''deeply concerned'' whether its approval of the initial application would result in an ''undue concentration of resources.'' It noted that:

> *Congress did not provide specific criteria* with respect to the size of acquisitions which should be disallowed to avoid an undue resources concentration. . . . It was the Board's judgment that approval of the original application, involving acquisition by the nation's largest bank holding company of a major consumer finance company with a nationwide network of offices, although a close question, raised issues of concentration in credit-granting resources that were inconsistent with the intent of Congress in enacting the 1970 amendments. [Italics added]

In its revised proposal BankAmerica offered to divest many of the finance company's assets and offices, especially in the western states. In view of these proposed ''extensive divestitures,'' the Board concluded that ''the possible dangers of an undue concentration of resources are significantly lessened and the Board no longer views this factor as warranting the degree of adverse weight initially assigned.''

In both the initial and revised proposals, the Board concluded that the proposed acquisition would likely result in public benefits such as: ''an overall strengthening and revitalization'' of the finance company, expansion of lending services to various categories of borrowers, and ''possible reduction in certain loan rates due to Applicant's easier access to funds, probably at lower cost.'' When it applied the balancing test, however, the Board concluded ''that Applicant's showing of public benefits had not outweighed the possible adverse effects of the proposed acquisition,'' and so the Board denied the initial proposal. Subsequently, when it applied the balancing test to the revised proposal (with its more extensive divestiture plans), the Board unanimously concluded that ''the reasonably expected public benefits from this revised proposal outweigh possible adverse effects.''

The preceding case summary demonstrates how:

- The Board of Governors evaluated a large BHC's proposal to acquire a large nonbanking firm.
- A BHC structured its proposals to include commitments to divest specific assets of the firm to be acquired.

This and subsequent decisions provide guidelines for officials who develop a BHC's acquisition strategies and proposals.

### The Chase Manhattan Corporation and Dial Financial Corporation

Soon after its BankAmerica-GAC Finance decisions, the Board denied a large BHC's proposed acquisition of "one of the nation's major consumer finance companies," Dial Financial Corporation.[20] The applicant BHC was the Chase Manhattan Corporation, the nation's second-largest BHC.

In its evaluation the Board concluded that the acquisition would only slightly eliminate existing competition between the two firms. It also concluded that "irrespective of the effect on particular markets, . . . consummation of the proposal would eliminate a substantial possibility" that the two firms would compete in the future.

The Board further concluded that the proposed acquisition:

> . . . involves the issue of concentration in credit-granting resources that was within the intent of Congress in enacting the 1970 amendments. *While the matter is not free of doubt and is one on which reasonable differences of judgment may occur*, the Board has concluded that, at a minimum, this factor weighs against approval of the application. [Italics added]

Finally, the Board specifically reviewed the extent to which the proposed acquisition, if approved, would likely produce public benefits. It concluded that:

> While the proposed acquisition would clearly lead to some public benefits, there is little indication that the . . . claimed benefits are not likely to be obtained in the absence of the acquisition. Accordingly, the Board concludes that overall public benefits asserted by Applicant do not outweigh the above described adverse effects.

On this basis the Board—by a 5-to-2 vote—denied the proposed acquisition. The minority, in a dissenting statement, summarizes its view that "the reasonably expected benefits to the public from this proposal considerably outweigh any possible adverse effects."

Soon afterward the Chase Manhattan Corporation again applied to acquire Dial Financial.[21] This application differed from the preceding one principally by containing "a proposal to lower to 30 per cent the maximum annual percentage rate charged by Dial for new loans." While it regarded this proposal as a public benefit, the Board concluded that "the aggregate public benefits that may reasonably be expected from the affiliation of Applicant and Dial do not outweigh the possible adverse effects" as

---

20. *Federal Reserve Bulletin*, February 1974, pp. 142-147.

21. *Federal Reserve Bulletin*, December 1974, p. 874.

enumerated in the Board's previous denial. Therefore the Board denied this revised application.

### First National City Corporation and Advance Mortgage Corporation

In 1974 the Board of Governors also denied the application by First National City Corporation, the nation's third-largest BHC, to retain control of Advance Mortgage Corporation, a nonbanking affiliate that it had acquired prior to the 1970 amendments.[22] (Under provisions of the amended Bank Holding Company Act, the applicant BHC needed Board approval to retain this nonbanking affiliate beyond year-end 1980.) Advance Mortgage was and is "one of the nation's major mortgage banking companies."

The Board regarded loss of some direct competition between the two firms "as an adverse factor weighing against approval of the application." The Board also found that the loss of "probable future competition between a substantial potential entrant [the BHC] and a major competitor [the mortgage banking firm] in various local markets as well as national markets for certain loans constitutes an adverse effect which weighs against approval of the application."

In addition, the Board expressed its "particular concern" that:

> The dangers which Congress feared might arise from an undue concentration of financial resources would appear to be present through the combination of one of the country's largest banking organizations with one of its largest mortgage bankers.
>
> . . . Another possible danger—though not the only one—arising from an undue concentration of financial resources lies in the potential for abuse of the power to grant credit, and thereby favor a holding company subsidiary over its nonbanking competitors.

The Board then specifically reviewed whether the overall public benefits of the affiliation "are sufficient to outweigh the substantial adverse effects of the acquisition," and it concluded that they were not. Therefore, by a 5-to-2 vote, the Board denied the application. Two governors each appended a concurring statement to this decision, and one governor filed a dissenting statement. These statements provide additional insights into how specific Governors analyzed the application in the context of their interpretations of the Bank Holding Company Act.

### Surveys of Nonbanking Operations by Bank Holding Companies

While it has denied some major nonbanking acquisitions by large BHCs, the Board of Governors approved many nonbanking acquisitions in which it

---

22. *Federal Reserve Bulletin*, January 1974, pp. 50-56. The Board of Governors subsequently reviewed this case, and it again rejected the BHC's application to retain Advance Mortgage Corporation. *Federal Reserve Bulletin*, April 1978, pp. 321-325.

determined that either there were no adverse effects, or if so, the probable public benefits outweighed them.

One author reviews how BHCs focused their initial nonbanking acquisitions on consumer finance and mortgage banking firms. "In consumer finance, BHCs usually have acquired relatively small or medium-size firms. In mortgage banking, however, BHCs have often acquired companies that were among the largest in the industry."[23] What motivated BHCs to enter these activities? At least in the early 1970s, the rates of return on equity from mortgage banking generally exceeded those from banking. Mortgage banking also seemed logically to extend the mortgage processing done by a BHC's large affiliate bank(s). BHC motivations for entering consumer finance are less clear. Although consumer finance companies face increasing competition from financial intermediaries such as credit unions, a BHC could develop an interstate network of consumer loan offices and thus position itself for "wider use of electronic funds transfer and perhaps eventually nationwide branch banking." Meanwhile, these offices can, and often do, offer a wide variety of loans, financial counseling services, and, in some states, various types of low-denomination, consumer-oriented debentures that are exempt from Regulation Q ceilings.

One author tests whether BHC acquisitions of mortgage-banking firms increase the flow of funds to mortgage markets. He finds that "mortgage banking firms affiliated with bank holding companies do not grow any faster than nonaffiliated mortgage bankers," and "commercial banks did not increase or decrease their mortgage lending relative to total lending subsequent to affiliation with a mortgage banker." He concludes that "these results taken together suggest that bank-holding-company acquisitions of mortgage bankers do not increase the flow of funds to the mortgage market and, therefore, should not generally be viewed as a public benefit."[24]

Two coauthors analyze whether there are significant differences in the performance of finance companies that are or are not BHC affiliates. Subject to the caveats that their study involves a limited sample and a brief post-acquisition interval, the authors conclude that their tests do not confirm the general claims by BHCs that "their entry into the consumer finance industry will yield numerous public benefits."[25] Another author also analyzes BHC entry into consumer finance and concludes that their "relatively poor profit performance so far, which is partly due to significant *do novo* expansion, may simply be the price that BHCs are willing to pay for

23. Samuel H. Talley, "Bank Holding Company Performance in Consumer Finance and Mortgage Banking," *The Magazine of Bank Administration*, July 1976, pp. 42-44. Also Peter S. Rose and Donald R. Fraser, "Bank Holding Company Diversification into Mortgage Banking and Finance Companies," *The Banking Law Journal*, November-December 1974, pp. 976-994.

24. Stephen A. Rhoades, "The Effect of Bank-Holding-Company Acquisitions of Mortgage Bankers on Mortgage Lending Activity," *The Journal of Business*, July 1975, pp. 344-348.

25. Stephen A. Rhoades and Gregory E. Boczar, "The Performance of Bank Holding Company-Affiliated Finance Companies," a Staff Economic Study summarized in the *Federal Reserve Bulletin*, August 1977, pp. 715-716.

longer-run benefits,'' such as developing interstate networks of nonbanking offices in anticipation of EFTS developments and possible interstate branching.[26]

A Governor of the FRS reports that by year-end 1974 BHCs and their nonbank affiliates accounted for the following percentages of receivables in these permissible activities: [27]

| *Industry* | *Percentage* |
|---|---|
| Consumer and sales finance (86 largest noncaptives) | 22 |
| Consumer and sales finance (105 largest, including captives) | 9 |
| Mortgage banking (100 largest measured by volume serviced) | 32 |
| Factoring (30 largest) | 50 |
| Leasing (estimate) | 10 |

Although some of these percentages may seem substantial, from another perspective, the assets of their nonbanking affiliates "accounted for only 3 percent of the total assets of 69 of the largest bank holding companies" (1973). From either perspective, the Governor suggests the need for regulatory caution and further study of BHCs, especially in the areas of: affiliate autonomy within a BHC, capital management and "double leveraging," and competitive behavior in various markets. The Governor reports that the FRS is "deeply involved in such a review."

In summary, to date there is only limited information about how the nonbanking activities of BHCs have affected—or are likely to affect—competition, concentration, and public benefits. In its recent review of studies in this area, the staff of the Board of Governors of the FRS concludes that:

> Only two activities have received attention at all in the published studies—mortgage banking and consumer finance—and here the evidence suggests little about the long run impacts of BHCs. Not only are the studies few in number, they also suffer from the weakness that they cover a short time span at the early phase of BHC involvement in the activity.[28]

---

26. Samuel H. Talley, "Bank Holding Company Performance in Consumer Finance and Mortgage Banking," p. 44.

27. Robert C. Holland, "Bank Holding Companies and Financial Stability," *Journal of Financial and Quantitative Analysis*, November 1975, pp. 577-587, especially Table 1, p. 580. Governor Holland reports that the source of these specific estimates is the Board of Governors of the Federal Reserve System.

28. "Bank Holding Company Study Completed," *Voice* (Federal Reserve Bank of Dallas), July 1978, pp. 9-13.

Yet, while the FRS encourages further analyses of BHC expansion, BHCs can proceed to plan their future expansion.

## PLANNING FUTURE EXPANSION BY BANK HOLDING COMPANIES

While they manage their firm subject to current laws and regulations, BHC officials also need to position their firm to benefit from probable changes in the laws and regulations.

Under its "go slow" policy, the FRS is slow to add new nonbanking activities to its "permissible" list; and it signals to BHCs that they ought generally to slow their rate of expansion and "to direct their energies principally toward *strong and efficient operations* within their existing modes, rather than toward expansion into new activities" (italics added). The FRS has communicated its go slow policy by means of public statements and by its recent denials of a larger proportion of BHC expansion proposals compared to those in the period shortly after the 1970 amendments. This go slow policy gives legislators and bank supervisory officials an interlude during which to evaluate the effects of initial BHC expansion, and it gives BHC officials time to digest past expansion and to prepare for future expansion opportunities.

As a first step, an expansionary BHC needs to focus its energies on "strong and efficient" current operations. This may require improved planning and control systems, higher capital ratios, and diligent attention to persistent problem areas (such as noninterest-earning loans) within its current banking and nonbanking affiliates. In contrast to a BHC that delays such internal improvements, a BHC that focuses on strong current operations will likely achieve a higher market valuation of its securities and position itself with a "clean slate" when it subsequently requests FRS approval of specific expansion proposals. Also to try to strengthen its subsequent applications, a BHC can specifically develop a record to show how its recent acquisitions have resulted in public benefits.

An expansionary BHC needs to monitor, and try to anticipate, changes in the FRS's go slow policy. In general, this go slow policy applies to all BHCs; it does not distinguish between expansion proposals by well-managed, conservatively financed BHCs and those by highly leveraged BHCs with operating problems.[29] When it starts to modify this policy, the FRS will likely become more receptive to expansion proposals by well-managed, conservatively financed BHCs while it continues to impede expansion by BHCs with major current or potential problems. If so, this modified policy will give additional incentives to BHCs that have "strong and efficient" operations and carefully prepared expansion plans.

To anticipate possible changes in the FRS go slow policy, a BHC has

---

29. *Federal Reserve Bulletin*, December 1974, p. 872.

its staff monitor trends within BHCs and trends in FRS statements and decisions concerning BHCs. One source is the "Law Department" section of the monthly *Federal Reserve Bulletin*. Initially, this section reported all such decisions by the Board of Governors. Since November 1972, it reports in full only decisions accompanied by a statement (majority, concurring, or dissenting), and it lists the other decisions that are published in full in the *Federal Register*. Also, within a BHC, some officers and staff people need to keep abreast of the banking and academic journals that regularly publish articles about BHCs and their changing legal-regulatory environment.

Recent and possible changes in federal laws will likely open new expansion opportunities to a BHC that plans ahead. The FRS recently obtained congressional authority to invoke cease and desist actions, if necessary, against BHC affiliates which the FRS believes are engaging in unsound financial practices that may jeopardize the BHC and/or its affiliates. Also, the FRS has received new powers to impose civil penalties for violations of the Bank Holding Company Act and to order a BHC to divest or terminate any nonbanking activity that endangers a BHC's affiliate bank(s). With these additional powers, the FRS can act more directly against specific problems within specific BHCs and thereby can deemphasize its use of general policies to deal with particular problems.

In anticipation of probable changes in the FRS go slow policy, an expansionary BHC will identify and evaluate potential markets that it wants to enter *de novo* or by acquisition. It thus positions itself to move promptly as new opportunities become available. In addition to focusing on acquisitions, an imaginative BHC needs to evaluate whether some voluntary divestitures would, on balance, open new expansion proposals. In some cases a BHC may conclude that by selling one or more nonproblem affiliates it will obtain funds that it can then redeploy to expand the BHC in other markets or activities. Also, when it develops a plan to acquire a firm engaged in a permissible activity, a BHC may decide that the probability of regulatory approval will increase sharply if it offers to divest some of the acquired assets.

Even as it thus prepares to expand via the BHC vehicle, an expansionary BHC simultaneously focuses on other paths by which its current affiliates can expand their domestic and international activities—often by way of new services, new branches, and new technology.

## SUMMARY

A BHC is likely to expand its nonbanking activities if it foresees net benefits from such activities and/or faces impediments to the expansion of its banking operations.

The Bank Holding Company Act authorizes the FRS to determine which nonbanking activities are permissible for BHCs. The FRS is to designate as permissible only those activities that are closely related to banking and that are likely to result in public benefits that outweigh possible adverse effects, such as anticompetitive effects. On this basis, the FRS made decisions that:

- designate an initial list of permissible activities
- allow BHCs to engage in interstate nonbanking activities
- expedite the processing of applications by BHCs that want to enter a permissible activity *de novo*

Within these initial guidelines, many BHCs promptly expanded their nonbanking activities after the 1970 amendments to the Bank Holding Company Act.

In 1974 the FRS initiated a go slow policy to limit BHC expansion, especially into new nonbanking activities. It did so in order to encourage BHCs to digest their previous expansion and strengthen their affiliate banks. This go slow policy remains in effect and thus constrains BHC expansion into new nonbanking activities.

Various studies examine the initial effects of BHC expansion into nonbanking activities. Two studies suggest that BHCs can achieve diversification benefits by engaging in permissible nonbanking activities. Several experts question whether a BHC can in practice control its risks by owning a set of legally autonomous affiliate firms. If a BHC affiliate encounters problems that jeopardize its creditors, then a court may pierce the corporate veil and rule that the coaffiliate firms, with their resources, are part of the same total entity. Even prior to such a court test, a BHC is likely to try to solve the problems of a troubled affiliate, but in ways that may jeopardize the resources of and/or confidence in its other affiliates.

Even if a large BHC can control its risks better than can small banking organizations, it is difficult to specify how much more risk a BHC can—or should—accept. Also, the question of risk management intertwines with questions of capital management by BHCs. The FRS emphasizes that a BHC should "serve as a source of financial strength for its subsidiary banks," and so it monitors the extent to which BHCs engage in double leveraging. It also scrutinizes how BHCs propose to service—and actually service—their debts. Some studies indicate that BHCs leverage their nonbanking affiliates beyond industry standards, and other studies are inconclusive as to whether financial markets impede possible excessive leveraging by BHCs. Therefore to position itself for future expansion, a BHC needs to manage its capital and debts in ways that will reduce possible criticism by the FRS and other bank supervisory agencies.

The FRS has to determine whether BHC entry into a nonbanking activity is likely to result in public benefits that exceed possible adverse competitive effects. The FRS uses this benefit-cost test to help define permissible activities and to evaluate specific BHC applications to engage in permissible activities. An applicant BHC bears the burden of trying to demonstrate how its proposal passes this test.

If it reviews past FRS decisions about BHC applications to engage in nonbanking activities, a BHC gains insights into how to structure its application(s) in order to increase the probability of FRS approval. As one strategy, a BHC may propose to divest, from the nonbanking firm that it proposes to acquire, selected activities that are likely to pose questions of anticompetitive effects. Also, it will enumerate specific ways by which its acquisition will likely result in public benefits, such as lower interest rates for borrowers. However, based on results of studies to date, despite their limitations, one has to document carefully assertions that BHC involvement in nonbanking activities will lead to major public benefits.

An expansionary BHC needs to position itself for an eventual change in the go slow policy of the FRS. It can:

- focus on building "strong and efficient" current operations
- develop a demonstrable record of how its current operations yield public benefits
- monitor and try to anticipate changes in the go slow policy
- monitor, and possibly influence, legislative changes that will open new expansion opportunities, such as across state lines
- identify geographical and permissible product markets that it wants to enter
- possibly redeploy some of its resources by voluntarily selling or spinning-off some affiliates

Yet even as it positions itself to expand its BHC activities, an expansionary banking system also evaluates its opportunities for multinational expansion.

# APPENDIX
## LIMITED OBJECTIVE ONE-BANK HOLDING COMPANIES

In contrast to large BHCs that seek to expand their banking and nonbanking affiliates, there are many limited-objective OBHCs, each of which owns a small or medium-sized bank and possibly a small nonbanking affiliate such as, in rural areas, a local insurance agency. These limited-objective OBHCs do not aspire to become large multiaffiliate BHCs; they can, however, provide important financial and tax benefits to their stockholders.

### MOTIVATIONS TO FORM LIMITED-OBJECTIVE ONE-BANK HOLDING COMPANIES

Formation of a limited-objective OBHC often occurs when a group of people wish to purchase control of a bank. In such a case the selling stockholders may own their shares free of associated indebtedness, and the bank itself may have no debentures. In contrast, a potential buying group (or individual) typically has to borrow part of the purchase price, usually by negotiating a bank-stock loan from a large correspondent bank.

One approach is for the new stockholders, as individuals, to purchase a bank's controlling shares and to arrange the bank-stock loans(s). To help service their loan, the new controlling owners receive from the bank various revenues in the form of salaries, fees, and dividends. From the bank's view, the salaries and fees are deductible expenses before taxes; the dividends are paid after taxes. From the controlling stockholders' view, they must pay income taxes on all these revenues and then use after-tax dollars to help service their bank-stock loan, of which the interest expense (usually up to $10,000 per year) is tax-deductible but the principal repayment is not.

An alternative approach is for the new controlling stockholders to organize a corporation that they control and which, in turn, buys control of the bank.[1] Instead of their directly borrowing funds to finance the purchase of the bank, the buyers have their new corporation arrange a loan secured by its controlling stock in the bank. If they are active in the bank, the new

---

1. For a more complete discussion of the motivations for and structuring of small OBHCs, see Carol C. Madeley, ''One-Bank Holding Companies Increase Rapidly,'' *Voice* (Federal Reserve Bank of Dallas), September 1978, pp. 14-17.

controlling stockholders can receive some salaries, fees, and possibly dividends. Yet they will likely prefer to have the bank pay fees and dividends to the OBHC, which in turn uses these revenues to service its bank-stock loan. When one corporation (the OBHC) thus receives dividends from another corporation (the bank), under current tax laws the recipient firm has to pay taxes on only 15 percent of this intercorporate transfer. (If it owns at least 80 percent of the bank, the OBHC can achieve additional savings by filing a consolidated tax return for the two companies.) Thus, compared to the situation where new owners, as individuals, acquire the bank, the OBHC can obtain from the bank a larger after-tax flow of funds by which it then can service its bank-stock loan.[2] As the OBHC retires its debt over time, the controlling stockholders' equity in the OBHC increases. Eventually the stockholders may choose to sell their OBHC and realize a long-term capital gain that is subject to advantageous tax rates compared to ordinary income.

## FEDERAL RESERVE REVIEW OF APPLICATIONS TO FORM ONE-BANK HOLDING COMPANIES

Despite its limited objectives, an OBHC is subject to the Bank Holding Company Act as administered by the FRS. Because it knows how use of an OBHC vehicle can benefit a bank's owners, the Board of Governors states that:

> In acting on one-bank holding company formations, the Board has been less restrictive than otherwise with respect to financial considerations in cases that involve a current or prospective owner-chief executive establishing a holding company to hold the individual's direct equity interest in the bank. The Board regards such a policy as being in the public interest in order to facilitate management succession on the community level at the Nation's many smaller, independent banks.[3]

While the Board of Governors thus makes a policy distinction between a limited-objective OBHC and other BHCs, an application to form a limited-objective OBHC remains subject to the criteria of the Bank Holding Company Act.

When it reviews an application to form a BHC, the Board of Governors applies the statutory banking, competitive, and convenience and needs factors. On this basis the Board readily approves many such applications.

Consider a typical applicant that is a new firm which has no subsidiaries, engages in no activities, and was organized for the purpose of

---

2. One study analyzes a large sample of banks that subsequently became affiliated with small OBHCs. It reports that, after their affiliation, the sample banks significantly increased their "upstream" payments (primarily dividends and fees) to the parent OBHC. Roger D. Stover, "The Single Subsidiary Bank Holding Company," *Journal of Bank Research*, forthcoming, 1980.

3. *Federal Reserve Bulletin*, July 1976, pp. 638-639.

becoming a BHC by acquiring a specific bank. Also, the applicant's principal stockholders do not control other banks. In such a case, the Board of Governors generally observes that consummation of the proposed acquisition "would not have any adverse effects upon either existing or potential competition nor would it increase the concentration of banking resources in any relevant area," and therefore "concludes that the *competitive effects* of the proposal are *consistent with approval* of the application" (italics added). Second, even if it contemplates no major changes in the bank's services, the Board concludes that "considerations relating to *convenience and needs* of the community to be served are *consistent with approval*" (italics added). Third, the Board reviews the applicant's financial resources and future prospects—especially its debt-servicing plans—and its managerial resources. Unless it finds these matters to be unsatisfactory, the Board will likely conclude that "considerations relating to *banking factors* are regarded as being *consistent with approval*" (italics added). Then, if all three factors are "consistent with approval," the Board is likely to judge that the proposed formation is consistent with the public interest and therefore approve it.[4]

In some decisions the Board states that the convenience and needs factor lends weight toward approval. In an illustrative case, the Board noted how the applicant's principals, since they, as individuals, had acquired the bank, had "initiated a more aggressive loan policy, with the result that Bank has become more responsive to the borrowing needs of the area." The Board further observed that this policy change did not injure the quality of the bank's loan portfolio, and so the Board regarded this expansion of lending services as a "positive factor" that lent weight toward approval of the proposed formation of an OBHC.[5]

In contrast, in some cases the Board finds that one or more of the three factors is adverse and therefore weighs against approval of a proposed formation of an OBHC. Concerning the competitive factor, the Board scrutinizes situations in which organizers of a proposed OBHC already control (either as individuals or through other BHCs) one or more banks in the relevant market. To illustrate, in one case in which it denied a proposed formation of an OBHC, the Board noted that the OBHC's "proposed acquisition involves an individual's use of a holding company structure to acquire control of an existing bank that is a direct competitor of another bank under the control of the same individual."[6]

Often when it denies the formation of an OBHC, the Board cites adverse banking factors. As it states about large expansionary BHCs, the Board cites "that a holding company should constitute a *source of financial*

---

4. These quotations are from a decision reported in the *Federal Reserve Bulletin*, November 1977, pp. 1014-1015. The Board uses similar wording in other decisions in which the circumstances are similar to those of this illustrative decision.

5. *Federal Reserve Bulletin*, October 1977, pp. 936-937.

6. *Federal Reserve Bulletin*, December 1977, pp. 1083-1085.

*and managerial strength* to its subsidiary bank(s), and that the Board will closely examine the condition of an applicant in each case with this consideration in mind''(italics added). On this basis, the Board scrutinizes such items as the resources of the principal stockholders of the applicant company, the prior management record of these principals, and the applicant company's proposed debt and debt-servicing plan. In its review of one such plan, the Board concluded that:

> Based upon more realistic earnings and growth projections, it is the Board's judgment that Applicant would not have the necessary financial resources to meet its annual debt servicing requirements, maintain adequate capital at Bank, and meet any unexpected problems that might arise at Bank. . . . In sum, the Board does not view Applicant's overall financial plan as one that would enable it to serve as a source of strength to Bank or one that would enhance Bank's prospects.[7]

When it evaluates an application that involves a bank that is part of a chain of OBHCs, the Board looks beyond the specific bank and analyzes the financial and managerial resources of the other banks in the chain. In such cases the Board adopts a multibank perspective and applies the standards that it uses for MBHCs ''because of the interdependence of the banks in a chain of commonly-owned one-bank holding companies and the distinct possibility that the financial and managerial resources of one or more of the banks in the chain may be used to support the operations of other members in the banking group.''[8]

Also in its review of the banking factors, the Board considers ''how business practices employed by the principals of a bank holding company in acquiring the stock of a bank reflect upon the managerial resources of the proposed bank holding company.'' Although it cannot deny a proposed acquisition solely because a BHC has made unequal offers to a bank's majority and minority stockholders, the Board reviews whether, in its judgment, a bank's minority stockholders have received sufficient material facts about their bank in order to make an informed decision whether to sell their stock to the principals who then apply to form a BHC. Although it disclaims ''primary responsibility for enforcing the securities laws,'' the Board claims the power, in assessing an applicant BHC's managerial resources, to ''take account of evidence indicating that management has violated legal or fiduciary obligations of fair dealing with minority stockholders.''[9]

---

7. *Federal Reserve Bulletin*, October 1977, pp. 934-935. Also see *Federal Reserve Bulletin*, December 1977, pp. 1082-1083, 1098-99.

8. *Federal Reserve Bulletin*, July 1976, pp. 638-639.

9. *Federal Reserve Bulletin*, November 1977, pp. 1009-1011.

## SUMMARY

Those who seek or have control of small banks can obtain financial and tax benefits if they control the bank indirectly via an OBHC. Organizers of a limited-objective OBHC are likely to receive FRS approval to acquire a specific bank if they *do not* control other banks in the same market and *do* demonstrate a realistic debt-servicing plan and a history of managerial competence and integrity. If the organizers control other banks, either as individuals or through BHCs, the Board will also evaluate the financial and managerial resources of these related banks and apply to this group the standards that it applies to MBHCs.

# 21

# MULTINATIONAL
# BANKING SYSTEMS

While they expand domestically by means of modern funds-transfer systems, branching, and/or BHCs, most large money-center banks also are expanding their international operations. This chapter introduces the principal:

- types of international banking transactions
- motivations for American banks expanding abroad
- strategies for international expansion
- returns, risks, and risk-control procedures for international banking

Even as American banks expand abroad, some large foreign-based banks have begun to expand their banking networks within the United States, leading to a prolonged public-policy debate as to the extent to which federal law should constrain such foreign-bank expansion.

## INTERNATIONAL EXPANSION: A FRAMEWORK

No matter what its size or location, a bank has customers who engage in occasional international banking transactions. These customers send funds to relatives or firms abroad, and they purchase some foreign currency for their foreign travels. An outlying bank meets this infrequent demand by using international banking services provided by its principal correspondent bank; it has little incentive to expand its own international operations. In contrast, a large money-center bank has to be able to provide efficient international banking services to outlying correspondent banks and to other clients that regularly engage in international transactions.

Exhibit 21-1 outlines the principal directions by which large money-center banks expand their international-banking activities and their networks of foreign locations. This schematic framework introduces the process by

**EXHIBIT 21-1**

**International Expansion: A Framework**

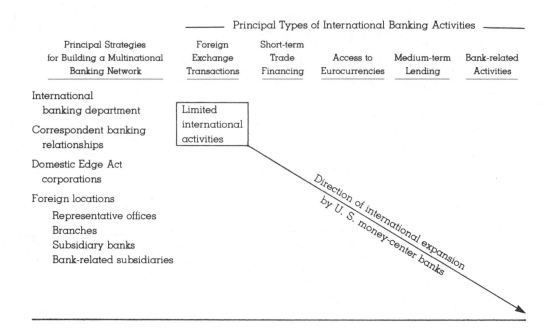

which individual banks and the American banking system have expanded—and continue to expand—their international operations.

## PRINCIPAL TYPES OF INTERNATIONAL BANKING ACTIVITIES

Some international banking activities, such as short-term trade financing, have long histories; others, such as intermediate-term Eurocurrency financing, emerged during the 1960s. In all cases, however, the banking system and individual banks have sharply increased their involvement in these activities. They have done so primarily to:

- service the rapid expansion of international trade and travel subsequent to World War II
- help meet the financing needs of corporate customers that have become increasingly multinational in their operations
- increase their returns by expanding their domestic and international loan portfolios, especially during periods when public policy tried to constrain such expansion
- control their portfolio risks and variability of returns by broadly diversifying their portfolios and other sources of revenues

The expansionary banks seldom achieved all these objectives, and some encountered setbacks that led senior banking officials and supervisory agencies to reevaluate the objectives and control procedures for international expansion.

## FOREIGN EXCHANGE TRANSACTIONS

Foreign exchange transactions arise because of travel, trade, and capital flows among countries that have different currencies.

Travelers engage in various foreign-exchange transactions. To illustrate, an American traveler who is about to depart for the United Kingdom (U.K.) may choose to exchange some dollars for pounds sterling prior to the departure. An international banking department will, for a small fee, sell pounds to the traveler. At any time there is an *exchange rate* between two currencies, and the current exchange rate is the *spot rate*. Over time the exchange rate can vary, and so an experienced traveler may choose to "speculate" in the foreign currency transaction. If, for example, he or she anticipates that the value of pounds soon will increase in terms of American dollars, the traveler will exchange most of the dollars for pounds prior to departure. Conversely, if he or she expects the value of pounds to decline, the traveler will defer purchasing most of the pounds until they are needed in the U.K.

Instead of carrying much of either foreign currency, the traveler can purchase travelers checks (denominated either in dollars or pounds) from a bank or other agent of one of the large issuers of travelers checks. The selling agent gets most or all of the fee paid for the travelers checks; the issuing firm benefits from the float that arises between its prompt receipt of funds for the travelers checks and its redemption of the checks when the traveler eventually cashes them.

Firms that engage in international commerce also engage in diverse foreign exchange transactions. For example, an American computer manufacturer sells a unit to a U.K. firm that agrees to purchase the unit for 500,000 pounds sterling payable in 60 days. The manufacturer can wait 60 days, collect the payment, and convert it to dollars at the then-prevailing exchange (spot) rate. The manufacturer thus exposes itself to the risks (and returns) of exchange-rate fluctuations. To avoid this type of risk, a firm can enter into a *foreign exchange contract* whereby two parties agree to exchange specific amounts of specific currencies at a specific date. In the example, the manufacturer would agree to exchange the 500,000 pounds that it will receive in 60 days for a total dollar amount to which the two parties agree today. The contractual dollar amount will reflect the price currently quoted in the 60-day forward market for the two currencies. Although the *forward exchange rate* can differ from the spot rate, the manufacturer knows exactly how many dollars it will receive in 60 days in exchange for the 500,000 pounds. The other party to the contract may be another firm that needs 500,000 pounds in 60 days and wants to hedge itself by buying them now for future delivery at an agreed dollar price. More likely, the other party is a speculator who expects the dollar value of pounds to increase over the 60-day period, or it is an international banking department of a large bank that regularly enters — and itself hedges — foreign exchange contracts as part of its ongoing operations.[1]

If it directly engages in foreign exchange operations, a bank has a trading room in which about half the people are *traders*, who directly conduct the foreign exchange transactions, and the others are support personnel who are involved in communications and record-keeping. The traders stand ready to service the bank's clients, and they trade for the bank's own account. They are expected to contribute to bank profits through their transaction spreads and fees and their occasional profits from correctly anticipating, and sufficiently unhedging, the bank's account in order to benefit from exchange rate fluctuations.

A bank's foreign exchange operations involve several risks, one of which is that the other party to a contract is unable or unwilling to fulfill its commitment. A bank can control this risk by analyzing the creditworthiness of the parties with whom it has foreign exchange contracts and by diversifying its contracts among many creditworthy parties. A second risk arises from unhedged spot or forward foreign-currency positions. If, for example, it agrees to deliver 10 million pounds at a specific dollar price 60 days from now, a bank has to deliver the pounds even if it then has to buy the pounds at a spot price (in dollars) that exceeds the price at which it had previously agreed to sell them. To control this risk, a bank can match its forward delivery contract with an offsetting forward contract in which it agrees to take delivery, at a specific dollar price, of 10 million pounds at about the time it has to deliver the same amount. Whether a bank trades for a client or for its own account, these risks are real — as attested by the publicized large foreign exchange losses by a major New York bank and a West German bank.

Two coauthors summarize how a bank can further control its foreign exchange risks if it has:

- "a professional staff of traders operating within clearly delineated rules provided by senior management as to currency position limits, credit limits, and transaction recording procedures
- "adequate support resources (i.e., employees, systems, and equipment) to capture, process, and summarize essential information
- "accounting and auditing systems that effectively measure profitability and monitor procedures"[2]

The *currency position limits* specify the authorized maximum long (and short) position in each currency traded; the *credit limits* specify the

---

1. For a more detailed discussion of foreign exchange markets and contracts, see Janice M. Westerfield, "Foreign Exchange Markets: Booming and Bustling," *Business Review* (Federal Reserve Bank of Philadelphia), September 1974, pp. 12-22.

2. Howard G. Johnson and J. James Lewis, "Keep Control of Foreign Exchange Operations," *The Bankers Magazine*, Spring 1975, pp. 79-83.

maximum contractual exposure to any one party, such as a trading firm or another bank. The support systems, most of which are computerized, enable the bank's senior officers to monitor whether the traders stay within their limits and to evaluate various return-risk measures of the trading operations.

## SHORT-TERM TRADE FINANCING

Some large money-center banks, especially in coastal cities, have long engaged in short-term financing for international trade. Especially since the 1950s, as more U.S. firms became involved in the rapid expansion of world trade, these banks and other money-center banks sharply increased their financing of international trade—in many cases by using specialized financial instruments.

### Letters of Credit

A bank's letter of credit, drawn for a specific client, specifies the conditions under which the bank—either directly or through the correspondent banking network—stands ready to make payments to another party.[3] These letters of credit expedite the flow of goods across national boundaries, and they provide fee income to issuing banks.

To illustrate, an American exporter receives a large order from a Dutch firm to which it is reluctant to ship goods on open account. Therefore the exporter asks the Dutch firm to arrange with its local bank to issue a letter of credit guaranteeing that the agreed sum will be paid to the exporter's account at its American bank as soon as the exporter meets specific conditions concerning the export transaction. A basic condition is that the exporter will deliver copies of the shipping documents to its bank, which confirms that this and all other conditions have been met. The American bank then credits the exporter's account, and in turn collects from the Dutch bank, which collects from or has collected from the importer. The sequence is reversed if an American importer arranges with its bank to have a letter of credit drawn to guarantee prompt payment to a foreign exporter once the exporter meets the agreed conditions.

### Bankers' Acceptances

Bankers' acceptances, which are direct extensions of commercial letters of credit:

---

3. Most letters of credit cover commercial transactions. However, a traveler who plans a lengthy, expensive foreign journey can have a large money-center bank prepare a letter of credit, which functions like a non-interest-earning passbook account. The traveler presents this document at the issuing bank's foreign offices or correspondents, identifies himself or herself with a passport and possible separate letter, and then draws funds against the letter of credit (account) at the current exchange rate and up to the maximum amount of the letter. The amount of each transaction is entered on the document, and it reduces the remaining balance. Most travelers find it more expedient—and for smaller sums more economical—to purchase travelers checks and/or to have funds transferred to a foreign branch or bank to be held until the traveler's arrival.

- arise primarily in international trade
- provide short-term financing (up to a maximum of 180 days)
- are negotiable money-market instruments

From a peak of $1.7 billion in 1929, outstanding bankers' acceptances fell to $110 million in 1944, after which they have grown, especially since the 1960s, to over $14 billion.

Exhibit 21-2 schematically summarizes the principal participants and steps in the process of creating and redeeming an illustrative banker's acceptance.

(a)  An American importer and a foreign exporter initially agree on their commercial transaction. Among the terms, they agree to use a letter of credit and a time draft that will become a banker's acceptance.
(b)  The American importer arranges for its money-center bank to issue a letter of credit for the pending transaction and subsequently to accept a ninety-day time draft on behalf of the importer. The issuing bank relays this information, via its foreign branches and/or correspondent banks, to the foreign exporter.
(c)  The foreign exporter ships the agreed goods.
(d)  The foreign exporter then draws a time draft, for the agreed amount, against the importer. The exporter presents this draft and supporting shipping documents to its local bank and receives prompt credit, probably at a discount or else for a fee. The exporter's bank in turn forwards the time draft and documentation to the importer's bank, which, after reviewing that all specific conditions have been met, accepts the time draft by writing, and signing, "Accepted" on its face. The "accepting" bank thus guarantees that the instrument will be paid on its due date. The accepting bank will, as instructed by the importer's bank, either hold the acceptance in safe keeping until the due date and then remit the funds or else discount the acceptance in the money market and promptly credit the importing bank with the discounted amount.
(e)  If discounted, the acceptance becomes a money-market instrument, primarily because it has been accepted (guaranteed) by a recognized money-center bank. (Subject to guidelines, the Federal Reserve Bank of New York has authority to buy eligible acceptances either outright or through repurchase agreements.)
(f)  By the due date the importer, which meanwhile has been able to process and/or market the imported goods, pays its money-center bank, which redeems the acceptance. If the importer fails to pay on time, the accepting bank remains obligated to redeem the acceptance.

By creating bankers' acceptances, an issuing bank services specific client needs, and it obtains fee income, customarily "a minimum of 1½ per cent per annum, or ⅛ of 1 percent per month, for accepting a draft on behalf

**EXHIBIT 21-2**

**Creation and Redemption of a Banker's Acceptance**

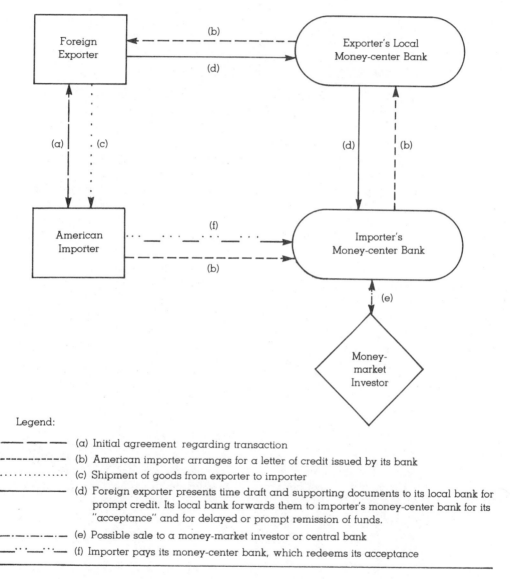

Legend:

——— ——— (a) Initial agreement regarding transaction

------------- (b) American importer arranges for a letter of credit issued by its bank

················· (c) Shipment of goods from exporter to importer

——————— (d) Foreign exporter presents time draft and supporting documents to its local bank for prompt credit. Its local bank forwards them to importer's money-center bank for its "acceptance" and for delayed or prompt remission of funds.

—·——·——·— (e) Possible sale to a money-market investor or central bank

—··—··— (f) Importer pays its money-center bank, which redeems its acceptance

of nonbank customers of the highest credit rating.''[4] An importer usually also pays—in the price of the goods—for the discount and/or fees that the exporter pays to its bank in the transaction.

---

4. Joy S. Joines, ''Bankers' Acceptances,'' from *Instruments of the Money Market* (edited by Timothy Q. Cook), 4th ed., Federal Reserve Bank of Richmond, 1977. This source describes other variants and uses of bankers' acceptances.

To control its risks in creating acceptances, an issuing bank evaluates the creditworthiness of the customer on whose behalf it accepts a time draft. Also, it establishes the maximum amount that it will accept on behalf of each customer. In addition to internal policy limits, if it belongs to the FRS, a bank cannot accept, on behalf of any one party, unsecured drafts in excess of ten percent of the bank's capital stock plus surplus.

### Other Services to Facilitate International Trade

A large money-center bank provides additional services to clients that engage in international trade. It:

- collects checks and drafts for them
- obtains credit information about current and potential customers based in other countries
- provides timely information about each nation's economic and social trends, especially as they may affect international transactions
- provides current information about each nation's laws and regulations that affect trade and capital flows

To perform most international trade financing activities, a large money-center bank needs only a head-office international banking department (IBD) that works through a network of domestic and foreign correspondent banks. The overseas correspondents process items at their end of transactions, and they gather and relay economic intelligence about developments in their areas. Thus, if it limits itself to foreign exchange transactions and short-term trade financing, there is little need for a large money-center bank to develop networks of overseas branches and/or subsidiaries.

## ACCESS TO EUROCURRENCIES

A *Eurocurrency* is a national currency that a foreign bank is willing to accept as a deposit. *Eurodollars,* for example, are U.S. dollar-denominated deposit liabilities of banking offices located outside the United States. Eurodollars are the principal Eurocurrency, of which others include Eurosterling, Euromarks, and various Eurofrancs. To become a Eurocurrency, a national currency has to be readily convertible into other major currencies and relatively free from exchange controls.

Starting in the 1960s, an increasing number of U.S. money-center banks wanted to improve their access to the rapidly developing Eurodollar market.[5] Initially, their principal motivation was to practice liabilities

---

5. For more information about development of the Eurodollar market, see Milton Friedman, "The Euro-Dollar Market: Some First Principles," *Review* (Federal Reserve Bank of St. Louis), July 1971, pp. 16-24. (This article was first published in *The Morgan Guaranty Survey*, October 1969, pp. 4-14.) Also, a three-part series of articles on "The Eurodollar Market," *Economic Review* (Federal Reserve Bank of Cleveland), March 1970, pp. 3-19, April 1970, pp. 3-18, May 1970, pp. 3-14.

management, especially during periods when the FRS's Regulation Q ceilings limited their ability to attract and/or retain large negotiable CDs. Faced with run-offs of their large domestic CDs, large money-center banks moved to position themselves to borrow conveniently short-term Eurodollars that were not subject to Regulation Q ceilings and that were not, until late 1969, subject to FRS reserve requirements.

Although it could borrow Eurodollars through the correspondent banking system, a large money-center bank typically concluded that it would have more dependable access if it had as a conduit its own foreign branch that could directly accept Eurodollar deposits or borrow interbank Eurodollars and in turn "lend" Eurodollars to the head office in the United States. Some large money-center banks decided to open a branch in London, a principal center of Eurodollar trading, but many others concluded that they could as readily engage in Eurodollar transactions by having a small offshore branch in Nassau (the Bahamas). This expansion of London and Nassau branches underlies much of the foreign branch expansion by U.S. banks between 1965 and 1969, when FRS member banks increased their number of U.K. branches (primarily in London) from 17 to 37 and their Bahamian branches from 2 to 32.[6]

Also, by having an overseas branch that had access to Eurocurrency markets, a large money-center bank positioned itself to service multinational clients that became increasingly subject to government restrictions on their funds transfers from the United States:

- One program, initiated as voluntary in 1964 and made mandatory in 1968, limited the amount of funds that a U.S firm could transfer to its overseas affiliates and also limited the amount of funds that such affiliates could retain for reinvestment overseas.
- Another program levied an interest equalization tax on American holders of foreign securities—thus impeding foreign issuers (including overseas affiliates of American firms) that wanted to raise funds in U.S. capital markets.
- The Voluntary Foreign Credit Restraint (VFCR) program, administered by the FRS, requested U.S. banks to limit their head offices from expanding their foreign lending beyond their historical levels or, later, beyond amounts related to a bank's size.

Faced with this network of constraints, multinational firms sought to raise funds in the Eurodollar and other Eurocurrency markets, and they turned to overseas offices of American banks for Eurocurrency loans and for advice in placing Eurocurrency securities offerings. Thus, to retain and build relationships with multinational clients and to develop new sources of profits, large money-center banks had additional motivations to establish and/or expand their overseas branch networks.

---

6. Allen B. Frankel, "International Banking: Part I," *Business Conditions* (Federal Reserve Bank of Chicago), September 1975, pp. 3-9.

Although some factors that triggered their development have changed, Eurocurrency markets continue; and U.S. banks have chosen to maintain and expand their access to these markets:

- Use of Eurodollars in liabilities management has become less attractive since late 1969 when the FRS first imposed reserve requirements and other rules on head-office borrowings of Eurodollars from overseas offices.
- Since 1970 the FRS has suspended interest-rate ceilings on negotiable CDs in excess of $100,000, thus eliminating prior differences in which Eurodollar liabilities were not subject to interest-rate ceilings as were large negotiable CDs. [7]
- In 1974 the U.S. government terminated its VFCR program, and it eased other impediments to international capital flows.

Yet by the time these changes had occurred, many American banks had:

- established an overseas presence
- acquired expertise in traditional international financing
- developed new procedures and markets for international operations, especially in international lending

## MEDIUM-TERM LENDING

As they have expanded their international loan portfolios to include new types of loans and new borrowers, American banks have had to reevaluate the returns, risks and risk-control procedures associated with these changing lending practices.

### Servicing Multinational Firms

In the 1950s and 1960s a growing number of U.S. firms developed overseas operations, and they turned to their principal bank(s) to help service their international transactions and financing needs. A bank that had no overseas branches initially could service these multinational clients by expanding its head-office international banking department (IBD) and by using its overseas correspondents. However, with the advent of the VFCR program and other capital controls, such a bank typically concluded that it needed to have at least one overseas branch from which it could more directly service its multinational clients.

With access to Eurodollars, a bank's overseas branch(es) can make both short-term and medium-term Eurodollar loans to its corporate clients. Although some are at fixed rates, many loans are *floating-rate Eurocredits*,

---

7. Initially the suspension applied to large CDs with maturities of 30-89 days; in 1973 the suspension was extended to include large CDs having maturies of 90 days or longer.

in which the interest rate floats in tandem with an interbank lending rate, such as the six-month London interbank offered rate (LIBOR). A prime borrower pays the smallest spread above this base rate, and other borrowers pay higher spreads that provide a risk-premium to the lender. Also, as they develop their loan portfolios, the overseas offices apply previous home-office innovations such as term lending (in some cases up to twelve years) and analyses of a borrower's anticipated cash flows as a measure of its debt-servicing capacity.

As it develops its capabilities, an overseas branch can compete for business of overseas-based multinational firms and, to the extent permitted by local regulations and custom, for business of local firms in its overseas market.

## Lending to Lesser-Developed Countries

As they competed to lend to multinational firms, overseas banks and offices reduced their lending terms such that between 1970 and 1973 the "normal" maturity of Eurodollar credits went from 3-7 years to 10-12 years and for prime borrowers the spread over the interbank rate narrowed from over 1 percentage point to a range between ⅜ and ⅝'s of a percentage point.[8] As they thus faced narrower margins, various banks looked toward new categories of borrowers. Among such potential borrowers were major oil-importing countries—such as Brazil, Japan, and Mexico—the economies of which felt the initial shock of the quadrupling of petroleum prices by the Organization of Petroleum Exporting Countries (OPEC) in 1973 and 1974. This action by OPEC triggered worldwide concern about whether and how the financial system could recycle the new trade surpluses (so-called petro-dollars) of the oil-exporting nations and whether and how various oil-importing nations could finance their purchases.

Initially, various banks increased their credit lines and loans to oil-importing countries and/or to lesser-developed countries (LDCs). One observer reports that "within the reduced total of international bank credit in 1975, the oil-importing LDCs . . . obtained over $8 billion in publicly announced Eurocurrency credits, as against some $4 ½ billion in 1974."[9] Moreover,

> during the three years following the oil price increase, the nonoil LDCs as a group obtained an estimated $60 billion in commercial bank credits. . . . Of this amount, publicly announced borrowings from the Euro-currency markets alone totaled nearly $30 billion, a sharp rise from the previous three years when total new Euro-currency credits were less than $10 billion. [10]

---

8. Frankel, "International Banking: Part I," p. 6.

9. Richard A. Debs, "Petro-Dollars, LDCs, and International Banks," *Monthly Review* (Federal Reserve Bank of New York), January 1976, pp. 10-17.

10. David C. Beek, "Commercial Bank Lending to the Developing Countries," *FRBNY Quarterly Review* (Federal Reserve Bank of New York), Summer 1977, pp. 1-8.

Ten nations accounted for most of the total bank borrowings by LDCs at the end of 1976. Brazil and Mexico accounted for almost half of the total, and eight other countries (Argentina, Chile, Colombia, Korea, Peru, the Philippines, Taiwan, and Thailand) accounted for most of the rest. These countries have been the principal beneficiaries of the recent explosion in bank lending to LDCs. In contrast, many poorer and more populous LDCs have had to rely primarily on loans and grants from international agencies and other countries.

When it lends to an LDC or to a foreign-government enterprise, a bank seldom does so on its own. It participates in a banking syndicate that is originated and administered by a lead bank that receives a syndication fee for its services. This syndication process allows banks to share the risks and returns of a large loan.

## Using the Asian Dollar Market

The Asian dollar market is a mechanism whereby banking offices accept deposits in convertible currencies, primarily American dollars, and they make loans and investments denominated in these currencies. The market originated in 1968; and it is centered in Singapore, the government of which provided various incentives for its development:

- "exemption of interest-withholding tax on Asian dollar deposits
- "abolition of liquidity requirement for foreign currency deposits
- "elimination of stamp duty on certificates of deposit and bills and exchange
- "reduction of tax on net income derived from offshore Asian-currency loans."[11]

From its modest beginnings, the Asian dollar market grew to over $12.8 billion by 1976, and over sixty banks—including some large U.S. banks—participate in it.

Banks involved in the Asian dollar market borrow from each other (interbank deposits), and they obtain deposits primarily from foreign corporations, governmental units, and wealthy individuals. The banks lend to each other (interbank deposits), to governmental units, and to local and multinational corporations. As in the Eurocurrency markets, banks and nonresident participants in the Asian dollar market face few governmental restrictions. The Asian dollar market is part of the international network of financial markets, and its rates generally move in line with money rates in the United States and in Eurocurrency markets.

## Managing Risks of International Lending

As it extends its portfolio into international lending, a bank goes beyond domestic risks of default and interest-rate fluctuations and adds risks of:

---

11. Anindya K. Bhattacharya, "Exploring the Asian Dollar Market," *The Bankers Magazine,* Summer 1977, pp. 74-78.

- repudiation or nonpayment of its debt by a sovereign nation
- foreign exchange fluctuations
- capital controls

There are strategies by which a bank can control the diverse risks of international lending.

**Default Risk** When they receive an application from a private firm, a bank's international loan officers have to evaluate the applicant's debt-servicing capacity. As with domestic loans, they focus on the firm's past and projected performance as computed from historic and pro forma accounting statements. The bank's credit analysts and loan officers can readily apply their computer programs and analytical skills to financial statements provided by American-based multinational firms and their affiliates. In contrast, they find that foreign-based firms provide financial statements that use different accounting conventions, and that legal requirements for a binding loan contract vary among nations. Faced with such intercountry differences, an American bank chooses either to have specialized personnel who can evaluate and structure loans to foreign borrowers or else to limit its lending to American-based multinationals.

In contrast, when they evaluate a loan request from a foreign government or its state-owned enterprises, bank loan officers use different analytical techniques; and they know that, under international law, a sovereign nation can repudiate its debts. Therefore the loan personnel evaluate a nation's:

- past and projected balance-of-payments figures
- current level of, and repayment schedule for, external debt
- international reserves, primarily in the form of foreign exchange and drawing rights against international credit agencies such as the International Monetary Fund
- domestic economic, social, and political developments

Even the preceding summary suggests the need for specialized economic analyses and forecasts. For example, one author notes that "full-fledged econometric models are available for some countries, and these can be used to project and determine whether the nation is heading for a trade surplus or a trade deficit." He also indicates how the concept of credit-scoring can be extended to develop a "country risk index" that combines "the quantitative variables from balance of payments and domestic economic analysis with subjective factors derived from social-political assessments."[12] The specific construction and application of country risk indexes vary among international lenders that use them as tools to aid decisions by experienced international loan officers.

A bank can have international loans guaranteed or insured by public or private parties. For example, to maintain its national integrity in world

---

12. A. Blake Friscia, "Creditworthiness of a Country," *The Bankers Magazine*, Spring 1974, pp. 31-36.

capital markets, a nation may require prior government approval before one of its large private firms or public agencies undertakes an international borrowing. Moreover, in some cases the government or its central bank also will guarantee the approved borrowings. Even in these cases, a lender has to evaluate the quality of the guarantee.

Other parties also guarantee or insure against specific risks associated with some types of foreign loans. The U.S. Export-Import Bank (Eximbank) will guarantee medium-term bank loans against default risk; and the Foreign Credit Insurance Association, acting as agent for a group of insurance companies and the Eximbank, will insure against such risk. As in domestic lending, if it plans to become involved in guarantee or insurance programs for its international loans, then a bank has to evaluate the expected net benefits of such programs and develop some in-house expertise in the use of such risk-control procedures.

**Interest Rate Risk**   As in domestic lending, a bank tries to protect itself against interest-rate fluctuations. Although its economists try to forecast interest rates in various loan markets, a bank basically protects itself by matching the maturity structure of its sources of funds and its portfolio of international loans and/or by making floating-rate loans in which the rate is closely linked to a bank's fluctuating cost of funds.

**Foreign Exchange Fluctuations**   A domestic bank is unconcerned about foreign exchange fluctuations when its assets and liabilities are all denominated in American dollars. When, however, it makes loans denominated in nondollar currencies, a bank has to evaluate the probable future dollar value of the nondollar loan repayments. To evaluate and to try to control this risk, a bank's economists and other specialists try to forecast future exchange rates among foreign currencies. Because such forecasts are inexact and at times incorrect, a bank also uses various hedging techniques to control foreign exchange risks:

- Denominate foreign loans in dollars so that the borrower assumes the risk of converting local currencies to dollars in order to service its dollar-denominated debt.
- Match loans and liabilities in nondollar currencies. For example, an American bank's U.K. branch may accept deposits in pounds sterling and then make similar-maturity local or Eurocurrency loans denominated in pounds. The branch thus hedges itself against foreign-currency and interest-rate risks and seeks to profit from the spread between its loan rate(s) and cost of funds—each denominated in pounds.
- Examine feasible ways to control its foreign exchange risks for medium-term nondollar loans by entering forward contracts to deliver the nondollar repayments in return for specific amounts of dollars or other currencies.

Although it can thus try to protect itself against foreign exchange fluctuations, at times a bank has a creditworthy foreign borrower that stands ready to service its debt but cannot do so because of governmental restrictions on its capital flows.

**Capital Controls** An international lender, both to private firms and to governmental units, has to have specialists who can interpret and operate within a changing maze of controls that nations impose on capital flows. To illustrate, many nations use foreign exchange policies, special taxes, and direct restrictions to try to control capital inflows and outflows. The U.S. has used an interest equalization tax and VFCR program, and other nations have used detailed programs to limit the amounts, types, and repayment terms of external debts incurred by their private and/or public firms.

Many countries continuously have capital controls; other countries at times impose such controls because of unanticipated adverse balance-of-payments developments. In such cases a specific debtor may have the resources and willingness to service its external debt, but it cannot do so because of newly imposed restrictions on capital outflows. Thus when it evaluates an international loan applicant, a bank has to project not only the applicant's debt-servicing capacity but also the probability that the applicant's country of residency will impose capital controls that impede loan repayments. Its use of a country risk index helps a lender to assign probabilities to the imposition of capital controls. Another way to manage this risk is to lend to multinational parent firms or to have a multinational parent cosign an affiliate's loan. This way, even if specific capital flows are blocked, the parent's worldwide resources are committed to servicing the debt.[13]

## BANK-RELATED ACTIVITIES

Until the 1960s American banks seldom extended their overseas operations beyond the traditional banking activities performed by large correspondent banks and some overseas branches. Then, as a logical extension of the domestic development of BHCs with their bank-related activities, large American banks began to focus on expected benefits from multinational expansion into bank-related activities:

- increase returns and the rate of expansion
- control risk via additional functional and geographical diversification and by operating through legally distinct affiliates
- sidestep some regulatory constraints
- offer the convenience of one-stop financial services to multinational clients
- thereby increase the market valuation of the firm

To expand its set of financial activities, a large multinational banking

---

13. For additional information about evaluating and managing risks of international lending, see Janice M. Westerfield, ''A Primer on the Risks of International Lending and How to Evaluate Them,'' *Business Review* (Federal Reserve Bank of Philadelphia), July-August 1978, pp. 19-29.

organization builds a network of overseas subsidiaries that engage in bank-related activities, such as:[14]

- consumer finance companies
- factoring
- financial advisory services
- investment banking
- leasing
- merchant banking, which combines banking, investment banking, and other financial services for corporations

As it faces FRS constraints on domestic BHC expansion, so does an expansionary banking organization face FRS constraints on its multinational expansion into bank-related activities.

## CONTROLLED EXPANSION OF INTERNATIONAL BANKING ACTIVITIES

Although it manages risks throughout its domestic operations, a bank accepts new types of risks as it expands its international activities. To illustrate:

- The Franklin National Bank of New York, at one time the twentieth-largest bank in the U.S., encountered serious problems in its foreign exchange operations. "Franklin, like many other banks, had expanded its international banking activities at a very rapid pace. In doing so, however, management control was not effectively maintained, and it was in this area that some of the more serious problems of the Franklin case came to light."[15] Franklin National subsequently was acquired by a group of large foreign banks.
- In 1974 several banks incurred "substantial losses" in foreign exchange operations, most notably due to the failure of a West German bank.
- Some large American banks have nonaccruing loans in their international portfolios, and they have had to restructure loans to specific LDCs, such as Peru and Zaire, as it became clear that these borrowers could not meet the terms of the initial loan agreements.

Thus, as it expands its international activities, a bank needs to have a comprehensive strategy for managing the new risks associated with such expansion.

A money-center bank first needs to develop a long-range plan for its international expansion. The plan can be revised over time, but it provides a

14. Steven I. Davis, "U.S. Banks Abroad: One-Stop Shopping?" *Harvard Business Review*, July-August 1971, pp. 75-84.

15. Richard A. Debs, "International Banking," *Monthly Review* (Federal Reserve Bank of New York), June 1975, pp. 122-129.

comprehensive framework by which the senior officials can evaluate the extent to which their bank should expand its international activities and the form and timing of such expansion. The senior officials can then evaluate and rank specific expansion proposals in the context of the long-range plan.

In order to service the growing international banking needs of its corporate clients and outlying correspondent banks, a money-center bank is likely to conclude that it needs to expand its international banking activities over time. Its senior officers then can evaluate three principal expansion strategies:

- expand the head-office international banking department (IBD) and further develop its ties with overseas correspondent banks
- identify subareas of international banking in which it can develop a comparative advantage over other international banking organizations
- build a diversified multinational banking system that engages in financial activities throughout many countries

For most regional money-center banks, the resource requirements (and risks) of the third strategy make it infeasible, except possibly as a long-range goal. Therefore they have to focus on the first two strategies, which are not mutually exclusive and in which the first strategy leads logically to the second.

### Expansion of Head-Office International Banking Department

This strategy enables a bank to build a head-office staff of specialists who can, either directly or through their relationships with large multinational correspondents, service most routine international banking transactions involving foreign exchange, short-term financing, and some medium-term financing. Because they are located in the head office, the senior officials and specialists can conveniently develop policies and control limits within which the specialists agree to operate. For example, to limit the bank's risks, foreign exchange specialists will agree not to operate with large unhedged positions; and the loan officers will focus on traditional short-term and medium-term lending to American-based multinational firms. Occasional exceptions to the agreed policies and control limits can be conveniently cleared with the senior officials. If they thus develop a head-office team of IBD specialists with whom they communicate and in whom they have confidence, the senior officials position their bank for subsequent controlled expansion.

### Identify and Develop Specialized Subareas of International Banking

Instead of trying to compete broadly against major money-center banks with their extensive resources, a regional money-center bank typically services clients within its own state and region. In many cases a regional bank can focus on servicing the specialized domestic and international banking needs of regional clients. As summarized by one observer:

Regional banks that are successful in foreign banking business are those that (1) capitalize on their close knowledge of their own home territories, especially for trade financing; (2) have specialized expertise in-house; (3) apply credit criteria to overseas business similar to those on domestic business—or all three.[16]

To illustrate these principles, the author cites case histories of banks that have identified and successfully developed their special niches in international banking, for example:

- a large Cleveland bank that concentrates on trade financing for the many export-oriented, heavy equipment manufacturers based in the Cleveland area
- a Pittsburgh bank that approaches its targeted returns on assets by "concentrating on export-import financing for its own trading territory plus occasional syndicated lending originated in-house"
- regional money-center banks in the Southeastern U.S. that are active in international trade financing for regional products such as tobacco, soybeans, and textiles

Another author cites cases in which affiliate banks of his regional bank holding company use letters of credit to service the specialized banking needs of client regional firms and outlying correspondent banks.[17]

If it thus identifies special niches and manages its risks by means of policy guidelines, control limits, and use of specialists, a regional bank can implement its long-range plan for controlled expansion of its international activities.

### Control Systems for Diversified Multinational Organizations

Comprehensive planning and control systems are especially necessary for a multinational banking organization that engages in diverse financial activities via a farflung network of branches and subsidiaries. This organization needs a strategic plan for controlled expansion, and it needs to develop a cadre of senior international-banking officers who manage the bank's specialists in foreign exchange, multinational lending, and bank-related activities.

A multinational banking organization especially needs policy guidelines and monitoring systems to control its exposure to *country risk*, whereby a nation's policies can impede the repayment of debt by firms operating within its jurisdiction. Such policies include special taxes, capital controls, devaluations, and nationalization. A survey of large money-center

---

16. Joe Asher, "Regionals Find Their Niche in Foreign Banking," *Banking*, July 1976, pp. 25-27 ff. Also "Three Regionals Find Their Niches," *Banking*, July 1978, p. 76.

17. Jerre R. Haskew, "How Regional Banks Can Become International Lenders," *The Bankers Magazine*, Autumn 1977, pp. 40-43.

banks reports that most compute their exposure in each country by aggregating the amount of assets (such as loans) and off-balance sheet items (such as commitments and letters of credit) that they have extended to entities domiciled in the country.[18] In addition, many reporting systems disaggregate the total exposure by type (e.g., loans, acceptances) and maturity. The survey summarizes the specific country exposure reporting systems used by several large money-center banks.

The federal bank supervisory agencies have developed a new supervisory approach to monitor international lending practices of U.S. banks. The new approach involves a standardized semiannual country exposure report and an examination process that has three principal parts:

1. "*Measurement of exposure* in each country where a bank has a business relationship. In turn, individual bank exposure would be consolidated to show the overall exposure of the United States banking system to each country abroad.
2. "*Analysis of exposure levels and concentrations of exposure* in relation to the bank's capital resources and the economic and financial conditions of each country in which the bank has outstanding credits.
3. "*Evaluation of the risk management system* used by the bank in relation to the size and nature of its foreign lending activities."[19]

This new supervisory process "reviews internal management systems and identifies certain concentrations of credit within the foreign loan portfolio that warrant management attention." It thus encourages multinational banking organizations to focus on portfolio diversification and to maintain internal systems to monitor and control their country exposure.

## BUILDING A MULTINATIONAL BANKING NETWORK

Congressional legislation has long permitted national banks to establish offshore branches (since 1913) and to invest in federally chartered corporations (since 1919) that engage in international banking and financial activities. State-chartered member banks have had to adhere to state law, which in states such as New York apparently did not impede potential overseas expansion. Despite this legislative flexibility—administered permissively by the FRS—by 1960 only eight banks had overseas branches and only fifteen banks had invested in international-banking affiliates.[20] This was the limited base from which American banks began to build multinational banking networks.

---

18. *Country Exposure Measurement and Reporting Practices of Member Banks*, Association of Reserve City Bankers, March 1977.

19. "A New Supervisory Approach to Foreign Lending," *FRBNY Quarterly Review*, Spring 1978, pp. 1-6.

20. Andrew F. Brimmer and Frederick R. Dahl, "Growth of American International Banking: Implications for Public Policy," *The Journal of Finance*, May 1975, pp. 341-363. (Table I)

## INTERNATIONAL BANKING DEPARTMENT

Any large money-center bank has a head-office international banking department (IBD) that services international financing needs of the bank's corporate clients and outlying correspondents. The IBD's senior officers supervise the department's specialists who conduct daily foreign exchange transactions and short-term trade financing. As it expands, a bank's head-office IBD adds more managers and more specialists who build the IBD's traditional operations and/or expand its activities into Eurocurrency transactions and diverse types of medium-term multinational loans. The head-office IBD sends out representatives to call on current and potential clients for multinational services, and it coordinates the activities of any overseas branches and/or affiliates.

## CORRESPONDENT BANKING RELATIONSHIPS

As in domestic banking, each bank develops a network of correspondent relationships with other banks. A large money-center bank provides specialized international banking services downstream to its outlying correspondent banks, and it exchanges services with other large banks in selected money centers in the U.S. and abroad. Thus a bank's IBD works with those of other money-center banks in such areas as: foreign exchange transactions, acceptances, letters of credit, economic intelligence, interbank Eurocurrency transactions, and loan participations. Through its network of domestic and overseas correspondents, a money-center bank can conveniently provide most international services that are needed by its corporate clients and smaller correspondent banks, and it does so without investing resources to build its own network of overseas offices.

## REPRESENTATIVE OFFICES

A bank's representative office (RO) neither accepts deposits nor makes loans; it is a vehicle by which a bank maintains a formal, but limited, presence in a foreign city.

An RO is a low-cost, low-risk method for a bank to operate in a foreign country. An RO usually operates from a small leased office, and its small staff develops new business for the bank's head office (or its offshore, full-service facilities) and keeps the head office informed about local developments. A bank faces minor regulatory and economic barriers to its opening—or closing—an RO.

There are four principal cases in which a bank uses an RO:

- in a country in which it would like to operate a full-service facility, but cannot do so because of the host country's prohibition of, or unacceptable conditions for, foreign-owned, full-service banking facilities
- as a transitional vehicle while awaiting regulatory approval and/or host country approval of its opening a full-service banking facility

- in a country where the expected business volume does not warrant the costs of a full-service facility
- in a country where the potential instability does not warrant investment in a full-service facility

To gradually expand its overseas network, a regional money-center bank can use ROs to establish initial formal representation in strategic cities. As the ROs in stable countries develop their clientele, the bank can then apply to convert them to more permanent, full-service facilities. Even banks with overseas networks of full-service facilities use ROs in selected countries where they cannot—or choose not to—have full-service facilities.

## OFFSHORE BRANCHES

In contrast to an RO, a branch accepts deposits, makes loans, and engages in other banking activities. If it has at least one offshore branch, a bank positions itself for convenient access to Eurocurrency markets and for controlled development of a multinational branch network.

Although the OCC and each state's banking agency have specific responsibilities concerning overseas branches of banks they supervise, the FRS has extensive statutory authority over foreign branches of all member banks. Regulation K provides that a member bank may, with prior approval of the FRS, establish a foreign branch. In addition, unless it is otherwise advised by the FRS, "a member bank that has branches in two or more foreign countries may establish initial branches in additional foreign countries after 60 days notice to the Board," and it may establish additional branches in a foreign country in which it already operates at least one branch. As with domestic branches, a creditor of a foreign branch has a claim against the bank of which the branch is an integral part.

An offshore branch provides an American bank with convenient access to Eurocurrency markets. A London branch places a bank at the center of these markets, but it requires approval from the Bank of England and substantial initial and continuing investment. Instead of a London branch— or in addition to a London branch—an American bank can apply for FRS approval of a so-called "shell" branch, usually in Nassau or the Cayman Islands. A *shell branch* is one at which "there is to be no contact with the local public at the branch" and at which the "quarters, staff, and bookkeeping may, at least in part, be supplied under contract by another party."[21] A bank uses such a shell branch primarily to participate in interbank Eurocurrency transactions and to participate in direct and/or syndicated Eurocurrency loans.

Once it accesses the Eurocurrency markets via a London and/or shell branch, a bank has to decide to what extent it will build a network of overseas branches. If it strategically develops such a network, a bank positions itself to:

---

21. Frankel, "International Banking: Part I," p. 7.

- promote its world-wide system of in-house, multinational banking capabilities
- develop profit centers in the world's major financial centers
- implement multinational tax-planning strategies

Not all of a bank's multinational branches are operational coequals. As in domestic branching, a multinational branch system involves strategically placed, full-service branches, such as in London, around which are clustered some satellite branches in the same country and/or in nearby countries.

In developing a long-range plan to build a network of overseas branches, an American bank has to evaluate some basic constraints:

- Some countries, such as Australia, do not permit entry of foreign branches; and other countries, such as Japan, have been slow to approve such entry.
- An American bank has to evaluate whether the expected long-run benefits of a foreign branch will exceed the probable costs of disrupting long-standing correspondent relationships with banks based in the foreign country.
- Both directly and because of the need for FRS approval, a bank's financial and human resources limit the rate at which it can develop a branch network.

To bypass some of these constraints, a bank evaluates its use of ROs and of nonbranch subsidiary organizations.

## EDGE ACT CORPORATIONS AND AGREEMENT CORPORATIONS

The Edge Act (1919) amended the Federal Reserve Act to permit American banks to invest in corporations that in turn engage in international banking and finance.[22] Congress passed this facilitating legislation so that American banks, through nonbranch subsidiaries, could match the services offered by banks in countries where banking laws are less restrictive than in the U.S. Congress gave the FRS broad powers to administer this legislation.

An *Edge Act corporation* operates under a federal charter granted by the FRS; either directly or through equity participations it can engage in international and foreign banking and in financial activities approved by the FRS. Although nonbanking firms can apply for a federal Edge Act charter, banking organizations account for most Edge corporations. A member bank's equity participation in an Edge corporation cannot exceed ten percent of the bank's capital stock and surplus.

An *Edge Act Agreement corporation* operates with a state charter, but, by agreement, remains subject to FRS regulation. It, too, can engage in

---

22. This section's legal-regulatory summary draws on Allen Frankel, "International Banking: Structural Aspects of Regulation," *Business Conditions* (Federal Reserve Bank of Chicago), October 1974, pp. 3-11.

international and foreign banking but not in broader financial activities. While they technically differ, Edge corporations and agreement corporations are subject to similar FRS regulations; and so, for brevity, the term Edge corporation often is used to refer to both types of corporations.

The FRS has authority to allow an Edge corporation to exercise those powers that the FRS judges usual ''in connection with the transaction of the business of banking or other financial operations in the countries, colonies, dependencies, or possessions in which it shall transact business.'' While it has latitude in permitting overseas activities by Edge corporations, by law the FRS cannot permit an Edge corporation to invest in a firm ''in the general business of buying or selling goods, wares, merchandise or commodities in the U.S.''

In deciding which nonbranch overseas activities it will allow U.S. banking organizations, the FRS considers three factors:

- ''What effect the overseas activity will have on the solvency of the U.S. bank;
- ''What effect the overseas activity will have on the concentration of economic power;
- ''What effect the overseas activity will have on the competitive position of U.S. banking organizations vis-a-vis their foreign competitors.''

To expedite its decisions and to provide guidance for expansionary bankers, the FRS has developed an approved list of overseas activities. This list includes some activities (such as consumer finance and equipment leasing) that are open to a BHC's bank-related domestic affiliates and some activities (such as investment banking and warehousing services) in which foreign banks usually engage but that are not permitted to a BHC's domestic affiliates. In addition, the FRS has ruled that it will not permit subsidiaries of American banks to engage in some activities, such as general insurance underwriting. Thus, as with domestic BHC activities, the FRS develops lists of activities that are approved or proscribed for overseas subsidiaries of American banks. Even if it applies to engage in an approved activity, a banking organization, usually through its Edge corporation, has to receive FRS approval of its specific expansion proposal.

To decide whether to use an Edge subsidiary to expand its multinational activities and/or geographical locations, a bank has to evaluate a set of factors:

- Under FRS guidelines, an Edge subsidiary has greater flexibility to engage in bank-related areas than does an overseas branch or an RO.
- If a host country prohibits branches of foreign banks, then an American bank can apply to enter the country via a separately chartered banking and/or bank-related Edge subsidiary.
- Moreover, if a host country insists that its citizens have an investment interest in banks and/or bank-related companies that operate within its

borders, then an American bank can apply to enter the country by using a non-wholly-owned Edge subsidiary in which the host-country's citizens also are investors.

- A multinational banking organization possibly can shield itself if serious problems arise within one of its separately chartered, legally autonomous Edge subsidiaries. As with domestic BHCs, however, this "corporate veil" is not invulnerable to legal piercing; and the parent banking organization is likely to conclude that its moral obligations and/or long-run economic interests require it to try to remedy problems within one of its subsidiaries.

- The costs of an Edge subsidiary can be less than those of a full service branch, especially if a bank joins a *consortium* of banks (and possibly nonbank firms) that jointly own a foreign banking subsidiary.[23] The participants in a consortium pool their financial resources and expertise to build a jointly owned subsidiary and to share in its returns and risks. Yet, to succeed, a consortium requires continuing commitment from its joint owners, who at times face conflicts: for example, whether to service a specific multinational client in-house or to direct the client to the consortium in which each is only a part owner.

Thus if it establishes an Edge corporation that invests in various banking and bank-related subsidiaries, a banking organization gains additional flexibility in its multinational expansion.

## OTHER STRATEGIES TO EXPAND OVERSEAS

Instead of—or in addition to—using an Edge corporation to invest in overseas subsidiaries, a bank can invest directly in foreign banks. Also instead of—or in addition to—a bank's expanding its overseas network, its parent BHC can be a vehicle for expansion. Subject to FRS approval, an American BHC can directly or through an Edge corporation invest in foreign banking and bank-related firms. No matter whether it uses a BHC, affiliate banks, and/or various subsidiaries to expand abroad, international expansion by a banking organization generally is subject to FRS policies and approval.

## DOMESTIC EDGE ACT CORPORATIONS

A bank also can develop a domestic network of banking Edge corporations that transact only international or foreign business. In contrast to an Edge corporation that primarily invests in overseas subsidiaries, the FRS, through its Regulation K, defines a *"banking" Edge corporation* as one that "is ordinarily engaged in the business of accepting deposits in the United States from nonaffiliated persons." A banking Edge corporation:

- can accept demand and time deposits that are incidental to international

---

23. Michael von Clemm, "The Rise of Consortium Banking," *Harvard Business Review*, May-June 1971, pp. 125-136.

or foreign transactions (deposits from foreign citizens are included in this category)

- is subject to the same required reserves and interest rate ceilings that apply to member banks
- cannot lend a single customer an amount that exceeds ten percent of its capital stock and surplus

Although subject to FRS constraints, a domestic banking Edge corporation is a vehicle by which money-center banks extend their multinational operations into other domestic money centers.

A large out-of-state bank can use a domestic Edge corporation to position itself in New York City. A New York Edge corporation has convenient access to world money markets, and it can help service the international banking needs of its parent bank's clients. Especially since the 1970s, however, large money-center banks have used domestic Edge corporations to enter such other traditional money centers as Chicago, Los Angeles, and San Francisco and such emerging regional money centers as Houston and Miami. Thus, while interstate branching is prohibited, large banks are developing interstate networks of banking Edge corporations.

Several surveys summarize the development of banking Edge corporations in regional money centers. A survey of banking Edge corporations in Miami reports their close ties to Latin American depositors. [24] A Miami Edge makes some direct loans within its loan limits, arranges loans to participate with its parent bank, and directs large loan requests to its parent bank. Seldom does it participate in loans with nonrelated institutions, and it does not actively engage in foreign exchange trading. A survey of banking Edge corporations in Houston cites how they especially service the international banking needs of Houston's petroleum-related firms.[25] A Houston Edge corporation, as part of its parent firm's multinational banking network, engages in loan participations and provides worldwide funds transfers, letters of credit, and economic intelligence. Its foreign exchange operations are not done in-house but instead are directed to New York.

## SUMMARY

Exhibit 21-3 schematically summarizes how a large American banking organization has many paths by which to develop a multinational network of offices. Many American banks use this flexibility to expand into new activities and locations. Yet, as they become increasingly multinational, American banks encounter large foreign banking organizations that similarly are building multinational networks that include banks and bank-related activities in the United States.

24. Donald E. Baer, "Expansion of Miami Edge Act Corporations," *Economic Review* (Federal Reserve Bank of Atlanta), September-October 1977, pp. 112-117. John E. Leimone, "Edge Act Corporations: An Added Dimension to Southeastern International Banking," *Monthly Review* (Federal Reserve Bank of Atlanta), September 1974, pp. 130-138.

25. "New Edge Offices Participate in Expanding International Banking Market," *Business Review* (Federal Reserve Bank of Dallas), March 1976, pp. 1-5.

**EXHIBIT 21-3**

**Building a Multinational Banking System**

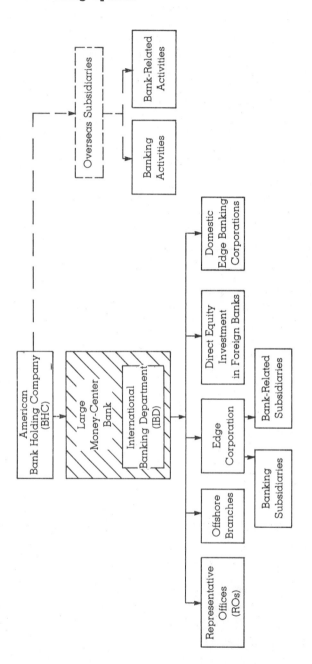

*Note:* In many cases the subsidiary and/or related firms can in turn operate with branches and/or subsidiaries.

# EXPANSION OF FOREIGN BANKS IN THE UNITED STATES

Some large banking organizations, especially those based in Switzerland and the United Kingdom, have long traditions of providing international banking services to residents and nonresidents. The Swiss banks primarily do so through their major offices within Switzerland; the U.K. banks do so in London and through extensive networks of overseas branches that historically were positioned throughout British colonies.

During the 1960s and 1970s, large banking organizations based in various industrialized countries have expanded their multinational operations, and many have chosen to enter the United States. Since late 1972, when the FRS first began collecting monthly balance sheet figures about them, the assets of U.S. banking offices of foreign banks increased from $18 billion to about $90 billion (1978). Thus, not only do foreign banking organizations compete with large U.S. banks that operate abroad, but they have been aggressively increasing their role in U.S. banking.

## MOTIVATIONS FOR FOREIGN-BANK EXPANSION IN THE UNITED STATES

Since the late 19th century, some large Canadian banks at various times have had offices in Chicago, New York, and several West Coast cities. These offices serviced foreign currency transactions and short-term financing for corporate clients, and the New York offices also gave their Canadian parents access to the New York money markets. During the 1920s some European and Japanese banks opened U.S. offices, the growth of which was stunted by subsequent worldwide economic conditions and war.

By the 1960s foreign banks again began to establish offices in the U.S., especially in New York City. A foreign bank's motivations for expansion in the U.S. often parallel some of the reasons why large American banks decide to expand abroad:[26]

- With strategically located offices, especially in New York City, a foreign bank can expand its in-house participation in foreign exchange transactions and short-term financing of international trade.
- A New York office gives it convenient access to dollar assets — such as money-market instruments and loans — so that the parent bank can hedge the Eurodollar liabilities of its European offices.
- At times the dollar deposits and other liabilities of its New York office provide a net source of dollar funds that the parent bank uses to make dollar loans to multinational clients and/or to manage its systemwide liquidity.

---

26. Fred H. Klopstock, "Foreign Banks in the United States: Scope and Growth of Operations," *Monthly Review* (Federal Reserve Bank of New York), June 1973, pp. 140-154. Joseph G. Kvasnicka, "International Banking: Part II," *Business Conditions* (Federal Reserve Bank of Chicago), March 1976, pp. 3-11.

- Its American office(s) enable a foreign bank to expand its in-house banking services to its multinational clients that include: American subsidiaries of foreign-based firms, and American firms whose overseas affiliates are serviced by the foreign bank.

Although most foreign banks thus expand to the U.S. in order to increase their direct role in multinational banking and finance, some foreign banks have additional motivations to expand to, and within, the United States:

- to develop U.S. offices that provide retail banking services to American ethnic minorities (Most notably, some large Japanese banks have networks of banking offices, especially in California, that direct their marketing toward Americans of Japanese descent.)
- to develop a major position in U.S. banking, in order to provide broader geographical diversification for their stockholders (To illustrate, recent large-scale entrants in the U.S. market include banking organizations with extensive networks in the Republic of South Africa or in Hong Kong, a British crown colony that is scheduled to revert to China in 1997.)
- to position themselves in key U.S. financial centers prior to congressional legislation that would ''grandfather'' their current operations but control their future expansion

The foreign banks have innovatively structured their expansion to and within the United States.

## EXPANSION STRATEGIES WITHIN THE UNITED STATES

Until 1978 there was limited federal supervision of foreign bank expansion in the United States. If it chose to expand indirectly via the BHC vehicle, then a foreign banking organization was subject to the Bank Holding Company Act as administered by the FRS. If, however, it chose to expand directly via additional offices in the U.S., then, because there were no federal licensing provisions, an expansionary foreign bank had only to receive approval from the relevant state banking commission. Many foreign banks thus positioned their networks of offices prior to congressional passage of the International Banking Act of 1978, which provides a more comprehensive federal policy for foreign bank expansion in the U.S.

A foreign bank can choose from among various forms of organizational structure.[27]

---

27. This section draws on ''Recent Growth in Activities of U.S. Offices of Foreign Banks,'' *Federal Reserve Bulletin*, October 1976, pp. 815-823. Also see Neil Pinsky, ''Edge Act and Agreement Corporations: Mediums for International Banking,'' *Economic Perspectives* (Federal Reserve Bank of Chicago), September-October 1978, pp. 25-31.

### Representative Offices

Although a representative office (RO) neither accepts deposits nor makes loans, a foreign bank may decide to have some ROs in the U.S., especially where state law precludes its having an office with more banking powers. A foreign bank thus can use ROs as a low-cost way to: maintain a presence in selected cities, provide limited services to current and potential corporate clients, and direct business to the parent bank's head office and/or full-service branch(es) in the United States.

### Agencies

An agency is a banking office that can lend and transfer funds but cannot accept deposits from domestic residents. Its exact powers depend on those granted by the state in which it is licensed to operate. California, for example, stipulates that if an agency accepts deposits from foreigners then it is subject to lending limits to individual borrowers.

There are various reasons why a foreign bank chooses to place an agency in some U.S. locations:

- Although it cannot accept domestic deposits, an agency is a vehicle to access the U.S. money markets and to service large multinational clients. An agency usually faces no legal limit on the amount that it can lend to any one borrower.
- State law may make a full-service branch infeasible. For example, New York law contains a *reciprocity provision* that prohibits a foreign bank from operating a full-service branch in New York unless banks chartered by New York can in turn conduct specific banking activities in the foreign bank's home nation.

For reasons such as these, foreign banks operate more agencies than branches in the United States.

### Branches

Where permitted by state law, a branch of a foreign bank can conduct full-service banking that includes acceptance of both foreign and domestic deposits. A branch usually faces a state-imposed legal lending limit to any one borrower, but the limit seldom is burdensome for branches of large foreign banks. In New York, for example, a branch's legal lending limit relates to the capital and surplus of its parent bank. Branches thus have deposit and lending flexibility, and the number and total assets of foreign branches have grown rapidly from a low initial base in the early 1970s.

### Subsidiaries

A foreign banking organization can own subsidiary firms that operate in the U.S. Most such subsidiaries:

- are state chartered
- engage in banking or bank-related activities
- are subject to the Bank Holding Company Act and associated FRS supervision

Especially where state law impedes its opening an agency or branch, a foreign bank may decide to acquire a subsidiary bank. In this case it usually applies to acquire or establish a bank. With its own charter and capital, a subsidiary bank has the legal flexibility of any bank operating within the state. It can:

- accept deposits
- make loans up to its legal lending limit
- provide trust services
- obtain FDIC insurance, which until late 1978 was not available to U.S. branches of foreign banks.
- choose to be a member or nonmember of the FRS

Most subsidiaries choose not to belong to the FRS.

A foreign banking organization is subject to the provision of the Bank Holding Company Act that requires FRS approval of a firm's application to acquire or establish a bank. Once it becomes a registered BHC, a foreign banking organization also is subject to the provisions of the Bank Holding Company Act that:

- prevent a BHC from controlling subsidiary banks in more than one state (except under some "grandfather" provisions)
- limit a BHC to controlling only banking and approved bank-related subsidiaries

Until enactment of the International Banking Act of 1978, a foreign banking organization had more latitude in its U.S. operations than did a large American bank:

- Although it could control a subsidiary bank in only one state, a foreign bank could also operate agencies and/or branches in other states; there was no federal control of these state-licensed offices. In this way some foreign-banking organizations developed *interstate networks of full-service offices* — an opportunity not available to American banks.
- If it had no subsidiary bank in the U.S., a foreign banking organization was not subject to the Bank Holding Company Act. It could obtain state licenses to operate offices in one or more states and also have nonbanking subsidiaries that engage in activities beyond those on the FRS's approved list for BHCs. In this way some foreign banking organizations controlled *investment banking subsidiaries* in the U.S., an avenue closed to American banks by the Glass-Steagall Act.

As foreign banking organizations have thus expanded their U.S. operations in ways closed to American banks, there have been proposals to broaden federal control of foreign bank expansion in the U.S.

## TOWARD FEDERAL REGULATION OF FOREIGN BANK OPERATIONS IN THE UNITED STATES

Throughout most of the 1970s Congress considered proposed legislation that would revise the ground rules for foreign bank expansion in the United States. This public-policy debate culminated in the International Banking Act of 1978.

### Principal Participants in the Public Policy Debate

The ranks of American banking were split in the debate about whether and how to control foreign bank expansion in the U.S. Major money-center banks in New York, California, and Illinois especially faced competition from nearby foreign banking offices that sought to service multinational clients and large U.S. firms. In most cases these offices were not subject to FRS reserve requirements or FDIC insurance assessments, and so they had a cost advantage over their American counterparts. Yet these major money-center banks held mixed views as to the extent to which there should be changes in the ground rules for foreign banks operating in the U.S. If they supported extensive new regulations on foreign bank expansion in the U.S., then their own overseas branch networks would likely face retaliatory moves from some foreign governments whose major banks would have to face the new U.S. constraints. Also, if such regulations did not take effect, then for a while the foreign banks would continue to have some competitive advantages in their U.S. expansion; but the expansionary money-center banks could then, on equity grounds, seek similar expansionary powers — especially for interstate operations. Thus, officials of the New York Clearing House Association, which consists of eleven major banks, testified in Congress that they favored preservation of foreign banks' privileges, such as their freedom from Federal Reserve membership and their right to operate offices in any state that permits them.[28]

Regional money-center banks and smaller banks generally supported new regulation of foreign bank expansion. These banks had little, if any, overseas operations that might be subject to retaliation; and they foresaw increasing regional and local competition from foreign banks and also from large money-center banks if they eventually got similar powers to expand interstate.

The bank supervisory agencies also differed in some views about regulation of foreign banks. The FRS proposed and supported a variety of

---

28. David C. Cates, "Foreign Banks Are Cracking the Facade of U.S. Banking," *Fortune*, August 28, 1978, pp. 94-96 ff.

legislation that would broaden its control of foreign bank expansion and that would require FRS membership by U.S. depository offices and subsidiaries of large foreign banks.[29] The FDIC was reluctant to extend FDIC insurance to U.S. offices of foreign banks. It pointed out the administrative difficulties of its evaluating and controlling its risk exposure when insuring deposit liabilities of multinational banking networks headquartered in other nations.[30] Therefore, as an alternative to requiring FDIC insurance, the FDIC favored a legislative provision that would require a foreign bank to protect its U.S. depositors via a surety deposit or a pledge of assets.

Although they generally supported new rules governing foreign bank expansion in the U.S., some state banking commissioners opposed federal legislation that would limit a foreign bank's office(s) to only one state. Under such a one-state constraint, most foreign banks would likely choose to operate in a traditional major money center and thus impede the development of new international money centers, for example, in some large Southern cities.

Faced with such diverse views, Congress debated proposed legislation for several years before it passed the International Banking Act of 1978.[31]

## International Banking Act of 1978

The International Banking Act (IBA) of 1978 sets comprehensive new rules for foreign banking firms that operate in the U.S. As its principal objective, the Act tries to have similar rules apply to the U.S. operations of foreign and domestic banking firms. To achieve this objective, the Act primarily extends domestic banking laws, regulations, and supervisory procedures to the American operations of foreign banks.

Among its principal provisions, the IBA:[32]

- requires registration with the FRS by any foreign bank that operates an agency, branch, or commercial lending company in the U.S.
- requires a foreign bank to designate one state as its "home state," and its deposits from outside this state are limited to the international deposits that are permitted to domestic Edge corporations
- prohibits a foreign banking firm from acquiring a subsidiary bank outside its designated home state

---

29. *Federal Reserve Bulletin*, September 1976, pp. 769-773.

30. Gary G. Gilbert, "Foreign Banking in the United States: The Congressional Debate," *The Magazine of Bank Administration*, October 1976, pp. 40-42.

31. The following items provide additional background about the public-policy debate. Kay J. Auerbach, "International Banking: Where Do We Go from Here?" Staff Report #10 (undated), Federal Reserve Bank of Minneapolis. Robert Johnston, "Proposals for Federal Control of Foreign Banks," *Economic Review* (Federal Reserve Bank of San Francisco), Spring 1976, pp. 32-39. Francis A. Lees, "Which Route for Foreign Bank Regulation?" *The Bankers Magazine*, Autumn 1974, pp. 53-57.

32. *Federal Reserve Bulletin*, December 1978, pp. 990-992. John P. Segala, "A Summary of the International Banking Act of 1978," *Economic Review* (Federal Reserve Bank of Richmond), January-February 1979, pp. 16-21.

- contains a grandfather clause that exempts from the above limitations all foreign bank operations that existed prior to July 28, 1978
- allows a foreign bank to apply for a federally chartered agency or branch in any state where it does not have a state-licensed agency or branch, *provided that* a state's law does not prohibit a foreign agency or branch
- permits, subject to FRS approval, a foreign bank to organize and/or acquire control of an Edge corporation
- provides authority for the federal banking agencies to supervise foreign banking organizations that fall within their jurisdiction (The OCC supervises federally chartered agencies and branches; the FDIC and the appropriate state supervise insured state-chartered branches; and the FRS has ''residual examining authority'' over all U.S. banking operations of foreign banks.)
- allows the FRS to set reserve requirements and interest-rate limitations for all federally chartered agencies and branches of foreign banking organizations that have total worldwide assets above $1 billion and, in consultation with the states, similarly to set such requirements and limitations for state-chartered agencies and branches
- requires FDIC insurance of all retail branches (those that accept deposits of less than $100,000) of foreign banks (To help protect the FDIC, the IBA requires these branches' parents to deposit assets or surety bonds with the FDIC.)
- extends the nonbanking and anti-tying provisions of the Bank Holding Company Act to the American operations of all foreign banking organizations
- contains a grandfather clause that allows the foreign organizations to retain their nonbanking activities, such as investment banking, that were in operation prior to July 27, 1978

In addition, the IBA requests the President of the U.S., in consultation with the bank supervisory agencies, to review—and to report to Congress about—the extent to which the McFadden Act is applicable to the current financial system. It also requires the FRS to review and revise its regulations that apply to international banking operations. These reviews and possible revisions in turn will likely lead to new rules for domestic and foreign expansion by American banks.

## SUMMARY

Banking has become increasingly multinational. Large American banks have expanded their international activities and overseas networks, and foreign banking organizations have expanded their operations to and within the United States. Because these multinational operations pose additional risks for individual banks and the banking system, bank officials and bank supervisory agencies have had to develop new procedures to control the special risks of international banking.

From a small initial base, American money-center banks rapidly expanded their international activities during the 1960s and 1970s. Many did so in order to service the financing needs of multinational firms, especially during periods when public policy forced such firms to rely heavily on offshore borrowings. America's multinational banks now engage in diverse foreign exchange transactions, short-term trade financing, Eurocurrency transactions, medium-term lending to private and public borrowers, and bank-related activities. In each activity there are procedures by which a bank can control its risks. As a basic strategy, a bank needs a long-run plan by which the senior officials maintain management control as their bank gradually builds a cadre of international banking specialists who expand the bank's international capabilities at home and overseas.

Over time, a bank builds a multinational banking network to a level consistent with its perceived opportunities, risks, and resources. First it builds its head-office international banking department and its correspondent relationships with large banks in world money centers. From this base it evaluates the feasibility and expected net benefits of adding representative offices, offshore branches, Edge corporation subsidiaries, and domestic Edge corporations. In some of its offshore subsidiaries, because of host-country law or by choice, a bank decides to share ownership with other parties.

Even as large American banks build their international operations, foreign banking organizations expand their operations to and within the United States. In most cases a foreign bank adds U.S. offices to its multinational system for reasons analogous to those of American banks expanding abroad. Until 1978 there was no comprehensive federal policy governing foreign-bank expansion to and within the United States; and so some large foreign banks developed interstate networks of full-service offices and engaged in nonbanking activities, such as investment banking, that were closed to U.S. banks and BHCs. After lengthy public-policy debate, the U.S. Congress passed the International Banking Act of 1978. Although this legislation establishes new rules to control foreign bank expansion in the U.S., some observers view the grandfathered interstate offices of foreign banks and the interstate expansion of domestic Edge offices as initial breaches in the long-standing barriers to interstate branching in the United States.

# 22
# FUTURE DIRECTIONS OF BANKING

This concluding chapter summarizes some probable future directions of banking. Its projections, which build on the prior chapters, are not presented as a complete planning guide. They are intended to trigger further analysis and discussion by bankers, banking scholars, and public officials who are concerned with banking and public policy.

## INCREASING ACCOUNTABILITY

Banks will find themselves increasingly accountable to current and potential investors, major depositors and borrowers, governmental supervisory agencies, and citizens' action groups. These parties have access to increasingly detailed reports and comparative information by which to evaluate the performance of individual banks and groups of banks.

To evaluate the financial structure and performance of banks, these parties will analyze the detailed reports that banks publish and/or file with their supervisory agencies and, in many cases, with the SEC. While they can directly analyze these reports, investors and uninsured depositors also have access to comparative financial analyses provided by:

- private firms that provide comparative banking statistics
- private agencies that rate the default risk of large CDs of banks and/or of debentures of bank holding companies
- securities analysts that specialize in risk-return analyses of banking securities
- trade associations that provide analytical information, such the BAI Index of Bank Performance and the ABA reports about High-Performance Banks
- analytical services that evaluate and rank the portfolio performance of bank trust departments and other institutional investors

To evaluate the social performance of banks, governmental agencies and citizens' action groups will monitor bank compliance with diverse consumer protection laws, the Home Mortgage Disclosure Act, and the Community Reinvestment Act.

As they anticipate how various parties thus will evaluate their bank's performance, a bank's senior officials will also focus on performance objectives and control systems for their organizations. They realize that their bank's financial and social performance will be compared to such standards as stated performance goals and/or actual outcomes for peer banks.

## EXPANSION OF COMPUTER-ASSISTED MANAGEMENT SYSTEMS

All banks will increasingly use computers in their operations and management systems. Therefore each bank will have to reexamine periodically the extent to which it uses in-house computer systems and/or computer services from other banks and nonbanking firms.

Each bank will increasingly use computer-based systems to:

- help develop and process its expanding set of required reports
- help develop timely internal reports for directors and senior officers
- process funds transfers and deposit accounts within the expanding subsystems of EFTS
- help cash-flow managers to monitor and project their bank's cash flows and to evaluate cash-adjustment procedures
- assist investments officers who structure and monitor the risk-return combinations of investment securities that the bank owns or that its trust department manages for its clients
- assist loan officers who evaluate credit risks and potential net returns from standardized consumer and home mortgage loans and from nonstandardized business, agricultural, and real estate loans
- assist senior officers and specialists who plan and evaluate a bank's capital, branch network, holding company activities, and international operations

Previous chapters document how bankers thus can expand their applications of computers to diverse operating procedures and to strategic planning and control systems.

Bank supervisory agencies similarly have increased—and will continue to increase—their use of computers to help them:

- publish extensive reports, such as *Bank Operating Statistics*, that are derived from computerized data files
- monitor and evaluate bank risk and performance via computer-based systems such as the National Bank Surveillance System and other statistical early warning systems

- project future outcomes, such as the probable levels, under alternative assumptions, of bank capital and the probable future banking structure(s) if changes were to be made in specific constraints on branching and/or holding company expansion
- evaluate the social costs and benefits of current and possible future legislation in such areas as consumer protection, detailed disclosure requirements, and selective credit policies

Bankers must prepare to operate within this increasingly computer-based supervisory environment.

## APPLYING PORTFOLIO PERSPECTIVES

Bankers already focus on the structure of a bank's total balance sheet and the interrelationships among the component elements. They will increasingly plan and analyze their bank's:

- rates of return
- net interest margin and spread-management strategies
- new opportunities to control interest-rate risk via floating-rate assets and liabilities and possible use of interest-rate futures

As part of these total-portfolio strategies they will also focus on principal subcomponents, such as deposit and nondeposit sources of funds, investments, loans, and capital.

Officials of multiunit banking organizations similarly can apply portfolio perspectives to their analyses of branch systems, holding company activities, and multinational operations. If they analyze risk-return combinations of various current and potential component units, these officials gain new insights into how to structure the total organization and how to revise the structure over time. Previous chapters demonstrate why and how expansionary banking systems thus must evaluate their expected returns, risks, and risk-control systems as they expand into new geographical and product areas.

## PROBABLE CHANGES IN SOURCES AND USES OF BANK FUNDS

As documented in previous chapters, bankers must anticipate major legislative changes that will affect the costs and pricing of sources and uses of bank funds. They can expect Congress to pass legislation that will:

- expand the "banking-type" services provided by nonbank financial institutions
- permit NOW accounts throughout the U.S. and/or permit other funds

transfer procedures that in practice will erode the prohibition of interest on demand deposits

- phase out Regulation Q ceilings on consumer time and savings deposits
- specify uniform required reserves for all—or all large—financial institutions that offer transactions accounts
- further increase consumer-protection regulations and compliance examinations.
- expand the use of variable rate mortgages

Congress is less likely to mandate a system of selected credit policies.

If they conclude that Congress will soon pass such legislation, bankers need to reexamine some principal operating strategies. They need to develop and/or refine their information about bank costs and about probable customer sensitivity to alternate schedules of explicit prices for banking services.

## CHANGES IN BANKING STRUCTURE

American banking will undergo further consolidation that will result in fewer banks, many of which will be large systems that operate throughout a region, the nation, or the world. Bankers, public officials, and citizens can evaluate the merits of this probable outcome. Meanwhile, no matter what the size of their bank, bankers need to develop strategies and contingency plans for the changing banking structure.

Nonexpansionary bankers, as defined in Chapter 17, will become more receptive to *controlled* expansion by expansionary branch and/or holding company systems. They will do so because of:

- the complexities of modern banking which, for banks of all sizes, involve increasing accountability, directors' liability, obligatory reports, and specialized personnel and systems
- the difficulties—especially in a high tax, inflationary economy—for small and medium-sized banks to build their capital accounts and for individuals to finance the transfer of control of these banks
- acquisition proposals in which expansionary banks offer purchase premiums and tax-deferred gains to stockholders of smaller banks and also employee benefits to managers and personnel of such banks

As more nonexpansionary banks are absorbed into large expansionary systems, this process numerically reduces the political constituency of remaining nonexpansionary banks. To strengthen their negotiating position, nonexpansionary bankers will insist on home office protection laws as a condition for their acceptance of reductions in barriers to branching and/or holding company expansion.

Expansionary banking systems similarly will anticipate and try to influence the constraints on their expansion. They need to refine their strategies for the following probable developments:

- gradual easing of branching and holding company restrictions in states that have such restrictions (However, they also need to monitor proposals to limit a banking organization's maximum proportion of banking assets or deposits within a state.)
- increasing interstate activities via computerized funds transfer systems and via domestic Edge corporations, loan production offices, trust affiliates, and other "nonbanking" offices
- possible state and/or federal legislation that would permit out-of-state banking organizations to enter a state under special conditions, such as reciprocity agreements between states or to salvage a large problem bank
- when permitted by changes in state laws, consolidations of multibank holding companies into branch systems
- an easing of the go slow policy by which the FRS has constrained BHC expansion within permissible nonbanking activities and into new, permissible activities
- further expansion of foreign bank operations in the United States

Yet even as they develop and refine their expansion strategies, large banking organizations will focus on the risks and returns of their current system and its components. As a result of these review processes, they will decide to close some branches—subject, however, to their accountability under the Community Reinvestment Act—and/or to divest some activities and/or affiliates that no longer fit into the system's future plans.

## SUMMARY

As they look ahead, bankers must plan for—and have contingency plans for—probable changes in their operating environment. They can anticipate that their banks will:

- face increasing accountability to investors, major customers, governmental units, and citizens' action groups
- expand their use of computer-based processing and decision systems
- expand their use of portfolio perspectives to help analyze and control the returns and risks of banking
- face changes in the costs and pricing of their principal sources and uses of funds
- operate within a banking system that will contain fewer banks, many of which will be large systems that operate throughout a region, the nation, or the world

While bankers factor such probable changes into their planning, banking scholars and public officials need to reexamine the extent to which public policy fosters—and ought to foster—major changes in American banking.

# APPENDIX

## BANK OPERATING STATISTICS, 1977,
## NATIONAL TOTALS,
## SELECTED TABLES

TABLE C
NATION
---REPORT OF CONDITION ANALYSIS---

REPORT OF CONDITION 12-31-77

| | UNDER 5.0 | 5.0-9.9 | 10.0-24.9 | 25.0-99.9 | 100.0-299.9 | 300 OR MORE | ALL BANKS |
|---|---|---|---|---|---|---|---|
| NUMBER OF BANKS | 1,197 | 2,593 | 4,911 | 4,464 | 822 | 425 | 14,412 |
| **SECURITIES MIX (PERCENT OF TOTAL SEC):** | | | | | | | |
| US TREASURY SECURITIES . . . . . . | 55.99 % | 46.64 % | 38.27 % | 34.66 % | 34.83 % | 36.17 % | 39.87 % |
| OBLIG OF US AGENCIES & CORPS . . . | 24.82 | 23.47 | 20.50 | 15.68 | 14.58 | 11.60 | 19.30 |
| OBLIG OF STATES & POLITICAL SUBDIVS. | 14.96 | 27.19 | 39.06 | 47.37 | 47.70 | 46.14 | 38.20 |
| OTHER BONDS, NOTES & DEBENTURES . . | 2.12 | 2.07 | 1.76 | 1.90 | 2.30 | 3.39 | 1.97 |
| CORPORATE STOCK. . . . . . . . . . | 1.36 | .51 | .39 | .37 | .42 | .84 | .50 |
| TRADING ACCOUNT SECURITIES . . . . | | .01 | | .02 | .17 | 1.86 | .07 |
| TOTAL . . . . . . . . . . . . . | 100.00 | 100.00 | 100.00 | 100.00 | 100.00 | 100.00 | 100.00 |
| TOTAL SECURITIES TO TOTAL ASSETS. . | 27.94 | 28.49 | 29.11 | 29.11 | 28.35 | 22.87 | 28.67 |
| **LOAN MIX (PERCENT OF TOTAL LOANS):** | | | | | | | |
| REAL ESTATE LOANS. . . . . . . . . | 24.03 | 29.46 | 34.13 | 37.26 | 37.19 | 29.71 | 33.46 |
| LOANS TO FARMERS . . . . . . . . . | 30.88 | 25.66 | 17.06 | 7.73 | 2.27 | 1.68 | 15.57 |
| COMMERCIAL AND INDUSTRIAL LOANS. . | 15.32 | 15.97 | 18.09 | 21.96 | 28.14 | 32.69 | 19.68 |
| LOANS TO INDIVIDUALS . . . . . . . | 26.89 | 26.74 | 28.53 | 30.58 | 28.50 | 25.44 | 28.61 |
| ALL OTHER LOANS. . . . . . . . . . | 2.47 | 2.14 | 2.14 | 2.46 | 3.90 | 10.48 | 2.61 |
| GROSS LOANS (AB) . . . . . . . . . | 100.00 | 100.00 | 100.00 | 100.00 | 100.00 | 100.00 | 100.00 |
| GROSS LOANS TO TOTAL ASSETS . . . . | 50.62 | 54.86 | 55.88 | 56.46 | 55.37 | 52.03 | 55.30 |
| **ASSET & LIABILITY RATIOS:** | | | | | | | |
| EARNING ASSETS TO TOTAL ASSETS . . | 87.10 | 88.78 | 88.96 | 88.30 | 86.76 | 82.26 | 88.25 |
| TOTAL DEPOSITS TO TOTAL ASSETS . . | 86.65 | 89.83 | 90.50 | 90.12 | 88.51 | 83.23 | 89.61 |
| CASH & DUE & US GOVERNMENT SECURITIES TO TOTAL DEPOSITS. . . . . . | 23.05 | 18.19 | 15.87 | 14.65 | 15.51 | 18.07 | 16.55 |
| NET LOANS TO TOTAL DEPOSITS. . . . | 56.41 | 58.97 | 59.39 | 59.93 | 59.90 | 62.58 | 59.36 |
| DEMAND DEPOSITS TO TOTAL DEPOSITS. | 43.27 | 36.12 | 34.87 | 34.35 | 35.66 | 40.15 | 35.83 |
| TOTAL BORROWED FUNDS TO EQUITY CAPITAL | 29.01 | 30.84 | 25.28 | 25.00 | 32.23 | 45.45 | 27.76 |
| SUBORDINATED NOTES TO EQUITY CAPITAL . | 25.98 | 19.44 | 19.53 | 18.30 | 20.52 | 20.40 | 19.31 |
| **DEPOSIT MIX (PERCENT OF TOTAL DEPOSITS)** | | | | | | | |
| **BY TYPE OF DEPOSIT:** | | | | | | | |
| DEMAND DEPOSITS. . . . . . . . . . | 42.98 | 36.12 | 34.86 | 34.35 | 35.66 | 40.11 | 35.80 |
| SAVINGS DEPOSITS . . . . . . . . . | 18.60 | 23.25 | 26.03 | 28.64 | 29.55 | 23.89 | 25.86 |
| TIME DEPOSITS. . . . . . . . . . . | 38.25 | 40.63 | 39.11 | 37.02 | 34.75 | 31.73 | 38.20 |
| DEPOSITS IN FOREIGN OFFICES . . . . | | | | | .04 | 4.22 | .13 |
| **BY OWNERSHIP:** | | | | | | | |
| INDIVIDUALS, PARTNER & CORPS . . . | 86.59 | 87.65 | 88.09 | 88.02 | 85.40 | 78.59 | 87.43 |
| US GOVERNMENT. . . . . . . . . . . | .53 | .88 | .98 | .93 | .70 | .97 | .89 |
| STATES & POLITICAL SUBDIVISIONS . . | 11.15 | 10.19 | 9.58 | 9.46 | 10.19 | 9.34 | 9.81 |
| DEPOSITS IN FOREIGN OFFICES . . . . | | | | | .04 | 4.22 | .13 |
| ALL OTHER DEPOSITS . . . . . . . . | 1.56 | 1.28 | 1.34 | 1.59 | 3.67 | 6.87 | 1.72 |
| **CAPITAL MEASURES:** | | | | | | | |
| EQUITY CAPITAL TO NET LOANS. . . . | 20.89 | 17.97 | 16.07 | 14.68 | 13.68 | 12.67 | 16.09 |
| EQUITY CAPITAL TO TOTAL ASSETS . . | 10.04 | 9.03 | 8.16 | 7.59 | 6.94 | 6.33 | 8.15 |
| EQUITY CAPITAL TO TOTAL DEPOSITS . . | 10.74 | 9.82 | 6.99 | 8.43 | 7.86 | 7.63 | 8.98 |

NATIONAL TOTALS

NATIONAL TOTALS

**TABLE D**
**NATION**
----REPORT OF INCOME ANALYSIS----

REPORT OF INCOME 12 MONTHS ENDING 12-31-77

------------INSURED COMMERCIAL BANKS WITH TOTAL ASSETS (IN MILLIONS)------------

| | UNDER 5.0 | 5.0-9.9 | 10.0-24.9 | 25.0-99.9 | 100.0-299.9 | 300 OR MORE | ALL BANKS |
|---|---|---|---|---|---|---|---|
| NUMBER OF BANKS | 1,197 | 2,593 | 4,911 | 4,464 | 822 | 425 | 14,412 |
| **RETURN ON:** | | | | | | | |
| TOTAL LOANS | 9.12 % | 9.25 % | 9.32 % | 9.41 % | 9.21 % | 8.90 % | 9.30 % |
| TIME BALANCES WITH BANKS | 7.39 | 6.44 | 6.47 | 6.45 | 6.55 | 6.61 | 6.53 |
| FEDERAL FUNDS SOLD & SEC PURCHASED | 5.99 | 6.21 | 6.52 | 6.74 | 6.57 | 5.95 | 6.48 |
| US TREASURY SECURITIES | 6.91 | 7.00 | 6.92 | 6.89 | 6.76 | 6.60 | 6.90 |
| US GOVT AGENCY & CORP SECURITIES | 7.42 | 7.41 | 7.28 | 7.17 | 7.07 | 6.94 | 7.25 |
| OBLIG OF STATES & POLITICAL SUBDIVS | 5.65 | 5.31 | 5.16 | 5.05 | 4.90 | 4.87 | 5.15 |
| AVERAGE ASSETS | .80 | .93 | 1.00 | 1.01 | .88 | .74 | .96 |
| AVERAGE EARNING ASSETS | .90 | 1.01 | 1.08 | 1.11 | .99 | .87 | 1.05 |
| **COST FACTOR ASSOCIATED WITH:** | | | | | | | |
| TIME DEPOSITS OF $100,000 OR MORE | 5.80 | 5.90 | 6.01 | 5.96 | 5.71 | 5.50 | 5.92 |
| OTHER SAVINGS & TIME DEPOSITS | 5.41 | 5.44 | 5.51 | 5.51 | 5.41 | 5.29 | 5.48 |
| FEDERAL FUNDS PURCHASED & SEC SOLD | 5.41 | 5.62 | 5.88 | 5.99 | 6.26 | 6.12 | 5.97 |
| OTHER LIAB FOR BOPROWED MONEY | 7.68 | 6.82 | 6.98 | 7.42 | 7.24 | 7.29 | 7.24 |
| SUBORDINATED NOTES & DEBENTURES | 7.64 | 7.58 | 7.75 | 7.57 | 7.28 | 6.93 | 7.52 |
| **INCOME CONCEPTS & RELATIONSHIPS:** | | | | | | | |
| OPERATING EXPENSES TO OPERATING INCOME | 86.71 | 85.68 | 84.55 | 84.34 | 86.37 | 87.81 | 85.05 |
| OPERATING INCOME TO TOTAL DEPOSITS | 8.35 | 8.46 | 8.46 | 8.52 | 8.48 | 8.70 | 8.48 |
| INCOME BEF SECURITIES TO TOTAL OF INC. | 11.15 | 11.92 | 12.68 | 12.84 | 11.49 | 10.01 | 12.33 |
| INCOME BEFORE SECURITIES TO ASSETS | .79 | .90 | .96 | .99 | .86 | .73 | .93 |
| INCOME BEFORE SECURITIES TO DEPOSITS | .81 | .97 | 1.05 | 1.09 | .97 | .88 | 1.02 |
| INCOME BEF SECURITIES TO EQUITY CAP. | 8.15 | 10.44 | 11.95 | 12.91 | 12.51 | 11.25 | 11.68 |
| NET INCOME TO TOTAL OPERATING INCOME | 11.49 | 12.34 | 13.12 | 13.20 | 11.79 | 10.21 | 12.72 |
| NET INCOME TO AVERAGE ASSETS | .81 | .94 | 1.00 | 1.01 | .88 | .74 | .96 |
| NET INCOME TO AVERAGE DEPOSITS | .83 | 1.00 | 1.09 | 1.12 | 1.00 | .89 | 1.05 |
| NET INCOME TO AVERAGE EQUITY CAPITAL | 8.35 | 10.77 | 12.32 | 13.24 | 12.86 | 11.44 | 12.01 |
| **OTHER:** | | | | | | | |
| DIVIDEND PAYOUT RATIO | 26.86 | 23.26 | 24.59 | 28.37 | 34.04 | 41.42 | 27.00 |
| NET CHANGE IN CAPITAL TO NET INCOME | 76.39 | 81.41 | 83.08 | 81.89 | 73.98 | 62.82 | 80.76 |
| NET CHANGE IN CAPITAL TO EQUITY CAP. | 8.42 | 10.72 | 12.41 | 12.91 | 11.23 | 8.67 | 11.75 |
| INDICATED TAX RATE (A4A/A3A) | 14.30 | 15.25 | 16.75 | 16.94 | 15.77 | 18.11 | 16.32 |
| EARNINGS PER THOUSAND OF COMMON STOCK. | $ 456.09 | $ 623.55 | $ 682.07 | $ 675.83 | $ 612.67 | $ 562.51 | $ 645.99 |
| BOOK VALUE PER THOUSAND OF COMMON STK. | 61,140 | 71,742 | 77,800 | 75,975 | 75,238 | 83,775 | 74,804 |
| AVERAGE SALARY & BENEFITS PER EMPLOYEE | 10,284 | 10,912 | 11,101 | 10,887 | 11,094 | 12,075 | 10,964 |
| NET INCOME PER EMPLOYEE | 5,736 | 7,660 | 8,724 | 8,532 | 7,418 | 6,746 | 8,110 |
| ASSETS PER EMPLOYEE | 508,380 | 771,898 | 875,126 | 877,027 | 858,936 | 909,981 | 833,411 |
| **LOAN LOSSES & RECOVERIES:** | | | | | | | |
| LOAN LOSS COVERAGE | 5.40 TIMES | 9.46 TIMES | 12.90 TIMES | -14.98 TIMES | 14.15 TIMES | 8.86 TIMES | 12.15 TIMES |
| VALUATION RESERVE TO TOTAL LOANS | .89 % | .85 % | .88 % | .91 % | .99 % | 1.07 % | .90 % |
| PROV FOR LOAN LOSSES TO TOTAL LOANS | .49 % | .45 % | .42 % | .39 % | .39 % | .47 % | .42 % |
| NET CHARGE-OFFS TO TOTAL LOANS | .22 % | .26 % | .29 % | .29 % | .31 % | .40 % | .28 % |

# AUTHOR INDEX

# SUBJECT INDEX

.

*About the Author*

Paul F. Jessup is a Professor of Finance and Banking at the University of Minnesota. He is a frequent contributor to, and reviewer for, finance and banking journals; and he also is the author of a companion book, *Modern Bank Management: A Casebook*, West Publishing Company, 1978.

Professor Jessup has served as a consultant to the Committee on Banking and Currency (U.S. House of Representatives), the Federal Deposit Insurance Corporation, the Federal Reserve Bank of Minneapolis, and various banking organizations.

†